ARSONIST

THE MOST DANGEROUS MAN IN AMERICA

NATHAN A. ALLEN

Griffins Wharf Productions LLC
Westport, Connecticut

ARSONIST
The Most Dangerous Man in America

Griffins Wharf Productions LLC
Westport, Connecticut

Copyright © 2011 by Nathan A. Allen

All rights reserved under International and Pan-America Copyright Conventions.
Published in the United States of America by Griffins Wharf Productions LLC.

First published by Griffins Wharf Productions LLC, July 2011.

www.griffinswharfproductions.com
www.jamesotis.net

ISBN-10: 0983644608

ISBN-13: 978-0-9836446-0-6

Printed in the United States of America

Tu ne cede malis sed contra audentior ito

CONTENTS

Overture
vii

Chapter One
The time is which we have long foreseen
1

Chapter Two
Storms & tempests are consequent
23

Chapter Three
I will kindle a fire
103

Chapter Four
the Resentor & the popular Conductor
135

Chapter Five
mad people have overturned empires
167

Chapter Six
Troubles in this Country take their rise from one Man
195

Chapter Seven
the Terror of Election
227

CHAPTER EIGHT
a damned faction
283

EFFECTS
333

CODA
341

PAMPHLETS WRITTEN BY JAMES OTIS
A Vindication of the Conduct of the House of Representatives
(James Otis, 1762)
343

The Rights of the British Colonies, Asserted and Proved
(James Otis, 1764)
381

Considerations on Behalf of the Colonists in a Letter to a Noble Lord
(James Otis, 1765)
445

Sources & Notes
467

Index
493

OVERTURE

The early founders of the United States, the rebels of the 1760s, were profoundly radical. The most radical of them were not merely opposed to particular laws or regulations, whether they be about taxes or imports. They were opposed to the strong centralized government that had existed in feudal form for about 1000 years, and in Boston this feudal government was most evident in the oligarchy that essentially ruled the province. The "government" was not simply concentrated in official offices and government employees but rather in the few men who, in conjunction with holding those offices, owned much of the land, controlled most of the major components of the economy, and maintained a hierarchical culture atop which they firmly stood. This government – so different from a modern government – had been only marginally modified for centuries. In every town and province, a few men controlled nearly every aspect of life, and that control was infused throughout the culture. Law, religion and custom alike reflected the tidy, stratified organization of society.

After the revolution, the trappings of feudalism – titles, deference, duels – were transmuted from chivalrous to barbaric. John Adams's suggestion that the president be called "His Excellency" was met with ridicule; Hamilton's duel with Burr was met with revulsion. That Hamilton and Burr, men of high esteem and status, had to sneak out of Manhattan at daybreak to duel on a riverside ledge in New Jersey is proof enough that what once was honorable was now taboo.

For the 50th anniversary of the Declaration of Independence in 1826, Thomas Jefferson wrote:

> May it be to the world, what I believe it will be, (to some parts sooner, to others later, but finally to all,) the signal of arousing men to burst the chains under which monkish ignorance and superstition

had persuaded them to bind themselves, and to assume the blessings and security of self-government. That form which we have substituted, restores the free right to the unbounded exercise of reason and freedom of opinion. All eyes are opened, or opening, to the rights of man. The general spread of the light of science has already laid open to every view the palpable truth, that the mass of mankind has not been born with saddles on their backs, nor a favored few booted and spurred, ready to ride them legitimately, by the grace of God. These are grounds of hope for others. For ourselves, let the annual return of this day forever refresh our recollections of these rights, and an undiminished devotion to them.

Jefferson was paraphrasing a famous 17th century speech from a scaffold by Hannibal Rumbold, who declared:

This is a deluded generation, veiled in ignorance, that though popery and slavery be riding in upon them, do not perceive it; though I am sure that there was no man born marked by God above another; for none comes into this world with a saddle on his back, neither any booted and spurred to ride him. …

Jefferson owned copies of English histories that reprinted Rumbold's speech. As Jefferson makes clear, the American Revolution was a signal "to the world," not a protest about any particular law or statute. Rumbold's speech is a denouement of a failed challenge to feudalism, whereas Jefferson's is a celebration of the first successful attempt to precipitate its demise. But how did we progress from Rumbold to Jefferson, from a scaffold in Edinburgh to a neoclassical home of a famed ex-President in Monticello? George Washington wrote in his Circular Letter of 1783, "The foundation of our Empire was not laid in the gloomy age of Ignorance and Suspicion, but at an Epoch when the rights of mankind were better understood and more clearly defined, than at any former period." How did "the rights of man" become "better understood"? What was the process? Who were the prime movers? The story of the Otis family elucidates some of the details of the journey.

History is not made in clearly opposed dichotomies – Whigs vs. Tories – but rather in dense thickets of entangled alliances and competing allegiances. James Otis and his father not only knew this grubby truth but also used it masterfully to their advantage. Seamless historical narratives constructed from two clearly delineated opponents are latter-day fabrications. The Revolution was no parade of romantic idealists marching toward an inevitable magical moment and serenaded with a symphony of liberty. In truth, the 1760s were improvised mayhem continually flirting with disaster. A few flourished in the cacophony and transformed what seemed like contemptible and chaotic stagnation into a beautiful mess.

Today, we stand on the shoulders on George Washington, and in 1783, Washington stood on the shoulders of the revolutionary generation of the 1760s. Few of those men made it into the new government, and that was probably for everyone's benefit. They were fighters, not compromisers. They were agitators, men who could convince the masses that they'd been wronged and provoke mobs to tear down private homes. These infantry soldiers brawled in the streets and in the media. They were not suited for the conciliatory mending that was needed after the war and in the new government. They were, quite literally, ready to die for their rights, and thus largely incapable of living with wrongs. If the rebels of Boston had been a part of the Constitutional Congress in 1787, no compromise on slavery would have been made, and thus no unified country would have emerged. The rebels were a necessary core ingredient to the conception of the country, the foundation on which everything else was built, and yet had no place in the country they conceived.

For it was these men – Otis, Sam Adams, Oxenbridge Thacher, Jonathan Mayhew, Thomas Cushing, Patrick Henry – who conceived the country. It was men such as Washington, Jefferson, Madison, and Hamilton who midwifed the country, and we raise it now. And yet this conception, so vital yet so ignored, occurred in the violent yet fertile grounds of Boston and Virginia in the 1760s. And no one was so instrumental to that conception as James Otis, Jr., the forgotten infantry soldier who made the general's glory possible.

While the Spirit of '76 burned for decades after the fact, in 1760 it smoldered in the hearts of few. Otis's arguments in the early years of that decade seem innocuous now because they were widely adopted a decade later; many of his most strident opponents in the early 1760s became hardened rebel allies by the end of the decade. Yet as Otis explored the meaning of "the rights of man" and attempted to apply that phrase to governance, he was attacked, labeled crazy, and ensnarled by whispers of sedition and treason. To be accused of being crazy wasn't new; John Adams too would later be accused of mental instability by none other than Benjamin Franklin and Alexander Hamilton.

Conjuring rumors questioning an opponent's mental health was a common political maneuver and every major political figure who had enemies, which is all of them, at some point was attacked with innuendo questioning his mental faculties. But Otis was unique in his fiery defense of principle and his unyielding application of ideas that struck at the very core of the West's *modus operandi* – feudalism.

Boston produced many rebels, trained as lawyers and reared in contentious New England politics, for whom all meaningful progress began with an argument. Consensus may have been the objective, even in Boston, but consensus was forged in fire. Otis, like John Adams later, usually prepared for every discussion by gathering kindling. In 1760s Boston, the opposing factions could meet at no middle ground because no middle ground existed. In order to construct the appearance of compromise, Otis could not position himself in some centrist position but rather planted one foot on each of the shaky extremes that were battling for power. The rebels viewed this as betrayal and the royal governor thought Otis only needed time to plant his second foot on the oligarchy's shaky bit of earth. Both were wrong. Otis's goal in this perilous straddling of extremes was the hope of destroying one before they moved so far apart as to destroy him. In 1794, Thomas Jefferson wrote "the consequent disgrace of the invading tyrants is destined ... to kindle the wrath of the people of Europe against those who have dared to embroil them in such wickedness, and to bring at length, kings, nobles & priests to the scaffolds which they have been so long deluging with blood." England was "the dead hand of the past," and Otis's objective was nothing short of putting feudalism in Rumbold's place on the hangman's scaffold of history.

It has been argued that the American Revolution "does not appear to resemble the revolutions of other nations in which people were killed, property was destroyed, and everything was turned upside down. ... The American revolutionaries seem to belong in drawing rooms or legislative halls, not in cellars or in the streets. They made speeches, not bombs; they wrote learned pamphlets, not manifestos ... They did not kill one another; they did not devour themselves." The idea that the Revolution was a proper affair conducted by gentlemen in drawing rooms is but an illusion, an historical slight-of-hand wherein the victors pull a cordial philosopher out of the fog of war. To be sure, the American Revolution was different from most. Serfs did not rebel. Slaves did not revolt. Rather, it was the wealthy, college educated – the very people who had the most to gain if nothing happened and the most to lose if their efforts failed — who tried to make something happen. If one were given to overgeneralizations, one could characterize the revolution as argued by Harvard trained lawyers, funded by global shippers, and sustained by the energy and gravitas of Virginian planters. In any iteration of a feudal system, these men were the lords and nobles, and yet it was this confection of the privileged who risked their lives to drive a stake into the heart of the feudal system.

And as referenced in that celebrated phrase, these men risked "our Lives, our Fortunes, and our sacred Honor." Misunderstood among that inventory is "sacred honor." While leveling the structure of feudalism, men of the 18th century could not escape the value of their family name. To risk one's "honor" meant to risk one's children, their ability to be educated, conduct business, and live successfully. The sins of the father were borne by their children and quite possibly for many subsequent generations. The rebels of the 1760s wagered their lives, homes, businesses and children, and Otis's story illustrates the devastating effects of that gamble. That the story is encapsulated in that brief phrase in the Declaration of Independence is evidence that Otis's wager was far from unique.

The Revolution was so radical precisely because it was so unlikely. And it was conducted by gentlemen philosophers and street brawlers alike. People were killed, private homes were destroyed, and everything was turned upside down. Mobs ruled streets and manifestos rolled off printing presses. And a few were consumed by the radicalism of the ideas they brought to life. The methods that brought forth the American Revolution are oft obscured because the society it created was unique to history. And yet battles, blood, passion, betrayal, high-minded idealism and ruthless acerbity — all the usual ingredients of revolution — were abundantly present in the American Revolution.

That the Revolution was focused on breaking the bonds of feudalism in general, and not only the bonds with England, can be gleaned from the fact that the English were the among the freest people on earth, and the colonists the freest among Englishmen. There were no bloodthirsty thugs, no murderous tyrants, no gulags, no "reform through labor" prisons. Taxes were not high in the colonies — in fact, they would have been considered very low for Europe. Laws were not particularly oppressive; most lived as they wished. There were no vast ecclesiastical organizations dictating rules, no priestly courts, extensive church taxes and immense church properties. There were no dukes taxing the profit out of the work of serfs, legislating against the merchant class, conspiring with the church to maintain their exclusive hold on property and wealth. The English colonists in North America had none of that oppressive feudalism with which to contend or even the remnants of feudal oppression for it had never existed in the colonies. They were utterly free of the usual systemic domination of feudal society and even largely free from its history. To argue that the colonists were rebelling strictly against the British would be to claim that a hand should be amputated for a splinter in the finger. The enemy was not England but feudalism. This explains why it was soon observed that Otis's works and the Boston rebels would shake "all four" continents. It was clear by the mid 1760s that the effects of Otis's argument would carry far beyond England. This further explains why in the 1780s the men who were constructing the new government knew their decisions would affect the world, and the country with which they were most concerned was France. It seemed so clear to them that a France free from feudalism could be a dynamic force in the world. It was inevitable in nearly every conversation about the debate with England that consequences beyond England were referenced. The colonists were very aware that the whole world – the feudal world – was listening to their discussion about *rights* and *consent*.

Otis's combustible ideas were not all consumed by the Revolution; they ignited over the next century whenever some aspect of feudalism would again stake its claim against modernity. The piecemeal death of feudalism was perhaps inevitable; the rapidity of its death was not. More importantly, because a cogent argument for feudalism's replacement was often not readily available to many other revolutions, they devolved into chaos or recursions into variants of feudalism.

It may be argued that inherited circumstances shape administrations, not vice versa, but for the death of a minor judicial figure to precipitate widespread rebellion takes a special kind of executive idiocy and a unique person to recognize and manipulate that idiocy to advantage. At least as far as Boston was concerned, by 1766, the Revolution was inevitable. The brilliant propagandists, manipulators and activists who conceived the revolution were not constituted to manage the brutal reality of war or to operate the compromising minutiae of peace. Yet in 1760, one man forced a discussion that few others desired. And when he was ignored, mocked and reviled, he retreated, gathered more kindling, and relit the discussion. The fire eventually caught until, in Jefferson's words, it began to "kindle the wrath of the people of Europe."

Traditional economic models that focus on labor, capital, population and technology cannot explain what happened in the West in the second half of the 18th century. Traditional political analysis likewise fails. They both neglect to take into full appreciation the fundamental operating system of the time. The breakdown of feudalism began at the edges, where men of middling means created businesses, began trading, and constructed a new paradigm for describing themselves and their activities. Such men had always existed, but in the 18th century, they began to be respected. They began to seek office to expand control over their lives; they built their own churches and schools and created their own communities. More than anywhere else, these were the men of Plymouth and Barnstable in Massachusetts Bay colony. Significantly more important than their purely economic or political activity, their ability to control their lives and ascribe to themselves dignity and import laid the foundation of a revolutionary era. The generations of the early 18th century moved into their new and liberated bourgeois roles timidly; they seemed to sense that their escape from the dominating force of feudalism was tenuous and depended on moving quietly so that the oligarchs would notice not – too much noise from the edge of the civilized world might wake the master. In the early 18th century, most of the British North American colonies were of little import to Britain and France and of practically no import to anyone else. The escape from feudalism depended on the situation staying that way.

But the children of these men who so boldly spoke of their small businesses with pride would not be quiet and refused to be unnoticed. Even more daring – or foolish, depending on how the history played out – these men would take up their middling educations and strike at the heart of the oligarchy. Refusing to wait for the oligarchy to find them, these rebels taunted the oligarchs and mocked their ideals. They would assert that the state did not grant *privileges* but rather God instilled *rights*; they would declare that governance required their consent.

Consent? One does not consent to the social structure; it was created that way from the dawn of time. And consent from men who sell wood for a living? who raise pigs? who grow apples to make cider so that their middling friends can drink enough to forget they don't matter? In a feudal world, all one needed to know is that a man who raises pigs or grows apples is hardly one to demand consent from a lord. Yet by the mid-18th century, these pig raisers and apple growers were becoming known as businessmen. Determination of their importance shifted from their social status to their citizenship status.

NATHAN A. ALLEN

The feudal world was not composed of free individuals but rather groups of people forming a stratum whose obligations in all regards depended on their relationship to the strata below and above them. The concepts of liberty, responsibility and consent as applied to individuals were nearly unknown, certainly outside of theoretical realms. The 17th century exploded with rational philosophers – Bacon, Descartes, Hobbes, Spinoza – who invariably sought an orderly neo-Platonic Republic that a middling class clamoring for *rights* and *liberty* could never deliver. Spinoza could have been Rumbolt's hangman, for it was Spinoza who believed all rights are derived from the state. The idea that apple farmers ought to control their destinies, assist in the operation of their governments, and had natural rights granted by God was not popular in the courts of law, the halls of Parliament, or at the desks of philosophers. At best, such ideas would have seemed foreign and undesirable, at worst, they would seem dangerous.

In 1778, *Samuel Johnson* made this characteristic late 18th century declaration: "Depend upon it, sir, every state of society is as luxurious as it can be. Men always take the best they can get." A century earlier, men would not "always take" anything. Lords took. "Men" received what was given to them. Only a man amidst the crumbling walls of feudalism could claim that "Men always take the best they can get." Sixty-eight years after the commencement of the revolution, Ralph Waldo Emerson observed, "...trade planted America and destroyed Feudalism; that it makes peace and keeps peace, and it will abolish slavery. We complain of its oppression of the poor, and of its building up a new aristocracy on the ruins of the aristocracy it destroyed. But the aristocracy of trade has no permanence, is not entailed, was the result of toil and talent, the result of merit of some kind ...." The trade practiced by small colonial merchants transformed religious vigor into a panoply of legal, political and philosophical apparati that were employed to disrupt and eventually destroy feudalism.

Life was good in Massachusetts Province in the summer of 1760. The economy had gone through a war boom, producing goods for the French and Indian war, and though the war was largely over, the economy was still strong. Crime was low, certainly lower than crime in most urban areas of Europe. Employment was high. Businesses were growing. Harvard College was thriving. And Boston was one of the more important ports of the world's greatest

Empire. Now with the French empire dismantled, the British controlled more of the world than anyone. The sugar and tobacco trades were booming, shipping was flourishing, manufactured goods and British woolens were traded world-wide. And the New England shipper-merchant was in the middle of it all.

The Otis family was a part of that success. Based in Barnstable, about 70 miles south of Boston, the Otis family were not part of the Boston ruling oligarchy, but they enjoyed increasing wealth and importance. The fifth generation of Otises, born in the 1720s-1740s, tended to be educated, had access to the corridors of power, and were members of the wealthiest family on Cape Cod. Colonel James Otis was the leading figure in the family in the 1750s: supplier of nearly 1,000 whale boats to the war effort against France, wildly successful lawyer, Speaker of the House, and holder of myriad minor government positions.

But by the end of the summer, everything would change. The fuse for the next great war, the American Revolution, was lit on September 10, 1760 when Massachusetts Bay Superior Court Judge Stephen Sewall died. Sewall wasn't particularly important, but the debate and appointment that followed would tear asunder the colony and create the conditions that nurtured the revolution. Superior court judges were appointed by the colonial governor, and in September 1760 the Massachusetts governor was Francis Bernard, who had just arrived the previous month, having been promoted from New Jersey governor. Bernard, above all else, wanted his tenure to be "quiet and easy." He was born to a middle-class family in Berkshire, England in 1712, spent seven years at Oxford, and was called to the bar at the Middle Temple. He married a well-connected woman who birthed numerous children, nine of whom survived childhood. Bernard studied law, recited Shakespeare from memory, and designed buildings. Harvard Hall was designed by him, as was Bernardston, a town in northwest Massachusetts. Bernard also named the Berkshire Mountains after the county of his birth. Bernard was intelligent, but he was also a pompous dilettante. He fashioned himself a renaissance man, meaning he was widely knowledgeable, largely impractical and mostly blind to his faults. Bernard's two years in New Jersey were easy but not very profitable. Bernard hoped for an equally eventless but much more profitable tenure in Massachusetts; after all, he had nine children, a wife who expected to live well, and the self-image of the patrician-genius. A man of his status certainly required and deserved a well-paying position. In England, Bernard would have been a middling striver, precisely the type that the aristocrats would have belittled, or, perhaps worse, ignored. But in the colonies Bernard could be the aristocrat, and he expected others to treat him as such.

Bernard's primary objective in all decisions was the path of least resistance. He came to Massachusetts to make money and bless the people with his genius, his Oxford education, and his artistic talents. He would design grand buildings and towns for them and entertain the ruling class with wit and poetry, but he was not interested in provincial politics. His administration included Lieutenant Governor Thomas Hutchinson and Secretary Andrew Oliver.

Given the Otis's wealth, the Seven Years' War victory, and the general elation that swept through the British colonies in the fall of 1760, what would drive the Colonel's 35-year-old son to threaten to set the province on fire? James Otis, Jr., born in 1725 and usually called Jemmy, was a successful Harvard educated lawyer and member of the state legislature. His family had been building bridges in Massachusetts Province – political, social, economic – for 150 years, and Jemmy was threatening to burn them all. He was frighteningly serious, and perhaps more alarming, exceedingly capable. Even his enemies, such as oligarch Peter Oliver, labeled Jemmy a genius.

By the winter of 1760 this provincial bourgeoisie, one of the wealthiest and most intelligent men in the British colonies, had become fully radicalized. He threatened to set the province aflame though, he confessed, he would likely be consumed in the fire. That his words – a promise and a prophecy – came to full fruition and his predictions about the province and his own life were entirely accurate would be unbelievable if it didn't actually happen.

CHAPTER I

the time is which we have long foreseen

The town of Glastonbury lies about 130 miles west of London and is most famous for being "Avalon," the presumed burial ground of King Arthur and his wife, Guinevere; King Arthur is credited with helping unify and establish the country of England. The famous Glastonbury abbey developed into an Arthurian cult. On November 30, 1611, another much less famous man was buried in Glastonbury: Richard Otis, an independent weaver who died in the local alms house. His will, dated the day before, listed his possessions: some clothes, a weaver's frame board, a chest and a bed. No gold crown and no Excalibur. His few possessions were split among his sons John, Stephen, and Thomas and his two daughters. John was 30 years old when his father died and inherited some of the clothes. He'd been married for nine years and had four daughters. In 1621, his wife gave birth to a son, who they named John Otis, Jr., and the family moved 70 miles west to Barnstaple, a small fishing village almost at the southwestern tip of the island of Great Britain. In 1630 the Otises moved again, paying £30 to captain William Pierce to take the family 3100 miles west to Bare Cove, just south of Boston. John Otis was fifty years old.

Why the seven-member John Otis family would move from Glastonbury and then from Barnstaple is not readily apparent. They did not appear to be members of any radical or new religious organization; in fact, the southwest of England – the "West Country" – was known for being fairly secular and generally immune to religious extremes. They raised a May pole, which had been banned in most Puritan towns. People worked on Sunday, and drunkards could be found on the streets every day of the week. And despite Richard Otis's seeming destitution, the family would have been considered "middle-class." Richard Otis apparently succeeded as an independent weaver, and he and his sons were literate. Further, John Otis could afford the £30 fare to the new world; few of the truly poor could afford the trip to Massachusetts Bay.

While the Otises were making their way to the new world, many families from Hingham, in East Anglia, were also making their way there. Hingham is about 100 miles northeast of London and 300 miles northeast of Barnstaple; Hingham's distance from Barnstaple was in both geography and culture. Unlike the West Country, East Anglia was given to religious extremes, and by the second decade of the seventeenth century had essentially viewed itself as a separate religious community; many towns in East Anglia had culturally isolated themselves, and the religious and political tensions that would explode into a civil war a few decades later were festering in East Anglia by 1600. Preachers in East Anglia were routinely convicted of non-conformity, and congregations and rebel preachers often met secretly.

East Anglia was also economically different from the West Country; while they too had a good number of farmers, the East Anglians were known for their weaving and other textile production. When the Otis family landed at Bare Cove, they found many families from East Anglia. These families usually travelled with their preacher; they tended to be what would have been considered radical Puritans and believed in the strong rule of law and morality. In England, they weren't so much religiously oppressed as perpetually harassed. When in 1638 Hingham's radical preacher Robert Peck departed the old world with nearly 120 of his rebellious congregation, the local chancellor celebrated; Peck and his non-conformist friends had been trouble-makers. And yet by 1640 the town of Hingham had petitioned the House of Commons that "most of the able Inhabitants have forsaken their dwellings and have gone severall ways for their peace and quiet and the town is now left and like to be in misery by reason of the meanness of the [remaining] Inhabitants." In the previous six years, forty families had left Hingham, and the concentration of these families in Bare Cove was such that the name was changed to their town of origin. The gentry had not left Hingham, England and not a single family on the poor relief roll had left Hingham. Rather, the entire middle-class, if the term can be used, had left to find "peace and quiet."

Hingham, about 18 miles south of Boston, grew tremendously in the 1630s, but its population never exceeded 2,000. A few had left England because of persecution or economic problems, but the vast majority – particularly the earlier settlers – left because they had a general sense that they weren't free to live as they wished, to form their towns as they wished and build communities as they wished. Specific religious persecution didn't really affect the East Anglia communities until the mid-to-late 1630s and didn't affect the West Country settlers at all. And most were reasonably well-off middle-class farmers, merchants and tradesmen; they had to be in order to afford the fairly high price of passage. So what drove them from their homes in England to the shores of a wild bit of land so remote that it didn't appear on maps two centuries earlier? What drove their sense that the choices in their lives weren't fully their own?

What's so astonishing about Hingham isn't any particular fact about the small farming village on the edge of civilization in the 1630s, but rather that we have so many facts. We have letters, diaries, voting records, court records, legislation, land records, receipts, marriage and death records, and everything in between. A highly literate group of middle-class farmers and craftsmen were deliberately and methodically rebuilding civilization, and they were focused on their middle-class needs and interests. A society was being constructed to support the middling farmer and small merchant, not kings or noblemen or warlords who needed to support their armies and castles and bureaucracies. It was a fundamental reinvention of civilization.

So what would bring the Otis family to the new world? Since they were the 17th century equivalent of middle-class and secular, then no particular economic or religious pressures drove them from their homeland. And though their churches were often chastised for not having a book of sermons or the latest translation of the Bible, the West Country towns were generally left to themselves – at least more so than other parts of England. West Country people were typically farmers, more so than much of the rest of England which tended toward animal husbandry and weaving, and cheap land is vital for a successful farmer. Of course, while the new world offered cheap land, it also had a smaller market for produce. John Otis probably knew some of the families in the new world; he'd probably heard of their experiences and may have sent letters letting them know that he'd soon be joining them. There were many other West Country families in the Plymouth area, and the Otis family seemed to be incorporated quickly into the new world society. And yet, none of that explains why a middle-class, secular family would leave their country. One can only assume that John Otis wanted more – more freedom, more opportunity, and more for his family than England could offer. Despite all that, John Otis clearly retained some lingering fondness for the Old World; he named a hill on his property "Weary All," the same name of a similar hill that sits alongside The Roman Way in Glastonbury.

Incredibly, many of the West Country settlers and East Anglican zealots got along in the new world, perhaps because they both sought the same goal: a community in which no authority intervened between the people and their king and God. This was a community devoid of pestering bishops and taxes originating outside of their town. Their town and church, the king and God formed their entire governing structure. Everything else was minimized. The East Anglia Puritans focused on theological debates, and the West Country men focused on acquiring land.

It wasn't long before the greater Plymouth area started to become crowded. A Puritan group from London had settled in Scituate, just five miles from Hingham, but by 1639 Scituate had become "too straite for their accommodation" and in their "lorded plea" to the Plymouth Governor for authorization to establish a town in another part of the province, Reverend John Lothrop confessed that "many greviances attend mee, from which I would be freed." His "greviances" consisted primarily of one of those predictable theological disagreements that plagued New England settlements that would transform into political discord a century later. In Lothrop's case, he was trapped between strident immersionists and vociferous latitudinarians, a conflict that had previously divided his London congregation. Bickering over theological minutiae may seem provincial, but it was this fervor that once filtered through the interests of the growing merchant class evolved into the legal and political passion for which the ensuing New England generations would be known.

The Plymouth Court sympathized with Lothrop's problems and terminated a conditional grant of the Barnstable district previously made to a Dorchester faction; Lothrop's group was then given authorization to move to Cape Cod and establish a town between the nascent villages of Sandwich and Yarmouth. The new town was called Barnstable. In September 1639, the Lothrop community arrived on the Cape with the "presence of God in mercy." The small number of the Dorchester settlers who still held legal title to their land welcomed the newcomers and provided shelter and food. In December, the newcomers elected two of the original Dorchester settlers, Thomas Dimmock and the minister Joseph Hull, as representatives to the Plymouth Court, and the new town of Barnstable – complete with a restaurant – was launched. Under Lothrop, the Scituate families assimilated smoothly with the Dorchester group with the exception of Reverend Hull. Whether the Scituate minister was the better preacher or politician is not known, but in 1640 Reverend Hull was excommunicated and thereafter disappeared from Barnstable, leaving Lothrop's Scituate congregation in control. The dual refinement that had taken place by the Lothrop congregation, initially in London and then in Scituate, ensured that only compatible people would have persevered. Physical isolation sheltered Barnstable from the swiftly developing diversity of towns such as Boston, and so from this foundation, Barnstable evolved and expanded while preserving an unusual level of cohesiveness.

Despite being small and cohesive, a hierarchy soon developed in Barnstable. Like all feudal stratification, the determination of status and vehicle for advancement was land. Originally, the grants for "seating a congregation" were made to a small group of leaders of the proposed community on the condition that they would distribute land to "such persons as may be fitt to live together there in the feare of God" in such "equall & fitt portions as the several estates, ranks, & quallities of such persons shall require." Barnstable's land was purchased gradually from the Amer-Indians with the shrewd disbursement of axes, coats, and fencing. The original nine Dorchester families had laid out house around the inlet at the mouth of Rendezvous Creek and around Coggins Pond. The new group from Scituate arranged lots in the same general areas; families were granted six to twelve acres with the restriction "that no inhabitant shall make a sale of his house or any of his lands until he has offered the same to the proprietors; and, in case the plantation buy it not, then he shall provide a purchaser whom the town shall approve." Families were required to construct houses on their assigned lots in order to secure dwelling rights, and within a few months, there were thirty-eight families recognized under this scheme, twenty-three from Scituate and fifteen from various other towns.

In 1642, the town contemplated issuing more lots "by common consent" to private landowners from public lands, and the assessment for measuring how much each Barnstable family received was determined by a traditional feudal formula: one-third for each lot already owned, one-third for each voting town member, and one-third "according to estate." This method of distributing public land into private hands was traditional but clearly biased for original settlers and the wealthy. Chiefly internal population growth required additional distributions of common lands according to the traditional method. By the end of the century, the increasing number of people receiving tiny disbursements of lands would protest the traditional method, but until then, it seemed fair.

John Otis's wife died in 1653, and the 76-year-old widower married Elizabeth Streame in 1655; multiple marriages resulting from death or divorce were not uncommon. The marriage only lasted two years, as John Otis, the man who dared to leave the old world, died in 1657 at age 76 in Hingham, Plymouth Colony. His will listed £20 in small loans to various men in town, so while he hadn't participated in politics, he made sure everyone owed him favors. His eldest son, John Jr., was 36 years old. An economic depression gripped Plymouth Colony during the 1640's while the Puritans were in control of England, hence significantly diminishing Puritan immigration to New England and therefore limiting the demand for new land, food and farming supplies; but once the depression ended in the 1650s, John Otis Jr. began an expansion of the family businesses that would last decades. Using his father's land, capital lent by his in-laws, and money invested with him by neighbors, he began to widely invest in real estate. He had the obvious challenge of converting an ever increasing amount of his farming operations, and their management, to employees. He also had to build the network of contacts necessary for the distribution of the commodities his farms produced.

The year following his father's death, John Jr. purchased over a thousand acres of land outside of Hingham, in Scituate, perhaps purely for investment but it's probable that tax considerations influenced his decision. Though John Otis, Jr. avoided formal politics, he did not abjure from political battles. He refused to pay Hingham taxes in 1650, even rejecting the town constable's demand for payment. Three years later he still refused to pay town taxes and took his case to the Plymouth General Court; the Court offered to substantially lower Otis's taxes if he'd only concede before the Hingham congregation that the town could levy them. The issue doesn't again appear in the records, and it's assumed that Otis agreed to this settlement; it's also possible the town decided to let the matter die as John Otis, Jr. – both feisty and wealthy – made for a formable opponent. The core problems were the tax payments that supported the church and tax exemptions for some of the well-connected. John Otis, Jr. again fights the exemptions in 1655 and is eventually joined by a few others. The majority of the town's voters was not convinced by Otis's arguments, as notions of tradition and deference allowed the few who commanded the apex of the social mountain to use their position to tax others and exempt themselves. The tax dissenters again stormed the gates of tradition and deference in 1661, and were again rebuffed. John Otis, Jr. left Hingham in 1662 for Scituate, taking with a wife and a five-year-old son, John III. In 1662 he took the compulsory oath of fidelity to New Plymouth and served the first of numerous jury duty assignments. Jury duty was one of the responsibilities of a landowner, and John Jr. fulfilled his responsibilities as a freeman of the Old Colony, but he never engaged in politics beyond this most local level. Over the next few years, John, Jr. would substantially increase his real estate investments; in 1664, he acquired a considerable interest in the quasi-corporate land company Conihasset Partners, with holdings near Scituate, an interest in sixty acres of land in Scituate, and, most importantly, in fall 1667, he purchased the John Smith farm in Barnstable.

John Smith, an original settler and brother-in-law of the future Plymouth governor, sold his "dwellinghouse and lands both upland and meddow Lying in Barnstable on the west side of a place Commonly called the bridge" to John Otis, Jr. on October 25, 1667 for £150. It is curious that John Otis would purchase land in the somewhat closed, religious community of Barnstable, and perhaps it's odder that Barnstable would sell such a fairly substantial piece of land to someone who was clearly not actively religious. But Otis had lived in Hingham and knew how to get along with religious communities, and, most likely, no one in Barnstable could afford the £150 price for the land that Otis offered. It is safe to assume that Otis wanted the Barnstable land because it was substantial, and the Barnstable proprietors permitted the land to be sold to Otis because the price was substantial. In fact, with the purchase of the Smith farm, Otis's total real estate holdings were valued at over £1000, making him the wealthiest man in all of Plymouth Colony. Despite the continuing development and diversification of New England society, Barnstable was a traditional, stable community, and the extraordinary exception was the social, religious and political approval of the Otis family.

John Otis was acceptable to the Barnstable community as he was admitted as an inhabitant before the purchase of the Smith land was finalized. It is possible that he forced the issue because there was no Barnstable man willing or able to match the substantial £150 offer, but the use of such pressure is highly improbable considering his swift integration into the social and economic life of the town. John must have lived on his recently acquired Barnstable farm at least temporarily because in October 1668 he served on a Barnstable Coroner's jury that concluded that young Isaac Robinson had drowned after ensnaring himself in seaweed whilst chasing geese on a Barnstable pond. John Otis, Jr. remained as feisty in Scituate as he'd been in Hingham, producing and selling cider from his apple orchards without a license. He was fined for the infraction and doubtless was annoyed at the perpetual reach of the law. Concurrently, John Otis, Jr. was assembling a base of operations and business network in Barnstable by other means. His daughter Mary married John Gorum, Jr., the namesake younger son of perhaps Barnstable's most prominent citizen, in 1674. Captain Gorum was a tanner and owner of the Barnstable corn and flour mill, and when he wasn't managing his small businesses, he was an untiring citizen-soldier. Also, like Otis and the new generation of upwardly mobile small merchants, Gorum was aiming for heights greater than those of his Pilgrim father, Ralph Gorum. Captain Gorum was conducting business with John Otis in Scituate by 1669, the year that he purchased a shipment of bark from Otis and Increase Clapp for his tannery, which inevitably devolved into a law suit. And yet this problematic bark transaction did not produce much hostility as their children married a few years later. The integration of the Otis family into the Barnstable community was concluded in 1683 when John Otis III married Mercy Bacon of Barnstable; she was the daughter of Nathaniel Bacon, the patriarch of a family that would spend much of the next century battling with and against the Otises. The Bacons were one of the town's foremost families, though not as prosperous as the Gorums. John Otis, Jr. was a man of progressive merchant interests wedded to the feudal objective of real estate accumulation, but the marriages of his children so shortly after the Otis family's introduction into the Barnstable community exhibit an unusual degree of diplomacy and compatibility, and, simultaneously, expansive consideration for the Otis future. New Englanders did not practice arranged marriages as many Europeans did, but parental approval was an essential element that involved not only social and religious compatibility but also property considerations. Interestingly, John Otis, Jr. returned to Scituate and died there in January 1684 at a comparatively youthful 63 years old, but he must have regarded Barnstable as the foundation of future Otis operations. In his will dated January 11, 1684, John Otis, Jr. left an estate of about £1500, designating him the wealthiest man in Scituate and perhaps Barnstable. John Otis, Jr. set a pattern for the family that would be pursued for the next century: assimilate with the community, marry well, and leave as much wealth as possible to the children. The exception to the pattern would be the escalating participation in politics that eventually became the major preoccupation of the 18th century Otises; John Otis and John, Jr. both avoided politics as much as they had avoided religion.

Though John Jr. had taken care of the financial needs of his children, he was leaving them to an exceptionally unpredictable world. The early 1680s was a decisive period for the New England colonies. The war with the New England Amer-Indians, King Philip's War, had taken a grave toll in lives and property, and engendered broad social disruption at its peak in 1675-76. John Gorum gained fame from leading a company of Plymouth soldiers in a decisive battle against the Amer-Indians on December 19, 1675. Though the war was fairly localized, it was one of the bloodiest wars in the history of North America and was largely centered on Plymouth, which suffered a blinding Amer-Indian counter-attack in January 1677, leaving more than a dozen houses burned and dozens of residents killed. John Otis, Jr. served in the town militia in the summers of 1675 and 1676, at the age of 55, and he was elected Scituate constable, the top law officer in town, in 1677, possibly because of a lack of available men to fill the position. John Jr. spent much of his life in conflict with the law without much consideration for who made or enforced the law, so the irony of the man who drew the constant attention of constables for infractions ranging from refusing to pay taxes to producing cider without a permit ending his life as a constable was perhaps instructive to his children; it's easier to obey the law if you're also making or enforcing the law.

The colony government under the indecisive non-leadership of Governor Hinckley was faltering, and the treasured rights granted by the colony's charter were to be challenged under the regime of Governor Andros. After suffering years of perpetual and somewhat aggressive insubordination, particularly in the lax enforcement of tariff and navigation acts, Charles II revoked Massachusetts's charter in 1684. Massachusetts's charter had been particularly advantageous to the colony because it bestowed an unusually significant degree of local control, which resulted in an unusually significant degree of laissez-faire government. Edmund Andros, the governor of the newly-minted Dominion of New England that eventually extended from Maine to New Jersey, was openly antagonistic to the colonists. He reinstated Christmas, which had been banned since 1659, and permitted Saturday night parties. He brazenly affiliated with the Church of England, permitted town governments to meet only once per year, enforced the Navigation Acts and limited legislative activity. Andros believed that the "Dominion" of the various colonies nullified their individual charters and by 1687 set out to visit each colony to physically seize its charter. Connecticut had a fairly laissez-faire charter that they wished to keep, so when Andros appeared in Hartford in October 1687, he was handed a forgery. With the real charter in their hands, the leaders of Hartford surely laughed at Andros and prayed for his downfall, which would come just 17 months later in April 1689. Andros's friend and benefactor the Catholic King James II was overthrown, the colonists violently rioted, and Andros attempted to sneak out of Boston dressed as a woman. According to legend, he would have succeeded if it weren't for his big feet. To this day, the state of Connecticut does not recognize Andros as ever having been governor as the state never surrendered its actual charter. And the Otises kept their distance from the affair; there is no record of the family being involved in the Andros episode in any regard. It's noteworthy that despite Andros's hostile attitude toward the colonies and complete disregard for whatever rights and privileges colonists may have had, the inescapable feudal notion of deference kept the oppressed from engaging in widespread armed rebellion.

The Glorious Revolution of 1688 in which the Catholic James was ousted by a united Parliament would reverberate powerfully in Massachusetts Province almost a century later. Parliament declared itself the final and absolute authority in the kingdom and could not be suspended or circumvented by the king. And while the king kept the navy – the "royal" navy – Parliament got the army, henceforth known as the "British Army" and not the "Royal Army." Though the regime of King James II was chased out of Massachusetts in a dress, the descendant of a Glastonbury weaver would challenge with devastating consequences whether Parliament really had absolute authority.

birth of the middle-class

As of 1689, Plymouth was an economic hinterland, with a tax base insufficient to support normal governmental operations and certainly inadequate to cover the continuous expense of securing the area from Amer-Indian attack. Plymouth's war debts were crushing, and estate taxes hit 17.5% in 1690. Barnstable, more remote than Plymouth, had escaped significant damage from the Amer-Indian war, but six of its men died in the war. Additionally, many leaders from the older generation such as Captain Gorum, John Huckins, Samuel Annable, Henry Cobb, and Thomas Huckins were buried. In 1678

Barnstable's minister, Thomas Walley, died and would not be replaced for five years. Barnstable was also experiencing a population explosion; between 1653 and 1690 the population grew from about 2,500 to about 10,000. It's no mystery why Barnstable's population exploded. Jobs were plentiful, and poverty was low, at about 7%. Land was owned by a wider demographic than in most of New England (and the world, for that matter). In Boston in 1689, the wealthiest 15% of the population owned 58% of the land. But in Barnstable, the top 15% owned only about 35% of the land. So while there was economic stratification in Barnstable, it was certainly less severe than in most other places. But a booming population in times of economic and social stress only exacerbates the problems; militia levies, increasingly onerous taxes, the inability to employ a full-time minister, and the general incompetence of the local government generated cause for concern south of Boston. The population explosion kept land prices high, but it also meant that the Barnstable community was certainly no longer a closed, insular operation. By 1698, Barnstable could not afford to maintain a permanent school teacher and crime and prostitution were on the rise.

Shortly after John III's marriage in 1683, Barnstable town hired Jonathan Russell, who with his son, Jonathan, Jr., were to command ecclesiastical affairs in Barnstable for nearly seven decades. Despite his ineptitude, Governor Hinckley acknowledged that Plymouth needed restructuring, and the colony was subsequently divided into three counties, with Barnstable as the principal town of the newly created Barnstable County, which encompassed all of Cape Cod. The principal town would be the seat of all government and judicial matters for the county. The town also planned a new main road; the old road had followed the Indian paths and stayed to the high grounds. The new road would run closer to the water and required a series of bridges. The new road made Barnstable more accessible and was near the large Otis farm. A new corn and flour mill was constructed in 1687, which perhaps was the first of the enormous windmills erected on Cape Cod. And Otis joined a small group of investors to obtain ten acres on the south side of the Cape to build a wool-cleaning mill.

Following the Andros upheaval, John Otis broke loose from the Otis paradigm of avoiding politics. Perhaps his wife, Mary, was the catalyst; she heralded from a family long engrossed in colonial politics. Her father, Nathaniel Bacon, had been a Barnstable deputy to the Plymouth Court for many years and had served as a court councilor for sixteen years. Otis may have concluded that as the area's wealthiest man he needed to ensure that his interests were being cultivated. After all, the recently departed Andros treated land deeds and contracts rather cavalierly, and a man with significant real estate holdings would likely want to be certain that no government again threatened the sanctity of such deeds and contracts. And John Otis may have concluded that merchant success required expanding his operations outside of bucolic Barnstable and into the larger cities, primarily Boston, which was now recognized as the undisputed political and commercial heart of New England. This conclusion was to be expected once the new 1691 charter joined Plymouth Colony to the Province of Massachusetts Bay. The spokes of the colonial economy inevitably realigned to the new axis indicated by the lines of governmental authority, and Barnstable was now entitled to representation in the General Court in Boston.

Whatever the source of Otis's new interest in government, he and his brother-in-law, John Gorum Jr., accepted the vote of the town of Barnstable as representatives to the first General Court of the Province of Massachusetts Bay in 1692. This was the first time an Otis was elected to major office and the beginning of four generations of Otis rule in Barnstable politics. The first session of the new Massachusetts House of Representatives produced a resolve claiming that the "house may use and exercise such Powers and Privileges here as the house of commons in England may and have usually done there allways having Respect to their Majesties Roy[al] charter ..." This new legislative body immediately staked claim to a position equivalent to the House of Commons and only subject to the King and charter. Parliament, of course, would reject the claim, but the issue was far from settled.

Governance in Massachusetts Province was broadly divided between the House of Representatives, the Governor's Council, and the Governor. The Governor was appointed from England. The Governor's primary power was his ability to appoint province officials, such as judges and sheriffs. Those who were connected to the Governor often would accumulate multiple lucrative appointments. The Governor could also call the House into session and suspend it at will. Confusing the Governor's control was the customs officials and the admiralty courts; while the divisions of power were not always consistent, provincial customs was typically controlled by a customs official appointed from London and whose authority was wholly separate from the Governor. And the admiralty courts, which by the late 1740s operated out of Halifax,

Nova Scotia but had jurisdiction over New England, were similarly outside of the Governor's purview.

Every town was permitted to elect representatives to the House, with Boston electing the most at four; these four Boston representatives would be known as the "Boston bench." While other towns could elect a representative or two, no town was required to send a representative, and every year a few dozen towns would send no representatives. Towns would decline to elect representatives for one reason: the town had to pay for all the representative's expenses. The House of Representatives would debate and pass legislation, write expenses bills, and pay the province officials. The House could withhold legislation, including spending bills, and could withhold or change the pay of provincial officials, such as judges. The House members were elected for one-year terms, and each year's election was typically held in May, at which point the newly elected members would vote for a Speaker who would generally manage House activities. The Governor could refuse to seat the Speaker, and, assuming he didn't need any money, could refuse to convene a session of the House altogether.

The Governor's Council was somewhat akin to a Senate; it was the smaller, more privileged upper house that typically advised the Governor. It served the useful function of making decisions on controversial matters for which the Governor alone did not want responsibility. The Council members were chosen by a vote of the House members and the outgoing Council members. If one was well-liked and had the support of the Governor, an election to the Council was often for life. The House would typically have over 100 members whereas the Council would have 28 at most. The Governor could refuse to seat a Councilor, though if the Governor were generally competent, he would be on good terms with the Council. As there were so few Councilors and most held multiple offices, the Governor's Council typically represented the most important 28 people in the province. The Council was often viewed as the governor's allies whose goal was to support Whitehall's agenda in a temperate and conservative manner. The Representatives and Councilors together were referred to as the "General Court." Though obviously they did not operate as a court in the modern sense, the General Court did hear appeals of court cases and a handful of other important judicial matters.

The route up the political ladder was fairly predetermined. First, it was an unspoken requirement that you were successful in private business; colonists did not often elect men who hadn't previously been successful landowners, shippers or merchants. In most towns, only a few families therefore qualified to hold public office. Those who aspired to political office would first attend town meetings so that their neighbors could hear their views. Attendance at town meetings was essential to building a base of constituents. Aspiring politicians would join town meeting committees that would address small town issues such as road designation, fence repair, and minor legal issues. The next step would be to get elected hogreeve, the official who keeps track of town hogs (and occasionally other town animals). Hogreeve was a lowly position, but it was the first step on the political ladder. Next would be warden, surveyor, and finally town meeting selectman, with the "first selectman" essentially acting as mayor. While climbing this ladder, one could also become a justice of the peace or an officer in the local militia. It was common for the particularly enthusiastic to hold several positions at the same time. After a period of proving oneself on the local level one could get appointed by the Governor to the lucrative positions such as sheriff, registrar of deeds, or judge of probate. These positions were valued at perhaps as much as £500 per year by the 1740s. One could also get elected to the province-wide legislature in Boston as a representative, and eventually, to the Governor's Council. One may also pick up more prestigious appointments such as judgeships, the most coveted of which was a seat on the province's supreme court. Of course, none of these offices required one to forgo one's daily business, and undoubtedly most of these offices significantly furthered one's opportunities, whether as a lawyer, merchant, shipper or landowner. It wasn't unusual for a judge to be a practicing lawyer, and for that judge to also be a sheriff and a councilmember.

Governor Hinckley had followed these very steps in his rise to power; though born in England, he emigrated to Scituate at the age of 17 and at 21 moved to Barnstable, where he would remain until he died in 1706. He was a deputy, representative, magistrate, court assistant, deputy governor, commissioner, councilor and governor. He was a paradigmatic colonial politician under the charter. But now governors were appointed from London, and political dynamics changed considerably; the recently minted Dominion of New England was converted in the separate colonies, with Massachusetts officially the "Royal Colony of Massachusetts." Concurrently, the perpetual skirmishes between the British and the French continued, as both battled for control of the world's seas. Piracy was rampant, particularly off North America's east coast and in the Caribbean, and to address that problem, authorities enlisted privateers, essentially private pirates legitimized by a government. Scottish born

New Yorker William "Captain" Kidd was one such privateer. Corrupt New York governor Fletcher, who was known to accept bribes from pirates among other indiscretions, was replaced by the Queen's Treasurer, Richard Coote, 1st Earl of Bellomont, and the new governor enlisted the aid of Captain Kidd to secure the coasts of New York and New England, of which Bellomont was also governor. Kidd sailed to England to receive a letter of marque from King William III, thus legitimizing his piracy – at least to the British. Sailing down the Thames in his huge, new ship, Kidd passed a Royal Navy ship and declined to salute, as the custom of deference required. The Navy ship fired a cannon at Kidd's ship, and Kidd's crew responded by saluting the Royal Navy with their derrières. Kidd then sailed for New York and supplemented his crew with a variety of New York thugs. Bellomont was an investor in Kidd's privateer enterprises, and when Kidd was implicated in piracy and landed in Boston to obtain legal aid from Bellomont, the governor had him arrested. Kidd was hanged in London and Bellomont lasted all of two years as Massachusetts governor. Life in the colonies was indeed chaotic.

John III served several terms as Plymouth's representative and in 1703 was elected to the prestigious Governor's Council, a position he held until his death in 1727. He was also a justice of the Court of Common Pleas for Barnstable County as of 1702, judge of probate as of 1714, and, if that wasn't enough, county treasurer, Barnstable town clerk, justice of the peace for the Mashpee Indians, and, with Gorum, co-commander of the Barnstable militia. So much like his father, John III was also often in court, but as judge rather than defendant. John also twice served on the extraordinary "oyer and terminer" courts that adjudicated the most serious matters, including piracy, murder, and witchcraft. It was oyer and terminer justice Increase Mather who concluded that "It were better that ten suspected Witches should escape, than that one innocent Person should be condemned." John Otis would later serve on a joint committee of the General Court to determine restitution for the victims of the witchcraft trials.

The evolution of John Otis and John Gorum as dominant forces in local governance is indicative of this seminal stage in the development of a political consciousness within the colonial merchant class. Otis and Gorum were characteristic of a new generation who operated in a transitional era between a seventeenth century wherein small businessmen were neither much respected nor particularly included in the political calculus to an eighteenth century wherein such men would increasingly wrest power from the feudal class. Another man indicative of the new generation of leaders was Reverend Jonathan Russell. While the same generation as Otis and Gorum, Russell was educated at Harvard. When Russell began his ministry in 1683, there were only seventy communicants, or full church members. Whether Russell's move to require that both parents be members of the church in full communion before their children could be baptized was purely driven by conviction cannot be known, but it was certainly far more orthodox than John Lothrop's liberal views of church membership. Russell's requirement was likely the catalyst for John Otis to enter into full communion in 1693 and resulted in a church membership that nearly doubled in ten years.

Otis, Gorum, and Russell embodied the attitudes of the new generation best characterized as energetic, prudent builders − of businesses, of churches, of government. This new generation began with the uncertainty of the 1670s and 1680s but found firmer footing in the Glorious Revolution and the new charter government of Massachusetts that was so vital to the optimism needed for builders to invest in the future. Otis's primary preoccupation was land, which is apparent in his involvement in town affairs between 1696 and 1703 when the final divisions of common lands were made: his name appears repeatedly as committee member, surveyor, arbitrator and grantee in Barnstable Town Records. Yet he was also constantly expanding his trading business beyond Cape Cod. Like Otis, Gorum also maintained his base of operations in Barnstable, but he appreciated the adventurous life of a soldier and was one of the early enthusiasts of amphibious warfare as commander of the whaleboat force in Maine in one of the interminable skirmishes with France. Gorum's Maine experiences caused him to start land speculating "to the eastward."

John III began with the Barnstable farm and then constructed the woolen cloth making mill in 1689 as the first of his manufacturing enterprises. He secured the approval of the town in 1696 to build a 1600 sq. ft warehouse near the center of Barnstable village at the mouth of Rendezvous Creek and not far from John Gorum's wharf. The warehouse and the wharf would be the heart of Barnstable's maritime ventures and fundamental to Otis's commercial enterprises, as both Barnstable and the Otis family rose with the rising tide of New England merchants. The term "New England merchant" covered a gamut of colonial society, starting with Boston dandies such as Charles Lidget and Samuel Shrimpton who wore powdered wigs, rode in horse-drawn coaches, and enjoyed economic and social symbiotic relationships with the oligarchs of London. Below the powdered wig princes of Boston were men such as Samuel

Sewall and Wait Winthrop, who had deep Massachusetts connections, but likewise earned their living from the London-Boston trade. Though he might conduct regular business in Boston and have a seat on the Governor's Council, John Otis III was still a country trader whose economic and social life was a world away from the powdered wig princes. It is possible that a man of Otis's ambition and abilities could have achieved the success of a Sewall or Winthrop, and his reasons for not making the attempt likely reveal the difference between the attitudes of Boston and Barnstable. John Otis choose to grow his business far removed from London and even Boston, thus distancing himself from direct contact with England, the source of great merchant prosperity. Barnstable's harbor was shallow, was mined with shifting sand bars, and certainly had no future as one of the world's great ports. Thirty ton sloops entered the harbor with trepidation, and ship captains much preferred to dock in Boston or even Plymouth. In consequence, John Otis's business typically focused on shipping modest quantities of pork, beef, fish, grain, wool, whale oil, leather, and other local products to Boston and returning with textiles, hardware, and imported manufactured goods to be either sold directly to customers on the Cape or distributed to country traders.

Profiting in this environment was likely more thorny than it had been thirty years earlier when competition was less relentless. By 1700, profitability required the cunning and nimble trading for which Yankees were to become famous – spices, tea, a bit of smuggling, and, above all, the ability to stay liquid by demanding quick payment from customers and delivering slow payment to suppliers. John Otis III mastered this business model. Shortages of currency and the declining availability of credit (one often triggered the other) was likely the source of more business failures than any other cause, and this lethal combination was in full effect at the beginning of the 18th century. The persistent scarcity of currency and the informal and slow judicial machinery together shaped a credit structure that favored the attentive and clever. County court records are crowded with law suits for unpaid invoices and requests for execution judgments, so despite its faults, the lumbering, archaic legal system provided an essential component to the expanding class of small businessmen. The courts compensated for a lack of currency and credit, and until the ladder problems were addressed, the former would remain indispensible. The debtor who could outmaneuver the creditor in the courts while quickly collecting outstanding invoices could achieve substantial liquidity. Of course, Barnstable, still on the edge of civilization, had no banks to extend credit lines to businesses, so this confection of business acuity and legal maneuvers – it probably can't be labeled a credit structure – provided the necessary capital and begat a component indispensable to the development of colonial merchant enterprise and political thought: the country lawyer. At the time, Plymouth colony did not have a single lawyer with formal legal training, so John Otis, like many of his fellow merchants, became a self-taught country lawyer out of necessity: first to file and argue his own collection suits and defend against similarly impatient creditors, then serving as attorney for other merchants who hadn't the time, ability or presence to handle their own cases. John Otis's legal work was always tangential to his merchant activities, but it coalesced with and informed his efforts as legislator, justice of the peace, and justice of the Court of Common Pleas and fulfills the image of a merchant renaissance man. Each vocation – merchant, farmer, politician, lawyer-judge, and militia officer – buttressed the others and confirmed his function as a principal force in the evolving southern Massachusetts economy. By committing himself to politics, he had broken the pattern established by his forebears, but he was unwilling or unable to make the decisive choice that would have been compulsory to achieve the life of a powdered wig prince: relocating to Boston. Everything known about John Otis indicates his great ambition, and it's unknown whether provincialism or discomfort with the Boston-London connection kept him in Barnstable.

The Otis family grew by four sons and two daughters between 1685 and 1702. His eldest son, John IV, was born in 1687 and his youngest son, James, was born in 1702. The eldest, Mary, married her cousin Isaac Little, who would be appointed to the Governor's Council in 1743. The other daughter, Mercy, married Jonathan Russell, son of the town's preacher and who would inherit his father's prominent position. For a man of John III's prominence, it was expected that one or more of his sons obtain that passport to prominence: a degree from Harvard College. John IV and a younger brother, Solomon, took their degrees at Harvard and were the evident choices to assume their father's influential role on Cape Cod. The heir to the Old Colony's greatest fortune married Grace Hayman, a very wealthy daughter of a Rhode Island merchant who was supplemented with a £2,000 marriage "settlement." John IV became both a lawyer and a doctor, but he apparently performed at less than the highest level in either profession. In the 1720s he practiced law in Barnstable, where his father was chief justice. The Superior Court named him King's attorney for a term in the absence of the attorney general, and he was appropriately appointed justice of the peace for Barnstable County in 1739 at age 52. The following year John IV became embroiled in the Land Bank that would be a recurring pock on the body politic for over a decade. He was elected to the Governors Council by the pro-Land Bank General Court in 1741, but Governor Belcher refused to seat Otis and a dozen other "pro Bank" men. The failure of the Land Bank, consequent successes in Louisburg, and the arrival of Governor Shirley combined to make John IV an acceptable Council member and he was elected again in 1747, completely bypassing the customary years of service in lower positions. He remained a councilor until his death in 1758 at age 71. Notwithstanding his position on the Council and his other offices, including justice of Common Pleas and judge of probate, John's life suggests that of an aristocratic dabbler; compared to his younger brother James, John seemed to drift through life relying on the cachet of being the eldest son of the county's wealthiest man and a Harvard graduate.

His brother and fellow Harvard graduate Solomon likewise was successful only to the degree that he could parlay his family's assets into pursuits that interested him. While he remained on good terms with his family throughout his life, Solomon certainly strained every connection he had. Solomon freely traded on the Otis name, opening lines of credit that he almost certainly couldn't pay. His young nephew, Samuel Allyne, was bemoaning his uncle's profligate ways as late as 1766, knowing that all Otis's had to honor a debt created by Solomon. Solomon's older brother John routinely invested in his dubious ventures and honored his debts, including one venture costing the enormous sum of £500. Unlike his father, Solomon was better at losing money than making it.

John III's youngest son, James, married a woman from Wethersfield, Connecticut; in the early 18th century, it would seem a bit odd to search so far from home for a bride, but the choice was based on family connections. Joseph Allyne, a descendant of one of Barnstable's founders, moved from the family farm a mile east of the Otis home to Plymouth and married Mary Dotey, a descendant of one of the Mayflower Compact's signers. While in Plymouth, Mary gave birth to two daughters, Elizabeth in 1700 and Mary two years later, but by 1705, when their third daughter was born, they had moved on to Wethersfield. And yet the Allynes were more than neighbors of the Otises; Joseph Allyne's older brother, Thomas, had married Elizabeth Otis, John III's sister, so James's far ranging search for a wife was no search at all. On May 14, 1724, twenty-two year old James Otis married twenty-two year old Mary Allyne before Elisha Williams, Connecticut legislator and Wethersfield tutor of the Yale students and soon to become rector of Yale at New Haven.

While James wasn't sent to Harvard as his older brothers were, evidence suggests he was his father's favorite, most likely because as James matured it became apparent he was quite like his father. Unlike his older brothers, James had the drive, intelligence, social skills and organizational ability to increase the merchant and political empire his family had been building for three generations. As his father's favorite, James was thus a favorable match for the Allynes. Joseph Allyne would inherit part of his father's Barnstable estate, but how much fell into Mary's possession is unknown. James would be heir to all of the Otis's Barnstable properties and businesses. The Great Marshes neighborhood, to which the bride and groom returned, had slowly become West Barnstable. In 1700 Governor Bellomont had mandated that the town militia be divided into two companies, with Captain Gorum leading the "first foot Company," and Captain John Otis the "second foot Company in said Town," the latter being the men of West Barnstable.

A similar separation divided the Barnstable church. Minister Jonathan Russell died in 1711, and at the subsequent town meeting John Otis, now a colonel, submitted the controversial proposal that the congregation be divided into two. Substantial disagreement ensued that may have involved the competency of Jonathan Russell, Jr., particularly as successor to his very accomplished father. The issue was eventually decided according to John Otis's proposal, and two new meetinghouses were constructed, the East Parish in 1716 and the West Parish in 1717. When the West Parish was completed, young Minister Russell chose to remain with the Otis family in the West Parish. Six years later his parishioners erected a steeple on their meetinghouse and crowned it with a gilded weathervane imported from England.

West Barnstable prospered in its new independent status. The neighborhood along the new county road was inhabited by the Otises, the Hinckleys, the Crockers, the Bacons, the Allynes, and the Howlands. Their homes were bordered by smaller houses, and on the outskirts at Scorton Creek, north of the Otis farm and near Cape Cod Bay, stood the huts of local Indians who had shunned the Mashpee reservation to work as servants and field hands. The Court House, taverns, wharves, warehouses, and most businesses were all to the east in the main town of Barnstable. West Barnstable then appeared to be a very isolated world, but it could not evade the English ideas of political deference and social status and the Puritan idea of hard work, and such ideas were all apparent in most of the Otises. The achievements and subsequent influence of this family were supported by the Englishman's focus on land ownership synthesized with the talent to succeed in an expansive range of economic pursuits. The merchant renaissance qualities of the Otis family's leaders seemed to have been perfectly designed to bridge the chasm from the early period when the son of a middling Glastonbury weaver stepped ashore, initially focusing on subsistence and survival, and the turbulent early eighteenth century when those who succeeded were clever, persistent generalists.

And yet the most significant evidence that the sands of history were quickly shifting is that we know so much about a small group of middling farmers eking out an existence at the edge of the civilized world. The families of Plymouth and Barnstable in the 17th century were highly literate, concerned with recording their transactions and ideas, wanted to implement a system of law and order, and boldly determined to create a fully functioning economy out of nothing. For the first time in the West, the driving force behind historical events was small farmers and tradesmen, not lords and clerics.

CHAPTER II

storms & tempests are consequent

When John Otis III died in 1727, he had accomplished exactly what his father before him had: tripling the value of the family's assets. He was one of the three wealthiest men in the county, owned three slaves that were listed with the "swine" in his estate inventory, was a member of the Governor's council, and had a real estate, merchant and shipping business that dominated lower Massachusetts. His sons were militia captains, registers of probate and deeds, and town clerks. And the minister who attended to his funeral was his son-in-law. Only the beloved youngest, James, seemed to be staying out of public office and public affairs.

James's wife, Mary Allyne, bore 13 children, only seven of whom survived infancy. This was the lowest survival rate of any Otis family since they arrived to the New World. The first was born on February 5, 1725 and was named after his father, James Otis, Jr. He grew up in the Otis family estate on the Great Marshes of Barnstable surrounded by relatives, indentured servants, farm hands, and slaves. He was an only child for barely a year when Joseph was born on March 6, 1726. His sister Mercy joined the boys two years later. In 1730, sister Mary was born, and in 1732 Hannah arrived. The next three children, Nathan, Martha and Abigail, all died in infancy. Elizabeth joined the group in 1739 and Samuel Allyne in 1740 – Samuel almost always included his mother's maiden name in his own. Sarah, born in 1742, did not live to see her first birthday and neither did another Nathan, born in 1743. When a final child was born in 1744, a girl, mother Mary refused to name her. The unnamed child soon died.

While James Jr., Mercy, Joseph and Samuel Allyne would become prominent members of the Barnstable clan, the lives of the children of Mary Allyne and James Otis would take every conceivable turn over the ensuing three decades. One would be the local brute, one the spinster, one the famous historian, one the urban playboy, one the insane revolutionary, and one the traitor. This family would perhaps have greater influence over revolutionary politics than any other family, and yet when the smoke cleared, they would have all but destroyed the mercantile empire started five generations earlier by the son of a Glastonbury weaver.

James Jr. was typically called "Jemmy," which was a nickname used not only in Barnstable but also during his years in Boston as an adult. Jemmy's childhood was probably spent catching alewives and trout in nearby Bridge Creek, helping the hired hands – perhaps local Indians – pick apples in the family's orchards to be fermented into cider, and shooting the innumerable ducks that populated the Great Marshes that abutted the family's West Barnstable farm. The Otis boys probably made more than one trip to Sandy Neck to watch the whalers painstakingly strip the sheets of blubber from the whale carcasses and witness the great iron kettles over blubber fed fires. It was a horrifically malodorous process, but the smell was one of prosperity, and the whale boats that were perfected on the Cape were to provide Jemmy's father with a valuable avenue to enter province affairs as well as cradles for a breed of mariner – the Capeman – who would become legendary a few decades later. And perhaps he caught a ride with his father on the family horse to Barnstable village to see the wharf, Otis's warehouse, or visit the Court House.

Jemmy was too young to appreciate the most significant event of his childhood: the death of his grandfather, John III, in November 1727. James Otis, Sr., though a young twenty-five, abruptly found himself in charge of the sprawling Barnstable businesses. While James held junior status in the family as the third son, his father had willed him his silver headed cane, a symbol of family authority. But this was no surprise to his older brothers; when the patriarch had made out his will three years earlier, he had made the executors his wife and his third son. It was clear to everyone who John III had expected to be most successful. Jemmy's life would be deeply influenced by the gifts and expectations bestowed upon his father by his grandfather.

John III had made sizeable gifts and loans to some of his children, but even with these deductions his estate was valued at almost £5000. The assessment was made in the spring of 1728 and recorded a business inventory of £60 and "Disperate" debts of about £1000, which are not numbers that appear to correlate to a vigorous business. The business was successful and continued to be so; the Otises had managed to nearly sell their warehouse bare by the end of the winter, much on credit, so the payments due that spring were considerable. At the same time the Massachusetts economy was depressed by currency devaluation; deteriorating currency values and cyclical currency instability was a permanent feature of business in Massachusetts colony and produced the vacillating values of all businesses. In 1727, James Otis was a mere 25-years-old, the head of a growing family, and the supervisor of a trading business and a large, diverse farming operation. Though his business was complex, James Otis remained a simple country trader by Boston standards. Moreover, he was expected to assume his father's position as a community leader. These were great expectations, and the fact that James Otis thrived amid such expectations reveals much about his determination and talents.

The Barnstable town meeting in the spring of 1724 had selected 22-year-old James Otis as its juror to serve at the Plymouth term of the Superior Court; it was a small honor but an honor nonetheless as petit jurors typically served on a series of juries during the Court's local term. After this introduction, civic responsibilities increased rapidly, and community affairs gave James Otis little respite. Just before his father died, James was selected by the town to join a committee to prevent "Indians, Negroes, and other disorderly persons" from frequenting taverns at night. The following year, James was selected to be a town surveyor and was asked to join a committee to "draw up something" about controlling stray animals on Sandy Neck, the large beach area that stretched between the marshes and Cape Cod Bay. In 1732, James Otis's escalating civic stature became evident when a small emergency erupted in the Barnstable school. On August 15th, James Otis was moderator of the town meeting for the first time; it was almost certainly not by accident that the foremost issue on the agenda was the town school because young Jemmy Otis had just reached the age when New England boys began some kind of formal education. The town was "Destitute of a School by Reason Mr. Bennet (with whom the Agents say they agreed) Neglects to keep School." The meeting appointed Otis chairman of a committee of sixteen to find a solution for their indolent teacher, and allotted £65 to pay for that solution – a considerable increase over the prior year's education budget.

While the Massachusetts Bay General Court had become concerned with education at an early date, a long tradition of inattention and neglect festered in the area south of Boston. As early as 1647, the Court ordered all the towns to employ teachers and additionally required the larger towns to establish "grammar schools" with masters capable of delivering an education that would produce applicants capable for admission to Harvard. The Court's order had been embraced with apathy in Plymouth Colony, which was conspicuously unpopulated with the college educated. It was 1658 before education was even mentioned officially in Plymouth colony, and then the Court merely announced that the towns "ought to take into their serious consideration" the problem of educating their young; it was a typical charter-era laissez-faire exercise of central authority – more suggestion than admonition and more admonition than regulation. Various tepid measures were attempted, such as the earmarking of the uncertain revenues from the Cape fishery, which amounted to nothing more than paying for education with nature's lottery; but eventually it was the incorporation of Plymouth into the Province of Massachusetts Bay and the concern of such men as James Otis that gave momentum to education funding and reform. Barnstable organized a common school to teach reading, writing, and some math at an unknown date. Any possible beneficial consequence from this modest beginning was frustrated when objections from residents on the south shore necessitated a division of the already fractional school year between north and south in 1714. New England towns such as Barnstable developed the archetype of the modern school board when they found it impractical to govern the day to day problems of the school in the town meeting. Matters of "settling" a teacher and arranging for school sessions in private homes was delegated to "Agents" and committees such as the one headed by James Otis.

By 1732, Jemmy's father was likely growing increasingly aware of his own academic limitations – he was the son who didn't attend Harvard – and thus began to insist on the best possible education for his first born. Not surprisingly, the Otis committee created a "grammar school" to supplement the problematic common school that had been theretofore Barnstable's educational system. The committee devised a complex schedule with the unreliable Mr. Bennet for rotating grammar school sessions in four locations, one of which was the John Howland home close to the Otis farm. The grammar school curriculum began with two years of "common" – meaning English – reading and writing, and then the students were immersed in Latin, and later Greek. By about the age of ten, the boys began Latin regardless of whether they were equipped to study the new language; it was an unsympathetic pedagogy but the survivors secured an education that would possibly satisfy the rigid entrance requirements of Harvard. The two or three month sessions at the traveling grammar school were hardly enough to give a student a depth of familiarity with Cicero, Virgil, Isocrates, and Homer, but fortunately Jemmy could call on his uncle, Jonathan Russell, Jr. to fill the gaps left by Mr. Bennet. Russell tutored Jemmy for college and by the summer of 1739 considered his 14-year-old student ready to undergo the rather grueling Harvard admissions process.

On June 21, 1739 the *Boston Weekly News-Letter* announced that the President and Tutors would "attend the Business of Examination" for those who desired admission to Harvard during a two day period in July. Of all the boys who began grammar school with Jemmy seven years earlier, only four students – John Crocker, William Bourne, Lothrop Russell, and Jemmy Otis – considered themselves college bound. Before the advent of packet boats, the trip from Barnstable to Boston was a two day ride on horseback, with an overnight stop in Plymouth town. It is likely that the anxious Cape Cod applicants made the expedition with their fathers. It is also probable that this was the first time these boys had been exposed to the bustling activity and powdered wig princes of the provincial metropolis, Boston.

The actual examination must have been an overwhelming affair for a country boy from Barnstable. The applicants presented themselves before President Edward "Guts" Holyoke and the four tutors. After something of an interview, the applicant would be thoroughly examined in reading and writing Latin and Greek – Virgil, Tully, the New Testament, the rules of prose and Greek noun and verb declinations. It was a remarkably comprehensive exam. Those who passed then acquired a copy of the College Laws that the president and tutors signed as evidence of admission. Then the newly admitted students's fathers paid five pounds to the steward and furnished a bond for an additional forty pounds against future bills for food, sweepers, and the glazier. In September 1739, Jemmy Otis, fourteen and a half years old, set out for Cambridge to begin a new life. He registered at the Buttery in Old Harvard Hall where the seemingly omnipotent steward held forth as registrar, dormitory officer, and man in charge of nearly everything nonacademic. Old Harvard, which stood on the site of the present Harvard Hall, contained not only the Buttery, but also the kitchen, library, a public hall, and rooms for two tutors and a dozen students.

At the same time that Jemmy was consumed with the Harvard application process, the entire province was consumed with the Land Bank scheme in which his uncle John had been involved. The Massachusetts Land Bank threatened the tear the province asunder, almost brought armed insurrection to Boston, and polarized New England to such a degree that it would be largely responsible for drawing the battle lines in the 1760s.

Up until the late 1730s, the province could issue paper money without approval of the Board of Trade in England provided that the money was issued to pay for government expenses. Such money was more equivalent to modern government bonds than to modern paper money. And just like modern government bonds, these colonial bills had expiration dates, at which point they were to be redeemed and their value cancelled, thereby paving the way for their replacement with new bills. But the colonial government had fallen into the habit of not redeeming the old bills and simply printing more. These bills could be bought from the government and then used to purchase anything in the province. Of course, the seller may refuse to accept colonial bills for payment, but hard currency – silver and gold – was fairly rare. Since a quickly growing and fluid economy requires a significant and growing money supply, the continual printing and lack of redemption of the bills provided this needed supply.

But in 1739, the royal government mandated that government bills of credit be redeemed on their actual redemption date. This meant that a significant number of bills of credit would be retired from circulation in the near future and all bills of credit in circulation in 1739 would be retired by 1741. There was widespread alarm, particularly in more rural areas where gold and silver were very rarely used in transactions. Making payments in commodities was common, chiefly for those outside of the Boston merchant elite who had access to gold and silver. Many even paid their taxes and other government expenses in commodities. But paper currency allowed for an elasticity that commodities didn't, and many firmly believed that their economic well-being depended on having access to paper currency.

While the colonial government could only make a limited contribution to paper currency, mostly in the form of tradable bonds, there was nothing prohibiting privately printing currency. Privately printed currency, usually in the form of "receipts" for precious metals on deposit, was pioneered by the Italian city-states more than two centuries prior, and, while banned some areas in favor of government monopoly on issuing paper currency, had grown to be a widely accepted practice in many parts of Europe. In the New England colonies, those who desperately needed such currency tended to be farmers whose primary asset was land, so the currency would be backed by land rather than by precious metals. This currency would be issued by a "Land Bank." Land would be used as collateral, and the value of the currency would be paid back in commodities — land and commodities was what the farmers of Massachusetts possessed.

Once the Land Bank's currency was circulating, farmers could buy what they needed with it and sell their products for it. The idea of a colonial Land Bank had been circulating for a few decades. So in 1739, Robert Auchmuty, William Stoddard, Samuel Adams, Sr., Peter Chardon, Samuel Watts, John Choate, Thomas Cheever, George Leonard and Robert Hale — some Boston merchants but mostly merchants and farmers from the towns outside of Boston — devised a Land Bank. They petitioned to receive official approval from the colonial government, though it seemed clear that no approval was required. The governor, the governor's council, and the elite Boston merchants aggressively opposed the Land Bank on the belief it would throw the province's economy into fiscal anarchy. The lines were drawn.

The Boston merchant elite devised their own plan to address the impending need for paper currency: a Silver Bank wherein bills of credit would be backed by silver. One hundred and six Boston merchants, headed by Edward Hutchinson and including James Bowdoin, Samuel Sewall, Hugh Hall, Joshua Winslow, Andrew Oliver, and Edmund Quincy, backed the silver scheme. Their combined investments exceeded the amount proposed to be issued and were reduced to keep within the limits of the proposed plan. And they too applied to the General Court for approval. The backers of the Silver Bank also pledged exclusive fidelity to currency backed by silver or gold, "We the subscribers therefore agree and promise, that we will neither directly nor indirectly, by ourselves, nor any of us, receive any bills that shall be emitted hereafter by the neighboring governments unless redeemable by Silver and Gold as aforesaid ... and that we will wholly refuse in all Trade and Business, and for all debts due, the notes that may be emitted by the subscribers to the bank commonly called the Land Bank. ..." The Silver Bank investors agreed to refuse to trade in Land Bank currency. In itself, this may not seem so monumental, but Silver Bank investors included most of the elite Boston importers, exporters, wholesalers and government officials. Clearly such a group united in opposition, together with the Governor and the Council, could make life very difficult for those who participated in the Land Bank.

The House took up the matter and was favorable to the Land Bank. When it was clear that the House would approve the Land Bank, the Governor's Council on June 12, 1740 referred both banks to a joint committee; the House agreed and appointed members to the committee, but the House committee members refused to meet with the Council committee members because they rightfully believed that the Council's primary mission was to kill the Land Bank. The proponents of the Land Bank weren't as opposed to the Silver Bank as they simply did not believe it would effectively alleviate the currency problems in the countryside; in contrast, the Silver Bank proponents aggressively opposed the Land Bank. As tension mounted and the currency crisis worsened, the debate became very public, and the publicity increased public support for the Land Bank and sympathy in the House. When the Land Bank held a meeting in Roxbury to select officers, 800 committed Land Bank investors attended. The directors agreed to move forward for although they hadn't secured the approval of the House, they knew the House supported the bank and would not interfere with its operation. And the strong support for the Land Bank in the House was evident given that six of the leading members of the House were bank directors and many House members were Land Bank investors.

With such support in the House, the governor and the Council were powerless to stop the Land Bank with legislation. When the Land Bank first approached the General Court for approval, there were fewer than 400 investors, but by the time it commenced operation on September 19, 1740, there were almost 1,000 investors. Powerless to act through legislation, the Governor resorted to the blunt force of his executive power. On November 5, the governor threatened to remove from office any appointed official who supported the Land Bank. The next day, he expanded the threat to include military officers.

Illustrating that the governor and his advisors were ignorant of the need for currency reform and arrogant, a wave of appointed officials pro-actively resigned after the early November threats. On November 10, William Stoddard, Samuel Adams Sr., John Choate, and Robert Hale resigned their positions as justices of the peace. Many more resigned and still more refused to disassociate themselves from the Land Bank. By November 19, 1740, the Governor realized that he was powerless to stop the wave of support that the Land Bank commanded. He wrote to the provincial lobbyist in London, "I believe nothing less than an Act of Parliament will put an end to it, the undertakers are so needy and violent in the pursuit of it." And so began the intense effort to persuade Parliament to outlaw the Land Bank.

But the political bloodbath would continue until Parliament acted. The governor had not acted on the November resignations, but on December 5, the same day the Land Bank formally requested that the Council consent to the Bank's existence, the Governor formally began dismissing all Land Bank supporters who held appointed government positions. Samuel Adams, Sr., William Stoddard, Samuel Watts, Robert Hale, and John Choate were dismissed as justices of the peace. In the following two weeks, justice of the peace and judge George Leonard was removed from office, justice Joe Blanchard was dismissed, and nine military officers tendered their resignations. And in the first week of January, justices John Burleigh, John Fisher, Elkanah Leonard, and Ammi Ruhamah Wise all lost their jobs.

The purge continued into the first few months of 1741, during which Isaac Little of Plymouth County, John Metcalf and Samuel White of Suffolk, Samuel Dudley of Worcester, Colonel Estes Hatch, Captain Adams and Captain Watts of Chelsea, eight lieutenants and one ensign were all dismissed from their positions. Colonels of regiments were instructed to investigate the officers subordinate to them for any Land Bank related activity. Justices of the peace were required to use their power both in court and as individuals to prevent circulation of Land Bank bills, and they were required to take into consideration whether the merchant would accept Land Bank bills as payment when granting merchant licenses. The register of deeds provided the Governor's Council with a list of Land Bank subscribers who took loans using their land as collateral, and a blank form of summons was prepared for use by the Governor's Council in cases where they wished to bring before it persons accused of passing Land Bank bills. The bills were entirely legal, but the council could still issue a summons and launch inquisitions.

The purge and inquisition intimidated a few, but it inspired anger and contempt among many. As Captain Kidd's crew saluted the Royal Navy with their derrières, several Land Bank supporters wrote to the Governor and the Council to openly express their scorn. Justice Henry Lee of Worcester wrote that his rights as an Englishmen were all he needed to justify his interest in the Land Bank, and that "As I act to my conscience, I regard being punished any way for differing in my opinion from the Council, to be civil persecution, and to be deprived of my office until I be proved unfaithful in it, or have violated the laws of the land, I look on as an invasion of my native rights." Justice Lee was removed from office.

Then on January 27, the Council leveled the most severe punishment it could by enacting a rule "That no person shall be admitted to appear and plead before this Board as an attorney and counsellor at law, on any pretence whatever, who shall pass, receive, or give encouragement to the bills called Land Bank or Manufactory Bills, but that notice he given hereof in the public prints." The Council acted as a probate and appeals court, and this vote meant that no attorney who even gave "encouragement" to the Land Bank, as gauged by the Council, could work on cases that came before it.

While the Governor, Council and elite merchants were attempting to drive the Land Bank out of business, several towns – in acts of overt defiance – were voting to accept Land Bank bills as official payment. On the same day that the Council refused to permit Land Bank encouragers in the chamber, Middletown voted unanimously to accept Land Bank bills for tax payments. The towns of Abington and Braintree soon followed with similar votes. Meanwhile, several groups in towns across the province were arranging their own Land Banks. Not only could the governor not terminate the Land Bank, but it now appeared that he couldn't even limit the problem to one land bank. At least three more land banks were being organized in the province.

While the province was engulfed in the Land Bank inferno, Jemmy was somewhat insulated at Harvard. Jemmy's exposure to the world was primarily through the faculty, which consisted of the president, two professors, four tutors, and two instructors. The four tutors taught most of the lessons, with each tutor assigned to a class with which he remained throughout the four year course. The two instructors taught Hebrew and French. Hebrew was required, and French was optional. Harvard President Holyoke was starting his third year in office in 1739, but his broadminded outlook was already making itself felt. President Holyoke's laissez-faire approach coincided effectively as the Enlightenment invaded Harvard. The philosopher's reverence for the classics was already well established at Harvard, and their preoccupation with the future – the idea of progress, scientific inquiry, critical examination – now flourished. Formal education would no longer be fixated on the past.

One example of the enlightenment flowering at Harvard is illustrated in Professor John Winthrop, a brilliant scientist who had assumed the professorship of Natural Philosophy in 1738. Winthrop, the great-great-grandson of the founder of the Massachusetts Bay colony, was a force in science from his appointment at Harvard in 1738 until his death in 1779. He used Newton's *Principia* as a guide and aggressively upgraded the mathematics and astronomy courses. He observed the transit of Mercury in 1740 and 1761 and led an expedition to Nova Scotia in 1761 to view the transit of Venus. He published extensively on the Lisbon earthquake of 1755, using computations rather than religion to explain the quakes, and is sometimes credited with being the father of seismology. Winthrop was the kind of academic who was teaching at the Harvard of the 1740s, and by 1742, the revamped curriculum had the students studying the latest ideas in geography, astronomy, and philosophy, including a considerable dose of John Locke. Of course, the core of the Harvard education was still Latin, Greek, Logic and Rhetoric.

The class of 1743 was large – forty students. When they entered Harvard there were about a hundred undergraduates in residence, plus a scattering of graduates who had chosen to stay at Cambridge to complete their studies for their Master's degrees, which were normally granted three years after earning an undergraduate diploma. The great majority of students took a second degree, but most completed their studies away from Cambridge. The student body during Otis's years included names that were to reappear frequently during his later career. Benjamin Prat, one of the later leaders of the Boston bar, was in the class of 1737 and served as college librarian. Oxenbridge Thacher of the class of 1738 was to ally with Otis in arguing some of the province's most famous legal cases. Samuel Adams graduated in 1740. Otis's own class included Samuel Cooper, the passionate minister of Boston's Brattle Street Church, and Royall Tyler, Otis's mentor in the application of pragmatic politics. Thomas Cushing and Jonathan Mayhew graduated a year after Otis. Mayhew would become minister of Boston's West Church and one of the elect in both John Adams's list of great patriots and Peter Oliver's "black regiment." The class of 1745 included James Bowdoin, at first Otis's political foe and later ally, and James Warren, a future brother-in-law.

Each February, the solemn feudal custom of importance was the "placing" of the class in "order." The president and tutors listed the members of the class according to a somewhat arbitrary view of the social and political standing of the students' families, and this ranking remained in effect until graduation regardless of any academic considerations. A governor's son would, for example, be ranked first without question, but when the faculty had descended to the level of country justices of the peace and minister's sons, the problem of ranking became complex. The president and tutors ranked Otis thirteenth in his class, just below William Bourne and Lothrop Russell, a clear indication that while James Otis, Sr. had certainly established his financial preeminence in Barnstable Country, he had yet to establish social supremacy.

Foster Hutchinson led the class; he was the younger brother of Thomas Hutchinson and heralded from perhaps the most powerful family in Massachusetts. The official ordering of the class doubtless made Jemmy truly aware of the expanse that separated the son of a Barnstable justice of the peace from Boston oligarchs such as the Hutchinsons. In 1741 and 1742, Otis roomed with Lothrop Russell in Stoughton 5 and Massachusetts 15, but there is no record of his residency during his first two years. The logical conclusion is that he resided alone. The faculty disciplinary records for Otis are blank for these first two years.

The most remarkable artifact of this period is the earliest known letter written by Otis, which he sent to his father at the beginning of his sophomore year:

> Cambridge September the 5th 1740
> Honoured Sir after my duty to you this comes to inform you that through the good providence of God I am in good health at presant pleast to give my love to brother and sister my duty to mother (which might have been first) and let Joseph write to me by every opertunyty I have got aunt Russels chocolate and have been at every shop in to Boston to get her bowls but cant as yet but I am going down to Boston tomorrow and will try again and if I cant get them I shall be glad to keep the money If you are willing if not I will return it I have also sent you recepte for all the money that I have paid away since I have been at colledge except the first payment, to Mrs Angier which the receipts for the last will clear and as for the last payment at the stewards which is in the receipt for part is because there was twelve shillings more then eight pounds but I could not very well spare the mony or else I would have paid it and I hope this is sufficient account of the matter if not please to send me word and I will corret it. Uncle Allen is looked for from Wethersfield every day and then he will

come to Barnstable with Aunt of if not shall myself Aunt remembers abunans of love to yourself and mother I have nothin else whorth a sendind so remain your obediend son

James Otis

The spelling, grammar, and handwriting are dreadful, even by eighteenth century standards. This can be partly explained by the fact that the writer is a fifteen-year-old boy who, though he could read Cicero, had been exposed to a minimum amount of common education and little formal English; he was simply unfamiliar with non-phonetic languages. The "Honoured Sir" and "Obediend Son" remain constant in form (though not in spelling) throughout Jemmy's life — so constant that the father assumes a stereotyped image of the "Honoured Sir." While the concept of "Honoured Sir" would hardly change over the next few decades, the definition of "your obediend son" would transform under the pressure of a dawning era; Jemmy's conception of "obediend" — to what? to whom? — would be profoundly challenged. He obviously missed Joseph and Mercy, but mentioned his mother only parenthetically. The expected "Uncle Allen" was Samuel Allyne, Mary Otis's younger brother after whom Samuel Allyne Otis was to be named at the time of his birth later that fall. The financial complexities were to be a recurring theme in all of Jemmy's Harvard letters.

There were more than visiting uncles and "amusement" in the fall of 1740; famed travelling preachers George Whitefield and Gilbert Tennent injected the Great Awakening into Cambridge when they rhapsodized before the Harvard students. The reaction these beguiling preachers elicited from the Harvard faculty was mixed, at least until Whitefield took it upon himself to harshly criticize the college. The college rebuked Whitefield several times; in 1745, the colony's first divinity professor, Harvard Hollis Chair Edward Wigglesworth, publically stated Harvard's position on Great Awakening preachers such as Whitefield:

> If we consider *the Nature of Enthusiasm*, which is to make a Man imagine, that almost any Tho't which bears strongly upon his Mind (whether it came into it by *Dreams, Suggestion*, or whatever other Way) is from the Spirit of God; when at the same Time he hath no Proof that it is; it will plainly appear to be a very dangerous Thing.

Wigglesworth proceeded to state that "Reason" and "good Conscience" should guide one's mind, and that if a thought not based on proof "rushes strongly into [one's] Mind," the result will be a "Shipwreck in a most surprising Manner." The Harvard overseers and faculty had become fully converted empiricists, and they claimed that Whitefield had missed the boat. Importantly, Whitefield also disagreed with two emerging trends in New England: the rise of Arminianism and the sense that slavery conflicted with New England ideals. Whitefield promoted slavery, particularly in Georgia, and split with John Wesley's Methodist Church over the issue of Arminianism, which signaled Whitefield as more of the strict Calvinist. Debates over the influence and interpretation of Arminianism may seem removed from the political inferno of the 1760s, but the young Otis witnessed these debates and they would fuel some of his core decisions in the political realm two decades later.

And yet if tutor Henry Flynt is to be believed, the Great Awakening preachers put the students "in great concern as to their Souls and Eternal State." A group of students that included Russell and Otis "prayed together sung Psalms and discoursed together 2 or 3 at a time and read good books." One of the concerned, Samuel Fayerweather, later to be a missionary of the Society for the Propagation of the Gospel in Rhode Island, even witnessed "the divil in shape of a bear coming to his bedside." Otis may have been absorbed in Whitefield's revivalist fervor – after all, he was only 15 years old – but as with so many sudden conversions, the effects were fleeting. Two years later Jemmy humbly reported to his father that he owed an old bill to the butler who fled Cambridge "in the height of his zeal," but had now returned to collect, "Having Preached himself out of money if not out of credit" – certainly not the comment of a convert.

While Enlightenment philosophy and science were generating new lines of inquiry and debate at Harvard, by the spring of 1741, the political tension caused by the Land Bank throughout the province was extreme; discontent and civil unrest were in the air. On May 2, the governor received an affidavit attesting that there was a "confederacy" in the countryside of about 5,000 men who were planning to converge on Boston to make their position in favor of the Land Bank abundantly clear. The governor appointed councilor John Quincy to investigate, and he confirmed that an insurrection was planned. Cryptic notices were being posted on meeting houses alerting the townsmen of the date of the insurrection: May 19. The towns of Hingham, Weymouth, Stoughton, Abington, Plymouth and Bridgewater seemed particularly engaged. The target was the elite Boston merchants who refused to conduct business in Land Bank bills. Though Parliament had been lobbied aggressively by the governor and the Boston oligarchs and though Parliament had enacted a law banning the Land Bank, the Governor felt the situation was almost out of control. On May 11, the governor wrote to Thomas Hutchinson, "I assure you the concerned openly declare they defye any Act of Parliament to be able to do it. They are grown so brassy and hardy as to be now coming in a body to raise a rebellion, and the day set for this coming to this town is at the election (27th instant), and the treasurer, I am told is in the bottom of the design, and I doubt it not. I have this day sent the Sheriffe and his Officers to apprehend some of the heads of the conspirators."

And per the governor's instructions, on May 14 the council issued warrants for the arrest of all persons who "have been concerned in a design and combination with a number of evil-minded persons to come into the town of Boston in a tumultuous manner tending to the disturbance and disquiet of the government and affright and terror of his Majesty's good subjects." The open discussion of insurrection and the governor's swift action for its suppression prevented any widespread protests. The generation that would lead the revolution was currently in college and would learn lessons about insurrection and protest from their parents.

House elections had just taken place, and Land Bank representatives won a majority of the seats. As the warrants for the arrest of the conspirators were being issued, the House elected Sam Watts as Speaker; Watts was a director of the Land Bank and had been fired as a justice. The governor refused to approve of the rebellious Watts, so the House then elected William Fairfield as House Speaker. Fairfield was an active supporter of the Land Bank. The governor detested the selection but realized there was nothing he could do, so Fairfield got the position. Then the House and Council voted on new Councilors, and 13 – nearly half – were active Land Bank supporters or investors. The reality quickly set in for the governor; the Land Bank was immensely popular. The governor dissolved the House and called for a new election.

The new election was on July 8. The House met and defiantly elected John Choate – original organizer of the Land Bank and fired justice – House Speaker. He was rejected by the governor. John Hobson was then elected and approved as speaker; Hobson was a friend of the bank but not an investor. On July 31, the newly elected Council, per its responsibilities, began to appoint civil officers, and promptly began to appoint Land Bank directors to various civil positions, including Sam Watts, who had been rejected by the governor as House Speaker just two months prior.

While all this was transpiring the colonists were fully aware that the Governor's lobbying efforts had borne fruit in an Act of the Parliament outlawing the Land Bank. Parliament asserted that the Land Bank was illegal under the 1720 Bubble Act, which regulated and required government approval of all stock companies. It mattered not to Parliament that the Board of Trade and the attorney general had both recently concluded that colonial Land Banks were perfectly legal and required no government pre-approval. The Act of 1741 falsely described the Land Bank as a stock company, and then declared its operation illegal. At first, the Land Bank participants brazenly ignored the Act. To the farmers and rural merchants, the Land Bank was an effort by law-abiding citizens to alleviate a great public problem through means that had been explicitly declared legal by the government, and the Act of 1741 was enforcing a 1720 Act on a company to which it didn't apply that operated in the colonies, to which the 1720 Act didn't apply. The 1741 Act falsely described the Land Bank as a joint-stock company, falsely applied an Act to the colonies, and applied that Act retroactively. The Act instantly made the Land Bank currency entirely valueless and made those who had issued the currency criminals, subject to imprisonment and forfeiture of estate. Anyone holding the valueless currency could bring an action, and the courts were compelled to apply the law. And as Parliament was the final arbiter of law, no one could appeal and defy the Act. Reality sunk in during the summer of 1741; if Parliament declared that the Land Bank's currency was valueless and those who funded it were criminals, even if based on falsehoods, even if retroactively, then it was true.

But it was soon apparent that the nullification of all Land Bank currency was causing fiscal chaos. In September, fierce Land Bank enemy Governor Belcher was replaced by William Shirley, who was sympathetic to the financial disaster that the Act created and the general sense of unfairness it engendered. Regardless, Governor Shirley had to acknowledge the absolute supremacy of Parliament and demand that the bank cease operations. Shirley's sympathetic position encouraged the Land Bank investors to meet on September 22 to devise a plan for settling all outstanding accounts. But the meeting was contentious and only a slim majority voted to cease operations. A large and vocal minority desired to pursue a novel route: defy Parliament, challenge absolute authority, and continue operating. The Land Bank was popular and it was generally conceded that bank proponents had been unfairly treated, but wholesale defiance of the government was not a generally acceptable position in 1741. And Governor Shirley's evident sympathy made defiance seem a bit more unreasonable than it may have otherwise seemed.

Of course, the Land Bank was powerless to effectively wind-down operations since its currency and contracts were all voided. But as many of its directors and investors were representatives, the bank could request the General Court to assist, particularly because the bank had been created as a solution to a public problem. On April 3, 1742, the General Court passed a resolve to form a joint committee that would pay off bank debts, destroy the bills it had created, and distribute all proceeds. Of course, the General Court was virtually recognizing the same bank contracts that Parliament had declared void, but there seemed no other way to address the issue without creating fiscal and legal havoc. At the time, there were no English laws that addressed such a predicament, and the Governor was forced to officially withhold his consent from the General Court's proposal that would effectively recognize Land Bank contracts. It seemed that Parliament had crushed a lawful enterprise and subsequently created a situation where it was unlawful to cease operations in an organized manner but failure to do so would lead many to fiscal ruin and many others to jail. Such a brazen use of Parliamentary supremacy was rare, so a collective response would take years to form. Later, Thomas Hutchinson wrote that, "The authority of parliament to control all public and private persons and proceedings in the colonies, was, in that day, questioned by nobody." Hutchinson overstated the case, as the Land Bank proponents, on the verge of ruin and imprisonment, contemplated defiance. And yet the Land Bank debacle taught a generation of Massachusetts colonists the exact meaning of Parliamentary supremacy. The Land Bank scheme also taught a generation the power of a small but determined group. The Land Bank officially had about 1,000 supporters – a fairly small number. And yet in the face of government retribution, threats, investigations and jail, the Land Bank's popularity grew, and its support in the popularly elected House was strong and remained so throughout the debacle. It seemed clear to everyone that the bank's support among the general population far exceeded the number of people who directly benefitted from the bank. Much of the bank's support was derived not from its customers but from those who resented the seemingly arbitrary power of the oligarchy that ruled Boston, and the Act of 1741 made clear that the ruling oligarchy extended from the merchant elite in Boston all the way back to Parliament and Whitehall in London.

The Land Bank was a formative event for the Massachusetts colonists, and Jemmy's years at college coincided almost precisely with the rise and collapse of the Land Bank and the messy cleaning up that occurred for years after. And yet despite its widespread popularity outside of Boston, Barnstable town held the unique position of not having a single investor and Barnstable county only had ten investors. The lack of investors was not because Barnstable was aligned with the Boston elite but rather quite the opposite: Barnstable was incredibly conservative and generally opposed to "schemes." In Barnstable, the basis of wealth was land, and if land had to be converted, the only acceptable currency was gold, silver, or commodities. So neither Jemmy Otis nor his father was directly involved in the Lank Bank on either side.

Harvard Commencement in 1743 was scheduled for July 6 and preparations occupied most of the spring. Commencement Day festivities at Harvard were traditionally not only for the graduates and their families but also for all eastern Massachusetts residents. Formal class work ended in March for the seniors, and they spent their time attending a few lectures and otherwise preparing for final examinations and commencement orations. The "obediend son" penned several letters to his "Honoured Sir" that spring regarding commencement plans and pleading for more money. The "Honoured Sir" apprised Jemmy that his mother, sister Mercy, and brother Joseph planned to attend Commencement and that graduation clothes would be sent from home, which smothered Jemmy's plans to buy a new outfit in Cambridge. The "Honoured Sir" also instructed his son to plan very little entertaining, which was also a severe disappointment, for the extravagance of one's commencement dinner had become an important status symbol. The reaction from the "obediend son" was plaintive: "I suppose you would be willing I should make some small Entertainment which will be in some measure necessary if I have no more company than some of our own family." At the same time he was sending the "Honoured Sir" receipts for a half gross of bottles and "barrell of Cyder." In estimating his final expenses, Jemmy listed five pounds for commencement dinner, three pounds for the butler, two pounds for the president, "and as much more as you think fit." Jemmy's final letter to his father prior to commencement is typical:

ARSONIST

BOSTON, *June the* 17th, 1743.

HONOURED SIR, — I wrote to you the 11th Currant, but omitted Some Things which I Shall now enumerate viz. 15 Shillings for Printing Theses, for three Quarters shoing 24 shillings, for a Sett of Buckles 15 shillings, and if I make any manner of Entertainment there will be a great many things to buy, tho I shall not put you to much Charge for that, not intending to keep much of a commencement and what I do will be with Russell. Pray Sir send me money Enough for I believe I Shall not write again before commencement. Your most Obedient Son,

JAMES OTIS

The continuous recitation of pounds, shillings, and pence is not as significant in itself as in the insight it provides into the dawning of post-feudal relationships. The ascension of the Otis family from middling weavers to merchant moguls had been based in large degree on meticulous accounting and a reluctance to part with a shilling without cause. That James Otis, Sr. adhered to these principles is clear from his frequent requests for an accounting of every shilling spent. Painstaking accounting was fairly standard among the merchant class in the colonies, and Jemmy's college expenses, while high, were not atypical. These nascent provincial capitalists were becoming expert accountants.

Presumably the Otis family returned to Barnstable at the close of festivities, James, Sr. to continue the climb up the economic and political ladder and Jemmy to immerse himself in a broader field of reading than had been possible during his undergraduate years. Jemmy's four years at Harvard brought a degree of maturation, yet at the same time the handwriting and syntax of his final letters still exhibited a marked lack of assurance. The picture that emerges is of an 18-year-old of intellectual brilliance and sensitivity, who, on returning to Barnstable, would be very likely to shut himself away with his books – both to satisfy his passion for participation in the captivating world of the Enlightenment that was developing before him and also to escape from what he must have considered the monotonous features of his father's world. He was clearly not suited to be a country trader.

After commencement the class of 1743 scattered; most would return to Cambridge three years later to deliver their disputations and receive their master's degrees. The second degree had been initially intended as a mark of distinction for those graduates entering the ministry, following English university practice, but by 1743 it was the customary concluding act for a Harvard education, regardless of intended occupation. There was neither a curriculum nor a residency requirement, and only four of Otis's classmates spent substantial time at Cambridge during the intervening period. Seven taught school, five were drawn into the great push against French Canada that culminated in the capture of Louisbourg, Nova Scotia in 1745, four embarked on business careers, three began studying law, three went to sea, and two began preaching. Drop-outs, expulsions, and death accounted for seven. Lothrop Russell, Otis's roommate, neighbor, and close friend, died in 1745 at the age of 21. The future ministers who attended Harvard concurrently with Jemmy are notable, particularly Samuel Cooper and Jonathan Mayhew. What Peter Oliver called the "black regiment" were very radical preachers who could use the platform and protection of the pulpit to make arguments that few others would make; Bostonians had feared an Anglican imposition of their rights longer than they had feared a Whitehall imposition, so preachers bred on suspicion were quick to translate their vigilance from the religious sphere to the political. Mayhew's 1650 sermon *Discourse Concerning Unlimited Submission and Non-Resistance*, given on the 100-year anniversary of the execution of Charles I, justified the execution of a king who greatly imposed on the people's liberties. Mayhew was not a great philosopher; his sermons were not tight logical arguments. Further, he was protected by the pulpit in part because such sermons were inherently passive; Mayhew was not a lawyer arguing cases or a politician drafting statutes that would affect the population; he was not a street organizer or mob leader or tax evader. Puritan ministers in England had been espousing somewhat inflammatory ideology for over two centuries, and the congregation and government had come to expect it and assumed that more often than not such rhetoric would come to naught. But Mayhew was more fiery than most, and he'd attended college with those who would become the leaders of the popular government.

Instead of venturing into the world, young Jemmy Otis returned to Barnstable, probably at his father's suggestion; one of Jemmy's final letters home before commencement was dated June 11, 1743 and contained a brief reference to this plan:

> If you can possibly Spare me Some money for to buy me some Books if it is but ten Pounds-worth for if I live at home next year in order to

follow my Studies I had as goode pretend to Run with my legs tyed as to make any Progress with what Books I have.

So the house on the Great Marshes became the place where Otis immersed himself in Enlightenment thought. The conditions must have been less than ideal, even if the "Honoured Sir" left him alone, for there was now a four year old sister, Elizabeth, the three year old Samuel Allyne, and two babies born who died shortly after birth. No reading list exists, but from his later writings it is evident that Jemmy acquired a thorough knowledge with not only the classic authors but also with the best literature of the preceding century. Quotations from most of the major political philosophers from the previous 100 years — Coke, Milton, Sydney, Locke, Filmer, Pope, and Harrington — would flow from his agitated pen in searing profusion, and his quotations were not decorative as were some of his contemporaries's references. He was an insatiable reader all his life, but his "Studies" during his stay in Barnstable in 1743-1744 likely laid firm groundwork upon which his continuing education would be built. It was a fertile yet frustrating time for an introduction to public law and moral philosophy. The age of Hobbes, Grotius, Pufendorf, and Locke was in its twilight by 1743, but the inquiries and challenges presented by the later English writers of the Enlightenment such as Addison, Steele, Swift, Trenchard, Bolingbroke, Hume, and Gordon introduced Jemmy to an expansive assortment of ideas and critical techniques. He read them all, and in John Locke he found many compelling theories. Locke's vague views on sovereignty, ideas of reasonable representation, and his enigmatic concept of the ultimate "appeal to Heaven" were to be oft repeated by Otis. Montesquieu was yet to come with his ammunition against the ruling oligarchy of Massachusetts Bay, but by the time Otis had taken up the formal study of law he was thoroughly grounded in the concept of natural rights.

While Jemmy was buried in books, his father was continuing his ascension to political and social supremacy. At a town meeting in 1744, Barnstable residents elected him as selectman, a distinct promotion from his earlier positions as hogreeve and town treasurer. A genuine opportunity presented itself the following year when his neighbors elected him as their representative to the General Court. His predecessor was Deacon Robert Davis, a respected cooper, and later a captain of one of the Barnstable-Boston packet boats. The reason for the change is not clear, but in view of the long and frequent sessions of the General Court, Deacon Davis may have decided that he could not afford to neglect his business. The 1740s and 1750s was a period of gradual shift from part-time delegates to something resembling professional politicians, a change not only significant for Barnstable but also for the Otis family. Davis was apparently a good deacon, a good cooper, and well liked, but in Boston he was insignificant. During his final one-year term as representative, Deacon Davis served on only one committee and that for an unimportant issue. In abrupt contrast, James Otis, Sr. served on twenty committees during his first term, some of them significant, and three of them chaired by Otis. During this period the House of Representatives consisted of only one standing committee, the Committee of War, and all ordinary business was conducted by temporary committees appointed by the Speaker, Thomas Cushing. The *Journal of the House* did not record debates and only rarely recorded votes, but an analysis of committee service provides an indication of the relative importance and competence of House members. An ambitious representative need not heed customs of seniority and could immediately demonstrate his determination. Such a man was James Otis, but he also benefited from current events; Otis arrived in Boston shortly after news of the capture of Louisbourg did, and though the victory was much celebrated, it had severely strained the resources of Massachusetts Bay. Fortunately Governor William Shirley was a man of both political sagacity and common sense, qualities in short supply in colonial governors.

Between Jemmy's graduation in 1743 and his father's election to the General Court in 1745, King George's War broke out. The war had its origin when a British sailor named Jenkin's lost his ear to a Spanish knife; King George, not known for his temperance, declared war on Spain. A few years later the French joined the fray and the War of Jenkin's Ear was renamed the War of Austrian Succession, and nearly every European power was fighting someone, somewhere. Most of the conflict was contained to Europe and the Caribbean until, for whatever reason, the French fort at Louisbourg in Nova Scotia decided to attack English towns in Nova Scotia. The attacks were largely unsuccessful as the French Louisbourg troops couldn't seem to coordinate and execute plans with much order, but Massachusetts Bay responded to pleas of assistance from British towns in Nova Scotia with enthusiasm, sending a large supply of troops, equipment, and ships. Not satisfied with merely defending English towns, the Massachusetts troops promptly attacked and seized French Louisbourg. The Massachusetts forces in Nova Scotia were significant enough that the French wouldn't bother them again, but the French troops in Canada did engage in several substantial raids in the Albany area in coordination with their Amer-Indian allies, leaving most of the English towns north of Albany abandoned. For Massachusetts, the taking of Louisbourg was a monumental feat at enormous expense; the conflict cost the province about 10% of its adult male population. A peace treaty was signed in 1748, and Whitehall returned Louisbourg to the French in exchange for Madras, India, which the French had captured in 1746. For the people of Massachusetts province, the battle of Louisbourg was a vital episode in the maturation of the colony; they proved to themselves and others that the province could act as a unified force, could project power, and could defend its territory. But the return of Louisbourg for Madras made the Massachusetts colonists unsure of the mother country's loyalty.

James Otis, Sr. also drew assignments to assist in the drafting of proposed statutes, and this was, of course, an outgrowth of his recognized status as a successful country lawyer. "Country lawyer" described men who taught themselves law and who had learned to operate the fairly informal and manipulatable judicial machinery of the province by observation and practice. Unfettered by precedent and scholarship, country lawyers had gone far in liberalizing the framework of English common law. By 1740, however, country lawyers had risen above the low estate assigned to practitioners by the early colonists; ironically, the New Englanders, who in their eager attempt to escape the petty practice of law they had known in the country courts of England effectively denied any significant role to lawyers in the new world, had in effect created the very conditions that caused the increase of professionals who had been viewed as nuisances and parasites.

James Otis Sr.'s generation represented a transition from the legal limbo that preceded it to the innovative professional lawyers who matured in the 1760s and added an essential ingredient to the Revolution. The growing complexity of commercial and real estate transactions that marked the first half of the eighteenth century made a more efficient and responsive judicial system desirable, and the merchants began to consider the law's technicalities to protect themselves. Importantly, commercial and real estate transactions were not only growing increasingly complex but were also becoming the central component in all economic activity; small farmers and traders were fueling the Massachusetts economy, not feudal estates and government monopolies. Hence, lawyers became the arbitrators, deal makers, and risk abators in this explosion of competition. Inevitably the most proficient and influential were employed by their friends and associates to represent them, and their increasing proficiency and influence began to be reflected in elevated professional standards at bench and bar. John Otis III, Jemmy's grandfather, left behind a well worn copy of that seventeenth century bible of country practitioners, Dalton's *Country Justice*, which attests that he had played the part of transitional lawyer. He had no formal education in the law, and yet there were no formally educated lawyers in the area, so men such as John Otis III greased the wheels of the growing mercantile machinery with much-needed legal advice.

According to tradition, James Otis Sr. was in court to argue one of his own cases — most likely an issue of collecting an overdue bill — when a merchant neighbor requested his assistance and thus was launched his legal career. It's very apparent that he was a successful lawyer, and the explanation for his success is equally clear. One of his friends who later became a formidable political opponent, Peter Oliver, explained it in far from flattering terms: "But as the People of the Province seem to be born with litigious Constitutions, so he had Shrewdness enough to take Advantage of the general Foible, & work'd himself into a Pettifogger; which Profession he practiced in, to the End of his Life. He had a certain Adroitness to captivate the Ear of Country Jurors, who were too commonly Drovers, Horse Jockies, & of other lower Classes in Life." Though Peter Oliver labeled James Otis Sr. an ambulance chaser, it must be remembered that few lawyers were held in high regard at the time and a parvenu like Oliver would likely have described nearly all lawyers in similarly unfavorable terms. And yet Otis was widely regarded as a good lawyer, as one biographer wrote, "His arguments were strong, lucid and impressive; no man had greater influence on the jury than he had; he would accommodate himself to their understanding ... and work himself into their affection as to gain an advantage of which no other man, among his contemporaries, could avail himself." There is no date attached to the account of James Otis Sr.'s first case, but the records of the Superior Court show that he was sworn in as an attorney before that court in 1731 at the age of 29, and that his practice grew rapidly both in volume and geographical scope. It could be difficult to envision how Otis could handle both his legal and commercial business, but court sessions were acknowledged meeting grounds for the important men of a county. So Otis journeyed from Barnstable to Plymouth to Taunton to attend the quarterly sessions of the County Courts and the annual sessions of the Superior Court, and he carried a copy of the Province Laws and his writs in one saddlebag, and his detailed business accounts in the other. By 1740, Otis was a widely known and successful lawyer, leading John Adams to later comment that Otis was "the undisputed head of the bar in the three counties of Barnstable, Plymouth, and Bristol." Sam Willis of Dartmouth wrote Otis a letter in 1741 begging the lawyer not to sue him; Sam White, a Harvard graduate and successful lawyer, insisted that Otis represent his client in Taunton – he would accept no other lawyer. By 1744, James Otis Sr. represented nearly half of all litigants in Barnstable Court and handled such a remarkable number of cases that his fees, including charges for "attendance," amounted to as much as £1200 a year – more than the governor's salary. It is little wonder that when he arrived in Boston as a member of the General Court in 1745, his network of acquaintances and his reputation as an energetic, tenacious lawyer helped him to quickly secure a leading position in the House.

In the 1730s and 1740s, the Massachusetts judicial system relied heavily on juries and even trivial two pound cases were tried with a jury in the County Inferior Courts of Common Pleas; further, the cost of litigation was so modest that the unsuccessful party frequently appealed to the Superior Court where the case was retried before another jury. In many cases a third and fourth jury trial was held under what were called "writs of review" or appeals. It was these aspects of the Massachusetts judicial system in the 1730s and 1740s that explain how an untrained though intelligent legal novice could rather quickly become a seasoned veteran. The ability to try a case three or four times helped a new lawyer learn the system, provided opportunities to correct mistakes, and, of course, increased his billable hours. In effect, the judicial system itself was designed to provide an education for nascent lawyers and to give a forum for small business owners to settle their differences; in both regards, the Massachusetts judicial system was quite the opposite of the English Inns of Court. These curious features were an expression of the Puritan ethos; the courts were quite accessible, not ostentatiously formal, and functioned on common sense. Further, such courts permitted the Puritans to progress toward their most cherished goal: independence. The southern colonies would often send their young men to England to train at the Inns of Court; the New Englanders would make their own lawyers.

And the New Englanders applied the concepts of accessibly and common sense to the developing Massachusetts judicial system in other ways. For example, the ability to retry and appeal cases multiple times was actually an improvement over the situation before 1692 when a final judgment was unheard of, and a law suit only died when those suing died, and sometimes not even then. London merchants complained to the Board of Trade that "they find more security and better and more speedy justice in the most distant provinces of the Ottoman Dominions from their Bashaws than they do in some of the American Colonies." The courts were increasingly becoming efficient and effective tools of the growing middling merchants.

The only London trained lawyers with whom the elder Otis came in contact were Benjamin Lynde, the chief justice of the Superior Court, who administered the attorney's oath to Otis, and Paul Dudley, also a justice of the Superior Court. Despite Massachusetts's aversion to formal English legal training, the Bay Colony produced a few excellent courtroom lawyers in the 1730s, but they were uncommon, so the traders, joiners, and tavern keepers who acted as counsel retained a strong position in the operations of the local courts until the late 1750's when the college trained men assumed undisputed command. By 1762, of the twenty-seven practicing lawyers named as barristers by the Superior Court, only three had not attended college: James Otis, Sr., James Hovey, and William Read.

Another interesting feature of eighteenth century court procedure in Massachusetts was the regular employment of referees or arbitrators. The courts worked rapidly, often disposing of twenty cases in a day and had little time to consider or patience for convoluted details. When a complex issue arose that required the evaluation of minutiae, a common procedure was to refer the matter to three referees, one chosen by each party and one chosen by the court. The referees would then informally convene with the parties and draft a report to the court that was generally approved. James Otis Sr. excelled in these informal arbitration sessions, which were often held in the local tavern.

Jemmy lived in Barnstable until the spring of 1745. He then packed his small library and trekked back to Boston, most likely accompanying his father who was to attend his first General Court session. In July, during an adjournment when his father had returned to Barnstable, young Jemmy wrote home that he had purchased six quarts of "Ruhm" and that "Claret Sugar and Ruhm" were "quite good cheap." The disjointed, cramped handwriting of his college years was supplanted by an elegant and confident script. Three months subsequent he was embellishing his salutation with flourishes worthy of a royal charter when he reported at length about the return of Louisbourg hero Captain Rouse from England, where he had sailed to deliver the report of the victory, instead of on "good cheap" rum. The news of England's reaction to that achievement was nearly as exciting to Boston as the news of the victorious campaign itself, and young Jemmy was basking in the derivative glory.

The Louisbourg campaign was a baptism for New England as it seemed to prove that it was no longer the edge of civilization but rather a participant in world affairs, and the resulting sense of triumph, community pride, and global importance can find no clearer expression than in James Otis Jr.'s glowing letter. Even the reserved Thomas Hutchinson said the Louisbourg victory was "without parallel in all preceding American affairs."

While awash in Louisbourg inspired ebullience, twenty-year-old Jemmy Otis began his formal legal education that summer of 1745. His father had arranged for an apprenticeship with a preeminent lawyer, and while it's unlikely that Jemmy had much input in the decision, the prospect of working with a brilliant Boston lawyer-scholar must have been appealing. The choice of Jeremiah Gridley was both natural and fortuitous; Gridley had the reputation of one of the finest lawyers in the province and professed a sophisticated scholarly and cultured philosophy of law and life that would have been engaging to the emerging intellectual. The agreement between James Otis, Sr. and Jemmy's new mentor most likely resembled the one used by Gridley twenty years later when he undertook to train Daniel Oliver "liberally in Law" for the sum of £10 sterling annually for three years. Contemporaneously, the elder Otis had been engaged with Gridley and his business partner, oligarch Peter Oliver, in their project to construct an iron works and slitting mill to make iron bars, rods and nails in Plymouth County, and that contact may have laid the groundwork for Jemmy's apprenticeship.

That same year, a 13-year-old George Washington was studying at a French school in the newly founded tiny village of Fredericksburg, Virginia. The school was led by Rev. James Marye and, it seems, the staff was entirely French, including Marye who had arrived from France in 1729. Marye's school was decidedly old-fashioned and distinctly Continental. One of the students's exercises was to copy a book with 110 "Rules of Civility." The book traces its origin to *Bienseance de la Conversation entre les Hommes* (*Good Manners of Conversation between People*), a 16th century etiquette book used at the College at Pont-à-Mousson. Washington's transcribed copy of 1745 closely duplicates the 16th century book; the 110 lessons include:

> 26. In putting off your Hat to Persons of Distinction, as Noblemen, Justices, Churchmen, &c., make a Reverence, bowing more or less according to the Custom of the Better Bred, and Quality of the Persons Amongst your equals expect not always that they Should

begin with you first, but to Pull off the Hat when there is no need is Affectation. In the Manner of Saluting and resaluting in words keep to the most usual custom.

29. When you meet with one of Greater Quality than yourself, Stop, and retire, especially if it be at a door or any straight place, to give way for him to Pass.

39. In writing or Speaking, give to every Person his due Title According to his Degree & the Custom of the Place.

40. Strive not with your Superior in argument, but always Submit your Judgment to others with Modesty.

The "Rules of Civility" focuses not on relationships between the genders (save for the two rules mentioning "parents," the female gender is not referenced at all) but rather on relationships between oneself and "Persons of Distinction, as Noblemen, Justices, Churchmen" and those "of Greater Quality than yourself." The world of the *Bienseance de la Conversation* is filled with voluminous gradations of status, and receiving an education entailed, in large part, being able to discern a person's status and to respond appropriately. While Otis received a progressive education at Harvard and began tutelage under Boston's leading lawyer-scholar, Washington was receiving a traditional Continental gentlemen's education, which focused on manners not metaphysics. It's not the least bit surprising that the 16th century etiquette book *Bienseance de la Conversation* is traced to the College at Pont-à-Mousson, for Pont-à-Mousson is in northeastern France, just south of Luxembourg and in the heart of feudalism. The instruction Washington received in Fredericksburg was customary across Europe outside of the few progressive centers of education that had been stricken by the Enlightenment, and that his 1745 "Rules of Civility" is almost an exact copy of *Bienseance de la Conversation* illustrates how for most, little had changed from the late 16th to the mid 18th century.

Jemmy's legal tutor, Jeremiah Gridley – usually called Jeremy – was far from an etiquette teacher. He had graduated from Harvard in 1725 and shortly thereafter held the position of "usher" at Boston's South Grammar School. At the same time, he became a member in Monsieur Langloiserie's worldly French club, recently begun by the Frenchman who would shortly thereafter teach French at Harvard for 18 months for being accused to espousing "unsound and dangerous doctrines" – which may allude to his latent Catholicism or, more likely, to his claims of having "Dreams and Visions." In addition to the colorful company of Monsieur Langloiserie, Gridley entered the world of *belles lettres* in 1731 by editing and publishing the *Weekly Rehearsal*, a literary magazine. Two years later he gave up all of it, took a trip to England, and returned to teach himself law. By 1742 he was talented enough either as a politician or a lawyer to win election by the House of Representatives as attorney general. This office was not under the legal purview of the House despite long continued efforts to intimidate the governor on the point; so for Gridley, as it was to be later for James Otis Sr., it was a hollow victory. Gridley then accepted pupils including Benjamin Prat, the morose, one-legged, former Harvard librarian; Prat became Boston's most financially successful lawyer and later chief justice of the Province of New York. After Prat, Gridley mentored Oxenbridge Thacher, whom John Adams considered "queer and affected," and who probably absorbed Gridley's legal lore along with Otis. Another of Gridley's prominent apprentices was William Cushing, who was ultimately appointed third chief justice of the United States Supreme Court by George Washington. Apprenticeship under a practicing attorney may have been the most suitable introduction into the profession, but its value depended almost entirely on the moods and methods of the mentor. The potential for vast disparities in legal education is illustrated in the comparisons made by John Adams between his apprenticeship under James Putnam at Worcester, and the intellectual delight and inspiration he received from his studies with Gridley. Regarding his two years with Putnam, Adams wrote:

> Now I feel the Dissadvantages of Putnams Insociability, and neglect of me. Had he given me now and then a few Hints concerning Practice, I should be able to judge better at this Hour than I can now. I have Reason to complain of him. But, it is my Destiny to dig Treasures with my own fingers.

A few years later, Adams commented on mentoring under Gridley:

> We began the 13th Title of the feudal Law De Alienatione Feudi and read three Titles. Gridley proposed that we should mark all those Passages, which are adopted by the English Law, that when we come to read Ld. Coke we may recur back upon Occasion, to the originals of our Law.

Gridley was both an unparalleled legal scholar and an attentive mentor; those who learned under him considered themselves fortunate. The drudgery of being an apprentice of the law was the daily work as a clerk, with its continual copying of declarations and pleas. It is probable that Adams's displeasure with Putnam arose from the nonstop copying Adams was required to do and from which he learned by rote the idiosyncrasies of pleading syntax, and yet his mentor lacked the time or the talent to explain the underlying legal basis for the declarations and pleas. Legal theory was Gridley's specialty, a feature that oft materialized in Jemmy Otis's later work, and Gridley thoroughly educated his apprentices – the revolutionary generation of lawyers – in an extensive range of legal thought.

The emergence of legal scholars such as Chief Justice Lynde, John Read, and finally Jeremy Gridley and his pupils, and the corresponding increase in the intricacy and quantity of commercial business transactions, had generated within a few decades a judicial system that was progressively modern. The justices of the Superior Court, though largely self-taught, were competent and committed lawyers, but they were forced to operate on two levels by obsolete procedures and litigious countrymen. The Inferior Court justices and lawyers ranged in abilities and ethics from petty scroungers reminiscent of the seventeenth-century County Courts of England rejected by the first settlers to barristers who could have performed admirably before the King's Bench.

While the philosophers of Europe were increasing the precision with which they addressed eternal questions, the lawyers of New England were applying that same precision to the law. In December 1746, in response to his father's request, Jemmy forwarded a form of declaration to be utilized in a defamation suit, a branch of law that was to become very familiar to Jemmy. "The following is a Declaration of Mr Prats Drawing," he wrote, "which I believe you will like better than mine as it includes the words of Defamation for one ground of Action which Mr Prat has since informed me can be Proved." It would have been expected for a country lawyer in the elder Otis's situation to seek assistance in an atypical case from a son who had access to a large law library and a broad knowledge of modern legal forms. James Sr.'s request was also indicative of the transformation occurring in the practice of law in the province. A declaration such as the one supplied by Jemmy was the nucleus of a legal action, and, with the dawning of precise and sophisticated pleading, if it were written imperfectly in any essential feature, then the plaintiff's attorney would find his writ abated and the case dismissed if the opposing attorney could demonstrate the fatal flaw to the court. The clever lawyers of the younger generation eventually made for better law, but until the entirety of the bench and bar became more adroit in the use of pleading minutiae, the Massachusetts judicial system would remain a venue for imprecise law and occasionally ludicrous results. Books of pleading forms, or "Precedents," were not only scarce but also limited in scope, and the practice of drawing, adapting, copying, and trading pleading forms grew widespread and essential. The objective of formal pleading was to condense an entire case to a single issue of fact or law. Typically, a well-pled case resulted in less time spent in court, but it required significantly more time in research and preparation, an impractical demand for lawyers like the senior Otis who practiced impromptu law from the saddle. Further complicating legal progress, litigants were reluctant to forfeit their full day in court, even in exchange for a better case. A formal argument over a legal technicality gave inadequate satisfaction to the litigious New Englander who wished to fully expose the perfidy of his adversary in the course of a courtroom drama; in an age with few of modernity's vast entertainment options, some simply did not wish to forgo legal theater. In this period of flux we find Jemmy, Ben Prat, Oxenbridge Thacher, John Adams, and other legal novices copying and treasuring forms of formal declarations and pleas, perfecting pleading syntax, and analyzing minute concepts of theory. Jemmy's generation was the catalyst for the transformation of colonial jurisprudence from John Winthrop's utopian dream of a society without codes or lawyers to the rather sophisticated organization that materialized with the new nation after the Revolution. They were building the foundation for the excellent pleaders of Daniel Webster's day, and at the same time compelling their elders to either adapt or retire. That access to the courts coincided with the increasing sophistication and precision of the law also created the legal system needed to handle the greater complexity of 18th and 19th century life, including the advent of the industrial revolution, increasingly intricate banking, and civil rights matters.

Jemmy took a break in legal studies for the Harvard commencement in 1746, when he and twenty-six of his classmates returned to Cambridge to receive their Master's degrees. All the candidates were to deliver oral arguments on questions of their selection, and Otis's argument was that an oath obtained by craft was not binding. The main event at this commencement was the presence of the heroes of Louisbourg, Admiral Sir Peter Warren and Sir William Pepperell, who were present to congratulate young Pepperell on earning his second degree. James Otis Sr. was now a Colonel in the Barnstable militia and was commonly called by his deferential title "Colonel." He spent considerable time in Boston attending the General Court and could presumably consult personally with his talented lawyer son, so there are few letters between them from the late 1740s. The Colonel's second oldest son, Joseph, was assisting in the operation of the Barnstable businesses, so the Colonel's presence was required less often in Barnstable. Joseph was only 13 months younger that Jemmy, so they were quite close in age, and yet they couldn't have been more different in personality. Jemmy and Joseph were both prepared for admission to Harvard by the same tutor, and while Jemmy clearly had the aptitude required for college work, Joseph just as clearly had no business attending college. His only academic virtue was legible handwriting, which in itself was a valuable trait but didn't warrant a college education. And while Jemmy was somewhat short and pudgy – a man who clearly intimidated with his mind, not his body – Joseph was a bit brutish. Both Jemmy and his youngest brother, Samuel Allyne, would leave Barnstable for college and thereafter spend most of the remainder of their lives in the big city, Boston. In contrast, Joseph seemed to prefer to be a big fish in a small pond and lived his life in Barnstable. Not only did Jemmy and Samuel Allyne never return to live in Barnstable permanently, but they did not often visit. It's clear that Joseph was very different from his brothers.

While Jemmy was beginning his legal career and the Colonel was climbing the ladder of Boston politics, Joseph was getting in trouble in Barnstable. Due to his good handwriting, Joseph spent much of the 1740s sending out demands for payment and other correspondence for his father's businesses, and, of course, signing his father's name since his own wasn't of much value. It's probable that Joseph caused a decent amount of minor trouble in Barnstable and occasionally major trouble. At the end of the decade, the Hinckley's black nanny became pregnant and suspicion fell on the Hinckley's son, Isaac Hinckley, Jr. Quick to deflect blame, Isaac accused Joseph of being the father. The Hinckleys brought the case to court. Depositions were taken. Joseph's Aunt Russell, wife of the Otis's pastor and tutor, asserted that the charge made no sense because "if Joseph Otis wanted a Negro they had one at home." The Hinckleys replied that "There was a Difference between a Clean whore and a Durty one." No one was defending Joseph Otis based on the idea that he simply wouldn't engage in such activity. And Joseph's defense seemed to entail admitting that he "had Carnal knowledge of the said Nannys Body" but asserting that many other men in town also had such carnal knowledge, which apparently was true as one, David Manning, came forth to personally confirm Joseph's assertion. The court found in Joseph's favor, as paternity couldn't be proved. Joseph's defense reveals the kind of reputation that Joseph had in Barnstable and the kind of behavior in which he engaged and which his brothers and father almost certainly found repugnant. The Colonel, with his immense resources, could have certainly made the case disappear, and yet the father permitted the case to proceed against his son and required his son to defend himself in court and on the record, knowing that his son may have been guilty.

designed, by Nature, for a Genius

In the late 1740s Plymouth County reported a population of about 20,000 people, almost 2,000 living in the town of Plymouth. The town's core structures – wharves, corn and flour mill, iron mill, blacksmith shop, meetinghouse – were located near the mouth of Town Brook as it emptied into the bay. In the center of Plymouth town stood the old "County House" that had been the seat of the Plymouth Colony government and after its absorption into the Province of Massachusetts Bay was used to accommodate town and county government offices, a courtroom, and a portico to shelter the marketplace. In 1749 it was razed, and a new "Town House" was constructed on the same site according to oligarch Peter Oliver's design; Oliver was also one of Plymouth's Inferior Court justices. Across the street was the home of the Warren family, then headed by Sheriff James Warren, Sr, and included his son James, the clerk of the court and future husband of Jemmy's sister, Mercy. So the Town House, designed by the pompous aristocrat Peter Oliver sat across the street from the Warren house, where 15 years later the first organized plot to overthrow the government was hatched.

In the fall of 1747 Jemmy began his law practice in Plymouth town, most likely as a compromise with his father: Plymouth was neither the home of Barnstable nor the remoteness of Boston. In Plymouth, Jemmy could live in some freedom but still utilize significant family connections. While Barnstable was the center of the Colonel's operations, Plymouth was the center of the four counties of Southern Massachusetts: Barnstable, Plymouth, Bristol, and Dukes. It would have been to the Colonel's obvious advantage to have a trusted assistant in Plymouth. The Colonel could usually be present to argue cases, but there were clients to be interviewed, writs to be drawn, and, once the case was tried, writs of execution to be placed in the sheriff's hands if one were successful or appeals to be prepared and appeal bond to file if one lost the case. Apart from the Colonel's own interests, Plymouth County would have been more familiar to Jemmy than even Barnstable County, which incorporated all of Cape Cod; further, there were familial and mercantile connections on both his father's and mother's side that would be valuable. Fortuitously, Plymouth was understaffed in the quality and quantity of its lawyers for a town of its size and importance. Jemmy rented living quarters and office space in a house built and owned by Colonel John Winslow on the main street just a block from the Court House. In 1748, the local tax bill assessed the young lawyer at "20 £ personal estate and faculty," and this rate was most likely volunteered by Otis so that he could vote in town elections and meet the criteria to act as a bondsman. So in this context, Jemmy arranged his table and chairs, unpacked his legal books, sharpened his quill pens, and awaited his first client.

The house in which Jemmy lived and worked faced the home of Lazarus LeBaron, Plymouth's appropriately named physician and seemingly permanent town meeting moderator. Though Plymouth had only one room for its judicial functions and though the colonists had vastly improved and simplified England's egregiously complex judicial structure, the County still played host to five separate judicial bodies. First there were the appointed justices of the peace who acted as individual magistrates over small civil cases and minor misdemeanors. A lawyer rarely would be involved at this level. The justices named to the quorum comprised the quarterly Court of General Sessions of the Peace. This Court functioned as the court of original jurisdiction over most crimes and as a Board of Supervisors, issuing licenses for taverns, managing building projects, and issuing warnings to the unruly and unwelcome. Another Plymouth County Court was Probate, presided over by a single appointed judge and a clerk. Operating in tandem with the Court of General Sessions was the Inferior Court of Common Pleas, the court of origination for most civil cases and the training court for novice lawyers. The court consisted of four justices, appointed by the governor with the advice and consent of the Governor's Council, of which any three constituted the necessary quorum to hear a case; typically, colonial courts operated with multiple judges or justices hearing a case so that they were more similar to a tribunal than a modern court. These judgeship appointments were of considerable local cachet and were thus often the subject of passionate patronage mêlées. When Jemmy opened his law practice in Plymouth, the ubiquitous Peter Oliver, John Cushing, Thomas Clap, and Nicholas Sever commanded the four seats of the

Inferior Court of Common Pleas. Judge Sever was the senior justice, a Harvard graduate and former minister, and somewhat infamous for his inability to suffer fools lightly. Judge Cushing was a member of an old Plymouth family that produced several lawyers and politicians; in February 1748, he was promoted to the Superior Court and continued his position on the Province Council. His seat on the Plymouth bench was assumed by Isaac Lathrop, Jr., the son of a former judge. Wealthy pompous Judge Oliver must have considered his position on the court to be temporary; a man with his superior assets demanded a superior position, and it was made so in 1756 when he was promoted to the Superior Court and ultimately to the Governor's Council three year later.

The fourth and foremost court was the Superior Court of Judicature, Court of Assize and General Goal Delivery, generally referred to as the Superior Court. The governor and Council appointed four justices and a chief justice who served at the pleasure of their patrons. The court appointed two clerks, one of whom typically remained in Boston while the other accompanied the court on circuit. The circuit included the entire province with the exception of Dukes County (Martha's Vineyard) and Nantucket cases, which were tried at Barnstable. The Court operated in each county at least once a year on a statutory schedule and had broad jurisdiction, original with serious crimes and cases in which the King was party, and appellate in cases originating in both the Courts of General Sessions and Common Pleas. Its probate jurisdiction was restricted to orders for the sale of real estate to satisfy a decedent's debts; other probate appeals and actions for divorce were heard by the governor and Council.

In criminal and civil cases in which the King was a party, the appointed attorney general represented the crown, but the attorney general rarely could be bothered to travel outside of Boston, and one of the first acts of any session of the court on circuit was to appoint a local lawyer to serve as the King's Attorney for the term. When Jemmy Otis first appeared before the Superior Court, it was made up of Chief Justice Paul Dudley, who had studied law at the Inns of Court, Richard Saltonstall, Stephen Sewall, Benjamin Lynde Jr., and John Cushing. John Overing was the attorney general.

Jemmy Otis's first case was typical in many aspects, primarily because it brilliantly illustrates coordination between the legal and political spheres, between Jemmy and his father, and between practical "country lawyer" application and theoretical new-generation erudition. In these many ways, *Russell v. Dillingham* proved prologue to the drama that would occur later. It would be instructive to Jemmy and his generation in the power that a combination of the legislative and the increasingly respected legal worlds could produce. Further, it exhibited Jemmy's remarkable elasticity and talent for research in examining mountains of legal theory and precedent in order to outmaneuver his opponents.

Jemmy's client was "John Russell of Pembrook in the County of Plymouth husbandman," and he must have knocked on Otis's office door as soon as the young lawyer had his books unpacked. It is probable that Russell had tried other lawyers without success or that he was a Colonel Otis client who had been referred to the son; he seemed desperate and quickly sought Jemmy's assistance. Russell's grievance was that John Dillingham, also of Pembroke, had "for value received" provided Russell with a "note" promising to "pay and deliver" to him on demand a hundred fence rails and half a load of fence posts. Now Dillingham "though often requested" refused to fulfill his contractual obligation. Otis and Russell likely discussed fees, though there were statutory fees for the attorneys that were taxed as costs, and the winning lawyer could collect his fee from the losing party. In difficult cases, additional fee arrangements were often made. Otis first needed to make a decision as to which of the three available forms of action – covenant, debt, or assumpsit – would most likely produce the desired result. The promissory note was not under seal, so covenant was automatically excluded as a possibility. Since the amount of money claimed as damages was not "a sum certain," debt would have been inappropriate. Assumpsit, so called from the Latin word in the earliest forms of the writ, was a variety of general writ of trespass. The original principle of assumpsit was intentional harm, but over the centuries it had come to include trespass writs covering unintentional and consequential injuries termed "trespass on the case." Other varieties of the ancient writ included in "trespass on the case in assumpsit" that was applied to recover monetary damages for breach of contract, but this was oft ignored in the colonies and commonly replaced with the phrase "trespass on the case" to cover everything from suits on promissory notes and bills of exchange to the determination of real estate titles. Otis was in the fore of colonial legal practice when he chose to argue Russell's action as trespass on the case. Instead of the present day practice of drafting and signing the complaint as a separate instrument, the colonial Massachusetts lawyer normally copied the declaration directly on the printed form. The "writ" thus was both the plaintiff's declaration and a summons to the defendant to appear and defend, attested by the clerk and served by the sheriff. The writ may also include an attachment which directed the sheriff to seize property of the defendant or, in the absence of such property, to arrest the defendant until bail was posted.

Dillingham retained the Harvard educated yet hapless Daniel Lewis as his attorney. Lewis excelled at neither law nor politics and died insolvent, but even Lewis could see an obvious defect in Otis's declaration: the suit was filed years after the statute of limitations had expired. The preamble of the relevant act, which became law in 1740, declaimed that "it is highly reasonable, and conduces much to the peace and welfare of the subject, that a certain and reasonable time should be set for the prosecuting of actions." Dredging up thirty-year-old misdeeds had occurred in New England, but the law was progressing and the increasing complexity of merchant life demanded reasonable legal limitations. The Massachusetts statute, the language of which had been borrowed from the basic English act of 1623, declared that "all actions grounded upon any lending or contract" must be brought within four years. Lewis indicated the agreed fact that the demand note originated in 1730 and therefore the statutory period had long expired.

The case came up for trial in the March term of 1748, just after Jemmy turned 23. Lewis's defense raised a pure point of law, but the court reserved any decision on the technical legal point and permitted the case to go to the jury, though likely with an instruction that the action should be voided due the statute of limitations. The jury delivered the predictable verdict for the defendant, and the court taxed costs of one pound and seventeen shillings against Otis's client. In the Massachusetts tradition, Otis appealed, posted a twenty pound bond, and then the clerk assembled the writ, pleadings, bill of costs, and statement of the Inferior Court judgment and waited for the arrival of the Superior Court on its circuit. Many years beyond the statute of limitations, *Russell v. Dillingham* was quite clearly an unwinnable case. But a clever lawyer could manufacture opportunities when a case required, and reflecting his meticulous training under Gridley, Jemmy had painstakingly researched the issue of limitations. Unlike many lawyers of the 1740's, Jemmy had obtained books of English statutes and legal reports. In comparing the Massachusetts statute of limitations to its English predecessor, Otis became convinced that the phrase "upon any lending or contract" in the province statute was not intended to apply to promissory notes or contracts for goods between traders or merchants, which were explicitly covered in the English act under a separate section that was not included in the Massachusetts act.

Jemmy would argue that the legal result was that no limitation existed in Massachusetts on actions based upon such notes or contracts.

The Superior Court of Judicature arrived at Plymouth for its annual term in July 1748. Otis was ready to argue the point anew. To lend substance to his aggressiveness, he directed Sheriff Warren to attach a chair belonging to Dillingham. Dillingham was perhaps annoyed at losing a chair, so he returned to court with Benjamin Kent, a leading Boston lawyer. He argued again that the statute of limitations voided the case, and the Court affirmed the earlier judgment. However, Jemmy Otis was not only tenacious but seemingly immune to failure; losing only fueled his desire to outwit or outmaneuver his opponent. And so it was no coincidence that on January 6, 1749, the speaker of the House of Representatives Thomas Hutchinson abruptly appointed Colonel Otis as chairman of a committee to "prepare the Draft of a Bill for Explanation of the Act Intitled *An Act for Limitation of Actions, etc.*" And with speed rarely witnessed in legislative bodies, the Otis bill was made law just three weeks later. Its long preamble explained how the 1740 act had been intended as a replica of the English statute, and how "some courts of judicature of this province" had expanded the scope of the act beyond its intended range, thus causing "great mischief and inconvenience in the trade of merchandize." The new act permitted creditors who had been barred by the misinterpretation of the 1740 act to seek a new trial. Jemmy Otis had changed colonial law with his first case, but how did Jemmy's legal discovery make it into law in record time, and in time to file an appeal?

At the exact moment Colonel Otis chose to introduce his "explanatory" bill that would allow his son to appeal and almost certainly win his first case, the House was intensely engaged in a critical debate on Massachusetts currency. Speaker Thomas Hutchinson was frantically attempting to cultivate the votes required to abolish the deflated bills of credit then constituting province currency and to refund the province war debt with silver coming from England as reimbursement payment for the Louisbourg campaign; of course, oligarchs such as Hutchinson would benefit most from such a bill. Colonel Otis, with his substantial following south of Boston, was key to accumulating enough votes to pass Hutchinson's currency reform, and support for Otis's bill would have been a small price to pay for his continued aid with the currency legislation. Additionally, Otis's bill, which favored creditors, would have appealed to Hutchinson's merchant constituency. There's no paper trail to prove a connection, but it's likely that Hutchinson rushed through Otis's bill in return for support of the currency reform. The Colonel was a master of political manipulation and influence peddling, skills his son would later grudgingly learn so well he'd exceed the master.

But Otis's client had given up. Otis wrote his father on January 3, 1750 from Plymouth telling him that he had not seen Russell, but requested that the Colonel procure the necessary writ from Chief Justice Paul Dudley. And in July the ten pound case – now raised to twenty-five pounds – was on the docket again. With the limitation problem out of the way, the case could be tried on the merits, but the court was in no mood to listen to a nearly 20-year-old argument about the value of fence posts, and promptly referred the case to an arbitration panel. No referees report appears either in the record or the court files, and it's most likely that some amicable settlement was reached out of court. The 1740 statute of limitations was a perfect example of the confusion that resulted when legislators untrained in the law attempted to state in layman's language an inherently technical legal concept. The case also demonstrates Jemmy's doggedness and technical genius, and the Colonel's role in the case cannot be disregarded. It was at about this same time that the Colonel's 23-year-old son Joseph was being accused of impregnating the neighbor's black nanny, and the Colonel made the decision to let the trial against his son go forward. The Colonel desperately wanted to support his children and would access any connection to do so, but he clearly had no tolerance for bad behavior. So while Jemmy was making legal history, his brother was being put through an experience that must have been humiliating. Despite Joseph's legal problems, the Colonel still used his connections to help him. The Colonel's significant political power secured for the Otis family the guardianship of the Mashpee Indians, which meant that the province provided funds via Otis to supply the Indians with necessities. Joseph would handle this work. The Colonel could also influence the assignment of liquor licenses, the appointment of justices of the peace, and the selection of other minor town officials. The Colonel's brother Solomon continued to hold the position of town notary. In 1750, Joseph was appointed town collector of excise taxes. The Colonel held the town's liquor license until 1753 when the license was transferred to Joseph. So despite Joseph's troubles, he wasn't excluded from his father's benevolence.

The *Russell v. Dillingham* case provides insight into the cooperative endeavors of Colonel Otis and his son. They likely had divergent ideas about the law and its practice, but the practical advantages of cooperation seemed to keep such differences submerged. For example, in June of 1748, Colonel Otis, then in Boston, wrote his son in care of Mr. Williams in Taunton, granting executor powers of "Messrs Bowdoin" for Jemmy to use in a pending case and advising him to claim fees for travel, attendance, and sheriff's charges; the Colonel also asked Jemmy to supervise one case and appear for him in others. Above all, Jemmy's first case illustrates his absolute tenacity in pursuing a victory, his ability for deft and meticulous research, and his creativity in prevailing over the status quo. These skills were sharpened on fence posts but would be used to much greater effect a few years later, and again in silent cooperation with the Colonel.

In January 1750, Jemmy returned to Plymouth after a Barnstable visit, asked his father about the effect of the explanatory amendment to the statute of limitations and petulantly complained about printer Kneeland's failure to send him copies of the "temporary Acts" and the second volume of the "perpetual Acts." A few days later Joseph wrote his father from Barnstable concerning various mercantile affairs, and repeated Jemmy's request for the law books. In excusing his brother's failure to write often, Joseph noted that Jemmy "has taken so close to his studies that he scarcely allows himself time to eat drink or sleep." Two months later a client wrote a long letter to Colonel Otis about a pending case, but directed that the letter be delivered "to his Son Mr James Otis" in the event the Colonel was not attending court. Despite these details, Jemmy was never an integrated part of the family's interwoven political, legal, and mercantile affairs; of all the sons, Jemmy alone would almost entirely exclude himself from the mercantile aspects of the family empire. Initially, Jemmy stayed fairly close to his Plymouth base aside from an occasional appearance at the Barnstable courts and at the Taunton court in Bristol County where in May 1750 he was formally admitted to practice before the Superior Court, after taking the oath before Chief Justice Paul Dudley.

At the time, law partnerships were unknown in Massachusetts and though significant cases frequently employed multiple lawyers, there seems to have been no consistent pattern in those temporary associations. When Jemmy and his father would meet on circuit, primarily at the Superior Court terms at Plymouth, the clerk would often note that one party was represented by "Colo Otis & Son," but with almost the same frequency, they would be on opposing sides of a case. These confrontations likely presented engaging theater for the local connoisseurs of court room drama with Jemmy's oratorical brilliance and legal scholarship pitted against the charm of the Colonel with his country jurors.

The peculiar and legendary *Samuel Veazie v. The Inhabitants of the Town of Duxborough* is the first of such dramas of which there exists a record. John Adams complained that "litigious as Braintree" had become an insulting province proverb, and Veazie was a Braintree native from a family distinguished for its litigiousness even in that litigious town. After graduation from Harvard, Veazie became the minister of the Duxbury church despite the enduring reservations of a sizeable portion of the congregation. The "Great Awakening" of 1740 made him "morose, dogmatic and furious," a change that annoyed many of his congregants. The Duxborough congregants grew weary of the Reverend's Great Awakening attitude and wished to dismiss him, but Veazie was under contract. The disagreement was over whether Veazie had fulfilled the contract, and he had once hired attorney Ben Kent to attempt to compel the town to pay his salary; that case apparently never progressed beyond posturing.

So in the spring of 1748, Veazie engaged Plymouth County's newest lawyer, James Otis, to file a law suit for the "morose" minister's salary; Otis named the inhabitants of the town as defendants "of which Ezra Arnold, Gentleman and a Deputy Sheriff of the said County is one." Otis was aiming to establish Arnold as a suitable agent of the town for the purpose of serving the suit. The declaration alleged that Veazie was employed as a minister of the town "upon their special instance and request, had preached and ministered unto them, the Defendants, the Gospel" from April to April, indicating the end of the town's salary payments to its minister. Otis chose to sue for "as much as he should reasonably deserve," which, the declaration continued, was one hundred pounds per year. At the May 1748 trial, the parties agreed to turn the matter over to three referees, and Veazie chose Ezra Whitmarsh, the town chose the peculiarly named Wrestling Brewster, and the Court named Colonel Benjamin Lincoln (whose son, many years later, would marry Otis's daughter). The agreement to use referees stipulated that Veazie would request, and the town would grant, the minister's dismissal. But in submitting the request for dismissal, Veazie stipulated his reason as "the want of a Support and Mearly that Want Hereof," which the town was disinclined to put on record. At this point the town hired attorney Timothy Ruggles, who was to suffer under the lash of Otis's invective in the years ahead. At the sputtering case's scheduled hearing in September, Ruggles offered a motion to dismiss the suit on the grounds that the sheriff had failed to leave a copy of the suit at the office of the town clerk of Duxbury. This was a petty technicality but an arguable legal point in 1748, and the Inferior Court dismissed the case without further proceedings and assessed costs of four pounds and fifteen shillings against Veazie. Otis swiftly appealed the decision to the Superior Court and, together with one of Veazie's Duxbury supporters, filed the required appeal bond. The appeal was docketed for the July term of the Superior Court in 1749. The Duxbury church, however, now thoroughly riled, employed the most powerful advocate available, Colonel Otis, and thus father and son came face to face; the church again won the case on Ruggles's technicality. The church proceeded to dismiss the dejected Veazie, and he preached a tearful concluding sermon. "Brethren," he said, "I shall probably not come to you again in this place until I come in the clouds!" To which one of the congregants reportedly replied, "Why, the creature does not expect to come again until it rains toads!"

The Veazie case was unique in its details but common in its attitude: religious differences cause a town to refuse to pay their minister, so the minister sues the town. New Englanders did not demur from friction; public squabbles, printed debates and lawsuits were common in almost every facet of life. And in this environment, Jemmy Otis rapidly became a leading lawyer in Plymouth. He played a significant role in bringing legal scholarship and refined procedure to the county. His complex argument in *Russell v. Dillingham* is but one instance, and the case of *Otis v. Turner* is another; in December 1748, the case of *James Otis, Junior v. John Turner* appeared on the docket of the Inferior Court, and it is probable that the justices had never seen anything like the five page declaration filed by the young upstart.

Over the centuries, the feudal basis of English real property law had become encrusted with formal procedures of such mind-boggling intricacy that an action to quit the title to real estate, or to deal with encroachments of various sorts, approached near impossibility. The relatively simple action of ejectment with its fictional tenant, John Doe, became the primary method of proving land ownership in England. To the untutored colonists, this legal chicanery was still enigmatic, but by the 1740s, the trend toward legal sophistication and courtroom cleverness led some of the younger lawyers to employ ejectment.

Refinement in the application of property law was balanced by refinement in the black art of conveyance, and the creation of entailed estates became the vogue among those grasping aristocrats of colonial society who dreamed of a feudal landed gentry. In feudalism, the sole true owner of real estate is the king; all others are tenants, the lords being "tenants-in-chief." To maintain order and ensure that the tenants-in-chief do not sell land that is putatively owned by the king, the land was held "entail" by the lords. Entailed estates could only be granted to direct heirs; they could not be sold, divided, left to illegitimate or indirect heirs, or, typically, even used as collateral. To combat the development of entailed – that is, feudal – estates in the colonies, Jemmy Otis grasped the opportunity to display the results of Jeremy Gridley's careful teaching by employing arcane and complicated English legal maneuvers. *James Otis, Junior v. John Turner* was in the form of the archaic Writ of Entry that had been largely abandoned in England by this time. Otis was not actually the plaintiff and Turner was not actually the defendant. "Ejectment" was a complicated legal means that developed out of medieval England to settle disputes over who owned a parcel of land; a person who felt he owned disputed land would hire an attorney to file an ejectment case in which a fictitious plaintiff would sue a fictitious defendant. A copy of the suit in the name of the fictitious defendant would be sent to any potential real defendant. The fictitious defendants would appear, or no defendants would appear, and eventually the case would be decided on behalf of the fictitious plaintiff, who would then convey title to the real plaintiff. It was an elaborate legal drama meant to give a plaintiff a trial regardless of whether any real defendant appeared in court.

So Otis was merely a nominal plaintiff, having no actual interest in the land in question. John Turner and his wife Mercy, long time friends and distant relatives of the Otis family, were nominal, or collusive, defendants – they were colluding with Otis to present the case. The intention of the suit, which is completely hidden by its multiple fictions, was a "common recovery," designed to both settle title to real estate and to exclude any other claims; a claimant appearing out of nowhere after an ejectment case would have difficulty asserting ownership to a piece of land since a court had already decided the matter. The Turners, with Colonel Otis as their attorney, asked to "vouch," or call in, their "warrantors" as defendants. At the next term the "vouchees" appeared, likewise represented by Colonel Otis, who then asked leave to "imparl" with the vouchees, who then, according to the legal ritual, disappeared. This legal theater repeated itself a few times until net result was a collusive judgment giving Jemmy Otis nearly perfect title to various "lotts" of salt marsh and upland in Duxbury. He would then convey his new title to the real plaintiff, who may have been the "Baily" who paid the Otises one hundred pounds "profits" for his "common recovery" the following year. One hundred pounds was a large fee, but if Baily had read the pleadings in *Otis v. Turner* he probably would have concluded that the fee was small compared to the complex legal chicanery his lawyer employed. Father and son split this fee, as they did many others during the Plymouth years. *Otis v. Turner* was profitable theater, but it and similar cases led these eager young legal scholars to imbed such technical and complex forms of action so firmly in Massachusetts law that they were still in use far into the 19th century. Importantly, this 1748 case was a small skirmish in the battle between modernity and feudalism and demonstrates a young Jemmy employing the law in a minor victory against the armies of aristocracy. Victories like these would coalesce with lessons from the Land Bank to instruct Jemmy's generation about the battles that lay ahead.

Otis won many cases, and he lost several as well. Though he was the brightest and best educated lawyer practicing in Plymouth, his scholarly superiority was no guarantee of courtroom omnipotence. He was to prove himself a superb orator, but his oratory was of a different variety than his father's and may have been less convincing to the "drovers and horsejockies" on the Plymouth juries. With perseverance, Jemmy could have risen to the top of the Plymouth bar, but he may have felt, either consciously or unconsciously, that his aspirations were greater than to be Plymouth's leading lawyer, and he may have been impatient because of his father's dominant position in the courtrooms of the region. In that hierarchical world he might have always remained "young Otis." He had been bloodied in the courtroom battles of Plymouth, Taunton, and Barnstable and had been admitted to practice before the Superior Court, so he was professionally qualified to take his place in the Boston bar. Jemmy had been financially independent since 1748 and his August 1750 relocation to Boston was an assertion of independence in a broader sense. The Superior Court Minute Book records the "young Otis" picking up writs of execution in Plymouth as late as August 1, and his account with his father was balanced off just prior to that; it was time to move on.

Jemmy Otis's time as a Plymouth lawyer was short but he'd clearly established an excellent reputation; in later years the inhabitants of Plymouth and Bristol Counties were quick to retain his services as he followed the Superior Court on circuit. And he had made a strong impression on Inferior Court Justice Peter Oliver as one "designed, by Nature, for a Genius."

the customs establishment & the leverage of juries

In August 1750, Jemmy Otis moved in with his maternal Uncle Allen in Boston, but for the next five years kept a low profile outside of legal circles, his name never appearing in town records or newspapers. His work would have been almost entirely centered around the Town House and the Exchange, the hub of legal and mercantile affairs in Boston. The classic brick Town House was built in 1713 and rebuilt after the devastating fire of 1747; it dominated the center of the town, standing directly at the intersection of King Street and Cornhill (now State and Washington Streets). It was near the dividing line between the North and South Enders who engaged in annual Pope's Day mêlées, and between the rougher dockworkers to the east and the gentry to the west. The Town House served every segment of society. The merchant's Exchange occupied all of the first floor except for an office in the northeast corner presided over by Nathaniel Hatch and Samuel Winthrop, the clerks of the Superior Court, and a similar nook in the northwest corner for Province secretary Josiah Willard. The second floor was divided into three rooms, each of which would present a stage for Jemmy Otis as he alternately played his roles as hero and villain. Overlooking King Street and the Long Wharf, the east room served as the Council Chamber; the largest room was in the middle and served as the meeting place for the House of Representatives, and the small room in the west end was the Court Room.

The daily routine of Boston's lawyers required them to rent offices near the Town House. Every lawyer spent considerable time at the "Change," or Exchange, where news, rumors, and clients could be found in the assortment of merchants, traders, sea captains, legislators, and lawyers gathered there. More time would be spent in "Hatch's Office" where writs were filed, executions issued, and returned writs examined. Otis lived and worked in a small neighborhood across King Street – an area no larger than Plymouth town or West Barnstable. To the north of the Exchange stood the Brazen Head Tavern and down the street were Benjamin Kent's office, the Exchange Tavern, and later the Customs House. Otis's residence and the British Coffee House were no more than a few blocks from any of these points of interest.

The Suffolk County Inferior Court in Boston handled almost four times as many cases as the Plymouth Court, and the £10 cases that engaged the country courts often swelled into £100 and £1000 cases in Boston. Duxborough congregation clients were replaced by litigants from London, Barbados, and Jamaica, and the Superior Court, while requiring only three days to work through a Plymouth county docket of cases, needed two extended sessions to complete its work in Boston. In the less populous counties of Plymouth, Bristol, and Barnstable, Otis had grown comfortable to a degree of legal dominance by his family; this feature of small town life was unexpectedly repeated in the metropolis, for often when Otis appeared in the Inferior Court of Suffolk County he found himself facing two justices named Hutchinson, one of whom also held the position of judge of probate. In 1750, the cousins Edward Hutchinson and Eliakim Hutchinson were justices of the Suffolk County Inferior Court, and Edward was also judge of probate. On Edward's death in 1752 his nephew, Thomas Hutchinson, essentially inherited both offices. Nothing was said about the apparent heredity of official offices at the time.

In May of 1750, Henry Lloyd, the merchant, wrote his father in New York that "we haveing a Dearth of good Lawyers here, a door may be open for Mr Fitch." Two weeks later he continued: "All our eminent Lawyers," he wrote, "being either Dead or incapable of doing much business, may open a door for Mr Fitch if he inclines to try his tallents in Boston." Otis exhibited a less optimistic outlook; just a few weeks after arriving in Boston, Jemmy wrote his father, "As to Business I have but little or none Aplin being engaged in everything that goes beside the cup of Dana - Goff who are very carefull to keep what case there is." Referring to Fitch, Otis reported, "A man from Connecticut that makes a noise here and being Recommended to the court & backed with a great many friends will help spoil the Business." Samuel Fitch seemed to be the hot new lawyer in town. One of Fitch's "many friends" was Justice Eliakim Hutchinson, Henry Lloyd Jr.'s brother-in-law. "Goff" was Edmund Trowbridge who for many years used the name of his guardian-uncle, Gaffe. "Aplin" is an obscure figure, apparently the Aplin whom John Adams later found to be as "tedious" as Robert Auchmuty.

Otis was excessively gloomy; albeit of substantial population and importance, Boston counted only five veteran lawyers engaged in full time practice. John "Father" Read, the celebrated generalist of the older generation, had died in 1749, leaving Jemmy's mentor Jeremy Gridley as the pre-eminent lawyer of the Boston bar. Gridley's peers were Richard Dana ("Dana") and his brother-in-law Edmund Trowbridge ("Goff"), both of whom had been practicing before the Superior Court for nearly two decades. The younger generation of lawyers practicing in Boston included Ben Kent and Ben Prat. And yet Otis informed his father that Prat was suffering one of his recurring bouts of illness, and Gridley was "on his Passage" to some unidentified destination. This left Dana and Goff in a preeminent position. The younger generation rapidly filled this vacuum; Otis and Samuel Fitch arrived in the fall of 1750, and Robert Auchmuty and Oxenbridge Thacher followed them soon after. This newly arrived younger generation effectively composed the Boston bar in the early 1750s.

Other conditions in 1750 made for a favorable climate to embark on a legal practice; though generating distress amongst the general population, economic uncertainty benefits lawyers. Thomas Hutchinson and Governor Shirley had finally succeeded in legislating currency reform, but even the business community that stood to gain the most was faced with a dilemma. The old bills of credit had been voided, but their silver replacements were either slow to appear in the channels of trade or swift to disappear. The merchants were accused of shipping all the silver back to England to pay their debts, and the newspapers were filled with accusations. Convoluted tables for converting "Old Tenor" and "New Tenor" bills to the new silver coinage were printed, and Bostonians were either amused or angered by an open accusation leveled at Thomas Hutchinson that he had engaged in prohibited and profitable transactions with New Hampshire bills of credit, to which Hutchinson published an admission and a convoluted, technical justification that disappointed his allies and stoked the fires of his enemies. The abrupt correction after the long inflationary binge and the resulting disruption of intercolonial trade produced a precarious economic, legal, and political climate. Lawyers thrive in such conditions, and, not surprisingly, the animosity against the mysterious art and its practitioners surfaced in a poem published in the Boston *Evening-Post*, February 5, 1750 that concluded:

> Then rather let two Neighbors end your Cause,
> And split the Difference; tho' you lose one half;'
> Than spend the whole, entangled in the Laws,
> While Lawyers sly, at both Sides laugh.

Despite his pessimism, Otis quickly established himself in Boston, arguing for an appeal in the Superior Court as early as February 1751 – just five months after relocating. He was particularly growing popular among the merchants;

he won a February 1751 case for merchant Joseph Waldo, a Harvard acquaintance and member of the faction opposing Governor Shirley and Hutchinson. Two months later, the Superior Court disclosed enough confidence in the young lawyer to appoint him "to act as Attorney for the King" – essentially the town prosecutor, and Otis performed commendably in securing convictions of two street fighters and a young arsonist. In August 1751, he won four affirmations of Inferior Court judgments in a row, an impressive feat for a 26-year-old. His success improved his reputation among merchants, and before the end of the year he was representing wealthy merchant Nathaniel Cunningham, Jr., who would in turn become his brother-in-law. A case by case examination of Otis's practice would demonstrate his climb to eminence, but two major cases occupied much of Jemmy's time and best illuminate his ability to out-research and outmaneuver his opponents. These cases also illustrate the droll synthesis of crudity and sophistication that permeated the law and its practice during this period of maturation in colonial law.

The first, *Fletcher v. Vassall*, was one of those extraordinary cases of which every lawyer dreams; it engaged many of Boston's leading lawyers and incorporated nearly every ploy known to colonial lawyers before it finally sputtered to a halt five years after it began. Most importantly, *Fletcher v. Vassall* laid bare the oftentimes gruesome innards of Boston high-society, merchant affairs, and legal machinations, an understanding of which would be highly valuable years later when Jemmy would manipulate and attack many of the same institutions.

In all probability, the case began in the bottom of several bottles of madeira wine at a small dinner hosted by William Vassall in August 1749 for the members of his "clubb," one of the many small informal social groups that dotted Boston society. Scion of one of the province's oldest families, Vassall had amassed a mostly inherited fortune in Jamaica sugar plantations. He graduated from Harvard in 1733, lived for a time on the family's Caribbean plantations, and, after the death of his father, returned to Boston where he lived fantastically on his immense plantation income. He had several faults not the least of which was what John Adams later termed as "garrulity," and at the dinner in question his usual garrulity included outrageously slandering a Boston merchant, William Fletcher. His guests included distinguished Boston figures Belcher Hancock, the Harvard tutor, Doctor Ebenezer Miller, Joshua Richardson, Joseph Royall, and Doctor Jonathan Mayhew, the influential minister of the West Church who, a few months later delivered his famously defiant sermon *Discourse Concerning Unlimited Submission and Non-Resistance*. So in Massachusetts in 1749, a minister of a major church could argue that the execution of a king is justified if the king abrogated the people's liberties, yet one wealthy merchant couldn't speak poorly of another wealthy merchant. The preacher's sermon was acceptable not because the idea of regicide was acceptable but rather because no one thought, in 1749, that such an argument had any practicable effect on his life or his government. To actually apply Mayhew's argument to the province or the empire was entirely inconceivable; however, Vassall's slander may have had a practicable effect and thus was taken quite seriously.

Fletcher's background is hazy, but in 1749 he seemed to be a typical, respected Boston merchant. At the time of the inauspicious garrulity, Fletcher was in England attempting to collect a debt, but upon his return to Boston the following summer he found that Vassall's garrulity had seriously injured his reputation and credit. All colonial merchants operated within the tenuous credit structure of demanding quick payment from customers and delivering slow payment to suppliers, and suggesting that a particular merchant was an unusually slow payer could destroy that merchant's ability to function. And as Fletcher later summarized, "Credit is undone in Whispers," and this was unquestionably accurate of the small New England merchant community where even the soundest men were in precarious positions caused by low liquidity. Vassall was not satisfied with whispers, and he frequently repeated his dinner party garrulity, describing Fletcher as "a very great Villain, a Rogue, a Scoundrell, a Bankrupt, not worth a Groat" and asserted that Fletcher was "not able to pay his Debts." Vassall repeated again that Fletcher was a "great cheat, a shuffling rascal," and that he had "Bottom'd a Ship for more than she was worth, and cast her away on Purpose to cheat the Bottomers." Coming from a wealthy and eminent merchant, this was warning enough to scare away any potential supplier, but Vassall's most serious charge was that Fletcher had "bought an old Ship that had been condemned, purely to send his Brother in it to be cast away, in order to get his Brother's Interest and Estate." Vassall's charges soon reached Fletcher's suppliers in Amsterdam, and anxious creditors began to demand payment up front or more security and to restrict sales to Fletcher. He decided to bring suit against the garrulous Vassall and chose as his attorney his close friend Goff — Edmund Trowbridge — who drafted a brilliant seven page declaration on an action of trespass on the case for defamation against Vassall. The writ was issued on October 5, 1751. After describing Vassall's numerous statements against his client and a general declaration of the resulting injury, Trowbridge asked for damages in the stunning sum of £8000. If Vassall had bothered to consult a lawyer in advance of his bouts of garrulity, he would have learned that merchants had special protection under the common law because of their unique vulnerability to slander and that to accuse a merchant of bankruptcy or dishonesty was actionable per se and required no proof that either was true. Trowbridge delivered the writ to Sheriff Pollard of Suffolk County who, in accordance with the plaintiff's wishes, arrested Vassall and jailed him until he could arrange bail. Trowbridge's declaration proved his reputation as Gridley's equal, and Vassall sought Gridley to represent him, but apparently Gridley was still "on his Passage" and unavailable.

In lieu of Gridley, Vassall retained Gridley's virtuoso apprentice, Jemmy Otis. Just before the January 1752 term, Otis filed his defense, which reflected nervous desperation and emulated the standard English model, first attacking the jurisdiction of the court, then the plaintiff's declaration, and finally the merits. In his "Plea to the Jurisdiction of the Court," Jemmy argued that the court was an inferior one and thus had no jurisdiction since the declaration failed to allege that the "garrulity" in question had occurred within the court's limited area of jurisdiction. Otis then added a three part plea for abatement predicated upon alleged defects in the writ and declaration. He argued that the writ was invalid on the technicality that it was directed to the Sheriff and not the "Sheriff or Marshall" as prescribed by statute. Further, he added that the declaration was invalid because it failed to be "endorsed with the Sirname of William Fletcher or with the Sirname of his attorney." Finally, Jemmy asserted that the declaration was faulty because the plaintiff had not stipulated "in what Language the said pretended Slanderous words, or any of them, were spoken." Notwithstanding all other issues, Jemmy pled "not Guilty in Manner and Form as the Plaintiff declares, and thereof puts himself upon the Country." This array of pleas was prescribed by the theory that once a party pled to the merits he waived the issues of jurisdiction and formal pleading defects. Though Fletcher's failure to endorse his writ with his surname was a solid technical point that could have resulted in abatement if the court had been sympathetic, it was a very minor technicality that was unlikely to persuade any judge, and yet it illustrates well the concept that when one has no great defense, one counters with every conceivable defense.

An advocate is bound to seek advantage in every possible defect, and the Massachusetts courts had dismissed cases for similarly minor technicalities;

but the court ignored Otis's objections most likely due to the gravity of the charge. Despite rescuing the case from technicalities, the court let it slip into the limbo of Massachusetts appellate procedure when it sent the case to the jury even though Fletcher produced no witnesses and no evidence. The jury very properly found for the defendant. This seemingly obtuse behavior by the plaintiff's attorney was a common legal tactic: now he could appeal to the Superior Court with minimum cost and effort while concealing the true nature of his case from his opponent. The appeal was docketed for February 1752 in the Superior Court, and by this time Jeremy Gridley was available to insert yet another technical plea: the plaintiff had failed to endorse the writ joining in the general issue proposed by the defendant. This formality was ignored more often than it was used, but Gridley and Otis had to assault the merits of Fletcher's case in every conceivable approach. But again the defendant's objection was ignored and again the case went to the jury with no evidence being introduced by the plaintiff.

As before, the jury brought in a verdict for the defendant. Now the wily Trowbridge secured from Justice Saltonstall a writ of review ordering, in effect, a new trial. Technically, a writ of review initiated a new case because it required a new summons to the defendant. Vassall had moved to Cambridge, so the duty to summon and arrest the defendant fell to Sheriff Richard Foster of Middlesex County, and just as Sheriff Pollard did, Foster arrested Vassall and jailed the big talker until he produced bail. The review case would have been heard at the August term of the Superior Court, but the pervasiveness of smallpox in Boston delayed the trial until November. Meanwhile, Fletcher engaged in the dubious act of writing to Justice Cushing on May 1, 1752 about gathering depositions and requested the judges's assistance in securing none other than Colonel Otis as a witness. According to Fletcher, Colonel Otis had been among the many who had demanded additional security or prepayment on behalf of Fletcher's creditors, and could thus testify to the adverse effects of Vassall's garrulity. That Fletcher would compose such a letter to a judge sitting on his case or that Cushing would entertain such a suggestion was of questionable propriety, and Cushing then declined to sit on the case. But the Colonel did make an appearance – not as witness but as co-counsel for the plaintiff.

On Thursday, December 7, the trial began in the Town House Court Room before the four remaining justices; Fletcher painted the picture:

The Case was open'd by Col. Otis of Barnstable in a very concise, genteel and intelligible Manner to the approbation of the whole Audience; and the Witnesses were produced by Mr. Fletcher in the manner following, all being critically cross examined by Mr. Vassall.

What followed was an extraordinary effort to bury the defense under such a volume of testimony that Otis and Gridley would find it impossible to fight back coherently and effectively. Now Trowbridge's strategy became clear: in forfeiting his case in the Inferior Court and in the first trial in the Superior Court, Fletcher's counsel had concealed his case until the last possible moment. Since the governing statute permitted only a single review at each level, Otis and Gridley could only respond to each bit of evidence on the spot. The plaintiff paraded what seemed like all of Boston through the courtroom, calling thirty-six witnesses ranging from such influential figures as Doctor Mayhew, Edmund Quincy, and Charles Apthorp, down to carpenters, sailmakers, and ship-joiners.

Within a few hours, the parade had attracted such a crowd of the curious that the Court was adjourned to Faneuil Hall, and the trial became public entertainment. The evidence showed decisively that Vassall had indeed comprehensively assassinated Fletcher's character – at his little "clubb" dinners, in "John Billings shop," where Vassall and his associates oft congregated during the day, and all across town. Additionally, letters from New Hampshire, New York, and English merchants were employed to establish Fletcher's reputation as a merchant and the damage that resulted from Vassall's slander. "On Friday morning young Mr. Otis began to speak for the Defendant," but he had nearly nothing but innuendo to offer. He called merchant Thomas Cushing to "fish out something" but failed. He called the reluctant register of deeds and extracted the fact that Fletcher had concealed some assets and liabilities through unregistered deeds and mortgages. He called the plaintiff's brother, Thomas Fletcher, to demonstrate that Fletcher's net worth was only about £530, and sought to question Thomas Fletcher about a seizure of the plaintiff's goods by the customs officers, but the Colonel arose and bellowed forth an objection that an evenly divided court upheld.

According to Fletcher, Jemmy Otis insisted throughout the trial that "there was not one Word in the Writ that was actionable in this Country" and concluded his defense "with some indecent reflections upon the Plaintiff, which was no Service to him or his Client." Re-examination of some of the witnesses commenced on Saturday, and on Monday each party was given the occasion to speak on his own behalf. Vassall read a ten page justification of his garrulity that desperately focused on currency depreciation on £10 worth of lottery tickets, Fletcher's handling of an escrow transaction which may or may not have been mismanaged, and other minutiae of doubtful relevance. The case, finally accompanied with evidence, was sent to the jury, which returned with the verdict for the plaintiff for £2000.

This verdict of what was essentially the third trial was just the beginning. Vassall was without further recourse in the colonial courts, but his counsel quickly filed for "an appeal to the King in Council," to which Fletcher replied with a similar motion. Both motions were granted. The province charter specifically provided for this procedure in personal actions involving more than £300 on the conditions that the appeal was prompt, the judgment was enforced, and bond was posted by the appellee to provide for the repayment of the judgment in case of reversal.

So Vassall paid Fletcher the £2000 judgment, and Fletcher posted a bond for £6000 in case the judgment was reversed. Vassall then collected attested copies of the Clerk's records and sailed for London to supervise his appeal. Vassall was doubtless a bitter man; Fletcher was hardly the model of virtue depicted at trial, and Trowbridge had indeed perverted the writ of review statute to his advantage. Perhaps persuaded by Vassall, Otis now brought a series of actions against sheriffs Pollard and Foster who, likely at Trowbridge's directions, had each arrested Vassall and held him in jail until he could post special bail. Plaintiff's lawyers routinely used writ of capias, which required the sheriff to arrest the defendant until bail was posted, but this harsh and arbitrary process had been regularly mitigated in practice by the use of fictional bondsmen, the omnipresent John Doe and Richard Roe, and the defendant merely signed a bail bond and was released. This practice was known as common bail. Trowbridge had, however, insisted on special bail, thus resulting in Vassall's temporary imprisonments. Otis now sued the hapless sheriffs for false imprisonment on the technically correct grounds that special bail was improper in defamation cases without an order from the court. Otis's co-counsel Gridley "utterly refused to be concerned" with these cases, almost certainly realizing that damages would be minimal and that the sheriffs – even if they had been aware of the legal technicalities – would hardly have dared to contest Edmund Trowbridge, the attorney general of the Province. The sheriffs employed attorney Ben Prat; Otis's argument was technically sound, and Prat's defense argued that the sheriffs were merely following orders, but Prat won both the Inferior Court and on appeal to the Superior Court. It was evident that the town's sympathies lay with Fletcher.

Meanwhile Vassall was proceeding with his appeal in London by retaining a London solicitor to draft a "Petition and Appeal" to file with the clerk of the Privy Council. The Council referred the case to the "Lords of the Committee" for hearing, and *Fletcher v. Vassall*, now known as *Vassall v. Fletcher*, was docketed to be heard "in the Council Chamber at the Cockpit, Whitehall, on Tuesday the Twenty-second Day of January, 1754, at Six o'Clock in the Evening." Vassall hired William Murray, then solicitor general of England and later to be better known as Lord Mansfield, chief justice of the Court of King's Bench and one of the giant figures in the history of English law. Murray was assisted by Alexander Forrester, another regular of the councilor bar. Fletcher responded with similarly impressive council; he hired Charles Yorke, counsel for the East India Company who later followed in Murray's footsteps as solicitor general. Counsel then prepared the "Appellant's Case" and the "Respondent's Case" respectively, and after a recitation of the facts of the case, the argument appeared in a section entitled "Reasons," which were disputations of the contested points. The "Appellant's Case" included all of Otis and Gridley's technical objections augmented by three additional assertions: the damages were excessive considering Fletcher's modest assets, the statute of limitations had expired, and Fletcher's failure to present evidence until the review of the case in the Superior Court had deprived Vassall of any effective means of defense.

The hearing took place before nine members of the "Lord's Committee" and is of particular interest because of Charles Yorke's notes, which provide a window into how the best legal minds of England viewed the best legal minds of Massachusetts. Yorke viewed Otis's plea to the jurisdiction of the Inferior Court and his pleas in abatement as frivolous, which they were. Yorke's comments on the laws regarding slander indicate how far the English judges had gone in liberalization since Coke and Rolle, on whom Otis had relied as authorities; importantly, these comments demonstrate that the English were entirely and systematically disregarding older law in favor of newer law, whereas Otis was far more elastic when he applied the law and could – and typically did – absorb and marshal law in a far broader context than did his peers in London. For the solicitors, law was a neatly organized linear progression; for Jemmy Otis, it was a messy confection of suggestion and theory that posed challenges more than instructions. The foremost concern that emerged during the London hearing focused on the correctness of reaching a decision on the merits of Fletcher's case in the face of what a majority of the Lords considered as a rank perversion of both justice and the intent of the Massachusetts writ of review statute. In the end, the majority view prevailed, and at a meeting of the full Privy Council on January 31, 1754, the King approved an Order in Council reversing the judgment of the Superior Court, ordering payment to Vassall of the full £2000 plus costs and interest but did not rule on the merits of the case, granting leave to Fletcher to again bring suit without regard to the statute of limitations or the earlier judgments.

At the May 1754 term of the Superior Court, Jemmy Otis submitted a motion that Vassall's bond on Fletcher's appeal be returned and that a writ of execution be issued. Now the Superior Court suddenly grew concerned with technicalities such as the possibility of using an execution on a judgment it had not made. The motion was continued for advisement, and in August an impatient Otis once again moved for execution, but the court again continued the motion, suggesting that it did not feel it could rule without a full bench; since Justice Cushing still refused to sit on the case, a special justice would need to be appointed. In the meantime, Trowbridge's surprise attack strategy was rendered illegal by a statute passed in April that prohibited writs of review for cases that had been lost in both the Inferior Court and Superior Court; it was the second time an Otis case resulted in statutory changes.

On September 17th, Vassall filed a petition with Governor Shirley for said appointment and three days later the governor appointed Thomas Hutchinson to the temporary vacancy. In November, with Hutchinson on the bench, Otis's motion was finally granted and writs of execution issued, but now Otis was not on the scene to supervise them, having left for Halifax, Nova Scotia for his next big case. Without Otis there to motivate them, sheriffs Pollard and Foster exercised less than their usual diligence on behalf of Vassall, and on their returns finally filed in February 1755, both claimed that they could find no property belonging to Fletcher on which they could levy. Personal arrest was impossible because Fletcher had won the Cambridge seat in the House of Representatives, which gave him immunity from arrest during sessions of the General Court.

At this juncture both Fletcher and Otis dropped out of this messy affair, with Fletcher leaving his wife behind and fleeing to the Caribbean and Otis sailing for Halifax, Nova Scotia and his next significant case. Jeremy Gridley assumed the position as Vassall's attorney and began proceedings against Fletcher's bondsmen. Because of a defect in the wording of the Tudor-Quincy bond a direct levy failed, and new law suits were necessary, but Tudor ultimately grew exasperated with Gridley's legal harassment and in March 1756 paid the judgment. Fortunately the glowing characterizations of Fletcher's uprightness that bondsmen Tudor and Quincy had provided at trial had not prevented them from insisting on security: a mortgage on Fletcher's Cambridge "mansion house." Tudor foreclosed on it, and Fletcher neither satisfied his obligation nor returned to Boston. Fletcher's voluminous correspondence with his lawyer Trowbridge reveals a man of many broken promises and dashed expectations. In June 1756 Fletcher asked Trowbridge to pay Ben Prat, "a good Cockpitt soliciter," and to retain Colonel Otis to assist in bringing a new action against Vassall; the action never got past the initial writ stage. One can reasonably conclude that Fletcher was never quite the merchant he represented himself to be and that perhaps Vassall's "garrulity" contained some truth.

Jemmy arrived in Halifax, Nova Scotia by November 1754; it was a purpose-built city, founded for the exclusive function of balancing the threatening French fortress 200 miles up the coast at Louisbourg. The colonists of Massachusetts Bay were shocked when fortress Louisbourg was returned to the French in 1748 in exchange for Madras, India, as the colonists believed that a strong presence on Nova Scotia was vital to the security of the entire region, and the British had no other fortress or major city in the area. The French had sent a fleet containing 11,000 men to reinforce fortress Louisbourg and still controlled much of the area, so it was clear that the French were not done fighting for control of the region – the land or the waters. Parliament agreed that a British presence was needed, and on June 21, 1749, the city and fortress of Halifax was established. Unlike most North American colonies, Halifax was fully funded by the Crown. But this new and substantial British presence on Nova Scotia brought new problems. Regulations regarding trading with French persons and vessels had existed but could hardly be enforced in a place so removed from the British establishment, but now with British courts and officers firmly established in a middle of the region, regulations would become more than mere suggestions. Trade with France – the enemy – would now bring an entirely new level of antagonism and friction to the region, particularly to those merchants and shippers who had previously traded freely with anyone who could pay in hard currency.

Otis's involvement in the Halifax case likely began on August 31, 1754 when Captain Lott Hall arrived in Boston from Halifax with newspapers that reported a "melancholy Affair." The Halifax *Gazette* story was reprinted without comment in the Boston *Evening-Post* two days later, and it told the tale of murder on the seas: two crewmen of the *H.M.S. Vulture*, a Sloop-of-War, were killed by the crew of a Boston trading sloop, John Harris's *Nancy and Sally*, in a remote cove on the north shore of the Bay of Fundy. The Boston crew members were in the cold, dark Halifax jail awaiting trial for murder. Captain Hall requested immediate legal assistance. John Harris, the small trader in Boston who owned the *Nancy and Sally*, had no known connection with Otis, but William Bourne, a Halifax merchant and justice of the peace, was a Harvard classmate and Cape Cod neighbor of Jemmy Otis; and the Halifax merchant firm of Ewer and Webb were clients of Otis in a case pending in the Superior Court against Benjamin Faneuil. Thus, Bourne or Ewer and Webb likely recommended Otis. Jemmy and a second lawyer, possibly Oxenbridge Thacher, sailed for Halifax on their mission impossible in early October 1754; the slow motion calamity that was the Vassall case probably seemed tidy and winnable compared to the imbroglio that awaited them. Concurrent with Otis's arrival, a ship from England docked and delivered Jonathan Belcher, Jr, the son of former Governor of Massachusetts and now a barrister with orders to establish a new Supreme Court of Judicature in the Province of Nova Scotia, ominous circumstances for anyone soon to attempt to win a case in provincial courts.

The events surrounding the *Nancy and Sally* and her seven man crew characterize a facet of the War for Empire that soon erupted in its concluding chapter, the Seven Years War. The Treaty of Aix-la-Chapelle of 1748 offered but a brief intermission for the principal antagonists, England and France, and not even that for the English settlers and soldiers in Nova Scotia or for the French trappers, settlers, and Jesuit priests of New France. The prickly question of boundaries between these provinces was to be settled by a committee in Paris, including Governor Shirley of Massachusetts, and the predictable lack of progress at these negotiations made much of Nova Scotia a somewhat lawless hinterland, particularly the north shore of the Bay of Fundy and the strategic neck that joined the area to the mainland. The English claimed the Bay of Fundy and its surroundings, but the territory was inhabited and controlled by people who were French in nationality and sympathy.

The situation was so tense and laden with unresolved problems that the colonists of New England had long concluded that another war with France was imminent; despite that, New England merchants were quick to place pounds above principles and carried on a profitable trade with all the French settlements. As the publisher of the Boston *Evening Post* explained: "By the vast Quantity of Provisions carried to Louisbourg from this Continent, one would be tempted to think, that the English take more notice of Saint Paul's Advice to the Romans, Chap. XII., ver. 20. than any other part of his writings, viz.— If thine Enemy hunger, feed him; if he thirst, give him Drink." The British governor of Nova Scotia was more pungent in his report to the Lords of Trade: "We have long suffered great inconveniences by the Boston Vessels trading so much with the French in the Bay of Fundy." In an attempt to stamp out this "iniquitous Commerce," the energetic governor had a Royal Navy vessel under his control cruising the Bay of Fundy to discourage Boston interlopers. Captain John Hovey of the *Nancy and Sally* had a Boston clearance, but he had posted no bond covering the enumerated sugar and tobacco he carried as cargo, and, in addition, he carried a number of hats that were absolutely forbidden commodities, even in intercolonial trade. Captain Hovey surreptitiously traded much of his cargo to the French at Beausejour at the head of the bay, and then attempted to evade the wrath of the *H.M.S. Vulture* by means of a feigned sale of the ship to the French, but on July 27, 1754, Commander William Kinsey of the *Vulture* trapped the *Nancy and Sally*, forcing it to duck into Musquash Cove, a haven near St. Johns too shallow for the much larger sloop-of-war. Kinsey ordered his sailing master, Joseph Marriott, and a midshipman, George Phillips, to take the *Vulture's* "barge" with a crew of nine men, and seize the elusive Boston sloop that was hiding in the back of the cove. As the *Vulture's* barge approached the *Nancy and Sally*, it fired a volley of musket shots in the air as a warning signal. Renegade Captain Hovey first ordered one of the sloop's swivel guns fired wide of the approaching barge as a return warning, but when the gunner took direct aim at the English boat, Hovey panicked and hide in his cabin with his fourteen year old son, the French pilot, and one of the crew. Three of Hovey's men took to fighting; Ben Street, Sam Thornton and John Pastree loaded the swivels and broke out muskets and muskatoons, which were muzzle loading guns that fired a variety of shot in a wildly inaccurate spread that was rarely lethal at its maximum range of about 50 yards, sort of a colonial version of a sawed-off shotgun. After threats and counter threats, the barge pulled alongside the sloop, and one of the Boston men fired his muskatoon at close range, killing one English sailor and mortally wounding another. In archetypal Royal Navy tradition, the *Vulture's* remaining able-bodied men stormed the sloop with cutlasses drawn and subdued the rebellious New Englanders. Unfortunately for the Boston men, the usually non-lethal musaktoon proved quite lethal.

H.M.S. Vulture, with the *Nancy and Sally* in tow and her crew in irons, sailed to Halifax where lawyers took over. The Halifax Vice-Admiralty Court seized the sloop and her cargo for violation of the Acts of Trade and put it all up for auction. William Bourne, Otis's classmate, bought the sloop "together with all her Guns Tackle, Apparel Ammunition [and] Furniture" for £75. Ewer and Webb, Otis's clients, bought the 1280 beaver pelts that Hovey had picked up in trade at Beausejour for £350 – half their London market value. The governor first wanted to try them as pirates before a special "commission" as provided by the English statutes governing pirate trials in the colonies, which provided for fast and brutal justice, but fortunately for the "pirates" the governor discovered that such a trial was impossible without a special commission issued by the King or the "admiralty in England," and this vital document had been overlooked in the hasty establishment of the new town a few years prior. There were two alternatives: send the prisoners to England for trial under an older statute, an expensive and time consuming procedure of dubious legality, or try them for common law murder in the province. While the governor was considering the choices, John Duport, a justice of the peace, took sworn depositions from four of the men in the *Vulture*'s barge, and unsworn statements from Hovey and his crew, before committing the entire Boston crew to jail pending action by the grand jury. Further complicating an already complicated situation, John Hovey, the master of the *Nancy and Sally*, escaped from jail with outside assistance and disappeared.

Into this mess walked the lawyers and judges. Though the governor and Belcher had their disagreements, the governor was probably glad to cede the pirate case to his new chief justice. On October 29, the first day of the Michaelmas Term, Chief Justice Belcher – in a scarlet robe – members of the Council, the tipstaff, and members of the bar in their gowns, began the first session of the term, which commenced at a tavern "where an excellent breakfast was provided," and, after heard the required sermon undoubtedly on some variation of justice. Full of food and preaching, they marched to the Court House where Belcher was formally commissioned. Belcher issued "Directions for the Conduct of Practitioners," and then empanelled the grand jury. Later that day the jury returned with an indictment for John Hovey stating that "not having the fear of God before his eyes … feloniously, willfully and of Malice aforethought and by … his Command … did kill and Murder said Isaac Jolly and John McDermott against the peace of our said Lord the King his Crown and Dignity." Of course, the absconded captain failed to answer "though thrice called," and Justice Belcher ordered that he should be prosecuted "to an Outlawry." This technical procedure for dealing with fugitive felons was of tremendous rarity in the colonies, and in view of the Halifax Court's failure to prosecute it seems likely that Belcher assumed Hovey would never be seen again. The grand jury declined to indict the French pilot, Hovey's son, and two other crewmen, but they did indict Street, Thornton, and Pastree for murder. But now the critically significant problem of jurisdiction had to be resolved. Crimes committed "on the seas" were traditionally within the jurisdiction of the Lord High Admiral and his Admiralty Court rather than with the common law court, and Admiralty Court adhered to the civil law wherein juries were optional and the crime of manslaughter was nonexistent; Admiralty Court was about judges and murder.

For a defendant who may plead to manslaughter or may plead for his life to a jury of his peers, the issue was far from a scholarly technicality. Under Henry VIII, a statute against piracy and other crimes on the seas had been enacted that required trial by a commission that included admiralty judges, but which proceeded "in the course of the common law," which included a full scope of juries. The escalation of American trade and American piracy rendered this system impractical because of the difficulty of transporting defendants and witnesses to England for trial. Thus in 1700 a new practical and efficient statute was enacted that established special commissions for the trial of pirates in the individual colonies, but to avoid the bias of local and sometimes pirate-friendly juries, these commissions were to follow the juryless civil law in the traditional admiralty pattern. The new practical and efficient act proved to be only new as it omitted murder as a specific crime and covered crimes "committed in or upon the sea, or in any haven, river, creek, or place where the admiral or admirals have jurisdiction" without defining "upon the sea," or "where the admirals have jurisdiction." These defects were compounded by the provision that the commission's jurisdiction was exclusive, meaning that only the commission could try cases within its unspecified jurisdiction. The traditional view that the Admiral had jurisdiction over bays and rivers up to the first bridge had been seriously challenged by Lord Coke in the course of his extension of the jurisdiction of the common law courts. By 1754 there was substantial precedent that bays and river mouths behind a line drawn "between the headlands" were "within the county," thus giving the common law courts at least concurrent jurisdiction in such places – a concurrent jurisdiction that was supposedly not possible. The prospect of a common law trial embittered Commander Kinsey who had lost two sailors and any share in the proceeds of the condemnation of the *Nancy and Sally* when Henry Newton, Halifax collector of customs, claimed the "informer's share." Now he could imagine the opportunity of a local jury acquitting the Boston men. Commander Kinsey wanted the Boston men tried as pirates, so he filed a "Memorial" with Chief Justice Belcher urging that the proceedings be delayed until authorization for a piracy commission could be obtained from England or that the prisoners be sent to England for trial under the statute of Henry VIII. Jemmy Otis argued vigorously in favor of local jurisdiction and a quick jury trial. For a defense lawyer to argue for a speedy trial is risky, but the possible alternatives, all of which entailed the term "pirate" and lacked the term "jury," were treacherous for defendants who clearly committed the crime. So Jemmy Otis enthusiastically urged Chief Justice Belcher to take jurisdiction, and not surprisingly, Chief Justice Belcher took jurisdiction.

Under common law each defendant was granted twenty peremptory juror challenges, which gave the Boston lawyers sixty opportunities to challenge jurors without cause. Since Halifax had been founded in 1748 in order to create a fortified port to counterbalance Louisbourg, Whitehall encouraged discharged English army personnel to settle there and fueled this encouragement with direct Parliamentary grants. But New Englanders were not immune to the prospect of free land, no taxes, and the proximity of the fish rich Grand Banks; a vigorous advertising campaign in the Boston newspapers informed the general population of this new Eden. The peremptory challenges permitted Jemmy Otis to cull relocated Bostonians from the discharged English army personnel. The number of peremptory jury challenges exercised is not known, but the effect was documented by Commander Kinsey when he commented indignantly that the twelve-man jury finally selected included ten New Englanders. Jemmy had done his work.

Acting Attorney General William Nesbitt made his opening statement and paraded the crown witnesses to the stand where they recited the now well-known story of the Battle of Musquash Cove. The clerk did not record the questions asked on cross examination, but the recorded answers divulge the theory of the defense. It was incontestable that men were killed. It was therefore necessary to establish some justification for the killing. The jury had to be persuaded that a barge sailing from a sloop-of-war flying the Royal Ensign and manned by a crew of Royal sailors was a pirate or Indian attack or doubt had to be fomented in the minds of the jurors about the legality or motivation of Commander Kinsey's mission. Doubt lurked in the questions *was the H.M.S. Vulture visible from the Nancy and Sally? how were the English sailors clothed? had Kinsey ordered the seizure in his capacity as a Royal Navy commander or as a customs officer? who fired the first shot?*

According to common law criminal procedure, the indicted could not testify in his own behalf, so Jemmy Otis called the French pilot and the seamen who had not been indicted to the stand, and the questions were asked. At the point that the waters were muddied to his satisfaction, Jemmy rested for the defense sending the jury to decide the fate of the three men. They returned quickly with a verdict of guilty – of manslaughter. Chief Justice Belcher was incensed but helpless. Without delay, the convicted prisoners "beg'd they might be allowed the benefit of the Clergy which was allowed them." The "benefitt of the Clergy " was a remnant of the middle ages originally designed to protect the clergy from the King's courts; by the 18th century it had become a significant ingredient in English criminal law by providing leniency for first-time offenders. Had the men been tried as pirates, "benefit of the Clergy" would have been unavailable to the convicted Bostonians since it was specifically excluded by the statutes. As it was, all Chief Justice Belcher could do was "to pass Sentence, that they ... should be burned in the Hand, and that they should remain in Prison for the space of Nine Months." And the court record concludes: "Pursuant to which Sentence the said Benjamin Street, Samuel Thornton, and John Pastree were in open Court, burned in the Left Hand with the Letter 'M' and ... given in Charge to the Goaler." Since a convict could only plead "benefitt of the Clergy" once in his life, pleading "benefitt of the Clergy" entailed being branded on the hand so that "clergy" couldn't be used again.

Given the evidence, the Musquash Cove case was nearly impossible to win, and the manslaughter verdict was greeted as total victory for the defense and abject failure for the prosecution – including the time spent in jail awaiting trial, the defendants received prison sentences of about a year each for murdering Royal Navy sailors. The two critical decisions were to vigorously press for a speedy common law trial and the selection of the jury. Perhaps all those peremptory juror challenges proved fruitful for Jemmy, but a supposedly safe jury can go astray if not offered a rationale for siding with the defense. The Musquash Cove case extended Jemmy's reputation across the region, heightened his awareness of the inconsistencies in the Acts of Trade and their enforcement, and gave him experience in felonies "upon the sea" that would prove useful fifteen years later when he and John Adams successfully defended another renegade sea captain, Michael Corbet.

As a result of the "melancholy Affair" in Musquash Cove, the Nova Scotian governor sent his able assistant to Boston on a secret mission. He met with the Massachusetts governor to plan and execute an armed attack on the French military base at Fort Beausejour, Captain John Hovey's illicit trading post, and the Massachusetts Assembly was finally goaded into enacting a tough statute forbidding trading with the French. Otis returned to Boston, probably with Captain Delap, a Barnstable neighbor of the Otises, landing on December 11th, and a week later Colonel Otis tersely informed Joseph that "your brother is well." Such was not the case with the Musquash Cove killers; on their release from jail they were seized by a Navy press gang and disappeared into the bowels of the Royal Navy. And while Captain Hovey disappeared from history, the *Nancy and Sally* reappeared in Boston the following month and sailed for the West Indies, still owned, or re-owned, by John Harris. The general conclusion in Boston is that men who resisted imperial customs with deadly force received nothing more than a slap on the wrist thanks to Boston attorney Jemmy Otis. Merchants, smugglers and rebels would all take note, but so would the customs establishment.

The period of 1745-1755 began with the lingering turmoil of the Land Bank that nearly tore the province asunder, only to be healed by the unifying battle for fortress Louisbourg. A young Jemmy Otis was just beginning his legal studies under Jeremiah Gridley while his father was first elected to the House of Representatives and his uncle sat on the Governor's Council. The period ends with the Colonel in firm and ever-expanding political control of the Barnstable county, and Jemmy as a Boston lawyer with an impressive reputation. His brother Joseph was successfully managing the Barnstable businesses. Halifax was a newly established town and fort of some substance that could provide security for British ships.

The Massachusetts coast was secure, but the Ohio valley was not. About six months before Jemmy returned to Boston from Halifax, on May 28, 1754, 120 Virginians crouched in the woods in Western Pennsylvania. At 6am, their commander gave the signal, and they attacked first with bayonets so as to be as quiet as possible. The Virginians stabbed at their sleeping foe in the dimness of early morning; shots were fired in defense, but within fifteen minutes, ten

French Canadians were dead, two more were wounded, and twenty-one were captured. As the French commander rose to read an order declaring the area the property of the King of France, an axe was driven through his skull. The victorious Virginians then followed their commander to a nearby meadow, in which they erected an outpost and named it *Fort Necessity*. The Virginian's commander then wrote home to his brother, "I can with truth assure you, I heard bullets whistle and believe me, there was something charming in the sound," and signed his name, George Washington. The Seven Years' War had begun.

※

concatenation of Incidents

Life went on. James Otis joined Saint John's Masonic lodge and the Boston Fire Club. He was one of the founders of a law club wherein Suffolk lawyers met regularly at the Bunches of Grapes tavern on King Street, a tavern at which one could buy drinks, concert tickets, slaves, art, and a number of other items. And Jemmy was known to play the fiddle at dances. *Fletcher v. Vassall* was tried again in the Superior Court, and Colonel Otis soundly thrashed his son. Correspondence among the Otis family members during the 1750s shows a continuing cooperative effort to advance the family's position in all respects. From Boston to Barnstable streamed legal advice and the latest rumors, "lemmons," "hatts for my Sisters," and "Goloshoes for my Mother" were sent, family members were updated on each others's lives. The mail from Barnstable to Boston brought requests for more letters and help with legal and political errands. In 1753, Jemmy purchased a card table for his sister Mercy that likely was an acquisition in preparation for her impending marriage to James Warren, Jr., of Plymouth. The marriage took place in 1754 while Mercy's much adored older brother was busy defending his "pirate" clients in Halifax. After living for a period on the Warren family farm on Eel River, the young Warren couple moved into the same house in Plymouth that Otis had occupied while practicing there. This marriage was an expected Otis alliance; there had been a longstanding and close relationship between the two families, and the Warrens held a dominant position in Plymouth just as the Otises did in Barnstable.

In 1755, Jemmy reached his thirtieth birthday and was now well established and financially capable of assuming the responsibilities of a family. According to tradition, the Halifax case had generated "the Largest fee that had ever been given to any advocate in the Province," though there exists no documentation regarding the actual amount and source. Jemmy was one of Boston's most eligible bachelors. One of Otis's first clients in Boston was Nathaniel Cunningham, Jr., who at that point had been acting as administrator of his father's flourishing merchant businesses. Captain Nathaniel Cunningham had been a fairly inconspicuous but very successful Boston merchant at the time of his death in 1748. Like most successful merchants of his day, he was a generalist, supplementing his trading activities with real estate ventures in Connecticut, New York, and Boston, which included a wharf, three warehouses, and two tracts of land on the Boston Common next to the Hancock's. His estate was assessed at £50,000, and after leaving sixty ounces of silver to the Old South church for a communion cup and £9,500 for the poor of the Church, he provided graciously for his family, leaving £10,000 sterling to each of his two daughters, Ruth and Sarah. While Mercy Otis was courting James Warren, young Nat Cunningham was pursuing Sarah Kilby, daughter of wealthy former province agent Christopher Kilby. After cautiously checking Cunningham's balance sheet, Thomas Hancock, Kilby's business associate and confidant, recommended the marriage to Kilby. Nat Cunningham and Sarah Kilby married in the summer of 1754 and moved into a magnificent mansion in what is now Brighton, leaving the widow Cunningham and her two daughters on their own. Ruth, then 25 years old, was thus single and wealthy.

Jemmy Otis and Ruth published their intention to marry March 18, 1755 and were married soon thereafter. Marriage, particularly to an heiress, dictated a substantial change in Jemmy's lifestyle, and in September 1755 he purchased his first real estate, a house on the north side of School Street just down the hill from King's Chapel, an ideal location just two blocks from the Town House and Old South, Ruth's church. In the immediate vicinity, the Otises had a church, a tavern, and a school for neighbors. The following February, Jemmy formally "owned the covenant" before the Old South congregation; Ruth did the same in April. In another move up the social hierarchy, the Otises had their portraits painted by Joseph Blackburn, an itinerant artist of some talent who was painting portraits of eminent Bostonians at that time. Formal portraits were very popular among the merchant class in the 1750s and those wishing to be immortalized on canvas had a wide choice of artists. In 1755 John Smibert was perhaps Boston's best portraitist; he painted Nat and Sarah Cunningham, Benjamin Prat, and many others. Robert Feke painted portraits of Jeremy Gridley and Oxenbridge Thacher. Ruth's portrait depicts her as no raving beauty. In 1763, Jemmy was described as a "plump, round-faced, smoothskin, short neck, eagle-eyed politician," and while he was not yet a politician in 1755, the description is accurately reflected in his portrait. The most intriguing feature of his portrait is the confident half-smile, an expression that was unique to the deadly serious portraits of the period of proper Englishmen secure in their abilities to conquer the world; his nearly smirking lips seem to draw the line between bold surety and knowing secrecy.

James Otis and his new wife were political opposites, and he would later describe her as "high Tory" and claimed that she gave him lectures about loyalty. "Ruthy" bore their first child, Elizabeth, in March 1757 and their only son, James, in July 1759. It is apparent that Jemmy Otis began to chart his way through the accepted framework of the Boston legal and merchant world. As the son of a well-known merchant, lawyer and politician, Jemmy had unfettered access to provincial Governor William Shirley and the corridors of power, and his own clientele's stature was growing nearly as quickly as Jemmy's reputation. In recognition of his rising position among the Boston elite, Governor Shirley appointed Jemmy Otis as a justice of the peace for Suffolk County in September 1756. It was not a significant position of patronage, but it was a first step in the rise to power. Notably, unlike his country father, Jemmy would never need to start that rise at town hogreeve.

No one could escape the impact of the war between 1755 and 1760, and despite the fondness of the House of Representatives to quibble over martial minutia, the war in America between the British and the French was a struggle for the survival of Massachusetts. The province was exposed to French attacks by land and sea, and the governor made the management of the war in the colonies his own personal project. Since his inauguration as governor in 1741, Shirley had been more attentive than most of his contemporaries of the inexorable strangling of the English colonies by French imperial ambition. Shirley was not a military man but he had a firm understanding of strategic concepts and oft warned the English colonies and policy makers of the urgent necessity of paring the Bourbon lilies.

Governor Shirley was nearly as perceptive in political strategy as he was in military affairs as he had not only observed but also abetted Governor Belcher's defeat and thus fully appreciated the value of a broad and loyal constituency in the Massachusetts Assembly. Shirley also understood that turmoil and security threats brought together a disparate collection of competing interests and unified them under his control. Shirley had wielded great power during George's War and the capture of Louisbourg, and another war would help him tighten his grip on authority. The Otis family was an important part of Shirley's constituency, and Shirley carefully cultivated Otis friendships and support with patronage, including the acceptance of John Otis IV as a councilor in 1747 and the appointment of Jemmy as a justice of the peace in 1756. And Shirley recognized that Colonel Otis was the key figure, and Shirley's move was the commission as Colonel of the militia in 1747. Such tokens of patronage probably helped the Colonel overcome doubts he had entertained about the governor's military and currency reforms, neither of which held much appeal to Colonel Otis's conservative country constituency.

The war came home to Boston in 1755. General Edward Braddock landed in Virginia with two regiments, and, accompanied by George Washington, marched to western Pennsylvania to confront the French troops who had reestablished control of the area. The British were surprise-attacked and routed. Braddock himself was mortally wounded and died not too far from the place of Washington's victory a year earlier. Braddock's men buried him in the middle of the road and marched over his body to hide the grave so that the French wouldn't desecrate the body. And before dying, Braddock gave Washington his general's sash, which Washington reportedly wore into every battle thereafter, including the battles for independence. But the news that most shook Boston and Governor Shirley wasn't of Braddock's death but rather of the death of a soldier who died alongside Braddock: William Shirley, the governor's young son. Shirley would now seek to consolidate support and execute the war against the French with zeal. He turned to the Otises for political support. The governor's succession to the office of commander in chief of British forces in North America also made Otis feel close to the seat of power. In February 1756, the Colonel wrote Joseph from Jemmy's School Street house detailing his plans to support the governor and the war and reported his efforts in keeping the House of Representatives in line "notwithstanding we have such a seditious stupid spirit that reigns in our House that everything is gained inch by inch" and then directed Joseph to "make no noise" but to buy six whaleboats and sets of oars "as cheap as you can." Aside from the usual necessities of war, Shirley made it clear that a prime target of his war efforts would be Louisbourg in particular and Nova Scotia in general. Louisbourg would be recaptured and the region secured so that no French would remain to demand the return of the fortress. Further, there would be need for patrols on upper New York rivers and lakes as the colonists recalled that the French, once defeated in Louisbourg, attacked aggressively and successfully via northern New York. The Colonel's supply of small whaleboats would be valuable to these efforts.

Joseph was also informed that the Colonel had "made way" at Jemmy's suggestion "for a captain's commission for Mr. White" who was to quietly enlist a company of whaleboat men with the understanding that when enlisted they would purchase their supplies from the Otis store. The Colonel also directed Joseph to recruit the sailors they would need for their own operations. The Colonel also secured a promotion for James Allyne, a relative of the Colonel's wife, "for the family's sake." Feeling confident of English reimbursement, Colonel Otis directed Joseph to advance the enlistment bounty money from Otis family funds. The Colonel was preparing to fully support Shirley's efforts in the Seven Years War with a small fleet, supplies and sailors, and this was precisely the kind of broad-based provincial support a successful politician needed.

Of course, the Hutchinsons and Olivers were also planning to profitably support the war. The province had slipped into a bit of chaos, and the economy had slumped after George's War had ended. When Peter Oliver heard that some French-Canadian Indians had attacked a frontier town in 1750, he wrote to the Colonel, "Pray set your Head and Heart on making Paper Money next Session .... Blessed Times! The Golden Age is returning. We shall all be Kings, Priests, and any Thing else we incline to." No war broke out in 1750, but the oligarchy that ruled Boston knew that war brought political unity and opportunity for profit. Colonel Otis would, for the first time, be a part of the elite's profitable support of the war.

Shirley executed the war plans with ferocity, and though he did not succeed in capturing Louisbourg during his brief stint as commander, he did execute the wholesale expulsion of over 12,000 suspected French supporters from Nova Scotia. Thousands more French loyalists died, and their land was offered to colonists who supported the British. When Louisbourg was recaptured, there would be no Frenchmen left on Nova Scotia to exchange it for Madras, India, if such an exchange were ever again considered. In return for his support, Shirley promised Colonel Otis the next vacancy on the Boston Superior Court and urged Otis not to seek a seat on the Council because of his value in the House; but when Richard Saltonstall resigned from the bench later that year,

Shirley appointed Peter Oliver. The Colonel must have suspected the problem: Shirley was losing his grip on power, and in order to solidify his support among the Boston ruling elite, he had to appoint the powerful and connected Peter Oliver. On August 9, 1756, Shirley returned to Boston from the humiliating ceremony in York where he turned over his military command to the better connected Lord Loudoun. Loudoun would fail miserably as governor of Virginia and commander of North American forces and would himself be replaced a little over a year later.

But conspiracy was afoot; Shirley had been governor long enough, and others coveted the position. James DeLancey, chief justice and de facto governor of New York, together with other New York merchants, were bitter that Shirley directed all war contracts to Massachusetts merchants. DeLancey surely wondered why New York rivers and lakes were being patrolled with Otis-made boats. The New York merchants colluded with a 34-year-old secretary and advisor named Thomas Pownall, who had recently arrived in New York from London and was keen to gain a position of power in the colonies. And finally, French forces had just taken and destroyed Fort Oswego, a vital British fort in upstate New York on Lake Ontario. Someone had to be blamed. And not by coincidence, Thomas Pownall would sail from New York to assist the members of Parliament in assessing who should bear the blame.

Jemmy, in writing to his father, exulted that "Shirley is arrived and like to remain Govr as long as he pleaseth." This was naïve; Shirley departed for England in October to defend his political life, leaving the Otis family and other Shirley supporters mired in political uncertainty. Spencer Phips, the ailing lieutenant to the governor who remained in Massachusetts to administer the province, died six months later; without leadership, government power rested on the Council where Hutchinson and other oligarchs warily jockeyed for position, and the government as an active force slipped into confused stagnation. If Colonel Otis had ever agreed with Shirley not to run for a Council seat, he was now not subject to such restrictions.

The governor was gone, and the family representative on the council, the Colonel's brother John Otis IV, was ailing and would die within a year at the age of 71. So sure was the Colonel of his own electoral success that he relinquished his seat in the House to his distant cousin, Edward Bacon, in the elections of May 1757. Bacon received much of the Colonel's largesse, including a promise from Shirley that Bacon would be appointed to the rank of captain in the local militia. But when the General Court met, Colonel Otis was stunned to discover that he was not the commanding figure he thought himself to be as he was "left out" when the votes were counted. For the first time in many years, the Otis family did not hold a seat in the province government. It was a devastating blow for the Colonel, but instead of conspiring to avenge he sulked in Barnstable. At about the time the new governor, Thomas Pownall, landed in Boston, Colonel Otis realized that he had been duped. A nameless "D G Esqr" had informed him that Hutchinson and Oliver were laughing at the "little Low Dirty things" the Colonel had accomplished for Shirley and that the governor "made use" of him "as a Tool." The "opposite Party" was pronouncing Colonel Otis and his country constituency finished. This revelation likely embittered the Colonel so much that he retired from public affairs for more than a year.

The new Governor Thomas Pownall sought to build a coalition that included important Shirley men, the Otises included, and Jemmy, perhaps drawn by Pownall's youth and energy, readily assumed the role of intermediary between Pownall and his father. In an effort to conciliate Colonel Otis, Pownall quickly appointed Jemmy as acting advocate general of the Boston Vice-Admiralty Court. The titular advocate general was William Bollan who had held the office since 1741, but Bollan had worked as province agent in London since 1745, and his position with the Vice-Admiralty Court had apparently been filled on a temporary basis. William Bollan's role as province lobbyist would later become one of the battle lines drawn by the revolutionary generation. In 1745, Governor Shirley wanted Bollan, his son-in-law, to be the province agent so as to solidify his control over the province's efforts in Westminster, and Shirley succeeded in securing Bollan's appointment with the help of Hutchinson and Colonel Otis. The agent who then lost his job had been supported by Hancock and the merchants. So the position of province lobbyist fell from merchant control to political control, and in typical colonial fashion, Bollan did not relinquish his old position as advocate general after being appointed as province agent.

Now a dozen years later, Jemmy Otis's appointment as advocate general was not only meant to secure Otis support but also was part of Pownall's attempt to diminish Bollan's influence in London because, as a Shirley appointment, he could be dangerous to Pownall's still shaky political position. What the appointment meant to Otis in terms of duties and fees is unknown because the Boston Vice-Admiralty Court is sometimes pictured as an engine of oppression grinding out forfeitures and condemnations of England merchant shipping, but in reality the work of the court during the 1750s was largely concerned with determining cases involving seamen's wages, salvage, prize laws, and marine insurance. The advocate general was equivalent to the attorney general in the common law courts and represented the Crown in seizure cases arising from Acts of Trade violations. Otis variously claimed his fees were as large as £200 a year and as small as two guineas, depending on the point he was trying to prove. More important than the duties or fees is that Jemmy was integrating smoothly into the group Hutchinson called "the friends of government."

While Hancock and Hutchinson had made a fortune during the Seven Years War, things were not going well for the Colonel. His whaleboat business had boomed from Thomas Hancock's four boat order in 1755 to General James Abercromby's 200 boat order in 1758, but payments were slower than usual. Shirley's old enemies in New York vengefully blocked payment of Otis's account, complaining about the quality of his boat crews. The very reason DeLancey supported Shirley's ouster was that war contracts were going to Massachusetts merchants, and now DeLancey found every reason he could to withhold payment for hundreds of Otis-made whale boats.

In an attempt to facilitate cooperation and a friendly relationship, Pownall wrote to the Colonel on August 25, 1757 because Pownall was very aware of Hutchinson's and the Olivers' power in Boston and of Hutchinson's designs on the governorship. Pownall wanted to solidify support in the country, and few were as politically connected outside of Boston as the Colonel. Pownall placed an order with Otis for 100 whale boats for New York, and asked Otis to meet him and Lord Loudoun in Plymouth to finalize the details. Pownall clearly believed that Otis's support was important to the war effort and had convinced Lord Loudoun of the same. But the Colonel would not leave Barnstable, not even at the prospect of a pre-paid boat contract, pleading gout and local court commitments. Jemmy was embarrassed and urged his father to "come in a chaise if necessary." It is doubtful if it offered any comfort to Colonel Otis, but Thomas Hutchinson was also mired in ennui. He was disappointed that he had not been appointed governor after laying such careful groundwork with Lord Loudoun, but he was strongly recommended to the position of lieutenant governor by Pownall. Hutchinson accepted the position but found the younger Pownall too actively pragmatic for his orderly tastes; the Governor's inability, or unwillingness, to delegate authority brought two tough minds into conflict as the lieutenant governor found himself with little authority or responsibility.

In May 1759 Colonel Otis made another attempt for a seat on the Council and was in Boston for the opening of the General Court, securing commitments for what he thought would be enough votes, but his handpicked successor in the House, his relative Edward Bacon, performed what in Colonel Otis's eyes was classic political betrayal. The Council consisted of twenty-eight men chosen annually by the House and the previous year's Council. The first eighteen were from the "Territory formerly called the Colony of Massachusetts-Bay," four were from Plymouth Colony territory, three from Maine, one from Sagadahock, and two at-large. John Otis had been one of the four from Plymouth Colony but Bacon persuaded Otis not to force the displacement of their friend and neighbor Sylvanus Bourne and pledged his support to the Colonel for one of the at-large seats. Bourne was safely reelected, and Bacon immediately deserted the Colonel and engineered his defeat in an attempt to strike at Barnstable's foremost resident for having "too much power." This time the Colonel was furious; he was determined to return but abandoned further attempts to reach the Council without a firmer base in the House.

While these complex political struggles were unfolding, Jemmy was working on a variety of legal cases including leases, bonds, recoveries, ejectments, and accounting disputes. In one case he represented the Selectmen of Roxbury who had been presented "at the Suit of the King" in the Suffolk County Court of General Sessions in 1756 for failure to maintain the bridge on the main road through the town. Attorneys were rare in such cases but apparently the selectmen were either intimidated or felt the matter to be of great import. They retained Jemmy Otis who argued that the offending bridge was in fact a county responsibility since all land traffic in and out of Boston passed over it, but the justices were not convinced and fined the town £4 and court costs. Otis immediately appealed the decision, and the annoyed Court required an appeal bond totaling the unusually high sum of £150. The appeal was successful with the jury deciding that the bridge was a county responsibility. In October 1758, he accompanied Gridley to the term at Salem, and in 1759 he ventured as far as Portland, Maine. So while he did travel on circuit with the Superior Court to Plymouth, Taunton, and occasionally Barnstable, the bulk of his practice was in Boston. His membership in the Masons began to produce clients, and his reputation amongst the merchants was strong.

In one noteworthy case Jemmy faced Oxenbridge Thacher; *Otis v. Leonard* probably arose as a result of the case Otis had handled for Thomas Flucker. On appeal, Otis obtained a judgment in Flucker's favor for £102 and costs, and collected it in the form of a packet of those old Land Bank bills that had nearly torn the province asunder almost two decades earlier. The bills carried a face value of £357, but their actual value was purely speculative. The defendant was doubtless pleased to dispose of the judgment with what was probably considered to be worthless paper, and Flucker probably received his judgment in lawful money from Otis, who in turn took possession of the bills on speculation. So even by the late 1750s, wretched Land Bank bills were surfacing. By 1758, the great bulk of the outstanding bills had been partially redeemed or discarded as worthless, but Otis now possessed some of these bills. But why would Jemmy pay Flucker over £100 for Land Bank bills that so many would have considered entirely worthless?

The bills had been issued by George Leonard, leader of the powerful Bristol clan, chief justice of the Bristol County Court of Pleas, friend of Thomas Hutchinson and member of the Council that had aided in the defeat of Colonel Otis's Council candidacy. It's surely no coincidence that Jemmy took an interest in these old bills as most would have little hope of ever collecting on something long discredited; an attorney armed with genius and persistence saw not worthless paper but rather an enormous opportunity. So in April 1758, Jemmy Otis faced Harvard friend Oxenbridge Thacher and won a judgment against George Leonard for the face value of the bills and accrued interest – £730. Per custom, Thacher appealed for Leonard, but the judgment was affirmed. Otis's first writ of execution to collect the sizable judgment was dated August 15, 1759 and was returned by the deputy sheriff "in no part satisfied." A subsequent attempt in January 1760 likewise yielded nothing, and the deputy accurately noted that he could not arrest Leonard because of his exemption as a councilor. A third attempt that December finally brought a partial payment by the "commissioners" designated "for finishing the land Bank" in the amount of £140; in order words, Leonard got the government to partially pay for the bills. A fourth levy squeezed another £125 from the same government source. A fifth, in September 1761, brought in nothing, but by now Colonel Leonard was exhausted by being constantly pursued by deputy sheriffs and the sixth execution in March 1762 brought him a personal note and supporting bond for every farthing of the balance. Thus by unconditional determination Otis was able to gain a return of nearly six hundred per cent on his £102 investment and at the same time humble one of the high and mighty councilors he was starting to detest. It is doubtful that he made many friends, but it is certain that he now felt skilled wielding the weapon of the law.

The Boston bar was transforming even more rapidly in the late 1750s. The men who dominated Boston legal practice during the first half of the decade – Gridley, Trowbridge, Dana, Kent, Prat, Otis, Thacher, and Auchmuty – were quickly joined by several young new lawyers as the practice of law increased in respectability and profitability. Robert Treat Paine and Jonathan Sewall were admitted to practice in 1757, and Samuel and John Adams were admitted the following year. While Gridley had continued to mentor lawyers, Jemmy either did not desire or could not attract apprentices in the law. Only Pelham Winslow seems to have mentored under Otis, and that was in 1754-55, so he had no apprentices for the remainder of the decade. John Adams had studied with James Putnam in Worcester, but when he decided to return to his native Braintree he had to be admitted by the bar to practice in the Suffolk County Inferior Court, a formality Adams approached with considerable anxiety. On October 24, 1758, Adams rode to Boston and went to Court to appear before the bar. He nervously "sett down by Mr. Paine att the Lawyers Table" and "felt shy, for awe and concern, for Mr. Gridley, Mr.Prat, Mr. Otis, Mr. Kent, Mr. Thatcher were all present looked sour." He next visited Jeremy Gridley and with his characteristic mood swings came away from the interview excited and with lists of the fields of study for a lawyer in the colonies, advice on not marrying too soon, and suggestions on the "pursuit" of law, "rather than the Gain of it." His interview with "Thatcher" (whose name Adams never learned to spell correctly) was depressing; Adams received a lecture the "Origin of Evil" and the overcrowding of the legal profession. At this time Adams's opinion of Jemmy Otis one of palpable admiration and perhaps even awe, and his aim was "to win the Applause and Admiration of Gridley, Prat, Otis, Thatcher &c." In one of his unique character sketches, Adams pictured Otis as "extremely quick and elastic. His apprehension is as quick as his temper - He springs, and twitches his Muscles about in Thinking." With Thacher, Adams was not so kind: "Thatcher had not this same Strength Elasticity. He is sensible, but slow of Conception and Communication. He is queer, and affected. He is not easy."

In reporting an endless courtroom dispute over a plea offered by Prat after an appellant's death, Adams quoted a typical Otis comment, "I will grant, Mr. Prat, very readily, that there has been a time since Wm. the Conqueror when this Plea would have abated this Writ in England. But I take it that

Abatements at this day are rather odious than favored and I dont believe that this Plea would abate this Writ at any time within this Century in Westminster Hall." Jemmy Otis was sharp, direct, and impatient. Further, he was very aware of the law's evolution, both in theory and practice, and strongly desired to be at the fore of that evolution. He could be brutally persistent as witnessed by his behavior in the *Fletcher v. Vassall* case and his dogged pursuit of Colonel Leonard, but he also refused clients and cases that he felt were flimsy or fraudulent. And in some cases he refused any fee as he did after the successful defense of a few teenage Pope's Day rioters in Plymouth.

At the same time James Otis was rising to fame in the British colonies in the 1750s, another man was rising to fame in England. Thomas Gray had been a bookish boy who attended Eton and Cambridge and was similarly bound for the law. But unlike Jemmy, Thomas couldn't pry himself away from Latin and Greek, and became a somewhat reclusive scholar and sometime poet; he taught at Cambridge for most of his life, spending more time with books than with people. In so many ways, Gray was an example of what James Otis could have been – if not propelled by his father, if not for the tremendous legal, merchant and political connections, and if not for the elevation of and newfound respect for lawyers and low regard for poets in the colonies. It was generally respectable for a man to follow his dreams in England, even if such dreams resulted in a life of no apparent utility; in contrast, the colonists seemed to be on a mission, fueled by the concept of progress and grounded in the notion that each generation has a burden to leave this earth wealthier, more efficient and more effective than they had found it. Such concepts did not brook dreams of no apparent utility.

So it seems that if Jemmy Otis had his druthers, he would have spent his life studying the classics; thus, it shouldn't be surprising that his first published work was academic. The vacant lot between the Otis home and King's Chapel had been the site of the Boston Latin School, previously razed and rebuilt across the street in order to extend the Chapel and erect a larger school. Jemmy Otis was known to spend considerable time at Boston Latin, and in 1759 he was a member of the town's official school visitation committee, which functioned as something of a school board and accreditation council. Otis's interests in education went beyond this somewhat honorary position; in 1760, he published his first work: *The Rudiments of Latin Prosody, with a Dissertation on Letters and the Principles of Harmony in Poetick and Prosaick Composition, Collected from some of the Best Writers*. It was originally intended to be a trilogy, but the section on Greek prosody was abandoned for the lack of Greek type among the province's printing presses; the two Latin volumes of the book were printed and sold by Benjamin Mecom, Benjamin Franklin's nephew. Scholars at the Latin School spent seven years learning Latin and Greek, spending the last two years translating Aesop's *Fables* and the Psalms in Latin verse. Otis sought to mend the deficiencies in the standard texts that tended to be of little help with the intricacies of Latin poetic rhythms and syllable duration, and his effort was part of progress in the science of language. *The Rudiments of Latin Prosody* was well received and was still considered the best book on the subject 50 years after its first publication.

As was Thomas Gray, the English sometime poet who locked himself away with his books, Otis was inclined to the scholastic and literary. Gray had risen to fame with the 1751 publication of *Elegy in a County Court-yard*, a somewhat short, melancholy poem that became a phenomenon. It was claimed that British General Wolfe read it to his troops before the battle of Quebec and lamented that he'd rather have written that poem than successfully take the city from the French. Gray would publish little other poetry. And while Jemmy was known to recommend Shakespeare, Milton, Dryden and Pope to students interested in poetry, he let his erudition and perhaps affinity for modern poetry slip one day. At one point Jemmy was cross-examining an attractive young witness who had testified against his client; he asked where she was from and educated, to which she replied a village not far from the courthouse. Jemmy then inquired where she had travelled, to which she plainly stated that she had never been out of the county. Impressed by the eloquence of the country girl, he tossed out a couplet from Gray's *Elegy*:

Full many a flow'r is born to blush unseen
And waste its sweetness on the desert air

Somewhere in the corner of the universe, Thomas Gray and Jemmy Otis broke bread, and just a glimpse of that rendezvous was revealed in a country courtroom when Otis threw off a Gray couplet from memory with astonishing poetic accuracy; doubtless Gray's few poems comingled with the thousands of lines of Latin and Greek poetry that abided in that part of Jemmy's mind that harbored what could have been. It can hardly be doubted that Jemmy was born to lead the life of a Thomas Gray and such a revelation renders the events of the following year even more inexplicable, for it would soon be apparent that James Otis was some bizarre confection of scholastic poet and fierce warrior.

So ends James Otis's his first decade in Boston. Otis possessed the qualities so needed in a successful trial lawyer: "brilliance," "elasticity," and a merciless pursuit of victory. He was safely apolitical, generally employing conservative country sensibilities but concurrently enjoyed access to the highest circles of provincial government and society. And with his appointments as justice of the peace and acting advocate general of the admiralty court, he had taken small steps to power. The family status was buttressed in 1760 when his father won his old seat in the House of Representatives, after which was elected Speaker of the House; Governor Pownall promptly approved the vote. The Speaker position conferred more raw power than a seat on the Council, but Speaker was beneath Councilor in the feudal scale of prestige that still operated in Massachusetts Province. As Shirley had, Pownall also promised the Colonel the next open seat on the Supreme Court.

And yet Jemmy was quiet in Boston politics; while future leaders such as Thomas Cushing, Royall Tyler, Oxenbridge Thacher and Sam Adams begin regularly appearing in Boston town records by 1758, Otis's name is entirely absent. The March 1758 town meeting witnessed the appointment of freeholders to the myriad town positions and committees; typically, there were over 120 such appointments that included Selectmen, Overseers of the Poor, Firewards, Treasurer, Clerks of the Market, Surveyors of Boards, Informers of Deer, Surveyor of Hemp, Fence Viewers, Hayward, Assaymasters, Sealers of Leather, Hogreeve, Scavinger, Clerk of Faneuil Hall Market, Cullers of Staves, Purchasers of Grain, Constables, Collectors of Taxes, and Assessors and numerous committee assignments that varied by circumstance. At the town meeting of March 13, 1758, Cushing was elected a Selectman, Tyler an Overseer of the Poor and Fireward, and Thacher to a committee to "Collect all the By-Laws & Orders of the Town now in force" so that they could be officially printed. Sam Adams was elected a tax collector after the first two men elected declined the appointment because of the low commission of six pence per pound collected that tax collectors received. On May 15, 1759, the town of Boston appointed Cushing, Tyler, Thacher and Adams to a committee to petition the General Court for tax relief; Thacher and Adams also served on the school visitation committee. Other familiar names, such as lawyer Ben Pratt and merchant Thomas Flucker, for whom Jemmy had previously won a court case, appear regularly in the records of Boston politics in the late 1750s.

Jemmy's name doesn't appear in the record until May 13, 1760, when he was named to a committee along with Thacher and Ben Kent to deal with a Dorchester petition requesting Boston's help in "rebuilding a Bridge over Naponsit river near Jackson's Mills" – Otis was becoming something of a recognized bridge expert, which is possibly why a man entirely absent from the political record suddenly appears on a bridge committee. And again on May 13, "James Otis Esq." is listed as having served on the school visitation committee of July 1759 along with 27 others, including Thomas Hancock, Foster Hutchinson, Flucker, Tyler and Thacher. To a significant degree, visitation committees were nothing more than the town's most important men gracing the schools with their presence and thus are more a minor recognition of one's importance than an official review of the schools. The vast majority of the Boston town meeting's work was tending to the mundane non-political operations of the machinery of town government: paving roads, operating schools, corralling hogs and, by 1764, solving the small pox epidemic.

Jemmy's court room victory in Halifax made "the young Otis" rather famous by the late 1750s; in merchant circles he was a hero but within the customs establishment he was a man of suspect ethics. Otis's literary work distinguished him as a gentleman scholar, his Boston connections indicated an increasingly firm social foundation, and his town meeting committee work displayed a sense – though quite minor – of civic duty. These seemingly ideal, stable circumstances were, however, coming within the dawn of what Peter Oliver was to call a "concatenation of Incidents" that would have a cataclysmic effect on not only the School Street household but also on the whole of the North American colonies. Jemmy's growing prosperity, stability, and brilliant future belie the events that he would next instigate, which Chief Justice Ruggles would accurately claim "has shaken two continents, and will shake all four."

Pownall's last official act as governor would be to approve the Colonel as speaker because just a few days later, on June 3, 1760, Governor Pownall said goodbye to Boston as he embarked at Long Wharf to assume the considerably more lucrative position of Governor of the Carolinas. Pownall left both Thomas Hutchinson as lieutenant governor and leader of the Council, and Colonel Otis as Speaker and leader of the House, to anxiously await the arrival of the new governor, Francis Bernard.

ARSONIST

In 1757, Jeffrey Amherst served the British in the Seven Years' War by protecting German territory in Hanover; upon being reassigned to North America, he regained Louisburg from the French with the aid of General Wolfe. Amherst and Wolfe then split to attack French Canada from different directions. Shortly after Wolfe read Thomas Gray's *Elegy* and attacked Quebec with combined forces of nearly 30,000, Amherst invaded from the south with a larger force to strike at the heart of New France in Montreal. On September 8, 1760, Commander-in-Chief Jeffrey Amherst led his army down the St. Lawrence River from Lake Ontario, in part in Otis whaleboats, and assaulted French positions at Montreal. French Governor Vaudreuil surrendered, but Amherst refused the customary "honors of war" and directed that all French flags be seized, at which point the French burnt their flags to keep them out of British hands. The fall of Montreal essentially ended the "War for Empire" in America and unified most of North America under British control. New France was dead. Two days later Stephen Sewall, the intelligent, moderate chief justice of the Massachusetts Superior Court, died. The following month on October 25, King George II awoke at seven, enjoyed a customary cup of hot chocolate, and promptly died. Of all these incidents the one of ostensibly least importance emerged as the catalyst for a radical change in the course of history.

CHAPTER III

I will kindle a fire

And yet life seemed good in Massachusetts Province in the summer of 1760. A visitor from Cape Cod to Boston report that Saturday, August 2, 1760 was a "fine pleasant day ... a pretty breeze" and "all the gentlemen and troopers" were "on to meet our new governor: Bernard." The governors of Boston had some wealth or some decent connections in England, but they weren't the wealthiest or best connected. Certainly, Boston wasn't New Jersey, but it also wasn't the South or the Caribbean, the sources of great agricultural wealth. A man with great wealth or substantial connections certainly never landed the position of Massachusetts Bay governor, but a man with great aspirations or limited ability – or both – might.

It was the combination of governors of middling wealth and influence and locals of reasonable wealth and great education that created a mixture ripe for combustion. A powerful governor with a voice heard throughout the kingdom and Portuguese gold johannes to spare could command respect and authority amongst a band of affluent rebel philosophers – affluent for a poor colony. But such a man was rarely appointed and would not have desired the position of governor of Massachusetts Bay. So it was left to the middling strivers to herd the cats of Harvard College, of Barnstable town, of the Boston printing presses and pulpits.

Pownall's informal style had irritated many, but he had been a good governor, and it is doubtful whether any politician could have gained the universal approval of the contentious New Englanders. Hostilities with France were concluding, the economy had boomed during the war years, and the political situation seemed calm by colonial standards. And so the air was full of excitement and optimism that August Saturday as Francis Bernard arrived from Dedham in a "vary Magnificent Manner" escorted by grandees and cheering crowds. The new governor's first visit was to the Chamber in the Town House where Secretary Oliver read aloud the royal commission, and Lieutenant Governor Thomas Hutchinson administered the oath of office. Crowds cheered and sang, bonfires lit the sky, guns fired, and the guest of honor was feted at "an elegant dinner" at Faneuil Hall. When Bernard retired that night, he basked in the afterglow of bonfires and smuggled wine, for a "quiet & easy administration" seemed assured, as he wrote to his cousin by marriage and patron, Lord Barrington. Bernard elaborated on his assurance, "I shall have no points of government to dispute about, no schemes of self interest to pursue." And a few days later he continued: "I have the pleasure to inform your Lordship that I have a very fair prospect of an easy Administration." This wishful thinking exposes one of Bernard's several faults: abundant naiveté.

Francis Bernard was educated at Oxford and practiced law for a few years, but his well-connected wife and eight children seemed to demand more than what the life of an average lawyer could provide. His wife's relatives got Bernard appointed governor of New Jersey in 1758, a position that was neither challenging nor lucrative. He clearly hoped that Massachusetts would be just as easy but more profitable, and to achieve his goal he claimed he would build a government "on the broad bottom of a collation." His theories regarding the proper ordering of an imperial structure were characterized by the same tidiness as his plans for Harvard Hall and were a reflection of a systematic, uncluttered feudal world that was quickly passing. Bernard was a man of many theories and little practical knowledge, and his shortcomings in the field of political realism relegated his neat imperial plans to the realm of historical curiosities.

The first Massachusetts test of Bernard's theories and "broad bottom" building was Judge Sewall's vacant seat on the Superior Court, and the facts surrounding this issue are unambiguous and generally uncontested. Stephen Sewall died Wednesday evening, September 10, 1760, and the next morning Jeremy Gridley met Lieutenant Governor Hutchinson on the street and stated that Hutchinson "must be the successor," and other members of the bar echoed this sentiment. On Saturday, Jemmy Otis arrived in town from Barnstable with a letters from Colonel Otis addressed to Hutchinson and Hutchinson's brother-in-Law and Province Secretary Andrew Oliver. The letters requested the "interest" of the addressees in the open seat on the Superior Court. In delivering the letter to Hutchinson, Jemmy Otis stated that if it was a "settled point that your Honor was to be Chief Justice," then his father would withdraw his consideration; this offer illustrates the Colonel practicing the well-established art of deference. While Colonel Otis had been promised the position by two previous governors, he was also a politician who proceeded cautiously. He would never demand the office but instead diplomatically suggested his availability.

Hutchinson's reply is the subject of some disagreement, but it was most likely ambiguous. When Jemmy Otis met with Secretary Oliver with the letter, he thought Oliver's response also demonstrated ambiguity. Oliver recommended that Jemmy confer with Charles Paxton, surveyor of His Majesty's Customs at Boston, crier of the Superior Court, marshal of the Vice-Admiralty Court, and his wife's uncle. Jemmy was probably confused by this suggestion because Paxton would have little or no input into the matter, but he visited Paxton anyway. Paxton advised Jemmy that "he had not the least to think his Honor [Hutchinson] had made any Interest to be Chief Justice," but that application should be made directly to Governor Bernard who was determined to make no appointment without "a Personal Application." This seemed like good news; Hutchinson was not particularly interested in the position and the governor wanted to personally interview the candidates. The Colonel was likable and well-spoken, so a personal interview would likely favor him.

Judge Sewall was buried that Saturday, and his fiery minister, Reverend Mayhew, delivered the eulogy on Sunday. On Monday, Jemmy mounted his horse and rode two miles south of Boston to Dorchester to get a boat to Castle William, the island fort protecting Boston's inner harbor and residence of Governor Bernard. During the horse ride to Dorchester a coach bearing Thomas Hutchinson and Charles Paxton overtook Otis going in the opposite direction. Was it a coincidence? Bernard was indecisive during Otis's visit, and Otis probably wrote his father suggesting he pursue the position personally. Hutchinson, exercising great caution, made no vocal appeal for the position; instead, the three surviving justices took up his cause, which isn't too surprising because they were all related to Hutchinson. Colonel William Brattle also had an interest in the position. And, of course, Colonel Otis had been twice promised the post; furthermore, Otis's friendship and appreciation would have done much to improve the new Governor's political "bottom." About six weeks after Sewall's death, the Colonel travelled to Boston to speak with Bernard. According to his son's recollection, Bernard told the Colonel that "he might be appointed as the youngest Judge of the Superior Court if the Lieutenant would relinquish his pretentions." So what had Hutchinson said to the governor?

Meanwhile, Bernard also needed to address Pitt's concerns. On August 23 – just a few weeks after Bernard's arrival in Massachusetts – William Pitt, whose vigorous and inventive execution of the war in America solidified his popularity in the colonies, issued a stern circular letter to the American governors referring to the "illegal and most pernicious" trade with the French enemy and required that the colonial governors bring all the "heinous Offenders to the most exemplary and condign Punishment." The implementation of his directive was gradual and irregular, but the colonial merchants were apprehensive and began to seek other means to maintain the free trade they had for so long profitably enjoyed. In a letter to Pitt dated November 8, 1760, new governor Bernard stated that he had made a few inquiries and was "fully satisfied" that Massachusetts was "quite free from" illegal trading. Bernard's inexperience, so quickly and thoroughly displayed, was but an omen of the administration to come.

Bernard took his time with the judicial appointment but eventually deduced that his political "bottom" entailed pushing back against both the Hutchinson and Otis factions, instead aligning with the small Tyng faction in the House. Bernard almost certainly thought that non-alignment would bring fairness into governance and perhaps make all parties more eager to please the governor, but the result was that Bernard simply had no strong allies. For the appointment of the new chief justice, Bernard made his decision by consulting the Council and the other justices, but there were also many other considerations. Peter Oliver clearly stated the first consideration, "The surviving Judges of the Bench also, not willing to have an Associate of such a Character to seat with them, applied to Mr. Bernard, the then Govr., who had the Nomination to that Office, asking the Favor to have such a Colleague with them that that Harmony of the Bench might not be interrupted."

Hutchinson was the leading figure on the Governor's Council. Hutchinson was also Andrew Oliver's brother-in-law. Most public officers or political appointees held or desired to hold multiple appointments, though the accumulation of offices by Hutchinson and the Olivers was extraordinary. It was common for a judge to also be a practicing lawyer or an elected official or a sheriff. Many lawyers were judges in multiple courts. And as practicing lawyers, it wasn't uncommon for the attorneys in a court case to also be judges. It wasn't uncommon for these same judges to enact legislation governing the courts, setting fines and fees, and regulating business. The legislative branch then could feed work to the lawyers, who would bring that work to the courts. Often, a cycle of legislation, regulation enforcement, levying fees, bringing a court case and delivering a verdict involved the same small group of people.

Whether or not holding multiple offices was ethical was not generally debated before 1761; the practice was viewed as both firmly entrenched and necessary. Most offices paid little or nothing, so an office holder must be permitted to have other means of earning an income. And most offices were not full-time positions, so it made little sense to pay someone a full-time salary for a part-time job. So if one had political aspirations, one typically vied for and often won multiple offices. The fact that this created significant conflicts of interest seemed comparatively unimportant to the necessity of having legislatures, bureaucrats, sheriffs, judges, customs officers and others required to operate a government. The system was the best anyone could envision and, even if an alternative was devised, the system of holding multiple offices was so entrenched that it was inconceivable that it could be dislodged. What, after all, could one do? If one brought a lawsuit, the judge hearing the case probably held multiple offices, as did the legislators being asked to consider changing the law, or anyone else who had the power to address the problem.

So while there were many offices to hold, typically few held them. And access to those offices was generally limited to the well-connected. In Massachusetts province, anyone who wished to climb out of the cellar of country politics usually needed connections in Boston or England. The real power in Massachusetts Bay was the ruling oligarchy in Boston, a tight-knit group of men who closely held power. The group was presided over by the governor, who was connected enough in England to get the appointment, but rarely did the governor do anything other than position himself as the leader of the entrenched ruling group. And since the ultimate source of the ruling group's power was the governor; the oligarchy welcomed him into their circle, feting him with grand dinners at Faneuil Hall, offering gifts and all courtesies. Power within the oligarchy was limited to a few families and typically if a position opened, someone's brother or brother-in-law or son got the appointment. The power of the oligarchy is that "Harmony of the Bench" to which Peter Oliver referred.

And if one wasn't born into the ruling class, one could marry into it, as Governor Bernard did. His wife's cousin was Lord Barrington, and it was he who secured Bernard the colonial appointment. Hutchinson's wife was the granddaughter of the Rhode Island governor. Andrew and Peter Oliver were the sons of a wealthy merchant and grandsons of the former Governor of Massachusetts, New Hampshire and New Jersey. Thomas Oliver was not related to these Olivers but got the job as Lt. Gov. after Andrew Oliver died because Hutchinson thought he was related. And, of course, Thomas Hutchinson was Andrew Oliver's brother-in-law. And, of course, most of them attended Harvard (Hutchinson, Andrew, Peter and Thomas Oliver).

These connections are to be expected. The oligarchy that ruled Massachusetts politics was ever striving to be more exclusive. Children of governors married the children of other governors, or judges, or wealthy merchants, or large landowners. Outsiders were not welcome. By the 1750s these patterns were well-established and firmly entrenched. The oligarchy would have a reasonable explanation for these relationships: there were few men with the appropriate education, temperament and means to devote their lives to public service. Therefore, it shouldn't seem odd that only a few men held office. A semi-literate apple farmer can't be expected to be a Superior Court judge, particularly when the bench probably doesn't pay as well as the fields. Judge Peter Oliver claimed that he spent £2,000 more than he was paid to cover the expenses of running his court in Boston. How could an average man have the time, money, education and temperament required to hold these offices?

Andrew Oliver, a descendant of the Olivers who lived in New York City in the mid-20th century, owned a painting of Peter Oliver. The painting is a typical late 18th century portrait of a wealthy and important man. Mr. Oliver would inform you that the portrait was painted by John Singleton Copley, and the reprint is often attributed to Copley. The attribution makes sense; Peter Oliver was one of the wealthiest and most important men in colonial New England, and Copley was the greatest painter in colonial New England, particularly of wealthy, important men. Copley painted John Hancock twice and famously painted Hancock's friend and co-conspirator Sam Adams (a painting for which Hancock paid). Copley also painted perhaps the most famous portrait of the time: Paul Revere holding the silver teapot. The portrait of Peter Oliver is unsigned, but one can certainly assume it was painted by the most expensive painter in the colonies because it's of an Oliver.

The attitudes of the ruling oligarchy are well described in Peter Oliver's history of the revolution. Peter was a judge for 25 years, was a Superior court judge throughout the entire turbulent 1760s, and eventually rose to chief justice of the Superior Court. Prior to becoming a judge, Peter served with his brother and Hutchinson in the upper house of the legislature. He was one of New England's wealthiest landowners and was firmly entrenched in the oligarchy. Much of Peter's wealth came from his iron foundry, which flourished from government and military contracts during the Seven Years War. The Olivers won those contracts because they were well-connected in Boston and lobbied for both the contracts and for the taxes to pay for them. After leaving the legislature, Peter's brother became Secretary then Lt. Governor of the province. Peter's wife, Mary Clarke, came from a wealthy family. And the Oliver, Clarke and Hutchinson families occasionally went into business together, particularly on shipping contracts. Peter's daughter Sara married Hutchinson's son. Peter knew well nearly every actor in the revolution drama. He was a judge at the Boston Massacre trial and a close advisor to the final two colonial governors of the province, Hutchinson and Gage. Few families controlled as much of the province's activities.

The oligarchy strove to keep power within the small group. So even though Hutchinson had no urge to seek a seat on the Superior Court, he was being seriously considered. He was already Lieutenant Governor, member of the Governor's Council, chief justice the Suffolk County Inferior Court, judge of Probate, and captain of the Castle. Though he had an often perceptive interest in the law, he had never received legal training and had never practiced. But Bernard had another very serious consideration: Hutchinson had repeatedly pointed out that financially a seat on the Superior Court would be meaningless to him, and it seemed obvious to all that his goal was the governor's chair. He had made a cautious move in that direction at the time of Governor Shirley's departure in 1756 in letters he sent to his confidante, Israel Williams. These letters are replete with references to the care he was taking to keep in Bernard's good graces and to protect his rear. Hutchinson's rear was the Colonel, and Hutchinson had effectively blocked his path to more power. Bernard's rear was Hutchinson, and he may have been determined to award the appointment to Hutchinson to curb his advances toward the governorship.

The third consideration was the upcoming cases that would be heard by the Supreme Court, particularly the writs of assistance case. A writ of assistance was a general warrant that a customs officer could use to search anybody, anywhere, at any time, for contraband. A crackdown on trading with France had recently been implemented and a crackdown on untaxed goods was on the way; in both cases, the ability of a customs officer to engage in unrestricted search was vital to the success of law enforcement. The merchants were growing upset with the issuance of general warrants, and the matter would soon need to be decided by the Supreme Court. The governor's basic ability to perform his job and receive compensation, as he earned a portion of the proceeds from auctioning seized cargo, depended on the ability of customs officers to search ships, warehouses, and houses of all sorts. With the opportunity to help shape the court, Bernard would certainly wish to be certain that his choice would steer the court toward deciding in favor of writs of assistance.

We have no way to discern whether this final consideration was paramount to Bernard, but writing nearly sixty years later John Adams, as he was synthesizing his views on the causes of the Revolution, tends to affirm that Bernard's primary concern was a favorable decision in any pending cases involving writs of assistance. Adams recalled that Bernard was warned that a major legal challenge to the general warrant was pending and defeating that challenge was paramount to Bernard's ability to perform his job and would substantially determine his income. So the naïve and newly arrived Governor Francis Bernard was being told by the Council and the other Supreme Court justices that someone within the ruling oligarchy needed to be chosen as chief justice, and Bernard knew and feared the machinations of the wealthy and well-connected Thomas Hutchinson; and perhaps most of all, he feared a court decision against general search warrants. So on November 13th, Bernard appointed Thomas Hutchinson as the new Chief Justice. The appointment would meet with the approval of the Boston powerbrokers and might satisfy Hutchinson's lust for more power. Above all, Hutchinson would certainly side with government against the merchants in any case involving search warrants.

The Colonel likely felt betrayed: Governor Shirley's departure, bitter defeats in his attempts to gain a seat on the Council, the realization that he had been held down by the Oliver "junto" – his term for the oligarchy. Behind all this the feeling on the part of the leaders of the Council was that Colonel Otis, though a successful leader with a large political following, was just not the type of man they wanted as a Superior Court Justice. The attitude could be viewed as sheer snobbishness, but in 1760 it was part of the pattern of deference and recognizing a person's position in the social strata. Colonel Otis had not attended Harvard and did not live in Boston; while he was a "friend of government," he was also a country bumpkin. Something more than wealth and political clout was required that the Otis family could not yet deliver: the breeding, culture, and point of view of the provincial aristocrats who controlled the Council and the Superior Court. That there was an oligarchy could hardly be denied, for on a functional level all of the justices of the Superior Court were probably the center of power of everything in the entire province. And Hutchinson, while relinquishing his Inferior Court seat to his half brother Foster, did retain his Probate judgeship. Justice Russell was also a judge of the Admiralty Court, and several members of the Council also held seats on the inferior courts of their counties. Control of the power in the province was vital and depended on keeping the oligarchy small.

On a personal level, the oligarchic tendencies were just as pronounced. Andrew Oliver, the province secretary and councilor, was Hutchinson's brother-in-law. The son of Justice Peter Oliver, Andrew's brother, married Hutchinson's daughter while Justice Lynde was father-in-law to Andrew Oliver's son. A small group of families inter-married and collectively held a majority of the most powerful seats and were the wealthiest merchants. This government of blood ties was an accepted fact of both English and colonial politics. Interestingly, while the Colonel wasn't a part of the reigning coterie, his son, Jemmy, increasingly was. Jemmy had attended Harvard, married a Boston heiress, and lived on School Street. Jemmy did not quite posses the wealth to join the ranks of the very elite, but he was close and getting closer.

Perhaps more remarkable, Jonathan Mayhew's published elegy on the death of Judge Sewall pointed out the problem of the oligarchy: it was creating in appearance if not in fact "undue influence." Sewall held the offices of Councilor and Judge, and Mayhew wrote, "But he himself made opposition to it; and this, partly at least, because he doubted the expediency of his being at once a judge of the court, and at the council table; thinking that, hereby he might be brought 'into temptation and a snare'; I or, in plain words, subject himself to undue influence." Mayhew was one of the few at the time to elucidate this issue, but the idea was to burgeon during the following years into one of the most potent of the rebellions against the oligarchy that dominated the Massachusetts government. The opposition to multiple office holding was but one small battle in the simmering war of the people and merchants against the oligarchy. This war can most succinctly be viewed as an effort to dislodge government from the people who controlled it. In the feudal conception of government, there was little difference between the oligarchy and institutions of authority; the lawyers and preachers of Massachusetts Bay were on the fore of modern thought by demanding that the two become uncoupled.

Bernard later claimed that prior to appointing the new justice, the Colonel ended his application interview by warning both him and Hutchinson that if the latter were appointed they would "repent it." This assertion wasn't made until 1763, when Jemmy Otis was Bernard's arch enemy. Doubtless, Bernard wanted to paint the Otis family as bitter, vindictive political enemies and that the catalyst for Jemmy's opposition to Bernard had little to do with rights and everything to do with politics. But it could have happened, as the Colonel wasn't threatening Bernard as much as alerting him that Hutchinson was a polarizing figure, and he'd regret appointing such a man to such a powerful position. Or the Colonel may have intended to remind Bernard that Hutchinson hadn't been trained in the law and had never acted as an attorney. One might regret putting a man with limited experience in the highest position in the province. Or perhaps Otis was reminding Bernard that Hutchinson already held numerous important offices and couldn't reasonably have the time for another. Despite what Bernard later claimed, it's highly unlikely that the diplomatic, deferential Colonel would have threatened anyone of Bernard's standing.

And there were many other arguments made against Hutchinson while Bernard tried to formulate a decision. First embodied in an unfinished piece, John Adams wrote urging the appointment of a man trained in the law, not in "Husbandry, Merchandize, Politicks, nay in science or Literature." It's unclear who Adams would have preferred, but he obviously viewed Hutchinson as a poor choice. At the time, it was generally agreed that Hutchinson got the appointment because he was well-connected, well-bred, and wealthy; the arguments for and against him tended to cite the same criteria. No one argued that Hutchinson got the position because of his superior legal acumen and training. So the debate over Hutchinson's appointment wasn't over whether one should get a position based on merit, but rather which "merits" were worth considering. The Old World of deference and status accorded merit to one's station; a man with the right friends, enough wealth, and of a certain status merited consideration for any position. After all, Bernard didn't become governor of New Jersey because he showed any aptitude for governance. Quite the opposite was true; Bernard's law career in England was mediocre at best and gave no indication that he was capable of managing anything.

But he – or, rather, his wife – knew influential people. There was no test of his capabilities; Bernard, by virtue of his station, which was largely composed of his connections, merited the position of governor.

But it was clear that there was growing resentment in Massachusetts over this feudal conception of merit. The New England colonists had long been paranoid that Old World institutions would take root in the New World; they perpetually fretted about the Church of England creating a bishopric in New England. They wanted nothing to do with royalty or aristocrats or bishops, so it wasn't surprising that there was some animosity created by the development of what appeared to be an aristocracy. Men were getting jobs not because they were qualified or needed the compensation but rather simply because of their station. Many, like John Adams, wrote about this growing animosity. Jemmy Otis went further. A few weeks prior to Bernard's decision, Jemmy Otis let all of Boston know that in no uncertain terms a political explosion was imminent. He said, "If Bernard does not appoint my father judge of the Superior Court, I will kindle such fire in the Province as shall singe the governor, though I myself perish in the flames." A little over two years later in the Boston *News-Letter*, April 7, 1763, Thomas Hutchinson recalls that Otis said he would "set the Province in a flame." Peter Oliver's recollection was "that if his Father was not a Justice of the superior Court; would set the Province in a Flame if he died in the Attempt."

This threat was reported with minor variations from many sources and sometimes included a benediction *Fléctere si néqueo súperos Acheronta movebo.* This bit of Latin is precisely something a literary and Latin scholar such as Jemmy Otis would append to a notice. It's Book VII, line 312 from Virgil's *Aeneid*, and it's usually translated as, "If I cannot bend Heaven, I shall move Hell."

※

moving hell – the Christmas Eve massacre

According to reports received by Bernard, these threats were "declared publickly with oaths." As Hutchinson was to ruefully admit in later years, "From so small a spark a great fire seemed to kindle." Jemmy Otis's plan for setting Massachusetts aflame was complex, and it started by using the skills he'd developed as a lawyer and the target was someone who probably did not expect to be set to the match. Charles Paxton was the epitome of the grasping, conniving bureaucrat and thus a favorite target of critics; he had been a customs officer in Boston since 1752 and had inveigled his way into Bernard's confidence by tipping off the new governor to auction prices paid for the accoutrements of the office that Pownall had left in Thomas Hancock's care to be sold to Bernard. Paxton also demonstrated his love of backroom politics and perfidious rumor-mongering by insinuating to his English patron, General George Townshend, that the Surveyor General of Customs, Thomas Lechmere, had clashed with the Collector Benjamin Barons and hinting that if either were expelled from office he would be pleased to fill the vacancy. The clash between the Customs Surveyor and the Collector had been partially due to Paxton informing Collector Barons that former governor Pownall had written to England defaming Barons, and Paxton let Barons assume that Pownall got his information from the Customs Surveyor Lechmere. By 1760, Paxton's reputation was as a perfidious rat, and he was the oligarchy's rat.

Perhaps the lines that divided the two sides of the Revolution were first drawn by Otis that fall when he renounced his commission as advocate general of the Vice-Admiralty court; it was a direct rebuke of the oligarchy and a clear signal of Otis's allegiance to the merchants. It was also a necessary maneuver before the fusillade that was coming. Otis's other problem was that Paxton was a relative by marriage; so Otis told Paxton beforehand of the plan knowing that Paxton could do nothing to stop it or protect himself. A month after Hutchinson's appointment but before receiving his commission, the first of Otis's incendiary moves was made public in the form of a "humble petition" to the Governor, Council, and House of Representatives by fifty-nine of Boston's leading merchants. The crux of the petition was that there had been "many Instances of Misapplication of the Province's Part of Seizures" in the Vice-Admiralty Court, and since province revenue improprieties were a public concern, the petitioners requested an opportunity to "be heard ... upon the floor of the House." Petitions were nothing new to the General Court, but it took no political wonk to appreciate that this petition was unusual. The House was under Colonel Otis's leadership, so it quickly granted the request for a hearing and scheduled it for December 24, 1760. The hearing consumed most of the day, and the petitioners "were fully heard by their Council upon the Subject-Matter of their Petition."

The petition was based on the enforcement of the Molasses Act of 1733, which had been created to protect the British sugar planters's interests by assessing a confiscatory duty on the importation of non-English sugar and molasses.

The Act's extremely high tax wasn't intended to generate revenue as much as it was designed to discourage the importation of any non-English sugar or molasses. The Act was recognized more in the breach than in the enforcement; customs officials would agree not to confiscate smuggled sugar and molasses in exchange for a fee. Violators were subject to forfeiture of cargo and ship in the Vice Admiralty Court with the seized cargo sold at auction, and proceeds disbursed equally to "the use of his Majesty… to be applied for the support of the Colony," the Governor, and the informer; all prosecution expenses were paid out of the King's share. So while customs officials made a decent amount permitting smugglers to operate, informers and the governor wanted contraband confiscated and auctioned.

The primary issue of the merchant's complaint was that the "informer" had been unfairly collecting the King's (that is, the province's) share by charging the province for prosecution expenses that were illegal and excessive and for "securing information" expenses that were similarly considerable and suspiciously vague. The merchants intended to prove that the province's chief informer was a thief; of course, that informer was Charles Paxton.

Otis had combed the Vice-Admiralty books and extracted the settlement figures for seven seizures made since 1753; the gross receipts from the sale of forfeited cargo totaled about £1822, but the province received a paltry £2, suggesting that someone was siphoning off province revenue. The House quickly voted for the formation of an investigatory committee. Two days later the merchant group repeated their claim before the Council, and six councilors were appointed to the joint committee. On January 13, 1761, the committee submitted a report to the House and the Council: £475 had been illegally deducted from the Province's account, and the Province Treasurer should collect that amount. If the amount wasn't collected within a month, the Province would file a suit.

Bernard, surely under pressure from the oligarchy to protect one of its own, raised a technical objection: the King's money was at issue, and any suit for its recovery should be either in the King's or province's name, not the treasurer's, and therefore the suit should be instigated by Attorney General Edmund Trowbridge. The committee replied that since the treasurer could sue to recover tax monies on behalf of the province, surely he could sue to recover this money. The committee was dominated by House members, the Speaker of which was Colonel Otis, and the real reason for the committee's position was that they rightfully feared that, left to the governor and attorney general, the money would likely never be collected. Further, they wanted to retain their own lawyer, that curse of the customs establishment, Jemmy Otis. Realizing he had been expertly outmaneuvered, Governor Bernard stalled the investigation by suspending the General Court.

It was probably not yet clear to Bernard that he'd made powerful enemies in the Otises, for they had proved that they could bring much of the provincial government to a halt when they wished. Jemmy Otis also brilliantly illustrated that the deference that men of high station demanded meant nothing to him; members of the oligarchy could and would be attacked by commoners. If Bernard had not yet realized that a new order was emerging, Hutchinson and the Olivers did. While none of them had any idea where it would lead, they also knew that in Jemmy Otis they were dealing with a man of immense capabilities.

How had Jemmy devised a case so perfectly that the mighty ruling elite could do nothing but watch as it was proved that one of their own was stealing from the people and that such activity was accepted by those in power? Otis seemed to have every bit of evidence and every detail nailed down before he walked into the chamber on December 24. Using Paxton as a target had its origin in the mind of Benjamin Barons, who had arrived in Boston in 1759 with a collector's commission in his pocket. He owed nothing to Governor Bernard, Paxton, or Surveyor General Lechmere and did not disguise his desire to make a fortune from his position by allying himself with the merchant community. This collaboration between tax payer and tax collector was not uncommon for the customs officers who were authorized by statute to enter into agreed settlements with importers on contested interpretations of the Acts of Trade. If the collector had an antagonistic relationship with the merchants, then he needed to monitor shipments, search for smuggled cargo, cultivate and pay informants, hire lawyers, curry favor with politicians, and a host of other burdens. However, if the collector collaborated with merchants, he would agree to leave them alone provided they pay him a pre-determined amount in taxes. This collaborative relationship is precisely what Barons cultivated.

The problem was that this collaborative relationship cut severely into the compensation of Lechmere, the Surveyor General of Customs, and his staff of informers. Lechmere had temporarily suspended Barons soon after his arrival in 1759, but Baron's collaborative efforts did not diminish, and private meetings with Bernard, Russell, Paxton, and Lechmere served only to further anger Barons to the point where he unreservedly sided with the "illicit traders" – a term that could be applied to most of the merchants of Massachusetts. Barons's anti-establishment position might have been ineffective had it not been for the strengthening merchants' organization, the informal "Society for Encouraging Trade and Commerce," which met regularly at the British Coffee House – a few blocks from Jemmy's School Street home. Barons met with the key merchants and their advisor, James Otis, and it was at the British Coffee House that Jemmy devised the first attack on the customs system. As advocate general, Otis had unfettered access to the Vice-Admiralty Account Book, so he could obtain all of the payment information from the past decade. After obtaining this information, Otis renounced his position as advocate general. And Barons had detailed knowledge of customs practices; together, they wrote the unofficial indictment for presentation to the committee. Though the merchants delighted in attacking Paxton, the suit was just the first phase of a much bigger plan.

Charles Paxton was the visible target of Otis's first assault, but the real targets were the Olivers, Thomas Hutchinson and Governor Bernard. Though the merchant petition raised a valid grievance, both Bernard and Hutchinson knew there was no legal remedy, at least by the method chosen by the Assembly. Collecting the £475 was a Vice-Admiralty matter, not a provincial common law matter. Otis was too good a lawyer not to know this, but a proceeding in the Vice-Admiralty Court would not serve his purpose as it would have involved a hearing on the nature of the collection of the information to be argued before Judge Russell who could, and probably would, have denied it; in short, the judge would have determined that Otis's collection of information from the Vice-Admiralty Account Book was perhaps illegal and not admissible in court. The only redress would have been an expensive, time consuming, and probably fruitless appeal to the High Court of Admiralty in Westminster. It's clear that Otis wanted maximum political effect, not the £475. And it's clear that Otis advised the merchants that to sue Paxton in court would be to request one member of the oligarchy to convict another member, which wasn't likely to happen. Instead, Otis directed the merchants to the democratic House of Representatives, a sympathetic body largely composed of merchants and men elected by merchants and led by his father.

Hutchinson was painfully aware that he was a target. "I have opposed the whole measure," he wrote to Israel Williams on January 21, 1761, "I knew the spring of it. I thought it a cruel thing to force the Governor into the measure ... But it is not a farthings matter what principle I acted on as long as I oppose a popular measure the clamour will be against me." And he realized that he'd been entrapped in a political snare; while Hutchinson had the money and experience to be somewhat inured to such problems, Governor Bernard began to panic. On January 19, 1761, Bernard wrote to his benefactor Lord Barrington, "Mr Barrons has plaid the Devil in this town. He has put himself at the head of a combination of Merchants all raised by him with the Assistance of two or three others to demolish the Court of Admiralty & the other Custom house officers ... he & his emissaries have turned the fury of his party against me."

The Paxton case had exploded publically, and now that Jemmy Otis had everyone's attention, he lit another match; he would argue that Lechmere's customs officials did not have the right to search for smuggled cargo without probable cause. Such an argument was considered absurd and dangerous at the time because it would render the entire customs structure incapable of operating, would severely deplete government revenue, and would make even greater enemies of very powerful customs officials.

Otis's plan for setting the province aflame was becoming clear: attack with a level of aggression that the oligarchy had never before seen, and attack simultaneously on multiple fronts. The assault would be new and astonishing to the oligarchy because they had built a cozy club amongst themselves; they didn't always agree, but they remained focused on increasing their wealth and power. Jemmy Otis would attack the argument and the person making the argument; he would use the colonial media to put faces to the arguments to make certain that the masses knew exactly who to blame, who to terrorize, whose house to smash to bits, whose effigy to hang from the Liberty Tree. He would simultaneously employ sophisticated legal, historical and philosophical arguments and personal scathing insults. The oligarchy was well-fortified, and Otis would strike at it with every weapon in his possession.

Otis began writing the Lechmere case while the Paxton case was still being investigated by the committee. The case that Otis was preparing would become one of the most famous legal cases in history and certainly the most famous case in the pre-revolutionary colonies. The *Petition of Lechmere*, as it was formally called, would permanently drive a wedge between the average merchant and the oligarchy, a wedge so enduring that Otis's argument would be written into the U.S. Constitution 26 years later as the Fourth Amendment. The *Petition of Lechmere* was scheduled for a hearing before the Massachusetts Superior Court on February 24, 1761.

Though general search warrants, usually called "writs of assistance," were not unknown to Massachusetts lawyers, this writ was an anomaly in English law in that it required no showing of "probable cause" and no "return" or report to the issuing authority. A further odd feature was that it was valid until six months after the death of the reigning sovereign. According to Hutchinson, Governor Shirley had issued the writs as an executive function until Hutchinson had suggested the impropriety of that procedure. Thereafter, commencing in 1755, the Superior Court had issued the writs upon proper petition by a customs officer; their issuance was considered a standard and necessary component of custom operations.

There were several reasons why Otis targeted the writs at precisely this time. First, the writs expired six months after the death of the King, and King George has just died, so all colonial writs were set to expire in April 1761. They would all need to be renewed, so the interim period was an ideal time to challenge their legality. Second, James Cockle, the new collector at Salem, had just requested a writ of assistance to be issued from the Superior Court. Records don't exist for this request, so it seems probable that Cockle made a verbal request to the Court, but the Court, disturbed by earlier expressed reservations about the legality of the writ, dissuaded him from filing a petition until they could further consider the matter. Furthermore, any writ issued would simply need to be reissued in a few months, so Cockle was persuaded to be patient. This gave Otis the pause he needed to attack.

Otis's strategy in the Lechmere case would set a pattern he would repeatedly employ, confusing contemporaries and historians for centuries. There were probably multiple issues that Otis considered, the first of which was that his family, particularly his father, the current Speaker of the House, was politically quite moderate. The Colonel usually did not take sides on issues and would position himself as the temperate voice of reconciliation. His son, while much fierier, understood the strategic advantage of appearing to be on neither side of an explosive issue. Secondly, Otis undoubtedly considered the nature of his opponent: the customs structure. Customs personnel ranged from appointed aristocrats and commissioned officers to paid informers and wharf thugs. The process of raiding ships suspected of smuggling, attempting to seize cargo, and enforcing the law against dockhands and sailors could be nasty and life-threatening; Jemmy would not have had much direct experience with the dirty business of customs enforcement, but he had certainly been warned, and his Halifax case, in which men were killed in the process of enforcing customs, certainly made the dangers clear. In successfully defending men who had murdered Royal Navy sailors attempting to enforce customs laws and in successfully proving that custom officer Paxton was a thief, Otis had already made enough enemies.

The strategy that Otis employed was simple but effective: he would convince his opponents that he was sympathetic to their position, or that he was approaching the issue objectively and siding with neither party, or that he was not advising either party. He would make statements that would seem to contradict what his opponents suspected. He would declare himself in opposition to a position that he'd previously taken. His opponents would be bewildered and rendered incapable of moving forcefully against him, as no single target existed at which to aim. A few of Otis's colleagues would also be confused, for the effectiveness of the strategy depended on its apparent authenticity. As long as Otis could keep his opponents guessing, he was relatively safe.

So the merchant committee proffered the first formal petition to the Court asking, "That they may be heard by themselves and Council upon the subject of Writs of Assistance." The petition was signed by sixty-three merchants, most of whom also had signed the Paxton petition to the Court, but with four more signatures, it seemed the "combination of Merchants" was growing. Jemmy Otis neither directly composed nor signed the petition, though he advised the merchants in every respect. Deftly, Otis's fingerprints were nowhere to be found on the actual petition filed with the court.

The appropriate lawyer to defend customs officers would have been the attorney general, Edmund Trowbridge, but Surveyor General Lechmere knew that Jemmy Otis was behind the assault and needed a lawyer who knew and could defeat Otis. Lechmere's choice was the man who taught Jemmy Otis the law, Jeremy Gridley. The merchant's petition was quickly matched by a "Memorial" filed by Lechmere that recited the filing of the "Merchants and Traders" petition and requested "that Council may be heard on his Majesty's behalf upon the same Subject: And that Writs of Assistance may be granted, as usual."

Otis first appeared in court soon thereafter but not as an attorney for either side. In his opening, Otis stated: "I was desired by one of the court to look into the books, and consider the question now before the court, concerning Writs of Assistance." The records do not indicate which justice asked Otis to conduct this research or when. In all likelihood, the court asked the then prosecutor for the vice-admiralty court to research the legality of general warrants months earlier when Cockle verbally requested one. So while it's a safe assumption that the lawyer who would prosecute customs cases would be asked by the court for his opinion on the legality of customs warrants, Otis quit the position before reporting to the court. It's quite possible that Otis's research into the general warrants was a primary catalyst for his decision to attack the oligarchy and that the Paxton case simply came up first because it was simpler and was heard before the General Court, not the Supreme Court. And while Otis probably had to renounce his position as the King's advocate in Admiralty courts prior to the Paxton case, it's also quite possible that he knew that he had to renounce his position if he was to side with the merchants against the customs establishment in the warrants case.

Otis then sought to establish his role as "not only in obedience to your order, but also in behalf of the inhabitants of this town." So Otis was appearing on behalf of the court and the town, not on behalf of either party to the case. And Otis even had more cover when Oxenbridge Thacher was joined with Otis "at the desire of the Court." When the hearing opened, Gridley faced two of his pupils across the table. As he was to admit later, "I hatched two young eagles, now they peck out my eyes." The arguments presented by these three lawyers illustrate the progress made by lawyers over the preceding decades as myriad mundane legal skirmishes had sharpened their logical powers, and Gridley's almost antiquarian curriculum developed in his apprentices an acute appreciation of theory and precedent; some of James Otis's law books still have marginal jottings on salient points, others still folded to a wide range of entries bearing both the central and peripheral points he argued. Jeremy Gridley began with an uninspired presentation of the basic English statute of 1662 that authorized the writs of assistance, and then progressed to the structure of the writ as set forth in a standard work on Exchequer practice. Next he reminded the court of the common practice of issuing writs in Massachusetts, and finally he reminded the court of the necessity of public taxes being collected efficiently and effectually. Gridley's theme throughout his argument was that the primary purpose of the court was to support the government. He conceded that general warrants may be unpopular and may occasionally infringe on the individual rights of the people, but the government's revenue depended on the warrants, and without revenue, the government could not defend itself against an "invasion of her foes, nor the tumults of ... her own subjects." The preservation of the government and safety of the people depended on the warrants. Gridley stressed that the court must uphold the preservation of the government above all else, because the "Necessity of having public Taxes effectually and speedily collected" was "infinitely" more important that "the liberty of any individual." Gridley was willing to concede that the choice was between survival of the government and individual liberty, which seems to be an astonishing admission, but perhaps Gridley was aware that Otis would present an even more astonishing argument.

Future president John Adams was taking notes and recorded that Thacher spoke next; his argument failed to rouse Adams's pen, for he took hardly any notes on it. Thacher made two arguments; first the technical ground that the writs were a matter for the Exchequer and that the Superior Court at least in part renounced its Exchequer jurisdiction; secondly, that unlike England, the officers in the colonies were not "under the Eye and Directions of the Barons [of Exchequer] and so accountable for any wanton exercise of power." Hence, Thacher argued that there were jurisdiction and uniformity of application problems.

Then James Otis spoke – for the court and the people of the town to defend principle, as he made it clear he was working for no party to the case and would accept no fees from anyone for his work. Adams recollected that Otis spoke for four or five hours, and Adams's observations of the argument cover six pages of scribbled notes, providing the outline of both the theory and content of the argument. Otis started:

> Although my engaging in this and another popular cause [the Paxton case] had caused much resentment; but I think I can sincerely declare, that I cheerfully submit myself to every odious name for conscience sake; and for my soul I despise all those whose guilt, malice or folly has made my foes. Let the consequences be what they will. I am determined to proceed. The only principles of public conduct that are worthy of a gentlemen, or a man, are, to sacrifice estate, ease, health and applause, and even life itself to the sacred calls of his country. These manly sentiments in private life make a good citizen, in public life, the patriot and the hero.

This statement was directed at judges, not at a jury, so Otis is essentially making clear that he's aware that his comfortable life as a "friend of government" was over. The former King's advocate general probably would never again be appointed to another high ranking government position, probably would never be a judge or on the council, probably could not advance his career any further. He knew he was making enemies of the people in power and made known his decision that he'd rather be a patriot than a judge. Further, his opening statement adroitly straddled the feudal and post-feudal world – "a gentlemen, or a man" – making clear that the "principles of public conduct" and the very concept of "public conduct" applied to all; the "principles of public conduct" were no longer restricted to the oligarchy. And finally, his remark that "to sacrifice estate, ease, health and applause, and even life itself to the sacred calls of his country" echoes rather clearly the oath from the Declaration of Independence: "we mutually pledge to each other our Lives, our Fortunes and our sacred Honor."

After affirming his allegiance, Jemmy launched an attack against the writs as "against the fundamental Principles of Law and The privilege of House." The "House" Otis referenced was not a legislative "House" but rather a person's private dwelling, which Otis argued was privileged. The only "Precedent" for such a writ, the one produced by Gridley, Otis denigrated by noting its origin during the reign of Charles II "when Star Chamber powers, and all Powers but lawful and useful Powers were pushed to Extremity." He then ascribed the form of the writ, which was cast in truly execrable Latin, "to some ignorant Clerk of the Exchequer," which was probably closer to the truth than even Otis realized. "But," he continued, "all Precedents and this among the Rest are under the Control of the Principles of Law ... Better to observe the known Principles of Law than any Precedent." In view of the hazy and questionable origins of the writ this was a persuasive argument, for use of the writ had grown unchecked and, as construed in Massachusetts, no longer complied with the generally accepted rules against unreasonable search and seizure. The argument that precedent was irrelevant once it contravened principle would resurfaced in debates over slavery.

But Otis wasn't done. He had never been one for compromises and was capable of taking arguments to logical extremes that few others even could fathom, and so he took a further step in his argument that has intrigued legal scholars ever since. He argued that, "As to Acts of Parliament. An Act against the Constitution is void: an Act against natural Equity is void: and if an Act of

Parliament should be made, in the very Words of this Petition, it should be void." The general warrant, and by implication Parliamentary supremacy, was "Tyranny" and the court should quickly proceed to "demolish this monster of oppression." If general search warrants were legal, then "a tyrant in a legal manner also may control, imprison, or murder any one with the realm." Any government bureaucrat who was fortunate enough to possess a writ was a *de facto* dictator, able to wield power arbitrarily and without constraint.

The argument was explosive, and it's possible – even probable – that such an argument hadn't been made in a court of English law for nearly a century; such words were potentially treasonous and certainly seditious. As Otis and all colonists were aware from the Land Bank Act, Parliament was the absolute and final arbiter of the law. There was no mechanism by which another person or body could contravene Parliamentary law, and Parliament could change or overturn its own laws at any time, hence Parliament was not even bound by its own precedents; the Land Bank imbroglio had made that clear. Otis was arguing that the tide of reform that had been sweeping across England for the previous century was erroneous, for while the legislative body certainly had legal supremacy over church law or the king, it could not make any law it wished because it was bound by common right and common sense. What Otis had done was to fuse 17th century English legal progress with 18th century radical English political theory to achieve an argument with revolutionary potential.

Otis derived authority for his argument, in part, from an entry in Viner's *Abridgment* based upon Lord Coke's opinion of the 1610 *Dr. Bonham's Case*. Legal scholars have suggested that Coke misused his authorities to support his opinion and that Coke had in mind not a true concept of a "higher law" limiting parliamentary acts but rather an overly broad rule of statutory construction. In 1610, Lord Coke was essentially arguing that common right and common sense have precedent over parliamentary law. At the time, "common right and common sense" was not codified in any single place – no written constitution or sole source – but rather existed in previous legal decisions, royal decrees, treaties and charters, common practice and the notion of "reasonableness." Parliament could not enact and enforce a law that contradicted these sources of common right and common sense. Otis applied this principle, as expressed in his *Abridgment*, to the question at hand, ignoring the tangled background of *Dr. Bonham's Case* and its subsequent demise as an authoritative precedent in English law. Otis ignored the *Glorious Revolution* and rise of

Parliamentary Supremacy and merged Coke's assertion with Locke's *natural rights* and Cicero's *recta ratio*, or "right reason," thus formulating not only a legal argument but the cornerstone of his emerging political theory. The *Petition of Lechmere* argument and this emerging political theory was of stunning importance as it was to be a recurring theme in the development of the revolutionary ideology to follow and a cornerstone of both the argument for independence and the argument for a written constitution.

It is precisely because James Otis was not trained at the Inns of Court that he was able to conceive of an argument that had as its premise a law higher than Parliament, for Parliamentary Sovereignty was accepted fact in the courts of England in the 1760s. And it is through this argument that a torrent of ideas would flow, which eventually coalesced into the theories of written constitutions and judicial review. The power to "pass such Acts into disuse," – that is, to nullify laws and statutes – which Otis insisted the courts possessed, was a single but important facet in the structuring of "higher law" that in turn became the theoretical basis for the Declaration of Independence. The Land Bank Act should never happen again because such arbitrary power – Parliamentary supremacy – was "tyranny."

After a lengthy digression in which Otis analyzed, one by one, the English Acts of Trade, he returned to the writs of assistance that, unlike any other search warrant, were "Universal," being directed to "all and singular" public officers; they were "Perpetual," requiring no report to the court; they were usable "At Will"; they had been and continue to be subject to gross abuse and were treated as assignable from one officer to another without permission from or report to the court. While Otis readily admitted that special writs of assistance issued under oath and probable suspicion to a particular officer for a particular search would be valid, everyone in the court knew that the writs had been used to conduct searches simply to harass, even though the customs officer conducting the search could argue that anyone could be (and nearly everyone was) a smuggler. Such general warrants were virtually abolished in England and otherwise not employed, but customs officials were relying on them with increasing frequency. For Otis, such lack of equal treatment was the hallmark of arbitrary and fickle power.

John Adams characterized Jemmy Otis on the night of February 24, 1761 as a "flame of fire!" Adams said that "Every man of an immense crowded audience appeared to me to go away as I did, ready to take arms against writs of assistance. ... Then and there the child Independence was born." Otis made an argument with which the justices couldn't possibly agree: that Parliament was not the supreme legal authority. Further, agreeing with Otis would effectively emasculate Massachusetts customs efforts and substantially diminish the government. And yet Otis's argument was so powerful and so logical that Hutchinson, the new chief justice, was paralyzed. Hutchinson therefore convinced his fellow justices to stall the case until he could determine how warrants were presently executed in England.

Thus the *Petition of Lechmere* was held in abeyance while the other justices permitted Hutchinson time to confirm the practice of issuing writs in England. If the practice in England was a legal issue, it would be incumbent upon the petitioning surveyor general to obtain verification from the Board of Customs Commissioners or the Lords of the Treasury. If the Court intended to take judicial notice of English procedure, then an inquiry should have been sent by either the provincial Governor to the Board of Trade or by the Court to the attorney general of England. But Hutchinson knew he was playing with fire and did not want to risk a report that would support Otis's argument, so he ignored these proper avenues of inquiry. Instead, Hutchinson made his inquiry in a letter to his close friend, William Bollan, the province agent in London. Bollan was also the man who lost his job as advocate general of the vice admiralty court to Otis. So Bollan was a "friend of government" but not a friend of the Otises. Hutchinson had his own doubts about the legitimacy of the writs and knew that a finding that favored Otis would effectively halt the province's custom tax collection efforts. The suspicion that Otis may have found a fatal defect in the colonial tax collection process caused Hutchinson to seek unofficial advice rather than an official determination. Otis would not forget Bollan's participation, but for now, the validity of Otis's argument was in Bollan's hands.

So the court waited for an opinion from England, and Otis returned to the Paxton case. While the Writs of Assistance case attracted much attention, the Paxton case attracted more attention in Boston, in large part because Charles Paxton was a polarizing figure. While Paxton was being investigated by the legislature, a somewhat coordinated media attack commenced; personal attacks in the newspapers were nothing new, but they would take on a vigor, virulence, and effectiveness in the early 1760s never before experienced. And Charles Paxton was the first in a long line of public targets that would lead right up to the revolution.

The first story appeared in the *Gazette* of December 15, 1760, timed for publication just before the merchant petition was filed. It was in the form of allegory and described a hollow wooden statue representing the government, which was inhabited by a rat, Charles Paxton, which gnawed at the vitals of government from within. Allegory was a common weapon in colonial papers. The story of the statue and the rat was embellished in an issue printed January 2, 1761 and again on February 2, when it was reported that the rat was infesting the ships, docks, and warehouses of Boston harbor, but that some cats had been secured. Even the reserved Boston *Evening-Post* expanded on the theme in a virulent poem. This allegory reached its crest in the *Gazette's* "A Short Sketch of the History of Charles Froth, Esq." published on March 2. The force of the piece is diminished because of the obscurity of the allusions, but "Sir Thomas Graspall, who was dictator general" is certainly identifiable as Thomas Hutchinson. A few years later such rhetoric would not have been too scandalous, and a decade later it would have seemed somewhat common, but in 1760 and 1761, it was shocking to publicly mock the men of the oligarchy and accuse the government of being infested with rats and dictators. Of course, in accordance with Otis's plan, the articles were all published anonymously. And of course, given Otis's threat to set the province on fire, he was the suspected author, but Jemmy denied it, and no proof of authorship has ever been discovered. Otis would later make heavy use of anonymous newspaper articles as a tactical weapon, attacking men and destroying arguments, and his close relationship and alleged "management" of Edes and Gill's *Boston Gazette* would become a formidable weapon in the rebel's arsenal not only in Boston but across the colonies. The *Gazette* would become widely known for the acerbity and accuracy of its reporting, and its articles were probably the most reprinted in all the colonies; within a few years, *Gazette* articles would appear regularly in newspapers from New Hampshire to Georgia.

The formal lawsuit in the Paxton case, *Gray v. Paxton*, was filed on March 18th for *indebitatus assumpsit* (essentially unjust enrichment) alleging that Paxton "had & received" £357 "for the use of the Province." Benjamin Kent, Paxton's counsel on this particular aspect of the case, filed a plea in abatement arguing that the plaintiff had established no promise on Paxton's part to pay anything, and that even if Paxton did owe the money, it was the Province, not the treasurer, who was the proper plaintiff. The Inferior Court overruled the plea, thus requiring Kent to argue the case. The jury found Paxton, province rat, guilty; he appealed, and the case came before Chief Justice Thomas Hutchinson and his colleagues in the August term at Boston.

For the second time that year, Hutchinson was the chief judge on a case argued by Jemmy Otis that attacked the customs establishment. Fearing the outcome, the Court would not let the case go to a jury but rather agreed with the appeal, thus overturning the jury verdict. The reversal was good law. The decision to bring the action in the common law courts instead of in Vice-Admiralty Court was made for two obvious reasons, expediency and political impact; Otis was clearly not concerned with actually winning the case. And the decision to sue in the name of Harrison Gray, province treasurer, rather than in the name of the province itself was made to keep the case out of the hands of Attorney General Trowbridge, who would almost certainly have taken control of a lawsuit made on behalf of the province. But as soon as the first judgment was overturned by Hutchinson, a new one was filed named *Province of Massachusetts Bay v. Paxton*. The lawsuit was filed on September 21, 1761 but various postponements delayed it into 1762 and into a different political climate and ultimate oblivion. Regardless of the legal outcome, the Paxton cases had one significant practical outcome: collection costs and informers' fees never again would be deducted from the province's share of any recovery, thereby making customs enforcement less lucrative for both the governor and the customs officers. Even though Charles Paxton never paid the judgment, his cases produced a new level of scrutiny and fiscal honestly in provincial customs practices, again making James Otis wildly unpopular within the customs establishment.

Otis was determined to set the province "in a flame," and he was not a man to use just one or two matches. Though juggling *Petition of Lechmere* and the various *Paxton* cases would be enough to keep Otis occupied, there was more to come. Six days after filing his writ in *Gray v. Paxton,* Otis filed *Erving v. Cradock*. The plaintiff was John Erving, a merchant, councilor, and father of a signer against the writs of assistance. A year before, Erving's brigantine *Sarah* had been seized for violation of the Acts of Trade by customs coastal watchman William Shaeffe and tax collector George Cradock. Fearing the loss of his ship, Erving entered into a settlement in the Admiralty Court for £555, half the value of the vessel's cargo, but now his lawyer filed a suit in the Suffolk Inferior Court to recover his payment plus damages, claiming the settlement was made under duress – reflective of Jemmy's master's thesis that argued that an oath obtained by craft was not binding. The defense conceded the futility of a full scale defense in the Inferior Court and merely pled the general issue, and two of the justices went so far as to direct the jury to find for the plaintiff to "give him for damages every farthing he was out of pocket." The jury was happy to comply and gave Erving his judgment. Otis had now launched another successful attack on the provincial government's primary means of collecting revenue, and now the customs establishment was abundantly aware that they were under full assault.

The judgment was of interest in England because Erving's ship was seized while Pownall was governor, meaning one-third of any finding for the plaintiff would be paid personally by Pownall since the governor received one-third of the value of the settlement. Pownall was now a general in the British army. Governor Bernard panicked, as he typically did, and wrote to the Lords of Trade in England that he feared this decision would be the first snow flake in a coming blizzard. In a letter to the Board of Trade on August 6, 1761, Bernard said that Otis's lawsuit had "an immediate tendency to destroy the Court of Admiralty and with it the Custom house, which cannot subsist without that Court. Indeed the intention is made no secret of." And in a letter to Pownall dated August 28, Bernard continued to blame Otis as the source of all of his troubles, writing, "Mr Otis, Junr is at the head of the Confederacy. If you are acquainted with the natural Violence of his temper, supposed it to be augmented beyond all bounds of Common decency." The leader of the "combination of Merchants" was now named, and as Otis had earlier predicted, he would no longer be considered a "friend of government" but rather an enemy of the established oligarchy.

Despite "harangues of the council for the plaintiff," the Superior Court directed the jury to find for the defense on appeal because the Admiralty Court's judgment was not subject to common law; typically, once an action was started in Admiralty Court, the case was immune from common law courts. Hutchinson "imagined their [the Court's] opinion upon what was a mere matter of law, would have the same influence with the jury as formerly in like case," but the jurymen, reminiscent of Captain Kidd's crew saluting the Royal Navy with their derrières, fully affirmed the judgment against defendant Cradock in the amount of £740, which included interest. Former governor Pownall was required to pay £247.

Cradock was granted an appeal to the King in Council, but in the meantime he was subject to jailing if he did not pay the judgment, a matter of some concern to Bernard. Cradock could certainly have his appeal heard back in England, a process that would take many months, but he'd either need to pay the entire judgment – an enormous amount – or spend those months in jail.

But, like the Paxton case, Erving's case had by February 1762 drifted into a different political scene and was quietly settled out of court.

Meanwhile, Barons was not content to sit idly. He was aware that the governor and Paxton were plotting his downfall as retribution for the customs information he provided Otis for use in the Paxton case. Barons redoubled his efforts to increase animosity between the customs officers and Boston merchants, mostly with threats, gossip, and promises; but in late April he attempted to physically block the seizure of a highly illegal shipment from New Orleans. This was too much for old Thomas Lechmere, and he suspended Barons again and appointed Cradock as acting collector. Barons thought the suspension was illegal and his "Confederate" Jemmy Otis promptly filed three lawsuits, against Lechmere for unlawful suspension, against Cradock for taking his position in the customs house, and against Cradock for going over Barons's head in complaining to Lechmere. The suit against Lechmere was for £10,000, and borrowing from Edmund Trowbridge's playbook, Otis demanded the much dreaded "special bail." Lechmere was to be either jailed or bonded. Luckily, Lechmere was bonded at the last minute by wealthy councilor Thomas Flucker.

But, of course, the governor and the top tax officials in the province would marshal a solid defense, and, as everyone knew, Barons was admitting he smuggled goods, so the suspension seemed quite justified. Otis let the case linger, and he knew that it almost certainly could not be won; he had achieved his goal of harassing "the government." Barons was without money and his health was failing. His merchant friends wrote to the governor, pleading his case, and the governor agreed to settle the matter, but Barons refused to drop the case. Barons would fade from the public scene as would Lechmere who was 78 years old and was drinking enough Madeira wine to fill "a 74 gun ship." Lechmere would die in 1765. The case was hanging over both their heads to the end.

The period of 1760 to 1765 was witness to a significant coalescence of the merchant community – the "combination of Merchants" – partly triggered by the growing power and aggressiveness of the tax officials, which in turn was triggered by London's increasing intolerance for tax evasion. The concern and cohesiveness of this group was doubtless heightened by British Secretary of State William Pitt's rigid positions on trade and taxation that revealed his increasing frustration with Massachusetts merchant activity, mostly trading with the enemy France. Customs tax racketeering – those private agreements between tax collectors and merchants – was certainly an aggravating factor, as was what the merchants felt was discriminatory treatment compared to that of "wide open" Rhode Island. The Boston *Gazette* published an article on December 7, 1761 that complained, "It is not notorious that the Acts of Trade are nowhere executed with Rigor but in the Province?" The merchants widely believed that Massachusetts was treated unfairly, and, unfair or not, the Acts of Trade were enforced in Massachusetts as nowhere else.

Of course smuggling was widespread, and smuggling and customs racketeering fed on each other, but the balance between the two had been thrown off as the two sides seemed to declare war on each other. The primary cause of the equilibrium being disrupted is most likely the Seven Years' War, which made many colonists, such as Hutchinson, very wealthy and significantly increased merchant activity yet made trade with the French treasonous. This combination of growing private sector activity and a perception that it needed to be controlled fueled the expansion of the power and wealth of the government and the oligarchy that controlled it. Boston merchants uniting under James Otis to fight customs tax cases directly foreshadowed the political battles of the 1760s and the war of 1776. The unification of the Boston merchant community was fairly novel in 1760, but it was clearly powerful, and no one would soon forget that unification produced results that none alone could.

Thomas Pownall had more pressing concerns than losing a few hundred pounds in a colonial lawsuit; he would soon be sent as a general of British troops to fight in Germany. But Governor Bernard was frightened that Jemmy Otis was destroying his easy, lucrative fantasy world. Barons was obviously greedy, rash, and vindictive, but without the intelligence or strength of character to do anything more than inveigle in and out of "confederacies" and "play the Devil." Charles Paxton was a very slippery and dishonest man. He nearly always managed to insert expenses for "procuring Information," sometimes for as much as £93, and the Admiralty Court almost always paid the amount, which almost certainly went straight into Paxton's pocket. Paxton secured his position by being a sycophant to Bernard, but it was a tenuous position that made him hated more than liked.

Jemmy's threat – "I will kindle such a fire" – had traumatic meaning for Bostonians with memories of the recent fire that burned the heart of the town. Otis followed his threat with a period of intense activity, employing weapons close at hand: Barons's unstable vindictiveness, newspapers that would publish anonymous screeds, the restless merchant "Society," and his own legal acumen. And while Paxton was a tempting initial target, it was obvious that the inevitable targets were Hutchinson, Bernard, and a government bureaucracy that was viewed by some as corrupted by rats and dictators. The *Petition of Lechmere* explosively expanded the issue, for though the target of Otis's argument was the crippling of the customs officers' efforts and the embarrassment of the oligarchy, there was a broader question that transcended the local world of political feuding, and thus Otis's argument against the writs of assistance exists on two levels. There can be little doubt that Otis eagerly sought confrontation with the new chief justice, but more significantly he wished to pit individual rights against oligarchic oppression. In his argument, Otis skillfully interwove the theme of natural equity rights with Locke's natural rights of the individual. The idea that one's rights were guaranteed not by a monarch or a government but rather by nature or God was fairly novel, but Otis's argument took a monumental leap by propelling that idea from the realm of philosophy and academic debate to practical application. Perhaps most importantly, Otis's argument at the Council Chamber in the Town House on the evening of February 24, 1761 built the philosophical and legal foundation for resistance to acts of Parliament. It wasn't just lawyers and judges who took note; Otis's argument against Parliamentary power would soon be repeated on the streets of Boston. And this result demonstrates how Otis had moved beyond the philosophical musings of Bolingbroke and Cato's *Letters* and into the world of practical application; it was no longer enough to speak of *rights* and *consent* and say that "An Act against the Constitution is void." Now in the courts, those seditious ideas would be put to action. And soon that action would be taken to government meeting rooms, newspapers and the streets. Otis was determined that Gray's *Elegy* – Full many a flower is born to blush unseen – would not apply to the concept of natural rights.

Otis must have known that Hutchinson would have been placed in a difficult position, but Hutchinson never cracked. Even as a judicial novice, he had doubts regarding the theoretical propriety of such a writ, but he was conscious of his duty as a "friend of government" and could undoubtedly understand the problems that would ensue if the validity of the writs were to be denied. He parried Otis's thrust by delaying the case, thus pausing the action while evaluating his options.

But was Otis just another lawyer arguing a case or an innovative patriot risking his life? Hutchinson, in retrospect, commented that "Otis's zeal in carrying on these causes was deemed as meretorious as if it had sprung from a sincere concern for the liberties of the people." Even Hutchinson, who largely blamed Otis for his own downfall and exile in 1776, could see no selfish motive in Otis's behavior. Of course, Hutchinson didn't label Otis a patriot either; he labeled Otis insane. Bernard's almost neurotic concern over Barons led him to lump all of them together as a conspiracy to wreck his peaceful administration. Otis may have begun his actions to strike directly at the oligarchy, but it's evident from his persistence and consistency that he earnestly believed in his cause. Perhaps he initially intended to set aflame the courts and Castle William, but it was clear by 1762 that the fire was spreading across the province.

CHAPTER IV

the Resentor & the popular Conductor

Prior to 1761, Jemmy Otis is only listed in town records as a member of the school visitation committee and on a temporary committee to address problems with the Naponsit Bridge. The customs battles of 1761 were merely one component of Otis's efforts; in order to "kindle such a fire," Otis moved to attack the oligarchy from behind enemy lines. To accomplish this, he tapped into two groups that operated beneath the surface of Boston's political structure: the Society for Trade and the "Caucas Clubb." By the fall of 1760, Jemmy was a *de facto* member, legal advisor and spokesman of the merchant group. In contrast, the "Caucas Clubb" would have no legal advisors or spokesmen; in fact, this political machine received little public attention prior to 1763 and left no documentation regarding its membership and operations. John Adams did not even know of its existence until 1763 when Boston assessor William Fairfield, register of the Vice Admiralty Court William Story, desultory tax collector Sam Adams, and town clerk William Cooper, were publically named as Caucas Clubb members. The group met in Thomas Dawes's immense Purchase Street house, filled the garret room with cigar smoke, and agreed on appointments for town offices such as Informers of Deer, Surveyors of Hemp, Fence Viewers, and House Representatives. According to John Adams, a "caucas" representative would then confer with the merchant society, after which the selections and town meeting strategy would be distributed throughout Boston's taverns, Masonic lodges, and occasionally by printed broadside. Despite the nefarious undertones of a political machine, the "Caucas Clubb" likely was borne as much from the necessity of filling some 130 town positions every year as from some wicked motive to control town politics. And given how apolitical most of Boston's town governance was prior to 1764 – mostly focusing on paving roads and corralling hogs – it seems that controlling such positions was an unlikely source of great graft. The entire Boston town budget typically did not exceed a few thousand pounds, so it's unlikely anyone viewed monopolizing local government as a means to great wealth.

On April 20, 1761, the Boston *Evening-Post* printed a statement that the "Society for Encouraging Trade" was "to meet at Mr. Ballard's in King Street" to undoubtedly discuss the upcoming May election of Representatives to the General Court. The "Caucas Clubb" was likely also meeting, though no notice was made publicly. Normally Boston representatives had performed a variety of minor town responsibilities before earning the privilege of being considered for the top honor the town could grant – a seat on the Boston bench in the House. Royall Tyler, Otis's Harvard classmate and rising politico, had served as Clerk of the Market, Fire Ward, and Overseer of the Poor before gaining his seat in the House. Otis could not claim such a record of longstanding public service, having served on a largely ceremonial school committee and offering some advice on a bridge. But something significant changed in the spring of 1761. On March 9, 1761, he is appointed to a committee to investigate the wisdom of improving the town dock, again apparently appealing to his interest in or knowledge of bridges. The following day Jemmy was appointed to committees to investigate whether the town should require building owners to purchase ladders to facilitate escaping from and extinguishing fires, to "consider of the best method for the repairs" to the recently burned Faneuil Hall and the method to fund those repairs, and to a committee to resolve the apparent traffic problems around Dock Square. Finally, he was appointed to Boston's permanent committee of 15 to negotiate the town's contribution of the province's tax revenue. Two of Jemmy's committees reported at the March 23 town meeting. The ladder committee stated that a regulation requiring the purchase of ladders would be "fruitless" and that it would be more efficient for the town to purchase "about Sixty good Ladders, to be distributed & deposited at convenient places in the Town." The town would then have "Fire Meetings" to coordinate the implementation of the ladder purchases. The traffic committee drafted a petition to the governor and General Court requesting regulations against "the standing of People with their Horses and Carts in and about Dock Square, and the Street round the Market Place."

In the spring of 1761, Jemmy had quickly moved into this world of ladder and traffic regulations and within a few weeks had crafted the resume it would have taken others years to produce. Certainly he had committed himself to this task, as no man of means and stature would have travelled this route involuntarily, and yet the two-week cavalcade of committee assignments had to be endorsed and promoted by powerful political forces; unmistakably, the "Caucas Clubb" and the "Society for Encouraging Trade" were building the preliminary earthworks for a much greater siege.

But winning a seat on the Boston bench required considering the incumbents, and since 1750, save for the 1760 purging of two "friends of government," Benjamin Prat and John Tyng, by the merchants, the Boston bench in the House had been extremely stable, and none of the incumbents in 1761 had received the town's reprobation. Royall Tyler and John Phillips, also a public servant of long standing, had replaced the purged members while Samuel Welles and Thomas Flucker held the other two Boston seats. Welles was about the same age as Colonel Otis and a justice of the Suffolk County Inferior Court, whereas Thomas Flucker was a wealthy merchant, an Otis client, and had held his seat since 1756. Tyler and Phillips were younger and faithful, so they certainly couldn't be replaced; Flucker was affluent and influential and likely had higher aspirations, yet he seemed friendlier to government than to the merchants, as he was the one who bailed Lechmere out of jail. But the "combination of Merchants" was eager to place "the head of the Confederacy" on the Boston bench, and so the slate that evolved for the 1761 election evidenced indications of a negotiated deal that entailed retirement for Welles and the promise of a seat on the Council for Thomas Flucker.

Otis received advice on the art of getting elected from Royall Tyler, including the suggestions to look sincere in meetings, institute family prayers before the servants, engage some home repair work just before election, and join the dock workers on their 11 o'clock break. Otis ignored the advice, and voter turnout was light at the Meeting of Freeholders on May 12, 1761 with only 334 votes cast. Otis came in third, behind Tyler and Phillips. Thomas Cushing, also running for Representative the first time, came in fourth. The Boston bench was now composed of Tyler, Philips, Otis and Cushing. John Adams later remembered that the 1761 election caused great anxiety in some quarters: "On the week of [Otis's] election, I happened to be in Worcester, attending the Court of Common Pleas, of which Brigadier Ruggles was Chief Justice, when the news arrived from Boston of Mr. Otis's election. You can have no idea of the consternation among the government people. Chief Justice Ruggles, at dinner at Colonel Chandler's on that day said, 'Out of this election will arise a damned faction, which will shake this province to its Foundation.' Ruggles's foresight reached not beyond his nose. That election has shaken two continents, and will shake all four."

It is doubtful Otis either needed campaign advice or used it because his political appeal was on a different plane. Like his forbears in Hingham and Barnstable, Otis would create a path in history supported by farmers and small merchants instead of by aristocrats and the government. Perhaps for the first time in America, a major politician's power would be wholly derived from below and not from above. Otis's ability to get elected without any support from above in itself proved to be an obvious new danger to the oligarchy. It seemed that growing segments of society – farmers and merchants – were becoming independent of the controlling forces of feudalism. The colonists had long since left behind the church, constantly resisted the meddling influence of lords, and now had supported and promoted a man whose power and approval existed outside the ruling elite. Approval of the ruling elite was a necessary act of deference in the feudal world as it served to acknowledge and consent to the social hierarchy; resisting that approval was a rebuke of the hierarchy, a demand for a new order, and an invitation to anarchy. A few in the Boston oligarchy would recognize this – Hutchinson seemed to on occasion – but most, such as Bernard, would be perplexed and dismayed at the lack of deference.

To illustrate how busy he was in 1761, Otis could not be present at the meeting that started his legislative career because he was arguing cases before the Superior Court on its circuit. On May 7 and 8, the court sat in Barnstable, where Otis won a reversal for Joseph Gorum against Samuel Sturgis, and on the second day he suffered a defeat at the hands of the Colonel. Sam Sturgis was the father of Mary Sturgis, the wife of Jemmy's younger reprobate brother Joseph; the colonial merchant world was quite small and the plethora of lawsuits did not necessarily generate animosity. This second week in May was also likely the occasion of the marriage that joined his sister Mary with John Gray, the brother of oligarch Harrison Gray, Treasurer for Massachusetts province. And three years later Harrison Gray's daughter Elizabeth would marry Jemmy's youngest brother, Samuel Allyne.

The Otis's family and business connections were expanding during this period. Joseph proved an able manager and was the force behind the significant expansion of the Otis shipping business. Various in-laws provided useful contacts that helped the Otis's expand their shipping and trading businesses to Philadelphia and the Carolinas. Samuel Allyne had taken his bachelor's degree at Harvard in 1759, and, like his older brother, his master's degree in 1762. And in another indication of the Otis family's rising stature, while Jemmy was listed at 13th place in the Harvard social rankings, Samuel was ranked second. After graduation, Samuel considered following his brother's footsteps into the law, but he changed his mind and began to "trade" in a small way. Yet just like Jemmy, Samuel Allyne wanted to live in the big city; he had no interest in carving out a life in Barnstable as Joseph had. In some ways, Samuel Allyne was much like his brother Jemmy: both were cerebral and drawn to the big city. In this sense, Samuel was nothing like Joseph, who probably seemed a bit like a country dolt to the Boston elite. But unlike Jemmy, Samuel Allyne was drawn to Boston high society, to fashionable parties and witty banter. In his letters home to his brother Joseph, Samuel Allyne comes across as a saucy, facetious playboy. And unlike Jemmy, Samuel Allyne is noticeably a man of privilege. It's not surprising that Samuel Allyne married into a wealthy, well-connected family. And after he graduated with a master's degree from Harvard and rejected the idea of going into the law, he borrowed a very large sum from his father and essentially opened a liquor store "on the South Side of the Town Dock" where he had "for Sale at the Lowest Rates, fine Jamaica and Barbados Rum, and Molasses." One gets the impression that Samuel Allyne was a bit of a rum expert. By May 1764, he was advertising across the page from Jolley Allen in the *Gazette*; he was still at "Store No. 5, Southside of the Town-Dock" and offered for sale "New Rice & Pork …Hogg's Fatt …Lisbon Salt" along with the usual "Rum, Molasses & Sugars" all "At the very lowest Rates by Wholesale and Retail." Samuel didn't offer the money-back guarantee that Jolley Allen did.

Of course, Samuel Allyne referred to himself as an importer, and, of course, much of his imports would have been smuggled. This new store formalized the informal trading he had been doing as the Boston branch of the Otis Barnstable operation. After starting with liquor, Samuel Allyne branched out, using his connections – mostly his father-in-law – to secure good deals; he specialized in buying large quantities of highly profitable goods, so his business went in the direction of the next great deal and included everything from Irish linens and whale oil, to rice and fish. From 1761 to 1765, brothers Joseph and Samuel Allyne would make trips to the Carolinas, Georgia, Jamaica and Guadeloupe to secure markets for beef, flour, rum and wood products. They sold cheap fish in the Caribbean and imported rice and hard currency into the province. The Otises also began a very lucrative business importing salt from Antigua. By the summer of 1763, Samuel Allyne was urging Joseph to expand their merchant and shipping businesses to the Mediterranean and was pushing for a trip to Bilbao, Spain; he wrote to Joseph to "think it a good Scheme much better than lounging here with my fingers in my mouth."

From the start Samuel Allyne and Joseph argued about the proper method of keeping accounts, with justification. There was the firm of James and Joseph Otis, plus the individual trading accounts of the father and his sons to keep straight, and often it was difficult to determine who owed whom what amount. It is apparent, however, that Samuel got his start with Barnstable capital; by June 1763 he acknowledged owing the sizable sum of £437 to the family firm. Samuel Allyne was about twenty years younger than his brothers Joseph and Jemmy, and he felt he was always treated like the baby. The Colonel and Joseph were complaining to Samuel Allyne about the way he conducted business, perhaps as pretext to deny his travel request to Spain, and Samuel replied that only God could make him obey their directions. But the addition of Samuel Allyne to the Otis operations proved profitable. Clearly more astute than Joseph, Samuel Allyne had an intuitive sense for commodity trading, and he wrote letters to Joseph explaining how very little family capital could be employed in shipping to generate substantial incomes. He rigged and manned the family's six large ships in Boston and helped coordinate the very profitable whaling expeditions. These operations produced almost £5,000 profit in the years 1762-1765.

Samuel Allyne certainly wasn't all business. Many of his letters to Joseph were sarcastic; he knew that Joseph wouldn't be certain whether or not the letters were to be taken seriously which, it seems, caused Samuel to delight even more in sarcasm. He suggested that women's brains be dissected in order to determine what they were thinking, and also suggested to Joseph that woman "are the best bed fellows in the world, so god bless them." And while he sought advice from Jemmy, not his father or Joseph, Jemmy mostly stayed out of the family business, and most business arguments were conducted between the Colonel, Joseph and Samuel Allyne. Neither Samuel Allyne nor Joseph was particularly interested in politics, except in how it affected their businesses. In that regard, they were similar to Hutchinson; the government existed to further their financial interests. Samuel Allyne's interest in politics typically consisted of expressing either amusement or alarm to Joseph about Jemmy's fireworks. In October 1761, Samuel Allyne wrote to Joseph, "Govr B__d is a busibody in S Davis's Affairs; tis true he says he is poor & wants to what money he can of us: but whether this is the case, or if tis whether he ought to oppress the industrious mercht to fill his pocket or gild his own Chariot with another's Gold; or aggrandizing his family with his neighbour's property: I dont pretend to say." And typically, that sentiment was the extent of Samuel Allyne's interest in politics in the early 1760s.

More Superior Court sessions kept the Otises from taking their seats in the House; the Court met on May 12-14 in Plymouth where Jemmy faced his father across the counsel table in seven cases; Jemmy won three of them. While in Plymouth, the Colonel and his son stayed in James and Mercy Otis Warren's home. James Warren would eventually surface as a rebel leader, and Mercy would be a radical of the Jeffersonian republican sort – too radical for many eminent Bostonians such as John Adams. One can only imagine what the Colonel, his son, daughter and son-in-law discussed at the dinner table in those May spring nights; the fire of independence would soon burn hot in the three younger diners, and it's undeniable that Otis's arguments – "An Act against the Constitution is void: an Act against natural Equity is void: and if an Act of Parliament should be made, in the very Words of this Petition, it should be void" – were almost certainly discussed. And it's probable that the Colonel – the wily politician who'd been rejected and humiliated by the oligarchy – counseled the younger generation in how to navigate the tumultuous political waters that lay ahead. Perhaps they were deliberating what it would mean to "shake the province to its foundation." Three years later the father and son would stay again at the Warren's house and hatch the plot that would spread the flame from Massachusetts to the other 12 colonies. They were consumed with their legal practices, but perhaps they also entertained foundation shaking scenarios over dinner.

The first session of the newly elected House opened in the Town House on May 27, 1761, and Colonel Otis again took his seat as Speaker by unanimous vote. Sitting in the Speaker's chair, the Colonel could look down the rows of benches that lined the walls and spy the famous Boston bench occupied by his son and his three colleagues. Was this the foundation shaking that Brigadier Ruggles so feared? The assured and composed Colonel was the archetypal country trader and lawyer and the undisputed master of his county, representing a confection of mercantile, legal, agricultural, and social interests that was incurably attached to Boston by the delicate threads of patronage and economics. The Colonel represented the practical needs and desires of the "combination of Merchants," not their theoretical positions. Conversely, the

Boston bench comprised of the arsonist Jemmy Otis, the steadfast Thomas Cushing, and the political operator, Royall Tyler, represented Bernard's feared "Confederacy," a group who increasingly sought to break those delicate threads of patronage and economics that tied the people's needs to the oligarch's desires.

Even this "Confederacy" – the Speaker and the Boston bench – consisted of only five of 123 men, many of whom were puppets whose strings were manipulated by powerful merchants or farmers and "the King's friends" whose primary purpose was to promote government policy in exchange for government patronage. Despite this, a number of powerful and independent minds also existed in the House. Colonel Choate of Ipswich was as skilled in parliamentary combat as Colonel Otis. Brigadier Timothy Ruggles, now of Hartwick in Worcester County and Elijah Williams of Hampshire County, one of the River Kings of the Connecticut valley, also held seats in the House. Then there was the mercurial Chambers Russell; a judge of Vice Admiralty and Superior Court justice, he had resigned from the Council the preceding month likely due to the mounting attacks on plural office-holding and the appearance of what Mayhew labeled "undue influence."

The Boston bench had, however, been the source of almost every instance of defiance ever since the elder Elisha Cooke rebelliously led the House as Speaker in the 1680s, and Boston's exceptional advantage of having four representatives in the General Court gave its bench strength beyond its numbers. The Council was elected each year by the new House and the previous year's Council; in theory, a unified House could determine Council membership. In practice, however, a combination of custom, perceived exclusivity, and feudal deference had preserved a Council overwhelmingly loyal to the governor and government; the Council held the prerogative of being "the King's friends." The resignation of Chambers Russell from the Council and the election of James Otis to the House were, however, harbingers of the erosion that would destroy this combination of custom, perceived exclusivity, and feudal deference. And as an omen, the new representative's first maneuver was to attempt to block Hutchinson's election to the new Council, but the effort was futile, and the voting produced no substantial shift in Council power. The radical's plan was too radical in 1761. And according to plan, Thomas Flucker was also elected to the Council.

The General Court, composed of the House and the Council, was now formally organized, and Governor Bernard gave the opening address, which wistfully reflected the era of Charles I more than recognized the quickly shifting sands of 1761. He asked the members "to lay aside all divisions and distinctions, especially those (if any there be) that are founded upon private views. ... Let me recommend to you, to give no attention to declamations tending to promote a suspicion of the civil rights of the people being in danger." There was no doubt in the minds of the audience that his remarks were directed to Jemmy Otis and the Popular Party, nor was there doubt in Bernard's mind as to the meaning of the House's reply that "your recommendation ... shall have its weight. It is our intention to see for ourselves. ..." Bernard was asking the General Court to be a friend of government; the Court was non-committal.

As did his father in his first term as a representative, Jemmy quickly emerged as a leader, serving on more important committees than any other member. The Colonel, as Speaker, had significant involvement in committee appointments, but there are no indications that his recommendations opposed the wishes of the House, and even Governor Bernard acknowledged the mounting prominence of "the head of the Confederacy." In reporting to John Pownall, the Secretary to the Board of Trade and brother of the previous Massachusetts governor, in a letter dated July 6, 1761, Bernard wrote: "The Assembly keeps in very good temper; all necessary business is properly done, notwithstanding an opposition is kept up (seldom raising the minority by one third) by Mr. Otis, Junr. who has been Mr Barrons faithfull Counselor from the first beginnings of these Commotions." Bernard was still wistfully hoping for his easy term as governor but knew that "Mr. Otis, Junr." lurked in the shadows.

Five days later Bernard suspended the General Court, and Otis seemed no nearer to vitiating the friends of government, likely because no issue yet presented itself that could be leveraged to increase the minority Popular Party to a majority. Otis targeted a message from the governor stating that during the recess – that is, after suspending the General Court – he had found it necessary to man the province ship so that it could protect the fishing fleet from French privateers. As there was no appropriation for this purpose, the governor had borrowed the necessary funds and now asked the House to repay the loans; the House commenced on a "long debate" and eventually acquiesced to the governor's request but would not let the issue rest for long.

Concurrent with the trials of *Gray v. Paxton*, *Erving v. Cradock*, and Benjamin Barons's ongoing saga, events were congealing to supply the awaited issue from which Otis could capitalize in order to increase the size of his "Confederacy." Heavy war expenditures in New England were sharply increasing the trade deficit with the mother country, and just as the trade deficit deteriorated for Massachusetts, the gold-silver price ratio in Europe shifted, thus generating unusually high demand on the already low supply of silver in the colonies. So the depletion of the silver supply aggravated the ongoing need for more silver. On August 28, 1761, Boston merchant John Rowe wrote his English agents that "The money which has been circulating in this Country begins now to be shipt off ... Abt Twenty thousand pounds were shipt p[er] the Chesterfield & should another man of war come here tis like a Larger sum may go." And merchant Thomas Hancock alerted his friend Thomas Pownall that sterling bills were commanding a premium of as much as seven percent. Sterling was being drained from the colonies at a frightening rate.

And yet another development was fuelling the fiscal crisis. In June 1761, a trader was caught passing counterfeit silver specie. The criminal was quickly convicted and sentenced to stand in the pillory where he was promptly besieged with rotten eggs. Reportedly, the most energetic participant was Dr. Seth Hudson, a notorious scoundrel who was in Boston only to answer charges of payroll fraud. A month after the counterfeit specie trial, Dr. Seth Hudson himself was jailed along with his accomplice, Josh Howe, for forging province notes. Hudson's scheme attracted far more attention than the counterfeit specie scheme because the amount ran into hundreds of pounds, and the victims were prominent men.

Just as the Seven Years War was reaching its conclusion, the counterfeiting problems were agitating the crowds; men desperate to climb out of debt or buoy their post-war-boom finances turned to desperate acts of counterfeiting. Samuel Allyne wrote to Joseph explaining the low prices at which he sold a warehouse of Cape Cod leather: "I can only inform you of the dulness of business is being swallowed up in the noise of war, this day the proclamation for war will be read when Shoe boys whores & fine Ladies will muster as thick as at the Hudsonick Shew." The "Hudsonick Shew" occurred on the day Dr. Seth Hudson was pilloried and whipped after his conviction for counterfeiting. Samuel Allyne concluded that business was difficult in uncertain times. A small counterfeiting problem was turning into a significant political crisis because of the increasing debt and decreasing availability of silver.

Governor Bernard was troubled enough by the counterfeiting schemes that he was finally able to disregard his obsessive documentation of Benjamin Barons's treachery and call the General Court into session on November 12, 1761. The governor's speech was a compilation of customary political clichés, but he stressed that the purpose for the session was "a particular Business that requires immediate redress." The "particular business," he stated, was counterfeiting, a problem that appeared to concern all equally, without regard to political affiliation. But Otis and his minority managed to craft the ostensibly non-partisan issue into *casus belli*.

After summarizing the crimes of the counterfeiters, the governor observed that there was no provincial statute that rendered the production of counterfeit province notes and private bills of exchange and notes a crime *per se*; the only applicable statute available for such cases regarded forgery, which Bernard claimed that when "compared with the mischief [was] little better than none." After criticizing the limited extent of the province laws and mild penalties afforded by them, Bernard proposed to recall all treasury notes in circulation and reissue them concurrent with the implementation of English laws on counterfeiting money instruments; Bernard concluded that enacting English counterfeiting laws for both English and other current coins would be "a terror to evil doers." But amidst Bernard's sermon on counterfeiting lurked a statement that gave "the head of the Confederacy" an opportunity: "In this country," Bernard commented, "where it is impossible to have a general currency of English money, such foreign Coin as is current by Law and is become legal tender is substituted in the room of the English coin, and the whole force of the reason of the penal Laws that has been applied in England to punish and prevent the counterfeiting the English Coin is equally applicable here to the common coin, whether English or Foreign that is current within the Province."

The House debated Bernard's message for a day, and then passed a series of guiding resolutions to be reproduced in proper form by a drafting committee led by the two Otises. One the other side, the Council submitted bills that were poorly drawn, and then after a bout of futile objections, finally deleted a provision implementing capital punishment for counterfeiting at the insistence of the House. But the House bills incorporated provisions considered objectionable to merchants such as Thomas Hutchinson, who had made a small fortune on the arbitrage of money instruments: the explicit acknowledgement of foreign gold coins as legal tender valued at predetermined and constant pound and shilling equivalents. A joint committee session lead by Jemmy Otis and Chambers Russell for the House and Hutchinson and James Bowdoin for the Council failed to produce a compromise. A battle of amendments continued for six days without a negotiated compromise. After sixteen days of political warfare, the frustrated governor conceded the obvious: "After more than a fortnight spent in fruitless debates," he announced, "I find myself obliged to prorogue this General Court without anything effectual being done." So activity in the General Court was again suspended.

But Bernard was sadly mistaken if he thought the Popular Party would waste the opportunity to officially meet on but one issue. On Wednesday November 18, the Superior Court occupied the Council chamber to entertain final arguments in the writs of assistance case — the *Petition of Lechmere* now titled *Paxton's Case*. As in February, Otis and Thacher opposed the writs, but now Gridley had Robert Auchmuty, Jr. as an assistant. John Adams, though just admitted to practice before the Superior Court, did not attend, but Josiah Quincy, Jr., a Harvard junior committed to the law, was present and took notes. From Quincy's observations the arguments appeared similar to those offered at the first hearing. Thacher made his argument more precise, emphasizing the divergence between Exchequer practice in England with its integral oversight of the customs officers and the practice in Massachusetts that lacked protections against exploitation of the broad powers a writ holder wielded. Quincy reported that Auchmuty added little, while Gridley remarked that "Quoting history is not speaking like a Lawyer. If it is the Law in England, it is law here." Clearly the remark was directed at Otis, and Otis's argument clearly indicated that the courts should reject the writs, regardless of whether Parliament made them law in England.

The Court now had a response from Bollan, but it was irrelevant because the court never could practically prohibit the issuance and employment of the writs. Tellingly, the court discreetly issued Paxton's writ two weeks later, but the "combination of Merchants" wouldn't let the issue quietly die. On January 4, 1762, the *Gazette* resurrected the subject of general warrants in an article that opened with "so great a lawyer as the Hon. Mr. H_tch_ns_n" – who was, of course, no lawyer at all – and concluded by warning that "such [customs] officers" with the "uncontroul'd power" of the writs of assistance could not be trusted; the article propelled the case from the court rooms to the coffee houses of Boston. The writs amounted to unchecked, unbalanced power, and as such were the instruments of tyranny. The author was anonymous but was almost certainly Jemmy Otis.

The legal decision proved nearly immaterial to the narrative arc; the people were being introduced to the argument that their government was working against them while the customs establishment was regulated more tightly, expenses were no longer being paid out of the people's account, and customs officials had to significantly diminish the previously strict rules of enforcement. The youngest Otis brother, Samuel Allyne, reported back to Joseph in May 1761 that Thomas Hancock now had no problems smuggling in Madeira wine, and Boston's printing presses proved that the Courts and the Town House would not be the lone venues for airing grievances.

Meanwhile, the problems of counterfeiting and the valuation and status of gold coins were unresolved; the nature of the argument became clearer after Bernard suspended the Assembly, and the battle moved to the newspapers. Unpredictably, it was the usually reserved Lieutenant Governor Hutchinson who drew first blood in what Jemmy called a "personal Challenge." Hutchinson explained his reasoning in a letter dated December 14, 1761 written to his friend and province lobbyist William Bollan:

> The House passed a Vote for making gold a lawful tender at the rate it passes. This would drive away our silver and eventually depreciated the Currency. I stood in the front of the opposition and it was with great difficulty the Council was kept from concurring and I am afraid of the next sessions as the Govr. at present is not sensible to the ill consequences of the proposal. If it should succeed I look it to be the first step of our return to Egypt. I think I may be allowed to call myself the father of the present fixed medium and perhaps a natural biass in favour of it. However I ventured to give my reasons for my conduct in print and if I am in error I should be glad you would let me know it.

It is remarkable that Hutchinson had to employ such efforts to maintain the governor's and council's allegiance; apparently, the House's committee, led by the Otises, had been powerfully persuasive and to Hutchinson's dismay the oligarchy had difficult holding firm. And what he labeled his "biass" for "fixed medium" was more of a decade old fixation that presented Jemmy Otis and the Popular Party a breach to exploit. Hutchinson's initial salvo appeared on the front page of the Boston *Evening-Post* on December 14, 1761 and was a dexterous and cogent presentation of an intricate topic. Hutchinson argued that silver was being rapidly drained from New England due to the complexities of exchange and an unintentional overvaluation of Portuguese gold johannes under a 1750 statute. Establishing gold as legal tender at its then inflated rate would only serve to exacerbate the current currency situation and a devaluation of gold was required to slow the silver outflow; he further explained that "Two metals as gold and silver cannot be the measure both together, and be both a fixed measure, because they are frequently changing their proportion." His argument recapitulated his own efforts to reform Massachusetts currency in 1749-1750, and he also recalled England's 1696 "Great Recoinage," directed by John Locke's unyielding monometallist theories, and thus closely followed Locke's theories in urging that silver be established as the "invariable standard," with a predetermined valuation of pounds to silver bullion. In contrast, gold coins would be considered a commodity and free to fluctuate in value according to market price. England and Massachusetts attempted to regulate this potential for fluctuation by placing maximum valuations on gold coins, but in all cases the par valuation had been set at the maximum valuation, thus resulting in overvaluation. And so Hutchinson argued for gold's devaluation to correct the imbalance and thus had to reject gold as legal tender valued at a fixed rate. The logic was sound, but he made his position increasingly politically unfeasible by sermonizing: "The plenty of money has produced luxury, luxury naturally tends to poverty, poverty will produce industry and frugality, industry and frugality will lessen the proportion of imports to exports and will bring money among us."

Only a man of the oligarchy could find Hutchinson's economic morality tale acceptable policy, and Hutchinson's analysis marked him as an aristocratic Englishman, whereas Jemmy Otis was progressively neither. Otis's reprisal in the *Gazette* on December 21 and 28, 1761 was swift and brutal. Jemmy opened with piercing mockery:

> A General Officer in the Army would be thought very condescending to accept from, much more to give a Challenge to a Subaltern. The Honour of entering the Lists with a Gentleman so much one's Superior in one View, is certainly very tempting; it is at least possible that His Honour may lose much, but from those who have, and desire, but little, but little possible be taken away.

Jemmy responded to Hutchinson's aristocratic Englishman mien with something that was clearly quite the opposite and as yet undefined. The consciousness of New Englanders had usually consisted of English conditional opposition – opposition to lords and bishops – but on the condition that they were nevertheless English; but now Jemmy seemed to be striking at the few threads that still tied the New World to the Old. After heaping scorn on the concept of deference, Otis defended the brave few who had "the resolution to think and act for themselves" though doing so entailed "opposing the Leviathan in power, or those other overgrown Animals, whose influence and importance is only in exact mathematical proportion to the weight of their purses." Otis continued to drub the oligarchy and the concept of deference for almost three columns, expanding on his theme that the government was controlled by beasts whose power is derived solely from their wealth. He launched an assault on the Hutchinson and Locke monometallist theory that promoted silver as standard coin and gold as commodity to fluctuate in value with market conditions. Jemmy asserted that gold should be legal tender "provided it be set at a proper rate." He dreaded that a gold valuation determined by freely floating market prices would enable very wealthy speculators to increase gold prices beyond what most could afford and thereby essentially create two classes of currency.

Jemmy reminded readers that Hutchinson had confessed to errors in the act of 1750 and "only it seems strange that there would be any mistakes in this Act, considering the great abilities of the gentleman, who at the time of making it, ruled our Councils, and was the Prime Conductor of all our public affairs." Of course, the Colonel was instrumental in getting the 1750 act passed in exchange for a clarification on the statute of limitations which helped Jemmy's legal career, but it was increasingly clear to all that Jemmy Otis was not marching in his father's footsteps; the Colonel had been the epitome of the compromising politician and had worked for years in a productive relationship with Hutchinson, the Olivers and whatever governor was in office at the time. It would seem that a fiery break with the oligarchy would strain his relationship with his father.

In his second article, Jemmy addressed a subject almost entirely overlooked by Hutchinson: the legal issue of provincial currency. Jemmy observed that Governor Bernard's initial affirmation of gold coin as legal tender was correct, and that the legitimacy of such coins ought to be affirmed by statute. Next Jemmy examined how a maximum valuation for gold was *de facto* its legal valuation, thereby demonstrating that the province had set a fixed gold value. In ending, Jemmy verbally smirked at Hutchinson's aristocratic homily. Hutchison's solution to the debt problem was to devalue currency and consume less, but Otis dismissed these prescriptions as high Tory notions that depended on a "wheel of fortune" that only the very wealthy would consider desirable. Hutchinson believed the colonists lived "too well" but Otis countered that "I do not think they live half well enough." Otis argued that Massachusetts should improve its economy not by reducing imports, as Hutchinson argued, but rather by increasing exports, observing that the province was mired in an absurd dilemma by still requiring imported wheat. In order to improve the debt problem, the province should focus growing the economy. Instead of fretting over luxury imports, "a very vague & loose term," the province should establish a bounty for domestic wheat and encourage local production of all necessities. Otis's arguments were persuasive in the House; a bounty for locally grown wheat was enacted during the next session.

Hutchinson's next article appeared in the *Evening-Post* the following week, on January 4, 1762. The Lt. Governor and Chief Justice of the Supreme Court began with a view of the oligarchy: "One would think that when members of a society by such enquiries are honestly pursuing a common interest, a difference in sentiments could give no just cause of offense." Members of the oligarchy didn't always share the same opinions, but they always shared the same goal: increasing their power and wealth. Hutchinson began to suspect that Jemmy Otis didn't share that goal. Hutchinson then reminded readers that in the great 17th century pamphlet debate between Locke and William Lowndes, Secretary to the Treasury, the adversaries "treated one another with great delicacy politeness" despite a "contrariety of opinion." He next proceeded to develop a monetary history of Massachusetts from the perspective of an oligarch, blaming payment in commodities – "country pay" – for the province's one-third overvaluation of English currency. Hutchinson concluded that since creditors will always be a minority and "in democratical governments generally there will be bias in the legislature to the number rather than to the weight of the inhabitants," overvaluation was unavoidable. So for Hutchinson, the source of currency problems was democracy itself because the majority will always be debtors, and that majority will also produce "bias in the legislature." By implication, Hutchinson suggests that such "bias" would be resolved if only citizens were represented by their "weight" – that is, their wealth. Hutchinson is typically reserved and politically savvy, so his tone deaf analysis of "bias" reveals a man of such aristocratic disposition that he can't hear the feudal leitmotif that ladens his position. The irony was certainly lost on Hutchinson when he concluded with a plea for reasonableness:

> I differ in sentiments from some whom I greatly honour and esteem, but as I know their views are as disinterested as my own, it shall never lessen the respect and value I have for them. I wish I had met with the same candor in such as profess to differ from me, and have thought fit to publish their thoughts on the subject.

Hutchinson purposefully never mentions Jemmy Otis or the *Gazette* article in which he was ruthlessly assailed. Hutchinson wrote to his friend William Bollan on January 11, 1762, a week after his "bias" article appeared:

> A Bear a successor of Jemmy Allen undertook to answer me but discovered so much brutality that my friends advised to make no reply and to publish something further on the same subject to show that I took no notice of him. I send it to you inclosed. ... The town is full of contention.

The "Jemmy Allen" referenced is James Allen, a wealthy Boston merchant known for his incorruptibility and independence. Jemmy Allen rose in the House along with Hutchinson in the 1740s, and when Hutchinson was Speaker from 1746-49, Allen energetically filled the role of chief antagonist to the "friends of government," which at the time included the Colonel. While Allen was considered intelligent and fiercely honorable, his hostility to the Speaker and Governor compelled the House to eject him in 1748. The people of Boston enthusiastically re-elected him, but the House refused to seat him for months. Allen was eventually permitted to take his seat and commanded 73 committee appointments. The oligarchy realized they could not minimize his influence through elections so instead relegated him to obscurity in the House; just four years later, Allen's 73 committee appointments shrank to 49 while the "friends of government" dominated committee work; the Colonel had 86 committee appointments, Samuel Welles 100 and Samuel White 108. In the private letter to Bollan, Hutchinson recognized Jemmy Otis as another James Allen, wildly popular and fiercely independent. Similarly, Hutchinson would know that a "democratical" government could not fix Jemmy Otis, and so he would either need to be co-opted into the "friends of government" or relegated to obscurity in the House. The problem, of course, was that

Jemmy's father, as Speaker, set the agenda and largely controlled committee appointments.

The final installment of Hutchinson's currency lecture appeared in the *Evening-Post* the following week on January 11. The same issue carried an article by a Hutchinson ally, "Y.Z.," who attacked Jemmy Otis with gusto but without Hutchinson's high Tory elitism. "Y.Z." was James Bowdoin, a fellow council member who later became a leading Hutchinson enemy and the second governor of the post-Revolution Commonwealth of Massachusetts. But in 1761-1762, before his break with the friends of government, Bowdoin was to defend the oligarchy against scurrilous attacks. Bowdoin started with a condemnation of Otis for indulging personal attacks. Regarding the content of the debate, Bowdoin supported Hutchinson's conclusions regarding gold's overvaluation, but he tepidly agreed with Otis's legal point that gold had been and should be in effect lawful currency. Bowdoin asserted that gold had a fixed rate of exchange in practice, so there was no need to formalize that fixed rate by legislation.

While Otis often sought to attach faces to his opponents' arguments, he also often attempted to disconnect himself from the issues and let the arguments stand on their own, thus obscuring the target for his opponents. For this reason he claimed to represent the people in the *Petition of Lechmere* case, not the merchants who wanted general warrants quashed, and he published his articles anonymously. Expanding his efforts to disconnect his positions from himself, he enlisted Oxenbridge Thacher to launch the newest attack against the oligarchy. Thacher printed a pamphlet in January 1762, after the publication of Bowdoin's piece. Thacher's pamphlet began with reprinting Hutchinson's article and then proceeded with a legal argument the echoed Otis's, rebutting Bowdoin's observations in the process. Thacher's pamphlet dismissed Hutchinson's and Bowdoin's academic remarks about the international currency markets and concluded with the observation that Portuguese gold johannes had been and continue to be valued at the maximum rate of 48 shillings. Thacher argues that formulizing a rate that already exists in fact would offer currency fluctuation protection to debtors.

Thacher then launched a new attack that would assail that prerogative of the members of the oligarchy: plural office-holding. Thacher had published an anonymous pamphlet the year before on the subject, but now the attack was much more fierce and direct; Otis had clearly provided the blueprint for how the oligarchy would be dismantled. "A Judge," Thacher wrote, "should be ever unmixed with all these political quarrels, that in such a State as ours, must be expected to arise." And yet Chief Justice Hutchinson was publically debating an unsettled politico-legal question. Plural office-holding was a ripe issue; it had been simmering below the surface for years, and Hutchinson and the Olivers were conspicuously guilty. Many worried that it was corrupting the government, and it was an obvious result of the oligarchy seizing power as most major government offices were held by increasingly few people. Otis knew it would be a theme that would resonate with the common people and would bog down Hutchinson and the Olivers in defensive positions while other attacks were being launched. Otis also knew his own father was just as guilty as anyone.

While the oligarchy was being attacked for multiple office-holding, Otis fired a salvo from an entirely different approach. In an article that appeared in the *Gazette* on January 11, the same day as Hutchinson's second currency lecture, Otis applied Montesquieu to Hutchinson's observation about "numbers" and "weight" in a "democratical government." Jemmy concluded that "mixed" government was ideal but cautioned that "It may happen in governments framed after this model, that in consequence of art and corruption, half a dozen, or half a score men will form an oligarchy, in favour of themselves; an aristocracy in favour of their families and friends." If Thacher's article wasn't clear enough, Otis just clarified it: Massachusetts was ruled by a corrupt oligarchy.

And in a special supplement to the January 11 issue of the *Gazette*, Jemmy brilliantly summarized the entire debate in two pages, complete with sarcastic deference to Hutchinson and a fierce attack on "Mr. Y.Z.,"

> I have suspected more than once whether this Mr. Y.Z. by his unmannerly and vulgar insinuations of a lawyers wilfully misrepresenting facts, and dealing in quibbles, mayn't be some leering assurance broker, piping hot from a counting house, by his scurrility against the profession and divine science of the law, expects soon to be deemed a very fit candidate for preferment.

The "assurance broker" to whom Otis referred was Foster Hutchinson, the lieutenant governor's brother and head of Jemmy's class at Harvard. Of course, "Mr. Y.Z." was Bowdoin, but Otis didn't know. Otis continued to the issue of plural office-holding as "Mr. Cooke, the Cobbler" – Jemmy's term for the average man – might not get energized over international currency debates, but he could be angered by the thought that a small group of men might "form an oligarchy" to enable "an aristocracy in favour of their families and friends."

Robert Treat Paine, who would later be the prosecutor in the trial of the British soldiers in the Boston Massacre, a signer of the Declaration of Independence, and a representative to the Continental Congress, wrote a letter to fellow Massachusetts lawyer Jonathan Sewall on February 17, 1762 about the simmering war. Asked by Sewall which side he takes in the "political controversies," Paine replied, "The right side." That seems non-committal. And when asked about the writs, Paine said he "Never was more in need of them. I shall soon apply for one to get a help meet." This was a joke; Paine had just been rejected for marriage and was supposing that a court warrant would help him secure a wife. But when asked about his opinion of Thomas Hutchinson, he referenced the Old Testament and observed that no man can know everything because no man is immortal, clearly questioning Hutchinson's sense of superiority. And Otis's friend Thacher? Again, the Old Testament reference: " ... as a serpent in the way that biteth the horse's heels, so that his rider falleth backward." Otis was the horse, and Thacher was the rider; the serpent was Hutchinson, Bernard, and the friends of government. And Otis? He is a mirror that "burns up everything that cannot be melted." Paine was politically astute and tread lightly on taking sides; he was no partisan in 1762, and yet he clearly identified Hutchinson as part of the oligarchy, the know-it-all serpent, and Otis as the arsonist, burning anything that could not be melted.

At the third session of the General Court of 1761-1762, Hutchinson had clearly lost the currency argument. After an extensive and at times pedantic debate, the Popular Party pushed through two acts that reformed the procedures for issuing province notes and established predetermined gold coin valuations according to the Otis-Thacher theory, and passed a comprehensive counterfeiting statute. The currency bills were too popular for even Bernard to ignore, so they became law. Bernard attempted to avoid alienating either side of the currency debates, and he certainly had no desire to anger the Otises again. But Bernard complained about the counterfeiting statute, saying "if you do not think proper to make counterfeiting the Treasurers Notes a capital Offense you had better not exact any punishment at all." The petulant Bernard didn't get everything he wanted, so he refused to sign the counterfeiting bill, and in sending the acts to London, he included a note to the Lords of Trade stating that the act establishing gold as legal currency "seemed unnecessary" as it merely acknowledged existing fact, but it was "very necessary to quiet the disputes in the Province."

Otis's legal attacks on the customs establishment depended in part on the supply of political fuel to keep them lit. One vehicle of attack comprised of the two Paxton cases was effectively stalled by the Superior Court. The *Erving v. Cradock* case had survived the Superior Court, but the prospect of defending an expensive appeal to the Privy Council tempered John Erving's enthusiasm, and that case was settled. Barons departure for England caused his case to wither for want of a plaintiff. Otis realized that while the judicial system that was controlled by his opponents likewise protected his opponents, they were vulnerable to town politics and the printing press. In the former forum he could at best convince judges and juries, but in the latter forums he could foment the support of the common people. Limiting himself to a jury of the few seemed inefficient when he could sway a jury of the many.

Otis also realized that the variety of issues that regularly confronted the House offered many possible weapons that could be employed against the oligarchy, and the currency controversy of the second and third sessions is one example of the options. In some cases the effect was direct and obvious, such as the legislative moves during the third and fourth sessions of Otis's first term to launch an inquiry into the law that established the Superior Court of Judicature and to examine the jurisdiction and powers that it exercised. It was a direct challenge to the elite judicial branch from the lowly House, and the House committee conducting the investigation was also charged to ascertain the "utility" of restricting the justices' commissions to "good Behaviour" rather than at the pleasure of the Governor and Council. Other direct attacks on the elite judicial branch were obvious: the usual Superior Court justice salary of £750 was reduced to £700, and the extra grant of £40 to the chief justice was ignored. When the justices formally complained about their decreased salaries, the House indefinitely postponed the matter just as the court had postponed Otis's customs cases. The House was attempting to make clear that the justices served them, not the other way around.

One of Jemmy Otis's 56 House committees was formulating a direct attack on the oligarchy in the form of a bill to prohibit the justices' from serving in the General Court, and even the Council joined the frenzy in a bill sonorously entitled "An Act for the better enabling the Officers of his Majesty's Customs to carry the Acts of Trade into Execution." The bill for an "Act for the better enabling" was amended by the House and would have reduced the dreaded writ of assistance to a special search warrant issued on an oath that stated the source of the officer's information – probable cause – and requiring a report back to the issuing agent. The House and the Council passed the act, thus indicating a significant fissure in the unity of the upper body. It also indicates the pressure the oligarchy was feeling by 1762 to pass legislation that the public perceived would curb the oligarchy's appetite for power and control. The Superior Court justices on the Council returned fire as best they could by aggressively lobbying Bernard, and despite passing both legislative bodies, Bernard vetoed the bill. It was a brazen display of the power of the few supplanting the will of the many, and it was also a heady portent of the restructuring of power.

The Popular Party, led by Jemmy Otis, explored every avenue to diminish the oligarchy's power. In January 1762 the Williams family of Hampshire County requested the immediate issuance of a charter for a "western academy" – later to be Williams College – in Hampshire County in memory of Ephraim Williams, a local landowner who was killed in the Seven Years War. The request was simple, but it presented the oligarchs, particularly Thomas Hutchinson, with a thorny dilemma. Israel Williams was a political ally and friend, but Hutchinson was an *ex officio* overseer of Harvard, and his fellow alumni indignantly opposed the establishment of a competing college in Massachusetts. So the lieutenant governor was carefully navigating these treacherous waters, and his inability to chaperone a small memorial through the General Court proved embarrassing. With the General Court at an impasse, Bernard proposed to issue a charter to the new college on his own authority. Otis then turned the issue into a constitutional debate; if the governor could issue such a charter without sanction from the House, then surely he could issue any charter without the House's consent. On March 8, a meeting of ministers, the governor and lieutenant governor, and the president of Harvard convened to discuss the charter; the ministers were concerned that the new college would provide an opening for Anglican bishops to assert their authority. The product of the meeting was a memorandum of objections drafted by Jonathan Mayhew. Similarly alarmed, the General Court requested that Bernard withhold the charter, which he did. It was a small matter but part of Otis's plan to assault and resist the oligarchy on every front possible, and it foreshadowed the ways in which the radical politicians and ministers could cooperate on shared issues.

Jemmy Otis's next maneuver may at first seem minor, but it was the first in a long line of actions that would confound both his contemporaries and historians, and yet it was precisely this line of masterful manipulation that eventually ruptured the body politic and enabled the revolution. By 1762, Bernard feared the Otises and certainly had no interest in provoking the "Confederacy." Hutchinson and the Olivers were annoyed, perhaps angry, but fearless. Further, Bernard was paranoid that Hutchinson desired the governorship. As the two parties – the suspicious fearful governor on one side and the grasping self-assured Hutchinson and Olivers on the other – differed in their views of the Otises, Jemmy took the opportunity to begin a prolonged and aggressive effort to drive a wedge between them.

As the war with France was ending, there was much agitation to draw new boundaries for Maine, Nova Scotia, and other points north, and there would be much interest in attracting settlers to those newly acquired lands. Conveniently, in January 1762 – the same time that Hutchinson was being assaulted in the currency wars and the Williams charter – Colonel Otis appointed his son to a committee to "select some Method" of establishing these new borders. Also conveniently at the same time, Governor Bernard was seeking financial help to cover the costs of securing his two commissions as Massachusetts governor, the original one of 1760, and the new one required after the death of George II. The House had just cut Hutchinson's salary as chief justice, which Hutchinson reasonably assumed Jemmy Otis had orchestrated. And now to drive the wedge between Hutchinson and Bernard, Otis supported and pushed through an enormous and likely profitable land grant for Bernard.

Jemmy proposed and convinced the House to support a grant of Mount Desert Island to Bernard; at 108 square miles, the island off the coast of Maine is the second largest island on the East Coast, after Long Island. Bernard could use the land to generate income and attract settlers to the north. He was elated and began to assail English officialdom with letters attempting to secure the compulsory royal approval. So at the same time that Jemmy pushed through a pay cut for Hutchinson, he orchestrated a significant land grant for Bernard. Some would be confused as to the reason Otis would be so generous to Bernard. The answer was that a land grant did not cost the Massachusetts tax payer anything, and it certainly gave Bernard pause to reconsider his alliances; perhaps Jemmy Otis wasn't so bad and perhaps the Popular Party and Boston bench were right about Hutchinson – after all, Bernard already had his own suspicions about Hutchinson's motives. That pause would enable Jemmy Otis to manipulate Bernard for some very substantial gains. The Mount Desert Island grant was a move of such manipulative genius that it almost certainly was conceived with the assistance of that political veteran Colonel Otis.

The next target for the popular party was William Bollan. Jemmy Otis was quite aware that Bollan and Hutchinson carried on an extensive private correspondence, and when Bollan, at Hutchinson's request, produced the verification of the English use of writs of assistance, his career as agent was finished. Bollan was Governor Shirley's in-law and protégé and had served as Massachusetts agent since 1745. He was an informed and effective agent, but after 17 years of service he was perhaps not quite as vigorous in executing his duties. He commanded a small salary, which at times wasn't even paid, but he often deducted commissions from grants he had coaxed out of Parliament and a parsimonious Treasury, a practice that was typical and to be expected. But Jemmy and the Boston bench often asked questions not previously asked, and to them the commissions should neither be typical nor expected. Bollan had been briefly dismissed in 1760, but there was no consensus on a replacement so he remained province lobbyist. But Jemmy Otis and the Popular Party had grown in numbers and organizational ability by 1761, and they had developed a strategy to strike at Bollan during the recess between the third and fourth sessions of the House. Hutchinson sent a warning to Bollan on March 31, 1762: "I have observed for some time the heads of a clan very busy and am satisfied they have some scheme projecting for the next session and am not without my apprehensions that you are the subject of it." Just as the defenseless Paxton had been warned about an impending assault, so too were Hutchinson and Bollan entirely cognizant of what was to befall them and yet utterly incapable of preventing it.

As a typical mid-April House session was ending and the representatives were preparing to go home, with no notice or prior debate, a motion was made to dismiss Bollan as province lobbyist; according to the Otises, Bollan's transgressions included his membership in the Church of England, taking commissions from province money, and private communication with oligarchs. The motion was hurried through by Speaker Otis who then appointed this son and two others to draft "a proper vote." The draft of the "proper vote" was presented with unusual speed, as if it had been coordinated in advance, and the vote was formally consummated the same day. To an uninformed observer it perhaps seemed like a one-act mystery play with the *deus ex machina* conveyed to the stage by Jemmy, but after so many viewings of Jemmy's stagecraft – in the courts, the papers, the pamphlets, and the halls of governance – Hutchinson was familiar with such theatrical tricks. He provided Bollan with a synopsis later in the week, writing on April 24, 1762, "My suspicions were well founded. Monday last the House sent up a vote to dismiss you from the Agency. I made what opposition I could but the Terror of Election which is just at hand prevailed over all other considerations and 11 votes carried it, against 10, for a concurrence with the house. Two lawyers of the same name carry all before them in the house. ..." Hutchinson was fixated on the problems with democracy – "the Terror of Election" – but the core issue was not "Election" in itself but rather a seeming disregard for proper deference by those elected. Hutchinson had witnessed this before in Jemmy Allen, the representative whose independence and sarcasm seemed so out of place in the late 1740s, and knew how to address the problem.

Concurrent with Bollan's dismissal, the colonies – and Massachusetts more than most – were growing alarmed at reinvigorated efforts by the mother country to govern and influence its territories. Customs enforcement was newly energized, new Acts were being formulated, and rumors were afoot of replacing colonial charters with royal governments. In Massachusetts, these concerns inevitably included the possible establishment of an Anglican bishop and a series of events seemed to confirm those fears: the promotion of a governor – Bernard – who was closely affiliated with the Anglican establishment, a new Anglican church in Cambridge and the appointment of the celebrated Reverend East Apthrop to lead that church, persistent gossip that the governor wanted to charter the Williams's new school as "Queen's College." Bollan was certainly a member of the Church of England, though there exists no evidence that he was engaged in some pending religious cabal. But Bollan's guilt or innocence was not relevant; he had supported Hutchinson's effort to maintain general search warrants, so he was an enemy. Bernard confirmed the removal of Bollan, in part because Jemmy Otis had just pushed through a huge land grant for him and in part because he did not want another fight.

After Bollan was dismissed, Bernard pushed for the appointment of Richard Jackson, the agent for Connecticut, a Member of Parliament, and Bernard's friend. The House, however, was in no mood to appoint friends of the oligarchy. Concurrent with these political battles, the Dissenters in the colonies, chief among them Mayhew, were battling the Anglican Church and the "Society for the Propagation of the Gospel in Foreign Parts." The Society was chartered in 1701 by King William III and its expressed purpose was to convert the heathen and forestall missionary efforts by the Jesuits. Yet by 1761, 66 of the society's 80 representatives in the New World were stationed in Philadelphia, New York, Boston and other northern cities, leaving only 14 representatives for the southern colonies and the Caribbean. For Mayhew, it was the clear that the society's purpose was political, not religious. He fought doggedly for the Society to focus on places that were populated with heathens or influenced by Jesuits, which certainly did not include Philadelphia, New York, and Boston. The politicization of the church and use of the Society to "Spye" on the Dissenters infuriated the Dissenter clergy in New England. But reformation of the Society seemed beyond their power, so the Dissenters of Massachusetts decided to pursue a plan to secure a charter for their own missionary society. A capable lobbyist in London would be required to secure such a charter.

For the new province agent, the House elected Jasper Mauduit, an elderly London wool wholesaler who likely secured the appointment due to the support of the "black regiment." Mauduit was a passionate religious dissident who was esteemed by Jonathan Mayhew and Charles Chauncy, two of Boston's most influential ministers. Chauncy had long communicated with dissenters in England and elsewhere and aggressively promoted colonial causes, not least of which was keeping Anglican bishops out of Massachusetts. Mauduit had been communicating with Mayhew for many years, and in 1755 sent to him "a box" containing the works of fierce anti-royalist Algernon Sidney who was executed in 1683 for plotting to kill King Charles II. Mauduit also supplied a box of Sidney's writings for Harvard. And while Boston's Black Regiment promoted Mauduit, he was neither aware of his election nor was he particularly interested. Mayhew wrote Mauduit a letter on April 26, 1762 urging him to accept the position:

> The most steady friends of Liberty amongst us, and all the Friends to the dissenting Interest (who are, I suppose, fifty to one throughout this Province) would be extremely sorry if you should decline this Service; thinking you will be much more likely to serve the Province in its most essential Interests, than a Gentleman of the Chh. of England tho' this is by no means the only objection that has

> been made against Mr. Bollan. The Chh. Party here, and perhaps *some Persons of distinguished Eminence,* may possibly, for their *own private Ends,* throw discouragements and stumbling-blocks in your way, in order to prevent your undertaking this Service.

Mayhew was quite clearly a man of political and religious interests and knew that a Church of England lobbyist would be disinclined to promote the Boston Dissenters's missionary charter. And Mayhew's reference to their opponents – *"some Persons of distinguished Eminence"* – plainly references the oligarchy. John Adams, in his *Diary*, noted that some critics cited

> the unfitness of Mr. Mauduit to represent this Province at the British court, both in point of age and knowledge. He is, as that writer says, seventy years old; an honest man, but avaricious; a woollen draper, a mere cit; so ignorant of court and public business, that he knew not where the public offices were, and that he told Mr. Bollan that he was agent of New England. He says that all the other agents laugh at this Province for employing him, and that all persons on that side of the water are surprised at us.

Mauduit, then, was the choice of the Black Regiment, not a seasoned lobbyist or diplomat, and his appointment struck fear in some of the oligarchy; Peter Oliver had accused Jemmy Otis of threatening "to secure the Black Regiment, these were his Words, & his Meaning was to engage the dissenting Clergy on his Side." The "dissenting Clergy" were suspicious of the oligarchy, particularly those from England who they feared would impose Anglicanism on the province. And rebel ministers such as Mayhew had been using the pulpit to criticize the oligarchy for over a decade. Peter Oliver knew that fiery preachers like Mayhew were usually harmless, but Oliver also knew that Mayhew could be wildly dangerous if anyone started taking him seriously or if he actually started effecting events – like the choice of province lobbyist.

Jemmy Otis was just as happy with his new agent as the Governor was with his new land grant. Otis wrote to Mauduit on April 23, 1762, "I have taken this early oppertunity to acquaint you that I have the merit of a small share in your election. Royall Tyler, Jno. Phillips, and Thomas Cushing, Esqrs., with whom I have the honour to represent the city Boston, are your staunch friends." Otis had just named the "damned faction, which will shake this province to its Foundation" that Judge Ruggles feared. Jasper Mauduit, a fiercely independent, not-very-wealthy, and not-well-connected Dissenter was exactly the type of lobbyist the Popular Party wanted precisely because Mauduit would never become a servant of the oligarchy. And for Bollan, he was now unemployed but still had his reputation for loyalty to those in power, so Bernard hired him as his personal agent in his quest to get his new land grant officially recognized as quickly as possible.

When Bollan was dismissed, the province was in debt to him for £4838 but was having great difficulty paying him. Attorney General Trowbridge wrote to Bollan on July 15, 1762, explaining that in his attempts to secure Bollan's pay, he "found the Town as much drained of silver as the Treasury was." The province's currency problems were perpetual. Trowbridge was informed that he could not get Bollan's "Money until the 28th of next June, as by the Agreements nothing more could be required than to pay the money at the End of the Year in Silver." Trowbridge then informed Bollan that he and "a Majority of the Council ... suspected [the delay] came from Otis." Trowbridge than expanded on the political situation in Boston:

> Coll. Otis's Son James raved against the Governor and his Conduct so loudly as that he sattisfied the People in Boston he was a proper person to represent them in the General Court, and they chose him accordingly, and he, together with a Number of other firebrands There presently set the Government into a Flame ...

And finally, Trowbridge informs Bollan that a core issue in his dismissal was "that our Dissenting Churches were in danger, that you being a Churchman were a very unsuitable Person ...." Just as Arminianism had coalesced with natural rights, the concerns about the "Society for the Propagation of the Gospel in Foreign Parts" coalesced with the promotion of rule by consent as ripe political issues. Concurrent with Bollan's dismissal, the separation of powers bill was brought out of Otis's committee for a vote on April 17; this bill would have prohibited Supreme Court justices from holding seats in the House or Council. Though this prohibition would have affected most justices, as they typically held seats in both the Supreme Court and the Council, this bill was clearly targeted at Hutchinson. It was defeated on a legal technicality with a handful of votes, but the bill proved that the issue of separation of powers was alive. Hutchinson was pessimistic about his political future; he sensed a threat to his world.

Thus ended Jemmy Otis's first year in office. On May 11, 1762, new elections were held; the Boston town meeting had a healthy attendance of 629 voters. After just a year in office, Otis was the recognized commander of the Boston bench and received 619 of the 629 votes cast. John Phillips received 613 votes, Royall Tyler 609, and Thomas Cushing 460. The following Monday the *Gazette* reported that the incumbents were reelected because of their "Zeal," and "particular Care" in preserving "the Religious and Civil Rights of the People." The confederacy was proving popular. Another *Gazette* article, likely written by Thacher in coordination with Otis, was published just before the selection of Council members and continued the barrage against plural office-holding, reminding the readers "that the Power of making and executing Laws in the same Persons were incompatible."

Abraham Williams, Jemmy's Harvard classmate and close friend of Colonel Otis, gave the opening sermon before the General Court on May 26, 1762, lecturing the politicians on the problem of "political schism." Nearly every General Court started with a lecture recounting the benefits of unity and the problems of divisiveness, and nearly every time, backroom deals divided the House nearly as soon as the opening sermon ended. Members of the Boston Bench felt good about their prospects, but events soon went horribly wrong: Colonel Otis declined his unanimous election as Speaker because "his living at such a Distance rendered his constant attendance very uncertain." A deal had been made, and certainly few – apparently not even Jemmy – were aware of it.

Like clockwork, Sylvanus Bourne resigned his seat on the Council, and Colonel Otis was elected to fill it; the "Distance" was not now so much of a problem. And before the Boston Bench could ascertain what was happening, that "friend of government" and fearer of "damned factions" Judge Ruggles was elected Speaker of the House. No evidence of the arrangement exists, but in all likelihood the governor, still giddy over his new vast land holdings, had warmed up to the Colonel. So when Councilor Bourne, who was quite old, suggested that he might retire, Bernard offered to secure the seat for his new friend Colonel Otis in exchange for Otis securing the Speaker seat in the House for a friend of government. The existence of an arrangement is further evidenced by Colonel Otis's boast that he received 112 votes, a total that must have included fairly solid support from the incumbent councilors who had just a year prior concluded that the Colonel was not oligarchy material and therefore should not be on the Superior Court. At long last, the Colonel would get a much-coveted seat on the Council. Bernard would strengthen a new friendship with the powerful Colonel Otis, and the friends of government would take back control of the House, which would enable them to limit Jemmy's committee assignments as they'd previously done to James Allen. Everyone would win.

Royall Tyler did not win. Ignorant of the deal that had been struck, the Popular Party put Tyler on the ballot as their candidate for Speaker of the House; the votes were already in for Ruggles. Peter Oliver told John Adams that he "never knew so easy an election." The governor wrote Secretary to the Board of Trade John Pownall that the election of Judge Ruggles for the Speaker position was "a great point in favor of government." Colonel Otis wrote to his son Joseph a report that explains the events as if they were the normal operations of a democracy. "They could not carry their point against the Great J_dg," he wrote, after reciting his resignation as Speaker. He noted that Judge Ruggles had beaten Tyler for the Speaker's chair by nine votes, as if Ruggles's election was not coordinated. Tellingly, the Colonel does not mention Jemmy in the letter. The Colonel's wife, Mary, infrequently visited Boston, but she did that May perhaps in anticipation – or foreknowledge – of her husband's election to the Council. It is likely on this occasion that the couple sat for John Singleton Copley, the premier painter of the era.

Judge Ruggles's role would not be forgotten. The Popular Party would be patient, as they had been with Bollan, but the response would be considerably more vicious. But first, the Popular Party had to comprehend the deal that cost them control of the House. A day after the Colonel had written home, Samuel Allyne also wrote to Joseph and reported the calamity as best he understood it: "You will be surprized when I tell you last fryday [May 28th] Jas Otis jr resign'd his seat in court & took leave of the members, he however resumed to it next but such a proceeding can by no means be justified, & is what has got him much dishonor, however he acts for himself & I resolved to think no more of politics...." So upon learning of the deal that put his father on the Council and Ruggles in the Speaker's chair, Jemmy resigned his House seat in protest and stormed out of the chamber. It seems clear that he didn't know about the arrangement, and the Colonel's silence in his letter to Joseph shows the tension that must have existed between the two.

It had been a demanding year for Jemmy, and he had not made much apparent progress in his crusade against the oligarchy. It's therefore conceivable that his political career might have ended in May 1762. He doubtless feared that his influence in the House would be curtailed by the obedient Ruggles. But Jemmy Otis's one day resignation of May 28, 1762 received little attention at the time precisely because it wasn't viewed as so bizarre; any man would have been shocked to learn of his father's betrayal. By the following day the episode seemed to have been forgotten, as the Popular Party regrouped and refocused its attention and Jemmy concluded that old issues could still be leveraged and new issues were appearing in the recently redrawn political landscape. The business of the first session of the General Court was fairly calm. Governor Bernard proposed that the province secure its 1760 parliamentary grant by drawing bills of exchange in London instead of shipping specie to the province; the shipment of such a large sum would have been extraordinary but more expensive. The proposal easily sailed through the House. And Bernard's proposal to survey the Saint Croix River boundary line similarly met with House approval. For the first time in over a year, Governor Bernard was optimistic that his easy and lucrative term might be a reality. On June 7, 1762 he gloated to his patron Lord Barrington about "the Credit I am in with the people. ... There never was greater Harmony in the Government than at present." The governor was still elated with his land grant and the election of Ruggles, and the co-opting of the Colonel seemed to signal a new beginning. "This island," Bernard continued, "proves to be so much more Valuable, than at first apprehended, that it becomes a Great object; especially to me."

What at first must have seemed like betrayal to Jemmy was now an important lesson; his father had easily manipulated Bernard to get the council seat he wanted. Jemmy and the Boston bench learned from this episode and would use Bernard's weaknesses to their advantage. In Bernard's letter to Lord Barrington, he reported as an afterthought that a French naval fleet had taken St. John's in Newfoundland and dispersed the Massachusetts fishing fleet. At the same time, Jemmy Otis informed Jasper Mauduit that the governor, despite falling "into some of the worst hands upon his first arrival," was now beginning "to be convinc'd whose view are nearly connected with the true interest of the province." Jemmy would take Bernard's new outlook and manipulate it to maximum effect.

CHAPTER V

mad people have overturned empires

A few in the oligarchy were apprehensive about Jemmy Otis's radicalism and Governor Bernard's naiveté. While riding circuit together, the young John Adams and the Superior Court justice Peter Oliver discussed the recent elections, and Oliver was a strident supporter of fellow oligarch Hutchinson. Oliver bemoaned that Otis "said not long since in the Representatives Room that all the superior Judges and every Inferior Judge in the Province, put all together and they would not make one half of a Common Lawyer" – clearly a strike at those judges such as Hutchinson who'd never practiced law. After some conciliatory comments from Adams, Oliver continued: "If Bedlamism is a Talent he has it in Perfection. ... I have the Utmost Contempt of him." The principal virtue of feudalism is order, and Oliver isolated the lack of that virtue as Otis's core vice. Adams and Oliver agreed that Jemmy was the master of Bedlam, and while that opinion was probably pervasive throughout the province, many would increasingly disagree over whether it was a character flaw or a successful tactic. Oliver was also aware of Otis's talent for manipulation. Writing of Otis and "the whole Pack" who followed him, Oliver observed, "They published the meanest, libellous Falsehoods against ... [Barnard] whom not long before they had caressed." Nevertheless, Oliver's "Contempt" had yet to negatively affect Jemmy's legal practice or growing popularity. It seems that Jemmy was absent from the May term of the Superior Court in Barnstable, but he was active in the Suffolk County Inferior Court, bringing suit against Stephen Brown for unpaid legal bills and sending writs to Falmouth. Ironically, Jemmy and Oxenbridge Thacher were ordered by the Boston selectmen to prosecute some bakers who had refused inspectors on the pretext that the inspectors had no warrant. Otis and Thacher were counsel for the town, so their position required them to defend these warrantless inspections.

Hutchinson and the Olivers were perfectly aware of Otis's efforts to move Massachusetts power away from the oligarchy; the oligarchy fought back in many ways, large and small. So while the war over whether the colonies would be an extension of the Old World or something entirely new occasionally witnessed major battles, most of the war was composed of small skirmishes. For example, in an effort to put more distance between themselves and commoners and to Anglicize the courtrooms, Chief Justice Hutchinson instituted the arbitrary rank of "barrister" at the August term of the Superior Court in Boston and those twenty-six lawyers who were selected for the new rank "appeared accordingly this Term in Barrister's Habits." The "Habits" included "Gowns and Bands and Tye Wiggs." The chief justice's efforts to make the court more formal and regal was certainly a strike at those who wished to create distance between the colonies and England, but it was also a part of a larger wave of Anglophilia sweeping over the outskirts of the Empire. Colonial newspapers regularly recounted royal events, and the King George's birthday was marked with cannon fire. Royal emblems and full-length portraits of Charles II and James II were being affixed to public buildings. In courtrooms, the justices's benches were being raised so that they peered down onto the courtroom; and two years after Hutchinson Anglicized the Boston courtrooms, the New York Supreme Court passed similar measures. So Otis's criticisms of Parliament steered clear of the Crown, and it probably seemed that each effort Otis made was rejoined with regalia.

Otis argued several cases that term including *Dudley v. Dudley et al.* and *Oliver v. Sale*. The Dudley case concerned an analysis of Governor Dudley's will in which an ambiguous statement could be interpreted as creating a fee simple or an entailed estate. Jemmy had some previous experience with fee simple and entailed estates and other vagaries of real estate law, particularly in cases such as *James Otis, Junior v. John Turner*, and he and co-counsel Gridley argued that Dudley's will created a fee simple in his son William, not an entailed estate. Entailed estates were a common law feudal creation that enabled estates to be passed down to heirs as a single unit, which the heirs are unable to sell, divide or otherwise alienate from themselves. It was a legal structure that ensured that entire estates remained within a family for generations and kept real estate from being divided into smaller parcels that middling class persons could afford. "Fee simple" real estate is the common legal structure in the modern world whereby real estate may be sold to anyone, divided, leased, used as collateral, and mortgaged. Jemmy made the forceful argument that public policy and the general nature of the colonies disfavored the feudal structure of entailed estates and that the courts ought to favor the more dynamic and less limiting concept of fee simple. His argument was countered by Benjamin Kent and Attorney General Edmund Trowbridge who supported the fee tail interpretation. The court sided with Otis and against entailed estates, which was another small step away from feudalism.

Oliver v. Sale was one of the early interesting cases addressing the uncommitted Massachusetts attitude toward slavery. According to plaintiff Oliver, defendant Sale had sold to him two mulatto boys "as slaves" but who apparently were in fact "free." At which point Oliver sued Sale for deceit, and Otis represented defendant Sale; Thacher represented Oliver. Jemmy submitted evidence showing that Sale had refused to sell the boys "for Slaves" but only transferred whatever rights to their "service" he may have had under an ambiguous oral indenture. Thacher replied that though slavery might not have been the issue *per se*, there was nevertheless a breach on Sale's part of an implied warranty that some service was due – otherwise, for what did Oliver pay? Otis won in every regard: the boys went free, Sale kept the money, and Oliver received a bill for costs and attorney's fees. The logic of Otis's developing political theory would cause him to soon address the slavery issue outside of the courtroom.

At the same time, Thomas Hutchinson was taking a "vacation" by going on circuit to Falmouth, Maine. He wrote the recently dismissed Bollan that he "was glad to get out of the way and shall be so until the Influence of Mr. Otis and men of his disposition is lessened," a reference to the efforts of a House newly controlled by the Court Party. The political tumult had subsided, and most of the political agitators were busy in the court, but the tranquility of the summer was deceptive, as Oxenbridge Thacher guessed; in a 1762 letter to Prat, Thacher wrote: "We seem to be in that deep sleep or stupor that Cicero describes his country to be in a year or two before the civil wars broke out. The sea is perfectly clam & unagitated whether this profound quiet be the forerunner of a storm I leave to your judgment."

With betrayal in the air and Court Party lackey Ruggles as House Speaker, it was simply a matter of time and circumstance before a storm erupted. A rumble of thunder growled in the distance during a short session of the Assembly that Bernard apologetically called for September 8th to attend to General Amherst's regular request for more troops; but again the hapless governor unintentionally provided the breach Otis needed. The Salem and Marblehead fishing fleets had panicked in June at the rumor of a French pirate ship operating near Breton and had requested government action. The provincial navy's main ship, the *King George*, was sailing to Newfoundland so Bernard, with the advice of the Council, had engaged the province sloop *Massachusetts* to search for the French pirates at an expense of £100. Bernard assumed that the House of Representatives would promptly approve an expenditure to protect the provincial fishing fleet from French pirates. But Bernard was long on naïve assumptions and short on memory because this identical issue had triggered a lively dispute the previous year before Otis's principled objections were overcome by practical expediency. Bernard's logic was simple: the cost of calling an emergency session to secure an appropriation in advance would hardly have been justified. This explanation was irrelevant to a House stirred by Jemmy's principled arguments about rights and separation of power, as was patent in the response Jemmy drafted, which was read aloud in the House:

> Justice to our selves, and to our constituents oblige us to remonstrate against the method of making or increasing establishments by the Governor and council.
> It is in effect taking from the house their most darling priviledge, the right of originating all Taxes.
> It is in short annihilating one branch of the legislature. And when once the Representatives of a people give up this Priviledge, the Government will very soon become arbitrary.
> No Necessity therefore can be sufficient to justify a house of Representatives in giving up such a *Priviledge; for it would be of little consequence to the people whether they were subject to George or Lewis, the King of Great Britain or the French King, if both were arbitrary, as both would be if both could levy Taxes without Parliament.*
> Had this been the first instance of the kind, we might not have troubled your Excellency about it; but lest the matter should grow into precedent; we earnestly beseech your Excellency, as you regard the peace and welfare of the Province, that no measures of this nature be taken for the future, let the advice of the council be what it may.

Reportedly, when the italicized portion was read, Representative Paine from Worcester declared, "Treason! Treason!" Some charged that Otis's remonstrance was evidence of "disrespect" toward the crown, and still others went further with "seditious, rebellious and traitorous," words that would be whispered by the oligarchs about Jemmy Otis from that day in September 1762 up until his death. Governor Bernard demanded that the part about King George being no better than King Louis if he ignored parliament be expunged from the records of the House; and, of course, with the faithful Ruggles as Speaker, the offending passage was deleted. On Saturday, September 18, Secretary Andrew Oliver presented himself at the door of the House chamber with a memorandum from the governor in "vindication" of his order to send out the province sloop prior to receiving appropriation from the House and then informed Speaker Ruggles that the governor "directed the attendance" of the House in the Council chamber. Realizing that the governor intended to suspend the General Court, Jemmy Otis quickly proposed two motions, one to print the governor's message in the *House Journal* so that it became part of the official record, and the other to appoint a committee to "prepare a reply" once the session was suspended. Both motions passed by a "large majority," but Ruggles took a play from Hutchinson's old playbook and appointed himself committee chairman along with Jemmy Otis and Royall Tyler. As Otis predicted, Bernard suspended the session, hoping to avert any further debate about "priviledge" and "right."

Bernard's "vindication" affirmed that it was the House's right to originate money bills, but he claimed there were two exceptions: the governor and Council had the lawful ability to issue money from the province treasury, and they could issue money without House approval in cases of urgent public necessity or very small amounts. Therefore, Bernard concluded, the deployment of the *Massachusetts* was wholly appropriate. Jemmy Otis was enraged by the governor's exemptions to the House's rights, his sanctimonious demeanor, and the tactic he employed to ensure that his position would be the final word. In a letter to Jasper Mauduit written on October 28, 1762, Otis revealed his anger at the oligarchs:

> The Governor very reluctantly consented to the choice [of Mauduit]. A dissenting agent is a bitter pill to an Oxonian, a bigot, a Plantation Governor, whose favorite plans are, filling his own pockets at all hazards, pushing the prerogative of the crown beyond all bounds, and propagating high church principles among good peaceable Christians. Perhaps you may wonder at this after the hopes I expressed in my first

letter that we should make a convert of the Governor but we are now convinced he is gone.

In the same letter, Otis elucidates the problem for Mauduit; the power brokers are:

> the Shirlean faction, a motley mixture of high church men, and dissenters who, for the sake of the offices they sustain, are full as high in their notions of prerogative as the churchmen. At the head of this party is the Lieutenant Governor who by the superficial arts of intrigue, rather than by any solid parts, by cringing to Governors and pushing arbitrary measures, has so far recommended himself to mr. Shirley and to our present Governor that by their means, tho' he was bred a merchant, he is now President of the Council, Chief Justice of the Province, Lieut. General and Captain of castle William, the Capital fortress in the Province, [and] Judge of the Probate of Wills for the County of Suffolk, the first County in the Province. Besides this he has filled the Supreme Court of Judicature with his friends, and the other Courts with his relations and dependants. How incompatible these offices are I need not tell you. ... Mr. Bernard was and I believe now is against Mr. Hutchinson, the Lieutenant Governor, from the motive of fear, lest he might thereby obtain the Government. He was for Mr. Jackson ... The Lieut. Governor had made himself dreaded by his enormous strides in power, ... [and] are firmly resolved to have Mr. Bollan or anybody else rather than a dissenter.

Otis was privately wondering whether Bernard could be manipulated and recognized that while Bernard may not side with the Popular Party, the anxious Governor feared Hutchinson, thus presenting the possibility that the Court Party could be turned against itself. But as had been the case during the currency controversy, the suspension of the General Court forced political arguments into the public sphere. Otis was not content to permit Bernard and "the prerogative of the crown" to dictate the possibility and pace of debate and would not wait for the third session of the General Court scheduled for January. Further, he wished to expand his analysis of "most darling priviledge of the House" beyond that which would reasonably be contained in a newspaper article. And so the following month, on November 11, 1762, *Gazette* publishers Edes and Gill advertised "This Day Published" the first of James

Otis's pamphlets, *A Vindication of the Conduct of the House of Representatives of the Province of the Massachusetts Bay, More Particularly, in the Last of the General Assembly.* Despite Jemmy's anger at the oligarchy for "pushing the prerogative of the crown beyond all bounds," *Vindication* was temperate. In a preface Jemmy offers a basic philosophical position:

> The world ever has been and will be pretty equally divided, between those two great parties, vulgarly called the winners, and the loosers; or to speak more precisely, between those who are discontented that they have no Power, and those who never think they can have enough.

Vindication begins by assembling the "record" of the Council and the House as contained in *House Journal*, including the House clerk's notes regarding the expunged language about King George being no better than King Louis if he ignored parliament. Otis launched into ten premises from John Locke's *Second Treatise of Government*, including the natural equality of men, the rule that kings and governors serve "the good of the people," the *de facto* arbitrary nature of governments, and that "the British constitution of government ... is the wisest and best in the world." These were ideas with which most would agree and established Jemmy's credentials as a full supporter of the king and the British government. Jemmy assured his readers that "the house intended nothing disrespectful of His Majesty, his Government or Governor."

Otis then argued that it was the constitution under which a king ruled rather than his "christian name," and thus to compare "George" to "Lewis" was a complimentary means of comparing the lives of "British subjects and the slaves of tyranny." Otis expanded on the theme:

> The first question that would occur to a philosopher, if any question could be made about it, would be whether the position were true. But truth being of little importance with most modern politicians, we shall touch lightly upon that topic, and proceed to inquiries of a more interesting nature.
> That arbitrary government implies the worst of temporal evils, or at least the continual danger of them is certain. That a man would be pretty equally subjected to these evils under every arbitrary government, is clear. That I should die very soon after my head should be cut off, whether by a sabre or a broad sword, whether chopped off to gratify a tyrant by the Christian name of *Tom, Dick* or *Harry* is

evident. That the name of the tryant would be of no more avail to save my life than the name of the executioner, needs no Proof.

The assertion was simple but novel: of primary importance was the constitution of the government not the people in the government. And further, the legitimacy of any government rested not in the names or labels affiliated with the government but rather in whether its actions were consensual or arbitrary. Jemmy then turns with biting sarcasm to the concepts of "indelicacy" when addressing "superiors" and the entire structure of the feudal hierarchy.

> Some fine Gentlemen have charged the expression as indelicate. ... The idea of delicacy in the creed of some politicians, implies that an inferior should at the peril of all that is near and dear to him (i.e. his interest) avoid every the least trifle that can offend his superior. Does my superior want my estate? I must give it him, and that with a good grace, which is appearing, and if possible being really obliged to him that he will condesend to take it. The reason is evident; it might give him some little pain or uneasiness to see me whimpering, much more openly complaining at the loss of a little glittering dirt. I must according to this system not only endeavour to acquire my self, but impress upon all around me a reverence and *passive obedience* to the sentiments of my superior, little short of adoration. Is the superior in contemplation a king, I must consider him as God's vicegerent, cloathed with unlimited power, his will the supreme law, and not accountable for his actions, let them be what they may, to any tribunal upon earth. Is the superior a plantation governor? he must be viewed not only as the most excellent representation of majesty, but as a viceroy in his department, and *quoad* provincial administration, to all intents and purposes vested with all the prerogatives that were ever exercised by the most absolute prince in Great Britain.

There would be no "Honoured Sir" from Jemmy. With respect to the "indelicacy" of the rebuke by the House, Jemmy struck at the heart of those oligarchs who required *"passive obedience"* from the masses:

> The votaries of this sect are all Monopolizers of offices, Peculators, Informers, and generally the Seekers of all kinds. It is better, say they, to give up any thing, and every thing quietly, than contend with a superior, who by his prerogative can do, and (as the vulgar express it)

right or wrong, will have whatever he pleases. For you must know, that according to some of the most refined and fashionable systems of modern politics, the ideas of right and wrong, and all the moral virtues, are to be considered only as the vagaries of a weak or distempered imagination in the possessor, and of no use in the world, but for the skilful politician to convert to his own purposes of power and profit.

Less than halfway through the pamphlet, Jemmy had disregarded one's name and the system of deference and championed the importance of a constitution and promoted individual – perhaps rebellious – thinking. Mocking the oligarchy was by now a common Otis theme; he had elevated Kidd's crew saluting the Royal Navy with their derrières to a philosophical position.

Otis reluctantly admitted to the truth of Bernard's contention that the governor and the Council had the authority to issue funds from the treasury, and he referenced previous instances of the House concurring with such issuances. But he correctly maintained "that without the aid of an Act of the province, the Governor and Council cannot legally take a shilling out of the treasury, let the emergency be what it may." Otis then asks, "But the Question is, Whether this power be limited?" He responds that this power is strictly limited by the charter to *"such Acts as are or shall be in force within our said Province."* If the governor illegitimately issued money, then what remedy was available? If the executive ignored the requirements of democracy, what could the people do in response? The governor could not be sued in the courts, so a rebuke in the House was the only action available. If that failed to stop the governor's actions, then the House could "stop a few Grants and Salaries," thereby depriving the governor of money. And if that did not "bring matters right," then there was the "last resort, but one; ... a dutiful and humble remonstrance to his Majesty." The "but one" was Locke's "appeal to Heaven, and the longest sword." Jemmy tempered this threat and undoubtedly accusations of sedition by adding: "God forbid that there ever should be occasion for anything of that kind." *Vindication* thus introduces an entirely new issue: the threat of armed rebellion. Injecting the right of revolution into the debate introduced what had been a radical theory thought not to seriously apply to anything other than perhaps the mostly bloodless Glorious Revolution of 1688. To suggest that an "appeal to Heaven, and the longest sword" might be a possibility, however remote, was to make clear the seriousness with which Otis approached the situation.

Vindication establishes in Locke and Montesquieu the cornerstone of American revolutionary thought: the right of the people to be taxed only by themselves or their popularly elected representatives. After stating that God made all men equal, Otis declares that "Kings were ... made for the good of the people, and not the people for them." And then, "No government has a right to make hobby-horses, asses, and slaves of the subject, nature having made sufficient of the two former for all the lawful purposes of man, from the harmless peasant in the field to the most refined politician in the cabinet, but none of the last, which infallibly proves they are unnecessary," which is quickly followed by "most governments are ... the curse and scandal of human nature." What makes *Vindication* exceptionally powerful is that Otis was not writing hypothetically or academically but rather to persuade people he knew and alter the government in which he worked. *Vindication* was intended to change minds at the British Coffee House and the Town Meeting, to get votes from the people in the annual elections and change the votes of the Representatives in the House. *Vindication* was created to justify and implement resistance to government.

One aspect of *Vindication* is often misunderstood. Otis's seventh "data" posited "The King of Great Britain" as "the best as well as most glorious Monarch upon the Globe" and referred to "his other royal virtues." His reign was "the *ne plus ultra* of human glory and felicity." Otis wrote of "his Majesty's Person, Crown, Dignity or Cause, all which I deem equally sacred" and that the King was "truly the most august Personage upon Earth." The catalog of royal virtues is lengthy, as there are references to the King's "wise and gracious administration," "the glorious revolution and the happy establishment resulting therefrom," and "the names of the three George's would doubtless have been immortal." When Bernard had viewed Otis's remonstrance as evidence of "disrespect" toward the crown, and others had termed it "seditious, rebellious and traitorous," Otis was shocked. His revulsion at the thought of treason may well have impelled him to publish his pamphlet rather than wait for the next session and likewise impelled him to establish his loyalty in the first part of the *Vindication* before turning to the constitutional merits of the question posed by Bernard's actions. Otis was very aggressive at positioning his argument: he was opposed to the government as embodied by Hutchinson and Bernard but not the nation as embodied by the King. Not only could one wish to overthrow the government while still remaining a patriot, but overthrowing the government could be an act of patriotism, as Locke argued. Otis's manifestation of this argument was to praise the king while threatening his government. Further, as regalia spread throughout the colonies, the court rooms became increasingly English, and the media fawned over George's every move, Otis had no choice but to draw a stark contrast between the target of his criticisms and the King. George III wasn't only untouchable for legal and philosophical reasons; criticism of him would have challenged the spirit of the times.

Vindication contains Otis's usual concerns, but it also introduces a cousin of the plural office-holding issue: separation of powers. Regarding Bernard's argument about "emergencies," Otis cautioned that "it is a very poor bargain, that for the sake of avoiding a session extraordinary" the people sacrifice "the right of being taxed by their Representatives." As for the executive branch co-opting the legislative's power to spend money, Otis observed: "I am as much for keeping up the distinction between the executive and legislative as possible. Happy, very happy, would it be for this poor province, if this distinction was more attended to than it ever has been." In arguing that a separation of powers was desirable, Otis was concurrently arguing against plural office-holding.

Otis ended his pamphlet with a moderate warning to the governor that reflects the traditional English politician's device of imputing the nation's troubles to unnamed rapacious ministers rather than to the King:

> I am convinced that if his Excellency will in all cases take the advice of the general assembly, (which however contemptably some may affect to speak of it, is the great council of this province, as the British parliament is of the kingdom) that his administration will be crowned with all the success he can desire. But if instead of this, the advice of half a dozen or half a score, who among their fellow citizens may be chiefly distinguished by their avarice, ignorance, pride or insolence, should at any time obtain too much weight at court, the consequences will be very unfortunate on all sides.

Here Jemmy offers Bernard an opening to assign blame to others – the oligarchs on the Council – for his intemperate actions. John Adams writing in 1818 enthusiastically claimed that "[*Vindication*] is a document of importance in the early history of the Revolution which ought never to be forgotten. . . . How many volumes are concentrated in this little fugitive pamphlet, the production of a few hurried hours?" Thomas Hutchinson had a different recollection, writing to John Cushing on January 3, 1763 that, "I never knew less notice taken of a pamphlet that contained so much slander which generally gives a run than there is of this and I am mistaken if he increases the number of his friends." But Hutchinson's "never knew less notice" was wishful thinking, for even he then comments that, "Brattle extols it to the skies and will not allow that a more sensible thing was ever wrote." Hutchinson hoped no one read the pamphlet because it threatened the unthinkable: the appeal to heaven and the longest sword. Hutchinson's peer on the Council and the bench John Cushing had sent remarks to the lieutenant governor about *Vindication*, and Hutchinson's January 3 reply reveals a glimpse of his honest assessment:

> You are less of a politician than I always before took you to be. ... I think O is a clever fellow. He was so unfortunate as to mistake before but he certainly has the right scent now. Pray do not stop him in his course. ... But to be serious ... it is whispered that great things are to be done next session.

Despite Hutchinson's complaint of "slander," Jemmy's *Vindication* was gentle compared to the views he had privately expressed weeks earlier and would publish two months later. A moderate tone may have been used in order to first establish Otis's patriotism; he knew that whispers of treason and sedition would be spoken, and he needed to assure his readers that one could oppose the government while still supporting the country. On November 8, just two days before the *Vindication* appeared, Jemmy and Ruth sold their home on School Street and rented a house on Queen Street (now Court Street) just up the hill to the west of the Town House. The purchaser of the School Street house was none other than Robert Auchmuty, Jemmy's successor as acting advocate general and opposing counsel in the second hearing in the writs of assistance case. At about the same time, the province was covered in two feet of snow and Jemmy trekked to Barnstable to consult with his father – perhaps about the "great things" to be done.

Meanwhile, both the political and religious dissidents were communicating with Mauduit. On October 12, 1762, Rev. Chauncy requested that Mauduit keep "my name a secret" and warned that "Mr. O-r [Oliver]... is a friend to those of most influence who are the friends of Mr. Bollan." And finally, Chauncy writes, "The Boston associated Pastors join with me in their compliments to you, and thanks for your endeavours to serve us." The radical pastors viewed Mauduit as their lobbyist too. On Nov. 17, 1762, a week after *Vindication* was published, Mayhew reported to Mauduit:

> I have had some conversation with several Gentlemen of his Majesty's council of this Province, respecting what you wrote to others as well as to me (and, as I understand, to the Government here also) about associating your worthy brother with you in the Agency.

This letter reveals Mayhew's direct efforts to influence provincial politics. It was increasingly apparent that Mayhew was very politically active and the Black Regiment actively attempted to influence government affairs.

The next session of the House commenced on January 12, 1763 and was rife with hostility; the Jemmy Otis led Popular Party thwarted repeated attempts by the Council to create joint committees with the House even though Colonel Otis chaired the Council delegation. The House wasn't simply rejecting the Council's efforts to cooperate; the House was rejecting the Colonel. The disagreement concerned the London agent; Mauduit was in poor health, and he had prudently suggested that his brother Israel be employed as an additional lobbyist. Jemmy and the Popular Party concurred with this suggestion as it would assure the continued irrelevancy of the oligarchy's favorite candidate, Richard Jackson. On October 28, 1762, Jemmy wrote Jasper Mauduit that "You may rely upon your friends doing everything that is possible to bring about his [Israel's] election as a joint agent with you" and further maintained "that this will finally take place I have no great doubt." Concurrently, Hutchinson informed Bollan that he could "scarce believe such a point can be carried but am not sure it will not." Jemmy Otis attempted to push Israel Mauduit's election through the House by using the parliamentary ploy of submitting the appointment as soon as a quorum was reached, but the appointment was approved only on condition that the addition of Israel Mauduit would require "no further Expense." The Council refused to budge, and attendance in the House had increased, so after further delays from the Council, Israel Mauduit's appointment was tabled. But the rebellious Otis faction in the House returned fire by finally placing in the record a moderate version of Jemmy's *Vindication*, refusing to grant any salary to Attorney General Trowbridge, and refusing to agree on instructions to the province lobbyist in London. The Popular Party was in a fighting mood.

In a sparsely attended House session on Saturday, January 29, Jemmy proposed a letter to be sent to lobbyist Jasper Mauduit informing him of the failure to elect Israel due to additional expense; the explanation wasn't true, but it would assure Mauduit of his support in the province and of the power of the Popular Party, which did not wish to reveal that they were being fiercely and sometimes successfully opposed by the Court Party at nearly every turn. The motion to send the letter passed, but on the following Monday the Council requested a joint committee to consider the letter only to be notified that Jasper Mauduit's letter had been "already answered." By the next day, several members returned to inquire about the letter, and it moved to reopen the previous vote. The Court Party led House insisted that the letter be produced, but Jemmy claimed that it was already sent to London. A quick review of the town newspapers, which regularly listed all ships entering and leaving Boston harbor, revealed that no ship had left in the interim; Jemmy narrowly escaped censure by an enraged Court Party.

Jemmy's name is thereafter absent from the *House Journal* until the closing sessions of the term; he may have refused to attend the Ruggles led sessions or may have been occupied with something else. During his absence, Attorney General Trowbridge's petition for a salary was moved for consideration, and Jemmy was excused from a committee investigating militia recruiting practices. The House seemed to be in turmoil, and Governor Bernard suspended the term on February 25. During the session Colonel Otis was awarded some of the patronage to which he was entitled as a member in good standing of the Governor's Council; his brother Solomon was granted a notary public's commission, and contrary to his standard country prudence, he was offered a share in the paper settlement of Murrayfield, a speculative venture that would create much pain and little profit.

Meanwhile, Jemmy's "Conscience" was alienating his legal associates. In one of the many attempts to limit petty law suits, the Boston bar agreed to four rules of practice that in effect barred plaintiffs not represented by sworn attorneys. On behalf of the Boston bar, Jeremy Gridley presented the rules of practice in open court for the expected approval of the judges, but suddenly and without warning, Jemmy Otis disrupted the *pro forma* proceedings declaring the rules to be "vs. the Province Law, vs. the Rights of Mankind," thus foisting upon the court his opposition. The court was stunned as they all thought the rules had been previously approved. John Adams wrote in his diary on February 5, 1763, "Thus with a whiff of Otis's pestilential Breath, was the whole system blown away." Thacher was particularly enraged, asserting "Whoever votes for him to be any Thing more than a Constable let him be Anathema maranatha. I pamphleteer for him again? No Ile pamphleteer against him." Auchmuty, who had recently purchased Otis's house, unleashed the rumor that Otis had originally supported the proposed rules in order to enroll some of the town's informal lawyers as apprentices but discovered that the prospective students were instead going to Auchmuty and Samuel Quincy; Auchmuty further opined that Otis's change of position was to protect his "tools and Mirmidons," the "Constables, Justices Story and Ruddock, &c." who practiced law as a hobby or part-time job. This explanation may have fulfilled the prejudices of someone such as John Adams, but it was too simple and belied the facts. Otis wanted the legal practice to become more professional, as they all did, but he realized that it was unfair and unrealistic to bar all but sworn attorneys from bringing a suit in the Inferior Courts, which is what the new rules would have accomplished. The courts may be tidier with the new rules, but effectively excluding everyone who couldn't afford an attorney from the plaintiff's table carried a whiff of the same oligarchy that Otis was attempting to exterminate. Further, at the time these proposals were being made, Jemmy had not had a legal apprentice for nearly eight years, and given his excellent legal reputation, the most likely explanation is that he was not interested in mentoring apprentices, and no evidence exists that he desired or attempted to engage apprentices. The first part of Auchmuty's explanation therefore seems to reflect ill-intentions by Auchmuty, whereas the second part of his explanation – that Otis wanted to maximize access to the courts – is likely closer to the truth. Auchmuty was and would continue to be a staunch royalist, eventually emigrating to and dying in England. He was also the firmest ally of the oligarchs and would later be implicated by Benjamin Franklin and Thomas Cushing in various loyalist conspiracies, so it is to be expected that he would rumor monger about Otis. Three years later in 1766 Jemmy Otis would make another strong move in the direction of increasing access to the corridors of power when he instituted a visitor gallery in the Assembly enabling anyone to witness the workings of government; it was perhaps the first instance in the world where the operations and deliberations of a legislative body was freely open to reporters and the public.

The early months of 1763 were very difficult times for Jemmy; it was a transitional period during which he fought the oligarchy while attempting to convince potential allies to join his small faction. A year later, he would begin to build the feared confederacy, but in early 1763, he was often alone. At about that same time, John Adams jotted down two shreds of altiloquence about his former hero:

> Recipe to make a Patriot. Take of the several Species of Malevolence, as Revenge, Malice, Envy, equal Quantities of scurrility, fear, fury, Vanity, Prophaneness, and Ingratitude, equal Quantities and infuse this Composition into the Brains of an ugly, surly, brutal Mortal and you have the Desideratum.

> The Life of Furio. In Croatia. His Descent. Education, at school, Colledge, at the Bar. Historians relate that he was greatly slandered, by a story of a Bastard of a Negro, his Wrath at Plymouth, at Boston he heads the Trade, brings Actions, fails, is chosen Representative, quarrells with the Governor, Lieutenant, Council, House, Custom house officers, Gentlemen of the Army, the Bar, retails prosody, writes upon Money, Prov. sloop.

These are the notes for satirical pieces that John Adams intended to write later but never did; apparently he changed his opinion of Otis. But at the time, Jemmy Otis seemed inscrutable to the young, impressionable John Adams. The reference to a "Bastard of a Negro" actually refers to Joseph Otis's involvement in the criminal trial involving a neighbor's slave girl in 1750. But by 1763, Jemmy's enemies were circulating the story with his name attached as the antagonist. "Furio" is probably a reasonable example of the opinion held of Otis by members of the bench and bar in early 1763. But part of the problem for Adams was doubtless that he was no sophisticated insider in early 1763; he did not know about the machinations of Boston politics and the ugliness of the exercise of power. Otis was fighting demons that did not yet exist for Adams. And the young Adams was also confused because it seemed as if Otis was attacking other members of the small group of highly influential men who controlled the province: the tight little club of Harvard graduates who worked with each other in the court and council rooms, who owned successful merchant businesses and farm land, who were part of the elite clique of provincial aristocrats. Adams saw the world much as Hutchinson did: there are differences of opinion amongst the group in power, but those differences could not be permitted to challenge the power of the group. Adams also still believed in the feudal constructs of deference and status. Disagreement was fine, polite disagreement in public was acceptable, but public feuds with other members of the group defied the ideas of deference and status.

Membership into the broader group in power was somewhat fluid; merchants came and went; new representatives from unknown families occasionally appeared on the scene. But the demons Otis was fighting included an increasingly powerful and indomitable ruling class determined more by heredity than merit, repeated attempts by the small ruling class to usurp power from the broader group in power, and a general apathy – or so it seemed – to these problems. Adams shared that apparent apathy; Jemmy's "Monopolizers of offices, Peculators, Informers, and generally the Seekers of all kinds" did not alarm Adams in 1763. In some ways, John Adams would always be a bit less savvy and a bit more aristocratic than his revolutionary peers.

※

a little paper war

Efforts to influence the debate through the media had previously occurred, but Otis's tactic using the media to pressure office holders and directly influence policy was revolutionary and increasingly powerful; by early January of 1763, both the Court Party and the Popular Party had begun to aggressively engage the media to influence public debate. "Media" in 1763 consisted mostly of newspapers and pamphlets, though it could be argued that hanging someone in effigy, lengthy courtroom summations, and giving speeches were similarly media events. Sometimes articles and pamphlets were published anonymously, sometimes with fictitious names, and sometimes with the author's real name. Sometimes people and places were named in print, sometimes fairly transparent allegory was used, and sometimes the piece was purely theoretical and philosophical. Pieces were often written quickly; newspaper articles were written longhand in just a few hours and delivered to the printer. Typically there were few or no revisions or editorial input. Sometimes it took months to compose a pamphlet, and yet some were dashed off in a few days. Often, an author would publish two or three articles in quick succession, expanding on ideas, correcting mistakes, clarifying issues. Articles by different authors were also often published in quick succession, debating points in the other's article, responding to questions and challenges, and incorporating events of the day. This media world was extremely fluid and fast-paced, and perhaps most unusual in such small circles of paper and pamphlet readers, many did not know the authors behind the anonymous or fictitious bylines.

On February 14, 1763, two letters started their six week cruise from Boston to London. In one, Hutchinson expressed despondency to Bollan: "I have no news to write. I am out of humor this fortnight by an infamous piece in one of our papers wrote by young Otis. ...Whether he has abused you or me the most I am at a loss. I have the satisfaction that people in general are very angry with him. I have no remedy but patience." In the second letter, Jemmy apologized to Jasper Mauduit for failing to secure his brother Israel's appointment as a lobbyist and for including Mauduit's name in "a little paper war."

"A little paper war" was an understated designation for one of the most ferocious and explosive public political battles ever witnessed in the colonies. In a letter to Edmund Quincy, Andrew Belcher described it as a "Bear Garden," and Samuel Mather gave a more straitlaced description to his son in a letter dated June 30, 1763, "The News Papers for a good many Weeks past have been filled partly with Mr Otis's wild and abusive Reflections on your Uncle [Thomas Hutchinson] and others; and partly with some satyrical Remarks on his Performances."

The genesis of the war was most likely the increasing frustration of the Popular Party due to the Council's entrenched position against Popular Party efforts and Court Party puppet Judge Ruggles's control of the House. Further aggravating the sense that the Popular Party wasn't making progress, the governor had suspended the General Court for most of the year, so it hardly met anyway. Debate in the usual forums was being stifled, and the Popular Party's message wasn't being heard; the momentum they had built up over the previous two years was waning, which was part of the Court Party's plan and an echo of the way in which Jemmy Allen had been relegated to obscurity in the 1750s. The Popular Party decided to reignite debate and hopefully energize its base with an unsigned article, almost certainly authored by Jemmy Otis, in the *Gazette* of January 17, 1763. The article praised Jasper Mauduit's work as agent, highlighting his low commission charges and his successes in obtaining reimbursement for the cost of maintaining troops at Louisbourg even though Bollan had advised against seeking such reimbursement. This article appeared at the culmination of the clash in the Assembly over the attempts to include Jasper Mauduit's brother as London lobbyist. The Court Party had previously either not responded to media attacks from the Popular Party or replied with very reserved, somewhat academic responses that one would expect from those who considered themselves aristocrats instilled with the concepts of deference and status; fighting for popular approval in public forums was beneath them. But in a sign that the Court Party believed they had lost the previous public battles and that public opinion was becoming an increasingly essential component to maintaining power, the response to Otis's fairly tame January 17th article was immediate and brutal.

The first attack was a crafty "notice" that appeared in the Court Party's paper of choice, the *Boston Evening-Post*. The printer's notice read: "A.Z.'s piece relating to Mr. Mauduit's being chose Agent," and his "Ignorance of public Affairs" was "not prudent to publish till the author discovers himself." The short, sarcastic notice was the talk of the town. Of course, the "A.Z. piece" was never printed nor ever intended to be printed, but its contents were soon the subject of debate; the printers, John and Thomas Fleet, even had a manuscript at their printing offices that they would reveal to anyone interested, including Jemmy Otis.

The fake notice was a sly but effective public relations stunt that created tremendous gossip. The Popular Party leaders were incensed by Thomas Fleet's ploy and a full assault against the *Evening-Post* and its writers swiftly developed. Jemmy opened the assault with an unsigned article in the *Gazette* targeted at Thomas Goldthwait, Bernard's newly appointed Secretary at War, for disparaging Mauduit on the floor of the House, and the following week Jemmy returned to attack Goldthwait as the "certain stuttering, sputtering Military Scribe, a notorious tool" who delivered the offensive "A.Z." essay to the *Evening-Post*. The primary target of this article, however, was lieutenant governor Thomas Hutchinson, whom Jemmy identified as the probable author of the "A.Z." article. Jemmy portrayed Hutchinson as "a tall, slender, fair complexioned, fair spoken 'very good Gentleman,'" whose "Beauty has captivated half the pretty Ladies, his Finess more than half the pretty Gentlemen." The attack on Hutchinson's feudal aristocratic accouterments was vicious and widely considered infamous. Otis had turned aristocratic characteristics from being positive attributes to blights on one's personality and manliness.

The "paper war" continued into the spring and grew increasingly malicious with each article, saturating the pages of the *Evening-Post* and *Gazette* with the usual allusion and allegory and a new dose of insinuation and slander. The Court Party realized that Jemmy Otis was a formidable opponent, and they were not willing to lose another public battle; the result of the Court Party's determination to win was to expose the Popular Party's caucus system and clubs – a secret John Adams discovered in the papers. These early merchant societies and proto-Sons of Liberty groups usually kept their public images low, but the Court Party revealed their existence in gossipy and sarcastic articles; the Court Party was suggesting to the people of Boston that the real danger to liberty was a small group of populists and merchants who controlled Massachusetts politics. The Court Party's other avenue of attack was leveled at Jemmy Otis personally; while some had previously suggested that only a madman would risk a successful future by expressing seditious and treasonous views, the Court Party writers made a concerted effort to plant those ideas firmly into the public consciousness: sedition, treason, madness. Repeatedly, publically and privately, Otis's mental health was questioned; the whisper campaign was aggressive and brutal. If the Court Party could not win the argument, they would destroy the person.

The *Evening-Post* Court Party writers, particularly "J," divulged the "Caucas" operations and labeled Otis "Bluster," Royall Tyler "Pug Sly," and Thomas Dawes "Adjutant Trowel." After Jemmy's disappearance from the public stage in early February, a scathing article by "J" provoked him anew, and he returned in the *Gazette* of February 28, occupying the entire front page and another column. He began by assailing the *Evening-Post* and lampooning the "master secretary at war." Then he confessed that since he supported "Liberty of the Press" he could not protest if others printed scurrilous articles about him and taunted his critics by saying "Go on then *Evening Posts, Pimps, Parasites, Sycophants, Predicting Parsons* and *Pedagogues*, I am ready for ye all." The "Predicting Parson" was probably East Apthorp, the new and heralded Anglican minister of Cambridge. East Apthorp was what Mayhew termed a "Spye" for the "Society for the Propagation of the Gospel in Foreign Parts," the "Foreign Part" being Cambridge. Technically, he was a missionary, but his presence was exactly what the Boston dissenters had hoped Mauduit would forestall. Mayhew was directly referencing Apthorp when he wrote to Mauduit in December 18, 1764, pleading for him to ensure "that no more Missionaries shall be sent to New England." The Pedagogue was John Lovell, Otis's friend and master of Boston Latin School who had angered Jemmy by publically criticizing his treatment of Hutchinson. Again, those within the broader group in power were confused and angered by attacks on people they perceived as belonging to their group, and nearly everyone wanted to believe that they belonged to same group as Thomas Hutchinson. And most believed they could curry favor within the group by defending and deferring to the powerful Hutchinson.

But Otis continued the attacks; he argued against plural office holding, "Projects for keeping the people poor in order to make them humble," province officers holding commissions at the pleasure of the "junto," and rumors of plans to keep a standing army in the colonies. And finally, he was speaking of himself when he mockingly invoked those who had the "unparalled impudence" to defend themselves against government infringement. He ridiculed the oligarchy's attitude by declaring, again referring to himself, that such people "shall be deemed seditious, libellous and traitrous; nay according to one wizard among the Benefactors, blasphemous." And the oligarchs should demand that "Every art shall be used to blacken the character of the supposed author of such a hint, to ruin his reputation and business, and deprive him, his wife and children, of their daily bread. When all other attempts fail he shall be represented as a mad man, in order if possible, to lay a train to get the guardianship of his person, and the possession of what little estate he may have." In ridiculing the oligarchs, Jemmy was taunting them to act.

The vicious whisper campaign continued when "J" in an *Evening-Post* article of February 21 referred to Otis's "mad rant" in the papers and opined that "a frenzy had seized the unhappy author." According to "J," even Jemmy's nine year old black servant boy referred to his master with "There goes the crazy Man." On March 7, the *Evening-Post* published a character sketch of Jemmy in the form of an allegorical execution of a "Hector Wildfire"; in his speech from the gallows, Mr. Wildfire admitted to being raised on tales of Wat Tyler and Masaniello of Naples and guilty of throwing stones at his father. Mr. Wildfire's post mortem was described in macabre specificity and concluded by observing that when Mr. Wildfire's corpse was fed to a pack of dogs, they all became insane. Some readers would know the references to Tyler and Masaniello (whose name is misspelled in the article); both these men led peasant uprisings and the invocation of their names was doubtless intended to insult Jemmy by associating him with men who forged chaos out of order by elevating the needs of the illiterate and unskilled. Tyler and particularly Masaniello were also labeled "mad" and unstable by their opponents. Both peasant revolts were largely successful, and both leaders died for their efforts and were thus elevated to a kind of martyrdom for rebel peasants. The allusion of throwing stones at one's father reveals the divergent attitudes toward the system of deference; Otis mocked the notion that Hutchinson and the oligarchs existed on an elevated plane whereas the Court Party adherents viewed this as assaulting a superior. And finally, there's the name – Mr. Wildfire – despite their jollity at mocking Jemmy, they certainly were aware of his intentions. And the oligarchs were not finished; John Lovell, the "Pedagogue" and master of Boston Latin School on School Street, declared that his former friend was "Solomon's Madman" who "threw about Firebrands, Arrows and Death," and waved "his Torch in Anger with Design, as he formerly threatened, to put all Things in a Flame." This time, the oligarchs attacked the man instead of the message. Everyone knew that Otis had threatened to inflame the province, and who but a madman would make such a threat?

Samuel Allyne wrote a letter to his brother Joseph on February 14, 1763:

> As to News & the political disputes father will give you a circumstantial Acct. of them. I think they run very high but as they dont affect your & my interest we will act as the Dutchmen have done all the war; look on & laugh, however if the[y] come to loggerheads, I shall by all means stand by Squire Bluster as he is an excellent fellow & ought not to be forsaken.

Like his brother Joseph, Samuel Allyne was interested in business, not politics, so he largely ignored the paper war; but he couldn't help but label his brother "Squire Bluster." A month later on March 8, however, the skirmish had evolved into a war and was starting to move from the printing presses to the streets. Samuel Allyne wrote again to Joseph and revealed his increasing anxiety:

> James Otis seems to have many enemies however his friends will stand by him – he was attacked the other day by six yanky officers but they did not strike him tho they threatened it, as had they done it it would have caused them a drubbing from the people of the town.

Before the Revolution, "Yanky" meant "cowardly." The "officers" were militia men angered by Otis's repeated public statements about not trusting full-time soldiers who were directed from London, rather than by a colonial legislature. So six militia officers threatened to beat or kill Otis. Did someone send them? Were they paid to deliver the threat? We don't know, but it wouldn't be the last time that, in the words of Jemmy's sister, an assassination attempt would be made. Hutchinson pled ignorance of any plot; as a good oligarch, he portrayed himself as existing above the fray. He wrote a friend on March 9, 1763 that "I am told nobody abroad understands our papers. ... I have always told my friends that it was the best way to treat such ribaldry with contempt but they would not bear it no longer and have broke out at once from all quarters and I really pity my enemy. He is indeed the strangest Creature in the world." An aspiring feudal lord responds with contempt to the man struggling to elevate the peasants.

The "J" critic was merciless, publishing an article in the *Evening-Post* of March 14 under the title "Mene, Mene, Tekel Upharsin," an omen from the Book of Daniel. Most of the Bostonians engaged in the paper war had studied Latin, Greek and Hebrew at Harvard and were entirely familiar with the omen. King Belshazzar was drunkenly surveying the gold and silver stolen from Solomon's Temple when a disembodied hand wrote on the wall "Mene, Mene, Tekel Upharsin," a prophecy usually left untranslated but roughly meaning "count and weigh your money" and implies "enjoy counting your money today, for tomorrow you will die." The writing on the wall appeared to King Belshazzar just before he was assassinated. Jemmy and the entire province would have known that the article's title alluded to an impending assassination, yet the irony is delicious and certainly unintended. While the allusion works as both the article and the omen have unknown authors – the Old Testament hand had no body – it fails in its reference; Belshazzar was a wealthy king who looted the poor, and the omen not only foretold his assassination but also the fall of the Babylonian empire. "Mene, Mene, Tekel Upharsin" would have been more appropriate for an anonymous article by Jemmy had he been interested in making veiled death threats. In the "J" article, the author explains the "Caucas" and its meeting place in "Adjutant Trowel's long Garrat." He described Otis's freedom of the press as nothing more than "a liberty, for every dabbler in politicks to say and print, whatever his shallow understanding, or vicious passions may suggest, against the wisest and best men: – a liberty for <u>fools</u> and <u>madmen</u> to spit and throw firebrands." Again, Jemmy is fomenting a peasant revolt and attempting to elevate those from whom the oligarchs should not hear.

Thus Otis was again threatened and labeled insane, and liberty of press was mocked as a means for "dabblers" to voice their opinions. The mockery of the caucus continued in the *Evening-Post* a week later on March 21 when "E.J." explained the difference between the "Grand Corkass" and the "Petty Corkass" and the method by which decisions for town meetings were made. Then "E.J." described the Boston town meeting of the previous week; the March meeting was of particular importance and typically the best attended because offices from moderator to hog catcher were filled, and the March 1763 gathering was much anticipated because it was the first to be held in the newly restored Faneuil Hall. Jemmy was elected moderator and promptly erupted in a "harangue on freedom and English liberty." His speech contained mostly the usual political clichés proclaiming "this is a proper Season" for the "Burial in everlasting oblivion" of "Prejudices and Animosities." And yet on the same day the *Gazette* published his brutal response to "J" that labeled him nothing more than "a Grub street bard" whose writing exposed "the crawling maggots of his mouldy brain." Rumor spread that Jemmy was writing pamphlets, and the following week – March 28 – the *Gazette* printed a notice that Jemmy would soon publish three pamphlets: "An Impartial History of the Last Session of the Court," "A full and true Account of the Grant of Mount Desert," and "The present political State of Province." The "Mene, Mene, Tekel Upharsin" article was published just as rumors regarding Jemmy's new pamphlets were spreading. Jemmy's pamphlets were never printed, and no trace of them appears in historical records; most likely, Jemmy burned the manuscripts for fear of his life after being advised by friends that his writings were likely treasonous and seditious. This would not have been the first time that Otis was warned that his publications and speeches may be considered seditious and treasonous, and *Mene, Mene, Tekel Upharsin* was almost certainly on his mind. The "full and true Account of the Grant of Mount Desert" was perhaps never actually written but rather was intended as a threat to lay bare the inner workings of the Court Party and the Governor. If the Court Party were going to reveal the Popular Party's secrets, then Jemmy would reveal the backroom deal that secured Mount Desert for Bernard.

The same day as the *Gazette* printed the notice of Jemmy's pamphlets, yet another smear appeared in the *Evening-Post* published under the name of Jehoshaphat Smoothingpain who concluded that Jemmy printed "bitter things against Judges … because thy Great-Grand-Father's Father's Cousin-German by the Father's side was not made a Judge." Sensing that they were losing, the Court Party now dragged Colonel Otis and the lost Supreme Court appointment into the fracas. Smoothingpain's article also contains the only other reference to Jemmy's altercation with the "six yanky officers" referenced privately by Samuel Allyne, and the reference suggested that Otis barely escaped a thorough beating – or worse.

An April 1763 series of articles between Thomas Hutchinson and Jemmy began with Hutchinson claiming that the root of the Popular Party's discontent lay with Colonel Otis's failure to be appointed judge in the fall of

1760. Jemmy Otis replied that the issue was hardly a significant concern in 1760 and certainly not an issue in 1763; of course, in 1763, the Colonel held a highly desirable seat on the Council, so Jemmy's assertion that no one now cared about a failed effort to be appointed judge appeared credible. It was fairly obvious that Hutchinson assumed he'd failed to win the substantive argument so he fabricated an issue out of an event that hadn't warranted comment for years.

Skirmishes continued with salvos fired by Philo Politiae, J. Philanthrop, Humphrey Plowjogger, U., L.S., S.A., A.Z., T.Q. and the ubiquitous J. "Humphrey Plowjogger" and "U." were John Adams, and his somewhat pedantic monologues did not garner much attention. By contrast, T.Q. – Oxenbridge Thacher's *nom de guerre* – published caustic criticisms of plural office holding printed just prior to the May elections that were forcefully targeted at destroying the Hutchinson-Oliver alliance in the council chamber.

The oligarchs had mustered all their weapons in the paper war, and Jemmy's radicalism was too provocative and unprecedented for many, so he was outgunned. Thacher's and Adams's articles were uncoordinated efforts that hit some of the same targets but provided no direct support to Jemmy. Most "friends of government" and former Otis allies believed that the madman had lost his support and alienated the people with his nearly treasonous attacks, yet the Boston town elections of May 1763 proved that the people of Boston resoundingly supported their beleaguered, threatened rebel. Jemmy Otis received 989 votes out of 1089 votes cast, more than anyone else and more than he had ever before received. Thomas Cushing received 899 votes, Royall Tyler 809, and Oxenbridge Thacher 716. It cannot be determined whether this astonishing victory at the ballot box was a spontaneous reflection of the people's will or the result of the merchants acting through the "caucus," but not only did it demonstrate enthusiastic support for Jemmy, but it also further radicalized the Boston bench with the replacement of the moderate John Phillips with the radical Oxenbridge Thacher. Phillips was ousted in large part because he had voted against the Popular Party in both the roll call votes of the fourth session. The Court Party almost certainly believed that they had benefitted from the little paper war in Boston, but the people of Boston resoundingly elected radical Popular Party stalwarts to represent them.

But there was a problem. While Jemmy and the Popular Party retained complete control of Boston, they were stunned to find that the Court Party still held a majority in the House. The Popular Party ruled Boston, but the Court Party still had considerable support in the countryside. The Court Party's revenge against the Popular Party was quick; Edes and Gill were dismissed as printers of the House Journal because of the Otis articles they had printed, and Samuel Cooper, the "silver tongued" Reverend of the Brattle Street Church – the rebels's church – and Jemmy's Harvard classmate, was dismissed as House chaplain. Colonel Otis came extremely close to losing his Council seat but was saved by Treasurer Harrison Gray's intervention, doubtless due to the close ties between the two families. Another friend of government, Sam White, replaced the divisive Ruggles as Speaker; but White was viewed as being more diplomatic and moderate than Ruggles. The Court Party wanted control, but they did not wish to repeat the cold war that broke out during the 1762-63 legislative term.

Jemmy assumed his party would be impotent and resigned; though popular in Boston, they could not seem to make progress in the bigger scheme of the province. Bernard did not celebrate the resignation; he wrote to Richard Jackson that "I doubt not" that Otis was scheming some attack on the oligarchy. And he was correct. Otis did have a plan. Repeating his earlier performance, he returned to the House the next day, apologized, and moved that the governor's salary be approved, a motion that Governor Bernard considered conciliatory. Bernard, Jemmy recalled, could be manipulated.

Otis's efforts to destroy the Court Party had failed – for now. As a political leader he had come close to destroying his own party by pushing hard for reforms without having the political power to achieve them. The paper war's political fallout resulted in complete polarization in the House as evidenced by the dismissal of publishers Edes and Gill and Reverend Samuel Cooper. Samuel Allyne wrote to Joseph Otis on June 18, 1763 commenting on the polarizing and heated sessions in which at least one representative had threatened another with a clubbing. The madness of revolt was indeed spreading. Jemmy had nearly damaged his relationships with the bench and the bar, and he had suggested that his legal practice was flagging. Scoffed at by his peers, Jemmy had become a "mad man" to the Boston elite. He clung to "Mr Cooke the cobbler" just as they seemed to cling to him, the drowning man and the life raft saving each other.

What inspired James Otis's radicalization in 1762-1763? He had been fighting against the oligarchy, against those in power and those who aspired to it, against plural office-holding and the aggregation of power in the hands of the few, and against "passive obedience." From Bernard sending the *Massachusetts* without the House's consent to the Boston courts's efforts to exclude non-lawyers, Otis had fought the accumulation of power and exclusion of the unprivileged at every step. And while such *Pimps, Parasites, Sycophants,* and *Pedagogues* were easily identifiable with the Olivers, Hutchinsons and Governor Bernard, it became increasingly obvious that these labels also described Jemmy Otis's own father. It was on May 26, 1762 that Colonel Otis declined his election as Speaker of the House supposedly because he was so infrequently in Boston, only to be appointed to a much-coveted seat on the Council. And the Colonel's position as Speaker was taken by that odious "friend of government" Timothy Ruggles, a thoroughly loyal Tory. Jemmy must have realized that his father was only slightly removed from Hutchinson and Bernard, and while the Colonel could never achieve Hutchinson's status, he certainly aspired to such socio-political heights.

In his opening statement for the Writs of Assistance case, Otis said, "The only principles of public conduct that are worthy of a gentlemen, or a man, are, to sacrifice estate, ease, health and applause, and even life itself to the sacred calls of his country. These manly sentiments in private life make a good citizen, in public life, the patriot and the hero." The mad man who was developing in 1762 and 1763 was a man torn between his country and his father, a man who could have chosen a life of ease and wealth but instead chose the path of patriot and hero. John Adams, James Bowdoin and many others would eventually join him on this path, but in 1763, Jemmy Otis just seemed like a crazy friendless traitor.

CHAPTER VI

Troubles in this Country take their rise from one Man

Governor Bernard was attempting to neutralize Jemmy Otis and the Popular Party using the customary method of purchasing peace, and the Colonel knew that Jemmy's paper war would make peace valuable to the Court Party. One component of Bernard's scheme was the Colonel's promotion to the Council in May 1762, but Bernard could not grasp that blatant patronage was precisely what so infuriated the Colonel's son. Naïve to this reality, the governor remained committed to his scheme, doubtless applying the only gambit he knew, and offered Colonel Otis additional appointments in Barnstable County in late 1763. Colonel Otis was quite willing to use his son's insolence to his advantage. According to Hutchinson, the Colonel approached him in the spring of 1763, at the height of the paper war, to offer a truce. Hutchinson reported the conversation to his friend Israel Williams on April 15:

> The former [Colonel Otis] just before the Court, rose desired to speak with me in the Lobby & mentioned that we used to think alike etc. I told him he could not be insensible of the injurious treatment I had received from his son & that the Monday before he had published the most virulent piece which had ever appeared, but if he would desist & only treat me with common justice & civility I would forgive & forget everything that was past. He replied it was generous. . . .

Of course, peace would not come cheaply; the Colonel would surely be compensated for silencing the pen of Jemmy Otis. On November 17, 1763, Hutchinson again wrote to Israel Williams and reported that Bernard's scheme was progressing as appointments were pending and both Otises "keep themselves silent." On February 1, 1764, Bernard appointed Colonel Otis as "first Justice" of the Barnstable Inferior Court and judge of Probate. These offices confirmed the Colonel's near total control of Cape Cod, and because they were appointed, not elected, positions, the Colonel would not need to continually campaign for reelection. By 1764, the Colonel held nearly every position of importance on Cape Cod and had a seat on Boston's highest deliberative body as he was a Councilor, chief justice of the Barnstable Inferior Court, judge of Probate, and Colonel in the militia. And collectively the Otis family power in Barnstable was formidable; his son Joseph was, until February 1764, sheriff of Barnstable County, militia captain, and justice of the peace, as was Solomon Otis, the Colonel's brother.

But Governor Bernard grossly misread Jemmy Otis's motivations. In a *Gazette* article published on February 28, 1763, Otis warned that his silence could not be bought, that he would accept no "office" in exchange for "good behavior." And his warning proved accurate. Bernard later observed that "no sooner were these patents sealed [offices granted to the Colonel] than Otis renewed his hostility against Government with fresh Vigor." The pressure of such political patronage must have been considerable on Jemmy. Almost certainly, his father and brothers felt that Jemmy's crusade against the oligarchy was damaging their business and reputations; his crusade was damaging his own law practice. And almost certainly Jemmy's Tory wife, Tory sister Mary and her Tory husband, and Samuel Allyne's soon-to-be father-in-law and the provincial treasurer, pleaded with Jemmy to forgo the little paper war lest it become a greater war. Imagine the family tension: Jemmy's little brother was married to the province treasurer's son; Jemmy's sister was married to the treasurer's brother – and Jemmy, up until now the superstar genius of the family, had declared war on the entire structure. Before 1764, Jemmy's political campaigning and philosophical explorations typically aimed at local targets. These first assaults focused on the local practical problems of customs abuses, plural office-holding and the corresponding issue of the separation of powers. The substantial exception to these local problems was Otis's battle against the writs of assistance in which he addressed the issue of parliamentary sovereignty and hence governmental power in general. Under immense pressure from all sides in 1764 – government, family, business – Jemmy almost achieved a comprehensive expression of his intricate political philosophy on an imperial scale. Now, Jemmy would integrate these issues into a comprehensive practical philosophy on the justification of authority: comprehensive in that its scope applied to all government authority and practical in that it was an academic philosophy chambered into a powerful weapon with a hairpin trigger.

The expansion of Otis's political philosophy may have been the natural progression of internal meditation on the issue of authority, but Otis was never purely academic and evolving circumstances in the Empire demanded his attention. First, the issue of plural office-holding was fatigued due to overuse and of limited credibility because Jemmy's own family held a significant collection of offices; it was an issue that reeked of hypocrisy and on which Jemmy was conspicuously vulnerable. Second, once Grenville assumed substantial control of the British government in the spring of 1763 as First Lord of the Treasury and Chancellor of the Exchequer, he was determined to ensure financial stability for the realm. Current revenues were inadequate and threatened the Empire's ability to maintain its global power as the interest payments on the Seven Years' War debt alone consumed over half of all revenue; further, total expenses did not appreciably decline with the end of the war. Domestically, the English were taxed as much as was feasible; real estate was taxed at rates perceived to be the maximum possible and taxes on cider were producing riots instead of revenue. It seems that the residents of England couldn't be taxed any more. While the English at home claimed to be over taxed, it appeared evident that the English abroad were under taxed. Lord Bute granted Grenville the authority to locate troops in the colonies, and though Grenville may or may not have considered that decision as such wise, financial support of the troops provided the perfect rationale to raise taxes on the colonists. And once an array of colonial taxation was established, however minimal the taxes may be, the administration could then raise those taxes with little opportunity for colonial protest.

While Grenville's office embarked on planning the implementation of colonial taxes, the Commissioners of Customs advocated a few immediate changes that did not require parliamentary approval. One such change required that all possessors of customs commissions perform their commission in person, rather than essentially leasing their commissions to oft corrupt proxies who would then engage in pre-arranged agreements with smugglers. This customs change did not so much alter the regulations as much as the official attitude toward their implementation; bending the rules would no longer be permissible. Further, the Royal Navy, enlarged by the war effort but increasingly available to assume non-military duties, was itself enlisted into the customs enforcement. Armed with customs commissions and authorized by Grenville's "Hovering Act" to seize vessels within two leagues – about six miles – off the American coast for Acts of Trade violations, the Royal Navy ensured that colonists grasped that the days of *laissez-faire* and largely untaxed trade were over. With the political climate as it was in England, and with a new, strict, ministry devising long term plans for the reordering of the empire, the London lobbyists for the colonies were very important men. Jemmy and his Popular Party had dismissed William Bollan out of spite and high cost and had supported his successor, Jasper Mauduit, despite ill health and lack of success. But the real reason for Bollan's dismissal and Mauduit's appointment may have been precisely what Peter Oliver feared: the Popular Party's political alignment with Boston's radical preachers. It seems clear that Mauduit was known to Boston's radical ministers in the 1750s but unknown to the Massachusetts political class. Jasper Mauduit was not so much the Popular Party's candidate as the Black Regiment's candidate, and the Popular Party's commitment to Mauduit was more a commitment to Mayhew and the radical preachers. The mystery of why the Popular Party would so defend a lobbyist who appeared less than fully competent is somewhat unraveled by the revelation that even Mauduit didn't particularly desire the position; in his reply to a letter of criticisms from the House, Mauduit reminds the House that he never desired the lobbyist position. So if Mauduit was fairly unknown to the Boston politicians in the early 1760s, was not qualified for the position, and did not desire the position, then why was he elected lobbyist? Peter Oliver had feared that the radical preachers would align with the radical politicians, and Mauduit was the proof that it had happened.

But none of those considerations necessitated competence; when Mauduit should have been alerting the General Court of taxes being considered in Whitehall, he was instead wrangling about parliamentary reimbursements and debating theological topics; in fact, he seemed more preoccupied with communicating with New England religious dissenters than with New England politicians. Jemmy had orchestrated Mauduit's selection and the rejection of the competent Richard Jackson because he was politically aligned with the Boston oligarchy. In April 1763, Mauduit had briefly remarked in a letter to House Speaker Timothy Ruggles that the issue of French molasses taxes had been "put off till another Year," a paltry detail compared to the extensive information available from Bollan or Jackson. As early as August

1763, Hutchinson was engaged in a personal exchange of letters with Jackson regarding possible taxes on French molasses. John Adams would later claim that "I know not why we should blush to confess that molasses was an essential ingredient in American independence." And while Jemmy claimed that "the fishery is the center of motion, upon which the wheel of all British commerce in America turns," molasses was the lubricant of New England commerce; myriad distilleries in Rhode Island and Massachusetts produced the rum from imported molasses that funded the fishing industry of the Grand Banks and slave trading in Africa, and these in turn enabled the financing that purchased and imported England's manufactures.

The Molasses Act of 1733 was a product of special interest lobbying that placed the exorbitant tax of six pence per gallon on non-English molasses with the objective of protecting British sugar planters. The Act's sole purpose was to tax foreign molasses at such a high rate that importers would only buy British molasses. But the supply of all sugar and molasses produced by the British islands never met the demand, and since distilleries respected neither law nor nationality, the Act was doomed from the beginning as French molasses flowed freely into the British colonies. Now Grenville proposed to convert this act from a trade regulation designed to prevent the importation of foreign molasses into a source of revenue by greatly reducing the tax while rigorously enforcing the law. Grenville attempted to arrive at a reasonably low tax rate by surveying the opinions of a range of advisors, but opinions differed by each advisor's position and connections.

By the late summer of 1763, Grenville clearly intended to raise revenue from the colonies by taxing molasses at a low rate and strictly enforcing the tax, and yet few in the colonies were as of yet troubled. Jasper Mauduit had not the temperament, knowledge, or connections to assist in Grenville's survey of opinions, and Mauduit received negligble support from his employer, the Massachusetts General Court, regarding questions to ask and answer. So in August 1763, Hutchinson and Jackson were discussing an issue that would not provoke Jemmy Otis and hence the general public until eight months later. Perhaps more frustrating, Bostonians learned of the ominous Hovering Act not from their London lobbyist but from their local newspapers.

It was Thomas Hutchinson who initially sounded the alarm; he informed Jackson on August 3, 1763 that a duty of one pence per gallon might be "generally agreeable" but cautioned, "But do they [the ministry] see the consequence? Will not this be introductory to taxes, duties and excises upon other articles, and would they consist with the so much esteemed priviledge of English subjects – the being taxed by their own representatives?" Even Bernard was distressed by the idea of a sugar tax, writing to Richard Jackson on August 23 that "if the Northern Colonies are not allowed to import molasses on Practicable terms, they will become desperate, for they really won't be able to live. ... I dread the consequences of such a resolution." Hutchinson, as a friend of government, would eventually publically support the tax, but he was initially opposed to any direct taxes on the colonies. Yet Hutchinson would make no public protestations against the tax in the summer of 1763. Oddly but perhaps predictably, Hutchinson's position caused some in the Popular Party to approve the direct tax; in October, Thomas Cushing, a Popular Party representative from Boston, admonished Mauduit "as a private person" and claimed that "Mr Bollan's Friends" suggested that Bollan would have forcefully objected to the Hovering Act. Cushing further claimed that "our trade must be distroy'd" if the Molasses Act were to be firmly enforced and advised that the new tax should be limited to one pence per gallon but reiterated that the official advice of the House was "to oppose any duty at all." And yet Cushing followed that letter with another to Mauduit on November 11, which stated that "if Parliament should think fit to lower the Duty to an half penny or a penny per gallon ... the Duty would be chearfully and universally paid." For Cushing, opposition was a tactic to negotiate a lower rate; unlike Hutchinson, Cushing had no philosophical problems with the proposed tax in 1763.

Thus as 1764 opened, there was no consensus in either the Court or the Popular Party on how to respond to the impending new tax; instead, there was little discussion and few opinions. Because of this apparent lack of interest and lack of unity, the Massachusetts lobbyist in London had little but vague advice, and consequently the House had no source of detailed information from Whitehall; Mauduit was not paying attention and the politicians in Boston weren't asking the right questions. On January 2, 1764 the Boston *Gazette* carried an announcement from the customs officers of Boston, Salem, Falmouth, and Piscatauqua that customs officers henceforth would board and inspect before docking all vessels carrying rum, sugar, or molasses. Despite anxiety over new customs inspections, Otis's expanding philosophy of rights took hold in other areas. On January 7, he submitted a bill in the General Court for the abolition of the slave trade in Massachusetts; the bill did not abolish slavery, but a prohibition against the slave trade would gradually eliminate slavery. A movement to abolish the slave trade would not develop in England for another two decades, and then it was largely promoted by the very religious, such as William Wilberforce, and manifested as a duty to their faith. For Otis, the abolition of slavery was a purely secular conclusion founded on the concepts of natural rights and consent. The bill was mostly ignored, but Otis persisted and introduced another bill for the abolition of the slave trade two years later on June 20, 1766. It likewise was ignored.

A week after the January 2, 1764 announcement of vigorous new customs inspections, the *Gazette* advertised an anonymous pamphlet, *Considerations Upon the Act of Parliament Whereby a Duty is laid of six Pence Sterling per Gallon Molasses, etc.* Grenville's new tax plan entailed lowering the duty at the exact same time as the customs taxes would be rigidly enforced; but the pamphlet suggested that rigid enforcement would begin first, while the customs taxes were still very high, and New England's merchant businesses would be impaired. This aroused the merchants, and the pamphlet reflected their anxiety, which was heightened by the Commissioners of Customs's February 27, 1764 announcement that henceforth customs "arrangements" as made notorious in *Erving v. Cradock* were strictly forbidden. Private deals or individual "understandings" with customs officials were no longer permitted. The law was to be applied without variation. By early 1764, the Massachusetts merchants began to panic; Whitehall's new regime was going to destroy their businesses. The politicians began to take notice as the merchants demanded a response. And yet, there was still no unified opinion as to the most appropriate response.

And yet more immediate problems were afflicting the General Court. The New Year brought yet another outbreak of smallpox. At a Boston town meeting on February 20, 1764, various petitions regarding small pox infections and "Inoculating Hospitals" were read, and a committee including Jemmy, Harrison Gray, Foster Hutchinson and others was formed to draft a plan to respond to the epidemic. Another committee that included Auchmuty, Ben Kent, Foster Hutchins, Sam Adams and Richard Dana was created to "examine the several Laws of the Principal relative to Infectious" diseases, the primary purpose of which was to determine whether and how infected persons could be kept from entering the town. And ironically, at that same town meeting, Jemmy was appointed to lead a committee to thank Rev. Whitefield for raising "a considerable Sum of Money in Great Britain for the distressed Sufferers by the great Fire in Boston" of 1760.

The small pox epidemic forced the General Court to relocate to Cambridge. The General Court had just unpacked their papers and begun the new term when their meeting place, Harvard Hall, caught fire and burned until nothing remained of Harvard's library and the Court records. Amongst the torched documents were official protests against the Molasses Act from the merchants of Boston, Marblehead, Plymouth, and Salem. The General Court had to move again, draw up documents anew, and request for the protests to be prepared and sent for a second time. Everything was running behind schedule, not least of which was the communication of various Molasses Act protestations to London. Massachusetts seemed to be in a losing battle with the twin threats of pox and fire. The Court relocate again even farther from the city to Concord.

It was obvious to all that Jasper Mauduit was not forcefully representing the Province, and thus an effort to appoint a special lobbyist commenced. The alleged objective of this effort was to have a special agent negotiate for Massachusetts in the upcoming discussions over the Massachusetts-Connecticut boundary. However, the special agent would certainly be asked to address the new sugar tax as well. The General Court was panicking a bit, and the Court Party must have felt pressure to address the problem since it controlled the Council and the House. A nearly full House passed the motion 46 to 40 and the Council quickly agreed. Thomas Hutchinson was then selected as the special agent; there were a mere eight dissenting votes in both the House and Council, three of which came from the Boston bench in the House: Jemmy, Royall Tyler, Cushing. It is difficult to ascertain the reason for the result, but it is likely that a majority believed that Hutchinson, as a member of the oligarchy, would be uniquely qualified to gain access and present the province's position to Whitehall. But Hutchinson's proposed trip to England never occurred; Hutchinson argued that he first needed permission from London, and the House, now dwindling in numbers and emboldened by Oxenbridge Thacher's return from illness, killed the mission. Again, history doesn't reveal whether the House actually agreed with Hutchinson or if the Popular Party persuaded a number of members to change their previous votes. But the General Court first voted to send a special agent to Whitehall and then declined to actually send one, which clearly indicates that no agreement existed on how to respond to the impending sugar tax; no single position had yet to consistently persuade a majority of the General Court.

Jasper Mauduit finally received assistance from his brother Israel, who prepared an appeal to present to the Treasury with the tepid support of Rhode Island, New Hampshire, and New York. But Grenville was constructing his master revenue plan with rapidity unusual for government bureaucracies, and the lack of any unified protests or lucid instructions rendered the colonial lobbyists impotent. At the merchants' insistence, the Massachusetts General Court finally transmitted instructions to their lobbyist in mid-February. Thomas Cushing summarized these instructions: "I find the Committee in general are of the oppinion that this Act [Molasses Act of 1733] is at this time put in rigorous execution in order to obtain our Consent to some Dutys being laid, but this is look'd upon of dangerous consequence as it will be conceeding to the Parliaments having a Right to Tax our trade which we can't by any means think of admitting, as it wou'd be contrary to a fundamentall Principall of our Constitution vizt. That all Taxes ought to originate with the people." The instructions crossed the ocean quickly but reached Mauduit only after the House of Commons had agreed on the "American bill."

Grenville "opened the Budget" in the House of Commons on March 9, 1764, and his able assistant Secretary of the Treasury Thomas Whately presented a series of resolutions addressing the issue of American revenue, including Molasses Act revisions and the key components of the Sugar Act. Whately also suggested that it might be "proper" to levy "Stamp Duties," but such a bill could only be considered after the other revenue bills had been finalized and enacted. Whately's proposals were printed without comment in the May 7 Boston *Gazette*. A week later "Nov. Anglicanus" authored a lengthy letter printed on the *Gazette's* front page scolding the Court Party controlled General Court for being in "a sound sleep" and for never sending clear instructions to Jasper Mauduit and refusing to employ Israel Mauduit to augment his brother's lobbying efforts. "Nov. Anglicanus" was mostly likely Sam Adams or Oxenbridge Thacher and likely reflected the views of many Massachusetts merchants.

The Boston town meeting convened the next day for annual elections. It was lightly attended largely due to the lingering small pox epidemic, but the Boston bench proved that its opposition to the Court Party was political successful as every incumbent was reelected. Of the 449 votes cast, Thacher received 430, Otis 423, Tyler 420 and Cushing 373. Thacher's vote count reflected the Boston electorate's taste for radicalism, as few were as rebellious as he. But Thacher had been ill in January and was inoculated with smallpox in February, yet he would never fully recover and had about a year to live.

The General Court seemed mired in bickering over the past year while Whitehall planned to extract revenue from the colonies; the people of Boston were demanding more from their representatives. While the town meeting of May 15, 1764 was preoccupied with its usual road paving, school master paying, and small pox inoculating issues, it also took the unusual step of appointing Sam Adams along with four others to a new and significant committee that gave Adams his first province-wide exposure. Adams had long been influential in the tavern clubs, and everyone knew him as a negligent tax collector since 1758 whose seeming disdain for his own job made him popular with all but the closest friends of government. But in a step that moved the town committee far beyond its typical preoccupations, Boston decided to transmit formal detailed instructions to its representatives in the House. Instructions were not new but usually encompassed only single issues; these new instructions were intended to be comprehensive, moving beyond reimbursement for municipal projects to more general, philosophical issues. This idea's genesis probably occurred in the mind of Sam Adams, and he maintained control of the resulting committee. Adams's father had been a Lank Bank director, and the young Sam Adams grew up in a house torn asunder by the Land Bank fiasco. Perhaps more than anyone else, Adams was raised in a house deeply affected by Parliamentary superiority and legislative absolutism. Though Jemmy was not an official member of the instructions committee, nor was any Boston representative, he had input into the finished product because of his status as a leading member of the Boston bench. The Boston bench likely had significant input into this committee's work, but their official absence from the committee was designed to affect a document that was to convey the town's objective opinion and could be employed as leverage in the General Court; Boston's representatives in the House could now demonstrate that the province's largest town and most significant revenue producer had taken a unified position. In a sign that indicated that Otis and Adams knew the instructions might be considered controversial, the town records of the May 15 meeting mention no specifics, only alluding to the "Instructions" in a few vague lines. Concurrently, Otis was working on a major pamphlet, and the Boston instructions reflected many of the concerns in the pamphlet, which would be published two months later.

The instructions were submitted to the adjourned meeting at 3pm, May 24, 1764 and reflect a noticeable break in town meetings records that had for years declined to produce grand statements. The instructions's first and primary concern is preserving "the invaluable Rights and Privileges of the Province ...; As well as those Rights which are derived to us by the Royal Charter, as those which being prior to it, and independent on it, we hold essentially as Freeborn Subjects of Gt. Britain." The critical distinction between rights "derived to us by the Royal Charter" and innate rights of "Freeborn Subjects" was fundamental to Jemmy's philosophy. The concept seems clumsily inserted into a basically Adams-produced document, which raises the possibility that it was a statement Otis authored and requested be included; further, it reflects the arguments that Otis was developing at that time. Listed next in the instructions, the Boston representatives were to "preserve that independence in the House of Representatives, which characterizes a Free People" by enacting an equivalent to the English "Place Act" that prevents judges from holding seats in the General Court. This was a variation of the oft repeated Otis-Thacher issue of plural office-holding and was essentially a re-vote on a measure that Otis had introduced to the House in early 1762. Tellingly, the issue of "independence" is raised with reference to the legislature; fundamentally, this would be the issue that propelled the colonies to independence.

The instructions then address public morals, stressing that the legislature should be greatly concerned with "Publick Happiness." The instructions then assert a position on public debt:

> You will remember that this Province has been at very great Expence in carrying on the late Warr, and that it still ly under a very grievous burden of Debt, you will therefore use your utmost endeavor to promote Publick frugaility as one Means to lessen the Publick Debt ...

The Boston representatives were further directed to minimize government expenditures in order to reduce debt. Regarding regulations, the Boston bench was told that they should "make it the Object of your attention to support our Commerce." Then the instructions confront the looming Sugar Act. The instructions committee conveyed its "surprize" that the lobbyist's "early notice" of new taxes had not produced a special session of the General Court and strongly recommended the representatives issue "a proper Representation" to Whitehall protesting the Act; this was a direct attack on Court Party leadership in the House and Council and a somewhat deceptive defense of Mauduit. The instructions ended with a characteristic Adams conclusion:

> But what hightens our Apprehensions is that those unexpected proceedings may be preparitory to new Taxations upon us; For if our Trade may be taxed why not our Lands? Why not the produce of our Lands and every Thing we possess or make use of? ... If these Taxes are laid upon us in shape without a Legal Representation where they are laid, are we not reduced from the Character of Free Subjects to the miserable state of Tributary Slaves.

After much debate, the instructions were ratified, and the Boston representatives left the smallpox ridden city and arrived at Concord for the opening of the General Court on May 30. The House elected the moderate friend of government Samuel White of Taunton as speaker, promoted Royall Tyler to "the Council board," and replaced his Boston bench seat with Thomas Gray.

Jasper Mauduit sent several official letters – five alone in March – to the General Court that required reading and deliberation. On June 1, the House appointed a committee consisting of Speaker White, Jemmy Otis, Thomas Cushing, Oxenbridge Thacher, John Worthington, Timothy Ruggles, and Judge Chambers Russell. Just a week later on June 8, the House Journal reports unusual activity:

> The Rights of the British Colonies in general, and the Province of the Massachusetts-Bay in particular, briefly stated, with Observations on the Act of the sixth of George the Second, called the Sugar Act. Read.

Just four days later, this "Rights of the British Colonies" was again officially read and then referred to the committee dealing with Mauduit's communications. The following day, the committee proposed a draft of a dispatch to Mauduit before the House; the House swiftly approved it. The dispatch to Mauduit angrily criticized him for granting that Parliament had the authority to levy any such taxes, tolerating Grenville's hollow gestures of friendship, and believing Grenville's professed interest "to consult the Ease, the Quiet, and the Goodwill of the Colonies." The House admitted that in practice Mauduit had sent warnings of the new tax plans, but in theory Mauduit had failed to understand or promote the province's principles. To help him better understand the province's principles, the dispatch concluded with: "Inclosed, you will have a brief State of the Rights of the Colonies, drawn by one of our Members, which you are to make the best use of in your power."

It was rare that a province's agent would be so harshly rebuked, particularly by his own employers. The Court Party was doubtless required to take such a firm position because as a majority in both the House and the Council, they were viewed as having botched the issue. And the Popular Party could admonish one of the Black Regiment members precisely because the Massachusetts Black Regiment, as characterized by Mayhew and Chauncy, were no less politically radical than Otis and equally fierce defenders of New England's political independence as they were of its religious independence, as evidenced by Mauduit sending Mayhew a collection of political radical Algernon Sidney's works; Sidney had written "... as death is the greatest evil that can befall a person, monarchy is the worst evil that can befall a nation," and, when sentenced to death for treason, declared that "We live in an age that makes truth pass for treason."

The document included in the dispatch to Mauduit was a version of the longer pamphlet Jemmy had nearly finished composing; that the House took the highly unusual decision of adopting and transmitting a political pamphlet to the province's agent as an official communication demonstrates how far that body had philosophically moved since Otis's rebuke of Bernard just two years earlier in which his comparison of King George to "Lewis" had so horrified Bostonians. Perhaps the House was moving toward a radical position out of conviction, or perhaps it was out of fear, or panic, or a feeling of helplessness in the face of Parliamentary absolutism. The Land Bank debacle had not been forgotten. Regardless of the reason, the Popular Party members in the House were in a fighting mood, and the Court Party members were under intense pressure from the merchants. The seeds that Otis had been planting for almost four years were starting to germinate, and almost certainly, the House's increasing radicalism reflected the general temperament of the province.

But the House was not satisfied with simply commanding their lobbyist to fight Whitehall; the House knew its options were limited to attempting to influence acts of Parliament, so they created a new option. The confederacy that Bernard so feared would form around Jemmy in Boston was now to be spread throughout the colonies; the House appointed Otis, Thacher, Cushing, Edward Sheafe, and Thomas Gray – the entire Boston Bench plus one – to a committee to write "to the other Governments to acquaint them with the Instructions ... and to the Agent of this Province, directing him to use his Endeavors to obtain a Repeal of the Sugar Act, and to exert himself to prevent a Stamp-Act or any other imposition." Per normal operating procedure, the Council invited the House to create a joint committee to draft Mauduit's instructions; though controlled by the Court Party, the House rejected the invitation. The practical limitations of plural office-holding benefitted the Boston bench as Hutchinson and the other Superior Court Justices then left the session early to hold their court term in York. With this core of oligarchic strength absent, Jemmy Otis could, and did, force his measures through the Assembly; the Popular Party was determined not just to alert their lobbyist to the *State of the Rights of the Colonies* but to incite other colonies. Governor Bernard was somewhat alarmed by the activities of this swiftly formed and radical interim committee and its communications with "other Governments." He had a vague premonition that it would "lay a foundation for connecting the demagogues of the several governments in America to join together in opposition to all orders from Great Britain." And for once, Bernard was prescient.

Fueled by the belief that too little had been done in the 1763-64 sessions, the House was aggressively and decisively communicating with their lobbyist in London. Ironically, one of Mauduit's few defenders was oligarch Hutchinson, who was troubled by "the most injudicious conduct" of the House in communicating so directly with the agent; Hutchinson firmly believed that protocol was principle and, in reality, he was protecting the Court Party's reputation as best he could. While Hutchinson was concerned with procedure and reputation, an invigorated Otis and his correspondence committee worked rapidly, sending letters to the other colonial assemblies by June 25. With the Court Party rendered impotent by the appearance of incompetence or apathy, Jemmy Otis and the Popular Party implemented plans with unbridled alacrity. On June 25, 1764 a letter written by Otis and sent to the Rhode Island Assembly called for "the united assistance of the several colonies in a petition against such formidable attacks upon ... the inseperable rights of British subjects."

Concurrent with these developments, Jemmy wrote his father a letter that in part said, "The new Act is come over which continues ye old one till Septr ... the time is come which we have long foreseen. I blame the people in England not half so much as I do our own. If we must be slaves I am only sorry tis to a pack of Villains among ourselves." It was probably quite obvious to both father and son that the list of members of the "pack of villains" was ambiguous; it certainly included Hutchinson, the Olivers, and Bernard, and probably included nearly all of the Council and the Supreme Court, but did it include that holder of so many offices, wealthy landowner and merchant, and Council member Colonel James Otis, Senior? The letter is vague enough to include the possibility that Jemmy was including his own father as one of the slavemasters. The reference to "the time is come which we have long foreseen" divulges the conclusion of the radicals in the Popular Party; a significant shift in the relationship between the people and the oligarchs had taken place, the battle lines were drawn, and the precipice that demarks periods in history was in view. "The time is come" to chamber Jemmy's academic philosophy into a powerful weapon with a hairpin trigger – that weapon would be the people.

Further suggesting that Otis intended this letter to implicitly include his father in the "pack of villains" are his apparent apathy to the looming stamp duties and his failure to disclose the explosive pamphlet that Otis was presently printing at Edes and Gill's press. Otis's omission of any discussion regarding the Stamp Act is striking because Otis was very aware of the Stamp Act preparations as his committee in the House had been considering Mauduit's letter of March 13, 1764. In a remarkable exhibition of ignorance of the House's anxieties, Mauduit had written:

> The Stamp duty you will see [the Whately resolves] is deferr'd till next Year. I mean the actual laying it: Mr Grenville being willing to give to the Provinces their option to raise that or some equivilant tax, Desirous as he express'd himself to consult the Ease, the Quiet, and the Goodwill of the Colonies.

Of course, this letter was addressed to Speaker Ruggles, a dogged Court Party advocate, and it likely infuriated Jemmy. Grenville's position as expressed by Mauduit was a condescending trinket of political subterfuge. As Jemmy viewed it, the "option" was a transparent deceit transmitted through a dupe to mollify the Boston bench into inaction. Thus it's clear by the omissions in Jemmy's June 1764 letter to his father that Jemmy did not compose this letter to discuss the news of the day or impending political issues; rather, the letter was an implicit indictment of his father and, perhaps, a warning that sides were being drawn, and it appeared that the Colonel was on the side of the oligarchy. Importantly, this letter shows that Otis was practically alone in 1764 in the belief that a conspiracy to suppress colonial rights and tax colonial revenues was afoot at Whitehall. The letter is ambiguous on many other matters; the tone suggests tepid resignation at first, then bitterness towards the oligarchy and the customs establishment, and lastly disgust toward the conspiring "ministry."

By late spring 1764, the absolutism of Parliament was about to be manifested again, the merchants were panicking, the House felt helpless, and the people seemed more willing than ever to entertain radical arguments. Under these circumstances, Jemmy began to write. On July 2, 1764 the *Gazette* carried an announcement: "Now in Press And Speedily will be published; The Rights of the British Colonies Asserted and Proved. By James Otis, Esq." Three weeks later the same paper announced that the pamphlet was for sale "This Day" at a price of "one Pistareen & Half," and thus was born the revolutionary philosophy whose lineage can be traced through every major revolutionary document, right up to the Declaration of Independence. Political pamphlets were not new, but Otis's *The Rights of the British Colonies, Asserted and Proved* is typically viewed as the first pamphlet of a long series of radical pamphlets that culminated in the Revolutionary War, and it is the first pamphlet to coalesce the possible responses to the new sugar tax into a unified, philosophically sound position. Its eighty pages contained the seeds of American revolutionary ideology: the people as the sole absolute power, the fiduciary nature of government, natural "inseperable" rights, equality created by nature, consent. It is a disjointed and hurried production, but these characteristics were common in the pamphlet genre as most pamphlets, and especially this one, were produced quickly in order to address current events. For nearly a year, the politicians of Massachusetts could produce no majority response to present to Whitehall either through their lobbyist or by special agent. *The Rights of the British Colonies* would provide the argument required to fight the power of Whitehall.

Jemmy probably began writing the actual pamphlet in May, though it was largely composed from pieces written over the previous year. Despite the grueling pace of work in the House during the first two weeks of June, Jemmy completed *Rights of the British Colonies* within six weeks, thus revealing that much of it was likely written extemporaneously. The work is divided into four "chapters" and an appendix. The fourteen page appendix consists of the Boston town meeting's instructions of May 24, 1764, and the "Substance of a Memorial presented to the House," which is the Otis statement as officially read to the House on June 8 and 12. This "memorial" outlines much of *Rights* but emphasizes arguments that would have a practical political effect – increasing merchant support. The first three chapters of *Rights* reflect a calm, scholarly approach that suggest they were first drafted long before the hurricane of activity in June. It's impossible to determine when this period of academic reflection might have occurred, but the March 1763 *Gazette* advertisement for three Otis pamphlets indicate that he was working on pamphlets 16 months earlier. The last of these March 1763 pamphlets, "The present political State of the Province of the Massachusetts Bay ... and a State of the Rights of the Colonists in general," may have provided the foundation of *Rights*.

The Rights of the British Colonies begins with a summation and analysis of contemporary theories regarding the basis of government authority and then proceeds to a meticulous and documented application of these theories to the much revered Glorious Revolution of 1688. Much of Jemmy's analysis referenced the works of early 17th century philosopher Hugo Grotius and late 17th century philosopher Samuel Pufendorf. Among Pufendorf's most significant works is a commentary and revision of Grotius's philosophy. In addition to being a proponent of theories of natural law, Grotius was also a proponent of Jacobus Arminius's theology; Grotius was 26 years old when his fellow Dutchman Arminius died and would develop and promote Arminius's heretical philosophy. Arminianism, as it was aptly called, confirmed the Calvinistic concept of preordination, but argued that God had preordained all souls, and salvation was at that point wholly determined by the will of the individual. This profoundly realigned the drama of salvation, for with Arminianism, the actor was not God but the individual. Grotius, Pufendorf and others discovered and developed an obvious and powerful relationship between the Arminian concept of salvation and an individual's natural rights; if it was an individual right to reject God, preordained or not, then such an individual could certainly reject anything less than God. Grotius was asked by the States of Holland to issue an edict in which he additionally argued that a government's purpose was limited to maintaining basic civil order; everything else should be left to the individual's conscience and effort. Grotius, along with his primary political supporter, Dutch statesman Johan Oldenbarnevelt, were arrested. Oldenbarnevelt was sentenced to death and Grotius to life in prison. After serving three years, Grotius escaped prison hidden in a large book chest, which cemented his reputation as a leader in the cause of individual rights. In Grotius and Pufendorf, Jemmy would find a highly combustible combination of natural law theory and Arminianism, which placed salvation squarely on the will of the person, not on decrees from God. Arminianism inverted the salvation hierarchy, making God the foundation and the will of the individual the apex. Salvation was not by works or grace but by will alone. Arminianism would spread rapidly in the colonies and, with a substantial contribution by John Wesley, became the dominant theological system of the United States by the 19th century.

After the review of Grotius and Pufendorf, Jemmy analyzes colonial rights and reviews the ways in which contemporary theories apply to the British North American colonies. This part challenges the reader with examples, allusions, and wit that is encyclopedic in its review of contemporary political thought. The essential contention – that the people are the absolute sovereign power and the authority of the government is primarily fiduciary – derives from John Locke. But Jemmy is unsatisfied with much of Locke, surprisingly considering him not radical enough to establish fundamental universal freedom; for that Jemmy looks to the Swiss legal scholar Emmerich de Vattel's 1758 *The Law of Nations or the Principles of Natural Law* – a copy of which would eventually land in the hands of George Washington. Otis used *Law of Nations* to substantially modify Locke's theories. In determining the "origins of government," Jemmy rejected Locke's theory of the social contract as the legitimating origin of social organization just as he dismissed "Grace" and "mere brutal power." Jemmy objected to the social contract theory for several reasons; first, it was impossible to define the parties to the contract, particularly parties who could not legally enter into contracts and parties of future generations who could be bound without consent to such contracts. Most importantly and uniquely, Jemmy dismissed Locke's focus on property rights as both a foundation and end for government as "playing with words." Otis rejected all efforts to legitimize a person's status or ability to participate in governance based on property; the entire notion that property ownership affected one's rights was the essence of the feudal system that Otis sought to raze.

In *Rights,* Otis agrees with James Harrington's "divine writings" – referring to his 1656 *Oceana* – that "Empire follows the balance of Property" though "the possessor of it may not have much more wit than a mole or a musquash." Here, Otis observes that property ownership – that is, wealth – does not require intelligence, so it is not inherently reasonable to bestow rights based on property. While property should not confer rights or imply virtue, a degree of fluidity maintaining a balance of property is necessary to establish a just government. In Vattel, Otis found the answer to the question of government's origin: "Such is man's nature that he is not sufficient unto himself ... since nature has constituted men thus, it is clear proof that it means them to live together." Jemmy then concluded that government's foundation and thus authority for operating was derived from "the unchangeable will of God, the author of nature." God, or nature, makes it "necessary that what we call matter should gravitate" and that the "different sexes should sweetly attract each other, for societies of single families." Thus societies form because of the nature of humans, which Jemmy summarizes as "Government is therefore more evidently founded on the necessities of our nature." Jemmy made an important distinction between social contracts and constitutions; he rejected the social contract as determinative to civil society and the formation of "simple democracy," but he pointedly supported the existence of constitutions – the "express compact" – to define the relationship between people and their government and delineate the scope of the government's power, particularly when it came to the problem of establishing the "two great powers of Legislation and Execution." Thus he considered the Convention Parliament of 1689 to be an express compact and attestation that the "community" is the "supreme power." In all cases, property and its ownership was removed from the equation.

Otis leveled new charges when addressing the "Colonies in general" and claimed that "Even the English writers and lawyers, have either intirely wav'd any consideration of the nature of Colonies, or very lightly touched upon it." This was largely true; the apologists of mercantilism had positioned colonies in subordinate relationships without seriously considering the legal and constitutional ramifications of such subordination. After criticizing those who considered the American colonies to be "little insignificant conquered islands," Otis offered his own definition: "A plantation or colony, is a settlement of subjects, in a territory disjoined or remote from mother country, and may be made by private adventurers or the public; but in both cases the Colonists are entitled to as ample rights, liberties and priviledges as the subjects of the mother country are, and in some respects *to more*." Otis's contention that colonies are entitled to certain rights not enjoyed by subjects in England was unique, and he had made a similar assertion earlier with respect to writs of assistance.

Jemmy then asserted that colonists have all the natural rights of anyone, stating that "The Colonists are by the law of nature free born ... as indeed all men are." In exhibiting his elasticity of mind that John Adams previously described, Jemmy followed this reasoning to the end – "white or black." And then Otis issued a statement on racial equality that borrowed from but improved on Montesquieu:

> Does it follow that tis right to enslave a man because he is black? Will short curl'd hair like wool, of christian hair, as tis called by those, hearts are as hard as the nether millstone, help the argument? Can any logical inference in favour of slavery, be drawn from a flat nose, a long or a short face.

The "law of nature" made all people free, and no law and no Parliament could change that; Otis's refutation of Parliamentary absolutism was thorough. No government, regardless of how or why it was constituted, could contravene the law of nature. The digression began by attacking first the slave trade and then the West Indian planters who flourished on it:

> Is it to be wondered at, if, when people of the stamp of a Creolian planter get into power, they will not stick for a little present gain, at making their own posterity, white as well as black, worse slaves if possible than those already mentioned.

Otis realized, as Jefferson later would, that a true break with the feudal past necessitated a break with systemic servitude. Translating that lofty philosophical conclusion into reality proved far more difficult than arriving at the conclusion and Boston rebels such as John Adams who lived to witness that break with feudalism held their own fiery radicalism in check on the subject of slavery in order to maintain a unified country. Adams, after all, had been good friends with slave owners; it's doubtful that Jemmy Otis would have held his tongue or quieted his pen on the subject had he lived beyond the creation of the Constitution. It's also doubtful Otis would have concluded that a United States with slaves would have been preferable to a separate New England with none. *The Rights of the British Colonies* was revolutionary because it entirely rejected the conception of the world as hierarchically ordered. And while Otis would follow every argument to its logical conclusion, his conclusions were often beyond the grasp of the year he published them; the colonial deferential relationship was a violation of nature, but it would be years before most agreed. Slavery was a violation of nature as argued by Otis in 1764, and yet even Jemmy couldn't bring himself to free his slave boy. His mind was working far ahead of the times and far beyond what was practicable in 1764.

The last chapter of the pamphlet is 34 pages, and its distinct change in style reveals it to have been hastily written, at times deteriorating into cryptic notes as the production of a mind so choked with ideas that they raced from his pen to breathe upon the page. The words raced to critique Thomas Pownall's *The Administration of the Colonies* that had just arrived from London. Crouching amongst the usual verbiage of criticism are explosive ideas. After praising the establishment of English liberties in 1689 – a "deliverance under God" – he makes a bold declaration of parliamentary power:

> All of them [the colonies] are subject to and dependent on Great-Britain; and that therefore as over subordinate governments, the parliament of Great-Britain has the undoubted power and lawful authority to make acts for the general good.

Jemmy knew that a concession of parliamentary power would be condemned by his fellow radicals, so he reasons that "'tis from and under this very power and its acts, and from the common law, that the political and civil rights of the Colonists are derived." He then heaps sacrilege upon apostasy by minimizing the importance of the colonial charters. These statements must have alarmed his Popular Party constituents, but, of course, he was setting up the reader for an even more audacious argument: it would be of no consequence if every colonial charter were extinguished because not "one of essential, natural, civil, or religious rights of the Colonists" would be impacted in the slightest for the same reason that no government could enslave a person. Fundamental rights are derived from God, not from any government or act of government or charter. Jemmy did not discard the importance of the charters as they were guarantees of special privileges, but they were prone to "annihilation" unlike "immutable natural" rights. Disparaging the charters actually established a position of parity with the mother country; the colonies were not dependant on Parliament for their rights, and the charters only established special rights, not basic rights. As such, the charters established extra rights for the colonists, as they already had the same basic rights as the inhabitants of England. The point was made by a quote from the *Aeneid* that Otis placed on the title page of the pamphlet, printed directly below the title: "et foederis aequas Dicamus leges, sociosque in regna vocemus" – *let us create an equal compact and let us invite them as partners to our government*. But given that colonial relationships in the 18th century were understood to be fundamentally subordinate, Otis was, perhaps somewhat inadvertently, arguing for colonial freedom. It was simply inconceivable that a colony could be considered equal to its mother country.

But Otis, while still maintaining his patriotism, argued that not only was a subordinate relationship undesirable, it was against God and nature. The European conception of the universe as hierarchically ordered was feudal in origin and thoroughly accepted in the 18th century; Otis aggressively rejected this conception on every level from race relations to empire organization. No piece of paper established a man's freedom, and the absence of that paper did not enslave him.

Repeating the charge made in his letter to his father, Jemmy criticized "a set of men" in the colonies that was subverting the colonists' natural rights and attempting to enforce hierarchies. The obvious reference is to Hutchinson, the Olivers, and the other members of the Boston oligarchy, but Otis was also likely referring to oligarchy in the colonies in general, as there were concurrent attempts to vacate the charters of Rhode Island and Pennsylvania and to put the administration of those colonies under the rule of appointed oligarchies.

Adopting the list from Locke's *Second Treatise of Government,* Jemmy then delineates the features of legislative power with respect to the colonies. But in his continuing efforts to modify Locke, Otis added a crucial amendment. Otis augmented Locke's declaration that the "legislative ... is unalterable in the hands where the community have once placed it" with "nor can a subordinate legislative [be] taken away without forfeiture or other good cause." Locke addresses the term "subordinate" but writes only "Of other ministerial and subordinate powers in a commonwealth we need not speak." In contrast to Locke, Otis sought to establish elected colonial assemblies on a solid theoretical foundation within the British Empire. Otis begins with the thesis that a subject has a natural right to representation in a legislative body. If a colonial legislative body was nullified by loss of or changes to its charter, then those colonists were entitled to representation in Parliament, though "it would be better if they had both." Otis supported direct colonial representation in Parliament as "a thousand advantages would result from it," and one of the primary advantages was that the system of "scandalous memorials ... privately cooked up ... and sent to the several boards" would be negated by official representation. Colonial representation in Parliament would also counteract the "vagabond stroller, that has run or rid post thro' America," referring generally to lobbyists and specifically to Benjamin Franklin. Otis had little tolerance for Franklin because of the latter's activities against the Pennsylvania charter. Franklin had spent most of the 1760s in London attempting to convert

Pennsylvania's government to a royal charter; he would soon support the Stamp Act and continue to lobby for a royal appointment up to 1771. The men of principle in Boston, including Otis and John Adams, went to their graves never forgiving Franklin for his backdoor treachery. Further, Franklin was a slave owner and though in theory he opposed slavery, in practice he never mobilized his tremendous reputation against the peculiar institution. Bostonians such as Otis viewed Franklin as a man whose first principle was himself and whose primary means of promoting that principle was by promoting the oligarchy through creating a royal government in Pennsylvania. More broadly, Otis had little tolerance for the myriad avenues of lobbying that layers of bureaucracy and indirect representation yielded.

Jemmy's view of the correlation between supreme and subordinate legislative bodies was developed from Lord Coke's views on the status of Ireland, which Otis considered to be a somewhat reasonable compromise and at least an improvement over the current situation. Ireland had its own parliament, yet was subordinate to the parliament of England. Otis argued that the colonies should, at minimum, enjoy the same status as conquered Ireland. This led Otis back to the lodestar of his revolutionary philosophy:

> To say the parliament is absolute and arbitrary, is a contradiction. The parliament cannot make 2 and 2, 5; ... Should an act of parliament be against any of his [God's] natural laws, which are immutably true, their declaration would be contrary to eternal truth, equity and justice, and consequently void.

Otis concluded that in such an event parliament would repeal "an act against any of his natural laws," but then he added that in the past "When such mistake is evident and palpable ... the judges of the executive courts declared the act 'of a whole parliament void.'" For Jemmy, this process of checks and balances was "the grandeur of the British constitution." The pointed irony of exhibiting this "grandeur" was that Parliament of the 18th century was neither checked nor balanced by any force external to Parliament as it had been previously; such "grandeur" existed prior to the establishment of parliamentary absolutism. Thus the system Jemmy described that combined the Convention Parliament of 1689, which placed government's authority in the hands of the people, with a parliament that cannot be "absolute and arbitrary" because of checks and balances was a system that existed nowhere save for in his own mind.

Otis then addressed Pownall's apprehension over colonial independence, the hazards of a regular army operating far from its civil leaders, colonial judges's purported ignorance, the salaries of colonial governors, the constant battle for jurisdiction between the common law courts and the admiralty courts, and the enormous expenses incurred by the northern colonies during the Seven Years War. He eventually arrives at the core issue: the constitutionality of the Sugar Act. Otis differentiated between the regulation and prohibition of trade and taxing it, the former foolish but constitutional, the latter foolish and unconstitutional. But markedly unlike his fellow political thinkers, Otis could not logically distinguish between internal and external taxes. Any tax on foreign trade is discriminatory, and so it may be constitutionally valid but morally unacceptable. In other words, the distinction is nothing more than circular reasoning: "Yet if taxes are laid on either, without consent, they cannot be said to be free. This barrier of liberty being once broken all is lost. If a shilling in the pound may be taken from me against my will, why may not twenty shillings; and if so, why not my liberty or life?" In the final analysis, all nonconsensual taxes were coerced payments, and it mattered not if parliament had the power, for if the taxes were coerced, that had not the right.

For Otis, the source of just action was consent; the exact nature of the action was irrelevant because if it was taken without consent, it was invalid regardless of its structure. John Marshall would later echo the idea in *McCulloch v. Maryland* when he wrote "the power to tax involves the power to destroy," but Otis, and Samuel Adams in his instructions on the same point, transformed this conclusion into an energizing political slogan: "No taxation without representation." The slogan did not differentiate between internal and external taxes. While for a majority of colonials, the "without representation" existed precisely because they could not be represented, Otis, in 1764 disagreed, writing, "When the parliament shall think fit to allow colonists a representation in the house of commons, the equity of their taxing the colonies, will be as clear as their power is at present of doing it without, if they please." The only logical solution to justify parliamentary taxation of the colonies was colonial representation in parliament.

In developing this proposal of colonial representation, Otis quoted from Jeremiah Dummer's rather famous 1721 book defending the colonial charters: "The legislative power is absolute and unaccountable, and King, lords and commons, may do what they please; but the question here is not about power, but right. ..." Dummer had been the Massachusetts agent and brother of the acting Massachusetts governor; Otis expanded Dummer's statement: the question concerns not only rights but also the source of those rights. For Otis, only nature, and therefore God, bestowed those rights; they were neither granted from nor could be taken by any human, elected or otherwise.

In a "sum of my argument" section, Otis offered a final summation of his most salient point:

> That this constitution is the most free one, and by far the best, now existing on earth: That by this constitution, every man in the dominion is a free man: That no parts of his Majesty's dominions can be taxed without their consent: That every part has a right to be represented in the supreme or some subordinate legislature: That the refusal of this, would seem to be a contradiction in practice to the theory of the constitution: That the colonies are subordinate dominions, and are now in such a state, as to make it best for the good of the whole, that they should not only be continued in the enjoyment of subordinate legislation, but be also represented in some proportion to their number and estates, in the grand legislature of the nation.

Court Party advocates and friends of government argued repeatedly that the colonists were represented in Parliament; the slogan "no taxation without representation" made no sense to them because the colonists in many cases, and certainly in the case of Massachusetts, directly elected their House Representatives, and it was the House that originated the majority of revenue bills. Further, everyone in the empire was represented virtually in Parliament; as had been frequently indicated by the friends of government, a great many people did not or could not vote, and yet Parliament represented everyone. In fact, the friends of government argued that this was superior to the "actual representation" that a few agitators desired because "actual representation" would result in a House of Commons that was full of nothing more than sectarian lobbyists attempting to drag back to their districts the largest pieces of government pork they could secure. As Parliament was then constituted, the members voted for whatever was best for the country as a whole, not for any particular faction.

Opponents of virtual representation not only rejected anything other than direct representation, but also typically rejected representation in Parliament because it wasn't local; as Otis put it, the members of Parliament were as far removed from New England as the savages of California; true representation must be done locally. And in every case, "representation" explicitly entailed consent; opponents of virtual representation often used the terms "representation" and "consent" interchangeably, meaning that they opposed representation without consent. Representative democracy, as envisioned by the Popular Party, entailed consent in its most literal and direct application. Virtual representation could not entail consent, and representation in distant London, even actual representation, was perverted by a lack of direct consent. For this reason, it wasn't unusual for local men to provide their local representatives with specific instructions on how to approach and vote on matters that were likely to come before the House.

And for Otis, it was irrelevant whether Parliament was absolute or not; this is why he often baffled his friends and enemies alike by sometimes disregarding the question of Parliament's power. Since the middle ages, English law and the constitution affirmed that taxation could only occur via the consent of elected representatives in the Commons. So for Otis, no degree of authority permits a government to tax without consent. Thus Otis could concede the issue of Parliamentary authority if it quelled the anger of the Court Party because, he would argue, Parliament was still obligated to obtain the consent of the taxed. On this, the Popular Party agreed; disagreement within the Popular Party existed over whether representation in Parliament, if even possible, was a solution. And yet if the colonists demanded consent, then representation in parliament was the only solution if they wished to remain within the British Empire. It's impossible to know what Jemmy thought on this subject other than his published writings, but he may have known at that time that such a solution was impossible for Parliament to accept, and yet the act of offering it put the onus directly on the Empire, and it would soon respond forcefully.

While it is unknown how many copies of the remarkable *Rights of the British Colonies* were printed at the time, it was dispatched to London the same day it appeared in Boston and was reprinted in England several times before the end of 1764. It was widely read by important government officials, many of whom praised or condemned it depending on their political persuasion. Joseph Harrison, a future Boston customs officer, wrote from London to John Temple, the Surveyor General of Customs in Boston, that "Mr Otis's Rights of the British Colonies has been reprinted here and I am told it gives great offence to the Ministry." The pamphlet was referenced in several Parliamentary discussions, and Lord Lyttelton and Lord Mansfield debated its import and impact in the House of Lords. Lord Lyttelton noted that "The Americans themselves make no distinction between external and internal taxes. Mr. Otis their champion scouts such a distinction," and Lord Mansfield observed that "Otis is a man of consequence among the people there" and though *Rights* "be called silly and mad, but mad people, or persons have entertained silly and mad ideas, have led people to rebellion, and overturned empires." Arthur Savage, a young Bostonian in London, reported that "opinions seem verry various in respect to Mr Otis jr. Some say it ought to be wrote in Letters of Gold – others think it is a Clam'rous Ill judg'd thing." Several London periodicals published essays about the pamphlet, and the *Critical Review* printed a lengthy assessment in its 1764 volume XVIII edition. The *Review* warned Otis against sowing the seeds of enmity in English towns that have no direct Parliamentary representation such as Birmingham, Halifax, Leeds and Sheffield. The *Review* then snidely remarks:

> We applaud Mr. Otis's zeal and should be glad that he had published a scheme of reciprocal independence between our colonies and Great Britain, which may be done in the way of a debtor and creditor, and which very possibly might awaken him and his vigorous friends from their visionary dreams of independency upon their mother country. There is nothing like a fair counter-reckoning, good Mr. Otis.

For some in England, it was clear by 1764 that Otis's political philosophy inevitably leads to independence, but the *Review* suggested that perhaps Great Britain would desire independence because then the colonies would be liable for all its own debts. A December 1764 meeting of the Board of Trade officially examined *Rights* and concluded that the "Acts and Resolutions of the British Parliament were treated with indecent disrespect and principles of a dangerous nature and tendency adopted and avowed." A lack of deference was nearly as serious a charge as treason, for it sprang from the same source: disrespect for authority. The Board referred the pamphlet to the Privy Council, which concluded that the offending documents should be presented to Parliament for action if the King concluded they deserved a formal response from the Empire.

Governor Bernard feared the worst, particularly after the recent "paper war," and was impressed by the moderate nature of *Rights*, sending the pamphlet to London with a note observing that though "the writer is by nature violent & vehement in his principles, this piece appears to us more temperate & decent than was at first expected...." Lord Mansfield's and Governor Bernard's assessments reveal the growing distance between the local understanding of the radicals and London's distant understanding; Mansfield declared "The book is full of wildness" while Bernard sensed that the Popular Party was capable of much more unbridled behavior than a pamphlet demanding *rights* and *consent*. And yet Bernard's apparent insight that political pamphlets were reasonably acceptable and thus the Popular Party was becoming friendlier to government would prove to be his ruin. *The Rights of the British Colonies* was the first major attempt by a knowledgeable American who was on, or rather in, the scene to present a comprehensive radical colonial view. *Rights* provided the logic and language needed for colonists to express radical thought and developed the idea that *rights* and *consent* were not granted by governments but instilled by God. The seeds of rebellion had been planted.

Two other pamphlets were published in 1764: Connecticut Governor Thomas Fitch's *Reasons Why* and Oxenbridge Thacher's *Sentiments of a British American*. Until 1764, Connecticut had been largely neutral in the battle over *rights* in Boston because of its small rum industry and hence negligible exposure to sugar and molasses duties and to the confidence they had in their competent lobbyist Richard Jackson. Governor Fitch's *Reasons Why* was the product of a state committee and hence an official document and was produced in response to an increasing awareness that the impending stamp duties – in contrast to sugar taxes – would affect Connecticut as much as any other state. In defense of Connecticut's narrow interests, *Reasons Why* made the argument that Otis completely rejected – that there was a substantial legal difference between internal and external taxes; the sphere of Britain's legitimate interests ended at Connecticut's borders, and all taxes within the state must originate within the state. Of course, Connecticut did not have the major import/export economy that Rhode Island and Massachusetts had.

Thacher had clearly been speaking to Otis about their pamphlets. In *The Rights of the British Colonies*, Otis remarked that "materials are collecting" to exhibit the extent of Massachusetts's "burden" in protecting British interests. The *Oxenbridge Thacher Papers* of the Massachusetts Historical Society in Boston contains a compilation of rough drafts Thacher's handwriting that has never been published. And in writing *The Sentiments of a British American*, Thacher undeniably had Otis's *Rights* before him, the bulk of which he adopted as the foundation of his argument; only after summarizing Otis's work does Thacher proceed to examine the issue surround the Sugar Act's enforcement provisions with particular stress on the worrisome swelling of the jurisdiction of juryless vice-admiralty courts.

Jemmy's *Rights* was the most undeniably forceful among these early revolutionary pamphlets. He alone surveyed a board array of political theory and adopted what was useful and uniquely modified much of what he adopted; his origins of government was a remarkable philosophy that roundly rejected most usual theories, just as he'd denied Locke's reliance on property and the typical distinction between internal and external taxes. And the "elasticity" of mind inevitably led to places logic could not deny: slavery was a corruption of natural rights, and consent through direct representation was the only solution for the Empire. His prescient rebuke of slavery would be quoted in Parliamentary debate over the next few decades. And he concluded that direct representation would "firmly unite all parts of the British empire, in the greatest peace and prosperity; and render it invulnerable and perpetual." The obvious implication is that a lack of direct representation would divide the empire and render it vulnerable and temporary. His examination of hierarchy as a series of subordinate governments that begins at the zenith with God as the originator of natural law and progresses down to the most modest social and political groups – the authority of each limiting the prerogatives of its subordinates – was a mosaic of complex political, theosophical, and legal considerations but was also a more effective and ultimately damning avenue of criticism than the typical internal-external dichotomous account of government relationships. Otis's reliance on natural law, conception of a balance of powers, and vision of a hierarchy of subordinate governments was a direct forebear of the Constitutional debates of 1787 and a structural forerunner of a supreme parliament of the Britannic Empire and the federal structure of the United States. The great difficulty in *Rights* results from its vast absorption of what is and what was, the post Glorious Revolution legal system and the Convention Parliament and the pre-1687 power balances, and Lord Coke's writings. He adopted Coke's view of the courts's function as sentinels of the common law and common sense while concurrently approving the parliamentary supremacy of 1689. As such, Jemmy was not describing a system of authority that presently existed. He had brilliantly detailed the problems and solution but had not yet devised a peaceful method to advance from the former to the latter. The legislative branch was supreme, except that it could not contravene the citizens' rights. The legislative branch had the power to contravene these rights, but such power must be curtailed. In both cases, some kind of court protected the citizens' rights and limited the legislative branch's power but not such that the courts would be more powerful than the legislative. The solution was in a written constitution and a complex kind of federalism that would make changing that constitution possible but difficult, and a legislative that authored all laws watched over by a court that suspiciously guarded against infringements upon the written constitution. Otis essentially described the features of such a system without describing the system itself, which was difficult – perhaps impossible – to imagine within the imperial structure as it existed in 1764.

Composing and publishing *Rights* was not easy for Jemmy, but he felt compelled, declaring, "I have waited years in hopes to see some one friend of the colonies pleading in publick for them. I have waited in vain." He was torn between his brothers and father who all apparently aspired to the oligarchy; he had fought in the trenches of local politics and suffered repeated defeats at the hands of the Court Party; the specter of an omnipotent ministry loomed over the colonies. The lurking ethos of *Rights* is an abiding, unshakable melancholy. Regarding his motivations, Otis wrote:

> should any thing have escaped me, or hereafter fall from my pen, that bears the least aspect but that of obedience, duty and loyalty to the King & parliament, and the highest respect for the ministry, the candid will impute it to the agony of my heart, rather than to the pravity of my will. If I have one ambitious wish, 'tis to see Great-Britain at the head of the world, and to see my King, under God, the father of mankind. I pretend neither to the spirit of prophecy, nor any uncommon skill in predicting a Crisis, much less to tell when it begins to be "*nascent*" or is fairly midwiv'd into the world.

Jemmy is, above all, a loyal and thankful subject of the Empire expressing "the agony of my heart," who does not wish a "Crisis," and yet who writes with melancholy precisely because he realizes that what must be cannot be – colonial representation in Parliament.

Otis's pamphlet first traveled to England in the same packet as the manuscript of another pamphlet that addressed every point in *Rights*. This manuscript asserted the supremacy of parliament, asserted that "tender regard" for "all rights natural and acquired" must be preserved, claimed that those not represented cannot be taxed, declared that there was no difference between internal and external taxes, and it rejected virtual representation. It was written by Thomas Hutchinson. Hutchinson's manuscript responded to the colonists' complaints by demanding actual representation as a prerequisite for taxation and seeking protection for all colonial rights. The man at the helm of the oligarchy was no dictatorial thug or advocate for strictly hierarchical, tightly controlled regimes. In fact, Hutchinson seems like a reasonable, fairly progressive, avuncular advocate for his province's rights. That Jemmy Otis consistently rejected Hutchinson's position *en masse* evidences the fierce radicalism of Otis and his *Rights*.

CHAPTER VII

the Terror of Election

A few merchants and politicians in London and Boston fretted about growing colonial resistance to Grenville's plans and the theories contained in *The Rights of the British Colonies Asserted and Proved*, but for most colonists, 1764 wasn't markedly different from the previous year. As usual, smallpox was a constant threat. Smallpox localizes in the skin, mouth and throat and results in characteristic rashes and blisters. The mortality rate could be as high as 35%, but the more common result was facial scars, which occurred in as many as 85% of survivors. Children were particularly susceptible, and child mortality rates were as high as 80%. George Washington became infected with smallpox on a visit to Barbados in 1751. Almost immediately after becoming the College of New Jersey's president in February 16, 1758, famed preacher Jonathan Edwards became a strong supporter of small pox inoculations and publicized his own recent inoculation. He died of the inoculation a month later.

So it wasn't surprising when, in the spring of 1764 as smallpox lingered in Boston, Otis's children, Polly, Elizabeth and Jemmy, became seriously ill. And that same spring, on April 23, the Boston *Gazette* published an article in which Otis family physician, Dr. Samuel Gelston, accused William Greenleaf, Jr. of selling adulterated drugs to the Castle William inoculation hospital causing "loss of life." Obviously accusing someone of supplying the King's (and governor's) hospital with diluted or fraudulent medicines when people were dying of smallpox caused quite a public outcry. So while the debate about the rights and consent of the governed continued, the colonists dealt with the omnipresent smallpox threat. That spring was probably difficult for

Jemmy as it seems that all of his children contracted the highly infectious disease. Luckily, by the summer, his children's health seemed to be improving, but Jemmy's marriage to Ruth was not improving; she was a stalwart loyalist who disapproved of the rebel activities and openly opined on the virtues of the British Empire.

The General Court's 1764 summer recess left serious questions unanswered, but it gave time for Otis to return to his law practice. He wrote notes to his father about a bill for costs in a pending case and revealed a suspicion that his mail was being illicitly read. He had also expressed this suspicion to Thomas Cushing who, in turn, questioned Jasper Mauduit about the possibility in a letter dated September 12, 1763: "I can't learn Mr. Otis of late received any of your favors. He suspects his Letters have been intercepted." A pervasive fear of conspiracy permeated the air on both sides of the Atlantic. The Boston Superior Court's 1764 August term was a diversion from the simmering political wars, just as it had been the previous summer, and again young Josiah Quincy was writing everything down. In one slave case, Jemmy argued about the competency of an administrator to testify about the condition of a decedent's estate, and whether recovery of stolen property's value could apply to a slave. In another case, Jemmy argued that the clothes owned by a woman before marriage could not be ordered sold by a court to cover her husband's debts. Chief Justice Hutchinson refused to condone the seizure and dissented from the majority of the court, which had concluded that all of a woman's personal property was legally owned by her husband upon marriage. More interesting than Otis's arguments in these two cases are that they reveal a sense of justice that is decades ahead of his time, but these cases also reveal a fellow traveler on the road to progressive justice: Chief Justice Hutchinson. The opinions he wrote clearly demonstrate that opponents of his appointment were correct: he was certainly unfamiliar with procedural points of evidence and pleading. But he also exhibits a sense of fairness unlike many of the other justices, which leaves us with the irony of a man who Otis depicted in the press as a greedy "Leviathan" who enjoyed "keeping people poor" quickly agreeing with his tormentor that it was unjust for a wife to "go naked." Newspaper articles and pamphlets give the impression that Otis and Hutchinson were enemies in all regards, but they worked rather closely in the courts despite their political differences. Reflecting an attitude that borders on playful friendliness, Hutchinson wrote Ezra Stiles on July 4, 1764, "I have had too great a share myself in our publick affairs for 30 years past to think of publishing that part of our History. I threaten Mr. Otis sometimes that I will be revenged of him after I am dead." Hutchinson had previously joked that he took political positions in order to keep Jemmy busy. Despite being political adversaries, their personal interactions were usually friendly and professional, and there are glimmers of personal admiration between them.

Meanwhile, tension between the colonists and Whitehall was increasing. The looming Sugar Act was sobering but omens from England about impending stamp duties – in essence, a sales tax on a variety of goods – was inflaming ever greater anxiety. On January 21, 1764, Francis Fisher of Philadelphia received forewarning from London, "The manner propos'd for Raising it [American revenue], is by a Stamp Duty, which however equitable, deprives us of a Liberty which Pennsylvanians have always enjoy'd & hope will ever Contend for. ....." On February 17, 1764, Stephen Sayre warned Isaac Sears in New York that "you'll soon have a parcel of Marmadonian Ravens who will feed upon, and rip up your very Vitals; such as officers of Stamp duties, Prizies of Lands, Houses, Furniture, &c. The Ministry are determined to make you pay for the peace which you like so well." Two months later, Eliphalet Dyer enlightened Jared Ingersoll of Connecticut that "Mr. Greenville strongly urged, not only the power but right of Parliament to tax Colonies & hoped in God's name as his expression was that none would dare dispute their Sovreignty." Within the first few months of 1764, widespread discussions regarding the pervasive stamp taxes were occurring.

Meanwhile in England, Thomas Whately, Grenville's industrious secretary, was rapidly assembling data and drafting instructions for the Stamp Act. In August 1764 he sent classified surveys to Boston Surveyor of Customs John Temple and Jared Ingersoll in Connecticut requesting information and input for features of the Act. Publically, Grenville kept the colonial lobbyists and legislatures in check by suggesting that the tax could be avoided if the colonies could produce similar revenue by other means. In response to this suggestion, Boston merchants and their representatives called for action, and on August 17, 1764, the Boston members of the House requested that Governor Bernard quickly call the General Court into session. Jemmy and the Popular Party suspected that Grenville's suggestion was merely a ploy to buy time and quiescence, but they were determined to organize resistance to the tax and dispatch more protests to Mauduit before Parliament convened in November. Bernard and Hutchinson were perfectly aware of the Popular Party's plans and wished to prevent the ruthless protests that the Popular Party was likely to demand in a House session.

A Boston town meeting was held on August 16, 1764, and Jemmy was again moderator. The usual issues of grammar schools and land improvement were addressed, and in a bit of sharp irony Jemmy was appointed to lead a committee directing the construction of an insane asylum to be funded by a £600 gift from Thomas Hancock, John's uncle, who had recently died. The following year, with Jemmy again as moderator, the town appointed the committee to establish Hancocks Hospital for "unhappy Persons" who had been deprived "of their Reason," with Jemmy on another committee to raise additional funds.

Meanwhile, Bernard tried to delay while waiting for more information from London – nothing could be worse than what Jemmy and the Popular Party expected – and to allow Court Party members enough time to travel to Boston; he wanted to be sure that Court Party attendance was at its maximum at the opening of the session lest Jemmy ram through another incendiary memorial right when a quorum was reached. Popular Party members took their annoyance about the delay to the press, and the *Gazette* unleashed a series of articles criticizing the delay that Bernard claimed only served to "inflame the people." On August 27, 1764, "T.Q." – probably Oxenbridge Thacher – published an explanation of the new strict customs system that included a description of the employment of the Hovering Act as nothing short of harassing coastal shippers. In the same *Gazette* issue, "Shearjashub Squeezum" published an article with references to possible corruption in the Salem customs house that resulted in the dismissal of Cockle, the customs officer who likely verbally requested the writ of assistance in 1760, and Governor Bernard's entanglement in some questionable business. Another paper war was simmering. And with Jemmy's principles detailed in *Rights* juxtaposed with the questionable activities of Cockle and Bernard, some Court Party disciples such as James Bowdoin began to lose their faith in the government. Eventually, Bernard agreed to call the General Court into session by mid-October, and following a meeting with Popular Party members, Bernard took refuge on his beloved Mount Desert Island. The *Gazette* published a rebuke on September 3, chiding that Mount Desert "must be very valuable; for we cannot suppose that a <u>trifling</u> matter would induce his Excellency to leave or postpone the most <u>Important Affair That Perhaps Ever Came Before A General Assembly</u>."

If Bernard was determined to delay political solutions, then the Popular Party and the merchants would implement market-based solutions; by October 1764, serious organization began for a boycott of British luxury goods.

Criticism in the press continued with intimations of incompetence, secret negotiations, perfidy, and speculation about Bernard being recalled to London and replaced by lieutenant governor Hutchinson. When the new session of the General Court finally opened on October 18, the Boston bench of Jemmy Otis, Thacher, Cushing, and Gray sprang to action. The morning consisted of procedural matters that included a lecture on moderation from the governor – it was impossible to tell whether he was attempting to instruct or begging, regardless, no one in the Popular Party cared to listen. After the lecture, Governor Bernard retreated to Castle William thus leaving management of the Council to Hutchinson. The afternoon consisted of a series of debates, and the next day the House decided "that an Address be prepared and presented to His Majesty in Parliament upon the State of the Province," and the entire Boston bench, moderate Speaker White and six others were appointed to the drafting committee, but the committee was a ruse because Thacher and Otis had drafted the "Address" well before Bernard gave his lecture on moderation. Three days later the "Address" was read into the record, accepted, and sent to the Council for concurrence. Hutchinson was opposed to the stamp taxes for both practical and philosophical reasons, so he favored an "Address," but he concluded that the Thacher-Otis creation was too aggressive to have any hope of being presented to the House of Commons. Hutchinson shepherded a rejection through the Council that generated a joint session without result. So a large joint committee was created, and by November 1 the "Address to the King in Parliament" had been attenuated to a "Petition ... to the Honourable House of Commons." Even some of the radicals hoped that Hutchinson would have some insight into how to get heard in an organization steeped in traditions of deference. The final point of contention rested on a single word. Whereas the House insisted on asserting their "Rights," the Council urged employing the term "Priviledges" with reference to parliamentary taxation exemption. The Court Party was eager to affirm their "Priviledges," which were bestowed by a superior and recognized a deferential relationship. The House and Council finally agreed on the term "Liberties." The petition was sent to Jasper Mauduit, and Bernard suspended the session with the sense that he'd luckily evaded a worse fate.

Hutchinson had argued that the Massachusetts petition's modest tenor would facilitate its effectiveness in the corridors of power, particularly when compared to the tactless petitions from Rhode Island and New York. William Bayard delivered a copy of the New York petition to Boston; it tackled the "rights" versus "priviledges" predicament directly, proclaiming "They nobly disdain the thought of claiming that Exemption as a Privilege. – They found it on a Basis more honourable, solid and stable; they challenge it, and glory in it as their Right."

The Massachusetts Popular Party was distressed that they had been persuaded to refrain from asserting their "rights." But the Boston oligarchy was strong, the Court Party was in control of the House and Council, and there wasn't much the Popular Party could do. Thomas Cushing sent a secret letter to Jasper Mauduit on November 17, delivered personally by fellow member of the House Bela Lincoln; Lincoln's brother Ben would years later officially accept Cornwallis's surrender at Yorktown. In Cushing's secret letter of 1764, he explained that the House "were clearly for making an ample and full declaration of the exclusive Right of the People of the Colonies to tax themselves … but they could not prevail with the Councill." Cushing further explains the House's predicament:

> in short they were reduced to this alternative either to join with the Council in the Petition forwarded you by the Secretary or to petition by themselves & considering they had wrote you fully upon the matter of Rights ye last session & had sent you a small tract entituled, The Rights of the British Colonies in general & of the Province of the Massachusetts Bay in particular briefly stated, which they then desired & expected you woud make the best use of in your Power, they thought it ye less necessary to remonstrate by themselves at this time …

In other words, the House members either wrote of privileges or liberties or nothing at all, and considering that they had previously forwarded Otis's *Rights* pamphlet to Mauduit, they felt that he was fully aware of their true position.

Though Jemmy Otis had been a member of all the drafting committees, it is not possible to determine what part he played in the final draft, though he likely conceded to the House's conciliatory impulses after realizing that the Council had no interest in the initial Thacher-Otis draft. Further, Jemmy was laying plans for an assault far greater than a letter to Parliament, and thus proceeded cautiously in the fall of 1764. During the hiatus before the General Court's winter session, the Otis family network would grow increasingly complicated. Samuel Allyne, probably through the social efforts of his sister and business associations of his father, had been acquainted to the Harrison Gray family and developed a relationship with Elizabeth Gray, the province treasurer's daughter. On November 14, 1764, they publicized their intention to marry, and the wedding was held on December 31. In reply to Harrison Gray's wedding invitation the Colonel pleaded "the season of the year and the health of our family" in excusing Mary Otis's absence. He also intimated that Joseph's health was questionable, though the reference may have been to Joseph's wife, Rebecca Sturgis, who would die a little over a year later. While Colonel Otis was certainly pleased with this marriage, another connection to a member of the Boston oligarchy surely complicated Jemmy's life. On December 5, 1764, Samuel Allyne wrote one of his usual jaunty letters to his brother Joseph urging him to attend the wedding, but in addressing his own circumstances, he suggested something ominous was looming: "And tho I launch out with a pleasant gale, tho my streamers all aboard betoken of my present prosperity; I dare not exult, & feel something which checks & seems to tell me: Storms & tempests are consequent."

One of the commercial enterprises that boomed during the war years was government money contractors, essentially private bankers that received money from the Parliament and distributed it to the troops, keeping a 2.5% commission. In the 1750s, Charles Apthorp, his son Charles and his son-in-law Nathaniel Wheelwright operated such a private bank in Boston. Charles Sr. died in 1758, and as the war ended, business decreased significantly. Charles Jr. dissolved the business in 1764 and moved to New York, where British troops were still stationed and the money contracting business was still profitable. Private banks such as Wheelwright's also issued private notes just as the province issued public notes. The public and private notes typically paid the same interest – "lawful interest" – of 6%, but the public notes had the distinct disadvantage of being monopolized by the oligarchs; those with few connections invested with private banks. Further, the parsimonious Massachusetts House was issuing fewer notes, just £138,000 in 1765. And so, private investors trusted their money with the same men Whitehall trusted. Upon Charles Jr.'s dissolution of the firm, investors were advised in the summer of 1764 to redeem their notes and otherwise settle accounts with Wheelwright. Charles Jr. conducted an audit of Wheelwright's books at the end of 1764, showing about £132,000 in debts and £154,000 in assets. The total value of all imports and exports between Britain and New England in the early 1760s did not exceed £300,000 annually, so Wheelwright's reported assets exceeded 50% of the entire value of annual Britain-New England imports and exports.

The month after Samuel Allyne's wedding, on January 16, 1765, Nathaniel Wheelwright did not open the doors to his counting house. The wartime economic bubble had burst, and New England's shaky credit structure that so many had attempted to stabilize was crumbling. Wheelwright's insolvency resembled that of any other colonial business: the precarious balance between creditors and debtors gave way when creditors demanded payment faster than debtors paid. Wheelwright simply could not maintain liquidity with the general economy slowing, Parliament issuing fewer money contracts, and Charles Jr. demanding the immediate transfer of about £92,000 while recommending that all clients settle open accounts. Charles Apthorp, Jr. again reviewed Wheelwright's books, and discovered his debt to Charles Jr. was over £92,000, his total debt exceeded £178,000, and his total assets, which included several accounts that Wheelwright was unlikely to collect, was £176,000. Businesses that had financing through Wheelwright closed; the courts were flooded with suits; merchants demanded payment in gold and silver and immediate payment on all open credit lines. Just two days before his 28th birthday, John Hancock, who had recently become a full partner at his uncle's firm House of Hancock, wrote his London agents on January 21, 1765 that "trade has met with a most prodigious shock. ... Times are very bad here; and take my word, my good friends, the times will be worse here." Merchant John Rowe, who owned the wharf next to Wheelwright's, reported his mind was "too much disturbed" to attend church. Governor Bernard wrote to London that Wheelwright's bankruptcy was "like an earthquake to the town; numbers of people were creditors, some for their all. Every one dreaded the consequences; lesser merchants began to fail; a stop to all credit was expected. ..." Jemmy similarly referenced an "earthquake" in his description to English clients on January 25, 1765:

> ... the failing of Mr Wheelwright which happened here last week and has given as great a shock to credit here as your South Sea Bubble did in England years ago. This Gentleman ... acquired such an undue Credit that he became next to the Treasurer, Banker General for the province and almost for the Continent his Notes passed at par with those of our province, which are as good as your Bank Notes ... I can compare it to nothing but the late Earthquake at Lisbon, such was the Consternation for some little time that people appeared with pale Horror and Dread.

As there was no credit structure to issue general credit to merchants or to guarantee Wheelwright's debt, Massachusetts's business from large shippers to small farmers slowed to a state of nearly schizophrenic panic. The General Court's winter term convened on January 9, 1765, and within a week, Wheelwright's bankruptcy colored every debate. On January 22, the House passed an Act to regulate the distribution of assets intended to curb the inevitable flurry of lawsuits by creditors. The House also proposed lowering the interest paid on public notes from 6% to 5% in order to decrease the burden on tax payers in uncertain economic times. But the Council, many of whom owned public notes and represented others who invested heavily in them, rejected the decrease. Through the end of January and into early February, the General Court considered several other proposals to avert bankruptcies and keep them orderly and out of the courts when they did occur. It was under these tempestuous conditions that the Sugar Act was being implemented, customs enforcement was taken to new levels of austerity, and stamp taxes were being deliberated. And it was under these conditions that calm debates about new taxes could be finessed into caustic action.

Jemmy had an idea but in order to implement it, he needed another Mount Desert Island, and he found it in much maligned lobbyist Jasper Mauduit. Mauduit was tired of Massachusetts politics and apprised the General Court that he no longer could act as lobbyist because of his failing health. The 73-year-old Mauduit had asked the Popular Party to find another lobbyist on October 31, 1764. Further, Boston's Black Regiment was growing doubtful of Mauduit's efforts. Mayhew wrote a letter on December 18, 1764 that questioned whether Mauduit was a *"double-minded* man – in a strait between *honesty* and the *wicked policy* of the times." A year before, on May 4, Chauncy wrote a letter to Mauduit expressing his displeasure that Mauduit had made no progress in getting the dissident's missionary society chartered. That same year, on June 1, Mauduit received a letter from another Black Regiment minister stating his displeasure that their charter "has met with such Opposition." The Court Party did not know that Mauduit had fallen from favor within the Black Regiment, and Jemmy realized the opportunity to play Mauduit's dismissal for maximum effect.

The two obvious candidates to replace Mauduit were his brother Israel and Richard Jackson, though a few people suggested that the Popular Party was considering Jemmy while the Court Party was pushing to reappoint

Bollan. The question proved to be immensely complex. On August 3, 1763, Hutchinson wrote a letter to Jackson, stating:

> For two or three years I have been the butt of a faction, and although they have missed their aim and have not hurt me in the esteem of the best people in the Province, yet I question whether the present assembly would give their vote in my favor, especially as I am not sufficiently satisfied myself of the expediency of it to make any interest for it.

Hutchinson had considered the position for himself. And in September 12, 1763, Cushing wrote a letter to Jasper Mauduit informing him that "Mr. Jackson had been already taken some notice of by the Court," so Jackson wasn't entirely loathsome to the Assembly and had long been considered for some sort of lobbyist position in London in addition to Mauduit. Complicating matters further, former lobbyist Bollan had apparently blamed the Court Party for his ouster, not the Popular Party. Pownall, the short-term governor prior to Bernard, had detested Bollan and was annoyed that the General Court kept him as their lobbyist while Pownall was in office; now, Pownall was apparently spreading rumors that it was the powerful Court Party who had control of the agency issue in 1761 and thus responsible for Bollan's dismissal. Further, Bollan was likely aware that Hutchinson was considering the position for himself. Hutchinson spent much of October and November of 1764 defending himself to Bollan:

> I did every thing in my power, more I am sure than any other member of the Court, to prevent your dismission, and when I failed in my endeavors, I intimated the true cause of it. I have never seen an opening since for doing you any service in the General Court.

Clearly, Bollan not only suggested that the Court Party was to blame for his "dismission" but also concluded that the Court Party had kept him from any colonial appointments. In a November 8 letter, Hutchinson continued to explain his actions:

> But it was not possible for me as a member of the legislature to agree to every measure without being a mere machine, and having no judgment of my own. A very few instances of disagreement, particularly my attachment to Mr. Bollan, who I really thought at that time the

> most fit person to serve the province, and with whom I had been in friendship for many years, occasioned a coldness and some very severe expressions before the Governor left the province, which other people resented more than I did. ... and whenever there shall be a new appointment of a governor, I shall choose to resign.

It was classic Hutchinson; he asserted that his sometimes inexplicable behavior, particularly in not supporting Bollan, was due to not wanting to be "a mere machine" and not because of his own aspirations. He goes further to assert that his friendship with Bollan cost him political capital and "some very severe expressions" from Pownall. Finally, he declares that he'll resign as Lt. Governor when a new governor is appointed, thereby attempting to assert some degree of principle and autonomy. The Popular Party believed none of this and Bollan increasingly grew doubtful as well. In a February 14, 1763 letter to Mauduit, Jemmy claimed that "Mr. Jackson ... will never be agent for this Province." This belief wasn't so much founded on faith in the Popular Party to keep Jackson out as on Hutchinson's habitual scheming to insert either himself or Bollan in the position if the Popular Party failed to elect their candidate.

According to Bernard, the Popular Party had decided on Israel Mauduit in late January 1765 and secured the votes to elect him, but Jemmy interrupted the vote to propose a three year term-limit on any lobbyist appointment. The term-limit motion was generally supported on principle, but some in the Popular Party disapproved of it in practice because it would make compromise candidates more tolerable since any such candidate, if he became undesirable to either party, was removed automatically in three years. The controversial term-limit motion passed, and now the Popular Party was split between the Black Regiment's candidate and Richard Jackson, who was generally viewed as effective and well-connected. In what Bernard concluded was "an overt act of Otis, designing to counterwork his colleagues," Richard Jackson was elected province agent. Jemmy even compelled a fellow Boston bench member, likely Cushing, to submit a private letter from Mauduit that affirmed Richard Jackson as the best man to promote rights and liberties. The letter was produced for the record in the last week of January 1765. It seemed as though Otis masterfully manipulated his own party to get one of Bernard's friends elected – a "counterwork" in Bernard's words.

Jemmy designed the "three year" term-limit to increase Jackson's support, not decrease Israel Mauduit's, as Jackson seemed to be the right man for the turbulent year 1765 already was and doubtless would continue to be. Many in the Popular Party supported Jackson but did not want to be stuck with him interminably, as they suspected they might because the Court Party appeared to have firm control of the Assembly. Though many in the Popular Party supported Jackson, Jemmy spun Jackson's election ingeniously; in a January 20, 1766 *Gazette* article, he accused the governor of electioneering for Jackson and in the process having "closeted, cajoled, threatened or persuaded the members of both houses." There is no ostensible answer for Otis's behavior other than he believed that the term of office should be limited, regardless of who held that office. His political maneuvering can seem bewildering until one considers that perhaps he was operating solely out of principle and not out of political considerations; after all, he did argue that slavery was against nature whilst owning a slave. And after all, a "counterwork" can work in both directions.

Regardless, Jackson was actually a popular choice, despite Jemmy blaming Bernard for manipulating the process. Even Hutchinson boasted to Jackson in a January 25, 1765 letter that he

> had desired every friend I had to vote for Mr. Jackson. You would otherwise have counted 68. There would have been a general vote if a blind bigotry had not influenced some who support none but a dissenter...

His assertions seem innocuous until it's considered that Hutchinson himself desired the position at times and he had professed his undying support to Bollan. In fact, Jackson's election was secured not with Hutchinson's efforts but with Jemmy's term limit proposal, and yet Hutchinson had no compunction about taking credit for the result. Hutchinson had long prided himself on being immune to Jemmy's "counterwork" efforts, and yet he would discover his vulnerability when William Bollan exacted revenge with brutal effect four years later.

But Jemmy's political plan was still unfolding. The recurrent issue of the Superior Court justices' salaries came to the floor of the House on February 1, and the House voted for £800, a raise for the Court in general, but no bonus for Chief Justice Hutchinson. Then, astonishing the Popular Party, Jemmy offered a motion to grant the chief justice a £40 bonus. After an unusual roll call vote, the motion passed by one vote with a split Boston bench; Jemmy and Gray – now an Otis relative by marriage – voting "Yea" and Thacher and Cushing voting "Nay." The "counterwork" was proceeding. On February 4, just three days after the vote, Speaker White abondoned his position in the House, and Jemmy Otis was elected speaker *pro tempore*. Perhaps more surprisingly, Governor Bernard consented to Jemmy's election. During this same month, the Stamp Act was being officially read in Parliament, the final reading occurring in March, and by March 22 the Stamp Act was a statute of the realm.

As the Stamp Act ascended to law in London, Jemmy ascended to power in Boston. Otis was instrumental in getting Bernard's friend elected as the province's lobbyist, and he then published criticisms of Bernard and Jackson; Otis voted for a pay bonus for Hutchinson and then is elected and approved by Bernard to be Speaker of the House. His tactics bewildered and frustrated nearly all involved, but he was maneuvering everyone into a position to answer that ultimate question: *What action can the colonies take if Parliament chooses to ignore their rights?*

※

The governor of Rhode Island, Stephen Hopkins, had published a pamphlet two months earlier in December 1764. His *The Rights of the Colonies Examined* follows Otis's arguments in *Rights of the Colonies Asserted and Proved*, and though no royalist, Hopkins was a good "friend of government," so he supported obedience to Parliament; despite the call for submission, Hopkins extensively tabulated the economic problems that would be created by the Sugar Act, stamp taxes, and the increasing authority of juryless vice-admiralty courts. He pointedly ignored the issue of direct colonial representation in Parliament and neglected to address that critical question: *What action can the colonies take if Parliament chooses to ignore their rights?*

Rhode Island excelled in acerbic political battles, even surpassing Massachusetts in that dubious honor. Factions in Rhode Island were stridently territorial and always prepared to brawl, and the Newport merchant faction's Martin Howard, a lawyer whose avocations included mocking Governor Hopkins, fully engaged in his hobby a month later. His scorn rolled off the presses on January 23, 1765, coyly titled *A Letter from a Gentleman at Halifax, To his Friend in Rhode-Island, Containing Remarks upon a Pamphlet, Entitled,*

The Rights of the Colonies Examined. The plodding, earnest Hopkins proved to be an easy target, and Howard comprehensively ridiculed Hopkins and his pamphlet from his perch atop the customary Tory worldview. For Howard, the charters "ascertain, define, and limit the respective rights and privileges of each colony," and he concluded with palpable impatience that he "cannot conceive how it has come to pass that the colonies now claim other or greater rights." *Halifax Letter* was a smart bit of Loyalist publicity that pursued standard Empire political theory in delineating rights into two camps: personal and political. Of the former, "life, liberty, and estate" are established at birth, but of the latter, their existence requires charters. Howard argued that rights and parliamentary power are derived from the same source, and just as parliamentary applies to all, Parliament represents all. He then observes the fact that many in England are not directly represented in Parliament but are taxed without protest, concluding that "The right of [direct] representation is but a phantom." The *Halifax Letter* then charges that Otis's *The Rights of the British Colonies Asserted and Proved* has "a tendency to embitter the minds of a simple, credulous, hitherto loyal people, to alienate their affections from Britain." But it was the inevitable reference to Jemmy as "Mr __ , who, though unhappily misled by popular ideas and at the head of the *tribunetian veto*, yet appears to be a man of knowledge and parts" that demanded a reply; the sarcastic compliment was clearly leveled at Jemmy as a "man of knowledge." The allusion to the *"tribunetian veto"* referred to the power of ancient Rome's lower house, which represented the commoners, to veto actions by the upper house particularly in response to infringements of legal rights. Oligarchs were forbidden to be members of the tribune, thus resulting in a legislative body that represented commoners and was composed of commoners. Tellingly, Howard clearly intended the *tribunetian veto* appellation to be insulting.

If Howard's lone ambition was to enrage James Otis, he succeeded brilliantly as Howard's insulting high Tory tone was certain to attract Otis's attention. Not surprisingly, two months later Edes and Gill advertised a new anonymous pamphlet, *A Vindication of the British Colonies Against the Aspersions of the Halifax Gentleman in His Letter to a Rhode-Island Friend.* Published without attribution, the pamphlet went on sale on March 18, 1765 and was Jemmy Otis at his most shockingly strident. The *Vindication* is a far-ranging work that ably exhibits Jemmy's ability to engage – or enrage – all parties. In *Vindication* the road from word choice commentary to human rights paeans is paved with a matchless command of language and an astonishing breadth of knowledge that carries the reader as if caught in an uncontrollable torrent of ideas. The Halifax *Letter* exhibits Tory gentility while Jemmy attacks with the brute force of his education unrestrained by the gilding of class. *Vindication* was designed to pummel Howard into resignation, and yet it also served to add another facet to a philosophy that never was out of sight of current political circumstances.

In *The Rights of the British Colonies Asserted and Proved*, Jemmy asserted that Parliament had the power to tax the colonies but not the right. In contrast, *Vindication* declares, "It is certain that the Parliament of Great Britain hath a just, clear, equitable, and constitutional right, power, and authority to bind the colonies by all acts wherein they are named." Just to further incite the fellow radicals, Jemmy makes it clear: "No less certain is it that the Parliament of Great Britain has a just and equitable right, power, and authority to impose taxes on the colonies, internal and external, on lands as well as trade." Parliament has the right but does not have the right? A contradiction is evident, but Otis employed multiple meanings with the term "right." Jemmy quoted Jeremiah Dummer in his first pamphlet when Dummer used "right" to mean fairness – doing what's *right*. In *Vindication*, however, Otis modified his definition of "right" to denote legal ability – having the *right* to do something. Now, whereas *power* indicated capability, *right* indicates legal ability. And Howard's deceptive argument about representation required Jemmy to address the difference between Great Britain's House of Commons and Parliament. In a sense, the colonies are represented in Parliament, but Howard's argument "was not of the sole and separate power and authority of the House of Commons but of the authority of that august and transcendent body the Parliament." To say that the colonies are represented in Parliament is not to say that they are represented in the House of Commons. To make the point clear, Jemmy adds:

> The supreme legislative indeed represents the whole society or community, as well the dominions as the realm; and this is the true reason why the dominions are justly bound by such acts of Parliament as name them. This is implied in the idea of a supreme sovereign power; and if the Parliament had not such authority the colonies would be independent, which none but rebels, fools, or madmen will contend for.

Of course Parliament controlled the colonies; if it didn't then the colonies would be independent. So Otis first agrees with the opposing argument that Parliament has full control over the colonies, and then he neutralizes it by redefining the primary operators. While Otis confirmed that the colonies were not actually represented in the House of Commons, he agreed that non-voting regions in England were "justly deemed as represented." Nonetheless, he asserted that the colonists were "as perfect strangers to most of [members of the House of the Commons] as the savages in California," and such government was, at least, impractical. Yet Otis veered again, concluding that

> 'Tis admitted the Parliament have the same right to levy internal taxes on the colonies as to regulate trade, and that the right of levying both is undoubtedly in the Parliament. Yet 'tis humbly conceived and hoped that before the authority is fully exerted in either case it will be thought to be but reasonable and equitable that the dominions should be in *fact* represented.

Howard had recommended that Parliament "frame some code and therein adjust rights of the colonies," to which Jemmy retorted:

> If I mistake not, there is in the air of this period the quintessence of a mere martial legislator, the insolence of a haughty and imperious minister, the indolence and half-thought of a *petit-maitre*, the flutter of a coxcomb, the pedantry of a quack, the nonsense of a pettifogger. A strange gallimaufry this .... Codes, pandects, novels, decretals of popes, the inventions of the d____l [devil] may suit the cold, bleak regions [of] Brandenburg and Prussia or scorching heats of Jamaica or Gambia; but we live in a more temperate climate, and shall rest content with the laws, customs, and usages of our ancestors, bravely supported and defended with the monarchy, and from age to age handed down.

And yet in this *Vindication* and in *Consideration*s, to be published three months later, Otis maintains the right to depose a ruler who attempts to establish a "tyranny" or "enslave" the people. But despite much analysis, Jemmy develops no means to limit parliamentary power, and perhaps he couldn't, for the establishment in England has issued a stern and definitive warning. To a significant degree, *Vindication* is as much Otis's response to Howard's *Halifax Letter* as it is to Blackstone's *Commentaries*. Blackstone was a failed lawyer-turned-Oxford professor who began to write down his lectures on English common law; the first volume of his lectures was printed in 1765 and quickly dispatched to the colonies.

Blackstone's objective in *Commentaries* was to buttress the establishment, and he was conscientious of offending those in power and sought to reassure them that their behavior was just and prudent. In 1761, as Blackstone was writing *Commentaries*, he was appointed a Kings' Counselor, a decade after Otis was appointed to a similar position in Massachusetts Bay colony. Also in 1761, Blackstone was elected to the House of Commons, where a few years later he would vote against the Stamp Act's repeal. Opposition in Parliament even then accused Blackstone of being an unthinking cog in the Whitehall machine, and when confronted with passages from *Commentaries* that seemed not to support Whitehall's positions, Blackstone rewrote the passages for the next edition. Blackstone's solicitude of the establishment was repaid when he was knighted and appointed Justice of the Court of Common Pleas in 1770.

So in many ways *Commentaries* was simply an apologia for the English legal system; Blackstone justified the system as it was, describing it as nearly perfect and providing plain explanations as to why the English legal system was reasonable and fair. The bulk of this reasonableness was built upon the foundation of medieval feudal hierarchies. According to *Commentaries*, "The Rights of Persons" is largely governed by their position in the hierarchy, starting with God and the King and working down to commoners. "Rights" were based on relationships: king/subject, husband/wife, master/servant, guardian/ward. "The Rights of Things" – property rights – is also primarily governed by feudal law. Colonial fealty to Parliament and the Crown were governed by "the law of nature" and could not be questioned or adjusted. Regarding "Public Wrongs," *Commentaries* vigorously defends English law and is notoriously brutal in its summation, "It is a melancholy truth, that among the variety of actions which men are daily liable to commit, no less than an hundred and sixty have been declared by Act of Parliament to be felonious without benefit of clergy; or, in other words, to be worthy of instant death." There can be no doubt that *Commentaries* is both a strident defense of Parliament's absolute authority and a somber reminder of the mortal consequences of disobeying that authority. That *Commentaries* was widely accepted as the authoritative and final exposition of the English legal system renders it an austere threat to those who questioned Parliament's supremacy.

While the English establishment maintained a philosophical desire to perpetuate feudal order, assigning seats in the House of Commons according to population – as was argued by some colonists, including Jemmy Otis – exposed a practical dilemma. England's population increased by 14% from 1701 to 1751, while in the same time period, the population of the colonies had surged almost 370%. In the 18th century, England's population would increase by 64% while the colonies' population would swell by 2,016%. Had seats in the House of Commons been apportioned according to population, the colonies would have been assigned 25% of them by 1770, 39% by 1800, and 53% by 1840, thereby snatching control of the empire from the mother country. In just the two decades from 1750 to 1770, the colonial population spiked 83%. The population demographics were transparently disadvantageous to England, and the colonies's 2,016% population growth in the 18th century was evident to all in the 1760s. Given the rapid and accelerating growth of the colonial population, it seemed that control from London was inevitably doomed; from that perspective, one could reasonably inquire as to whether the colonies would someday exert control over England. This dilemma left Blackstone little room but to promote feudal hierarchy as the only means to order the empire.

As the first attempt to systematize English common law, *Commentaries* was widely referenced; as the foundation for the application of English law, the four volumes became the standard text for law students and the customary source of citation for lawyers on both sides of the Atlantic. *Commentaries* would be oft quoted during America's Constitutional Convention, in Federalist papers (No. 69 and 84) and by anti-Federalists such as Patrick Henry. Stamp Act Congress attendee John Dickinson later applied Blackstone in his responses to Madison's concern about the Constitution. *Commentaries* was the preeminent articulation of English law. It could not be ignored. Otis clearly needed to contend with the emergence of this authoritative compendium of the law and legal structures, and he quoted *Commentaries* in *Vindication* in order to assure his readers that the new work was read and understood; those readers would include many in Parliament and Whitehall.

Blackstone's austere summation of the consequences of challenging Parliament's power is unquestionably at least partly in response to Otis's pamphlets, which were typically promptly shipped to England and widely distributed. Blackstone responded to some of Otis's arguments thus:

And, because several of the colonies had claimed a sole and exclusive right of imposing taxes upon themselves, the statute 6 Geo. III. c. 12 expressly declares, that all his majesty's colonies and plantations in America have been, are, and of right ought to be, subordinate to and dependent upon the imperial crown and parliament of Great Britain; who have full power and authority to make laws and statutes of sufficient validity to bind the colonies and people of America, subjects of the crown of Great Britain, in all cases whatsoever. And this authority has been since very forcibly exemplified, and carried into act, by the statute 7 Geo. III. c. 59, for suspending the legislation of New York; and by several subsequent statutes.

His response left no room for uncertainty or inquiry. And regarding Otis's argument about the source of rights, Blackstone declared:

Charter governments, in the nature of civil corporations, with the power of making bye-laws for their own interior regulations, not contrary to the laws of England; and with such rights and authorities as are specially given them in their several charters of incorporation.

Rights are given to the governments through their charters; the position was a direct refutation of Otis's argument that charters were inconsequential because basic rights were innate in the people, not granted by a charter. And as the Parliament is without peer, the king is infallible:

That the King can do no wrong, is a necessary and fundamental principle of the English constitution. ... The king is not only incapable of doing wrong, but even of thinking wrong: in him there is no folly or weakness.

Blackstone's and the establishment's unequivocal position was that as long as the colonies were bound to England, Parliament was the supreme power. Otis agreed, thus making the choices implicitly clear: obedience or rebellion. Otis had begun his earlier pamphlet *The Rights of the British Colonies* with an epigraph from Virgil's *Aeneid*: "let us draw up a treaty fair to / Both sides, and invite them to partner us in the kingdom." *Commentaries* exclaimed the establishment's position that there would be no partnership, only feudal subjugation. Blackstone even pointedly rebutted Otis's use of Lord Coke and *Dr. Bonham's Case* in *Rights*; Otis asserted that, as Coke did, courts could rule laws unconstitutional, and such judicial review was necessary to moderate the power of the legislative branch. Blackstone utterly rejected the notion of judicial review: parliamentary decisions were final and unreviewable.

Many rebels such as Jemmy Otis in the north and Thomas Jefferson in the south learned the law by reading the works of the early 17th century English judge and lawyer Edward Coke, particularly Coke's commentary on the 16th century judge Thomas Littleton's work. Coke was an outspoken critic of the king and, when summoned to appear before James I in 1616, told the king to his face that the law and parliament limited the king's power. Coke lost his position as Chief Justice. In Parliament, Coke contributed to *The Petition of Right*, a proto-declaration of independence for the parliament arguing for taxation by consent, against unlawful searches and seizures, and requesting standard enforcement of property rights and due process. With Coke in the lead, Parliament forced a king desperate for revenue into submitting to the *Petition of Right*. It is not curious why the rebels would denounce Blackstone and defend Coke. Coke was everything Blackstone was not; Coke, too, was a rebel.

In contrast, Blackstone thought it appropriate to restrict voting to property owners and declared the colonies "subject ... to the control of the parliament." And regarding the colonists scrutinizing their legal relationship to England, Blackstone made clear the opinion of the establishment: "It is well if the mass of mankind will obey the laws when made, without scrutinizing too nicely into the reasons of making them." Though *Commentaries* supported many of Otis's and the colonists' positions, including individual rights, a prohibition on taxation without consent, and the importance of jury trials, Blackstone represented nothing more than the long-established demand – or threat – that the colonies acquiesce to the absolute authority of Parliament. Blackstone was treated as Moses descending from the mountain, and Coke was Baal, once god now false idol.

At first, *Vindication* seemed to be a political catastrophe. Though wounded by Jemmy's pamphlet, Martin Howard pounced on the "Boston writer" for his apparent abdication of his previous views of *rights* and *power* in *A Defence of the Letter from a Gentleman at Halifax to his Friend in Rhode-Island* published just a month later. Howard took a few more shots at hapless Rhode Island ex-governor Hopkins, bashed the Boston *Gazette* and Oxenbridge Thacher for their unhelpful and belligerent comments, and then focused on his main target.

Howard labeled *Vindication* "a dreary waste of 32 pages" and accused Jemmy Otis of being one of the "false brethren" who would sooner abandon Hopkins and the clamor for *rights* than forgo "a single ray of his superior discernment." Howard quoted the Otis section on "right, power, and authority" and then called out his hypocrisy: "Here he will certainly appear, in the opinion of his associates and adherents, to have surrendered up all at discretion, and betrayed his whole party." Strong words, indeed. Surely Thomas Cushing and other Popular Party leaders wondered too if *Vindication* amounted to betrayal. Howard further asserted that *Vindication* "contains a most unreserved and solemn recognition of the absolute, unlimited authority of parliament over the colonies. The warmth of the expression, and the care taken to shun all ambiguity, indicates the zeal of a convert." Unlike Hutchinson and at times Bernard, Howard did not realize that Jemmy was capable of, in Bernard's words, "designing to counterwork his colleagues." Howard even went so far as to observe that *The Rights of the British Colonies* was generally condemned "at home" and sarcastically absolved and applauded Jemmy "on the happy conviction of his errors." It's doubtless that Blackstone's *Commentaries* was part of the condemnation Howard referenced.

Otis wished to make manifest the choice now before the colonies: total submission to Parliamentary authority or resistance on threat of death; Otis also wished to make known to Whitehall that he wouldn't commit – at least publically – any of Blackstone's 160 crimes that resulted in "instant death," though he did insist that the people have a right to depose a ruler who attempted to establish a "tyranny" or "enslave" the citizenry, even in the face of Blackstone's claim that the king is infallible. But the skirmish between Otis and Howard spawned chaos among the Popular Party faithful. On April 22, 1765, the Boston *Evening-Post* printed a letter from "Veritas" that harshly criticized the useless spectacle that was the Honourable Artillery Company parade, and the following week a *Gazette* article labeled the "Veritas" letter a "Grubstreet Piece" whose author would better be identified as "Virulentus." The *Evening-Post* was not Jemmy's paper, and the "Veritas" piece was clearly not his work, but even Jemmy's own *Gazette* seemed unsure of whose position he supported. Everyone was tense and, more importantly, no one could locate Jemmy Otis's allegiance. Just two weeks later, on May 6, 1765, the *Gazette* advertised another Jemmy Otis pamphlet, *Brief Remarks on the Defence of the Halifax Libel on the British-American Colonies*, and mocked their most prolific author and ardent supporter by claiming that Otis "will be busy some Time in drawing a Piece he intends to call T'other Side of the Question, another to be called Both Sides of the Question. ... After these he hopes to be free from all public Concerns, and political Connections, and at full Liberty to begin a new System." Edes and Gill undoubtedly questioned Otis's bewildering motives.

Prior to the publication of *Brief Remarks* in May, the colonists received a new pamphlet: *The Regulations Lately Made Concerning the Colonies and the Taxes Imposed upon Them, Considered.* The pamphlet itself isn't as remarkable as the assumption that is had been composed by none other than the First Lord of the Treasury, George Grenville. If Blackstone's *Commentaries* wasn't warning enough, Whitehall issued a direct admonition to the colonial rebels. Though the actual author was Grenville's secretary, the leviathan Thomas Whately, it was a sign that the ministry read and disapproved of Otis's pamphlets. In *Vindication,* Otis conceded that the colonies were represented in the "transcendant" Parliament yet forcefully rejected that they were represented in the House of Commons. The ministry disagreed, asserting that the colonists were as represented in the House of Commons as were the residents of Birmingham and Guernsey.

And so in *Brief Remarks,* Jemmy labeled the author – perhaps the Prime Minister – of *Regulations* "very ingenious, learned, polite and delicate," despite having previously mocked Pownall's *Administration of the Colonies.* And Jemmy concluded about *Regulations* that he had "the honor also to agree ... that the colonists are virtually, constitutionally, in law and in equity to be considered as represented in the honourable house of commons." But he was not satisfied with simply contradicting his previous assertion about representation. In *Rights of the British Colonies,* Otis had made an issue of the right to "give his sentiments to the public, of the utility or inutility of any act whatsoever, even after it is passed, as well as while it is pending." But since, Blackstone had cautioned that the colonists should "obey the laws when made, without scrutinizing too nicely into the reasons of making them." Jemmy confirmed that he'd heard the warning: "Nor shall I presume to say a single word on the expediency and public utility of this measure [the impending Stamp Act], after the administration have so long had it in contemplation. I humbly, dutifully, and loyally presume, ... that the supreme legislative of Great-Britain do, and must know infinitely better what they are about and intend, than any without doors." Whitehall, perhaps at the urging of the Boston oligarchy or at the King's direction, had entered the paper war and declared it over. In the short-term, is seemed that incendiary pamphlets would more likely risk one's life than yield political progress.

But Jemmy would have one last shot, and *Brief Remarks* is more invective and intimidation than philosophy. Howard's Newport faction is described as a "little, dirty, drinking, drabbing, contaminated knot of thieves, beggars, transports, or the worthy descendents of such, collected from the four winds of the earth, and made up of Turks, Jews and other infidels with a few renegade Christians & Catholics." Newport specifically and Rhode Island in general were notorious for pervasive lechery and lawlessness, so doubtless this description was more accurate than not; further, it would not have been shocking to hear their cantankerous governor utter such words – but they were beneath a well-born, well-bred Harvard lawyer to put in print. Jemmy further diagnosed Howard with having "the conscience of a highwayman, the heart of an assassin and the impudence of a billingsgate [worker in the seedy London fish market]."

The "counterwork" in *Brief Remarks* operated quickly, moving from riling the mobs to soothing the oligarchy in just a few lines. After the "contaminated knot of thieves," Jemmy pleads, "If there is any thing offensive in either pamphlet, I am heartily sorry, and am well assured the author never intended any such thing, and has given me authority in his name, humbly to ask pardon for the least iota that may have displeased his superiors, humbly imploring … that they would candidly impute any slip the "agony of heart, rather than to the pravity of his will." The operation of a "counterwork" need not suffice as the only explanation. If strung together, comments about Jemmy from others are enlightening:

> John Adams: "extremely quick and elastic. His apprehension is as quick as his temper - He springs, and twitches his Muscles about in Thinking."
>
> Governor Bernard: " …the head of the Confederacy. If you are acquainted with the natural Violence of his temper …"
>
> Peter Oliver: "…genius."

Brief Remarks displayed not only a "counterwork" to assure all factions that he was on their side – a ploy he'd used since the Writs of Assistance case four years earlier – but also exhibited his true nature. And yet the indelicacy of *Brief Remarks* provides one of the most direct clues for answering the question of Jemmy's elusive connection to the mobs. Cushing may have thought

Brief Remarks was beneath a man of Otis's stature; Hutchinson surely would have found it extremely distasteful; but the men of the Boston mobs would have concluded that Jemmy was – at least on paper – a brawler. Given what happens later in the year, it cannot be discounted that the mob men – dock workers, tanners, carpenters – would gather in taverns, share a few drinks, and howl in delight at Jemmy's mudslinging. They would have written no differently – if they were into writing articles. If Whitehall were to quiet the paper war, then Jemmy would remove himself from the print shops and relocate to the taverns, and the rebellion would follow.

The Rights of the British Colonies, *Vindication*, and *Brief Remarks* offer no single philosophy; attempting to extract a comprehensive political position would only result in confusion and contradiction. They cannot be understood apart from the circumstances that enveloped them, both before, during, and after. The ministry had issued two firm rebukes, and Otis's political enemies judged Otis's opinions to be treasonous and seditious, and he probably regarded these warnings with some seriousness. Howard had directly referenced the trouble Jemmy would be in with the ministry if he persisted. Further, it was clear that progress would require more than political pamphlets. In *Brief Remarks* Otis is almost desperate to learn the source of information and the identity of various pamphlets authors's – he wanted to gauge the degree to which he should fear for his safety. Otis most likely believed *Regulations* was a direct warning from the ministry, and whether the author was Grenville or Whately, it was likely causing him to wonder whether the accusations of treason and sedition were more than political smears. Did Jemmy entertain the thought that Whitehall was preparing charges of treason? Did Jemmy's many Tory friends and relatives advise him that such a danger was possible? Jemmy Otis was widely considered in both the provinces and England to be the colonies' most radical thinker and politician. He likely assumed that he could be one of Grenville's targets. But a man seriously concerned about offending those in power would not have proceeded the way Otis did. And if he were insane, he likely would not have had the mental capacity to do what he did next. The most likely explanation is that Otis was intentionally easing his enemies's apprehensions, coaxing them to let down their defenses, so that he could implement the answer to that ultimate question: *What action can the colonies take if Parliament chooses to ignore their rights?*

And what was the cause of this masterful stroke of political manipulation? The probable answer is that it was no event, but rather a person, the greatest political operator that Jemmy knew – his father. The relationship between son and father had been cold since the Colonel's ascendency to the Council; most in the Popular Party, Jemmy included, viewed the Colonel's new position as a betrayal. Jemmy had stormed out of the House and resigned his seat. The Colonel taught Jemmy a lesson with the Mount Desert Island grant to Bernard: an opponent will respond better to your argument if they don't think of you as an enemy. The Colonel had always been a master of compromise; recall that he'd helped push through Hutchinson's currency reform bill in 1750 in exchange for the debt collection clarification that helped Jemmy prosecute a case. And as John Adams later claimed that Jemmy's writs of assistance argument was the first shot of the Revolution, a meeting that would soon take place between Jemmy and his father would result in a thorough bombardment of the oligarchy. And that meeting was likely not the first between the two; the planning had probably ensued over months and perhaps began when Jemmy and his father spent that previous cold November together in Barnstable. The Colonel had likely told his son that if he desired his own Council seat, then he should grant his enemies a Mount Desert Island. Jemmy's apparent apostasy was a vital ingredient to the plan, as was the fact that Jemmy, now Speaker of the House, chaired 45 committees and sat on another 102 – a vast increase over the 14 chairs and 49 committee assignments he'd held the previous year.

Meanwhile, confusion reigned in the Popular Party, with John Adams later recalling that, "There was an appearance of coalition between Hutchinson and Otis, which had wellnigh Otis's popularity and influence forever. The rage against him in Boston seemed to without bounds. He was called a reprobate, an apostate, and a traitor, in every street in Boston. ... But I then suspected and believed that Otis was corrupted and bought off. ... This was the general opinion." Significantly, Adams failed to recognize that Popular Party members expressed the same "rage" when the Otises shepherded through the Mount Desert Island grant in 1762; the Colonel got a Council seat and was roundly condemned for being "bought off." Governor Bernard seemed to forget the details of the Mount Desert arrangement as well; he wrote John Pownall on May 6, 1765:

> The author of the Rights of the Colonies, now repents in Sackcloth & ashes for the hand he had in that book & in the printed Letter to the Agent. In a pamphlett lately published he has in the humblest manner asked for the pardon of the Ministry & of the parliament for the liberties he took with them. This Confession, which is sincere, is

likely to cost him his seat in the Assembly altho' he had evry Vote at the last Election.

Francis Bernard's naiveté was in no short supply, and his assurance to Pownall that the "Confession ... is sincere" exemplifies what the Otises surely knew and what Thomas Hutchinson feared: Bernard was blinded by his desperation for "Easy" and lucrative years in Massachusetts. The newspapers were quiet other than a jibe in the *Gazette* that Otis was now "free from all political Connections." The annual town elections were scheduled for Tuesday, May 14, and the buzz on the streets echoed Governor Bernard's opinion that Jemmy Otis would not be reelected. But on the day before the election, the two major newspapers published articles that swayed public opinion. Samuel Waterhouse, an anonymous pamphleteer and customs official known for his invective, published a cruel poem under the name "Peter Minim" in the *Evening-Post* meant to be sung to the tune of the old English satirical ballad *Lillibullero*. Waterhouse's burlesque was entitled "Jemmibullero: A Fragment of an Ode to Orpheus" and filled an entire column, and, in part, reads:

> And Jemmy is a silly dog, and Jemmy is a tool;
> And Jemmy is a stupid cur, and Jemmy is a fool;
> And Jemmy is a madman, and Jemmy is an ass,
> And Jemmy has a leaden head, and a forehead spread with Brass.
>
> And Jemmy's a malicious dog, – you see it in his look,
> And Jemmy's scribbled politics, and Jemmy's burnt his book.
>
> And Jemmy is a sorry jade, – Ah Jemmy hasn't mettle
> And Jemmy pleads his bloody nose when quarrels he should settle
>
> So Jemmy rail'd at upper folks while Jemmy's DAD was out,
> But Jemmy's DAD now has a place, so Jemmy's turned about.
>
> And Jemmy wrote the Letter too, and Jemmy's now afraid,
> But Jemmy needn't scare himself, –– THEY know what's Jemmy's trade.

Lillibullero is a British ballad that mocked Irish hopes of expelling English troops; the title is likely a garbed version of the Irish for "Lilly was clear and ours was the day" – the "lilly" a reference to both the Bourbon Lillies and a popular 16th century prophet who foretold of a Catholic English king. The irony of ridiculing Otis with a song that mocked the hopes of a people who wished to be free from British oppression with the aid of the French could not have been appreciated at the time. Yet the general idea was not lost on the people of Boston, and this bit of derision effected the opposite of its author's objective because it implied that Jemmy had not decamped in the Court Party. This is the second time that labeling Jemmy a "madman" only served to rouse public support in his favor. Also on that Monday before elections, the *Gazette* printed an appeal from James Otis addressed to the "Freeholders and other Inhabitants of Boston," claiming in part,

> There lives not a man who can say I ever asked his vote or his interest. ... I am, ever have been, and expect ever to be, a poor man. . . . I have given up £200 a year sterling. ...I know not where to go for any part of this money. Should my children want it, and their daily bread, I hope it will be some consolation to them, that their father lost part of his in a vain attempt to serve his country. ... I have sacrificed peace, quiet, real friends and every tempting allurement of man, naturally and constitutionally inclined to social pleasures. Tell me once dear friends, what have I got by all this, besides the curse causeless, of thousands, for whose welfare my heart has bled yearly, and is now ready to burst. ...

More than anything, Otis pleaded that he was not a part of the oligarchy. He was poor, not motivated by self-interest, not driven by social connections. This was certainly not an argument that Hutchinson, the Olivers, Bernard or Colonel Otis would present; all of them would have been embarrassed to makes such claims. After this declaration of his anti-oligarchy position, the pleading stopped, and the rebel returned:

> What would it avail for me to tell you, that were it lawful and possible, to get at my deeply entrenched fellow commoner, who I know to be the cause of all your calamities, I would leap like a Roe, not to run away but to pay part of the purchase of your ransom with my life or his? Possibly I need not leave America to find him.

Jemmy never uttered the word "independence" and sometimes decried mob action, but he more than once stoked the fire of violent uprising. Here, on May 13, 1765, he publically stated he would kill or be killed purchasing the ransom – the freedom – of the people of Boston. How long would it be before the people of Boston agreed with this sentiment? Jemmy also requested a "half an hour's talk" before the town meeting on election day, and apparently his words were sufficiently convincing. There were 641 votes cast that Tuesday. Thomas Gray got 570, Thomas Cushing 538, Oxenbridge Thacher 427 and James Otis 388. Obviously a significant number of people were unsure what to make of Otis's seeming new friendship with Bernard, but enough found faith in the "poor man" to return him to the Boston bench, and he was chosen as moderator. Samuel White was again elected Speaker, and the Court Party again seemed to effectively control the Assembly. Interestingly though, immediately after the votes were tallied, Jemmy was "unanimously chosen" as town moderator. The low vote count seems to reflect some trepidation, but the election as town moderator belies such a conclusion. The power brokers seemed to know perfectly well Otis's plans and were determined to affirm their support with a unanimous election to the moderator position. Otis was repeatedly chosen as moderator over the next few years.

The plot of which Hutchinson was all too suspicious but of which Bernard was all too ignorant had begun to unfold. Jemmy had simultaneously placated Bernard and enflamed the people. Later that month the Superior Court convened in Plymouth, and Chief Justice Thomas Hutchinson was informed that a mysterious meeting had taken place across the street from the Plymouth court house. The Warren family – a son had married Mercy, Jemmy's sister – had hosted Jemmy and the Colonel, and discussions had taken place. A decision – whose exactly we don't know – was made that the colonies should take united action against the Stamp Act. This unification would enable "the demagogues of the several governments in America to join together in opposition to all orders from Great Britain." Jemmy had led the efforts to unite the colonial assemblies a year before in opposition to the new sugar tax, and that effort – and its lack of result – must have been fore in his mind. It's likely he'd been planning this new move since then, and he'd been positioning Bernard so that the governor couldn't blunt the new efforts that were required to make this unification effort successful. Finally, he was going to answer the question: *What action can the colonies take if Parliament chooses to ignore their rights?*

The "Black Act," as John Rowe branded The Stamp Act, had become a statute of the realm on March 22 with a November 1, 1765 effectuation date. The Stamp Act was much more than a simple revenue act; it was Parliament's effort to lay comprehensive regulations on the Colonies, and, to a significant degree, the first such effort. The Act dictated the manner in which many businesses and private persons could interact and increased the ways in which ordinary daily interactions could be illegal. Nearly everything that pertained to paper was now regulated, and such regulations not only applied to the obvious, such as newspapers, but also to official documents of all sorts. A liquor business could be fined if its permit was not properly stamped; a wide variety of legal documents would be void if they lacked the appropriate stamps. And, as legislatures are sometimes wont, Parliament impregnated an ostensive revenue bill with special regulations for newspapers, pamphlets and books. First, the penalty for printing without stamps was steep:

> the Author, Printer, and Publisher, and all other Persons concerned in or about the printing or publishing of such Pamphlet, shall, for every such Offence, forfeit the Sum of Ten Pounds

But the Act went further; not only were all those associated with an unstamped publication fined, but they lost their copyright to the publication, such that

> any Person may freely print and publish the same, paying the Duty payable in respect thereof by virtue of this Act, without being liable to any Action, Prosecution, or Penalty for so doing.

The effect of such regulation would be to cool the hot colonial presses as every publication would now incur the additional expense of a stamp or a fine, and face the possibility of forfeiting ownership of the publication. But Parliament went further to cool the presses, particularly the heated political debates and paper wars, by banning anonymous publications:

> And it is hereby further enacted by the Authority aforesaid, That no Person whatsoever shall sell or expose to Sale any such Pamphlet, or any News-Paper, without the true respective Name or Names, and Place or Places of Abode, of some known Person or Persons by or for whom the same was really and truly printed or published, shall be written or printed thereon; upon Pain that every Person offending therein shall, for every such Offence, forfeit the Sum of Twenty Pounds.

All slanderous remarks and seditious observations must now have a name and "Place or Places of Abode" attached to them; it was clear to all that such a regulation not only permitted pervasive enforcement of the Black Act but also facilitated prosecution of anyone not a "friend of government." The Stamp Act's purpose went far beyond generating revenue; it inserted government regulation into the far reaches of private colonial activity and attached potentially significant liability to critiquing the government and government officials. And the colonists feared the Act was merely a prelude to greater regulation.

Otis and the Popular Party likely had been distressed by the variation that bordered on discrepancy reflected in the petitions the colonial assemblies had sent to England, and Otis had experienced during the paper war how little one man could accomplish. Further, given how easily Whitehall could target one man, he would have feared the impotence of any abrupt attempt by one colonial legislature and would have equally feared disparate efforts likely to result in nothing but more regulation. The Otis family conclave that occurred in May 1765 at the Warren house in Plymouth decided that a united colonial congress was the necessary solution to the inadequate efforts at colonial collaboration of the past year. They also concluded that such united cooperation was the foundation of any successful action the colonies could employ against Parliament. It was a daring, innovative idea that could only be safely nurtured by men who were viewed as friends of government. To have any likelihood of success, the unification effort had to be concealed as an inside job.

The newly elected General Court first met on May 24, 1765, and Governor Bernard gave the usual state of the province address in which he confessed to the "novelty" and the "disagreeable" features of the new "regulation," but strongly advised "respectful submission" for "there must be a supreme Legislature, to which all other Powers are subordinate." The speech could have been plagiarized from Jemmy's *Vindication* and *Brief Remarks*; while the Popular Party thought Otis's last pamphlet betrayed their beliefs, Otis had, in effect, written a script for Bernard to follow. And amazingly, Bernard was following it. Regardless of Jemmy's well laid plans, the Popular Party was determined to play the antagonist, first by attempting to deny a Council seat to Andrew Oliver, the newly designated stamp distributor and the eternally irritating Hutchinson; their efforts almost succeeded this time. Meanwhile, the newly government-friendly Jemmy and his father lobbied the moderate Assembly members to support a meeting of the colonies. So a committee began meeting on June 6; while the meetings weren't exactly secret, the House took the extremely unusual measure of withholding all official reports of the meetings from being printed in the House Journal until final decisions had been reached, which severely limited Bernard's knowledge of and ability to impede the meetings. Finally on June 25 – after all necessary meetings were concluded – the House voted to disclose these furtive meetings in the pages of the *Journals of the House of Representatives*, and they read in full:

> On a Motion made and seconded, *Ordered,* That all the Proceedings relative to the sending a Committee to *New-York,* be printed in this Day's Journal as follows, *viz.*
>
> *In the House of* Representatives, *June* 6, 1765.
>
> The House taking into Consideration the many difficulties to which the Colonies are and must be reduced by the Operation of some late Acts of Parliament; after some Time spent.
> On a Motion made and seconded, *Ordered,* That Mr. Speaker, Brigadier *Ruggles,* Col. *Partridge,* Col. *Worthington,* General *Winslow,* Mr. *Otis,* Mr. *Cushing,* Col. *Saltonshall* and Capt. *Sheaffe,* be a Committee to consider what Measures had best be taken, and make Report.
> The Committee appointed for that Purpose, reported as follows.
> The Committee appointed to consider what dutiful, loyal and humble Address may be proper to make to our gracious Sovereign and his Parliament, in relation to the several Acts lately passed, for levying Duties and Taxes on the Colonies, have attended that Service, and are humbly of opinion:
> That it is highly expedient there should be a Meeting as soon as may be, of Committees from the Houses of Representatives or Burgesses in the several Colonies on this Continent to consult together on the present Circumstances of the Colonies, and the Difficulties to which they are and must be reduced by the operation of the late Acts of Parliament for levying Duties and Taxes on the Colonies, and to consider of a general and humble Address to his Majesty and the Parliament to implore Relief.
> And the Committee are further of opinion that a Meeting of such Committees should be held at *New-York* on the first Tuesday of *October* next, and that a Committee of three Persons be chosen by this House on the Part of this Province to attend the fame.

And that Letters be forthwith prepared and transmitted to the respective Speakers of the several Houses of Representatives or Burgesses in the Colonies aforesaid, advising them of the Resolution of this House thereon, and inviting such Houses of Representatives or Burgesses to join this with their Committees, in the Meeting, and for the Purposes aforesaid.

And that a proper Letter be prepared and forwarded to the Agent of the Province on these Matters in the mean time.

Read and accepted, and *Ordered,* That Mr. Speaker, Mr. *Otis.* and Mr. *Lee,* be a Committee to prepare a draft of Letters to be sent to the respective Speakers of the several Houses of Representatives in the Colonies, and make Report.

The Committee appointed for that purpose, reported the following draft.

Province of *Massachusetts-Bay. Boston, June* 8. 1765.

SIR;

THE House of Representatives of this Province in the present Session of the General Court, have unanimously agreed to propose a Meeting, as soon as may be, of Committees from the Houses of Representatives or Burgesses, of the several *British* Colonies on this Continent, to consult together on the present Circumstances of the Colonies and the Difficulties to which they are and must be reduced by the Operation of the Acts of Parliament for levying Duties and Taxes on the Colonies ; and to consider of a general and united, dutifull, loyal and humble Representation of their Condition to his Majesty, and the Parliament, to implore Relief. The House of Representatives of this Province have also voted to propose that such Meeting be at the City of *New-York,* on the first Tuesday of *October* next, and have appointed a Committee of three of their Members to attend that Service, with such as the other Houses of Representatives or Burgesses in the several Colonies may think fit to appoint to meet them: And the Committee of the House of Representatives of this Province are directed to repair to said *New-York* on said first Tuesday of *October* next accordingly. If therefore your honorable House should agree to this Proposal, it would be acceptable, that as early Notice of it as possible might be transmitted to the Speaker of the House of Representatives of this Province.

SAMUEL WHITE, Speak'r,

Read

Read and accepted, and *Ordered,* That the Speaker sign the same, and transmit it to the respective Speakers of the several Houses.

It being, agreeable to the Order of the Day, *Resolved,* That the House proceed to the Choice of a Committee of three Persons to meet the Committees from the several Houses of Representatives at the proposed Convention at *New-York,* the first Tuesday in *October* next.

Ordered, That Judge *Ruggles,* Mr. *Foster* of *Plymouth* and Col. *Bourn,* be a Committee to fort and count the Votes, who reported that *James Otis,* Esq; Col. *Worthington* and Col. *Partridge* were chosen by a majority of Votes. Col. *Worthington* having excused himself from that Service, the House came to the choice of a Person in his room, and the Committee reported that Brigadier *Ruggles* was chosen.

In the House of Representatives, *June* 20. 1765.

Whereas the House at their present Session made Choice of *James Otis, Oliver Partridge* and *Timothy Ruggles,* Esqrs, their Committee, to meet the Committees from the Houses of Representatives or Burgesses in the several Colonies on this Continent, that may be convened on the first Tuesday of *October* next at *New-York.*

Resolved, That there be paid to the said Committee out of the public Treasury, the Sum of *four Hundred and fifty Pounds,* to enable them to discharge the important Trust to which they are appointed; they upon their return to be accountable for the same.

In the House of Representatives, *June* 24 1765.

On a Motion made and seconded, *Ordered,* That Mr. *Cushing* of *Boston,* Capt. *Sheaffe.* Mr. *Dexter* of *Dedham,* Mr. *Woodridge* and Mr. *Foster* of *Plymouth,* be a Committee to prepare Instructions for the Committee of Congress, and make Report.

Read and accepted, and *Ordered,* That the Speaker sign the same.

> On a Motion made and seconded, Ordered. That Mr. *Cushing* of *Boston,* Capt. *Sheaffe* and Mr. *Gray,* be a Committee to prepare the Draft of a Letter to the Agent, and make Report.
>
> The Committee for that purpose appointed, reported the draft of a Letter to the Agent.
> Read and accepted, and *Ordered,* That a fair draft thereof be signed by the Speaker, and forwarded to the Agent as soon as may be.

Thus on June 6, the House agreed to create a nine member committee to assess the province's "difficulties." The key to making the plan a success was convincing the moderate members to participate, and why not participate in a plan championed by the newly moderate Jemmy Otis? Though Jemmy and Cushing represented Boston and Popular Party ally Edward Shaeffe represented Charleston, the committee was dominated by moderate and Court Party figures including John Worthington, Oliver Partridge, Samuel White and the much reviled Court Party stalwart Timothy Ruggles. And again with rapidity so unusual for government that one can only suspect that the work had been previously completed, the committee issued a statement the same day as it was created. The statement concluded that "it is highly expedient there should be a Meeting as soon as may be, of Committees from the Houses of Representatives or Burgesses in the several Colonies on this Continent to consult together on the present circumstances." The committee's statement included all the details; the "Meeting" should be held on the first Tuesday of October in New York, and Massachusetts should send three representatives. Speaker White, Otis and Lee were assigned to draft letters to the other colonies, and again with suspicious rapidity the draft was produced and adopted just two days later. The meeting's stated purpose was guarded and deferential, suggesting only to assemble "to consider of a general and united, dutiful, loyal and humble Representation" to the King and Parliament. The Court Party dominated the election of delegates to the proposed meeting; the vote tally revealed that staunch loyalists John Worthington and Colonel Oliver Partridge and that apparent new friend of government James Otis were selected. Worthington "having excused himself from that Service," and was replaced by the even more ardent loyalist Brigadier Timothy Ruggles.

June 25, the day the report of the House committee meetings was published, was the last meeting day of the session; the General Court was suspended until mid-August – though that date would be severely missed. Governor

Bernard had been alerted to the committee meetings, but with the Court Party firmly in control, confessed to the Lords of Trade on July 8, 1765 that "It was impossible to oppose this Measure to any good purpose and therefore the friends of government took the lead in it; & have kept it in their hands." And yet he assured the Lords of Trade that "of the Committee appointed . . . Two of the three are fast friends to government of Great Britain. It is the general Opinion that nothing will be done in consequence of this intended Congress; but I hope I may promise myself that this province will act no indecent part therein." This was precisely the situation required in order for Bernard to view the "meeting" in New York as reasonably innocuous.

Jemmy's recent moderate pamphlets resulted in Otis appearing pacified, and Bernard had concluded that the Court Party had kept the explosive issue "in their hands." So while the Court Party felt in control, the Boston rebels renewed their activities. Their plans were fueled in part by the publication of the "Virginia Resolves" in the July 1, 1765 *Evening-Post*, which included those passed by the Virginia House of Burgesses and two additional resolves that had been proposed by Patrick Henry but discarded from the final draft by the Burgesses. The rejected resolves were confrontational and controversial, denying the colonies were "bound to yield Obedience" to Parliament and declaring "an Enemy" anyone who rejected the idea that the sole right to levy taxes on Virginians rested with the Virginian Assembly. The loyalist oligarchy was not nearly as strong in Virginia as it was in Massachusetts.

Predictably, Governor Bernard labeled the resolves originally debated in Virginia as "an alarmbell to the disaffected." John Adams later evoked a dying Oxenbridge Thacher proclaiming "Oh yes – they are men! they are noble spirits! It kills me to think of the lethargy and stupidity that prevails here. I long to be out. I will go out. I will go out. I will go into court make a speech, which shall be read after my death, as my dying testimony against this infernal tyranny." Thacher never made his great speech; he died a few days later on July 9, 1765. Jemmy had realized, probably with the assistance of his father, that the Popular Party's agenda could never be advanced by employing the Thacher or Virginia approach. Despite the differences in oligarch power, it is not surprising that the fiery Virginia approach did not work in Virginia and several other colonies. The governors of Virginia, North Carolina, Georgia, New Jersey and Delaware refused to convene their assemblies and thus obstructed official attendance to the "Meeting" by delegates from those colonies. The New Jersey and Delaware assemblies were undaunted and sent unofficial delegates.

In light of the Virginia Resolves, the *Gazette* lambasted the Massachusetts petition as a "tame, pusillanimous, daubed, insipid thing." But predictably, Hutchinson reported that Otis, unlike many of the rebels, had labeled the Virginia Resolves treasonous. Otis had worked his way into the confidences of the most important Court Party members. After his election to the House in May 1765 and to the New York Congress delegation, Otis once more took up his pen. *The Objections to the Taxation of our American Colonies by the Legislature of Great Britain briefly Considered,* an English pamphlet by member of the Board of Trade and amateur wit Soame Jenyns, was a chic little publication expounding the validity and superiority of virtual representation. In a series of articles in the *Gazette*, which were published later that year in London as *Considerations on Behalf of the Colonists in a Letter to a Noble Lord*, Otis responded to *Objections* first by characterizing the noble Lord's opinions as the "half-born sentiments of a courtier" and "the crudities of a ministerial mercenary pamphleteer." *Letter to a Noble Lord* took exception to Jenyns's flippant attitude toward the colonies's political problems. Jemmy stated plainly that the "king, lords and commons conjointly, as the supreme legislature, in *fact* as well as in *law*, represent and act for the realm, and all the dominions, if they please," but this obvious observation did not render the arrangement equitable, and he continued to distinguish between representation in Parliament and representation in the House of Commons. The colonies enjoyed the former in a virtual or transcendent sense; they clearly did not have the latter. Jemmy scorned Englishmen who offered as proof of representation the "everlasting changes to the colonists on the cases of Manchester, Birmingham and Sheffield, who return no members." Otis's argument was simple: if Manchester, Birmingham, Sheffield and Boston were not represented in fact, then "they ought to be" because it "is a pity" that Britain's actual body of voters was so limited. Jemmy observed that:

> The Great love pillows of down for their [the oligarchy's] own heads, and chains for those below them. Hence 'tis pretty easy to see how it has been brought about, that in all ages despotism has been the general tho' not quite universal government of the world. No good reason however can be given in any country why every man of a sound mind should not have his vote in the election of a representative. If a man has but little property to protect and defend, yet his life and liberty are things of some importance.

The philosophical arguments remained: only representation in fact was representation, and the basis of government was life and liberty, not Lockean property. Property ownership was foundational to the feudal system, so its importance must be diminished in order to free the general population. And by pounding the point of actual representation in the House of Commons, Jemmy was continuing to employ the undeniable leverage of colonial demographics to force the inevitable conclusion.

Otis directly references the demographic argument and essentially declares that England economically needs the colonies more than the colonies need England.

> The [colonial] consumer ultimately pays the tax, and 'tis confessed on all hands, and is the truth, that America, in fact or eventually, consumes one half the manufactures of Britain. The time is hastening when this fair daughter will be able, if well treated, to purchase and pay for all the manufactures her mother will be able to supply. She wants no gifts, she will buy them, and that at her mother's own price, if let lone.

Then he expands on the demographics argument:

> That I may not appear too paradoxical, I affirm, and that on the best information, the Sun rises and sets every day in the sight of five millions of his majesty's American subjects, white, brown and black. ...The period is not very remote when these may be increased to an hundred millions. Five millions of as true and loyal subjects as ever existed, with their good affections to the best civil constitution in the world, descending to unborn miriads, is no small object.

The population of the colonies is exploding, and "if let lone," not only will England reap the financial benefits, but:

> Revolutions have been; they may be again; nay, in the course of time they must be. Provinces have not been ever kept in subjection. ... Why it is of little importance to my master, whether a thousand years hence, the colonies remain dependant on Britain or not; my business is to fall on the only means to keep them ours for the longest term possible. How can that be done? Why in one word, it must be by

nourishing and cherishing them as the apple of your *eye*. All history will prove that provinces have never been disposed to independency while well treated.

Jemmy also spills substantial ink in *Considerations* criticizing what he viewed as the likely cause of the oligarchy's "lust of power and unreasonable domination." The Empire's massive debt, continued spending, and perpetuation of power through "bribes and pensions" was fueling its irrational pursuit of revenue:

> The national debt is confessed on all hands, to be a terrible evil, and may, in time, ruin the state. But it should be remembered, that the colonists never occasioned its increase, nor ever reaped any of the sweet fruits of involving the finest kingdom in the world, in the sad calamity of an enormous overgrown mortgage to state and stock jobbers. No places nor pensions, of thousands and tens of thousands sterling, have been laid out to purchase the votes and influence of the colonists. They have gone on with their settlements in spite of the most horrid difficulties and dangers; they have ever supported, to the utmost of their ability, his majesty's provincial government over them, and, I believe are, to a man, and ever will be, ready to make grants for so valuable a purpose. But we cannot see the equity of our being obliged to pay off a score that has been much enhanced by bribes and pensions, to keep those to their duty who ought to have been bound by honour and conscience.

Of course, jobs and pensions costing "thousands and tens of thousands sterling" have been spent "to purchase the votes" of Englishmen, but Otis perceives no reason why the colonists should pay for such "bribes and pensions." The solution for those oligarchs who've plundered the treasury or invested heavily in government bonds?

> A few jobbers had better be left to hang and drown themselves, as was the case after the South Sea bubble, and a few small politicians had better be sent after them, than the nation be undone. This would, in the end, turn out infinitely more beneficial to the whole, than imposing taxes on such as have not the means of paying them.

In the midst of the Wheelwright bankruptcy that fueled a credit and liquidity crisis, Whitehall wishes to tax and spend more; Jemmy found this not only untenable but also dangerous:

> In the way revenue has been sometimes managed, the universe, would not long set bounds to the rapid increase of the national debt. If places, pensions, and dependencies shall be ever increased in proportion to new resources, instead of carefully applying such resources to the clearing off former incumbrances, the game may be truly infinite.

If Whitehall were permitted to tax according to what it wishes to spend, and neither the rights of tax payers nor the magnitude of the debt limited its spending, then the government's ability to tax and spend "may be truly infinite." Otis observed that the people's ability to limit taxation is directly connected to their ability to limit government and the ability to tax without direct consent and without regard for its debt conferred unlimited power to the government. Consent continued to be the lodestar; little else was important. "No Englishman, nor indeed any other freeman," Otis argued, "is or can be rightfully taxed, except by own actual consent." No colonial writer appeared as well-read or closely acquainted with language as did Otis, who was just as capable of meticulous literary analysis as he was bombast:

> ... when a man in Europe or America votes a tax on his constituents, if he has any estate, he is at the same time taxing himself, and that by *his own consent;* and of all this he must be conscious unless we suppose him to be void of common sense.
>
> No one ever contended that "the consent of the very person he chuses to represent him," nor that "the consent of the majority of those who are chosen by himself, *and* others of his fellow subjects to represent them," should be obtained before a tax can be rightfully levied. The pitiful chicanery here, consists wholly in substituting *and* for *or.* If for *and,* we read *or,* as the great Mr. J _____ s himself inadvertently reads it a little afterwards, the same proposition will be as strictly true, as any political aphorism or other general maxim whatever, the theorems of Euclid not excepted; namely, *"that no Englishman, nor indeed any other freeman, is or can be rightfully taxed, but by his own actual consent in person, or by the majority of those who are chosen by himself or others his fellow subjects to represent the whole people."*

"If let lone," England will forestall revolution; Otis makes clear that history demands liberty or independence. The colonies should be treated as "apple of your *eye*," as the financial and demographic dynamo that they clearly were because "Provinces have not been ever kept in subjection." No clearer statement of the position he likely spent a year developing had been made: direct representation in Parliament or revolution. The first was demographically impossible, and the second was historically probable. Miraculously, he made this entire argument after repenting in "Sackcloth & ashes" according to the governor, after he was assumed harmless enough to be elected to the Stamp Act Congress by a Court Party controlled House.

Aggressive declarations of "rights" were replaced by a persuasive discussion of demographics, the people's ability to limit government, and consent, and these discussions formed an astonishingly precise description of America's future Constitution – a description that perhaps was not so astounding to the radicals of 1765. Otis's words were later echoed in 1832 when England increased voting rights and generally aligned parliamentary representation with population, so that the newer large cities had more members of Parliament.

In *Vindication* and *Noble Lord*, Otis addresses Blackstone's position of Parliamentary supremacy. In its August 19, 1765 edition, the *Gazette* asked Otis to explain this passage from *Noble Lord*:

> True it is, that from the nature of the British constitution, and also from the idea and nature of a supreme legislature, the parliament represents the whole community or empire, and have an undoubted power, authority, and jurisdiction, over the whole; and to their final decisions the whole must and ought peaceably to submit.

The *Gazette* asked, "If the Parliament should decree away the Property, Liberty, and Life of every Member of the Empire that was not a Member of Parliament, ought we in that case peaceably to submit?" The question perfectly made Otis's point: Parliament is the supreme power, and what can the colonists do when Parliament exercises its power without the their consent and against their will? Otis and Sam Adams would later be accused of being the *Gazette*'s "managers," so one must wonder whether Otis was asking this question of himself.

Otis concluded that if Parliament's will is absolute and unreviewable, and in the final analysis the colonies are under the sole control of Parliament, then the only solution to the problem of structuring the empire is direct colonial representation in Parliament. Otis broached the subject in *Vindication* and attempted a "Defence" of it. Yet by *Noble Lord*, he admitted the idea had little support on either side of the Atlantic. Otis observed that Jenyns "has made himself quite merry with the modest proposal some have made, though I find it generally much disliked in the colonies, and thought impracticable, namely – an American representation in parliament." The "some" who had previously proffered this proposal refers to Otis himself, previously writing anonymously. Otis's tactic was twofold: first, to illustrate and confirm that the establishment's position, as expressed via Blackstone, only left "American representation in parliament" as a solution; second, to project a colonial position that was reasonable and ostensibly cooperative. If the only logical solution to the problem, given Blackstone's position, was "American representation in parliament," and Parliament rejected that position, then who was being unreasonable? Otis knew that representation in Parliament would be – and had to be, given the colonies's population explosion – firmly repudiated by Parliament and Whitehall, but publicly entertaining the topic advanced the rebels's observations from the coffee houses and publishing offices and into the public square. Blackstone's solution was no solution at all, and it was Parliament and Whitehall, not the colonists, who were unreasonable and uncooperative. This shift – such deft legerdemain that it could be unnoticed – was seismic and structural in effect; now, the colonists could believe that it was the rebels who were reasonable and Parliament who was capricious and contradictory. Now, all the conspiracy theories began to take root.

Otis maintained the tension between assuring the oligarchy that his "Confession" was "sincere" and stoking the fire. He would apologize one day and declare the next that taxation required consent. The atmosphere in Boston was taut with apprehension just as Otis had seemed to convince Bernard that the friends of government had everything under control and "nothing will be done" at the meeting in New York. And just as Otis was publically declaring his sincere "Confession" and debating American representation in parliament, privately, the colonists were preparing a different kind of response to Blackstone. Almost certainly under the direction of "The Loyal Nine" – the high command of the subsequent Sons of Liberty – Ebenezer McIntosh and his well-coordinated mob orchestrated nights of terror in August. James Freeman recorded the events in notebooks written at the time.

Augt 14. The effigies of the distributor of stamps, pendant, behind whom hung a boot newly soled with a Grenville sole, out of wc. [which] proceeded the Devil was exhibited on the great tree in main street. The spectacle continued ye whole day wh .out the least opposition. About evening a no. of reputable persons assembled, cut down the effigies, placed it on a [wagon?] , and covering it with a sheet, they proceeded in a regular solemn manner, amidst the acclamations of the populace thro the town, till they arrived at ye Court House, where after a short pause, they pass'd, & proceeding down King's Street, soon reached a certain edifice then building for ye reception of stamps wc they quickly leveled with ye ground it stood on & wh the wooden remains there from march'd to Fort Hill, where kindling a fire the [they] burnt the effigies. The gentleman who was to have been the distributor of the stamps had his house near the hill, & by that means it received from the populace some small insults, such as breaking the windows of his kitchen which would have ended there, had not some indiscretions been committed by his friends within, wc so enraged the people, that they were not to be restrained from entering the house; the damages however was not great.

According to a letter Cyrus Baldwin sent to Loammi Baldwin the next day, the mob had written "It's a glorious sight to See a Stamp-man hanging on a Tree" on the left arm of Andrew Oliver's effigy. And, as Freeman notes, Oliver's effigy was paraded through town, decapitated and burnt. The governor ordered drummers to sound a general alarm, but the drummers were too busy destroying Oliver's house. And, according to Baldwin, "tho the Sheriff with another Officer or two went and askd liberty to take it down but to no purpose." Baldwin summarized the mob's attitude on the night of August 14th thus: "I beleve people never was more Univassally pleasd not so much as one could I hear say he was sorry, but a smile sat on almost every ones countinance." The soirees of August 14 and 26 forced Oliver's resignation as stamp distributor and rendered his store building and house ghastly heaps of contorted and smashed lumber and glass. William Story, the deputy register of the Vice-Admiralty whose juryless courts were about to assume substantial jurisdiction, watched as a mob demolished his home, ruined his important papers, and marched away with anything of value. Benjamin Hallowell's impressive home in Roxbury was gutted, and all the wine in his voluminous cellar eagerly guzzled. The mob had put Jemmy's words into action. It was only natural that sooner or later Thomas Hutchinson would feel the wrath of the people who had for so long been educated in Otis's philosophy.

Firebrand preacher and Colonel of the Black Regiment Jonathan Mayhew couldn't resist, and on Sunday, August 25, he delivered a sermon on tyranny and slavery, arguing that subjugation of any kind was enslavement. The jeremiad was a Mayhew classic; what it lacked in solid philosophical foundation, it made up for in an archetypal Puritan fire-and-brimstone screed with the government assuming the place of the devil. Mayhew's church was the congregation of choice for the Sons of Liberty and other men "of the Mob," and his choice of terms used in his speech – tyranny and slavery – knowingly and precisely echoed Otis's two pamphlets published a few months earlier. The night after Mayhew's "tyranny and slavery" jeremiad, August 26, Hutchinson's house was nearly obliterated, silver and money stolen, and his priceless collection of historical documents and personal papers were dumped in the street and scattered. James Freeman recorded the events:

> Augt 28th. Gov'r issues another proclamation, in wc. [which] he says, That on 26th of Augt towards evening a great no. of persons assembled them-selves in Boston armed wh clubs & staves, and first attacked Wm. Story's house, broke his windows, damaged & destroyed great part of the furniture, & burnt & scattered the books & files of the court of admiralty. After wh they proceeded to Benjan. Hallowell's house / comptroller of the customs / broke down the fence before it, broke his windows, enter'd his house, damaged & destroyed the furniture, drank his liquors, took away his wearing apparel, broke open his desk & trunks, & took all his papers and about £30 in money. The same night they attacked Gov'r Hutchinson's house, entered it, broke down & destroyed the wainscot & partitions, broke & destroyed every window with all the furniture, destroyed or carried off the wearing apparels jewels, books, & papers of every kind, took away or destroyed all the liquors, & carried off about £900 sterling in money, & all the plate, and cut down the cupola on the top of the house & uncovered great part of the roof.
> The same people continued assembled the whole night, committing outrages, threatening the custom house, & several dwelling houses. Three hundred pounds offered for the discovery of the leaders, and £100 for assistants.

In Peter Oliver's words:

> ... the Mob of Otis & his clients plundered Mr. Hutchinsons House of its full Contents, destroyed his Papers, unroofed his House, & sought his & his Children's Lives, which were saved by Flight. ... The Mob, also, on the same Evening, broke into the Office of the Register of the Admiralty, & did considerable Damage there; but were prevented from an utter Destruction of it. They also sought after the Custom House Officers; but they secreted themselves ... it was in vain to struggle against the Law of Otis, & the Gospel of his black Regiment ... Such was the Frenzy of Anarchy ...

Peter Oliver claimed his brother Andrew was forced to resign his office as stamp master under oath "on pain of Death." Boston was in a state of astonishment at both the mob's audacity and the possibility of unseating the oligarchy. Jemmy Otis moderated a hastily arranged town meeting on August 27th that passed a resolve declaring the "utter detestation of the extraordinary & violent proceedings of a number of Persons unknown" – given Jemmy's deft employment of "counterwork" over the past year, nothing short of official condemnation could be expected. More importantly, the meeting put on the record that the perpetrators were "Persons unknown." The meeting then stated it would assist "in the Suppression of all Disorders of a like nature that may happen when called upon for that purpose." It is an artfully attenuated bold statement – "that may happen when called upon." No affirmative action taken or proactive steps employed, no investigation, all "Persons unknown" and "may" and "when." Josiah Quincy recorded Hutchinson's appearance and speech in the Superior Court the same day, writing,

> The Distress a Man must feel on such an Occasion can only be conceived by those, who, the next Day, saw his Honour the Chief Justice come into Court, with a look big with the greatest Anxiety, cloathed in a Manner which would have excited Compassion from the hardest Heart, his Dress had not be strikingly contrasted by the other Judges and Bar, who in their Robes. – Such a Man, in such a Station, thus habited, with Tears starting from his Eyes, and a Countenance which strongly told the inward of his Soul.

Despite Otis's quick repudiation of the violence, the members of the oligarchy knew that "Mr Otis, Junr is at the head of the Confederacy." Peter Oliver ascribed the sacking of Hutchinson's house to "the Mob of Otis & his clients" and said the affair was "a Joy to Mr. Otis." Those "clients" were the merchants who Otis repeatedly represented against the customs establishment, and it was no coincidence that offices of the customs and admiralty administrations were targeted. Bernard did not accuse Otis of actually directing of the mob but laid the destruction at his door: "It is very Fair (without penetrating into the Secrets of the Cabinet) to impute that inhuman Treatment of him [Hutchinson] to such professed resentment: especially when the Resentor & the popular Conductor is the same person." Bernard had already consented to Otis as Stamp Act Congress delegate, so being labeled the "Resentor & the popular Conductor" wasn't of much concern to Otis now; Bernard could hardly rescind his consent without direct evidence of Otis's involvement in the mob activity, of which there would never be any. It is noteworthy that in labeling Otis "the Resentor & the popular Conductor," Bernard claimed that Otis was behind the incendiary paper war – "Resentor" – and the mobs – "popular Conductor." The clever James Otis would never provide Bernard with the incontrovertible evidence he would need to damn him and publically Otis only professed shock and disgust at the destruction of Hutchinson's and Oliver's homes – at least for now.

The oligarchy almost uniformly suspected Otis was the "Conductor" of the attacks; was he? And to what extent were the efforts of the mobs, Sam Adams, Jemmy Otis and Jonathan Mayhew coordinated? There is no evidence that Jemmy Otis actually directed the mobs, and there is no evidence that Otis coordinated the events of the summer of 1765 with Adams and Mayhew, but to suggest that what appeared to be orchestrated was actually all coincidence is to ignore the direct line of communication from Otis to Adams and Mayhew and from Adams and Mayhew to the mobs. Otis and Mayhew knew each other well, and Otis and Adams worked closely together on articles and in the House, and Adams was well-connected to the mobs. While the events of 1765 may not have been entirely planned, it defies logic to suggest that Otis, Adams, Mayhew and the mobs were ignorant of each other's activities. Otis, perhaps more than others, knew the explosive nature of the situation in Boston; he would later write to his sister that he was holding the town together and that without him, anarchy would erupt. His letter to his sister essentially claimed that he was coordinating everything and walking the fine line between rebellion and anarchy. And, according to his plan in which the less savory aspects were delegated to others, Mayhew and the mobs played their roles perfectly. So that he wouldn't be targeted, he required accomplices, a role that Mayhew and Adams filled flawlessly. And the Harvard educated lawyer would never get his hands dirty destroying a house; the mobs, too, played their role. The rebellion had to be a decentralized effort; one man could be arrested and jailed and hanged. Regardless, Otis was rightfully labeled the "Conductor."

The contagion was not limited to Boston and the militia's control seemed negligible. From James Freeman's notebooks:

Sep'r 16.
Mr Messervey distributor of Stamps for prov. Of N. Hampsh. resigned his employment in Boston. This occasioned great joy among the people. The morn'g ushered in wh. Ringing of bells. Train of artillery march'd down King street, fired several rounds &c. Towards evening a guard of men armed belonging to the militia were posted near Liberty tree to present disorders from the concourse of people. Bonfires in Charles-town & Cambridge.

By August of 1765, New England society's foundation had been so destabilized that it did not regain its solidity until after the Revolution. Public displays of government authority almost entirely vanished and government operation proceeded under the Loyal Nine's invisible guiding hand. The government issued generous bounties for the mob leaders, but no one came forward. Of course, the "Persons unknown" were quite known, and Bernard ordered well-known mob leader Ebenezer McIntosh arrested, but he was released once it became clear that no one would offer evidence against him. Further encouraging Bernard's cooperation, the sheriff reported that the citizens would decline their duties as armed night watchmen if mob leaders were jailed. The total mob control of Boston is exemplified in its ability to maintain peace and unleash mayhem at will.

Bernard hoped to delay the meeting of the General Court until Whitehall approved moving the Court out of Boston. In an August 18, 1765 letter to Board of Trade Secretary John Pownall marked "private," Bernard asserted that the Court would "neither be free from Terror on the one hand, nor undue Influence on the Other" if it remained in Boston. He continued, "The mobs are bad but the Politicians are worse." Whitehall declined; nevertheless, the governor hoped that moderate representatives would supply a calming influence when the fall session of the General Court opened on September 25,

1765 – six weeks after it was originally intended to convene. After all, the Court Party still controlled both houses.

Governor Bernard sat before the General Court that late September morning and opened with, "I have called you together at this unusual Time in pursuance of the unanimous Advice of a very full Council, that you may take into Consideration the present State of the Province, and determine what is to be done at this difficult and dangerous Conjuncture. I need not recount to you the violences which have been committed in this Town ..." Then he staked out the safest position he could in response to the Stamp Act: "I shall not enter into any Disquisition of the Policy of the Act: It has never been a Part of my Business to form any Judgment of it ; and as I have not hitherto had any Opportunity to express my Sentiments of it, I shall not do it now." Importantly, not only did Bernard fail to defend the Stamp Act, but he distanced himself from it, doubtless an admission the radicals's and mob's strength. Bernard vacillated between insisting and begging the House to fully reimburse those whose property was destroyed by the mobs. Despite aggressively remaining neutral on the subject of the Stamp Act, he added, "And I trust that the Supremacy of that Parliament over all the Members of their wide and diffused Empire never was and never will be denied within these Walls."

Bernard then illuminated an obvious problem:

> The Right of the Parliament of *Great-Britain* to make Laws for the *American* Colonies, however it has been controverted in *America,* remains indisputable at *Westminster.* If it is yet to be made a question, who shall determine it but the Parliament? If the Parliament declares that this Right is inherent in them, are they like to acquiesce in an open and forceable Opposition to the exercise of it? Will they not more probably maintain such Right, and support their own Authority? Is it in the Will or in the Power, or for the Interest of this Province to oppose such Authority? If such Opposition should be made, may it not bring on a Contest which may prove the most detrimental and ruinous Event which could happen to this people?

It's almost as if Bernard were a covert radical as he made a fairly radical observation: the only body that could decrease Parliament's power is Parliament, and why would Parliament ever decrease its own power? A governing body never voluntarily abdicates power; it can only be forcefully taken. Bernard's argument might have held sway over Jemmy and the House radicals who often proclaimed their undying fealty to Great Britain – if only they had meant what they said. Bernard was shrewd enough to admit Otis was capable of a "counterwork" but still too naïve to believe it.

Bernard then referenced the problems that Wheelwright's bankruptcy had caused, saying that some "argued from the inexpediency of it at this Time, and the inability of the Colonies to bear such an Imposition" – the Stamp Act could be acceptable if only the province could afford it. Bernard did not refute this claim, acknowledging that none of the radicals actually held this position. Finally, Bernard asserted that obedience to the Stamp Act was required for the province's basic functioning, as the Courts and legal documents in general all required stamps.

> When the Courts of Justice are shut up, no one will be able to sue for a Debt due to him or an injury done to him. Must not then all Credit and mutual Faith cease of Course and Fraud and Rapine take their Place? Will any ones Person or Property be safe when their sole Protector the Law is disabled to act?

In the end, Bernard resorted to maintaining that compliance with the Stamp Act was a necessary bulwark against a tsunami of anarchy. The radicals duly noted Bernard's concerns about safety and would soon offer their own solution. And they would too soon have a response to Bernard's observation that Parliament alone can make taxes "a question," and Parliament alone can decrease its power. Bernard ended his late September morning speech with, "This Province seems to me to be upon the Brink of a Precipice," an observation on which he and the radicals would agree, though they'd differed on whether leaping into the abyss was resignation to anarchy or resistance to tyranny.

The next day, Bernard sent formal notice to the house that "*A Ship is arrived in this Harbour with stamped Papers on board for the King's Use in this Province; and also with other stamped Papers for the like Use in the Province of New-Hampshire and Colony of* Rhode-Island." And Bernard begged the General Court for assistance in what to do with the shipload of stamps "As Mr. Oliver *has declined the Office of Distributor of Stamped Papers*. ..." The House replied the same day that they did not have any "interest themselves in this matter." The House did not even consider reimbursing the oligarchs whose houses, businesses, and properties were destroyed. Rather, they occupied their day with mundane matters such as approving the sale of estates in probate to settle the deceased's debts. The Boston town meeting also had dealt with Oxenbridge Thacher's July death by electing someone no less radical. Voting was tight, but on the second ballot, Samuel Adams defeated John Ruddock and John Rowe and became the newest member of the Boston bench. While Sam Adams was no more radical than Thacher – doubtless anyone could be more radical than Thacher – Adams was a better writer, had a stronger philosophy of rights, and perhaps most importantly, had strong connections to the mobs that ruled Boston. Thacher was radical but not particularly effective; Adams was both. Bernard, realizing that the House was determined to be unhelpful and that the Stamp Act's flames of rebellion begun to burn amongst the moderates, suspended the session of the General Court after just two days.

Preparations for the "general Congress" in New York commenced, the three Massachusetts delegates withdrew their expense money of £150 each, and the meeting that Bernard doubted would occur evolved into an impressive congregation of the greatest and most radical colonial minds. The conservative *Boston Evening-Post* mustered interest in the New York gathering, printing on September 9, 1765, "We hear that the Meeting of the Commissioners from the several provinces will be general to the great pleasure of every Inhabitant of this [province], where it was first proposed." The August 26 *Gazette* printed a story about the choice of Christopher Gadsen, Thomas Lynch, and John Rutledge as the commissioners from South Carolina. The *New-York Mercury* reported from Philadelphia on September 30 that "The Gentlemen appointed by [the Pennsylvania] Assembly [John Dickinson, John Morton, and George Bryan] to assist at the General Congress at New York, we hear set out this Day [September 19] for that Place." The same *New-York Mercury* issue printed another story proclaiming that "those from Boston and Connecticut are daily expected" and that the "Commissioners from Pennsylvania and Rhode-Island" had arrived. The idea of a colonial convention had electrified the public imagination.

Jemmy moderated a tumultuous Boston town meeting on Wednesday, September 18, 1765, and the meeting again issued "Instructions." Otis, as Boston's representative to the New York "Meeting," received specific direction "to contribute the Utmost of his Abelity, in having the Rights of the Colonies stated in the clearest vein." In its instructions, the town warned against "arbitrary unconstitutional Innovations" that the Stamp Act relied upon and asserted that "It is certain we were in no sense represented in the Parliament of Great Britain." These were strong words; the town meeting had clearly moved beyond road paving and hog corralling. It addition to "unconstitutional Innovations," the town was deeply concerned about the expansion and employment of "Courts of Admiralty without a Jury." Given Jemmy's history of winning customs cases, the town knew that juryless courts would be widely utilized to prosecute resistance. The town blamed England for the recent war that "brought upon themselves a Debt almost insupportable" and was of "very little if any advantage" to the colonists. The war and its consequences resulted from Whitehall's not Boston's policies. And finally, perhaps the most significant issue the rebels had with the tax, was that "if carried into Execution, will become a further Grieveance to us as it will afford a Precedent for the Parliament to Tax us in all future Time, and in all such Ways and Measures, as they shall Judge meet without our Consent," which clearly abrogates "the Inherent unalienable Rights of the People." In a final act of united rebellion, the town meeting then "Voted unanimously" to approve the instructions. Delegate Ruggles had also received private instructions from Governor Bernard, who wrote a letter to Ruggles on September 2, 1765 confirming that he was to act as a "friend of government" and insisting that he permit nothing short of submission to the Stamp Act in order to rescue Massachusetts from "Ruin." So as Otis was told to be alert to rights, Ruggles was told to be alert to ruin.

The Massachusetts delegation and John Cotton, the House of Representatives's clerk whom the delegates had coerced into acting as Secretary of the Congress, departed for New York on the Old Post Road on October first. They arrived in New York six days later and secured rooms at the Kings Arms, an inn popular with many of the delegates. Despite the absence of Virginia, North Carolina, and Georgia, the collection of 27 colonial representatives was novel. John Watts reported to General Robert Monckton on October 12, 1765 that the "Committees are met" and "to do 'em justice, I believe they have deputed some of their best people, and I imagine the fruits of their deliberations will be sensible and moderate enough." New York Lieutenant Governor Cadwallader Colden ignored the Congress, refusing to recognize the delegates or their "Meeting." The commander of British forces in America, General Thomas Gage, was circumspect, writing to Secretary of State Conway that the delegates were "of different Characters & Opinions, but it was to be feared that the Spirit of Democracy was strong amongst them"; however, curiosity got the best of Gage, and he threw a dinner party. David Meade, a young Virginian who was in New York with John Randolph as part of a grand tour of the colonies, was one of the "very numerous" attendees at Gage's soiree and penned a sketch of the Massachusetts delegation.

> Of the company... were three deputies from Massachusetts, viz, General Ruggles, Col. Partridge, and the distinguished champion of his country's rights at that time, Mr. Otis. ... Mr Otis, of the year '65, appeared to be a modest sensible man, who was no stranger to good company, of middle stature, inclining to be fat, little (if any) over middle age. Brigadier Ruggles was, to appearances, not less than seventy years of age, very tall, very taciturn, and of aspect neither engaging nor patrician. Col. Partridge was a pert little man, with the coat of a gentleman, he a complete clown in his manners, manifested the most entire ignorance of the usages which prevail in polished societies.

Gossip spread from the dinner party and the "Meeting," and Governor Bernard wrote to Pownall on November 5, 1765 that he'd received information claiming Jemmy declared "the Province of Massachusetts would never be in order, until the Council was appointed from Home" while at Gage's party. It's evident why Gage feared "Spirit of Democracy was strong amongst them." According to Otis, it was only local, actual representation that would calm the mobs – the very mobs that the Boston oligarchy assumed Otis controlled.

The members of the "general congress" first formally met on October 7 in City Hall. The Massachusetts lawyers could compare their homegrown scholarship, legal and speaking skills with those trained in English Inns of Court such as Pennsylvania's John Dickinson and South Carolina's John Rutledge, and the other delegates could meet the rather famous Boston lawyer, writer and agitator about whom they'd heard so much. Since the congress was a Massachusetts creation, it was agreed that the chairman should be from that province. "The clown" Colonel Partridge was not even considered, and according to New York delegate John Watts, "Otis aimed at it and would have succeeded, but they thought as he had figured much in the popular way, it might give their meeting an ill grace." The congress members knew they needed an official who would lend credibility and sanction to the meeting, as they were very aware that many governors and "friends of government" viewed the congress with suspicion and disdain. Otis, though an obvious choice, was in the minds of the oligarchy too closely allied with the rebels and the mobs, and his reputation outside of Massachusetts was still that of a fiery radical. There was really only one logical choice: Ruggles, the Court Party stalwart, who would give the imprimatur of legitimacy to the entire proceeding.

In his first action, Ruggles appointed a committee to produce a declaration of congress's resolves and selected the meeting's youngest delegate John Rutledge as chairman. Ruggles may have thought that the young Southerner would prove timid and thus moderate. But Rutledge was more than capable, and John Dickinson and James Otis served with him on the committee. The two weeks spent discussing the resolves embodied a pivotal historical moment wherein the colonies needed to choose between maintaining their individual identities or surrendering a bit of that independence for a unified voice and – perhaps they perceived this – a greater independence. Delegate Gadsden wanted a pronouncement on the rights of Englishmen, whereas Livingston argued for concession on the issue of Parliament's sovereign legislative power, and Johnson believed the charters offered reasonable protection. Caesar Rodney observed that finding common ground – for the first time amongst the colonies – proved difficult; writing home on October 20, 1765, Rodney said the debates were "one of the most Difficult Tasks I ever yet see Undertaken. ... However After arguing, and Debating two weeks on Liberty, privilege, Perogative &c &c in an Assembly of the greatest Ability I ever yet saw, We happily finished them." Despite Ruggles's likely intentions, the triumvirate of Rutledge, Dickinson and Otis proved to be a committee of some of the most learned and capable ever assembled in the colonies. Rutledge recalled that Otis was one of the leaders, and Delegate McKean of Delaware claimed that Otis was "the boldest and best speaker." The precise role of any participant is unknown, but Jemmy clearly made an impression.

The fourteen restrained yet firm resolves were adopted on October 19, recognizing reasonable subordination to Parliament but declaring that taxation without actual representation violated the colonists's rights while declining Otis's suggestion to request direct American representation in the House of Commons. Again, Otis was doing his conspicuous best to appear reasonable. The resolves repeated the widespread objection to the expanding jurisdiction of the juryless vice-admiralty courts. With the resolves established, appointments were made for Livingston, Johnson and Murdock to draft an address to the king; Rutledge, Tilghman, and Philip Livingston to draft a memorial and petition to the House of Lords; and Thomas Lynch, McKean, and James

Otis to draft a petition to the House of Commons. On Monday, October 21, the committees submitted their drafts, which were debated and returned to the committees for editing. The drafts were finally approved, and the final issue loomed. The majority of delegates officially presented credentials that echoed Otis's letter of invitation, but there were variations. A few delegations, such as Connecticut's, could not formally consent to any decisions prior to receiving approval from their colonies's assemblies, and the delegations from New Jersey and Delaware were entirely unofficial. Due to this menagerie of protocols, the congress concluded not to disclose the documents until all represented colonial assemblies reviewed them. A motion was then made to sign the documents, thereby formalizing their status as official products of the congress. Ruggles promptly moved that the documents first be approved by the colonial assemblies prior to anyone placing a signature on them, and with that suggestion, Ruggles refused to sign anything. The delegates agreed to keep secret Ruggles's refusal to sign so that "he would not have travel'd through N. England in safety had the fact been known." Ruggles then departed New York before the others in order to return to Boston before the countryside discovered that he had refused to sign the resolves, but all the delegations left Boston just a few days later, on October 24.

The resolves, address, memorial, and petition made no shocking claims – certainly nothing that Bernard and Whitehall hadn't seen in print a hundred times before – but did articulate moderate colonial opinion. Bernard, in an atypically and likely accidentally insightful observation, stated precisely the precedent set by the Stamp Act Congress when he wrote to Richard Jackson on November 7: "they have come to a set of resolutions much like those of separate Legislatures." The resolutions weren't new, but the Stamp Act Congress had acted as a prototypical national legislature. The paper products of the meeting were hardly the most significant results; rather, the meeting laid the foundation for colonial communication and eventual unification. These disparate colonies had never before met to unify their efforts and synthesize their thoughts in application to a common problem. Their existence up to that point had typically ricocheted from pointed apathy to sibling rivalry to affably brutish provocation and back again. The October 1765 "Convention at *New-York*" conceived the essence of a national consciousness and produced a model for colonial communication and unification efforts up through the revolution.

James Otis returned to Boston to witness years of revolutionary agitation coming to fruition against an intransigent government. It was November 1, and the Stamp Act officially went into effect. The Boston he returned to was fully engulfed in the flames of revolution. The terror of the mobs drove Governor Bernard to Castle William, but the rebels recalled Bernard's late September question: "Will any ones Person or Property be safe when their sole Protector the Law is disabled to act?" The courts were closed, but the Loyal Nine, the high command of the increasingly large "Sons of Liberty" mob, maintained order in the streets. As church bells tolled, a throng of Bostonians marched peacefully past the Town House to the gallows where effigies were hung of George Grenville and John Huske, who was rumored to have lobbied for the passage of the Stamp Act in the House of Commons. According to James Freeman's notes from that day:

> Nov'r 1st. being the day the stamp act <u>was to</u> take place, the morn'g was ushered in by the tolling of bells, & the vessels in the harbor displaying their colours half- mast high in token of mourning. Liberty tree adorned with the effigies of George Grenville & John Husk. The figures continued suspended whout molestation till 3 o'clock in afternoon, when they were cut down amid the acclamations of several thousand people of all ranks, & being placed in a cart were with great solemnity & order followed by the multitude, formed into regular ranks to the Court House, were the assembly was then sitting: from thence proceeding to the N. End of the town, & then returning up middle street they passed back thro' the T. [town] to the gallows, where the effigies were again hung up, & after continuing some time were cut down, when the populace, in token of their detestation of the men they were designed to represent, tore ym in pieces & flung their limbs with detestation into the air. This being done, 3 cheers were given & every man retired quietly to his own home, & the evening was more remarkable for peace & quietness than common

Freeman underlined "was to" in his notes; it was far from obvious whether the government could implement the Act. To further the mob's absolute control of the town, the Sons of Liberty negotiated a peace and mutual cooperation treaty between the North End and South End mobs; the agitation efforts of these street brawlers were focused on "Liberty" rather than wasted protesting the pope and Guy Fawkes. The treaty was celebrated by the new banker to the radicals, John Hancock, buying a round of drinks for the town. Bernard wrote home to Pownall that the mob was dancing to "Otis's tune," singing the words, "Who will Seize Merchants Goods, what Judge will condemn them, what court will dare to grant Writs of Assistance now." In a letter to Secretary Conway on November 25, 1765, Bernard admitted that he was only nominally the governor; the rebels ruled the mobs, and the mobs ruled the streets. Jemmy started signing his letters *Anno Liberatus Primo* – the first year of liberty.

CHAPTER VIII

a damned faction

The General Assembly was called into session on October 23, and the following day issued a lengthy reply to Bernard's September speech that read like a summary of Jemmy's pamphlets, asserting "that there are certain original inherent rights belonging to the people, which the parliament itself cannot divest them of ... among these is the right of representation in the same body which exercises the power of taxation." The House repeated the theme throughout the letter, referencing repeatedly the "rights which are derived to all men from nature." Near the end of the letter, the House refused to reimburse those whose property mobs destroyed, claiming that they "cannot conceive why it should be called an act of justice" for taxpayers to pay for the damages. Sam Adams was one of the primary drafters, and his work exhibited all the hallmarks of a thorough education in radical thought. On October 29, Sam Adams led the House in issuing their own "Sett of Resolves ready cutt & dried" that were replete with invocations of *rights* and *consent* and far more incendiary than those of the New York congress.

On the afternoon of Friday November 1, the Boston House of Representatives reported that "*James Otis*, Esq; returned from *New-York*, making his Appearance in the House, laid upon the Table the Proceedings of the Commissioners of the Congress at *New -York*." The House unanimously approved the resolves the next morning. The government that James Otis had threatened to set aflame was now a charred relic; the oligarchy went through the motions of governing, but in reality the radicals and mobs controlled Boston. Ruggles made it home alive but was officially sanctioned by the House for refusing to sign the Stamp Act resolves after testimony was given by "*James Otis*, and the *Oliver Partridge*, Esq'rs of their Conduct at the late Congress at *New-York*." The House appointed special agent Dennis De Berdt to Parliament to promote the resolves. In a letter to John Pownall on November 5, Bernard wrote that Jemmy, upon learning that the Council approved additional expenses to safeguard the stamps at Castle William, delivered a speech to the House "so mad & devilish that they all stood astonished & no one durst contradict him" and labeled the Council "a cursed Septemvirate (7 being a quorum) that endeavored to destroy the liberties of the People." Of course, Jemmy's own father was on the Council. The House promptly elected Jemmy chairman of a committee appointed to formally rebuke the Council and governor for approving province funds to protect the stamps. The committee's reprimand, adopted by the House, declared it "astonishing" that additional province funds were spent at the same time that "very heavy additional taxes, external and internal, have been imposed on them by the British Parliament, without their consent."

A week earlier at a Boston town meeting held the evening after his return, Otis gave an "inflamatory Harangue" that Bernard reported in a letter dated November 12, 1765; Otis "hoped no one would call pulling down 2 or 3 two penny Houses rebellion." Did Otis regret mob rule? Did he truly condemn the destruction of Hutchinson's house and Oliver's business? Publically, he could condemn violence but then turn around and incite the mob again. It seems most likely that he was the master manipulator who could work into the confidences of opposing factions, telling each what they desired to hear, and then position himself to get what he wanted. Otis knew and well-described the problems, and he offered various solutions. But the path from the problem to the solution was unclear; it seems that he knew that revolution was the only possible answer; he'd hinted at that conclusion several times. But his heart was that of an Englishman, and it was nearly inconceivable to entertain a future apart from the great empire. Nearly.

The opposing opinions that held sway in Otis's mind were revealed in a letter he wrote to William Samuel Johnson on November 12, 1765 regarding riots that were sweeping the colonies.

> God only know what all these things will end in, and to Him they must be submitted. In the meantime, 'tis much feared the Parliament will charge the Colonies with presenting petitions in one hand, and a dagger in the other.

The dagger was part of the reorganized Popular Party; the revolution that had begun in the courtrooms and print shops had now moved to the streets. The "Black Act," as it was called, was being openly defied. Newspapers continued printing without stamps, businesses operated, and mobs ensured that the absence of stamps didn't shut down the city. But it did shut down the courts, which couldn't operate without the stamps. On December 20, the town asked John Adams, Gridley, and Otis to plead with the Governor and Council to open the Courts with or without stamps. John Adams made the argument that the Stamp Act was unconstitutional and therefore "utterly void." The same Adams who had written Otis off as insane a few years prior was now making the same argument that Otis had made. While Adams reached back to an Otis argument of a few years prior, Otis made an even older one: the refusal to operate the courts was an abdication of government, suggesting that either the Popular Party operate its own courts or the province revert to a state of anarchy. Bernard would have been quite aware that this argument had been made against James II almost a century earlier, and it was used to depose the king and justify the English revolution of 1688. Again, Otis could denounce mob action but then employ the same argument against the English that the English had used to depose a king – and to what end was Otis suggesting the people take his argument? He was too clever to ever state an answer, but it almost certainly terrified Bernard; both Bernard and Otis knew he'd built a party capable of revolution. On April 11, 1766, Jemmy wrote to his sister:

> Dear sister, for near two years I have not had it in my power to spend any time for myself; it has been taken up for others and some of them perhaps will never thank me. The time however I hope is at hand when I shall be relieved from a task I shall never envy any man who in performing it shall pass the anxious wearisome days and nights which I have seen. This country must soon be at rest, or may be engaged in contests that will require neither the pen nor the tongue of a lawyer. ... If we are to be slaves the living have only to envy the dead, for without liberty ... I desire not to exist ...

He then went on to reveal his fears, concluding that he could not leave Boston because he was the moderating force holding the empire together.

> Besides till matters are settled in England I dare not leave the Town, as men's minds are in such a situation that every nerve is requisite to

keep things from running to some irregularity or imprudence, and some are yet wishing for an opportunity to hurting the country.

Without his steady hand guiding the party, the radicals would assume control, and the city would be engulfed in anarchy. In a letter to Otis on December 5, 1767, John Dickinson, the rebel from Philadelphia who Jemmy had met at the Stamp Act congress, expressed gratitude for Jemmy's cautious approach to rebellion.

> This Subject Leads me to inform you with Pleasure, because I think it must give you Pleasure, that the Moderation of your Conduct in composing the Minds of your Fellow-Citizens, has done you the highest Credit with us; you may be assured I feel a great satisfaction in hearing your praises.

At the time, moderate Tory Quakers, who mostly had no interest in rebellion, controlled Pennsylvania politics; Dickinson's rebelliousness was thus necessarily tempered by Quakers intolerant of radicalism. New England had been born and bred in fiery religious zealotry that approached the world with an active effort to shape it; in contrast, Quakers were greater dissenters, but could hardly be described as a people consumed with righteousness. Their grasp of principle was a firm tepidity with one foot always planted on the solid ground of caution. If it appeared that the rebels were inciting violence in Boston, Dickinson knew the cause would gain no traction in Philadelphia. Jemmy's cautious approach and outward rejection of violence enabled rebels in other colonies to promote the cause. Dickinson pleaded with Otis in that December 5 letter that Massachusetts be the first to "kindle the Sacred Flame" of liberty. In another letter from Dickinson shortly thereafter, he refers to Otis as "deservedly placed at the Head of such excellent Citizens." Dickinson's writings were very influential in the colonies and were reprinted in nearly every colonial paper, and yet Jemmy and the Boston radicals set the example for other colonies of how to translate words into action and how to develop a rebellious consciousness among the general population; despite Dickinson's popular writings and Boston's example, Philadelphia wouldn't become a rebellious city until 1775.

Perhaps the most illuminating comment about Otis's relationship to the radicals – the Sons of Liberty and the mobs – is contained in a private letter dated September 6, 1769 that Dr. Thomas Young wrote from Boston. Dr. Young was a radical's radical; he was the first signer of the Albany Constitution of the Sons of Liberty in 1766, moved to Boston, and then advocated completely abolishing the oligarchy and redistributing their wealth. By 1769, Dr. Young was one of the most prominent members of the Sons of Liberty, openly managing the organization under the supervision of Sam Adams. As with all other radicals with direct and obvious connections to the street mobs, Young would have only limited contact with Otis, so it's curious that in a letter to a friend, Young casually referred to Jemmy Otis as "our chairman." This title is curious for two reasons. First, the letter was written in 1769, a time when many historians assume that Otis's importance was negligible. By 1769, the Popular Party was long thought to have been under the control of the new group of radicals that included Sam Adams, Joseph Hawley, Hancock, Cushing and Bowdoin. Second, the only organization to which Dr. Young belonged is the Sons of Liberty. It's assumed that Otis was a member of that group, though "membership" was not exactly an official process. But most historians have assumed that Otis's interaction with the Sons of Liberty was, at most, tangential. He knew many of the active members well, particularly Sam Adams, but Otis didn't rally the mob in the streets or sing drunkenly at the Liberty Tree. So to have a high-ranking member of the Boston Sons of Liberty refer to Jemmy Otis as "our chairman" challenges commonly held conclusions about Otis's position in 1769 radical circles.

Perhaps Dr. Young is referring to Otis as chairman of various committees to which Young was appointed. On June 14, 1768 – over a year before writing the letter – the Town of Boston appointed Young to a committee. The Town of Boston would create many such committees that were almost exclusively composed of Sons of Liberty members. The committee members weren't necessarily members of the House or otherwise politically active; such committees were essentially a method of legitimizing the radical group and giving them official business. The 1768 committee's purpose was, in essence, to go to Roxbury and harass Bernard. It was something the Sons of Liberty may have done anyway, but now their work was official. The chairman of this committee was, technically, James Otis. The effort to legitimize and incorporate the Sons of Liberty into the Massachusetts political landscape included the creation of many such committees, including the Committee of Correspondence created on November 2, 1772, of which Otis was also chairman. And yet Jemmy's title was more honorary than indicative of his role on the committees, for he rarely engaged in any of their activities. Historians tend to dismiss as paranoia the oligarchy's belief that Otis was the leader of the rebels because

Otis often publically moderated or contradicted his radical positions and publically criticized mob activity. And yet the radicals seemed to agree with the oligarchy; in Dr. Young's 1769 letter, no Otis-chaired Sons of Liberty committee had recently met and Young's letter mentions no committee or related work. He wasn't referring to Otis as the chairman of any particular committee but rather to his generally perceived position within the Sons of Liberty; James Otis was "our chairman."

The winter swept in to Massachusetts in late 1765, all stamp distributors had resigned, and the stamps were secured in Castle William like some *plague bacillus* that no one dared touch. Customs and court houses ceased operation due to lack of stamps, effectuating a near government shut-down. Governor Bernard, earnestly considering Otis's abdication of government argument and fearful that any misstep on his part would invite another wave of violence, declared the arguments for opening the courts without stamps "very good" and asked the Superior Court to consider the matter. Meanwhile, both the Probate and Inferior Courts in Boston opened, even without stamps. Otis took to the pages of the *Gazette* to further the progress of his answer to the question *What action can the colonies take if Parliament chooses to ignore their rights?* Importantly, Otis had moved the debate of this question from the taverns and halls of government to the public sphere. Writing under the pseudonym "Hampden" in a December 30, 1765 *Gazette* article, Otis confessed:

> I am fully satisfied any kind of American representation in parliament would be universally disagreeable to the colonists, and from their distance, poverty, and other circumstances, is justly tho't impracticable. That this topick was never handled, but principally as argumentum ad huminem ...

Parliament is the supreme power, so the people have a right to be represented in it. Yet the option of American representation is by late 1765 acknowledged by all to be unfeasible. Otis then moves on to the next possible solution:

> If in the nature of things, and in some future age, a plan of a general union of all parts of the British empire under one equal and uniform direction and system of laws be possible to be carried into execution, yet it must be on such noble, generous and disinterested principles, that it is ten thousand to one if any such thing ever takes place —

So Otis quickly moved on to some kind of imperial federation of equally balances parts and just as quickly dismissed Britain as capable of having the principles required to create "any such thing." Otis positions the rebels as being the reasonable party constantly exploring solutions, and repeatedly claims that the "friends of government" are inflaming the problems.

Bernard opened the House's January session with a speech asserting that "the disordered state of the province had affected its very councils," thus suggesting that the government had become as radical as the mobs and that the August riots were being transformed from aberration to policy. Recognizing the Popular Party's power yet concluding it ephemeral, Bernard wrote to the Board of Trade on January 10 that the "system of Mr Otis" was fueling "Notions of Independency." Bernard labeled Jemmy "The King of Massachusetts Bay" and asserted that he would challenge the King of Great Britain, though he would be alone, because most of the radicals were ultimately feckless and "would tremble, if they saw it like to be brought to a test."

After Bernard's opening speech, the House created a committee with Otis as chairman to respond. While the committee's report, issued January 21, squarely blamed government attitude and action for inciting the mobs, it largely ignored Bernard's speech; instead, the committee's report focused on Bernard's actions in November and December. It castigated the governor and Council for even officially printing the Stamp Act and chastised Bernard for holding regular secret meetings. Most importantly, the report reiterated Otis's argument that closing the courts was an abdication of government. The House then voted on January 24, 81 to 5, in favor of a resolution stating that all courts should operate, with or without stamps. Bernard continued to believe that, despite the overwhelming majority in favor of ignoring the Stamp Act, the House was controlled by a few extremists employing thuggish intimation to secure votes. On January 25, Bernard wrote to Conway, the new Secretary of State for the Southern Colonies, a detailed description of the intimidation tactics he believed was being employed. Meanwhile, Jemmy wrote to his father on January 30 that he'd received a letter from Conway attesting that the "Stamp Act must be repealed," though Conway fretted about how to achieve this without appearing that the colonies had "conquered Britain." The Council declined to even vote on the House resolution, with Hutchinson calling the House's rejection of the Stamp Act "extra judicial." Eventually, the Council decided that a meeting of judges should decide whether or not to open their courts. "The King of Massachusetts Bay" and his allies viewed the Council's refusal to reject the House's resolution as total victory.

Yet even with victory, Jemmy was relentless. Writing under the pseudonym "Freeborn Armstrong" in the January 27 edition of the *Gazette*, Otis relayed his synopsis of events for all of Boston to read:

> The Resolve was the same Day sent up the Hon. Board for their Concurrence, when the Hon. Thomas Hutchinson, Esq; Lieutenant Governor and Chief Justice of the Superior Court, who on this Occasion also sits as President of the Council, a Place he has usurped, after engrossing all the Places of Honor and Profit in the Province, moved to give it the go-by, saying it was Impertinent, and beneath the Notice of the hon. Board or to that Effect.

Lambasting Hutchinson both for his vast collection of offices and his demand for deference, Otis paints a picture of an aloof aristocrat. Hutchinson was livid and insisted that *Gazette* printers Edes and Gill formally identify the author, though everyone knew it was Jemmy. The Council refused to issue Hutchinson's demand to Edes and Gill, arguing that if the author were imprisoned, the mob would quickly free him. Further, Hutchinson had hoped that once the identity of the author were known, the House would reprimand him, but the Council did not wish to pick a fight with the powerful and rebellious House, thus confirming that they knew the author was a powerful member of the House. Writing to Thomas Pownall on March 8, Hutchinson said he found the Council's unwillingness to defend him "dishonorable" and thereafter refused to attend Council meetings for the remainder of the session.

By March, the Popular Party's near complete control fueled rumors that the Prime Minister would capitulate, and the Black Act would be repealed; Hutchinson refused to be present in Superior Court, and the court declared that it would hear all cases attorneys initiated, with or without stamps. The Popular Party was now unquestionably the lone force in Massachusetts politics, exhibiting a solid philosophical foundation in Otis's pamphlets, and enjoying a reputation for slaying giants among the population. Bernard summarized the opening months of 1766 in a March 10 letter to John Pownall thus: "The Great Leviathan (Otis I mean) has frequently & lately given his Testimony of the Equity & Mildness of my administration; at the same time he was doing all he could to embarrass it." And throughout these months, Jemmy continued to push his arguments about colonial rights vs. Parliamentary supremacy. In responding to an *Evening Post* article that claimed the radicals desired independence, Otis wrote in the January 27, 1766 edition of the *Gazette*:

> Where is the policy ... of putting wicked dangerous tho'ts into young people's heads? Are not such tho'ts but too apt to obtrude themselves? For shame, let this string be no more saw'd, lest it be cut asunder in good earnest!

Otis continues to establish two related arguments: first, that the Boston radicals were the more reasonable and responsible party; second, that should efforts toward independence ever erupt, the catalyst will be a push from Whitehall and the Court Party, not a pull from the radicals.

The Stamp Act was repealed on March 18, 1766, though the colonists would not learn of the repeal until after the May elections. The repeal occurred fewer than five months after it was intended to go into effect, though it never truly went into effect. The bureaucracy and enforcement organizations required to implement and enforce such a tax simply did not exist. The Stamp Act, which was in essence a sales tax, was intended to be too pervasive to enact in the face of mass resistance. But as Parliament repealed the Stamp Act, they replaced it with The Declaratory Act, which plainly stated that Parliament "had, hath, and of right ought to have, full power and authority to make laws and statutes of sufficient force and validity to bind the colonies and people of America ... in all cases whatsoever." In theory, the colonists should have been pleased that the Stamp Act was repealed, and some were, but the Declaratory Act of 1766 was an echo of the Dependency of Ireland on Great Britain Act of 1719, which made Ireland wholly subservient to England. Had the issue been about taxes, then the colonists all would have rejoiced. Instead, Sam Adams, Jemmy Otis and others were as opposed to the Declaratory Act as much as they'd been to the Stamp Act because both were predicated on the concept that Parliament could create taxes without the people's consent. Otis's arguments had not been primarily about taxes but about consent and Parliamentary absolutism – "An Act against the Constitution is void" – and replacing the Stamp Act with the Declaratory Act did not resolve the problem. Parliament, of course, was quite aware of Otis's arguments, and the Declaratory Act was its response.

Three days before the Stamp Act was repealed, Governor Bernard issued a desperate proclamation to "all Justices of the Peace, all Sheriffs and Deputies, and all Civil Officers in their several Districts and Departments" to "use their utmost Endeavors" to enforce the Acts of Trade. Further, Bernard promised fifty pounds to any person "who shall inform against or discover any one or more concerned in these riotous and unlawful Proceedings." Additionally, Bernard promised that any informer "shall receive his Majesty's Pardon" if the informer is also an accomplice. The proclamation, which revealed an anxious governor making a final attempt to reestablish government control over the province, was printed in the *Boston Gazette* of Thursday, March 18, 1766 – two days after the Stamp Act was repealed. The same issue was filled with advertisements for imported goods for sale, mostly undoubtedly smuggled, including an advertisement for "Choice Dumb FISH, a Few Bushels of HEMP-SEED, – Also Newcastle Case and Quart BOTTLES: – To be Sold by – Samuel A. Otis, At Store No 5. Just below the Swing-Bridge." It is safe to assume that more were interested in Samuel Allyne's "Choice Dumb FISH" than Bernard's bounty.

The General Court's session had been set to adjourn on Wednesday, April 9, but on the Saturday before, Bernard issued a proclamation immediately dissolving the Court. In Monday's *Gazette*, Otis argued that such a move was an act of arbitrary government and called for a meeting of the House on Wednesday. Only about a dozen members showed, and Bernard ignored their request to postpone dissolution until more members arrived. The members in attendance then left, but Bernard notes in a letter to the Board of Trade on April 10, it was a "daring and dangerous" provocation by Otis. He had attempted nothing short of severing the Crown's control of a colonial legislature. Bernard postulated that had Otis succeeded in producing a quorum, the colony's charter would almost surely have been revoked. Further, Otis's actions "subjected the persons of all the members joining therein to the highest penalties of the Law," by which he meant one of Blackstone's "hundred and sixty have been declared by Act of Parliament to be felonious without benefit of clergy; or, in other words, to be worthy of instant death." In short: treason.

The May 1766 elections would serve as a referendum on the expected repeal of the Stamp Act: was the issue about taxes or rights and consent? If the issue were about taxes, then Bernard would be proved right, and the Court Party would regain many of the seats it had lost; while the colonists did not yet know that the Act was repealed, they expected it to be. The Popular Party launched the first province wide political campaign in Massachusetts history. The 32 Court Party members of the House seeking reelection were tagged as

Black Act supporters and targeted for defeat; Otis's efforts focused on using the media to cultivate a sense of American nationalism and a consciousness of resistance against imperialism. Predictably, the Court Party concentrated its attacks on Otis, with the *Evening Post* launching weekly assaults in April and early May on the man they labeled a "double-faced Jacobite-Whig." In late April, Bernard reported that Otis had declared that if Parliament doesn't repeal the Stamp Act, "We will repeal it ourselves."

Only 11 of the 32 Court Party incumbents were reelected as the Popular Party swept the elections. Hutchinson was shocked by the people's response and the campaign's efficacy; he claimed the success of the "plebian party" was the result of Otis's ability to bring the rural voters and the Boston voters together in unified opposition to Parliamentary rule. The Popular Party's first act in power was to elect Jemmy Otis Speaker of the House. The Popular Party then purged the Governor's Council of Court Party stalwarts: Lt. Governor Hutchinson, Secretary Andrew Oliver, his brother Superior Court Justice Peter Oliver, and Attorney General Trowbridge. Only Province Treasurer Harrison Gray retained his seat, most likely because he was now related to the Otises through two marriages.

Governor Bernard continued his long record of imprudence and poor diplomacy; he vetoed the selection of James Otis as Speaker, an action only one previous governor had ever dared do. Bernard then vetoed the men selected to replace the Court Party Council members who had been purged. Bernard then vetoed the reelection of Colonel Otis to the Council. In letters dated May 30 and 31, Bernard gloated that he had "humbled" Otis and that his vetoes engendered "universal satisfaction" to Boston's "principal people." The vetoed men "sunk down in part of their own insignificance & others in the effect of their own Machinations." Despite Bernard's proclamations of victory, it was clear that the Popular Party had cultivated the will to stand their ground. Bernard informed the House that Colonel Otis would have his Council seat if Bernard's four "friends" – Hutchinson and company – could regain their seats. Jemmy Otis responded for the House that the time for compromise had passed. Bernard labeled the Popular Party's maneuvers "an attack upon government," and Otis responded that the only attack on government would be not to implement the people's wishes. Bernard refused to approve the Popular Party members to the Council, and the Popular Party refused to elect new members to the Council. In result, the credibility and power of the Council withered. The Popular Party decisively won the House and, with Bernard's assistance, relegated the Council to irrelevancy. Since Otis was unable to secure Bernard's approval as House Speaker, he was replaced by his Boston bench friend Thomas Cushing. In some ways, Cushing was no less radical than Otis, but he wasn't a beacon for revolution as Otis was, and Bernard knew that the House was now full of radicals, and he couldn't reject them all for the Speaker position. And in sanctioning the election of Thomas Cushing, Bernard approved the man who would lead the House as Speaker right up to the Revolution.

By 1766, the fire had been lit and could not be extinguished. The ruling oligarchy went through the motions of exercising authority, but they knew they were one rebel speech away from another night of terror by Sam Adams's gang. They knew they were one mistake or misunderstanding away from riots, destroyed houses, and widespread looting. Otis, by infiltrating the Court Party, had managed to permanently loosen its control of Massachusetts Province. The oligarchy could be challenged and intimidated, and that lesson would soon be applied to the greater oligarchy that ruled from London.

The Colonel was of the previous generation, so he hoped for compromise, to regain his seat on the Council, and to restore normalcy and stability. The Colonel openly rejected some of the Popular Party's most radical positions. He objected when his son rendered Locke obsolete by arguing that a man's greatest asset was his liberty not his property, and therefore a government's primary purpose was to protect liberty. Thus, a government could not make slaves of anyone. And consequently, a man in possession of his liberty had a stake in government and must be permitted to vote, regardless of whether he owned property. The Colonel, reflecting feudal attitudes of the centuries before Jemmy Otis, firmly believed that voters should have property qualifications and reaffirmed that belief publicly in Barnstable town meetings.

Reverend Mayhew wrote a letter to Jemmy on June 8, 1766 that illustrates his interest and involvement in Popular Party politics. In the letter, Mayhew advises that "Cultivating a good understanding and hearty friendship between these colonies, appears to me so necessary a part of prudence and good policy, that no favorable opportunity for that purpose should be omitted. I think such an one now presents." Mayhew was to attend an Ecclesiastical Council the following day and suggested to Otis that the colonies create a "communion of colonies" just as there was a "communion of churches." The council that Mayhew was to attend settled disputes in and among churches and acted as an objective source of advice in all church affairs. "It is not safe for the colonies to sleep," he advises, "for it is probable they will always have some wakeful enemies in Great Britain." In order to organize a "communion of colonies" without arousing the government's suspicion or anger, Mayhew suggested that issuing invitations to the other colonies to join the communion be "conceived ... in terms of friendship and regard, of loyalty to the king, filial affection towards the parent country ...." Mayhew made clear that he felt compelled to commit "these hints" to paper because he was going out of town and didn't expect to return for over a week.

Mayhew's letter demonstrates that he saw Otis regularly and did not often write letters, particularly ones that contained "hints," and hence Mayhew's need to explain why he was writing. Mayhew appears very involved in politics and is clearly "hinting" at coordination not just between the radical preachers and the Popular Party, but among rebels in every colony. Mayhew also stated in the letter that he'd already "had a sight of the answer to the governor's last ... speech." Mayhew was an insider, an advisor, and as a popular and influential minister, a potent compatriot of the rebels's cause. Jasper Mauduit, that old friend of Mayhew, was almost certainly appointed province lobbyist to ingratiate the Popular Party with the Black Regiment. It wasn't long before the alignment between the political and clerical rebels was openly acknowledged; in an allegorical dialogue printed in the *Gazette* of July 25, 1768, one of the characters comments, "But Otis says, he could not carry his points without the aid of the black regiment." And while the rebels's every move in church and government may not have been coordinated, there can be little doubt that Bernard's 1761 accusation that Otis "was at the head of the Confederacy" was accurate. After the Ecclesiastical Council, Mayhew returned home riding through rain on horseback. He grew ill and developed a fever and died on July 9, 1766, a month after he'd sent that letter to Otis.

Bernard essentially held his breath until the May 1767 elections; he would ensure the government would do as little work as possible until he could return his "friends of government" to office. Bernard reported that one of his associates in the House had declared that he "knew the time when the House would have readily assisted the Governor in executing the Laws of Trade." Otis replied that "the times were altered; they now knew what their rights were, then they did not." The times were altered too much for some. Bernard understood the Colonel and his generation; he understood the spoils of office and flattery. Bernard did not understand Jemmy Otis and Sam Adams. And so the governor responded to the Popular Party's power the only way he knew how: to panic. According to Judge John Cushing, a friend of Hutchinson, the governor was "promising almost Everybody" rewards and commissions in return for their support. The paranoid governor also alerted Lord Shelburne that Jemmy Otis was orchestrating a campaign to impugn Bernard's standing in Whitehall. Bernard was correct.

The Stamp Act was not the only statute being ignored in 1766; with the Popular Party in control of the House and the streets, they decided to disregard whatever revenue statutes they felt were unfair. Daniel Malcolm, a member of the Sons of Liberty, was officially referred to as "captain" but only because "smuggler" and "antagonist" weren't official designations. Malcolm not only smuggled alcohol into Massachusetts, but he did so brazenly. In the late summer of 1766, he smuggled in 60 casks of French brandy protected by a mob of club wielding thugs, undoubtedly lent to him by the Sons of Liberty. The shipload was transferred from boat to basement without declaring a single drop. The customs establishment, if it was to remain an establishment at all, had to confront such a blatant disregard for the law. So in September 1766, customs officers were sent to Captain Malcolm's house to search his cellar and, not surprisingly, Captain Malcolm refused to admit them and declared that he'd shoot anyone who entered his house without his permission. A crowd assembled and the mobs were informed that the bells of North Church would ring if Malcolm required their assistance in expelling customs officials from his house. The officers then went to court to obtain a writ of assistance – that general warrant that would permit them to search wherever they liked. And not surprisingly, Captain Malcolm hired famed writs defense attorney Jemmy Otis. Customs officials sought Bernard's assistance, and he passed the problem off to the Council, which, fearing the power of the mobs, promptly declared that their assistance did not "appear at present to be needful." But the Council and governor did proceed to take depositions, at which point the Boston town meeting elected Otis to chair a committee to demand the names of Malcolm's accusers and copies of the depositions. Several New York merchants began writing to Jemmy and the Boston radicals requesting their assistance in defying New York trade regulations.

While Thomas Hutchinson was ousted from the Governor's Council, he still sat as Chief Justice of the Superior Court. Dan Malcolm's case illustrates that the mob roaming the streets of Boston actively promoted Jemmy's customs causes and supported his argument against external taxes. Just a few years prior, many had argued that Parliament could levy external taxes – customs taxes – but not internal taxes such as sales taxes. But now, in flaunting the customs taxes, the rebels made it clear that they wanted all taxes originating from their local representatives. Jemmy Otis, the *de facto* representative of the anti-customs movement, unloaded another aggressive court room argument against the constitutionality of general search warrants, an argument that was vindicated when William de Grey, the Attorney General of Great Britain, voided their issuance the following month. The general search warrant was dead, and the customs establishment had been crippled. The Townshend Acts of 1767, of which the Revenue Act was one, would revisit and attempt to revive the general search warrant, which was so clearly required for any possibility of effectively implementing customs taxes. The Acts expressly directed the superior courts of the American colonies to issue general search warrants and the new Board of Customs Commissioners on how to acquire and employ such warrants.

The political issue that kept boiling to the surface after the May 1766 elections was reimbursement of those whose property was destroyed in the August 1765 riots. The Council and governor continued to press the House on the issue. Many General Court members from the country rejected reimbursement because they viewed it as a Boston problem. Many Popular Party members rejected it because they did not wish to set a precedent, which made it clear to all that they thought that the August riots may not be the last. By December 1766, the Popular Party got the bill they wanted: province-wide payment for reimbursement and amnesty for all suspected rioters, probably all of whom were Popular Party members. The bill passed the House 53-35, with many Court Party members voting against it. Otis led a committee to draft and present a resolution to Bernard making clear that the reimbursement was a result of their "loyal and grateful regard to his Majesty's most mild and gracious recommendation" and not because they felt legally compelled because the "suffers had no just claim or demand on the province." Again, they wanted to ensure that the reimbursement was not perceived to set a precedent. Back in London, the Privy Council was peeved by the amnesty portion of the bill and disallowed it, but disbursements had already been paid by Bernard from the treasury, so the House could do nothing in response.

Concurrent with the reimbursement battle, Otis sought to further purge the government of conflicts of interest. Thought Hutchinson had lost his Council seat, he still attended Council meetings in his capacity as lieutenant governor, and thus Hutchinson directly influenced all three branches of government. The governor had a seat on the Council and could send a deputy in his stead, but Otis asserted that the executive branch occupying more than one Council seat abrogated the separation of powers and the House's message to Bernard declared the situation an "impropriety" that was "repugnant to the constitution." The House and the Council passed a resolution forbidding Hutchinson from occupying a Council seat while Bernard was present, and Hutchinson, knowing he was defeated, let Bernard know that he would further refrain from attending Council sessions. Bernard, however, was not one to know when he was defeated. He dispatched a letter to Secretary of State Shelburne requesting clarification. Shelburne wanted no part of the matter and informed Bernard that the Council should determine its own rules. The Council had already declared Hutchinson *persona non grata*, and Hutchinson had concurred, so Bernard was left to stew in another defeat.

Indicating the coordination between political veteran and young firebrand, the Colonel advised Jemmy in a January 24, 1767 letter to "keep exactly to Last Year's Plan & Choose the same Councillors yt was last year Chosen unless there was a fair Chance to Drop a few of the Torrey Part." The Colonel was willing, though likely begrudgingly, to forgo his Council seat in order to advance the Popular Party's escalating grip on power. The Colonel's other bit of advice in the same letter was that Jemmy and the Popular Party should "keep to strick Truths" in their campaigns because "there is enough of them" to win elections. The issues favored the Popular Party, and the Colonel strongly recommended that its campaigning and electioneering "be so Canvassed that they may Bear a Thorough Examination." The Court Party spent much of 1766 and early 1767 promising patronage in return for votes: small rural positions, officer ranks in the militias, whatever someone in the House desired in exchange for loyalty to the government. Court Party member John Cushing complained to Hutchinson in a December 1766 letter that the governor was "Gitting into office Scandalous & unfit persons & Throwing abt Commissions & promising almost Everybody." The *Gazette* followed up the charge on April 27, 1767, declaring that Bernard "is at his old Trade of rubbing up old Tools, and making new ones against the ensuing Election" and charging that commissions "are shamefully prostituted to obtain as many that shall be subservient to his Designs." The Court Party also resorted to outright threats, sending an anonymous letter to Jemmy in February that read in part, "if your Assembly will suffer themselves to be led by that absur'd ignorant Firebrand, he may bring them into a worse scrape than they can imagine."

On February 27, the House formally declared the anonymous writer "an Enemy to this Province," effectively passing their own charge of treason. Collectively, Court Party members believed that the fire raging in the Province would burn out, some men would come to their senses and others could be bought, and that normalcy would return by the May 1767 elections.

They were wrong about the May 1767 elections. Jemmy increased his vote totals from 86% in 1766 to 93%. Sam Adams was re-elected with 90% of the votes cast, and John Hancock was re-elected with 100%. The wave of optimism that the Court Party rode into the election was not quickly realized to be fantasy, for on June 15, 1767, the *Evening Post* held a wake for Jemmy:

> Epitaph for Jemmy
> A Life of slander, scrawl and quarrel past,
> Here JEMMY hides his envious head at last.
> Beneath the pressing Turf the Troubler's laid,
> While fern and brambles rise, a junto shade!
> His restless Spirit fled, close here we'll pin him;
> Unless he'd quiet now—the DEVIL'S in him!

"The King of Massachusetts Bay" and the Popular Party quickly exerted their control, again electing the same six Councilors that the previous year had been vetoed by Bernard. They went further and rejected one of Bernard's more moderate friends, Israel Williams. Bernard again vetoed all but one, permitting moderate Popular Party member Nathaniel Sparhawk to take a Council seat. Bernard felt compelled to explain to the Council that he vetoed the powerful and seemingly moderate Colonel because "the Father's Principles and the son's were both a Like But the father was not so open." Writing to Jemmy on June 12, 1767, the Colonel mocked Bernard for now becoming "a Searcher of Hearts," regardless of one's actual behavior and voting record. But the Colonel comforted Jemmy that he was "Perfectly Easy" to follow his conscience instead of his political ambition. The Colonel now seemed converted to the cause.

Writing to Jackson on June 30, 1767, Bernard asserted that Jemmy's "reign" was over. He had been wrong about the 1767 election and would be again about the 1768 and 1769 elections. Thomas Hutchinson would never again be elected to the Governor's Council. The governor's friends were so repeatedly rejected that by 1769 only 16 of the 28 Council seats were filled, and the Council was nothing more than a weak group of government puppets. From 1766 until the Revolution, the Popular Party consistently controlled at least two-thirds of the House. The 1766 elections proved not to be an aberration. The wedge that Otis had driven through the oligarchy beginning with the Mount Desert Island grant was taking full effect; Bernard blamed Hutchinson, and Hutchinson blamed Bernard. Bernard was inept but not hated; Hutchinson was hated but effective. As they grew to mistrust and despise each other, the Popular Party tied each to the other like political weights around their necks.

And in 1767, Parliament threatened to suspend the New York assembly because it refused to implement the Quartering Act. In an article in the *Gazette*, Otis again made the point that the issue was not about taxes or representation, but consent. Otis wrote that if "our legislative authority can be suspended whenever we refuse obedience to laws we never consented to, we may as well send home our representatives, and acknowledge ourselves slaves." The 1,500 British soldiers who had arrived in New York City in 1766 were forced to stay on their ships, and when the New York assembly refused to comply, Parliament suspended the governor and legislature. On August 10, 1767, the Boston *Gazette* continued to print rumors that the ministry's solution was to essentially remove the oligarchy from any control by local assemblies, including appointing Hutchinson and Andrew Oliver to custom board positions that would hold broad powers not subject to any local control and whose salaries would be paid directly from England. In the words of the *Gazette*, the oligarchs would then be "rendered independent of the people." On August 17, the *Gazette* printed *The Petition of Right* of 1628, the Coke influenced declaration of independence for the parliament arguing for taxation by consent, against unlawful searches and seizures, and requesting standard enforcement of property rights and due process. Coke was the rebel's response to Blackstone's orthodoxy. For a year, the *Gazette* had been issuing warnings about the ministry's intentions to remove officials from the purview of local assemblies, particularly the authorization and administration of salaries, and the *Gazette* had been entirely correct. Such a move by the ministry would be a direct abrogation of the primacy of consent.

The issue of consent, regardless of whether the taxes were internal or external, exploded in late 1767 as Parliament attempted to implement the Revenue Act, a series of duties on imported items. Parliament believed that since the tax was external – on imported items only – it would be accepted by the colonists. But Otis had years earlier abolished the distinction between internal and external taxes, and the rebels were not interested in entertaining the new tax. And yet at a Boston town meeting on November 20, the day the Revenue Act went into effect, Jemmy made a shocking speech that, in reporting to the Secretary of State the next day, Bernard claimed was "entirely on the side of government. He asserted the king's right to appoint officers of the customs, in what number and by what denominations he pleased." Many at the time and later were baffled by Otis's strategy, which operated on two levels. First, it was the continuation of the "counterwork" to ingratiate himself to the oligarchy; second, it operated to crystallize the issue of Parliamentary control for the colonists. The second level is made clear by a point Bernard claimed Jemmy made in that November 20 speech: opposition to acts of Parliament should be unified or not at all. By asserting that the government and king had the power and the right – under the law – to operate customs without the consent of the colonists, Jemmy was pushing for a more fundamental change. The entire structure of the empire was defective, and disparate acts of defiance would do little to ameliorate those structural problems. Burning effigies and derrière salutes would amount to no more than another Land Bank debacle; opposition would need to be both united and directed at the causes, not merely the effects. Jemmy's November address also stressed that the mobs remain orderly; he knew that the push for *rights* and *consent* could easily devolve into anarchy. The *Evening Post* continued to mock Jemmy, publishing on November 30 an updated version of *Jemmibulero* entitled *The Jemmiwilliad* that ended with:

> And may kind Heaven joint exit bring,
> And their fond hopes, and ours fulfill;
> Nor quit this life without full swing!
> May Jemmy Split and Cooper Will!

The "williad" and "Cooper Will" are references to Boston's rebellious town clerk William Cooper, brother to Jemmy's Harvard classmate and member of the Black Regiment Samuel Cooper. Both were close friends of Jemmy's, and Will Cooper was so beloved that he held his position of town clerk for 49 years. *The Jemmiwilliad* was followed by the considerably more malevolent *Jemmyicumjunto*, published on January 11, 1768, which continued the oligarchy's assertion that a mad junto had taken control of Boston and was precipitating its ruin. *Jemmyicumjunto* was a direct attack on the Popular Party's and Jemmy's efforts to coordinate the merchants in boycotting taxed imports and to encourage an increase in domestic manufacturing. While the Court Party was mocking the House's embargo and manufacturing Resolves, merchants in England were taking them quite seriously. The merchants were suffering from the end of the Seven Years War and various other small embargoes and were ever anxious that a serious colonial embargo would severely impede their sluggish economic recovery. Lord Shelburne questioned Boston merchant Nathaniel Rogers while Rogers was visiting London, and Rogers reported back to Hutchinson that the Resolves had caused "great umbrage" in London and that Shelburne was concerned about whether the Resolves would be widely implemented. In volume 17 (1767) of London's *Gentlemen's Magazine*, an article complained that any embargo and manufacturing resolutions would forestall an economic recovery because "some vain pernicious ideas of independent and separate dominion, thrown out and fomented by designing spirits in that country." The article concluded by urging Parliament to declare embargoes illegal.

The ministry was devising its own plans for removing the oligarchy from control of the people. Thomas Pownall wrote to Thomas Hutchinson on September 9, 1767 "that you shall have a handsome salary fixed as Chief Justice, as soon as the American revenue shall create a fund." The revenue would be derived from the Revenue Act. The plans, though, were known to the rebels, and they widely publicized them in order to repeatedly defeat Hutchinson's appointment to the Governor's Council and to discredit the Ministry's plans for removing control of local officials's salaries from the legislature. Lord Hillsborough was appointed first Secretary of State for the Colonies, a new office replacing the Board of Trade that coincided with the newly created Board of Customs Commissioners. In explaining his repeated defeats, Bernard wrote to Lord Hillsborough:

> ... two chief heads of the faction (Otis and Adams) told the House that the Lieutenant Governor was a pensioner of Great Britain, and averred that he had a warrant from the Lords of the Treasury for two hundred pounds a year out of the new duties which they were then opposing. This being urged in a manner which left no opportunity or time for refutation or explanation, gave a turn against him, so that, upon the second polling, he had ten votes less than before.

The pressure on the oligarchy was increasing, and despite Bernard's enduring optimism that the rebels's progress would soon flag and fade away, their rejection of Hutchinson seemed to be gaining support. Perhaps more disconcerting, Otis and the Boston rebels were gaining widespread support and sympathy, not only from other colonies but also from England. Catharine Macaulay, whose progressive views on women and British history were scandalous in her home country, sent Jemmy, who she titled "the great Guardian of American Liberty," a copy of her radical history of Britain. She signs her letter to Jemmy: "with high admiration for your Virtues." From within Parliament and without, Otis was increasingly viewed as the champion of the people's rights.

Most of the new members of the customs establishment arrived on a ship from England on November 5, 1767. Henry Hulton, the first commissioner of customs, had been a clerk in the Plantation Office in London for the previous five years; Hulton's sister recounted that when the customs officials arrived, a "mob carried twenty devils, popes, and pretenders through the streets, with labels on their breasts, Liberty, and property and no commissioners." Like a good oligarch, Hulton reportedly "laughed at 'em with the rest." November 5 was "Pope's Day," wherein the Protestants celebrated the fact that they weren't Catholic, but the festivities's overt politicization was an indication that "the times were altered." The popes and pretenders would be heaved into a giant bon fire; the devil was left on the doorstep of Hutchinson's house. It would take Hulton three years to learn just how altered the times were.

Bernard delayed convening the General Court until late December, hoping to avoid any hostile resolutions to the new customs commissioners and the Townshend Acts. When the Townshend Acts went into effect and the new commissioners arrived in early November, Jemmy urged caution, and the Boston town meeting approved his message and adopted a resolution denouncing mob activity. When the General Court finally convened, it appointed a large committee to draft letters and petitions to various officials on the state of the province. The letter were polite – praising the King and constitution – but insistent that all taxation must originate with the local legislature. They further rejected accusations that they sought independence and would "by no means be inclined to accept of an independency, if offered ...." And yet the flurry of conciliatory letters and the petitions produced by the House at the end of the year only seemed to be setting the stage for a greater drama to come.

Under the leadership of Otis, Cushing, and Sam Adams, the House then decided to make perhaps the most audacious pre-1776 gambit; they would issue what amounted to a summary of Otis's earlier pamphlets in an official declaration. Otis writings, called everything from "Letters of Gold" to the ramblings of a treasonous madman, would now be the official proclamation of the people of Massachusetts. And furthering Otis's objective to increase communication and cooperation among the colonies, the letter would be directed not to the colonist's lobbyist, Parliament or the King as the Stamp Act Resolves were, but rather the letter would be directed to the people's assemblies of the other colonies. The letter was soundly defeated in the House by a two to one margin, with many members fearing that Whitehall and the King would conclude that the letter sought to establish a government outside of Britain's control. Two weeks later, many House members had left to go home; Otis and Sam Adams quickly moved first to vote again on the letter and then to vote to expunge the record of the previous vote. Both passed, and the result was issued on February 11, 1768 with the laborious title "A circulatory Letter, directed to the Speakers of the respective Houses of Representatives and Burgesses on this Continent ; a Copy of which was also sent to Dennis DeBerdt, Esq; their Agent, by Order of the House, that he might make use of it, if necessary, to prevent any Misrepresentations of it in *England*." Bernard quickly dispatched a letter to Lord Shelburne, writing on February 18 that the House's Letter was "calculated to inflame the whole Continent."

The Letter has the hallmarks of a typical Otis "counterwork." It begins innocently, stating its purpose to address "a common concern" and its goal that the colonies "should harmonize with each other." Then it quickly confirms that "his Majesty's high Court of Parliament is the supreme legislative power over the whole empire," which echoes Otis's declaration from *Considerations* confirming that Parliament and the King are "the supreme and universal legislature of the whole empire." After these assurances, the Letter makes its brazen declaration:

> That it is an essential unalterable right in nature, ingrafted into the British constitution, as a fundamental law, and ever held sacred and irrevokable by the subjects within the realm, that what a man hath honestly acquired is absolutely his own, which he may freely give, but cannot be taken from him without his consent : That the American subjects may therefore, exclusive of any consideration of

charter rights, with a decent firmness, adapted to the character of free men and subjects, assert this natural, constitutional right.

This statement is in essence a summary of Otis's previous positions regarding natural rights, the irrelevance of the charters, and the necessity of consent. The Letter quickly performs a "counterwork" and asserts in the same paragraph that this is "their humble opinion, which they express with the greatest deference." Otis in *Rights* makes a similar claim to natural rights "with all humble deference," and in all his pamphlets asserts his opinion with humility.

The Letter continues to hammer the point about natural rights and consent: " ... imposing Duties on the people of this province, with the sole and express purpose of raising a revenue, are infringements of their natural and constitutional rights, because, as they are not represented in the British Parliament, his Majesty's Commons in Britain, by those Acts, grant their property without their consent." Representation in parliament is the only solution, as Jemmy had observed, and yet, "This House further are of opinion, that their constituents, considering their local circumstances, cannot by any possibility be represented in the Parliament." The only solution is "That his Majesty's royal predecessors, for this reason, were graciously pleased to form a subordinate legislative here." In 1702, the first session of the new Massachusetts House of Representatives with John Otis as one of its leaders produced a resolve claiming that the "house may use and exercise such Powers and Privileges here as the house of commons in England may and have usually done there allways having Respect to their Majesties Roy[al] charter. ..." This new legislative body in 1702 immediately staked claim to a position equivalent to the House of Commons and subject only to the King and charter, which was just as quickly rejected by Parliament. And so almost seven decades later the issue was revisited, and yet the demographic characteristics and national debt made representation in Parliament or local control dead issues. Otis, Cushing and Adams almost certainly knew this, and yet, again employing Jemmy's strategy, they needed to appear reasonable and offer solutions along with making claims. A component of appearing reasonable included listing grievances specific enough so that the referent was clear to all readers yet general enough so the grievance applied to all colonies. The crowning complaint of the short list was "officers of the Crown may be multiplied to such a degree, as to become dangerous to the Liberty of the people." Inherent in this complaint was that the size of government, regardless of purpose or justification, must be limited in order to protect the "Liberty of the people." The Letter made clear the dire consequences of not heeding the House's warning, as it advised that the Ministry should "take notice" in order to prevent "mutiny." It was as close as any official document had come to invoking the specter of independence.

The remarkable Circular Letter was not only a nimble summation of Otis's previous pamphlets, but it was also a bridge from those early rebellious pamphlets to the Declaration of Independence issued seven years later. The "essential unalterable right in nature, ingrafted into the British constitution, as a fundamental law, and ever held sacred and irrevocable" became the "certain unalienable Rights" in the Declaration. "The consent of the people" became "the consent of the governed" and "imposing Duties ... without their consent" became "imposing Taxes on us without our Consent." Tellingly, Jefferson's draft of the Declaration employed "consent" twice among the 1,685 words that comprise the body. When edited, chiefly by John Adams, 363 words were deleted, rendering the Declaration 22% shorter, and yet the emphasis on consent was increased, and the word was inserted a third time just to be certain that no one could misunderstand the source of government authority.

Perhaps the most direct connection from Jemmy's early pamphlets to the Declaration is the latter's treatment of property. For many, the Lockean notion of "property" had provided both the foundation for and justification of government. Jemmy took great pains to abolish a direct connection between government and property; while in *Rights*, he stated, "The *end* of government being the *good* of mankind, points out its great duties: It is above all things to provide for the security, the quiet, and happy enjoyment of life, liberty, and property," he quickly averred that government by consent directly results in the protection of property. Therefore, as long as government authority is founded on consent, property rights are protected, thus rendering "property" and "consent" redundant. In *Considerations*, Jemmy observed, "If a man has but little property to protect and defend, yet his life and liberty are things of some importance," thus illustrating that government's focus should be the "happy enjoyment of life, liberty." Perhaps the most astonishing aspect of the Declaration is that while Jefferson's draft contained but a single reference to property, Adams and the drafting committee excised this single reference so that it did not once directly refer to property. A document that failed to reference property cannot properly be called a child of Locke, and this was a philosophical position Otis initially staked out in the colonies in 1762.

The Declaration replaced "property" with a phrase that seems so curious to the modern mind: "the pursuit of Happiness." And yet the phrase employed as the people's interest and the government's objective was not remotely exotic to the Massachusetts rebels. The Circular Letter makes clear that a problem of corrupt governments is that they "endanger the happiness" of the people. And "the pursuit of Happiness" is a phrase that directly echoed Jemmy's *Considerations*, in which he declared that the principal purpose of his political activism was that "The inhabitants ... of the dominions of the British crown ... who I hope e'er long to see *united* in the most firm support of their Prince's true glory, and in a steady and uniform pursuit of their own welfare and happiness." People pursuing "their own welfare and happiness" connoted a small government that derived authority through consent. It's not happenstance that Jemmy employed some variation of "happiness" 34 times in *Vindication, Rights* and *Considerations*.

The Declaration referenced the "patient sufferance of these Colonies" and asserted that "In every stage of these Oppressions We have Petitioned for Redress in the most humble terms. ..." Such a statement was made possible by both Jemmy's repeated assertions of humility and the Circular Letter's proclamation that its firm message was delivered "in the most humble terms" – the precise phrase that's repeated in the Declaration. The Massachusetts House's Circular Letter of 1768 is as a remarkably prescient predecessor to the Declaration of Independence as it is a summation of Jemmy's radical pamphlets.

The Circular Letter was also transmitted to the province's lobbyist "to prevent any Misrepresentations of it in *England*" precisely because the House had long suspected that Governor Bernard was sending letters to the ministry impugning their motives and distorting their objectives. After the issuance of the Circular Letter, the House demanded copies of Bernard's letters; expectedly, Bernard refused, and the rebels took this as an admission of guilt, a conclusion with which the Boston papers largely concurred. The *Gazette* judged Bernard "totally abandoned to wickedness." The Council deemed the article "impudent libel" while a House committee that included Otis and John Hancock affirmed freedom of the press as a foundation of liberty. Bernard, apoplectic as usual, asserted that Jemmy "behaved in the house like a madman" in defense of the *Gazette* article and admonished the Council members against pursuing the matter lest they jeopardize their political futures. The Council and Bernard declined to indict anyone involved with the *Gazette* article for libel doubtless out of fear; Bernard knew that "two of the chief leaders of the faction in the House (Otis and Adams) are the principal managers of the *Boston Gazette*." Indictment of a sitting House member for libel was not only legally dubious but also existentially foolish. Between the August 1765 nights of terror that destroyed homes and businesses and the May 1766 statewide political campaign that castrated the once powerful Council, the oligarchy feared any official moves against Otis and Adams. Hutchinson, though, saw no reason not to move against Edes and Gill; the chief justice argued for a grand jury indictment, hoping to shutter the *Gazette* and "eradicate the absurd notion of the liberty of the press," as he confessed was his goal in a March 23 letter to Richard Jackson. Out of a probable confection of fear and loyalty, the grand jury refused to indict anyone.

And just as the House had never previously formally issued a summation of Jemmy's pamphlets, the ministry had never formally declared such words seditious. In April, a mere two months after its issuance, the whispers of sedition could be no longer ignored. On April 21, the Secretary of State for the Colonies Lord Hillsborough, upon direct order from King George, sent a copy of the Massachusetts Circular Letter along with a list of "his Majesty's commands" to all colonial governors. He reported that the Letter would "encourage an open opposition," and each governor was to "exert your utmost influence to defeat this flagitious attempt to disturb the public peace by prevailing upon the Assembly of your province to take no notice of it, which will be treating it with the contempt it deserves." Hillsborough, and by direct implication the King, challenged the colonial assemblies to prove "their reverence and respect for the laws, and of their faithful attachment to the constitution" by "showing a proper resentment of this unjustifiable attempt to revive those distractions which have operated so fatally to the prejudice of this kingdom and the colonies." If any assembly exhibited anything other than contempt for "this seditious paper," then it was the governor's "duty to prevent any proceeding" by suspending or dissolving the assembly. And so upon the King's command, Governor Bernard had no choice but to attempt to obtain the rescission of "this seditious paper." A week before the rescission vote, Jemmy delivered a rousing speech against the oligarchy and deference. He observed that "the unthinking multitude are taught to reverence .... as little deities" the men of the oligarchy while the oligarchy looks down upon everyone else as "vulgar." And yet, he questioned why such men were esteemed, for "there are no set of people under the canopy of Heaven more venal, more corrupt and debauched in their principles." He urged the Bostonians not to revere the

English oligarchs for their Cambridge and Oxford educations, as such places teach little other than "whoring, smoking, and drinking." Otis's harangue transformed Captain Kidd's derrière salute into a political position, an issue of freedom of speech and of the press. And "his Majesty's commands" as communicated in Hillsborough's letter transformed what could have been akin to a local Land Bank fiscal crisis into a continental emergency. "His Majesty's commands" would ensure that Massachusetts's bold claims about "natural and constitutional rights" and "consent" would not "waste its sweetness on the desert air."

Of the 109 House members in the 1767-68 legislative year, only 17 conceded to Bernard's request and voted for rescission. The "Glorious 92" who brazenly rejected "his Majesty's commands" were celebrated throughout the colonies. Bernard obediently dissolved the assembly, several other assemblies approved the Circular Letter in some fashion, and the disparate colonies previously tepid to the Boston rebels's talk of *rights* and *consent* and repeated efforts to "harmonize with each other" transformed into an energetic and increasingly unified group dedicated to resisting authority. The dissolved House then petitioned the king to have Bernard removed from office; shockingly, the cowed Council concurred. Bernard believed that given the direction that Massachusetts politics had taken, he wouldn't be able to find 10 supporters in the House the following year – and that was perhaps optimistic. There was no doubt that the Court Party was dead.

The "Glorious 92" "Anti-Rescinders" were celebrated throughout the colonies. Paul Revere smithed a silver punchbowl engraved with the names of the 92, and the bowl was baptized in rebellion when 18 of the "Anti-Rescinders" including Otis, Adams, Hancock and the notorious smuggler Daniel Malcolm drank from it on August 1, the same day that Sons of Liberty mobs roamed the streets of Boston strictly enforcing the non-importation of many British goods. Parties were held in Newport and Marblehead; in Philadelphia, the lyrics of the official march of the Royal Navy were changed, thus transforming "Heart of Oak" into the "Liberty Song." Before the end of the year, every colonial legislature save for New Hampshire had in some way concurred with the Circular Letter. In Pennsylvania, Governor Penn observed that "even those persons who are the most moderate are now set in a flame and have joined in the general cry of Liberty."

The Circular Letter wasn't rescinded, but neither was the tax. To enforce the tax, Whitehall created the American Board of Customs Commissioners and three additional juryless Vice-Admiralty Courts; one of the new courts would be in Boston, where the Board of Customs would be headquartered. And the man chosen to direct the Board of Customs was none other than the most hated customs official in the colonies, Charles Paxton. The first recorded opposition to the Revenue Act in Boston was a town meeting chaired by Jemmy Otis. The meeting concluded that the response to a new tax on imported goods would be not to import the goods. The non-importation movement's slogan as printed in the *Gazette* on November 30, 1767 was "No Mobs and Tumults, let the Person and Properties of our most inveterate Enemies be safe – Save your Money and you save your Country." Of course there would be no public approval of mob violence, but the mobs would certainly encourage merchants to comply with the non-importation pact. And to which "Country" did the slogan refer? At the meeting, Otis urged calm and reminded the assembled crowd that a previous generation had to petition Charles I for fifteen years "before they would betake themselves to any forceable measures." On January 12, 1768, the House sent the argument to their London agent in a letter Otis wrote: "We are taxed, and can appeal for relief, from their final decision, to no power on earth; for there is no power on earth above them." Otis could not bring himself to print the logical conclusion, but perhaps it need not be printed. Years earlier, Otis had already referenced the final resort: an appeal to heaven and the longest sword. And the reference to the "fifteen years" was an uncanny coincidence, for it would be fifteen years from what John Adams labeled the first shot Jemmy fired in the court room at the Writs of Assistance case to the shots fired at Lexington and Concord.

The Customs Commissioners concluded that Otis's Circular Letter refuted their basic authority and was blatantly seditious; they requested that Whitehall send armed men to assist in the collection of taxes. Bernard agreed that any enforcement of taxes would be futile without a significant police force but feared making any official request himself. He asked the Council to make the request in a secret poll, but the Council members unanimously declined. The mob responded to the Commissioners's presence by hanging an effigy of Commissioner Paxton on the Liberty Tree, near Boston Common, on March 18, the anniversary of the Stamp Act's repeal. On June 8, the ministry finally concurred and Hillsborough ordered General Gage to send at least one regiment to Boston. Otis noted that the presence of armed men escorting customs officers and marching down the streets would only serve "to hasten on with great rapidity events which every good and honest man would wish delayed. ..." He still couldn't say independence, but the conclusion was clear. Bernard agreed that the news of the troops impending arrival may only "hasten" riots, so he plotted to withhold official proclamations until the troops were already in Boston. In September, Gage sent a deputy to Boston to make arrangements for the troops. Bernard informed the Council that he had private knowledge of the troops's arrival but did not have any official information. The news quickly spread throughout Boston, and a town meeting was scheduled for September 11, 1768. Bernard then learned that a barrel of turpentine had been affixed to a pole in Beacon Hill and was to be lit when the British troops arrived in order to alert the mobs. Bernard asked the Council to address the issue, and the Council asked the town's Selectmen to address the issue. The Selectmen refused, and the Council next asked the Sherriff to remove the barrel, which he did.

On September 11, a large town meeting was held with Jemmy as moderator and the Court Party in abeyance. The crowd demanded "a head," a massacre, and to "take all the power into their own hands." The argument was made that liberty was life, and one may defend one's life by taking another. Bernard feared the worst. In a September 16 letter to Hillsborough, Bernard reported that a plot was "reported & believed" to have been developed by the radicals to seize Castle William by force on September 18. It is highly unlikely that such a plot was seriously considered at that time, but the letter illustrates the fear that had gripped Bernard and the oligarchy. Eventually, Jemmy soothed the crowd with a plan to form a delegation that would demand information from Bernard. Bernard informed the committee that he had no official information regarding troops, and the town sensed an outright lie. The next day, another town meeting was held, and as the crowd swelled to 3,000 – nearly all the able-bodied adult males of Boston – it was reconvened to Old South Church. Bernard could not fathom that the overwhelming support of the Popular Party was genuine and reported to Hillsborough that "a Set of Speeches by the Chiefs of the Faction and no one else, which followed one another in such an order & method, that it appeared as if they were acting a Play ... everything ... seeming to have been pre-concerted before hand." According to the official meeting minutes, Jemmy was again chosen as moderator and proposed the two-fold course of action. First, the town would submit a "proper application" of their grievances to the authorities. However, if the authorities failed to adequately address the problems, there would be "nothing more to do, but gird the Sword to the Thigh and Shoulder the Musquet." And so the town called for a convention that would operate outside of the purview of the General Court and for the citizens to arm themselves. While Jemmy's efforts to convene an extra-legal assembly failed the previous year, now the call for a similar assembly received unanimous approval from the town. A convention of the towns of Massachusetts met on September 22, with most towns sending their House representatives as delegates. It was a representative assembly wholly outside of Britain's control, and as such, Bernard demanded that it disband immediately. The Convention asked Bernard to explain the laws under which the assembly was illegal, and Bernard refused to even receive the request. The Convention produced several letters and petitions that declared its intention to resolve the problems amicably and yet demanded solutions. While Bernard was surprised by the Convention's moderation, he was nevertheless convinced that the rebels aimed to "Seize the Governor & Lieut Govr, and take Possession of the Treasury and then set up their Standard." He suggested that the leaders, primarily Otis, Cushing and Adams, be forbidden from holding any government office. Both Houses of Parliament passed resolves condemning the town meeting that approved the convention, declaring it illegal and "Calculated to excite sedition and insurrections." Augustus FitzRoy, the 33-year-old new Prime Minister, requested King George's permission to employ a Henry VIII statute that enabled the ministry to arrest and transport suspected traitors to London for trial. The king brushed aside the request and questions raged in Parliament and throughout the colonies whether Otis, Cushing and Adams were guardians of liberty or guilty of treason.

Many were not convinced that the Convention solved anything, and debate erupted in myriad skirmishes across the province. The second floor of the British Coffee House in which Otis and the merchants held meetings years before was occupied by John Mein, a Scottish immigrant who operated a circulating library out of his King Street office and published the *Chronicle* out of a print shop on Newbury Street. Mein was a fierce loyalist and hardened antagonist; he openly ignored non-importation schemes and published the names of merchants suspected of importing banned goods, thus exposing alleged hypocrisy. Mein's exposés were dubious as he conveniently neglected to distinguish between imports that had merely arrived on a ship and those that had actually been signed and delivered, between permitted and banned imports, and between imports signed by Boston merchants and those signed by merchants from outside of Boston who merely used the harbor as a point of entry. In January 1768, "Americus" published an article in the *Gazette* criticizing Mein. Furious, Mein stormed over to the *Gazette* offices on Court Street

ARSONIST

and demanded to know the identity of "Americus." *Gazette* owners Ben Edes and John Gill refused to provide that information; Mein returned the next day and again demanded the identity of "Americus" to be met again with the same response. Mein then demanded a fight in the street; Edes and Gill again refused, at which point Mein declared he'd beat the *Gazette* owner he next saw in the streets.

Ben Edes was the large brash agitator whereas his partner John Gill was a slight, quiet man who worked hard at printing Boston's most prominent newspaper. So as luck would have it, shortly thereafter Mein met the slight John Gill in the street and hit him with his cane, assaulting both Gill's person and his status, as a blow from a gentleman's cane is a demand for deference. John Gill then hired the mysterious "Americus" to sue Mein, and, of course, Mein appeared in court to hear James Otis argue that this was an assault, not an act of self-defense. Otis's primary evidence was that Mein was a huge man while Gill was quite the opposite. Otis won the case; Mein was fined 40 shilling for criminal assault and ordered to pay Gill damages of £75 plus costs. Perhaps predictably, the loss inspired Mein to take the *Chronicle* to new heights of aggression. Mein continued to rail against the rebels, the embargo and the supposed hypocrites who used the embargo to increase prices.

Jemmy reported in a letter to a London client on November 26, 1768 that Boston was quiet save for the constant "military musters, and reviews and other parading of the red coats." Gage had given stern orders that the troops in Boston be well behaved, and so when one marine accosted Jemmy in late November, he was confined to his quarters as punishment. It seemed that every incident in 1768 and 1769 was mined for a possible violation of the colonists' rights; as Otis had earlier proclaimed, "they now knew what their rights were, then they did not." And now the people were alert to discovering and demanding their rights. Shortly after the 1768 Mein assault, Michael Corbet, a Marblehead sailor, shot and killed Lieutenant Henry Panton of the H.M.S. *Rose*. Panton had boarded Corbet's ship, asked about smuggled contraband, then attempted to impress some of Corbet's crew. Panton was clearly a royal officer, from a royal ship, engaging in official business. But Panton was aggressive, Corbet was frustrated, and shots were fired. John Adams and Jemmy Otis formed Corbet's defense team. First, Otis argued for a jury trial instead of a juryless admiralty trial knowing that a jury would never convict a patriot like Corbet. Chief Justice Hutchinson denied the request for both legal and practical reasons; with a jury of his peers inside the courthouse and undoubtedly a mob outside, Corbet would be sainted before being convicted. Now faced with convincing a judge with the evidence in admiralty court, the defense team of Adams and Otis proved that Lt. Panton had neither a customs warrant nor an impressment warrant, so his presence on Corbet's ship constituted an act of trespass. And due to the aggressive nature of the trespasser, lethal force was justified. The defense was brilliant; the prosecutor could not then prove that Panton had any legal reason to be on Corbet's ship. The trial did not help the Court Party in the 1769 elections, as the Court Party had been shackled to the ministry and the customs establishment. Lieutenant Panton fit neatly into the narrative of Court Party attempts to infringe and usurp rights.

The 1769 elections proved to Bernard that "the times were altered" and could not be reversed. Of the Glorious 92 House members who refused to rescind Otis's seditious Circular Letter, 81 were re-elected. The Popular Party firmly controlled the House, and the Council was *persona non grata*. Almost immediately, the House appointed Otis to chair a committee to demand that Bernard remove military forces from Boston, arguing that "military guard with canon pointed at the very door of the state house" constituted an affront to the people. Bernard replied that he had no such authority. Finally, on June 1, 1769, Bernard conceded the obvious, writing to Pownall that "Otis, Adams, etc, are now in full possession of the government." That summer, rumors spread throughout the province that Whitehall was planning to repeal the Revenue Act. And exactly two months after Bernard conceded the government to Jemmy Otis and Sam Adams, Governor Francis Bernard sailed back to England, never again to see Boston. Bernard asked the House to pay his salary prior to leaving, and in a parting shot, Otis chaired the committee that replied to the request, stating that the House was "bound in duty at all times; and we do, more especially at this time, cheerfully acquiesce in the lawful command of our Sovereign." Otis was certain King George would not want Bernard to be paid, so the request was denied. But Boston did finally get Bernard's long wished for puppet government, as none other than Thomas Hutchinson assumed the governorship.

Just prior to Hutchinson's ascension to the governorship, Lord Hillsborough dispatch a circular letter to the colonies assuring them that all Townshend duties would soon be repealed – except for the one on tea. The extra-legal town meetings continued, as merchants and other town members debated the news and its affect on non-importation agreements. By early August, the meetings concluded not only to continue the embargo on British manufactures but also to strengthen them. The town members agreed that Britain only agreed to drop taxes on goods that the colonies had begun to manufacture domestically, and the colonists wished to promote local manufacturers. Finally, the town members agreed to publish a list of merchants who defied the boycott and branded them "Enemies." Predictably, John Mein's name was prominent on the "Enemies" list. In a letter to the recently departed Bernard on August 8, Hutchinson reported that Jemmy was "smiling at his success."

At least one person in the province refused to believe that the times were altered. Ruth Otis's loyalty to the royal government was tartly steadfast; she seemed to delight in antagonizing her husband and his associates. Hannah Winthrop, a good friend of Jemmy and his sister Mercy, wrote a letter to Mercy in 1769:

> I went to see Mrs. Otis the other day. She seems not to be in a good state of health. I received a Visit lately from Master Jemmy [Jemmy and Ruth's 10-year-old son]. I will give you an anecdote of him. A gentleman telling him what a Fine lady his mama is & he hoped he would be a good Boy & behave exceedingly well to her, my young Master gave this spirited answer, I know my Mama is a fine Lady, but she would be much finer if she was a Daughter of Liberty.

We can only surmise that life in the Otis home was exceedingly difficult, though the Colonel made an attempt to temper the turmoil. By 1768, Jemmy's political career consumed his days, and his law practice had suffered. He had begun writing to his London clients to inform them that he would be no longer accepting cases "in order as soon as possible to retire from business." In a November 26, 1768 letter informing London merchant Arthur Jones of his impending retirement from business, Jemmy added, "Our Fathers were a good people and have been a free people, and if you will not let us remain so any longer, we shall be a free people." While Ruth brought a substantial inheritance to the marriage, it is doubtful that it could have funded the family for so long. The obvious question about the source of Jemmy's financial resources is revealed in a discreet transaction conducted in early 1768. The Colonel purchased Jemmy and Ruth's first house on School Street; they had left the house after a few years and had been renting since. Samuel Allyne wrote to his brother Joseph on February 8, 1768 that while the Colonel did not divulge his reasons for purchasing the house, it was most likely intended to be a gift for Jemmy. And so it seems the Colonel agreed that the "Fathers were a good people and have been a free people," and he wished the same for his children.

※

assassination

John Robinson was a powerful man. He was the king's customs officer sent by Lord Grenville to patrol the high-traffic and high-crime waters off New England, a position with incredible authority and immense opportunity for profit. This thought must have crossed Robinson's mind as a jeering mob paraded him on April 12, 1765, six miles from Dighton, on Narragansett Bay, to the Taunton, Massachusetts jail. The sheriff led him, and the mob danced around him, swords drawn. His Majesty's customs officer was getting a treatment usually reserved for only the most dangerous and despised criminals.

The February 27, 1764 Commissioners of Customs's announcement forbidding customs "arrangements" took the merchants by surprise and dismayed many customs officers. They'd had an easy income through their "understandings" or by essentially leasing out their posts. Newport, Rhode Island was a major port under the control of Thomas Clift, but Clift had never visited the colonies and had no intention of doing so. Instead, he leased the post and collected regular payments. By early 1764, it was clear to Clift that he'd need to bestow the post to someone willing to actually sail to the colonies and engage in strict enforcement in person. John Robinson was that man.

So why was Robinson being paraded and jeered on a dirt road to Taunton? Foolishly, Robinson attempted to enforce the law in, of all places, Rhode Island. When Robinson arrived to claim his commission, the Assembly forbade the governor from administering an oath of office; the people of Rhode Island would take no part in establishing law enforcement. So John Temple, Surveyor General, had to travel from Boston to administer the oath personally. While Temple was in Providence and amidst the confab of customs officers, a ship arrived from Surinam. Cargo was unloaded. No customs were paid. A Rhode Island superior court judge owned the ship. There were reasons why Rhode Island was oft times referred to as "Rogue's Island." And when a ship was confiscated, the court would often call the case for immediate hearing in Providence while the customs officer was busy in Newport – not by accident. Or the province prosecutor would fail to show, and the case would be dismissed for lack of evidence. Or the smuggler would be convicted, and his ship confiscated and auctioned by the court for a minimal fee, often sold right back to the smuggler. Usually, the worst case scenario was comparable to a modern-day parking ticket. And if customs officers boarded a ship at sea, the crew often interpreted this action as the Royal Navy's invitation to fight, not a cargo inspection. Corbet's case was not unusual. Customs officers often boarded ships to search for smuggled cargo, and failing to find any, to impress young men into the Royal Navy. Swords and guns were common responses to a customs officer's questions.

John Robinson's determination to reform Rhode Island was put to the test when the sloop *Polly* sailed into Newport on April 2, 1765 with cargo from Surinam. Her captain reported 63 casks of molasses, the ship's owner paid the tax, and the *Polly* sailed out of Newport for Dighton. But John Robinson resented being taken for a fool, and on April 4 decided that a large sloop like the *Polly* would certainly carry far more than 63 casks. So Robinson sailed up to Dighton, personally inspected the *Polly* on April 6, and discovered that her cargo was double what was reported. He seized the ship and the undeclared cargo in the name of the king. Robinson would then have had the *Polly* sail to Newport to be condemned by the court and auctioned if only he could find a few Dighton sailors to take the sloop to Newport. No one would, so Robinson left the *Polly* in Dighton under the watch of a servant and a customs assistant. The next day, Sunday April 7, the servant and the assistant rowed ashore to get a drink from a seaside tavern, and as night fell, a few dozen locals disguised in old clothes and blackened faces rowed out to the *Polly*, unloaded her cargo and everything else that could be removed. The servant and the assistant witnessed all of this from shore, but a few men from the tavern let them know that responding wouldn't be healthy. The two hapless men asked the justice of the peace to make an arrest and were told that an angry mob had been looking for them; the servant and assistant then decided it was time to leave Dighton.

Upon hearing what happened, Robinson returned to Dighton with 70 soldiers and sailors to find the *Polly*, her cargo, rigging, and everything else gone, and her hull drilled with holes. Robinson's prize was nearly worthless. Certain that the cargo and rigging would be found in the ship owner's home, Robinson was ready to find the owner's house and reclaim the cargo but was instead served with a warrant and arrested. The ship's owner claimed that he was prepared to defend himself in court and retake possession of his ship and cargo, which was in the custody of Robinson. But while in Robinson's custody, the ship was nearly destroy and the cargo and rigging was stolen; Robinson was responsible and the owner wanted him held liable. The audacity of the owner – to steal his own cargo and rigging and scuttle his own ship, and then to have Robinson arrested for it – may have shocked the customs officer, but there was nothing he could do. So he was arrested and marched six miles to the Taunton jail.

Obviously a jailed customs officer would find no one in Taunton to post bail, so Robinson sent a letter to the Surveyor General of Customs John Temple, and two days later, bail arrived. Meanwhile, Robinson was told that the ship's owner was willing to come to an "accommodation," meaning the lawsuit would be dropped if Robinson dropped his smuggling charges. Robinson would have none of it, called the owner a "Wretch" and said he would be "Inflexible" in applying the law. And so he sat in jail for two days, likely ridiculed the entire time. And while Robinson sat in jail, the illicit casks of molasses disappeared into the mercantile network of New England. Meanwhile, the famous Boston rebel Jemmy Otis was defending men who murdered customs officers, decrying the customs regime as tyranny, and comparing the writs of assistance to enslavement. Otis had and would continue to publish attacks against Robinson's friends and colleagues in Newport, calling them a "little, dirty, drinking, drabbing, contaminated knot of thieves" from whom proceeded "every evil work that can enter into the heart of man." And when Robinson's friends were hung in effigy in Newport, it was often Otis's words that were pinned to their burning bodies.

Robinson spent the next three years battling smugglers, pirates and mobs in Newport, often living on a boat offshore because he feared the Newport mob. In 1768, he was made Commissioner of Customs in Boston, and Otis and the Sons of Liberty made him a target. It was under Robinson's watch that Otis and John Adams successfully defended Mike Corbet, the smuggler who murdered a Royal Navy lieutenant. The Boston propaganda machine accused Robinson of being a fortune hunter and bribe taker and intimated that he was a rapist; it's unlikely that all the charges were true and yet equally unlikely they were all false. And it was under Robinson's watch that Otis and Sam Adams took "full possession of the government." The new customs board of which Robinson and Paxton were members had quickly targeted the rebels's banker John Hancock, only to utterly and publically humiliate themselves. Hancock's ship *Liberty* entered Boston harbor on May 10, 1768, paid duties on 25 casks of Madeira wine, and docked at Hancock's wharf. Hancock was certainly a smuggler, and the rather large *Liberty* certainly held more than 25 casks, so the Customs Board seized the ship on June 10. But they were so blinded by the overwhelming evidence of Hancock's overt smuggling that they failed to collect any evidence specific to the *Liberty*'s May 10 cargo. By the first week of June, the ship had been fully unloaded of wine and reloaded with whale oil and tar. The mobs promptly rioted, causing the customs commissioners to flee Boston for the *HMS Romney*, the naval ship under the guns of which Hancock's *Liberty* was now anchored. The mob then sacked the homes of two of the commissioners and carried a private boat of a third commissioner all the way to Boston Common and put it to the match. A few days later, the mob gathered again under the Liberty Tree and was persuaded to join a meeting at Faneuil Hall. The Hall proved too small for the enormous gathering, so they reconvened to Old South Church, the same church that Jemmy and Ruth officially joined in February 1756. At the meeting, Otis was chosen moderator and took to the pulpit and, according to Hutchinson, "harangued" the crowd with a classic Puritan jeremiad, and then convinced the Bostonians in attendance to approve a petition – believed to have been composed by Otis – that insisted that "no man shall be govern'd nor taxed but by himself or Representative" and continued to assert that Bostonians had been burdened with "Laws and Taxes" without their consent. The petition concluded that the town nearly felt "as if War was formally declared against it," and though war was "a most shocking and dreadful Extremity," surrender was unimaginable. Otis was then chosen as chairman of a committee of 21 to present the acerbic petition to Bernard, who was pleasantly surprised to be approached with a petition and not a dagger. Bernard stated that he appreciated the petition but had no authority over a ship of war and thus could to nothing about the 50-gun *HMS Romney*.

The fearful commissioners graciously agreed to return the *Liberty* as long as Hancock provided a bond and then would await trial. Hancock agreed, but his advisors – Jemmy and Sam Adams – convinced Hancock to leverage the issue for maximum political effect; Otis and Adams had limitations, but they were matchless in the art of crafting pandemic political crisis out of bureaucratic bumbling. So then Hancock refused the deal, the British unloaded the whale oil and tar and condemned the *Liberty*, which was promptly converted to a British customs enforcement vessel. A monumental problem confronted the customs board: it had no evidence and now Otis and Adams had escalated the *Liberty* case into a cause célèbre. The talented and seasoned lawyer Otis probably knew the case was weak, but he could not have known that it would weaken the entire customs structure. At trial, the Customs Board offered a primary witness who, it was apparent to everyone, had perjured himself. A Suffolk county grand jury indicted the witness for perjury without delay, but he was given a customs job and secreted away, therefore dodging the charge. The trial then ended curiously; Judge Auchmuty opened court on March 26, 1769 by reading his commission as judge for one of the new vice-admiralty courts – a customs job – thereby ending his tenure as judge of the *Liberty* trial. The attorney general, Jonathan Sewall, was likewise awarded a judgeship in one of the new vice-admiralty courts. Without a judge or attorney general, the case was dropped. Had the Customs Board limited the price of prosecuting a weak case to three customs jobs, they probably would have considered the situation a minor bump on the road to an effective customs administration. Of course, the rebels would be sure that the Customs Board was hoist by its own petard. The Board was publically ridiculed and lost whatever credibility it had. The House demanded rent for the ten weeks that the Board had spent sequestered at Castle William while the mobs rioted in protest of the seizure of the beloved Hancock's sloop. The officers were sued for charging fees higher than Massachusetts law permitted, and then the Board members were charged an "income tax" on their salaries. By the end of the year, a Suffolk county grand jury ordered the attorney general to indict the recently departed Governor Bernard, the entire Customs Board, and a variety of customs officials for slandering the residents of Boston. The following year Hancock's *Liberty*, while patrolling Rhode Island waters for the Customs Board, was seized and set afire by a mob.

The Customs Board was thoroughly discredited, and yet more damage was to be done. In August, a ship from London delivered purloined copies of letters and memorials written between February and July 1768 by Customs Board officials and sent to various ministry officials and Parliament members. The letters were sent to the rebels from London by none other than William Bollan, previously the bête noir of the Popular Party. Fueled by rumor and subsequent events, Bollan had grown suspicious of the Court Party. He knew Pownall and Bernard disliked and distrusted him, but he also witnessed how the Popular Party flatly rejected Bernard's lobbyist choice and selected Mauduit, and then when Mauduit proved ineffectual, they selected Jackson and later added De Berdt as a special agent. It appeared to Bollan that the

Court Party made no particular effort to get him reappointed to any position and that Hutchinson was treacherous, only Bollan's friend when Bollan could be useful, as he was in affirming the use of writs of assistance in England. Jemmy's term limit proposal that cemented the election of Richard Jackson resulted in the Court Party to appear selfish and scheming, and certainly no friend of William Bollan.

The letters Bollan sent directly accused Jemmy Otis and his accomplices of leading a rebellion and provided evidence to encourage and enable the ministry to arrest and indict Jemmy for treason. Of course, copies of the letter were promptly made and distributed among the Popular Party, and the entire Customs Board fiasco fueled the theories that the Ministry and customs establishment was actively conspiring to impugn the rebels's reputations, confiscate their property and imprison their leaders. The *Gazette* had been warning of precisely these dangers for years, and such speculation proved shockingly accurate. A few months later, the Town Meeting issued a formal examination and condemnation of the letters. The Town Meeting spent much time addressing Bernard's inconsistencies, as when he blamed the rebels for the riots but "The Governor himself owns that 'the Selectmen of the Town' and 'some others' and even the Gentlemen who dined at two Taverns near the Townhouse upon the occasion of the day 'took great pains that the festivity should not produce a Riot.'" The town meeting questions Bernard's credibility when he asserts that the same people who promoted the riots, in this instance the riots that exploded after the seizing of Hancock's *Liberty*, also stopped the riots. Regarding the *Liberty*, the town further asserted that "opposition was made, not at all to the seizing of the Vessel by the Officers of the Customs but wholly to the manner in which it was secured." The *Liberty* was not seized through legal channels but rather by a ship of war; for the colonists, this represented an act of war, not an act of customs enforcement. The town observed that "The Commissioners say in plain terms that 'there had been a long and extensive plan of resistance to the authority of Great Britain,'" which, of course, they denied, though the observation was entirely accurate. The town's issue with the statement was that there was simply no direct evidence of this, and such an accusation lodged without evidence "shows the Combination, and the settled design, of the Governor and the Commissioners to blacken the character of the Town." The assertion – "Combination" and "settled design" – were intended to demonstrate that the conspiracy was entirely concocted by the oligarchy to target the townspeople. The town meeting again eviscerated Bernard's credibility, quoting his statement that a Sons of Liberty meeting placard read "an invitation of the Sons of liberty to meet at six O'Clock to clear the land of the vermin which were come to devour them," when in fact it read:

> Boston June 13 1768 The Sons of liberty request all those who in this time of oppression and distraction wish well to and would promote the peace, good order and security of the Town and Province, to assemble at Liberty Hall under Liberty Tree on Tuesday the 14 Instant, at 10 O'Clock precisely.

The actual placard showed a group interested in "peace" and "security." The town then corrected Bernard's account of a mob descending on Commissioner Robinson's house to harass and perhaps injure him; in fact, what had occurred amounted to no more than a group of drunken boys eating Robinson's fruit from his trees. At the time, Robinson was hiding in Castle William, and everyone knew he wasn't at his home in Roxbury. The town chided Bernard for noting that everything at the town meetings seemed "to have been preconcerted" by "the Chiefs of the Faction, and *no one else* followed in such *order & method*." The town mocked Bernard for mistaking a united town for a town under the strict control of a few.

The town also cited a letter Bernard had sent to Lord Hillsborough that recounted an episode at the Town House during which the Selectmen ordered the town arms be brought to the townhouse, cleaned and openly displayed, and only then "were deposited in Chests, and laid upon the floor of the Town Hall *to remind the People of the use of them.*" The town meeting didn't deny that this event had occurred; they simply observed that they did not think it incredibly remarkable, as cleaning and displaying the town's arms had been done previously, though not for a nearly a decade. The town meeting concluded that the letters were a "Monument of disgrace" to Bernard and others.

But Otis and Adams would not wait for the town meeting's formal rebuke; they demanded a public meeting with the Customs Board members at the British Coffee House. Henry Hulton and Charles Paxton sensed a trap and wisely declined the invitation, but John Robinson could not resist. He met with the rebels, exchanged invectives and resolved nothing.

And so Sunday September 3, 1769 was a busy day for Ben Edes and John Gill; the *Gazette* was due to be distributed Monday morning, as usual. John

Adams, his cousin Sam and Jemmy had dinner with John Gill at the *Gazette* offices in the townhouse two doors down from the Court House on Court Street. Then they watched as Gill rushed to prepare the presses that Sunday night – "working the political Engine," as John Adams would write. As Adams reported it, the night seemed ordinary. But the *Gazette* edition that was going to press to be distributed the next day printed excerpts from the Customs Board letters for all to see, including the Board's accusation that Jemmy led a "Confederacy" that sought to conquer the customs system and that he was given to "talk with great disrespect of, and threats against the GOVERNMENT." In that same issue, Jemmy printed a few choice words directed at the customs commissioners:

> Whereas I have full evidence, that *Henry Hutton, Charles Paxton, William Burch,* and *John Robinson,* Esquires, have frequently and lately, treated the characters of all true North Americans in a manner that is not to be endured, by *privately* and publicly representing them as *traitors* and *rebels,* and in a general combination to revolt from Great Britain; and whereas the said *Henry, Charles, William* and *John,* without the least provocation or colour, have represented me by name, as inimical to the rights of the crown, and disaffected to his majesty, to whom I annually swear, and am determined at all events to bear true, and faithful allegiance: for all which general, as well as personal abuse and insult, satisfaction has been personally demanded, due warning given, but no sufficient answer obtained ....

The day after Boston's uneasy population read that edition of the *Gazette*, Tuesday, September 5, 1769, John Robinson was socializing after work at the British Coffee House on King Street – the same Coffee House in which Benjamin Barons and Boston merchants had met with Jemmy Otis to devise the first attack on the customs establishment nine years earlier. That Tuesday night, Robinson was surrounded by customs colleagues, all subordinates, and some military personnel. The Coffee House was crowded and lively. Despite the reports and the testimony that followed, no one could be certain why John Robinson did what he next did. Perhaps it was those two nights in the Taunton jail. Perhaps it was all those nights he had to sleep aboard a customs ship because he feared the mobs of Newport. Perhaps he was angry that he needed to arm himself in Boston for fear of attack. Perhaps he was angry that Jemmy Otis defended men who murdered customs officers or at Jemmy's role in embarrassing the Custom Board. Or perhaps it was being surrounded by a group of subordinates who looked up to him and who followed his example. Perhaps he felt he had something to prove. Whatever the reason, when Jemmy Otis walked into the British Coffee House at about 7:30 that evening, "John Robinson ... insulted and fell upon him ... with the assistance of half a dozen or more such scoundrels as himself [and] nearly murdered him before he escaped their hands." Otis was left crumpled on the floor with a bloody head, which was believed to have been hit with a metal object, though debate raged whether it was a cane or a sword. Robinson and the witnesses, nearly all Robinson's friends and colleagues, described it as a defensive "drubbing." Jemmy's friends and relatives described it as an assassination; the *Gazette* argued that a fully orchestrated murder plot was afoot. Even Hutchinson seemed to believe that it was an "attack," though he suggested that Otis had provoked it with his newspaper articles. Curiously, the Court Party's *Evening Post* published an account almost identical to the *Gazette's*. According to these accounts, several men held Otis, and others chanted "Kill him! Kill him!" while he was being struck with canes and swords. John Gridley, Jeremy's nephew, was the only other Popular Party man at the fight, and he left with a broken arm. Once the crowds from outside swarmed into the coffee house, Robinson and his men fled. Two Boston surgeons later testified that the cut on Jemmy's head was so deep that it must have been made by a sharp object, and other testimony described a number of bludgeons and a scabbard found on the Coffee House floor after the assailants had escaped, thereby drawing a picture of a premeditated assault. Some measure of the varying accounts was a confection of propaganda and wishful thinking, but the *Liberty* fiasco and the letters to England accusing Jemmy of treason had painted the Customs Board members as lying, vindictive conspirators and, as such, highly vulnerable to any accusation. One man was arrested, and the loyalist working in his office above the Coffee House, John Mein, put up the arrested man's bond. The mob tired of Mein's antics and attacked his office the following month and Mein, fearing for his life, took to a ship in Boston harbor and sailed for England.

If it was an assassination, it was thoroughly effective because John Robinson accomplished in a few minutes what the British Empire failed to accomplish in a decade. Though Jemmy would physically survive, he was now what the Court Party had previously tried in vain to brand him: insane. He wrote to Lord Hillsborough, the Colonial Secretary, urging him to read the Bible. He smashed the windows of the Town House. He delivered the address at the Boston Massacre victims's public funeral in a toga. He fired off his guns on Sundays. His family confiscated his guns, and the court judged him insane in

November 1771. Samuel Allyne was appointed Jemmy's legal guardian and tried to care for him in Boston, but Jemmy faded in and out of insanity, occasionally appearing lucid and other times needing to be transported against his will, bound hand and food. He was clearly so insane and potentially dangerous that his family decided to confine him, first to the Otis's Barnstable compound and then to a friend's farm in the small rural town of Andover. In a June 18, 1775 letter, James Warren wrote to his wife and Jemmy's sister Mercy, "Your brother Jem dined with us yesterday, behaved well till dinner, was almost done and then in the old way got up went off where I know not." Though Jemmy was 50 years old, "behaved well till dinner" suggests they were dealing with a little boy. And "then in the old way" suggests that perhaps over the course of the year he had appeared more sane, and perhaps they were optimistic that he could recover his sanity, but in mid 1775 he seemed to be "in the old way" – not well behaved, wandering off in the middle of dinner. And concurrent with the Declaration of Independence, in July 1776, Jemmy seemed to have forgotten how to spell his name, signing official forms "James Oates." It's impossible to determine whether such misspelling was wholly involuntary, but in the same month that the colonies found their identity as the United States of America, Jemmy had thoroughly lost his.

Newspapers up and down the coast reported the "assassination." John Robinson was soon on a ship back to England. Boston voters were accustomed to James Otis being labeled insane, and they re-elected him to the Boston bench in the May 1771 elections. Except this time, he truly was insane and would spend some time "unwillingly detained" in Barnstable in the mid 1770s with his father, and, after his father died, most of his time limited to the Osgood's Andover farm, drinking, mumbling, lost in a fog. Titles were commonly bestowed on the important, and as his father was referred to as a colonel, Jemmy was now oft referred to as "Patriot Otis" and the "Chairman." In 1772 he was given the position as Chairman of a committee "to ascertain the Sense of the People," as Sam Adams wrote, but such positions were largely recognition of Otis's importance to the cause; his contributions now were chiefly ceremonial.

Otis's influence on revolutionary politics is obvious; in forcing the ideas of *rights* and *consent* into the colonists' consciousness, he created the platform to envision independence from Britain, from slavery, from government. His fight was not so particularly against a regime that oppressed him; he was wealthy and more a part of the ruling oligarchy than different from it. His fight was against a regime that oppressed anyone, not just by obvious tactics – as Hutchinson often argued the oligarchy in Boston did not – but simply by the way in which society was structured. A practical philosopher and a rebel, James Otis provided the means by which the people could free themselves from the feudal hierarchy that had shackled them for a thousand years.

George Hewes, a poor and mostly unskilled shoemaker and cobbler, was thought to be one of the last surviving participants in the events that preceded the Revolution, so he was interviewed often in the 1830s as the states celebrated various anniversaries of those events. Hewes tells one story of being invited to visit John Hancock after repairing one of his shoes. Hewes washed himself, put on his best clothes, and walked to Hancock House. A servant answered the door and told Hewes to wait in the kitchen. A few minutes later, Hancock appeared and invited Hewes into the sitting room. Hewes was scared "almost to death." Hewes gave a "pretty" little speech that he had prepared, announcing how honored he was to be in Hancock's presence and complimenting the merchant on everything Hewes could imagine. Hancock pressed a coin into Hewes' hand and thanked him for the compliments. He called for wine, and they each had a glass, clinking them together to make a toast, an act that Hewes had never before witnessed. Still horrifically frightened of Hancock, Hewes thanked him and attempted to leave as quickly as possible. He bowed, repeated his compliments, and, before he could run out, Hancock asked him to visit again next year. Hewes said he would but never did.

That was early 1763; Hewes – grateful, frightened, mystified – played perfectly the role of deferential commoner to Hancock's feudal lord. But Hancock had no reason to meet with Hewes, yet did so and invited Hewes to meet again. It was as if Hancock were aware that though now they were nearly lord and serf, someday soon they would be equals. The times would be altered, and as banker to the revolution, John Hancock would press coins into the hands of many rebels so that one day a man like Hewes could visit a John Hancock without being overcome with fear and trembling.

Sixteen years later, the still greatly impoverished Hewes got a job on the ship *Hancock*. But before the ship sailed out, he walked by the ship's Lieutenant on the street. The Lieutenant demanded that Hewes remove his hat; Hewes rejected this act of deference and refused to sail with any man who required it. So Hewes quit that ship and found another job. It was 1779, and George

Hewes refused to remove his hat for any man. The times were indeed altered. The ideas of *rights* and *consent* had infiltrated the colonists's consciousness. The chains of the feudal social structure had been broken, and a poor man like George Hewes could now confidently refuse to sail on the *Hancock*. One suspects the ship's owner knew perfectly well that his coins pressed into the right hands would lead to such a result. George Washington had copied his "Rules of Civility" from the 16th century *Bienseance de la Conversation,* demonstrating how little had changed over centuries. But now, just three decades after young Washington spent his days transcribing "In putting off your Hat to Persons of Distinction, as Noblemen, Justices, Churchmen, &c., make a Reverence, bowing more or less according to the Custom of the Better Bred," *Bienseance de la Conversation* died in the streets of Boston.

Henry Hulton, that Custom Board commissioner who had stepped off the boat on November 5, 1767 and haughtily laughed at the parading mob, soon too discovered that the times were altered. Writing in February 1770, he observed that colonials's attitudes were disconcertingly and increasingly different from those of England's residents:

> The servant will not call the person he lives with, Master; and they have the utmost aversion to wearing anything in the shape of a livery, or performing any office of attendance on your person, or table; We have however a Coachman, who had the fortitude to drive us in spite of the ridicule of his Countrymen, who point & look at him, with contempt, as he passes by.
>
> The people are very inquisitive, and what we should call impertinent; they never give one a direct answer, but commonly return your question, by another; and if you fall in with them on the road, or at a public house, they will directly inquire of you, who and what you are and what is your business.

These people seemed to Hulton to be a new breed incapable of acknowledging an innate hierarchy in society and mocking those who did. The "Coachmen's" countrymen were not pointing and ridiculing a man as he passed by; they were ridiculing feudalism. Jemmy's repeated efforts to maintain order amidst the chaos recognized that the rebellion was not merely against a political structure but against the entire social structure, and such a fundamental alteration in the source of authority for both institutional and interpersonal relationships could so easily slide into anarchy.

As Jemmy Otis surveyed the early 1770s landscape, he perceived the possibility of unstoppable, impending anarchy. "Cursed be the day I was born," he told his doctor. As Otis observed just a few years earlier, the presence of armed customs protection and enforcers only served "to hasten on with great rapidity" the rebellion, and the fire did indeed spread quickly. The Boston Massacre, 1770. North Carolina armed rebellion, 1771. Colonial Committees of Correspondence, 1772. Attack and torching of a British customs ship off Rhode Island, 1772. Tennessee declares itself semi-autonomous, 1772. Sons of Liberty expand operations down the coast, 1773. Boston Tea Party, 1773. Intolerable Acts, closing of Boston Port, effective revocation of Massachusetts charter, and widespread quartering of British soldiers in colonial homes, 1774. British military under General Gage take control of Boston, 1774. Gage begins to confiscate gun power and weapons, 1774. Battles of Lexington and Concord, 1775.

In 1815, John Adams asked, "Who shall write the history of the American Revolution? ... Who can write it?" Reflecting on the stages of history that he shared with so many and probing for the decisive act that mobilized the lumbering gears of revolution toward their inevitable conclusion, one cold night in February 1761 eclipsed all else; Adams denied any plan to "make a speech for" Jemmy but then proceeded to make several about the night of February 24 that Jemmy Otis birthed "the child Independence." In 1816, John Adams observed that "1760 to 1766, was the purest period of patriotism ... the revolution was complete, in the minds of the people, and the union of the colonies, before the war commenced in the skirmishes of Concord and Lexington ...." In gauging the importance of the participants, Adams declared that "the characters the most conspicuous, the most ardent and influential in this revival, from 1760 to 1766, were, first and foremost, before all and above all, James Otis; next to him was Oxenbridge Thacher; next to him, Samuel Adams; next to him, John Hancock; then Dr. Mayhew ...." And in assessing Otis, Adams concluded that "if Mr. [Patrick] Henry was Demosthenes and Mr. Richard Henry Lee, Cicero, James Otis was Isaiah and Ezekial united."

Writing in the late 1770s, Peter Oliver did not yet know the rebellion's outcome. He did not know that he would never return to the colonies nor retrieve his property. His letters from the late 1770s show a man not so much embittered as perplexed, for he had so quickly plummeted from Boston Brahmin to refugee. And he blamed one man: the "young Mr. Otis, as he was the first who broke down the barriers of Government to let in the Hydra of Rebellion." Bernard, too, blamed Jemmy Otis, writing to Secretary of State Petty on December 22, 1766 that "Troubles in this Country take their rise from, and owe their Continuance to one Man." Bernard, Oliver and Adams had quite divergent opinions about the causes of the American Revolution, but they agreed on one detail: James Otis, Jr. started the fire.

※

revenge

The *Jersey* was a British man-of-war stuck in the mud in Wallabout Bay, a small Brooklyn bay near the present-day Williamsburg Bridge. She had been stripped of her rigging and fittings; there was no sail, and no way to sail her. But the British preferred that the *Jersey* wasn't sailable. She was a prison ship.

The British seemed to perfect the concept of the prison ship during the war. The first ship, the *Whitby*, was a cattle ship converted to hold men. They could keep their clothes and bedding but were given nothing else. They were fed once every few days, and the food they were given was whatever was too rotten for the British soldiers to eat. They were provided no medical care. The colonial prisoners aboard the *Whitby* set fire to the ship in October 1777 knowing that they would die: being burned alive was preferable to the torture of being caged on the prison ship. By all appearances, the almost certain death that occurred to the prisoners of the *Whitby* was by design.

Conditions aboard the *Jersey* were considered worse. Food was brought aboard every three days; some days, the prisoners were given raw meat and not permitted to cook it. There were no fruit or vegetables. The ship was never cleaned, and sometimes the men were kept below deck all day. On hot summer days, the heat and stench were horrifying. Scurvy, yellow fever, smallpox and dysentery ravaged the 400 to 1200 prisoners kept aboard. Prisoner Christopher Vail kept a journal: "we suffered very much for food and fresh air. We were ... all put down between decks. At sun down there was as many people lay on deck as to touch each other all round the deck ... And the fore part of the ship full of sick prisoners with the fever. There was only one passage to go on deck at a time. And if a man should attempt to raise his head above the grate he would have a bayonet stuck in it. Many of the prisoners was troubled with the disentary and would come to the steps, and could not be permitted to go on deck, and was obliged to ease themselves on the spot. And the next morning for 12 feet around the hatches was nothing but excrement. ..."

Each morning, the men were awakened to the sound of a British soldier yelling, "rebels, turn out your dead." The corpses would be sometimes just thrown into the water, sometimes buried in shallow graves just on shore. Bodies would float around the ship and colonial women would rebury them on higher ground. Between 1780 and 1783, about five corpses were turned out each day for a total of almost 12,000 — more than all the colonial causalities in all revolutionary war battles combined. To be sent to the *Jersey* was to be sentenced to death.

Famous prisoners of war and officers, such as Ethan Allen, were sometimes paroled into Manhattan. They knew they couldn't leave and agreed to remain on the island and not cause trouble; British officers sometimes invited them to dinner. It was the everyday soldier who was kept on the prison ship – or the subject of revenge. One day not unlike any other day during the war, the British soldier on duty called out, "rebels, turn out your dead." One of the five corpses dragged up to the deck was familiar to the soldiers; it was Master Jemmy, the only son of the famous rebel leader. The British surely knew that James Otis was the *Resentor & the popular Conductor* and the rebel leader. It was no accident that his 18-year-old son, once captured, was sentenced to death on the *Jersey*.

What James ever knew of his son's fate — or anything at that point — is questionable. In late 1782 Jemmy's nephew, Samuel Allyne's son Harrison, brought his uncle from Andover to Boston. The Otis house in Boston was abuzz with visitors, invitations, and hopes that he had recovered. John Hancock, now governor of the state of Massachusetts, visited and insisted that his old friend attend a large party. Jemmy did, and after his condition deteriorated. He made his will and, at his brother Samuel's suggestion, returned to the Andover farm. His will beings, "In the name of God, Amen. –I James Otis, being in no kind fear of death, though by some called the king of terrors, and by old Bannister in his will a sergeant, I make this my last will and testament." The will is dated "31st day of March, in the year of Jesus Christ one thousands seven hundred and eight three and of the assumption of declaration of the Independence of the thirteen United States of North

America, the seventh year." Precisely six weeks after his return to the farm, on the afternoon of Friday May 23, a brilliant thunderstorm was sweeping across New England. The insane rebel walked to the doorway of his room of the Osgood farm house in Andover, Massachusetts. As the rain poured down and the thunder boomed, Jemmy was drawn to the yard, and the "Isaiah and Ezekial united" who set the continent aflame was struck down with fire from the heavens. Mr. Osgood rushed to him but nothing could be done. The bolt of lightning had killed Jemmy Otis instantly.

Later that summer, King George's representative signed the Treaty of Paris, which begins:

Article 1
His Britannic Majesty acknowledges the said United States, viz., New Hampshire, Massachusetts Bay, Rhode Island and Providence Plantations, Connecticut, New York, New Jersey, Pennsylvania, Delaware, Maryland, Virginia, North Carolina, South Carolina and Georgia, to be free, sovereign and independent states, that he treats with them as such, and for himself, his heirs, and successors, relinquishes all claims to the government, propriety, and territorial rights of the same and every part thereof.

EFFECTS

Exactly one month after the "assassination" of James Otis, John Robinson married Anne Boutineau, whose older sister was married to the Lt. Governor of Nova Scotia. The ceremony took place at Boston's Trinity Church. Otis filed a lawsuit against Robinson for the assault to the staggering sum of £3,000 – recall that Otis recovered £75 in damages the previous year for Mein's assault on John Gill. Otis won £2,000 in damages plus costs, and Robinson posted a bond and sailed for England on March 16, 1770, the week after the Boston Massacre. Robinson returned to Boston in August 1772, acknowledged his fault and begged forgiveness. Otis accepted the apology and discharged the damages. Robinson paid court costs and once again returned to England.

Colonel Otis died in 1778, at 76 years old. Like the three generations of Otises before him who died in America, he left his children far wealthier than his father had left him. But that wealth wouldn't last much longer. Just as the residents of Barnstable were not much interested in the Lank Bank, they also were not much interested in independence. They were known as the only town in Massachusetts not to vote for immediate independence in 1776. Joseph and Samuel Allyne, like their father, remained moderate in their views and focused on the family businesses. But when the war began, Joseph and Samuel Allyne marshaled the vast resources of the Otis business empire to support the effort. Joseph was elected to the House and took control of the Barnstable militia, even mustering and marching toward Lexington when news of that battle reached Barnstable. The Colonel convinced the town to withhold all tax payments from Gage's government. Joseph sent uniforms for 80 soldiers to his cousin, Jonathan Otis, in Newport in February 1775. Samuel Allyne joined the war department and procured supplies from the Otis warehouses. Supplying all it could in the early years of the war and suffering from naval blockades, Cape Cod soon endured severe shortages of war materiel and basic necessities. In 1778, rebel government leader and future president of the Massachusetts Senate Jeremiah Powell informed Joseph Otis that he could let the prisoners of war starve to death in order to reserve enough food for Cape Cod residents. Every household on Cape Cod was expected to contribute whatever food, money, clothing, or weapons it had; total war had come to Cape Cod.

Barnstable would remain intransigent. They rejected the Articles of Confederation and eventually the war. Barnstable did not want to support any centralized organizations of control outside of Barnstable. For Barnstable, independence did not mean transferring power from Britain to Boston. By 1782, Barnstable even refused to pay state taxes. Samuel Allyne wrote of Barnstable that after opposing the "infringement of their liberty and property from abroad, will suffer them to be overturned by licentious abandoned people at home, is to suppose like causes produce directly contrary effect." Barnstable viewed taxation from both Britain and Boston as "like causes."

Samuel Allyne's decision to support the war could not have been easy; his wife was the daughter of Harrison Gray, Province Treasurer under the royal governors. But when the war began, he focused on increasing the money supply, even offering to melt down his own silver belt buckles to increase the circulation of hard currency. He raised supplies for the troops including providing 18,000 uniforms. He would take Jemmy's place on the Boston Bench, eventually rising to Speaker of the House. "All revolutions are founded in blood," he wrote in 1782, as he was concerned that Massachusetts quickly return to peace and prosperity. By 1783, both Samuel Allyne and Joseph were impoverished. Joseph refused to sell the Otis farm or sue those who owed him money. By 1785, Samuel Allyne's creditors were getting restless, and he deeded his Boston real estate to his children and pled poverty. On Samuel's advice, Joseph Otis likewise deeded the Otis estates in Barnstable to his children. By September of 1785, Samuel Allyne was officially bankrupt and owed £30,000 to creditors. Without credit, the Otis mercantile businesses were ruined.

On April 8, 1789, two days after the newly created United States Senate achieved its first quorum, vice-president elect John Adams convinced the members to elect his friend as their chief legislative, financial, and administrative officer, the first Secretary of the United States Senate. Twenty-two days later, Samuel Allyne held the Bible on which George Washington swore to uphold the Constitution. Samuel Allyne, then 48 years old, had a long list of service to the new government: Quartermaster of the Continental army,

Speaker of the Massachusetts House of Representatives, member of Congress under the Articles of Confederation, and John Adams's longtime ally. He had fully transformed from a businessman apathetic to politics to a political insider. In those early days of the government, the Secretary proved unusually influential as he was the chief negotiator between the Senate, the House and George Washington. It wasn't before long that Washington's cabinet secretary desired the surprisingly influential position of Senate Secretary and asked Washington to have Otis removed, but Washington declined, as did the Virginians when they swept to power in 1800. Though the Federalists were resolutely turned from power in the 1800 elections, Samuel Allyne was kept on precisely because the new government was so unstable and fractious and a peaceful transition so uncertain. Southern Republicans and northern Federalists alike mongered rumors of secession and nullification, and Hamilton had been conspiring to raise an Army to not only enforce radical Federalist doctrine but to 'liberate' all of the Americas from European influence. Nearly everyone recognized that the diligent, steady, non-partisan Samuel Allyne Otis was an invaluable asset if the new government was to have a chance of surviving. And so Samuel Allyne provided the order and stability that the new government so desperately required and was Secretary until his death in 1814; his 25 years as Secretary is a record that still stands, and he was known for never missing a day of work. His optimism in the new federal government led him to invest every penny he could scrounge together in U.S. bonds, and he remade much of the wealth he'd lost in the war. Samuel Allyne's eldest son, Harrison Gray, named for the loyalist provincial treasurer, was a U.S. Senator from Massachusetts, the Mayor of Boston, a U.S. Representative from Massachusetts, Massachusetts District Attorney appointed by Washington, and, by today's standards, a billionaire.

Jemmy's sister, Mercy Otis Warren, became a rather famous poet and America's first female playwright; in the 1770s, she wrote anti-loyalist plays. After the war, she wrote a well-received history of the Revolution that was much more Jeffersonian and egalitarian than her blue-blood peers in Boston would have preferred. She remained close friends with John Adams till the end, though Adams occasionally wrote snarling letters to her complaining about his lack of prominence in her histories. Mercy died in Plymouth six months after her brother Samuel Allyne, in October 1814, at the age of 86. It was at Mercy's and her in-laws' houses in Plymouth that the Stamp Act Congress was conceived. It seems appropriate that the dawn of English settlements in New England occurred in the same place as did the dawn of the new nation, and there's some poetic truth in Plymouth's claim to being America's Avalon, that the fourth great grandson of a weaver from that mythical town of King Arthur conceived the new nation in that town on Cape Cod Bay. And that hill on the original Otis property in Hingham that John named "Weary All," the same name of a similar hill that sits alongside The Roman Way in Glastonbury, was renamed "Otis Hill" and it currently rests alongside "Otis Street."

Jemmy's sister Mary, who had married John Gray, brother of Province Treasurer Harrison Gray, remained loyalist and left for England when war erupted in 1776. She would never see Jemmy again. She and Samuel Allyne both married into the Gray family, and the war put an ocean between them.

Ruth Cunningham Otis, that heiress who'd marry the most brilliant lawyer in the province, was widely despised by the other Otises, particularly Jemmy's sister Mercy, who in 1776 wrote of "a weak Infatuated Woman who has heretofore Brought innumerable Difficulties upon her own Family." It had been suggested that Ruth was partially to blame for Jemmy's insanity or, at least, his inability to recover. Regardless, Ruth was bitter to the end, blaming problems seen and unseen on the rebellion and asserting to her dying day that the British government was preferable to the new government. Ruth and Jemmy's daughter Elizabeth married a British officer and moved to England, probably to the delight of her mother. Her father never forgave her and left her a paltry five shillings in his will. Their other daughter Polly married Benjamin Lincoln, Jr., who probably would have delighted her father. Polly's father-in-law was General Lincoln, the man who acted as a referee in the *Veazie v. The Inhabitants of the Town of Duxborough* case of 1748, one of Jemmy's first cases, and who officially accepted Cornwallis's surrender at Yorktown in 1781; Lincoln would become the new nation's first Secretary of War and Lt. Governor of Massachusetts. Ruth died in 1789. It was Polly who informed John Adams that she "had not a line from her father's pen." According to Polly, her father took "great pains" to collect everything he wrote and, as with the continent and eventually himself, "committed them all to the flames." Was it fear that the true role of "our chairman" in the "Confederacy" would be discovered? That charges of sedition and treason would be brought? Or madness?

Nathaniel Wheelwright, the great private banker whose insolvency in January 1765 proved fertile ground for rebellion, fled Boston in March 1765 – less than two months after his insolvency. He left behind three sons, one living with the reverend of King's Chapel, one with his maternal grandmother and one with his paternal uncle. He also left behind his wife, Ann Apthorp, his business partner's sister. Disgraced, Wheelwright hopped a ship to Central America, never to return. He died in 1766 in Guadalupe of yellow fever. His business partner, Charles Ward Apthorp, had purchased a bit of real estate upon moving to New York – 50 blocks of the Upper West Side, from 89th to 99th streets, from Central Park to the Hudson river. Charles's death inaugurated law suits – beginning in 1799 – that would last over 100 years. The primary dispute seemed to be whether the city should compensate the landowners when it created city streets on what had been entirely private land. By the early 1900s, the suits were valued at $125 million.

Capt. Dan Malcolm, that smuggler who had flaunted the rebels's control of Boston by openly importing brandy without paying taxes and drank from Paul Revere's "Glorious 92" punchbowl, died in 1769. The British did not forget him. His gravestone reads, "A TRUE SON OF LIBERTY A FRIEND TO THE PUBLICK AN ENEMY TO OPPRESSION AN ONE OF THE FOREMOST IN OPPOSING THE REVENUE ACTS ON AMERICA." The gravestone still stands at the old North Burying Ground, covered with the marks of the musket balls that British soldiers fired at it when they used the North Burying Ground as a military camp at the opening of the war. Around the same time, British soldiers also cut down the Liberty Tree.

Francis Bernard, the man who only wanted an easy administration and to make some money, really never knew what hit him. Naïve and clumsy as he was, he had Whitehall and Parliament on one side and Otis and the rebels on the other; it's doubtful anyone could have prevented the inevitable collision. Bernard went back to England and was appointed to the Board of Revenue for England, which is ironic because it was precisely the issue of revenue – Molasses Act, Stamp Act, etc. – and the Declaratory Act that echoed the oppression of Ireland and ignited the widespread rebellion. Once the war broke out, he lost his beloved Mount Desert Island. John Adams would later label King George III "the mad idiot" and in the midst of stabilizing the new country declare that George's "idiocy is our salvation." Adams had witnessed the gift of executive idiocy decades earlier in Francis Bernard; Adams was keenly aware that such "idiocy" was key to manipulating a successful outcome, just as he had seen the Colonel and Jemmy Otis use Bernard's idiocy to their advantage. As a token of appreciation to a faithful ally of the Revolution, the western half of Bernard's beloved Desert Island was granted to John Bernard – Francis Bernard's son.

Andrew Oliver, the high ranking member of the oligarchy and stamp distributor whose business and house were destroyed during the Stamp Act riots of 1765, became Lt. Governor in 1771 when his brother-in-law, Thomas Hutchinson, became governor. Andrew died of a stroke while in office on March 4, 1774, and Peter could not attend his brother's funeral because he feared the mobs that controlled the streets. Andrew's son Stephen would flee to England when the war broke out; in 1801, he married 27-year-old Sarah Hutchinson, daughter of the last British governor of Massachusetts. The vast fortunes of both Thomas Hutchinson and Peter Oliver were confiscated. Both wrote books about the colonies, and both believed they had acted honorably and reasonably and were the victims of an inferno of insanity that swept through the colonies.

Timothy Ruggles, the loyalist sent to the Stamp Act congress to ensure that what happened didn't happened, only to creep his way back through New England to find the House had censured him for not signing the Stamp Act resolves, remained a staunch loyalist. Ruggles created the "Ruggles Covenant," a loyalist pledge to oppose any colonial congress and to remain loyal to the king. Once the war broke out, Ruggles crept his way to Nova Scotia, leaving his daughter Bathsheba behind enemy lines. Ruggles was much despised, but nothing could be done as he'd escaped. But his daughter made herself a viable target when she plotted with two AWOL British soldiers to have her husband killed. The murder was successful; the cover-up was not. Bathsheba begged for leniency as she was five months pregnant, but the leader of the Massachusetts Executive Council, John Avery Jr., signed her death warrant anyway. Bathsheba was hanged July 2, 1778 before a crowd of 5,000 in Worchester. She was the first woman executed in the United States. John Avery Jr. was a member of the Loyal Nine, the high command of the Sons of Liberty.

Brutal righteousness swept from the villages of Massachusetts to the highest offices in the rebel nation, as Major John Andre would discover in 1780. A highly regarded British officer of flawless comportment, Major Andre was caught attempting to facilitate Benedict Arnold's treachery. Washington's officers, most notably Hamilton, recommended that Andre be held prisoner for the length of the war, a sentence befitting a man of his rank. But Washington knew what John Avery and the townspeople of Worchester knew and what many others, again notably Hamilton, had failed to yet appreciate: the war Washington's army waged wasn't merely against the British; it was against feudalism. A criminal's sentence would be determined by his crime, not his rank or lineage or gender. Washington's officers protested; at the least, they argued, Andre should be shot as an officer. Yet Washington, like Jemmy Otis, possessed an uncanny ability to sense a larger picture even when the picture was apparent to few others. He ordered Major Andre to be hanged as a commoner, and he was the next day.

Ironically, it was Nova Scotia, the land that Massachusetts Province had fought so hard for in the 1740s, that provided refuge for fleeing loyalists such as Timothy Ruggles. The Louisbourg campaign of 1744 had been a powerful unifying force for the province, and the return of Louisbourg in exchange for Madras, India had planted a seed of doubt about the mother country's loyalty to the province. And now, that stretch of land was a haven for those disloyal to the cause.

And that single student who studied law under Jemmy Otis in 1754? Pelham Winslow would become Major Pelham Winslow, British Commander of Castle William, Britain's primary fort during the siege of Boston and a place of refuge for loyalists. The fort was soon taken and would subsequently be renamed Fort Independence.

James Bowdoin started as a loyalist and was the author "J" in the paper war, roundly criticizing Otis and defending the oligarchy. And yet by the mid 1760s he would largely agree with Otis's earlier radical positions, becoming a great critic of Hutchinson, who would reject Bowdoin's appointment to the Council in 1769. Bowdoin would become the Massachusetts constitutional convention's president, delegate to the first Continental Congress, and governor of Massachusetts in 1785 – a full convert to Otis's incendiary position. Thomas Cushing could, at best, be described as a tepid supporter of the rebels, but he too eventually became an advocate of independence. Along with John Hancock, Bowdoin and Cushing took turns as the first governors of the state of Massachusetts.

And what of Charles Paxton, the odious omnipresent Commissioner of Customs who in 1760 directed his deputy to ask the court for a writ of assistance? John Adams later wrote of Paxton that he was "the essence of customs, taxation, and revenue," and that he appeared at one time "to have been governor, lieutenant-governor, secretary, and chief justice." Rebels hung his effigy on the Liberty Tree more than once, though on one special occasion it was hanged between those of the devil and the pope. He was driven by angry mobs to take up protection at Castle William. He and his family escaped Boston in 1776 and went to Halifax, Nova Scotia, and, shortly thereafter, England. He died in obscurity in 1788, living at the house of a fellow tax collector. Paxton's legacy lives on in the town named after him about 50 miles west of Boston. Paxton, Massachusetts was incorporated in February 1765, a month before Parliament passed the Stamp Act. The bell that still rings from the Paxton, Massachusetts Meeting Hall was cast by Paul Revere.

CODA

John Singleton Copley, the most famous colonial painter of his day, painted portraits of the Colonel and his wife Mary Allyne, their daughter Mercy Otis Warren, her husband James, Elizabeth Gray Otis, John Hancock, Andrew Oliver and Sam Adams. The portraits of Mercy and James Warren, John Hancock and Sam Adams hang in the Boston Museum of Fine Arts, as does Peter Oliver's portrait. The Boston Museum also has a group portrait of the Oliver brothers – Peter, Andrew and Daniel – painted when they were young adults. Elizabeth Gray Otis's portrait hangs with her husband Samuel Allyne's portrait in the National Gallery of Art in Washington, D.C. Samuel Allyne's portrait was painted by Gilbert Stuart, another famous artist whose portrait of George Washington graces the one dollar bill. Andrew Oliver's portrait also hangs with Elizabeth and Samuel Allyne in the National Gallery. In life, the Colonel and his wife Mary Allyne were always deemed to be rural folk, and in death they are still far from the madding crowd; their portraits hang in the Wichita Art Museum.

Jemmy Otis midwifed the philosophical concepts of *rights* and *consent* into the world of practical politics, a world whose feudal spirit was both horrified and intrigued by "the child Independence." The man who promised to "kindle such a fire" oft stood alone amidst the flames in 1762 and 1763, and the now assumed wisdom of the separation of powers and "unalienable rights" began under a cloud of sedition and doubt. In those early years of apprehension and rejection, Jemmy employed newspapers and pamphlets to affect elections and government that has molded the way media operate, and by late 1765 he had persuaded thousands to risk their lives, fortunes and sacred honors to raise that child. The concept of judicial review bears the imprint of his theories about the role of the judiciary in the legislative process. He helped modernized the practice of law and politics while maintaining that the credibility of both rests on their access to all. His argument against general search warrants is enshrined in the Fourth Amendment to the U.S. Constitution.

The fire he lit is immortalized in the Statue of Liberty, who holds the flames of freedom high to enkindle the world. Lady Liberty's head is encircled with a halo of seven rays, signifying that the torch is to ignite all seven continents just as Jemmy's 1761 election would "shake all four." She holds a tablet of the law inscribed with an updated confirmation of Jemmy's *Anno Liberatus Primo* – JULY IV MDCCLXXVI – and the chains of feudalism lay broken at her feet. His insistence – at times bombastic, at times menacing – on the primacy of individual rights and the inevitable absurdity of slavery and voter property qualifications reverberated long after he lay lifeless on a rain soaked yard in Andover; it was as if he saw the future and couldn't wait to get there and failed to understand why others were dawdling. His dogged pursuit of *consent* indeed shook "all four" continents. This "Isaiah and Ezekial united" had a tempestuous life, charged with passion and fury and fueled by a burning pursuit of solutions to problems that few knew existed. And his faith in the pursuit and belief in the solutions fused wholly with the consciousness that led to rebellion and created the republic.

Joseph Blackburn, the artist who trained the great Copley yet received little recognition for his own work, painted James Otis's portrait. Blackburn slipped into the murky depths of history in the mid-1760s and is assumed to have died about a decade later, but his date and place of death are unknown. His portrait of Jemmy Otis hangs in no museum; its location is unknown.

A Vindication of the Conduct of the House of Representatives (1762)

THE PREFACE

The following Vindication, was written in order to give, a clear View of Facts; and to free the House of Representatives, from some very injurious aspersions, that have been cast upon them, by ill-minded people out of doors. Whether the writer has acquitted himself as becomes a candid and impartial vindicator, is submitted to the judgment of the publick; which is ever finally given without Favour or affection; and therefore the appeal is made to a truly respectable and solemn tribunal? At the same time that a sincere love is professed for all men, and the duty of honour and reverence towards superiors is freely acknowledged, it must be allowed that one of the best ways of fulfilling these Duties, is in a modest and humble endeavor, by calm reason and argument, to convince mankind of their mistakes when they happen to be guilty of any. The more elevated the person who errs, the stronger sometimes is the obligation to refute him; for the Errors of great men are often of very dangerous consequence to themselves, as well as to the little ones below them. However it is a very disagreable task, to engage in any kind of opposition to the least individual in Society; and much more so when the opinions of Gentlemen of the first rank and abilities, and of publick bodies of men are to be called in question.

The world ever has been and will be pretty equally divided, between those two great parties, vulgarly called the winners, *and the* loosers; *or to speak more precisely, between those who are discontented that they have no Power, and those who never think they can have enough.*

Now, it is absolutely impossible to please both sides, either by temporizing, trimming or retreating; the two former justly incur the censure of a wicked heart, the latter that of cowardice, and fairly and manfully fighting the battle out, is in the opinion of many worse than either. *All further apology for this performance shall be sum'd up in the adage.* Amicus Socrates, amicus Plato, sed magis Amica veritas.

A VINDICATION & c.

A *Quporum* of the house of representatives of the *Province* of the *Massachusetts-Bay,* being met, on the 8th of Sept. A.D. 1762. according to prorogation, informed his Excellency the Governour by a committee chosen for that purpose, that they were ready to proceed to business. The committee returned that they had delivered the Message. Mr. Secretary came down soon after with a message from his Excellency, directing the attendance of the House in the council chamber. Mr. Speaker with the House immpediately went up; when his Excellency was pleased to make the following Speech; of which Mr. Speaker obtained a Copy, and then with the house returned to their own Chamber.

His Excellency's speech is as follows. Viz.

"Gentlemen of the Council, and

"Gentlemen of the House of Representatives,

"I have been always desirous to make your Attendance to this General Court as unexpensive to your Constituents and as convenient to yourselves as the Nature and Incidents of the public Business will allow. But, as, whilst the War continues, this Province, however happy in the Operations being re-moved at a Distance, must expect to bear some Share of the Trouble and Expence of it: It will sometimes unavoidably happen that I must be obliged to call you together at an unseasonable Time. I HAVE now to lay before you a Requisition of His Excellency Sir JEFFERY AMHERST, who, observing that the great and important Services on which His Majesty's Regular Troops are now employed, and the Uncertainty of their Return, render it absolutely necessary, that Provision should be made in Time for garrisoning the several Posts on this Continent during the Winter, desires that you would provide tor continuing in Pay the same Number of Troops that remained during last Winter; that is, Six Captains, Thirteen Subalterns, and Five Hundred and Seventy Two Privates, amounting in the whole to Five Hundred and ninety one Men.

I MUST observe to you that the Necessity of this Request arises from the present vigorous Exertion in the *West-Indies;* which promises effectually to humble the Pride of our Enemies, and pave the Way to Peace. As this glorious Expedition cannot but have your entire Approbation, I doubt not but you will readily embrace this Opportunity to give a public Testimony of it.

THE *French* Invasion of *Newfoundland* must give you great Concern upon Account of the National Loss which the Interruption of the Fishery there must have occasioned, although this Province will not, in its own particular, greatly suffer thereby. But I am persuaded that the Reign of the *French* in those Parts is by this Time near over; and I flatter myself that this Government will have some Share in the Honour of putting an End to it.

Gentlemen of the House of Representatives,

THE great Alarm which spread itself over the Country upon the *French* getting Possession of a strong Post in *Newfoundland,* obliged me with the Advice of Council to take some cautionary Steps which have been attended with Expence. But as these Measures were advised with an apparent Expediency, and have been conducted in the most frugal Manner, I doubt not but what has been done will have your Approbation. I shall inform you of the Occasion of these Expences, and order the Accounts thereof to be laid before you.

Gentlemen of the Council, and
Gentlemen of the House of Representatives,

As I have called you together at this Time with Reluctance, so I shall be desirous to dismiss you, as soon as the public Business shall have had due Consideration. This, I apprehend, will take up not many Days; after which I shall be glad to restore you to your several Engagements at your own Homes with as little Loss of Time as may be.

Council-Chamber,
Sept. 8, 1762.　　　　　　　　　　　　　　　FRA. BERNARD.

This speech (with General Amherst's Letter therein referred to) being read, the Consideration thereof was appointed for the next morning at nine of the clock.

September the 9th, the house agreable to the order of the day, entered into the Consideration of his Excellency's speech. In the course of the debate the following speech was made, as nearly as can be recollected by memory;

"Mr. Speaker,

This Province has upon all occasions been distinguished by its loyalty and readiness to contribute its most strenuous efforts for his majesty's service. I hope this spirit will ever remain as an indelible Characteristick of this People. Every thing valuable is now at stake. Our most Gracious Sovereign, and his royal Predecessor, of blessed memory, have for some years been engaged in a bloody and expensive, but most just and necessary War, with the powerful Enemies of their Persons, Crown and Dignity; and consequently of all *our* invaluable civil and religious Rights and Priviledges. The Almighty has declared the justice of this War, by giving us the most astonishing series of Victories and Triumphs recorded in ancient or modern story. From these

Successes we had reason to hope that the War would have ended last year in a glorious peace. Our King and Father has condescended to tell us that his Endeavors for that purpose were frustrated by Gallic Chicanery and Perfidy. The King of Spain has been prevailed upon to break his Neutrality, to forsake his alliance with Great Britain, to turn a deaf Ear to the Interest and Cries of his own Subjects, and to attach himself to the Party of France and of Hell. But Heaven still smiles upon his Majesty's Arms. We have within this Hour received undoubted Intelligence of a memorable Victory obtained by Prince Ferdinand of Brunswick; and of the Reduction of the Havannah, the Key of the Spanish Treasury. Besides an immense Value in specie we have taken and destroyed one quarter of the Spanish navy. This has been done at a bad Season of the year and in Spite of as Gallant a defence as ever was made of a strong Hold. *Mr. Speaker,* the Fate of North America, and perhaps ultimately of Great Britain herself depends upon this War.

Our own immediate Interest therefore, as well as the general Cause of our King and Country, requires that we should contribute the last peny, and the last drop Of Blood, rather than, that by any backwardness of ours, his Majesty's Measures should be embarrassed; and thereby any of the Enterprizes, that may be planned for the Regular Troops miscarry. Some of these Considerations, I presume, induced the Assembly, upon his Majesty's Requisition, signified last Spring by Lord *Egremont* so cheerfully and unanimously to raise thirty three Hundred Men for the present Campaign; and upon another Requisition, signified by Sir *Jeffery Amherst,* to give a handsome bounty for inlisting about nine Hundred more into the regular Service. The Colonies we know, have been often blamed without Cause; and we have had some share of it. Witness the miscarriage of the pretended Expedition against Canada in Queen Anne's Time, just before the infamous Treaty of *Utrecht.* It is well known by some now living in this Metropolis, that every Article, that was to be provided here, was in such readiness, that the Officers, both of the army and navy, expressed the utmost Surprise at it upon their arrival. To some of them no doubt it was a Disappointment; for in order to shift the Blame of this shameful affair from themselves, they endeavoured to lay it upon the New-England Colonies. I remember, that by some, who would be thought faithful Historians, the miscarriage at Augustin in the last War, has been attributed to the neglect of the Carolinians. But it is now notorious to all, that the ministry of that Day never intended that any good should come of that Enterprize; nor indeed to any other, by them set on foot, during the whole War. The Conduct of that War, so far as the ministry were concerned, has been judged to be one continued abuse upon the Sovereign and his People. Thank God, we are fallen into better

Times. The King, the ministry, and the People are happily united in a vigorous pursuit of the common good. Surely then if *We* should discover the least remissness in his Majesty's Service, as we should be truly blame-worthy, we may depend upon having matters represented in the strongest light against us, by those who delight to do us harm.

I am therefore clearly for raising the men, if Gen. *Amherst* should not inform us, by the return of the next mail, that he shall have no occasion for them. But as his Letter is dated the 4th of *August,* before even Moore Castle was taken, and since the Reduction of the Havannah, a number of the Regulars are returned to New-York, it is possible the General may have altered his Sentiments, as to the necessity of these Provincials.

Waiting 2 or 3 Days however can't make any odds in this Business, as our Troops are all inlisted to the last of October. Upon the whole *Mr. Speaker,* I am for a Committee to take the Governor's Speech and the present Requisition into Consideration, and make report." This being seconded, *Mr. Speaker, Mr. Otis, Mr. Tyler,* General *Winslow,* and *Mr. Witt,* were appointed a Committee to take said Speech and Requisition into Consideration, and make report. The Committee waited a few Days for the Return of the Express, but hearing nothing further about the men it was taken for granted that the General expected them. The Committee therefore without debate unanimously reported to the House in favour of raising them at the bounty of Four Pounds each, that is, ten Shillings more than was given in the Spring. This Report was likewise almost unanimously accepted, and the men are now inlisting.

Here is another instance of the readiness of this Province to do every thing in their Power for his Majesty's Service. This Spirit notwithstanding many ungenerous Suggestions to the contrary, has remarkably discovered itself in most if not all the British Colonies during the whole War. This Province has since the year 1754, levied for his Majesty's Service as Soldiers and Seamen, near thirty Thousand men besides what have been otherwise employed. One year in particular it was said that every fifth man was engaged in one Shape or another. We have raised Sums for the support of this War that the last Generation could hardly have formed any Idea of. We are now deeply in debt, but should think our selves amply rewarded if *Canada* should be retained.

The House did not enter into a particular Consideration of the latter part of the Governor's Speech, at this Time; as it is general; and an explanatory message was expected, with particular accounts of all the expences alluded to. Accordingly Sept. the 14th Mr. Secretary came down with the following message, from his Excellency, Viz.

Gentlemen of the House of Representatives,

"SOON after the French Invasion of *Newfoundland*, the Inhabitants of *Salem* and *Marblehead*, who were concerned in the Fishery North-West of *Nova-Scotia*, were alarmed with Advice that a *French* Privateer was cruising in the Gut of *Canso;* and petitioned for protection for their Fishing Vessels then employed in those Seas.

AS the *King George* was then out on a Cruize, and the *Massachusetts-Sloop* was just returned from *Penobscot*, I fitted the latter out in the readiest and most frugal Manner I could. I put on board her twenty-six Provincials, which I had within my Command, and augmented her Crew which was established at six Men, to twenty-four; and having compleately armed her, sent her to the Gut of *Canso,* to the Protection of the Fishery there.

FROM thence she is just now returned, after a Cruize of about a Month; in which she saw no Enemy, although she heard of a *French* Pirate being in those Seas, and looked after him; and has in some Part Answered her Purpose, by encouraging the Vessels there to stay to compleat their Fares.

SHE now waits for Orders; and before I disarm her, and reduce her Crew, it may deserve Consideration whether it may not be advisable to keep up her present Complement, 'till the *King George* is discharged from the Service she is now engaged in; which I refer to your Deliberation."
Council-Chamber,
Sept. 11, 1762.   FRA. BERNARD.

A little paper only, accompanied this message, with a short account of the Difference to the Province by the Governor and Council's inlarging the Establishment, which amounted to about Seventy two Pounds. But no notice was taken of the Commissary's and other Bills which must finally swell this account much higher. However it was neither the measure, nor the expence of it, that gave the House so much uneasiness, as the manner of it; that is, the inlarging an Establishment without the knowledge of the house, and paying it without their privity or consent. The Council minute relating to this Affair stands thus.

"At a General Council held at the Council Chamber in Boston upon Monday the 9th Day of Dec. 1761.
Present
His Excellency the Governor.

Hon. *Thomas Hutchison,* Esq; Lieutenant Governor. Mr. *Danforth,* Judge *Lynde,* Brigadier *Royal,* Capt. *Erving,* Brigadier *Brattle,* Mr. *Bowdoin,* Mr. *Hancock,* Mr. *Hubbard,* Mr. *Gray,* Mr. *Russell,* Mr. *Plucker,* Mr. *Ropes.*

Upon representation made to his Excellency the Governor from a Number of Persons Inhabitants of the Towns of *Salem* and *Marblehead,* for some protection to be afforded to the Fishery, they having received an account of a French Privateer in the Gut of *Canso.* Advised that his Excellency give orders for fitting out the Sloop-Massachusetts, in order to proceed on a cruize, to the Gut of *Canso,* and Bay *Vert,* for the protection of the Fishery and to continue her said cruise not exceeding one Month; and as his Excellency proposes to put on board twenty-six Provincials, and ten men out of the Ship King George, provided she arrives seasonably, towards manning of the said Sloop: Advised that her proper Crew be augmented to twenty-four men, officers included, upon the following Wages, viz. Captain £.5 6 8. per Month, Lieut. £ .4 0 0. Master £.4 0 0. Master's mate £.368. Boatswain £.3 6 8. Boatswain's mate £.3 0 0. Gunner £.368. Gunner's mate £.30 0. per Month, and each Private £.2 13 14. per Month; and that the Commissary General put in Provisions for said Cruize accordingly."

The Protection of the Fishery is undoubtedly a very important object and the Province at the beginning of the War built a Ship of twenty Guns, and a Snow of sixteen Guns, for the *immediate* protection of the Trade. I wish the Interests of Commerce were more attended to by those who have it in their Power to cherish them. The trade in the opinion of some has never received a Benefit from those Vessels equal to the Tax Trade alone has paid for their Support. However if more are wanted, when that necessity appears, doubtless the assembly will establish more, in the mean time, no more can be lawfully established at the publick Expense. There has been an Instance or two of the Governor and Council's taking upon them in the recess of the Court to fit out the Province Ship, in a very unusual and unconstitutional manner, as appears by the following Extracts from the Council Records.

"11th of September 1760. Present in Council the *Governor, Lieutenant Governor, the Honorable Jacob Wendell, Samuel Watts, Andrew Oliver, John Erving, James Bowdoin, William Brattle, Thomas Hancock,* and *Thomas Hubbard, Esqr's.*

His Excellency having communicated to the board some Intelligence he had received of five Privateers being cruizing off the *Southern Provinces* in Lat. 39. 28. and asked the advice of the Council with respect to manning the Province Ship King George. Advised that his Excellency give Orders for immediately compleating the Ship's Complement of Men, by directing Captain Hallowell to beat up for Volunteers upon the Encouragement of eight Dollars per man for the Cruize over and above the Wages agreable to the Establishment. Advised and Consented that a Warrant be made out to the Treasurer to pay unto Captain Hollowell the Sum of One Hundred and sixty Pounds sixteen Shillings, to pay the Bounty of said Men, he to be accountable."

To the Honour of General *Brattle* he was single in his Opposition to this Resolution.

"21st of May 1761. In Council,

Present the *Governor, Lieutenant Governor, the honorable John Osborne, Jacob Wendell, Andrew Oliver, John Erving, William Brattle, Thomas Hancock,* and *Thomas Hubbard, Esqr's.*

Whereas Intelligence has been received of two Privateers cruizing off Block-Island which have already taken divers Vessels bound to and from the Colonies, and the Ship King George having no more than thirty men belonging to her, Officers included, and there being no prospect of any further men inlisting upon the present *Establishment,* and the *appropriation* for the Service of said Ship being exhausted, and his Excellency having proposed to put fifty men of the new raised Troops on board said Ship to serve for one Cruize only; therefore in order to compleat the Complement of Men; advised that his Excellency give orders to Captain Hallowell to send the Ship down to Nantasket without Delay, and to impress from all inward bound Vessels, coasters and Provincial Vessels excepted; also to inlist Volunteers upon a Bounty of ten Dollars each; provided the money can be procured; and for that Purpose it is further advised that a Warrant issue upon the Treasurer for seven Hundred Dollars, to be paid out of such Sums as shall be subscribed by any Merchants or other persons, for the above services, upon the credit of a Reimbursement *to be made by*[1] the General Court at their next Session."

There had been some other Proceedings that were very much disrelished by former Houses, e. g. In three Days after the Heirs of Lieutenant Governor Phipps had received a Denial from the House to bear the Expence of his Honor's Funeral, the Governor and Council paid it. Some other extraordinary accounts had also been allowed contrary to the known and express Sense of the House. All these matters together alarmed the present House, and they thought it high time to remonstrate. Accordingly when the Governor's Message relating to the Sloop Massachusetts was read, (upon a motion made and seconded) it was ordered as an Instruction to the Committee to answer it, to remonstrate against the Governor and Council's making and increasing Establishments without the Consent of the House. Tho' no Notice is taken of this Instruction in the printed Votes of the House. The Journal stands thus, "Read and Ordered, that Mr. Otis, Mr. Tyler, Captain Cheever, Col. Clap

---

1   I wish the words had been, "to be recommended to"

and Mr. Witt, take said message under consideration, and report an answer thereto."

Sept. the 15th, The committee reported the following answer and Remonstrance,

Viz.

May it please your Excellency,

"The House have duly attended to your Excellency's message of the 11th, Instant, relating to the Massachusetts *Sloop,* and are humbly of opinion that there is not the least *necessity* for keeping up her present complement of men, and therefore desires that your Excellency would be pleased to reduce them to fix, the old establishment made for said Sloop by the General Court.

"Justice to our selves, and to our constituents oblige us to remonstrate against the method of making or increasing establishments by the Governor and council.

"It is in effect taking from the house their most darling priviledge, the right of originating all Taxes.

"It is in short annihilating one branch of the legislature. And when once the Representatives of a people give up this Priviledge, the Government will very soon become arbitrary.

"No Necessity therefore can be sufficient to justify a house of Representatives in giving up such a *Priviledge; for it would be of little consequence to the people whether they were subject to George or Lewis, the King of Great Britain or the French King, if both were arbitrary, as both would be if both could levy Taxes without Parliament.*

"Had this been the first instance of the kind, we might not have troubled your Excellency about it; but lest the matter should grow into precedent; we earnestly beseech your Excellency, as you regard the peace and welfare of the Province, that no measures of this nature be taken for the future, let the advice of the council be what it may."

Which being read, was accepted by a large majority, and soon after sent up and presented to his Excellency by Captain Goldthwait, Mr. Otis, Captain Taylor, Mr. Cushing and Mr. Bordman.

The same day the above remonstrance was delivered, the Town was alarmed with a report that the House had sent a message to his Excellency reflecting upon his Majesty's person and government, and highly derogatory from his crown and dignity, and therein desired that his Excellency would in no case take the advice of his majesty's council. About five of the clock P. M. the same day Mr. *Speaker* communicated to the house a Letter from the *Governor* of the following purport.

"SIR,

I have this morning received a message from the house, which I here inclose, in which the King's name, dignity, and cause, are so improperly treated, that I am obliged to desire you to recommend earnestly to the house, that it may not be entered upon the Minutes in the terms it now stands. For if it should, I am satisfied that you will again and again wish some parts of it

were expunged; especially if it should appear, as I doubt not but it will, when I enter upon my vindication, that there is not the least ground for the insinuation under colour of which that sacred and well-beloved name is so disrespectfully brought into Question.
September 15th. To the
Honourable Speaker of the
House of Representatives.
Your's, etc.
FRA: BERNARD."

Upon the reading of this letter, it was moved to insert these words, to wit, "with all due reverence to his Majesty's sacred Person and Government, to both which we profess the sincerest attachment and loyalty be it spolen" "it would be of little importance," &c. But a certain member crying "*Rase them,*" "*Rase them,*"[2] the proposed amendment was dropped, it being obvious, that the remonstrance would be the same in effect, with or without the words excepted against. These dreadful words, under which his Excellency had placed a black mark, were accordingly erased and expunged, and the Message returned to the Speaker.

In the course of the debate a new and surprising doctrine was advanced. We have seen the times when the majority of a council by their words and actions have seemed to think themselves obliged to comply with every Thing proposed by the Chair, and to have no rule of conduct but a Governor's will and pleasure. But now for the first time, it was asserted that the Governor in all cases was obliged to act according to the advice of the council, and consequently would be deemed to have no Judgment of his own. In order to excuse if not altogether justify the offensive Passage, and clear it from ambiguity, I beg leave to premise two or three *data*.[3] I. God made all men naturally equal.

---

2 Meaning that part of the remonstrance which is in Italick.

3 The natural liberty of man is to be free from any superior power on earth, and not to be under the will or legislative authority of man; but to have only the law of nature for his rule. The liberty of man in society, is to be under no other legislative

power, but that established by consent in the common wealth; nor under the dominion of any will, or restraint of any law, but what that legislature shall enact according to the trust put in it. Freedom then is not what Sir *Robert Filmer* tells us, O. A. 55. A liberty for everyone to do what he lists, to live as he pleases, and not to be tied by any laws. But freedom of men under government, is to have a standing rule to live by, common to everyone of that society, and made by the legislative power erected in it; a liberty to follow my own will in all things where that rule prescribes not, and not to be subject to the unknown, unconstant, uncertain, arbitrary will of another man; a freedom of nature is to be under no restraint but the law of nature. This freedom from absolute arbitrary power, is so necessary to, and closely joined with a man's preservation, that he cannot part with it but by what forfeits his preservation & life together. For a man not having power over his own life, cannot by compact or his own consent enslave himself to anyone, nor put himself under the absolute, arbitrary power of another, to take away his life when he pleases: no body can give more power than he has himself. He that cannot take away his own life, cannot give another power over it. *Locke's* DISCOURSE on GOVERN'T. Part II,
CH. IV.
The legislative, whether placed in one or more, whether it be always in being, or only by intervals, though it be the supreme power in every common-wealth, yet in the utmost bounds of it, it is limited to the public good of the society, it is a power that hath no end but preservation; and those can never have a right to destroy, enslave or designedly to impoverish the subjects.
These are the bounds to which the trust that is put in them, by the Society, and the laws of God and nature, have set to the legislative power 01 every common wealth, in all forms of government.
First, They are to govern by established promulgated laws, not to be varied in particular cases; but to have one rule for rich and poor, for the favourite at court, and the countryman at plough.
Secondly, These laws ought to be designed for no other end ultimately, but the good of the people.
Thirdly, They must not raise taxes on the property of the people, without the consent of the people, given by themselves or deputies.
Fourthly, The legislature neither must nor can transfer the power of making laws to any body else, nor place it any where but where the people have. *Id.* Ch. XI.
Where the legislative and executive power are in distinct hands, as they are in all moderated monarchies and well formed governments, there the good of the society requires that several things should be left to the discretion of him that has the supreme executive power. This power to act according to discretion for the public good, without the prescription of Law, and sometimes even against it, is that which is called *PREROGATIVE.*
This power, while employed for the benefit of the community, and suitably to the trust and ends of government, is undoubtedly Prerogative, and never is questioned. For the people are very seldom or never scrupulous or nice in the point, they are far

from examining Prerogative whilst it is in any tolerable degree employed for the use it was meant, that is, for the good of the people, and not manifestly against it. But it there comes to be a question between the executive power and the people, about a thing claimed as a prerogative, the tendency of the exercise of such prerogative to the good or hurt of the people, will easily decide the question. Prerogative is nothing but the power of doing public good without a rule. The old question will be asked in this matter of Prerogative, But who shall be judge when this power is made a right use of? I answer, between an executive power in being with such prerogative, and a legislative, that depends upon his will, for their convening, there can be no judge on earth, as there can be none between the legislative and the people. Should either the executive or legislative, when they have got this power in their hands, design or go about to destroy them, the people have no other remedy in this, as in other cases, when they have no judge upon earth, but to appeal to heaven. Nor let anyone think that this lays a perpetual foundation for disorder, for this operates not 'till the inconveniency is so great that the majority feel it, and are weary of it, and find a necessity to have it amended. But this the executive power or wise Princes never need come in the danger of; and it is the thing of all others, they have most need to avoid; as of all others the most perilous.

Id, Ch. XIV.

"Fatherly authority, or a right of fatherhood in our Author's sense (i. e. Sir *Robert Filmer*) is a divine unalterable right of sovereignty, whereby a Father, or a Prince, (and a Governor might have been added) hath an absolute, arbitrary, unlimited, & unlimitable power over the lives, liberties and estates of his children and subjects; so that he may take or alienate their estates, sell, castrate or use their persons as he pleases they being all his slaves, and he Lord proprietor of everything and his unbounded will their law."

Locke on Govt. B. I. Ch. II.

He that will not give just occasion to think that a~1 government in the world is the product only of force and violence, and that men live together by no other rules but that of beasts, where the strongest carries it, and so lay a foundation for perpetual disorder, mischief, tumult, sedition and rebellion, (things that the followers of that hypothesis, i.e. *Filmer,* and the advocates for passive obedience, so loudly cry out against) must of necessity find out another rise of government, another original of political power, and another way of designing and knowing the persons that have it, than what Sir *R. Filmer* hath taught us."

Locke on Govt. B. II. Ch. II.

This other original Mr. *Locke* has demonstrated to be the consent of a free people. It is possible there are a few, and I desire to thank God there is no reason to think there are many among us, that can't bear the names of LIBERTY and PROPERTY, much less that the things signified by those terms, should be enjoyed by the vulgar. These may be inclined to brand some of the principles advanced in the vindication of the house, with the odious epithets *seditious* and *levelling.* Had any thing to justify them been quoted from Col. *Algernon Sidney,* or other British Martyrs, to the liberty of their

2. The ideas of earthly superiority, preheminence grandeur are educational, at least acquired, not innate. 3. Kings were (and plantation Governor's should be) made for the good of the people, and not the people for them. 4. No government has a right to make hobby horses, asses and slaves of the subject, nature having made sufficient of the two former, for all the lawful purposes of man, from the harmless peasant in the field, to the most refined politician in the cabinet; but none of the last, which infallibly proves they are unnecessary. 5. Tho' most governments are *de facto* arbitrary, and consequently the curse and scandal of human nature; yet none are *de jure* arbitrary. 6. The British constitution of government as now established in his Majesty's person and family, is the wisest and best in the world. 7. The King of Great-Britain is the best as well as most glorious Monarch upon the Globe, and his subjects the happiest in the universe. 8. It is most humbly presumed the King would have all his plantation Governors follow his royal Example, in a wise and strict adherence to the principles of the British constitution, by which in conjunction with his other royal virtues, he is enabled to reign in the hearts of a brave and generous, free and loyal people. 9. This is the summit, the *ne plus ultra* of human glory and felicity. 10. The French King is a despotic arbitrary prince, and consequently his subjects are very miserable.

---

country, an ourtcry of rebellion would not be surprising. The authority of Mr. *Locke* has therefore been preferred to all others, for these further reasons. 1. He was not only one of the most wise, as well as most honest, but the most impartial man that ever lived. 2. He professedly wrote his discourses on Government, as he himself expresses it, "To establish the throne of the great restorer king *William,* to make good his title in the consent of the people, which being the only one of all lawful governments, he had more fully and clearly, than any Prince in christendom, and to justify to the world, the people of England whose love of liberty, their just and natural rights, with their resolution to preserve them, saved the nation when it was on the brink of slavery and ruin." By this title, our Illustrious Sovereign GEORGE the III. (whom GOD long preserve) now holds. 3. Mr. *Locke* was as great an ornament, under a crown'd head, as the church of England ever had to boast of. Had all her sons been of his wise, moderate, tolerant principles, we should probably never have heard of those civil dissentions that have so often brought the nation to the borders of perdition. Upon the score of his being a Churchman however, his sentiments are less liable to the invidious reflections and insinuations that High-flyers, Jacobites, and other stupid Bigots, are apt too liberally to bestow, not only upon Dissenters of all denominations, but upon the moderate; and therefore infinitely the most valuable part of the Church of England itself.

Let us now take a more careful review of this passage, which by some out of doors has been represented as seditious, rebellious and traiterous. I hope none however will be so wanting to the interests of their country, as to represent the matter in this light on the east side of the atlantick, tho' recent instances of such a conduct might be quoted, wherein the province has after its most strenuous efforts, during this and other wars, been painted in all the odious colours that avarice, malice and the worst passions could suggest. The house assert, that "it would be of little consequence to the people, whether they were subject to George or Lewis, the King of Great Britain or the French King, if both were arbitrary, as both would be, if both could levy taxes without parliament." Or in the same words transposed without the least alteration of the sense.

"It would be of little consequence to the people whether they were subject to George the King of Great-Britain, or Lewis the French King, if both were arbitrary, as both would be, if both could levy taxes without parliament."

The first question that would occur to a philosopher, if any question could be made about it, would be whether the position were true. But truth being of little importance with most modern politicians, we shall touch lightly upon that topic, and proceed to inquiries of a more interesting nature.

That arbitrary government implies the worst of temporal evils, or at least the continual danger of them is certain. That a man would be pretty equally subjected to these evils under every arbitrary government, is clear. That I should die very soon after my head should be cut off, whether by a sabre or a broad sword, whether chopped off to gratify a tyrant by the Christian name of *Tom, Dick* or *Harry* is evident. That the name of the tryant would be of no more avail to save my life than the name of the executioner, needs no Proof. It is therefore manifestly of no importance what a prince's christian name is, if he be arbitrary, any more, indeed, than if he were not arbitrary. So the whole amount of this dangerous proposition may at least in one view be reduced to this, viz. *It is of little importance what a King's christian name is.* It is indeed of importance that a King, a Governor, and all other good christians should have a christian name, but whether Edward, Francis or William, is of none, that I can discern. It being a rule to put the most mild and favourable construction upon words that they can possibly bear, it will follow that this proposition is a very harmless one, that cannot by any means tend to prejudice his Majesty's Person, Crown, Dignity or Cause, all which I deem equally sacred with his Excellency.

If this proposition will bear an hundred different constructions, they must all be admitted before any that imports any bad meaning, much more a treasonable one.

It is conceived the house intended nothing disrespectful of His Majesty, his Government or Governor, in those words. It would be very injurious to insinuate this of a house that upon all occasions has distinguished itself by a truly loyal spirit, and which spirit possesses at least nine hundred and ninety nine in a thousand of their constituents throughout the province. One good natured construction at least seems to be implied in the assertion, and that pretty strongly, viz. that in the present situation of Great Britain and France, it is of vast importance to be a Briton, rather than a Frenchman; as the French King is an arbitrary despotic Prince; but the King of Great Britain is not so *de jure, de facto,* nor by *inclination;* a greater difference on this side the *Grave* cannot be found, than that which subsists between British subjects, and the slaves of tyranny.

Perhaps it may be objected that there is some difference even between arbitrary Princes in this respect at least, that some are more rigorous than others. It is granted, but then let it be remembered, that the life of man is as a vapour that soon vanisheth away, and we know not who may come after him, a wise man or a fool; tho' the chances before and since Solomon, have ever been in favour of the latter. Therefore it is said of little consequence. Had it been *No* instead of *little,* the clause upon the most rigid stricture might have been found barely exceptionable.

Some fine Gentlemen have charged the expression as indelicate. This is a capital impeachment in politicks, and therefore demands our most serious attention. The idea of delicacy in the creed of some politicians, implies that an inferior should at the peril of all that is near and dear to him (i.e. his interest) avoid every the least trifle that can offend his superior. Does my superior want my estate? I must give it him, and that with a good grace, which is appearing, and if possible being really obliged to him that he will condesend to take it. The reason is evident; it might give him some little pain or uneasiness to see me whimpering, much more openly complaining at the loss of a little glittering dirt. I must according to this system not only endeavour to acquire my self, but impress upon all around me a reverence and *passive obedience* to the sentiments of my superior, little short of adoration. Is the superior in contemplation a king, I must consider him as God's vicegerent, cloathed with unlimited power, his will the supreme law, and not accountable for his actions, let them be what they may, to any tribunal upon earth. Is the superior a plantation governor? he must be viewed not only as the most excellent representation of majesty, but as a viceroy in his department, and *quoad* provincial administration, to all intents and purposes vested with all the prerogatives that were ever exercised by the most absolute prince in Great Britain.

The votaries of this sect are all Monopolizers of offices, Peculators, Informers, and generally the Seekers of all kinds. It is better, say they, to give up any thing, and every thing quietly, than contend with a superior, who by his prerogative can do, and (as the vulgar express it) right or wrong, will have whatever he pleases. For you must know, that according to some of the most refined and fashionable systems of modern politics, the ideas of right and wrong, and all the moral virtues, are to be considered only as the vagaries of a weak or distempered imagination in the possessor, and of no use in the world, but for the skilful politician to convert to his own purposes of power and profit.

With these,

> *The Love of Country is an empty Name,*
> *For Gold they hunger: but n'er thirst for Fame.*

It is well known that the least "patriotic spark" unawares "catched," and discovered, disqualifies a candidate from all further preferment in this famous and flourishing order of knights errant. It must however be confessed they are so catholic as to admit all sorts from the knights of the post to a garter and Star; provided they are thoroughly divested of the fear of God, and the love of mankind; and have concentrated all their views in *dear self,* with them the only "sacred and well-beloved name," or thing in the universe. See Cardinal *Richlieu's Political Testament,* and the greater Bible of the Sect, *Mandaville's Fable of the Bees.* Richlieu expresly in solemn earnest, without any sarcasm or irony, advises the discarding all honest men from the presence of a prince, and from even the purlieus of a court. According to Mandeville, "*The* moral virtues are the political offspring which flattery begot upon pride." The most darling principle of the great Apostle of the order, who has done more than any mortal towards diffusing corruption, not only thro' the three kingdoms, but thro' the remotest dominions, is, "that every man has his price, and that if you bid high enough, you are sure of him".

To those who have been taught to bow at the name of a King, with as much ardor and devotion as a papist at the sight of a crucifix, the assertion under examination may appear harsh; but there is an immense difference between the sentiments ·of a British house of commons remonstrating, and those of a courtier cringing for a favour. A house of Representatives here at least, bears an equal proportion to a Governor, with that of a house of Commons to the King. There is indeed one difference in favour of a house of Representatives; when a house of Commons address the King, they speak to their Sovereign, who is truly the most august Personage upon earth: When a house of Representatives remonstrate to a Governor they speak to a fellow subject; tho' a superior, who is undoubtedly intitled to decency and respect; but I hardly think to quite so much Reverence as his master.

It may not be amiss to observe, that a form of speech may be, in no sort improper, when used *arguendo,* or for illustration, speaking of the King, which same form might be very harsh, indecent and even ridiculous, if spoken to the King.

The expression under censure has had the approbation of divers Gentlemen of sense, who are quite unprejudiced by any party. They have taken it to imply a compliment rather than any indecent reflection, upon his Majesty's wise and gracious administration. It seems strange therefore that the house should be so suddenly charged by his Excellency with *Impropriety, groundless Insinuations,* &c.

What cause of so bitter Repentance, *again* and *again,* could possibly have taken place, if this clause had been printed in the Journal, I can't imagine. If the case be fairly represented, I guess the province can be in no danger from a house of Representatives daring to speak plain English, when they are complaining of a grievance. I sincerely believe the house had no disposition to enter into any contest with the Governor or Council. Sure I am that the promoters of this address had no such view. On the contrary, there is the highest reason to presume that the house of Representatives will at all times rejoice in the prosperity of the Governor and Council, and contribute their utmost assistance, in supporting those two branches of the legislature, in all their just rights and preheminence. But the house is and ought to be jealous and tenacious of its own priviledges; these are a sacred deposit intrusted by the people, and the jealousy of them is a godly jealousy.

But to proceed with our narration; on Saturday about a quarter before one of the Clock, Mr. Secretary came down with his Excellency's vindication, which is as follows.

"*Gentlemen of the House of Representatives,*

I have received an Answer from you to a Message of mine; informing you of my having upon a sudden Apprehension of Danger, fitted out the Province Sloop to protect a considerable and very interesting Fishery, belonging to this Province: Upon which Occasion you are pleased to observe, that the Method of doing this, which you call *making or increasing Establishments is taking from the House the Right of originating Taxes, annihilating one Branch of the Legislature,* and tending to make *the Government arbitrary.*

These are hard Words: and the Consciousness of my own Integrity will not permit me to submit in Silence to such Imputations. I know what the Priviledges of the People are, and their Nature and Bounds: and I can truly say that it has never been in my Thoughts to make the least Invasion of them. If therefore you think proper to send such a Charge as this to the Press; I must desire that my Vindication may accompany it.

In Order to which I shall first consider what the legal and constitutional Powers of the Governor and Council are, then state the Fact in Question, and by Application of the one to the other, see whether the Conclusions before mentioned will follow. In this Disquisition I shall not inquire *whether any Necessity can be sufficient to justify a House of Representatives in giving up the Priviledge oj originating Taxes;* as I do not believe that such a Cession was ever desired by any Person concerned in the Government, or that any Governor and Council since the Revolution attempted or ever will attempt to tax the People.

The Business of originating the Taxes most certainly belongs to the Representatives of the People, and the business of issuing Money out of the Treasury, as certainly belongs to the Governor with the Advice of the Council. In general all Votes and Orders for the Charge of the Government originate in the House of Representatives, and the Money for defreying such Charges is issued by Warrant of the Governor with the Advice of Council, without any further Reference to the House of Representatives.

But as it is impossible that the General Court should provide for every Contingency that may happen unless they were continually sitting; there will sometimes be Cases in which the Governor, with the Council, is to be justified in issuing Money for Services not expresly provided for by the General Court: Of these there are two very obvious.

The one is, where a Danger arises so immediate and imminent that there is no Time for calling together the Assembly. In this I apprehend there is no other Limitation of Expense, but'in Proportion to the Evil impending: For the Safety of the People being the supreme Law, should at all Events be provided for.

The other is, where the Expence of some necessary Service is so inconsiderable, as to be not worth the while to put the Province to the Charge of the Assembly's meeting for that Purpose only, at an Expence perhaps ten or twenty Times more than the Sum in Question.

This I take to be the Law and Usage of every Royal Government on the Continent. In that over which I formerly presided, where the people were very averse to frequent or long Sessions of the Assembly, I have upon an Emergency, with Advice of the Council only, raised Three Hundred Men at a Time, and marched them to the Defence of the Frontiers; and when the Assembly has met, have received their Thanks for so doing.

Now let me state the Case in Question. Most of the principal Merchants in *Salem* and *Marblehead,* who were considerably interested in a Fishery near the Gut of *Canso,* in which I am told upwards of One Hundred Vessels from this Province were employed, received Advice that there was a French Privateer or Pirate cruizing in those Parts. It has appeared since, that this Alarm was not peculiar to this Province: It reached *Quebec,* from whence an armed Schooner was fitted out to look after this Frenchman. It reached *New-York,* from whence General AMHERST advised me of this French Vessel. These Merchants therefore applying by their Deputies to me for an immediate Protection of their Fishery, I laid the Matter before the Council, and it happening that the Province Sloop was just returned from *Penobscot,* it was advised by the Council, that she should be immediately fitted out to go to the Protection of this Fishery: this was done in the most frugal Manner possible; out of the Fifty Men put on board the Sloop, only twenty-four were charged to the Province, the rest were drawn out of the Provincials employed at *Castle-William,* and in the recruiting Service; the Ammunition and Military Stores were taken from the Castle, to which they have been restored without Loss or Expense; the Men were engaged only for one Month, after which they were not to be continued without the Advice of the General Court. This is the true State of this Transaction; and surely I may say it deserved a very different Animadversion than what it has had.

Now to apply it to the Censure it has met with: This was an Act which the Governor with the Council had a Right to do; it was a legal and constitional Exercise of the Powers vested in them; it was an Exertion of the Executive Power of the Government, distinct from that of the Legislature. If it was wrong and ill advised (which I don't mean to admit) it could amount to no more than an improper Application of the public Money, by those who have lawful Authority to apply such Money to the public Purposes. When this Distinction is considered; how can this Act, whether right or wrong, be applied to the Right of originating Taxes, annihilating one Branch of the Legislature and making the Government arbitrary?

As for the discretionary Part of the Act, after I have had the Advice of the Council, and the Approbation of my own Judgment and Conscience, I shall not enter into any further Argument about it, than just to observe; That if the Governor and Council legally acting in the Executive Administration, and determining to the best of their Judgment and Skill, with a conscientious Regard to the Good of the People, shall be liable to be called to account for Difference of Opinion only, the Government will be very much weakened. But I shall persuade myself that a steady Attention to the Peace and Welfare of the Province, which you recommend to Me, will always sufficiently justify my Conduct: and in that Confidence I hope I shall never fail to exert the Powers which have been committee to Me for the Defence and Protection of the People of this Province, by all lawful and constitutional Means.

Province-House,
Sept. 18, 1762.   FRA. BERNARD."

This being read, the Secretary instantly informed the Speaker, that his Excellency directed the attendance of the house in the council chamber.

The two houses had finished the publick business; and before this the house of Representatives had by a committee asked a recess, so it was presumed the house was sent for to be prorogued, as it turned out. The Speaker rose to go up to the council, without desiring the house to attend him, the usual and regular form, which it is presumed was forgot. But it was moved that his Excellency's vindication, according to his desire, should be printed in the Journal. This motion was seconded, and passed in the affirmative by a great majority. Then a motion was made and seconded, for a committee to prepare a Reply to this vindication in the recess of the court, and to make report at the next session; this also passed in the affirmative by a considerable majority, and Mr. *Speaker,* Mr. *Otis,* and Mr. *Tyler,* were chosen a committee for said purpose. Then the House immediately attended his Excellency in the Council-Chamber. When his Excellency, after giving his assent to two or three bills, prorogued the court.

It was wished, at least by the moderate part of the house, that his Excellency had thought fit so far to give up the point, as to wave any contest about it, by assuring the house, that if his right was ever so clear, he would not exercise it, if grievous to the people. A like condescension crowned heads have practised, and found their account in it; as I am persuaded his Excellency would, if the unanimous vote of thanks from the whole representative body of this people is worth any thing. This I guess he would have had: And as it is a maxim that the King can do no wrong, but that whatever is amiss is owing intirely to those about him; so, with regard to his Excellency, we ought to presume the best; and that it is to be charged to the account of some weak or wicked advisers, that this business did not end happily. However, the matter is now become very serious, by his Excellency's vindication; which we shall next consider.

The Charter of the province of the Massachusetts-Bay, has invested the Governor and Council with power to issue (without the concurrence of the House, as it is now construed, or rather as the genuine sense of the Charter has been waved by former Houses) the monies out of the treasury. But the Question is, Whether this power be limited? If it is unlimited, the priviledge of levying taxes by originating them in the House of Representatives, is of little value. What Representative would plume himself upon the priviledge of originating taxes, if the money could be squandered away at pleasure; which in other words -may happen hereafter to be just as the tools and sycophants of power shall advise. This power therefore, in the nature and reason of the thing, should seem to be limited by some usage or custom, if not by something more explicit. The words of the Charter are, "And we do for us, our heirs and successors, give and grant, that the said General Court or Assembly, shall have full power and authority to name and settle annually, all civil officers within the said province, for the time being; and to set forth the several duties, powers and limits of every such officer to be appointed by the said general court or assembly; and the forms of such oaths, not repugnant to the laws and statutes of this our realm of England, as shall be respectively administered unto them, for the execution of their several offices and places; and also to impose fines, mulcts, imprisonments, and other punishments; and to impose and levy proportionable and reasonable assessments rates and taxes, upon the estates and persons of all and every the proprietors or inhabitants of our said province or territory, to be issued and disposed of by warrant, under the hand of the Governor of our said province, for the time being, with the advice and consent of the Council, for our service, in the necessary *Defence* and support of *our* government of our said province or territory, and the protection and preservation of the inhabitants there, according to such acts as are or shall be in force within our said province." Here seems to be an express limitation of the power. Nothing is left to usage or custom, much less to discretion. It is manifest from the Charter, that the *Acts* of the province are the only legal and constitutional justification to the Governor and Council, in issuing any money out of the treasury: *"According to such Acts as are or shall be in force within our said Province,"* are certainly no unmeaning words.

It is clear from hence, that without the aid of an *Act* of the province, the Governor and Council cannot legally take a shilling out of the treasury, let the emergency be what it may. It is agreed with his Excellency, that in issuing Money from the treasury, as the charter has of late years been construed the Governor and Council are meer executive officers. They are controllers general of the Treasury, i. e. the treasurer cannot pay without their warrant; but then they are as much bound by the acts of the province, as the treasurer himself. He, the Treasurer, indeed may be called to an account, but they can't, being in other respects two branches of the Legislature. The only remedy therefore is a remonstrance, and when that proves ineffectual, the house may and ought to refuse to supply the Treasury, and stop a few Grants and Salaries; which would soon bring matters right without any dangerous shock to Government, or weakening thereof; but what the whole world must impute to a Governor and Council, that would oblige a House to have recourse to the last resort, but one; I mean as we are a dependent Government, a dutiful and humble remonstrance to his Majesty.

The Parliament of Great-Britain have as the last resort, been known to appeal to Heaven, and the longest sword; but God forbid that there ever should be occasion for any thing of that kind again; indeed there is not the least danger of it since the glorious revolution, and the happy establishment resulting therefrom. It was formerly the custom for the Speaker of the house to sign all warrants upon the treasury, but this was at last either tamely given up, or at least waved.

It may be objected, that tho' our supply bills appropriate by far the greatest part of the sums raised, yet something is always expresly left for contingencies, and the Governor and Council ma and must in the nature of the thing apply this at discretion. I answer, 1. Even this is issued by force of an act, and not by virtue of any general power in the Governor and Council, independent of the act. 2. Neither custom nor usage suppose that this sum appropriated for contingencies could be applied to the fitting out of men of war, and making establishments for them; for armed vessels is one express appropriation in our acts, which shews that this is not considered as a contingency, and that the assembly do not expect any further charge for this

article, than they have appropriated.[4]

3. All our Governors and Councils have not always confined themselves to the appropriation for contingencies, but some have drawn for what they deem'd contingencies when they have known the appropriation to be expended, and in short have not confined themselves to any appropriation in payment; whatever they may have done in the form of their warrants. 4. If the Governor and Council can fit out one man of war, inlist men, grant a bounty and make establishments, why not for a navy, if to them it shall seem necessary, and they can make themselves the sole judges of this necessity. The rumour in the case of the Massachusetts was that fourteen privateers instead of one *pyrate* were cruizing off Canso. What could this one poor sloop have done against such odds? *Salus populi est suprema Lex.* Why then did not the Governor and Council fit out fourteen men of war, or at least enough to take

---

4   This Vessel's Expence was drawn for upon the Appropriation for armed Vessels, as appears by the Warrant and Roll.

fourteen privateers? It has been said that there were no privateers among the fishermen, but that when they discovered the sloop, she was taken for one, and that many of the fishermen ran home in a fright, and lost their fares. How true this is I can't say, but have heard it reported, and believe there is at least as much ground for it as there was to believe the story of fourteen privateers. The Governor and Council doubtless meant well as to the protection of the fishery, and had there been no unjustifiable extension of their power, everyone would have thankfully acquiesced. The money for fitting out this sloop might have been raised by the Governor and Council's promise to recommend a reimbursement to the assembly. They might perhaps have borrowed it of the Treasurer upon the same terms, and the priviledges of the House thereby would have been preserved. It would be a very easy thing to raise twenty times the sum wanted to fit out this sloop upon the credit of a like recommendation. This method was taken in fitting out the King George in 1761, as appears by the vote of Council, and the Govenor's message afterwards to the house of Representatives, and their vote thereupon, which last are as follows,

"*Gentlemen of the House of Representatives,*

"The provision made the last session for manning the King George was soon found insufficient for the purpose, and after bearing up for a month the crew amounted to but thirty men. In this condition the ship remained, when I received advice that there were two French privateers on the coast and that there were several more to be expected: I immediately called a Council; at which attended a committee of the merchants. The council were of opinion, that the ship should be immediately fitted out: and in order to do it with more expedition, I offered that if the crew could be quickly compleated to an hundred men, I would put fifty provincials on board for a short cruize. It was therefore "advised to raise seventy men, and to give ten Dollars bounty: But there was no fund in the Treasury to *resort* to for this purpose. It was therefore concluded to order the Treasurer to borrow seven hundred Dollars of the merchants on the credit of the province, *(not on the credit of a recommendation, as it should have been and perhaps was meant)* which was accordingly done; and I must desire you would take care for the repayment
thereof."

The House, after long debate, and divers referrences, on the second of June, voted, "that the province treasurer be directed to repay the seven hundred Dollars borrowed of the merchants *on the credit of the province* for bounty, in order to man the ship King George."

I want to know why the same method of raising the money might not have been taken the first time of fitting out the ship King George, and in fitting out the sloop Massachusetts.

However, even this method of supplying the treasury by the Governor and Council's ordering subscriptions upon the credit of the province (by which it is presumed a recommendation to the assembly is meant) is by no means a justifiable practice.

The Governor and Council have naturally a great influence in all Houses of Representatives, and when the money is once taken up and applied, it would seem hard to make the subscribers lose it; and so in time it would come to be a thing of course, for the House to reimburse all expences the Governor and Council should be pleased to create in the recess of the assembly; and after a course of tame acquiescence in such a practice, the House would become as some desire to have it, a very insignificant, unimportant part of the constitution.

It is therefore the indispensible duty of the House of Representatives, to be very cautious how they allow or approve of any expences incurred even in this way.

His Excellency is pleased to wave any inquiry "whether any necessity can be sufficient to justify a House of Representatives in giving up the privilege of originating taxes?" for this reason only expressed; viz. "I don't believe (says his Excellency) that such a cession was ever desired by any Person concerned in the government, or that any Governor and Council since the revolution, attempted or ever will attempt to tax the people." I wish I could exercise as much charity towards former Governors and Councils, as for his Excellency and the present honourable Council; but I can't. I am verily persuaded, that we have had some Governors and some Councellors, since the revolution, that would gladly have been as absolute as Turkish Bashaws; and that the whole tenor of their actions has given convincing proof of such a disposition.

A tax upon the people in form, by issuing a tax bill, and ordering an assessment, I believe has not been attempted by a Governor and Council since the revolution. This would be too alarming. The vulgar are apt to be forcibly affected with names and appearances, rather than by realities. If the money can be drawn out of the treasury without any regard to the appropriations, made by the acts of the province; and the House whenever called upon, will without murmuring supply the treasury again; they serve the purpose of a very convenient machine to quiet the people; and the money flows in with greater ease and plenty than if the Governor and Council were, *ad libitum,* to collect and dissipate the public treasure.

It is observable, that in France and other despotic governments, 'tis often with great difficulty, and sometimes with hazard, that the revenue is collected. Had *Richlieu* and *Mazarine* convinced the parliaments that it was a great priviledge to be allowed to vote as much money as was called for, and for any purpose the court might want it, the government would have had the appearance of liberty under a tyranny; which to those ministers would have been a vast ease and security. But those great politicians either never thought of this refinement, or, the parliaments were too stupid to be convinced, of the utility of such a plan.

His Excellency proceeds, "The business of originating the taxes most certainly belongs to the Representatives of the people; and the business of issuing money out of the treasury, as certainly belongs to the Governor and Council." To say nothing of the doubt that might justly be made, whether a non-claim, waver, or even an express concession by any former house, of the priviledge of joining in a warrant, for issuing the money, can be binding upon their Successors? Would not a stranger to our constitution be lead to think, from this general assertion of the Governor, that he with the Council, could issue money without regard to the acts of the province, and the *appropriations* thereby made; and that the house indeed, had no *right* to appropriate, but only to lay the burden of taxes on the people? Especially when his Excellency in the next period says, that "in general, all votes and orders (and acts might have been added) for the charge of the governments, originate in the House of Representatives; and the money for defreying such charge, is issued by the Governor, with the advice of the council, without *any further reference* to the house of Representatives."

That this is true in fact, to wit, that after the money is raised, his Excellency and their Honors have no further *reference to, or regard* for the house, is possible. But that they have had some regard to appearances is certain from the form of their warrants,

Province of the *Massachusetts-Bay*.

By his Excellency the Governor.

You are, by and with the Advice and Consent of his Majesty's Council, ordered and directed to pay unto A. B. the sum of
Which sum is to be paid out of the appropriation for
For which this shall be your warrant.

Given under my Hand at Boston, the   *Day*
   Of   176   ,in the   *Year of His*
   Majesty's Reign.   F. B.

To Mr. Treasurer.
By Order of the Governor, with the Advice and Consent of the Council.
                  A. O. *Secr'y.*

Now, if after the house have supplied the treasury, the Governor and Council have a right to issue the money without further regard to the house of Representatives; why are the words *Out of the appropriation for,* &c. inserted, but to salve appearances? Otherwise it might run thus, *"Out of the public money in the treasury."* "But as it is impossible, (says his Excellency,) that the General Court should provide for every contingency that may happen unless they were continually sitting; there will sometimes be cases in which the Governor & Council is to be justified in issuing money for services not expressly provided for by the General Court; of these there are two very obvious. "The one is, when a danger arises so immediate and imminent, that there is no Time for calling together the assembly. In this I apprehend there is no other limitation of expence, but in proportion to the evil impending. For the safety of the people being the supreme law, should at all events be provided for. The other is, where the expence of some necessary service is so inconsiderable, as to be not worth the while to put the province to the charge of the Assembly's meeting for that purpose only, at an expence perhaps of ten or twenty times more than the sum in question." Frequent and long sessions I know are burdensome to the people, and many think they had better give up every thing, than not have short sessions. But let these consider that it is a very poor bargain, that for the sake of avoiding a session extraordinary, sacrifices the right of being taxed by their Representatives; and risques ten or twenty times the sum in the end, to be levied by a Governor and Council. I know too, that some gentlemen in order to lessen the weight of a House of Representatives, are constantly exclaiming against long and frequent sessions; the people are gulled with the bait, and the house when they meet, are often in want of time to compleat the public business, in the manner that they would wish, and the nature of some affairs requires. What is the consequence? Why, it is become a very fashionable doctrine with some, that in the recess of the court, the Governor and Council are vested with all the powers of the General Assembly. It is costly and unpopular to have frequent and long sessions; therefore they shall be few, short and hurried; and in the mean time, the Governor and Council shall have a right to do what they judge "the supreme law," the good of the common-wealth, requires, and no limitation or bounds are to be set to the money they expend, but their sovereign judgment of the *quantum* of the impending evil; for, "the safety of the people being the supreme law, should at all events, and by all means *(but that of calling an assembly together)* be provided for." This is a short method to put it in the power of the Governor and Council, to do as they please with the men and money of the province; and those Governor's who can do as they please with the men and money of a country, seem to me to be, (or at least are in a pretty fair way soon to be) arbitrary; which in plain English means no more than do as one pleases. As to those inconsiderable services, not worth while to put the province to the charge of an assembly; it seems to be of no great importance whether they are performed or not. 2. There is always an appropriation for contingencies, great and small. If this sum should be exhausted, sufficient might always be procured upon the credit of a recommendation from the Governor and Council, for a reimbursement. 3. Any particular service had better suffer, and the province suffer, that way, than lose such a priviledge as that of taxing themselves; upon which single priviledge evidently depends all others, *Civil and Religious.*

His Excellency tells us of "the law and usage of every royal government upon the continent;" and that, "in that over which he presided formerly, he had upon an emergency, with the advice of the Council only, raised three hundred men at a time, and marched them to the defence of the frontiers, and when the assembly has met has received their thanks for so doing."

Whether the assembly of this province equal the assembly of *New-Jersey,* in gratitude or any other virtue, I shall not presume to determine. But this I am sure of, that this province has been more liberal in their grants to his Excellency, than to any of his predecessors. Instead of any debate about *his salary,* three grants have been made in less than two years, amounting to near three thousand pounds sterling in the whole, besides the very valuable island of Mount Desart which the province thought they had a right to grant subject to his Majesty's confirmation; and which his Excellency doubtless will have confirmed to him. All this with the ordinary perquisites, besides *the full third* of all seizures, must amount to a very handsome fortune, obtained in about two years and two months. His Excellency has not been pleased to tell us, whether the assembly paid the expence of this extraordinary march, or whether the Governor and Council ordered it to be paid? Now if the assembly paid it, as they doubtless ought, after thanking his Excellency, and thereby admitting the utility of the measure, their priviledge was saved. But if the Governor and Council paid it out of the treasury, and the House acquiesced in the infringement of their priviledge, it cannot be produced as a precedent for us, let it be ever so royal a government. His Excellency has a right to transport any of the militia of this province to any part of it, by sea or land, for the necessary defence of the same; and to build and demolish forts and castles, and with the advice of the council in times of war, to exercise martial law upon the militia, but then it is with the House to pay the expence, or refuse it as they please. No man by charter can be sent out of the province but by an act of the three branches of the legislature. The King himself applies to parliament to support his army and navy, and it is their duty to do it, and they ever have and will do it; and the supplies for these ever originate in, and are appropriated by the House of Commons; in whose money bills the House of Lords won't presume to make any amendment; consent or reject in the whole is all the power they exercise in this particular.

His Excellency next proceeds to state "the case in question," by which I suppose is meant the facts relative to fitting out the sloop Massachusetts. The facts mentioned, I take it for granted are in the main true, but the most material one seems to be omitted, namely, that the Governor and Council made an establishment; in consequence of which the expense of this fitting out, or a great part at least has been paid out of the Treasury, by warrant from the Governor and Council. There is also a small mistake in his Excellency's saying the sloop was then returned. She was expected, but her return was uncertain. Had the sloop been sent and the payor reimbursement referred to the House, there might have been no complaint as to this particular step. But the main question is not as to the right of sending the sloop, but of making, or increasing her establishment, and paying it out of the publick monies without the consent of the House; not only in this, but in a number of late similar instances, that have induced the House to question the right of the Governor and Council to draw monies out of the treasury in this way. Or more properly, as it results from the remonstrance of the House, and his Excellency's vindication: The question is in effect, whether the House have a right to appropriate the money they agree to levy upon their constituents?

It being pretty evident I hope by this time, that if the Governor and Council can issue what they please, *and for what* they please, that the House has no right to appropriate; and it is as clear that if the right of appropriation is of any avail or significancy, the Governor and Council cannot issue the monies from the treasury for what they please; but are bound and limitted by the appropriations and establishments made by the acts of the province, to which by the way they are two parties *of* three in the making.

His Excellency having given us his state of the case in question, proceeds "to apply it to the censure it has met with" as his Excellency is pleased to express it. By which I presume his Excellency means the application he had promised in the beginning of his vindication. "I shall consider, says his Excellency, what the legal and constitutional powers of the Governor and Council are; then state the *fact* in question, and by the application of the one to the other, see whether the conclusion before mentioned will follow."

Here again there seems to be some little obscurity, by reason of these words, *"fact in question"* ; there being no question about the facts, but about the right, not so much about the right of fitting out the vessel, as the Governor and Council's right to pay for it out of the treasury, without the consent of the House. What question can there be about facts? There is no doubt but that the vessel was sent, and that in consequence of an application from Salem and Marblehead gentlemen.

I therefore presume to read the second paragraph of his Excellency's vindication according to the sense and spirit, (tho' not strictly agreable to the letter.) thus, "In order to my vindication (dele *to which*) I shall 1. Consider what the legal and constitutional powers of the Governor and Council are. 2. State the facts. 3. By application of the legal and constitutional powers of the Governor and Council to the fact, see whether the conclusions before mentioned will follow." According to this division, which in the spirit, tho' not in the letter, is a *very good one;* his Excellency has given us his sense of the legal and constitutional powers of the Governor and Council. His Excellency is undoubtedly as well acquainted with the nature of these powers, as "what the priviledges of the people are, their bounds and their nature." I presume his Excellency also has the same thorough knowledge of "what the priviledges of the House of Representatives are, their nature and their bounds;" which last are more immediately the subject of inquiry, than those of the people. Tho' it is true, that the priviledges of the House are the great barrier to the priviledges of the people, and whenever those are broken down the people's liberties will fall an easy prey.

His Excellency having finished his state of facts, proceeds according to the method premised to the third and last *head* of discourse, which is, with his Excellency the *application;* not "of the case in question, to the censure it has met with,"tho' the latter words seem to import this; but of the legal and constitutional powers of the Governor and Council, to the facts, in order to make his conclusions. This is evidently his Excellency's meaning. The application is mental. The conclusions are expressed. The first his excellency is pleased to make is in these words. "This was an act which the Governor with the Council had a right to do." I am no great admirer of the syllogistic form of reasoning, and this dress is very uncourtly, yet all conclusive reasoning will bear the test of the schools. Let us try an experiment. His Excellency's whole vindication may nearly in his own words be reduced to this categoric syllogism.

"All the money for defreying the charges of the government *is* issued by warrant of the Governor with the advice of Council, without any further *reference* to the house of Representatives."

The principal merchants in Salem and Marblehead were frightened with a rumour of a privateer; upon their application the Governor and Council took the alarm, fitted out an armed vessel, and by their warrant defreyed the charge out of the treasury without any reference at all to the House of Representatives."

Therefore,

1. "This was an act which the Governor with the Council had a right to do." No man in his senses to be sure can deny the major proposition, for the word *is* plainly implies a right; according to *Mr. Pope* and other great authorities, "whatever *is* is right." The minor is a bare recital of *notorious* facts; therefore the way is clear to follow his Excellency in the rest of his inferences. 2. Inference. "It was a legal and constitutional exercise of the powers vested in them." 3. "It was an exertion of the executive power, distinct from that of the legislative." 4. If it was wrong, &c.

His Excellency then proceeds to ask the House a very important question. But before we consider what answer may be given to that question, and probably would have been given, had there been time before the court was prorogued; I beg leave to make a few observations upon his Excellency's three last inferences. I have carefully examined the Charter, and the laws of this province, and think I may challenge any man to show any thing in either, that gives the least colour of right to the Governor and Council, to fit out an armed vessel to cruize upon the high seas, at the expence of the province, or to grant a bounty for inlisting the seamen, or to impress them when they won't inlist fast enough, as in the case of the ship King George, or to make an establishment for the officers and seamens wages, much less to issue the money from the treasury for defreying these charges by warrant of the Governor and Council, without any *reference* to the House of Representatives, who must upon supposition of such powers be strangers, total strangers to the expense thus brought upon the province.

But we are told that *"this* is an exertion of the executive power of the government, distinct from the legislative."

I am as much for keeping up the distinction between the executive and legislative powers as possible. Happy, very happy, would it be for this poor province, if this distinction was more attended to than it ever has been. I am heartily rejoiced however, that his Excellency seems here to discountenance and explode the doctrine that some among us have taken great pains to inculcate, viz. that in the recess of the general assembly the whole power of the three branches devolves upon the Governor and Council. If I may compare small things with great, without offence, this doctrine is as absurd as if a man should assert that in the recess of parliament, the whole power of parliament is devolved upon the King and the House of Lords. Had such a doctrine always prevailed in England, we should have heard nothing of the oppressions and misfortunes of the *Charles's* and *James's;* The revolution would never have taken place; the genius of *William* the third would have languished in the fens of Holland, or evaporated in the plains of Flanders; the names of three George's would doubtless have been immortal; but Great-Britain to this day might have been in chains and darkness, unblessed with their influence. I take it for granted therefore, his Excellency must mean by "power of the government," not the power of the whole province in great and general court assembled, but only the executive power of the Governor and Council, distinct from the legislative, as just explained by him. Names are sometimes confounded with things by the wisest of men. It is however of little importance what the power is called, if the exercise of it be lawful. If the power of taxing is peculiar to the general assembly, if the charter has confined it to the general assembly, as I think it evidently does, and this act of the Governor and Council is a tax upon every inhabitant, as it clearly is, being paid out of money raised by their representatives upon them for other purposes, which must remain unsatisfied; and so much more must be raised upon them as is thus taken away: It follows that as all taxation ought to originate in the House; this act of the Governor and Council is so far from being an executive act peculiar to them, that it is evidently taking upon them in their executive capacity, or what other name else, you are pleased to give it, a power not only confined by the charter, law and constitution of the province, to the general assembly or legislative body of the province, but so far confined to one branch of that body, that it can lawfully and constitutionally originate only in the House.

If therefore this act was wrong and ill-advised, which I think has been abundantly proved, whether his Excellency will be pleased to admit it or not; it *could* "amount to more than an improper application of the publick money by those who have lawful authority to apply such money to the publick purposes." It is granted, should the treasurer without warrant do such an act, it would be no more than an improper application of the public money by one who has lawful authority to apply such money to the publick purposes, by warrant from the Governor and Council. Should the treasurer act without such warrant, he would be accountable. But when he has the Governor and Council's warrant, that perhaps will justify, or at least, ought to excuse him, be the warrant right or wrong; because it would be hard to make him answerable for the conduct of his superiors, and to expect him to set himself up as a judge against the Governor and Council, one of which joins in his choice, and the other has an absolute negative upon him. But upon supposition the Governor and Council act wrong, and misapply the monies of the province, which his Excellency seems to concede, is at least a possible case. What is to be done? I agree with his Excellency that they are not liable to be called to an account, and it would be a ridiculous vanity and presumption in the House to think of *any* such thing. We have no body to institute a suit against the Governor and Council; no court to try such a suit; all that would be left therefore in so unhappy a case (if the priviledge of the House of joining in all issues from the treasury has been given up by former assemblies, and that is binding upon their successors, "which I don't mean to admit") is to remonstrate. This method the House have taken in the present case, rather than at this juncture reclaim their ancient priviledge of joining in all warrants for the issues from the treasury. However, I conceive that the right of joining in such warrants can never die. But to confine ourselves to his Excellency's inferences, let us for a moment concede that this act by the Governor and Council, at most is only a misapplication of the publick monies. The conduct of the House is certainly to be justified. The Governor and Council of the province misapplying money, is a grievous event, a terrible misfortune, and a dreadful example to inferiors. It would be enough to infect seven eighths of the petty officers in the community. Whenever a peculator, great or small, should be called to an account after such an event repeated, and passed unnoticed by the House, he would at least console and comfort, nay even plume himself with such like reflections as these. "My betters have done so before me. They make what applications they please of the publick money, without regard to law, or the duty of their trust, and so will I." Tho' with regard to the present Governor and Council, it is presumed a misapplication can proceed only from an error in judgment, which the wisest are in a degree subject to, not from any supposed pravity .of inclination; yet it would be of dangerous tendency, and therefore a proper subject of remonstrance. A remonstrance is not an insolent and presumptuous "calling a Governor and Council to an account for difference of opinion only", nor any charge of wilful evil, but only of error in judgment, and a humble endeavour to point it out; relying always upon their known goodness and wisdom, that whenever they shall discover the truth, they will readily follow it. The House of Commons remonstrating (as they have sometimes done) I believe would be astonished to hear their humble petitions to the Throne called *"hard words and groundless insinuations,* &c. and viewed as calling the King to account. It is true, that the Governor and Council may do many things, if they are so disposed, which they cannot be called to an account for in this world; but this will hardly prove that they have a right to do them, especially after the whole body of the people by their Representatives complain of them as grievous. It is by no means a good inference in politicks, any more than in private life, or even in a state of nature, that a man has a right to do every thing in his natural power to do. This would be at once to make a man's own will and his power, however obtained, the only measure of his actions.

But in answer to his Excellency's grand question, it will appear that this act, and the like instances complained of, are more than a bare misapplication of the public money; they are what the house called them "a method, (and they might have added a lately devised method, the first instance almost being in the case of the ship King-George, in 1760) of making and increasing establishments by the Governor and Council," in effect taking from the House their most darling priviledge, that of originating all taxes." "In short (i. e. a short method for) annihilating one branch of the legislature."

And it remains infallibly true, when once the Representatives of a people give up this priviledge, the government will very soon become arbitrary, i. e. the Governor and Council may then do every thing as they please.

His Excellency asks, "When this distinction is considered, how can this act, right or wrong, be applied to the right of originating taxes, annihilating one branch of the legislature, and making the government arbitrary." His Excellency, thro' his whole vindication, seems to speak of the single act of fitting out the sloop, and don't once mention the establishment made for her, or the payment thereof; much less the two instances of fitting out the ship King George: All which the house had in view, as is manifest by their saying, that, "had this been the first instance, they might not have troubled his Excellency about it." However, if this was the only instance that ever had happened of such an exertion of the executive power by the Governor and Council, it seems to be very applicable to the right of originating taxes, and to have a tendency to make the Governor and Council of the province arbitrary. If the Governor and Council have a right to draw what money they please out of the treasury, under a notion of discretion which they are to exercise, as executive officers of the government; it follows, that for so much charge as the government incurs by the exercise of this discretionary power, by so much the province is taxed by the Governor and Council, without any privity or consent of the house; so much charge then as is incurred by this discretionary power, the house cannot be said to originate. Their right of originating taxes therefore is so far taken away; their power as to this ceasing and coming to nothing, by the Governor and Council exercising it themselves, without the house, may be said to be annihilated. And when the power and priviledge of any branch of the legislature ceases, is taken away and annihilated, then the government is so far arbitrary. The house are so modest as only to say, "that in such a case it will soon become arbitrary."

Can any man be so unreasonable as to contend that the province is not as much taxed by the Governor and Council's paying for this sloop out of the money already raised, as if the house had voted it? What is the difference? The people pay the reckoning whether the Governor and Council take upon them to arm vessels out of money raised for other purposes, or the house vote to raise money for arming vessels. When the money is gone out of the treasury for arming vessels, the debts of the province contracted by the three branches of the legislature must nevertheless be paid, and other monies must be levied instead of those taken away by the Governor and Council. And as according to his Excellency's distinction, there is no limitation of the discretionary expence, so long as the good of the whole, in the opinion of the Governor and Council shall require it; they may spend every farthing in the treasury, and for what they please. Suppose his Excellency should judge it expedient and absolutely necessary upon the apprehension of some imminent and immediate danger (of which he is in fact absolutely by the charter the sole judge) to march all the militia to the frontiers. This he can do without even the advice of the Council. Suppose the Council, tho' not consulted, as they need not be, as to the utility of the march, should place such absolute confidence in his Excellency's wisdom as to sign a warrant for drawing every farthing out of the treasury for the paying and subsisting this armament. Could not as much be said for all this, as is said for fitting out the sloop?

The House of Representatives, should they presume to remonstrate, might with the same propriety be given to understand that "there was not time to call *them* together", that "the danger was immediate and imminent, and in such a case there is no limitation of expence, but in proportion to the evil impending;" "for the safety of the people being the supreme law, should at all events be provided for." Furthermore, "this was an act the Governor and Council had a right to do:" "It is a legal and constitutional exercise of the powers vested in them". "It is an exertion of the executive power of the government, distinct from the legislative." Nay let us go but one step further, and I think the reasoning will be compleat on the side of his Excellency, or on the side of the House. All things are possible, and when his Excellency and the Council we are now blessed with, are taken from us, we may have a Governor and Council, that after they have given out orders to array and march the militia, and by warrant drawn all the money out of the treasury, may alter their minds as to the imminent danger, lay by the expedition, but instead of replacing the money in the treasury, divide and pocket it among themselves.

The reader no doubt starts at such a supposition, 'tis only a bare possibility as stated. The House might possibly remonstrate in such a case. But I hold that upon the principles advanced by his Excellency, it would be wrong in them so to do, and that it ought to be taken for a satisfactory answer, That "if it were wrong and ill advised in the Governor and Council (thus to convert all the treasure of the province to their own use, which they might not mean to admit) yet it would amount to no more than a *very improper application* of the publick money, by those who had lawful authority to apply such money to the publick purposes."

"When this distinction is considered, how could such an act, whether right or wrong, be applied to the right of originating taxes, annihilating one branch of the legislature, and making the government arbitrary." Perhaps such future Governor not understanding law distinctions so well as his Excellency our present Governor, might expresly add, and so good Messieurs Representatives you have nothing to do but to supply the treasury, again, tax the *many headed monster*[5] once more, and when you have done it, the first moment I think fit I'll draw it all out again, under colour of some sudden imminent danger; and if you don't like it, you may e'en go h-g yourselves, as they *at least* most certainly would richly deserve who should tamely submit

to such usage.

To conclude. Would all plantation Governors reflect upon the nature of a free government, and the principles of the British constitution, as now happily established, and practice upon those principles, instead (as most of them do) of spending their whole time in extending the prerogative beyond all bounds; they would serve the King their master much better, and make the people under their care infinitely happier.

Strange it is, that when King's and many of her mighty men have fallen in their attempts upon the liberties of the people of Great Britain, that plantation Governor's don't all consider the Act of 13th of George the second, Chapter vii. which is a plain declaration of the British parliament, that the subjects in the colonies are entitled to all the privileges of the people of Great Britain. By this act of parliament even Foreigners having lived seven years

---

5   An opprobious Name by some given to the People.

in any of the British colonies, are deemed natives, on taking the oaths of allegiance, &c. and are declared by said act to be his Majesty's natural born subjects of the kingdom of Great Britain, to all intents, constructions and purposes, as if any or every of them had been, or were born within the kingdom. The reasons given for this naturalization of foreigners, in the preamble of the act are, that "the *increase* of the people is the means of advancing the wealth and strength of any nation or country, and that many foreigners and strangers, from the *lenity* of our government, the *purity* of our religion, the *benefit* of our laws, the *advantages* of our trade, and the *security* of our property, might be induced to come and settle in some of his Majesty's colonies in America, if they were made partakers of *the advantages* and *priviledges* which the natural born subjects of this realm do there enjoy." Nor is any new priviledge given by this act to the natives of the colonies, it is meerly as to them a declaration of what they are intitled to by the common law, by their several charters, by the law of nature and nations, and by the law of God, as might be shown at large, had I time or room.

All settled attempts therefore, against the liberty of the subject, in any of the plantations, must and in the ruin of the Governor who makes them; at least they will render his administration as uneasy to himself, as unhappy for the people. It is therefore the indispensable duty of everyone, and will be the sincere endeavour of every honest man, to promote the utmost harmony between the three branches of the legislature, that they may be a mutual support to each other, and the ornament, defence and glory of the people Providence has committed to their care.

I am convinced that if his Excellency will in all cases take the advice of the general assembly, (which however contemptably some may affect to speak of it, is the great council of this province, as the British parliament is of the kingdom) that his administration will be crowned with all the success he can desire. But if instead of this, the advice of half a dozen or half a score, who among their fellow citizens may be chiefly distinguished by their avarice, ignorance, pride or insolence, should at any time obtain too much weight at court, the consequences will be very unfortunate on all sides.

Had the writer of these sheets any thing to ask or fear from his Excellency, for himself, a very slender modern politician would quickly perceive the incompatability of this performance with a court interest. That he has done every thing he could in his small sphere to make his Excellency's administration prosperous to him and happy for the people, abundant proofs have been given; and they will one day be convincing to his Excellency. He has never opposed his Excellency in any thing but what he would have opposed his own

Father in. And he takes this opportunity publickly to declare, that in all his legal and constitutional measures, his Excellency shall find him a fast tho' humble friend and servant: But the Liberty of his country, and the Rights of mankind, he will ever vindicate to the utmost of his capacity and power.

FINIS.

ERRATA.

Page 12. Line 6. for *Dec.* 1761. read *August* 1762. Page 20. line 5 from bottom, for *inviduous* read *invidious.* The candid Reader is desired to correct any others with his Pen.

Advertisement.

All anonymous Reflections upon this Performance, will be treated with neglect. But if the writer is wrong in the Principles advanced, and any Gentleman will condescend to refute them, and give his Name to the Public, as Truth only is sought after, the Obligation to the Discoverer shall be gratefully acknowledged.

The Rights of the British Colonies Asserted and Proved (1764)

INTRODUCTION
OF THE ORIGIN OF GOVERNMENT

The origin of *government* has in all ages no less perplexed the heads of lawyers and politicians, than the origin of *evil* has embarrassed divines and philosophers: And 'tis probable the world may receive a satisfactory solution on *both* those points of enquiry at the *same* time.

The various opinions on the origin of *government* have been reduced to four. 1. That dominion is founded in *Grace.* 2. On *force* or meer *power.* 3. On *compact.* 4. On *property.*

The first of these opinions is so absurd, and the world has paid so very dear for embracing it, especially under the administration of the *roman pontiffs,* that mankind seem at this day to be in a great measure cured of their madness in this particular; and the notion is pretty generally exploded, and hiss'd off the stage.

To those who lay the foundation of government in *force* and meer *brutal power,* it is objected; that, their system destroys all distinction between right and wrong; that it overturns all morality, and leaves it to every man to do what is right in his own eyes; that it leads directly to *scepticism,* and ends in *atheism.* When a man's will and pleasure is his only rule and guide, what safety can there be either for him or against him, but in the point of a sword?

On the other hand the gentlemen in favor of the *original compact* have been often told that *their* system is chimerical and unsupported by reason or experience. Questions like the following have been frequently asked them, and may be again.

"When and where was the original compact for introducing government into any society, or for creating a society, made? Who were present and parties to such compact? Who acted for infants and women, or who appointed guardians for them? Had these guardians power to bind both infants and women during life, and their posterity after them? Is it in nature or reason that a guardian should by his own act perpetuate his power over his ward, and bind him and his posterity in chains? Is not every man born as free by nature as his father? Has he not the same natural right to think and act and contract for himself? Is it possible for a man to have a natural right to make a slave of himself or of his posterity? Can a father supersede the laws of nature? What man is or ever was born free, if every man is not? What will there be to distinguish the next generation of men from their forefathers, that they should not have the same right to make original compacts as their ancestors had? If every man has such right, may there not be as many original compacts as there are men and women born or to be born? Are not women born as free as men? Would it not be infamous to assert that the ladies are all slaves by nature? If every man and woman born or to be born has, and will have, a right to be consulted, and must accede to the original compact before they can with any kind of justice be said to be bound by it, will not the compact be ever forming and never finished, ever making but never done? Can it with propriety be called a compact original or derivative, that is ever in treaty but never concluded?"

When it has been said that each man is bound as soon as he accedes, and that the consent may be either express or tacit, it has been asked. "What is a *tacit* consent or compact? Does it not appear plain that those who refuse their assent can not be bound? If one is at liberty to accede or not, is he not also at liberty *recede* on the discovery of some intolerable fraud and abuse that has been palm'd upon him by the rest of the high contracting parties? Will not natural equity in several special cases rescind the original compacts of great men as effectually, as those of little men are rendered null and void in the ordinary course of a court of chancery?"

There are other questions which have been started, and a resolution of them demanded, which may perhaps be deemed indecent to those who hold the prerogatives of an earthly monarch, and even the power of a plantation government, so sacred as to think it little less than blasphemy to enquire into their origin and foundation: while the government of the supreme *ruler* of the universe is every day discussed with less ceremony and decency than the administration of a petty German prince. I hope the reader will consider that

I am at present only mentioning such questions as have been put by highflyers & others in church and state, who would exclude all compact between a Sovereign and his people, without offering my own sentiments upon them; this however I presume I may be allowed hereafter to do without offence. Those who want a full answer to them may consult Mr. Locke's discourses on government, M. De Vattel's law of nature and nations, and their own consciences. "What state were Great Britain, Ireland and the Plantations left in by the abdication of James II? Was it a state of nature or of civil government? If a state of civil government, where were the supreme legislative and executive powers from the abdication to the election of William and Mary? Could the Lords and Commons be called a complete parliament or supreme power without a King to head them? Did any law of the land or any original compact previous to the abdication provide, that on such an event, the supreme power should devolve on the two houses? Were not both houses so manifestly puzzled with the novelty and strangeness of the event, and so far from finding any act of parliament, book-case, or precedent to help them, that they disputed in solemn conference by what name to call the action, and at last gave it one, as new in our language and in that of parliament as the thing itself was in fact?"[6]

If on this memorable and very happy event the three kingdoms and the dominions fell back into a state of *nature,* it will be asked, "Whether every man and woman were not then equal? If so, had not everyone of them a natural and equitable right to be consulted in the choice of a new king, or in the formation of a new original compact or government, if any new form had been made? Might not the nation at that time have rightfully changed the monarchy into a republic or any form, that might seem best? Could any change from a state of nature take place without universal consent, or at least without the consent of the *majority* of the individuals? Upon the principles of the original compact as commonly explained and understood, could a few hundred men who before the dissolution of the government had been called, and in fact were, lords, knights and gentlemen, have lawfully made that glorious deliverer and defender W. 3. rightful king"? Such an one he certainly was, and such have been all his illustrious successors to the present happy times; when we have the joy to see the sceptre sway'd in justice, wisdom and mercy, by our

---

6   On King James's leaving the kingdom and *abdicating* the government, the lords would have the word *desertion* made use of, but the commons thought it was not comprehensive enough, for that the King might then have liberty of returning. The Scots rightly called it a forfeiture of the crown, & this in plain english is the sense of the term *abdication* as by the convention and every parliament since applied. See the history and debates of the convention and the acts then made.

lawful Sovereign George the Third; a prince who glories in being a Briton born, and whom may God long preserve and prosper.

"If upon the abdication all were reduced to a state of nature, had not apple women and orange girls as good a right to give their respectable suffrages for a new king as the philosopher, courtier, petit maitre and politician? Were these and ten millions of others such ever more consulted on that occasion, than the multitude now are in the adjustment of that real modern farce, an election of a King of the Romans; which serves as a contrast to the grandeur of the antient republics, and shows the littleness of the modern German and some other gothic constitutions in their present degenerate state?

"In the election of W.3, were the votes of Ireland and the plantations ever called for or once tho't of till the affair was settled? Did the lords and commons who happened to be then in and about Westminster represent, and act, for the individuals, not only of the three kingdoms, but for all the *freeborn and as yet unconquered possessors and proprietors of their own money-purchased, bloodpurchased plantations, which, till lately, have been defended with little or no assistance from Great-Britain?* Were not those who did vote in or for the new model at liberty upon the principles of the compact to remain in what some call the delectable state of nature, to which by the hypothesis they were reduced, or to join themselves to any other state, whose solemn league and covenant they could subscribe? Is it not a first principle of the original compact, that all who are bound should bind *themselves?* Will not common sense without much learning or study dictate obvious answers to all the above questions? —and, say the opposers of the original compact and of the natural equality and liberty of mankind, will not those answers infallibly show that the doctrine is a piece of *metaphysical* jargon and *systematical* nonsense"? Perhaps not.

With regard to the fourth opinion, that *dominion is founded in property,* what is it but playing with words? Dominion in one sense of the term is synonimous with property, so one cannot be called the foundation of the other, but as one *name may* appear to be the foundation or cause of another.

Property cannot be the foundation of dominion as synonimous with government; for on the supposition that property has a precarious existence antecedent to government, and tho' it is also admitted that the security of property is one end of government, but that of little estimation even in the view of a *miser* when life and liberty of locomotion and further accumulation are placed in competition, it must be a very absurd way of speaking to assert that *one* end of government is the foundation of government. If the ends of government are to be considered as its foundation, it cannot with truth or propriety be said that government is founded on *anyone* of those ends: and therefore government is not founded on property or its security *alone,* but at least on something else in conjunction. It is however true in fact and *experience,* as the great, the incomparable *Harrington* has most abundantly demonstrated in his *Oceana,* and other divine writings, that Empire follows the balance of *Property:* 'Tis also certain that *property* in fact generally *confers* power, tho' the possessor of it may not have much more wit than a mole

or a musquash: And this is too often the cause, that riches are fought after without the least concern about the right application of them. But is the fault in the riches, or the general law of nature, or the unworthy possessor? It will never follow from all this, that government is *rightfully* founded on *property,* alone. What shall we say then? Is not government founded on *grace?*

No. Nor on *force?* No. Nor on *compact?* Nor *property?* Not altogether on either. Has it *any* solid foundation? any chief corner stone, but what accident, chance or confusion may lay one moment and destroy the next? I think it has an everlasting foundation in the *unchangeable will of* God, the author of nature, whose laws never vary. The same omniscient, omnipotent, infinitely good and gracious Creator of the universe, who has been pleased to make it necessary that what we call matter should *gravitate,* for the celestial bodies to roll round their axes, dance their orbits and perform their various revolutions in that beautiful order and concert, which we all admire, has made it *equally* necessary that from *Adam* and *Eve* to these degenerate days, the different sexes should sweetly *attract* each other, form societies of *single* families, of which *larger* bodies and communities are as naturally, mechanically, and necessarily combined, as the dew of Heaven and the soft distilling rain is collected by the all enliv'ning heat of the sun. *Government* is therefore most evidently founded *on the necessities of our nature.* It is by no means an *arbitrary* thing, depending merely on *compact* or *human will* for its existence.

We come into the world forlorn and helpless; and if left alone and to ourselves at any one period of our lives, we should soon die in want, despair or destraction. So kind is that hand, tho' little known or regarded, which feeds the rich and the poor, the blind and the naked; and provides for the safety of infants by the principle of parental love, and for that of men by Government! We have a King, who neither slumbers nor sleeps, but eternally watches for ur good; whose rain falls on the just and on the unjust: yet while they live, move, and have their being in him, and cannot account for either; or for any thing else, so stupid and wicked are some men, as to deny his existence, blaspheme his most evident government, and disgrace their nature.

Let no Man think I am about to commence advocate for *despotism,* because I affirm that government is founded on the necessity of our natures; and that an original supreme Sovereign, absolute, and uncontroulable, *earthly* power *must* exist in and preside *over* every society; from whose final decisions there can be no appeal but directly to Heaven. It is therefore *originally* and *ultimately* in the people. I say supreme absolute power is *originally* and *ultimately* in the people; and they never did in *fact freely,* nor can they *rightfully* make an absolute, unlimited renunciation of this divine right.[7] It is ever in the nature of the thing given in *trust,* and on a condition, the performance of which no mortal can dispence with; namely, that the person or persons on whom the sovereignty is confer'd by the people, shall *incessantly* consult *their* good. Tyranny of all kinds is to be abhor'd, whether it be in the hands of one, or of the few, or of the many. —And tho' "in the last age a generation of men sprung up that would flatter Princes with an opinion that *they* have a *divine right* to absolute power"; yet "slavery is so vile and miserable an estate of man, and so directly opposite to the generous temper and courage of our nation, that 'tis hard to be conceived that an *englishman,* much less a *gentleman,* should plead for it:"[8] Especially at a time when the finest writers of the most polite nations on the continent of *Europe,* are enraptured with the beauties of the civil constitution of *Great-Britain;* and envy her, no less for *the freedom* of her sons, than for her immense *wealth* and *military* glory.

But let the *origin* of government be placed where it may, the *end* of it is manifestly the good of *the whole. Salus populi supreme lex esto,* is of the law of nature, and part of that grand charter given the human race, (tho' too many of them are afraid to assert it,) by the only monarch in the universe, who has a clear and indisputable right to *absolute* power; because he is the *only* One who is *omniscient* as well as *omnipotent.*

It is evidently contrary to the first principles of reason, that supreme *unlimited* power should be in the hands of *one* man. It is the greatest *"idolatry,* begotten by *flattery,* on the body of *pride",* that could induce one to think that a *single mortal* should be able to hold so great a power, if ever so well inclined. Hence the origin of *deifying* princes: It was from the trick of gulling the vulgar into a belief that their tyrants were *omniscient,* and that it was therefore right, that they should be considered as *omnipotent.* Hence the *Dii majorum et minorum*

---

7   The power of GOD almighty is the only power that can properly and strictly be caled supreme and absolute. In the order of nature immediately under him, comes the power of a simple *democracy,* or the power of the whole over the whole. Subordinate to both these, are all other political powers, from that of the French Monarque to a petty constable.

8   Mr. Locke.

gentium; the great, the monarchical, the little Provincial subordinate and subaltern gods, demi-gods, and semidemi-gods, ancient and modern. Thus deities of all kinds were multiplied and increased in *abundance;* for every devil incarnate, who could enslave a people, acquired a title to *divinity;* and thus the "rabble of the skies" was made up of locusts and caterpillars; lions, tygers and harpies; and other devourers translated from plaguing the earth![9]

The *end* of government being the *good* of mankind, points out its great duties: It is above all things to provide for the security, the quiet, and happy enjoyment of life, liberty, and property. There is no one act which a government can have a *right* to make, that does not tend to the advancement of the security, tranquility and prosperity of the people. If life, liberty and property could be enjoyed in as great perfection in *solitude,* as in *society,* there would be no need of government. But the experience of ages has proved that such is the nature of man, a weak, imperfect being; that the valuable ends of live cannot be obtained without the union and assistance of many. Hence 'tis clear that men cannot live apart or independent of each other: In solitude men would perish; and yet they cannot live together without contests. These contests require some arbitrator to determine them. The necessity of a common, indifferent and impartial judge, makes all men seek one; tho' few find him in the *sovereign power,* of their respective states or any where else in *subordination* to it.

Government is founded *immediately* on the necessities of human nature, and *ultimately* on the will of God, the author of nature; who has not left it to men in general to choose, whether they will be members of society or not, but at the hazard of their senses if not of their lives. Yet it is left to every man as he comes of age to chuse *what society* he will continue to belong to. Nay if one has a mind to turn *Hermit,* and after he has been born, nursed, and brought up in the arms of society, and acquired the habits and passions of social life, is willing to run the risque of starving alone, which is generally most unavoidable in a state of hermitage, who shall hinder him? I know of no human law, founded on the law of *nature,* to restrain him from separating himself from the species, if he can find it in his heart to leave them; unless it should be said, it is against the great law of *self-preservation:* But of this every man will think himself *his own judge.*

The few *Hermits* and *Misanthropes* that have ever existed, show that those states are *unnatural.* If we were to take out from them, those who have made

---

9   Kingcraft and Priestcraft have fell out so often, that 'tis a wonder this grand and ancient alliance is not broken off forever. Happy for mankind will it be, when such a separation shall take place.

great *worldly* gain of their *godly* hermitage, and those who have been under the madness of *enthusiasm,* or *disappointed* hopes in their *ambitious* projects, for the detriment of mankind; perhaps there might not be left ten from *Adam* to this day.

The form of government is by *nature* and by *right* so far left to the *individuals* of each society, that they may alter it from a simple democracy or government of all over all, to any other form they please. Such alteration may and ought to be made by express compact: But how seldom this right has been asserted, history will abundantly show. For once that it has been fairly settled by compact; *fraud force or accident* have determined it an hundred times. As the people have gained upon tyrants, these have been obliged to relax, *only* till a fairer opportunity has put it in their power to encroach again.

But if every prince since *Nimrod* had been a tyrant, it would not prove a *right* to tyranize. There can be no prescription old enough to supersede the law of nature, and the grant of God almighty; who has given to all men a natural right to be *free,* and they have it ordinarily in their power to make themselves so, if they please.

Government having been proved to be necessary by the law of nature, it makes no difference in the thing to call it from a certain period, *civil.* This term can only relate to form, to additions to, or deviations from, the substance of government: This being founded in nature, the super-structures and the whole administration should be conformed to the law of universal reason. A supreme legislative and supreme executive power, must be placed *somewhere* in every common-wealth: Where there is no other positive provision or compact to the contract, those powers remain in the *whole body of the people.* It is also evident there can be but *one* best way of depositing those powers; but what that way is, mankind have been disputing in peace and in war more than five thousand years. If we could suppose the individuals of a community met to deliberate, whether it were best to keep those powers in *their own* hands, or dispose of them in *trust,* the following questions would occur – Whether those two great powers of *Legislation* and *Execution* should remain united? If so, whether in the hands of the many, or jointly or severally in the hands of a few, or jointly in some one individual? If both those powers are retained in the hands of the many, where nature seems to have placed them originally, the government is a simple *democracy,* or a government of all over all. This can be administered, only by establishing it as a first principle, that the votes of the majority shall be taken as the voice of the whole. If those powers are lodged in the hands of a few, the government is an *Aristocracy* or *Oligarchy*.[10] Here too the first principles of a practicable administration is that the majority

rules the whole. If those great powers are both lodged in the hands of one man, the government is a *simple Monarchy,* commonly, though falsly called *absolute,* if by that term is meant a right to do as one pleases. – *Sic volo, sic jubeo, stet pro ratione voluntas,* belongs not of right to any mortal man.

The same law of nature and of reason is equally obligatory on a *democracy,* an *aristocracy,* and a *monarchy:* Whenever the administrators, in any of those forms, deviate from truth, justice and equity, they verge towards tyranny, and are to be opposed; and if they prove incorrigible, they will be *deposed* by the people, if the people are not rendered too abject. Deposing the administrators of a *simple democracy* may sound oddly, but it is done every day, and in almost every vote. A.B. & C. for example, make a *democracy.* Today A & B are for so vile a measure as a standing army. Tomorrow B & C vote it out. This is as really deposing the former administrators, as setting up and making a new king is deposing the old one. *Democracy* in the one case, and *monarchy* in the other, still remain; all that is done is to change the administration.

The first principle and great end of government being to provide for the best good of all the people, this can be done only by a supreme legislative and executive ultimately in the people, or whole community, where God has placed it; but the inconveniencies, not to say impossibility, attending the consultations and operations of a large body of people have made it necessary to transfer the power of the whole to *a few:* This necessity gave rise to deputation, proxy or a right of representation.

A Power of legislation, without a power of execution in the same or other hands, would be futile and vain: On the other hand a power of execution, supreme or subordinate, without an *independent* legislature, would be perfect despotism.

The difficulties attending an universal congress, especially when society became large, have bro't men to consent to a delegation of the power of all: The weak and the wicked have too often been found in the same interest, and in most nations have not only bro't these powers *jointly,* into the hands of one, or some few of their number; but made them *hereditary,* in the families of despotic nobles & princes.

The wiser and more virtuous states, have always provided that the representation of the people should be *numerous.* Nothing but life and liberty are

---

10   For the sake of the unletered reader 'tis noted, that Monarchy means the power of one great man; Aristocracy and Olargarchy that of a few; and Democracy that of all men.

naturally hereditable: this has never been considered by those, who have *tamely* given up both into the hands of a tyrannical Oligarchy or despotic Monarchy.

The analogy between the natural, or material, as it is called, and the moral world is very obvious; God himself appears to us at some times to cause the intervention or combination of a *number* of simple principles, tho' never when *one* will answer the end; gravitation and attraction have place in the revolution of the planets, because the one would fix them to a centre, and the other would carry them off indefinitely; so in the moral world, the first simple principle is *equality* and the power of the whole. This will answer in small numbers; so will a tolerably virtuous *Oligarchy* or a *Monarchy*. But when the society grows in bulk, none of them will answer well *singly,* and none worse than absolute monarchy. It becomes necessary therefore as numbers increase, to have those several powers properly combined; so as from the whole to produce that harmony of government so often talked of and wished for, but too seldom found in ancient or modern states. The grand political problem in all ages has been to invent the best combination or distribution of the supreme powers of legislation and execution. Those states have ever made the greatest figure, and have been most durable, in which those powers have not only been separated from each other, but placed each in more hands than one, or a few. The *Romans* are the most shining example; but they never had a balance between the senate and the people, and the want of this, is generally agreed by the few who know any thing of the matter, to have been the cause of their fall. The *British* constitution in theory and in the present administration of it, in general comes nearest the idea of perfection, of any that has been reduced to practice; and if the principles of it are adhered to, it will according to the infallible prediction of *Harrington,* always keep the *Britons* uppermost in *Europe,* 'tis their *only* rival nation shall either embrace that perfect model of a common wealth given us by that author, or come as near it as *Great Britain* is. Then indeed and not till then, will that rival & our nation either be eternal confederates, or contend in greater earnest than they have ever yet done, till one of them shall sink under the power of the other, and rise no more.

Great Britain has at present, most evidently the advantage, and such opportunities of honest wealth and grandeur, as perhaps no state ever had before, at least not since the days of *Julius Caesar,* the destroyer of the roman glory and grandeur; at a time when but for him and his adherents both might have been rendered immortal.

We have said that the form and mode of government is to be settled by *compact,* as it was rightfully done by the convention after the abdication of *James II,* and assented to by the first representative of the nation chosen afterwards, and by every parliament, and by almost every man ever since, but the bigots, to the indefeasible power of tyrants civil and ecclesiastic. There was neither time for, nor occasion to call the whole people together: If they had not liked the proceedings it was in their power to controul them; as it would be should the supreme legislative or executive powers ever again attempt to enslave them. The people will bear a great deal, before they will even murmur against their rulers: But when once they are thoroughly roused and in earnest, against those who would be glad to enslave them, their power is *irrestible*.[11]

At the abdication of King *James,* every step was taken that natural justice and equity could require; and all was done that was possible at least in the wretched state in which he left the nation. Those very noble and worthy patriots, the lords spiritual and temporal of that day, and the principal persons of the commons, advised the prince, who in consequence thereof caused letters to be "written to the lords spiritual and temporal, being protestants, and other letters to the several counties, cities, universities, boroughs and cinque ports, for the choosing such persons to represent them as were of right to be sent to parliament, to meet at Westminster upon the 22d of January 1688, in order to such an establishment, as that their religion, laws and liberties, might not again be in danger of being subverted.' See W & M. sess. 1. C. 1.

Upon this elections were made, and thereupon the said lord spiritual and temporal and commons met, and proceeded to assert their rights and liberties, and to the election of the Prince and Princess of Orange to be King and Queen of England, France and Ireland, and the dominions thereto belonging. The kingdom of Scotland agreed in the same choice: These proceedings were drawn into the form of acts of parliament, and are the basis of the acts of union and succession since made, and which all together are the sure foundation of that indisputable right which his present Majesty has to the Crown of *Great Britain* and the dominions thereto belonging; which right 'tis the greatest folly to doubt of, as well as the blackest treason to deny. The present establishment founded on the law of God, and of nature, was began by the convention, with a professed and real view, in all parts of the *British* empire, to put the liberties of the people out of the reach of arbitrary power in all times to come. But the grandeur, as well as justice, equity and goodness of the proceedings of the nation on that memorable occasion, never have been nor can be so well represented as in the words of those great men who composed the convention; for which reason partly, but principally because they shew the rights of all

---

11   See Mr. Locke on the Dissolution of Government.

British subjects, both at home and abroad, and should therefore be in as many hands as possible, I have transcribed the following clauses.

1 Wm. & M. sess. 1. Chap. 1 preamble & sec 1 – entitled –

"An act for removing and preventing all questions and disputes concerning the assembling and sitting of this present parliament.

For preventing all doubts and scruples which may in any wise arise concerning the meeting, fitting and proceeding of this present parliament; be it declared and enacted by the King's and Queen's most excellent Majesty's, by and with the advice and consent of the lords spiritual and temporal, and commons, now assembled, and by authority of the same:

IIdly. That the lords spiritual and temporal, and commons, convened at Westminster, the two and twentieth day of January A. D. 1688, and there sitting the 13th of February following, are the two houses of parliament, and so shall be and are hereby declared, enacted and adjudged to be, to all intents, constructions, and purposes whatsoever, notwithstanding any want of writ or writs of summons, or any other defect of form or default whatsoever, as if they had been summoned according to the usual form.

1 of W. & M. sess. 2. Chap. 2. sec. 3,4, 5, 6, 11, 12.

An act declaring the rights and liberties of the subject, and settling the succession of the Crown.

Whereas the lords spiritual and temporal, and commons, assembled at Westminster, lawfully, fully and freely representing all the estates of the people of this realm, did upon the 13th of February A. D. 1688, present unto their Majesties, then called and known by the names and stile of William and Mary, Prince and Princess of Orange, being present in their proper persons, a certain declaration in writing, made by the said lords and commons in the words following; viz.

Whereas the late King James the second, by the assistance of divers evil councellors, judges, and ministers employed by him, did endeavour to subvert and extirpate the protestant religion, and the laws and liberties of this kingdom.

1. By assuming and exercising a power of dispensing with and suspending of laws, and the execution of laws, without consent of parliament.

2. By committing and prosecuting divers worthy prelates, for humbly petitioning to be excused from concuring to the said assumed power.

3. By issuing and causing to be executed a commission under the great seal for erecting a court called, The court of commissioners for ecclesiastical causes.

4. By levying money for and to the use of the crown, by pretence of prerogative, for other time, and in other manner, than the same was granted by parliament.

5. By raising and keeping a standing army within this kingdom in time of peace, without the consent of parliament, and quartering soldiers contrary to law.

6. By causing several good subjects, being protestants, to be disarmed, at the same time when papists were both armed and employed, contrary to law.

7. By violating the freedom of election of members to serve in parliament.

8. By prosecutions in the court of king's bench, for matters and causes cognizable only in parliament; and by divers other arbitrary and illegal courses.

9. And whereas of late years, partial, corrupt and unqualified persons, have been returned and served on juries in trials, and particularly divers jurors in trials for high treason, which were not freeholders.

10. And bail hath been required of persons committed in criminal cases, to elude the benefit of the laws made for the liberty of the subjects.

11. And excessive fines have been imposed; and illegal and cruel punishments inflicted.

12. And several grants and promises made of fines and forfeitures, before any conviction or judgment against the persons, upon whom the same were to be levied.

All which are utterly and directly contrary to the known laws and statutes, and freedom of this realm – .

And whereas the said late King *James* the second having abdicated the Government, and the throne being thereby vacant, his highness the prince of Orange (whom it hath pleased Almighty God to make the glorious instrument of delivering this kingdom from popery and arbitrary power) did (by the advice of the Lords spiritual and temporal, and divers principal persons of the commons) cause letters to be written to the lords spiritual and temporal, being protestants, and other letters to the several counties, cities, universities, boroughs, and cinque-ports, for the choosing of such persons to represent them, as were of right to be sent to parliament, to meet and sit at Westminster upon the two and twentieth of January in this year 1688, in order to such an establishment, as that their religion, laws and liberties might not again be in danger of being subverted. Upon which letters, elections having been accordingly made:

And thereupon the said lords spiritual and temporal and commons, pursuant to their respective letters and elections, being now assembled in a full and free representative of this nation, taking into their most serious consideration the best means for attaining the ends aforesaid; do in the first place (as their ancestors in like case have usually done) for the vindicating and asserting their ancient rights and liberties, declare,

1. That the pretended power of suspending of laws, or the execution of laws, by regal authority, without consent of parliament, is illegal.

2. That the pretended power of dispensing with laws, *or* the execution of laws, by regal authority, as it hath been assumed and exercised of late, is illegal.

3. That the commission for creating the late court of commissioners for ecclesiastical causes, and all other commissions and courts of like nature, are illegal and pernicious.

4. That levying money for or to the use of the crown, by pretence of prerogative, without grant of parliament, for longer time, or in other manner, than the same is or shall be granted, is illegal.

5. That it is the right of the subjects to petition the King; and all commitments and prosecutions for such petitioning are illegal.

6. That the raising or keeping a standing army within the kingdom in time of peace, unless it be with consent of parliament, is against law.

7. That the subjects which are protestants, may have arms for their defence, suitable to their conditions, and as allowed by law.

8. That election of members of parliament ought to be free.

9. That the freedom of speech, and debates, or proceedings in parliament, ought not to be impeached or questioned in any court or place out of parliament.

10. That excessive bail ought not to be required, nor excessive fines imposed; nor cruel and unusual punishments inflicted.

11. That jurors ought to be duly impannelled and returned; and jurors which pass upon mens trials for high treason, ought to be freeholders.

12. That all grants and promises of fines and forfeitures of particular persons before conviction, are illegal and void.

13. And that for redress of all grievances, and for the amending, strengthening, and preserving of the laws, parliaments ought to be held frequently.

And they do claim, demand, and insist upon all and singular the premises, as their undoubted rights and liberties; and that no declarations, judgments, doings, or proceedings, to the prejudice of the people in any of the said premises, ought in any wise to be drawn hereafter into consequence or example:

To which demand of their rights they are particularly encouraged by the declaration of his Highness the Prince of Orange, as being the only means for obtaining a full redress and remedy therein – .

Having therefore an entire confidence, that his said Highness the Prince of Orange, will perfect the deliverance so far advanced by him, and will still preserve them, from the violation of their rights, which they have here asserted and from all attempts upon their religion, rights and liberties.

III. The said Lords spiritual and temporal, and commons assembled at Westminster, do resolve that William & Mary Prince and Princess of Orange be, and be declared, King and Queen of England, France and Ireland, and the dominions thereunto belonging, to hold the crown and royal dignity of the said kingdoms and dominions to them the said Prince and Princess, during their lives, and the life of the survivor of them; and that the sole and full exercise of the regal power be only in, and executed by the said Prince of Orange, in the names of the said prince and princess, during their joint lives; and after their deceases, the said crown and royal dignity of the said kingdoms and dominions to be to the heirs of the body of the said princess; and for default of such issue, to the princess Anne of Denmark, and the heirs of her body; and for default of such issue, to the heirs of the body of the said prince of Orange. And the Lords spiritual and temporal, and commons, do pray the said prince and princess to accept the same accordingly.

IV. Upon which their said Majesties did accept the crown and royal dignity of the kingdom of England, France and Ireland and the dominions thereunto belonging, according to the resolutions and desire of the said lords and commons, contained in the said declaration.

V. And thereupon their Majesties were pleased, that the said Lords spiritual and temporal, and commons, being the two houses of parliament, should continue to sit, and with their Majesties royal concurrence, make effectual provision for the settlement of the religion, laws and liberties of this kingdom; so that the same for the future might not be in danger again of being subverted; to which the said lords spiritual and temporal, and commons, did agree and proceed to act accordingly.

VI. Now in pursuance of the premises, the said lords spiritual and temporal and commons, in parliament assembled, for the ratifying, confirming and establishing the said declaration, and the articles, clauses, matters and things therein contained, by the force of a law made in due form by authority of parliament, do pray that it may be declared and enacted. That all and singular the rights and liberties asserted and claimed in the said declaration, are the true, ancient and indubitable rights and liberties of the people of this kingdom, and so shall be esteemed, allowed, adjudged, deemed, and taken to be: and that all and every the particulars aforesaid, shall be firmly and strictly holden and observed, as they are expressed in the said declaration; and all officers and ministers whatsoever shall serve their Majesties and their successors according to the same in all times to come.

XI. All which their Majesties are contented and pleased shall be declared, enacted, and established by authority of this present parliament, and shall stand remain and be the law of this realm for ever; and the same are by their said Majesties, by and with the advice and consent of the Lords spiritual and temporal, and commons, in parliament assembled, and by the authority of the same, declared, enacted, and established accordingly.

XII. And be it further declared and enacted by the authority aforesaid, that from and after this present session of parliament, no dispensation by *non obstante* of or to any statute or any part thereof, shall be allowed; but that the same shall be held void and of no effect, except a dispensation be allowed in such statutes, and except in such cases as shall be specially provided for by one or more bill or bills to be passed during this present session of parliament.

12 & 13 of William 3d, Chap. 2. sec. 3 & 4.

"Whereas it is necessary that further provision be made for securing our religion, laws and liberties, after the death of his Majesty and the Princess Anne of Denmark, and in default of issue of the body of the said Princess, and of his Majesty respectively; it is enacted,

That after the said limitation shall take effect, judges commissions be made *quandiu se bene gesserint,* and their salaries ascertained and established; but upon the address of both houses parliament, it may be lawful to remove them:

That no pardon under the great seal of England be pleaded to an impeachment by the commons in parliament.

Whereas the laws of England are the birth-right of the people thereof, and all the Kings and Queens, who shall ascend the throne of this realm, ought to administer the government of the same according to the said laws, and all their officers and ministers ought to serve them according to the same; all the laws and statutes of this realm for securing the established religion, and the rights and liberties of the people, and all other laws and statutes now in force, are by his Majesty with the advice and consent of the lords spiritual and temporal, and commons, ratified and confirmed."

I shall close this introduction with a passage from Mr. Locke.

"Tho', says he, in a constituted common wealth, standing upon its own basis, and acting according to its own nature, that is, acting for the preservation of the community, there can be but one supreme power which is the legislative, to which all the rest are and must be subordinate; yet the legislative being only a fiduciary power, to act for certain ends, there remains still, *"in the people, a supreme power to remove, or alter, the legislative when they find the legislative act contrary to the trust reposed in them."* For all power given, with trust for the attaining an end, being limited by that end, whenever that end is manifestly neglected, or opposed, the trust must necessarily be forfeited, and the power devolve into the hands of those who gave it, who may place it anew where they shall think best, for their safety and security. And thus the *community* perpetually retains a supreme power of saving themselves from the attempts and designs of any body, even of their legislators whenever they shall be so foolish, or so wicked, as to lay and carryon designs against the liberties and properties of the subject. For no man or society of men having a power to deliver up their preservation or consequently the means of it to the absolute will and arbitrary dominion of another; whenever anyone shall go about to bring them into such a slavish condition, they win always have a right to preserve what they have not a power to part with; and to *rid* themselves of *those* who invade this fundamental, sacred and unalterable law of self preservation, for which they entered into society.

And thus the community may be said in this respect to be always the supreme power, but not as considered under any form of government, because this power of the people can never take place, till the government be dissolved." Locke on Government, B. II. C. 13.

This he says may be done, "from without by conquest; from within, 1st. When the legislative is altered. Which is often by the prince, but sometimes by the whole legislative. As by invading the *property* of the subject, and making themselves arbitrary disposers of the lives, liberties and fortunes of the people; reducing them to slavery under arbitrary power, they put themselves into a state of war with the people, who are thereupon absolved from any further obedience, and are left to the common refuge which God hath provided for all men, against force and violence. Whensoever, therefore, the legislative shall transgress this fundamental rule of society; and either by ambition, fear, folly or corruption, endeavour to gain themselves, or put into the hands of any other an absolute power over the lives, liberties and estates of the people, by this breach of trust, they forfeit the power the *people* had put into their hands for quite contrary ends, and it devolves to the *people,* who have a right to *resume* their original liberty, and by the establishment of a *new* legislative (such as they shall think fit) provide for their own safety and security, which is the end for which they are in society." Idem Chap. 9

NATHAN A. ALLEN

Of Colonies in general

This subject has never, been very clearly and fully handled by any modern writer, that I have had the good fortune to meet with; and to do it justice, would require much greater abilities than I pretend to, and more leisure than I ever expect will fall to my share. Even the *English* writers and lawyers, have either intirely wav'd any considerations of the nature of *Colonies,* or very lightly touched upon it, for the people of England never discovered much concern for the prosperity of the *Colonies,* 'till the revolution; and even now some of their great men and writers, by their discourses of, and conduct towards them, consider them all rather as a parcel of *little insignificant conquered islands,* than as a very extensive settlement on the continent. Even their law-books and very dictionaries of law, in editions so late as 1750, speak of the *British* plantations abroad as consisting chiefly of islands; and they are reckoned up in some of them in this *order – Jamaica, Barbados, Virginia, Maryland, New-England, New-York, Carolina, Bermudas.* At the head of all these *Islands* (for there is no distinction made) stands *Jamaica,* in truth a *conquered* island; and as such, this and all the other little West-India islands deserve to be treated, for the conduct of their inhabitants and proprietors with regard to the Northern Colonies: Divers of these colonies are larger than all those islands together; and are well settled, not as the common people of *England* foolishly imagine, with a compound mongrel mixture of *English, Indian* and *Negro,* but with freeborn *British white subjects,* whose loyalty has never yet been suspected.

There is a man now living, or but lately dead, who once was a secretary of state; during whose *wonderful* conduct of national affairs, without knowing whether *Jamaica* lay in the Mediterranean, the Baltic, or in the Moon, letters were often received, directed to the Governor of the *island* of New-England. Which *island* of New-England is a part of the *continent* of North-America, comprehending two provinces and two colonies; and according to the *undoubted* bounds of their charters, containing more land than there is in the three kingdoms. But I must confine myself to matters of more importance than detecting the geographical blunders, or refuting the errors of dead, superannuated or any otherwise stupified secretaries of state, who are now all out of place.

If I were to define the *modern* Colonists, I should say, *they are the noble discoverers and settlers of a new world;* from whence as from an endless source, *wealth,* and *plenty,* the means of *power, grandeur* and *glory,* in a degree unknown to the hungry chiefs of former ages, have been pouring into *Europe* for 300 years past: In return for which those Colonists have received from the several states of *Europe,* except from *Great-Britain,* only since the revolution, nothing but ill-usage, slavery and chains, as fast as the riches of *their own* earning, could furnish the means of forging them.

A plantation or colony, is a settlement of subjects, in a *territory disjoined* or remote from the mother country, and may be made by private adventurers or the public; but in both cases the Colonists are entitled to as *ample* rights, liberties and priviledges as the subjects of the mother country are, and in some respects *to more.*

Of the natural Rights of Colonists.

Those who expect to find any thing very satisfactory on this subject in particular, or with regard to the law of nature in general, in the writings of such authors as *Grotius* and *Pufendorf,* will find themselves much mistaken. It is their constant practice to establish the matter of right on the matter of *fact:* This the celebrated Rousseau expressly says of *Grotius,* and with the same reason he might have added an hundred others. "The learned researches into the laws of nature and nations are often nothing more than the history of ancient abuses, so that it is a ridiculous infatuation to be too fond of studying them"[12]. "This was exactly the case with *Grotius*".[13] The sentiments on this subject have therefore been chiefly drawn from the purer fountains of one or two of our *English* writers, particularly from Mr. *Locke,* to whom might be added *a few* of other nations; for I have seen but a few of any country, and of all have seen, there are not ten worth reading. Grotius B. 3 C. 1. sec. 21. discoursing of confederates on unequal terms according to his manner says, "to the inequality in question may be referred some of those rights which are now called right of protection, right of patronage, and a right termed *mundiburgium;* as also that which mother cities had over their colonies among the Grecians. For as *Thucydides* says, those colonies enjoyed the same rights of liberty with the other cities; but they owed a *reverence* to the city whence they derived their origin, and were obliged to render her respect and certain expressions of honor, *so long as the colony was well treated."*

Grotius de jure belli, &c. B. 1. C. 3. 21.

"Hitherto also (says he) may be referred that separation which is made when people *by one consent,* go to form colonies. *For this is the original of a new and independent state. They are not content to be slaves, but to enjoy equal privileges*

---

12   Marquis D' A.
13   Rousseau.

and freedom says Thucydides. And King *Tullius* in Dion. Hali. says, *we look upon it to be neither truth nor justice, that mother cities ought of necessity and by the law of nature to rule over their colonies."*

B. 2. C. 9. sec. 10.

"Colonies, says Pufendorf, are settled in different methods. For either the colony continues a part of the common-wealth it was sent out from, or else is obliged to pay a dutiful respect to the mother common-wealth, and to be in readiness to defend and vindicate its honor, and so is united to it by a sort of unequal confederacy, or lastly is erected into a separate commonwealth, and assumes the same rights with the state it is descended from."

Pufend. B. 8 C. 11. 6.

"Different common wealths may be formed out of one by common consent, by sending out colonies in the manner usual in old Greece. For the Romans afterwards when they sent a colony abroad, continued it under the jurisdiction of the mother commonwealth, or greater country. But the colonies planted by the Greeks, and after their method, constituted particular commonwealths, which were obliged only to pay a kind of deference and dutiful submission to the mother commonwealth."

Pufend. B. 8 C. 12. sec. 5.

From which passages tis manifest that these two great men only state facts, and the opinions of others, without giving their own upon the subject: And all that can be collected from those facts or opinions is, that Greece was more generous, and a better mother to her colonies than Rome. The conduct of Rome towards her colonies and the corruptions and oppressions tolerated in her provincial officers of all denominations, was one great cause of the downfall of that proud republic.

Dr. Strahan says, "there is a great affinity between the British colonies and those of the Spaniards and other nations, who have made settlements among the Indians in those parts: For the grants made by our Kings, of tracts of lands in that country, for the planting of colonies, and making settlements therein, appear to have been made in imitation of grants made by the Kings of Spain to the proprietors of lands in the Spanish colonies, upon the very same conditions, and in consideration of the same services to be performed by the grantees. So that the *government* of the Spanish colonies and the rights of the proprietors of lands therein, depending chiefly on the rules of civil and feudal law, as may be seen by the learned treatise of Solorzanus, *de indiarum jure,* the knowledge of the said laws must be of service likewise for determining any controversy that may arise touching the duties of forfeitures of the proprietors of lands in our English colonies.

Pref. to translat. of Domat.

With submission to so great an authority as Dr. Strahan, tis humbly hoped that the British colonists do not hold their lands as well as liberties by so slippery a tenure as do the Spaniards and French. The will of the Prince is the only tenure by which *they* hold; and the government of the Spanish and French settlements is in every respect despotic. 'Tis well known that the first American grants were by the Bulls of the Popes. The Roman Pontiffs had for ages usurped the most abominable power over princes: They granted away the kingdoms of the earth with as little ceremony as a man would lease a sheep-cot. Now according to Dr. Strahan's logic, it may be inferred, that the canon law, and the Pope's Bulls, must be of *service likewise, for determining any controversy that may arise, touching the duties or forfeitures of the proprietors of lands in the British colonies.* And indeed it must be owned, if we were to judge of some late proceedings[14] by this rule, we must allow that they savor more of modern Rome and the Inquisition than of the common law of England and the constitution of Great Britain.

In order to form an idea of the natural rights of the Colonists, I presume it will be granted that they are men, the common children of the same Creator with their brethren of Great-Britain. Nature has placed all such in a state of equality and perfect freedom, to act within the bounds of the laws of nature and reason, without consulting the will or regarding the humor, the passions or whims of any other man, unless they are formed into a society or body politic. This it must be confessed is rather an abstract way of considering men than agreeable to the real and general course of nature. The truth is, as has been shown, men come into the world and into society at the same instant. But this hinders not but that the natural and original rights of each individual may be illustrated and explained in this way better than in any other. We see here by the way a probability, that this abstract consideration of men, which has its use in reasoning on the principles of government, has insensibly led some of the greatest men to imagine, some real general state of nature, agreeable to this abstract conception, antecedent to and independent of society. This is certainly not the case in general, for most men become member of society from their birth, tho' seperate independent states are really in the condition of perfect freedom and equality with regard to each other; and so are any number of individuals who separate themselves from a society of which they have formerly been members, for ill treatment, or other good cause, with express design to found another. If in such case, there is a real interval, between the separation and the new conjunction, during such interval, the

---

14   Of some American Courts of Admiralty, if the reader pleases.

individuals are as much detached, and under the law of nature only, as would be two men who should chance to meet on a desolate island.

The Colonists are by the law of nature free born, as indeed all men are, white or black. No better reasons can be given, for enslaving those of any color than such as baron Montesquieu has humorously given, as the foundation of that cruel slavery exercised over the poor Ethiopians; which threatens one day to reduce both Europe and America to the ignorance and barbarity of the darkest ages. Does it follow that tis right to enslave a man because he is black? Will short curl'd hair like wool, instead of christian hair, as tis called by those, whose hearts are as hard as the nether millstone, help the argument? Can any logical inference in favour of slavery, be drawn from a flat nose, a long or a short face. Nothing better can be said in favor of a trade, that is the most shocking violation of the law of nature, has a direct tendency to diminish the idea of the inestimable value of liberty, and makes every dealer in it a tyrant from the director of an African company to the petty chapman in needles and pins on the unhappy coast. It is a clear truth, that those who every day barter away other mens liberty will soon care little for their own. To this cause must be imputed that ferocity, cruelty and brutal barbarity that has long marked, the general character of the sugar-islanders. They can in general form no idea of government but that which in person, or by an overseer, the joint and several proper representative of a Creole[15], and of the D—l, is exercised over ten thousands of their fellow men, born with the same right to freedom, and the sweet enjoyments of liberty and life, as their unrelenting task masters, the overseers and planters.

Is it to be wondered at, if, when people of the stamp of a Creolian planter get into power, they will not stick for a little present gain, at making their own posterity, white as well as black, worse slaves if possible than those already mentioned.

There is nothing more evident, says Mr. Locke, than "that creatures of the same species and rank

promiscuously born to all the same advantages of nature, and the use of the same faculties, should also be equal one among another, without subordination and subjection, unless the master of them all should by any manifest declaration of his will set one above another, and confer on him by an evident and clear appointment, an undoubted right to dominion and sovereignty." "The natural liberty of man is to be free from any superior power on earth,

---

15   Those in England who borrow the terms of the Spaniards, as well as their notions of government, apply this term to all Americans of European Extract; but the Northern colonists apply it only to the Islanders and other of such extract, under the Torrid Zone.

and not to be under the will or legislative authority of man, but only to have the law of nature for his rule." This is the liberty of independent states; this is the liberty of every man out of society, and who has a mind to live so; which liberty is only abridged in certain instances, not lost to those who are born in or voluntarily enter into society; this gift of God cannot be annihilated.

The Colonists being men, have a right to be considered as equally entitled to all the rights of nature with the Europeans, and they are not to be restrained, in the exercise of any of these rights, but for the evident good of the whole community.

By being or becoming members of society, they have not renounced their natural liberty in any greater degree than other good citizens, and if tis taken from them without their consent, they are so far enslaved.

They have an undoubted right to expect, that their best good will ever be consulted by their rulers, supreme and subordinate, without any partial views confined to the particular interest of one island or another. Neither the riches of Jamaica, nor the luxury of a metropolis, should ever have weight enough to break the balance of truth and justice. Truth and faith belong to men as men, from men, and if they are disappointed in their just expectations of them in one society, they will at least wish for them in another. If the love of truth and justice, the only spring of sound policy in any state, is not strong enough to prevent certain causes from taking place, the arts of fraud and force will not prevent the most fatal effects.

In the long run, those who fall on arbitrary measures, will meet with their deserved fate. The law of nature, was not of man's making, nor is it in his power to mend it, or alter its course. He can only perform and keep, or disobey and break it. The last is never done with impunity, even in this life, if it is any punishment for a man to feel himself depraved; to find himself degraded by his own folly and wickedness from the rank of a virtuous and good *man*, to that of a brute; or to be transformed from the friend, perhaps father of his country, to a devouring Lion or Tyger.

The unhappy revolutions which for ages have distressed the human race, have been all owing to the want of a little wisdom common sense and integrity in the administration of those, whom by their stations, God had in kindness to the world, rendered able to do a great deal, for the benefit of mankind with the exertion of a small portion of private and public vertue.

Of the Political and Civil Rights of the British Colonists

Here indeed opens to view a large field; but I must study brevity—Few people have extended their enquiries after the foundation of any of their rights, beyond a charter from the crown. There are others who think when they have got back to old *Magna Charta*, that they are at the beginning of all things. They imagine themselves on the borders of Chaos (and so indeed in some respects they are) and see creation rising out of the unformed mass, or from nothing. Hence, say they, spring all the rights of men and of citizens. . . . But liberty was better understood, and more fully enjoyed by our ancestors, before the coming in of the first Norman Tyrants than ever after, 'till it was found necessary, for the salvation of the kingdom, to combat the arbitrary and wicked proceedings of the Stuarts.

The present happy and most righteous establishment is justly built on the ruins, which those Princes bro't on their Family; and two of them on their own heads—The last of the name sacrificed three of the finest kingdoms in Europe, to the councils of bigotted old women, priests and more weak and wicked ministers of state: He afterward went a grazing in the fields of St. Germains, and there died in disgrace and poverty, a terrible example of God's vengeance on arbitrary princes!

The deliverance under God wrought by the prince of Orange, afterwards deservedly made King Wm. 3rd. was as joyful an event to the colonies as to Great-Britain: In some of them steps were taken in his favour as soon as in England.

They all immediately acknowledged King William and Queen Mary as their lawful Sovereign. And such has been the zeal and loyalty of the colonies ever since for that establishment, and for the protestant succession in his Majesty's illustrious family, that I believe there is not one man in an hundred (except in Canada) who does not think himself under the best national civil constitution in the world.

Their loyalty has been abundantly proved, especially in the late war. Their affection and reverence for their mother country is unquestionable. They yield the most chearful and ready obedience to her laws, particularly to the power of that august body the parliament of Great-Britain, the supreme legislative of the kingdom and in dominions. These I declare are my own sentiments of duty and loyalty. I also hold it clear that the act of Queen Anne, which makes it high treason to deny "that the King with and by the authority of parliament, is able to make laws and statutes of sufficient force and validity to *limit and bind* the crown, and the descent, limitation, inheritance and *government* thereof" is founded on the principles of liberty and the British constitution: And he that would palm the doctrine of unlimited passive obedience and non-resistance upon mankind, and thereby or by any other means serve the cause of the Pretender, is not only a fool and a knave, but a rebel against common sense, as well as the laws of God, of Nature, and his Country.

—I also lay it down as one of the first principles from whence I intend to deduce the civil rights of the British colonies, that all of them are subject to, and dependent on Great-Britain; and that therefore as over subordinate governments, the parliament of Great-Britain has an undoubted power and lawful authority to make acts for the general good, that by naming them, shall and ought to be equally binding, as upon the subjects of Great-Britain within the realm. This principle, I presume will be readily granted on the other side of the Atlantic. It has been practiced upon for twenty years to my knowledge, in the province of the *Massachusetts-Bay*; and I have ever received it, that it has been so from the beginning, in this and the sister provinces, thro' the continent.[16]

I am aware, some will think it is time for me to retreat, after having expressed the power of the British parliament in quite so strong terms. But 'tis from and under this very power and its acts, and from the common law, that the political and civil rights of the Colonists are derived: And upon those grand pillars of liberty shall my defence be rested. At present therefore, the reader may suppose, that there is not one provincial charter on the continent; he may, if he pleases, imagine all taken away, without fault, without forfeiture, without tryal or notice. All this really happened to some of them in the last century. I would have the reader carry his imagination still further, and suppose a time may come, when instead of a process at common law, the parliament shall give a decisive blow to every charter in America, and declare them all void. Nay it shall also be granted, that 'tis barely possible, the time may come, when the real interest of the whole may require an act of parliament to annihilate all those charters. What could follow from all this, that would shake one of the essential, natural, civil or religious rights of the Colonists? Nothing. They would be men, citizens and british subjects after all. No act of parliament can deprive them of the liberties of such, unless any will contend that an act of parliament can make slaves not only of one, but of two millions of the commonwealth. And if so, why not of the whole? I freely own, that I can find nothing in the laws of my country, that would justify the parliament in making one slave, nor did they ever professedly undertake to make one.

---

16 This however was formally declared as to Ireland, but so lately as the reign of G. 1. Upon the old principles of conquest the Irish could not have so much to say for an exemption, as the unconquered Colonists.

Two or three innocent colony charters have been threatned with destruction an hundred and forty years past. I wish the present enemies of those harmless charters would reflect a moment, and be convinced that an act of parliament that should demolish those bugbears to the foes of liberty, would not reduce the Colonists to a state of absolute slavery. The worst enemies of the charter governments are by no means to be found in England. 'Tis a piece of justice due to Great-Britain to own, they are and have ever been natives of or residents in the colonies. A set of men in America, without honour or love to their country, have been long grasping at powers, which they think unattainable while these charters stand in the way. But they will meet with insurmountable obstacles to their project for enslaving the British colonies, should those, arising from provincial charters be removed. It would indeed seem very hard and severe, for those of the colonists, who have charters, with peculiar priviledges, to loose them. They were given to their ancestors, in consideration of their sufferings and merit, in discovering and settling America. Our fore-fathers were soon worn away in the toils of hard labour on their little plantations, and in war with the Savages. They thought they were earning a sure inheritance for their posterity. Could they imagine it would ever be tho't just to deprive them or theirs of their charter priviledges! Should this ever be the case, there are, thank God, natural, inherent and inseperable rights as men, and as citizens, that would remain after the so much wished for catastrophe, and which, whatever became of charters, can never be abolished *de jure*, if *de facto*, till the general conflagration.[17] Our rights as men and free born British subjects, give all the Colonists enough to make them very happy in comparison with the subjects of any other prince in the world.

Every British subject born on the continent of America, or in any other of the British dominions, is by the law of God and nature, by the common law, and by act of parliament, (exclusive of all charters from the Crown) entitled to all the natural, essential, inherent and inseparable rights of our fellow subjects in Great Britain. Among those rights are the following, which it is humbly conceived no man or body of men, not excepting the parliament, justly equitably and consistently with their own rights and the constitution, can take away.

1st. *That the supreme and subordinate powers of the legislation should be free and sacred in the hands where the community have once rightfully placed them.*

---

17   The fine defence of the provincial charters of Jeremy Dummer, Esq.; the late very able and learned agent for the province of the Massachusetts Bay, makes it needless to go into a particular consideration of charter priviledges. That piece is unanswerable, but by power and might, and other arguments of that kind.

2dly. *The supreme national legislative cannot be altered justly 'till the commonwealth is dissolved, nor a subordinate legislative taken away without forfeiture or other good cause.* Nor then can the subjects in the subordinate government be reduced to a state of slavery, and subject to the despotic rule of others. A state has no right to make slaves of the conquered. Even when the subordinate right of legislature is forfeited, and so declared, this cannot affect the natural persons either of those who were invested with it, or the inhabitants,[18] so far as to deprive them of the rights of subjects and of men—The colonists will have an equitable right notwithstanding any such forfeiture of charter, to be represented in Parliament, or to have some new subordinate legislature among themselves. It would be best if they had both. Deprived however of their common rights as subjects, they cannot lawfully be, while they remain such. A representation in Parliament from the several Colonies, since they are become so large and numerous, as to be called on not to maintain provincial government, civil and military among themselves, for this they have chearfully done, but to contribute towards the support of a national standing army, by reason of the heavy national debt, when they themselves owe a large one, contracted in the common cause, can't be tho't an unreasonable thing, nor if asked, could it be called an immodest request. *Qui sentis commodum sentire debet et onus,* has been tho't a maxim of equity. But that a man should bear a burthen for other people, as well as himself, without a return, never long found a place in any law-book or decrees, but those of the most despotic princes. Besides the equity of an American representation in parliament, a thousand advantages would result from it. It would be the most effectual means of giving those of both countries a thorough knowledge of each others interests; as well as that of the whole, which are inseparable.

Were this representation allowed; instead of the scandalous memorials and depositions that have been sometimes, in days of old, privately cooked up in an inquisitorial manner, by persons of bad minds and wicked views, and sent from America to the several boards, persons of the first reputation among their countrymen, might be on the spot, from the several colonies, truly to represent them. Future ministers need not, like some of their predecessors, have recourse for information in American affairs, to every vagabond stroller, that has run or rid post thro' America, from his creditors, or to people of no kind of reputation from the colonies; some of whom, at the time of administring their sage advice, have been as ignorant of the state of the country, as of the regions in Jupiter and Saturn.

---

18 See Magna Charta, the Bill of Rights. 3 Mod. 152 2. Salkeld 411. Vaughan 300.

No representation of the Colonies in parliament alone, would however be equivalent to a subordinate legislative among themselves; nor so well answer the ends of increasing their prosperity and the commerce of Great-Britain. It would be impossible for the parliament to judge so well, of their abilities to bear taxes, impositions on trade, and other duties and burthens, or of the local laws that might be really needful, as a legislative here.

3dly. *No legislative, supreme or subordinate, has a right to make itself arbitrary.*

It would be a most manifest contradiction, for a free legislative, like that of Great-Britain, to make itself arbitrary.

4thly. *The supreme legislative cannot justly assume a power of ruling by extempore arbitrary decrees, but is bound to dispense justice by known settled rules, and by duly authorized independant judges.*

5thly. *The supreme power cannot take from any man any part of his property, without his consent in person, or by representation.*

6thly. *The legislature cannot transfer the power of making laws to any other hands.*

These are their bounds, which by God and nature are fixed, hitherto have they a right to come, and no further.

1. *To govern by stated laws.*
2. *Those laws should have no other end ultimately, but the good of the people.*
3. *Taxes are not to be laid on the people, but by their consent in person, or by deputation.*
4. *Their whole power is not transferable.*[19]

These are the first principles of law and justice, and the great barriers of a free state, and of the British constitution in particular. I ask, I want no more —Now let it be shown how 'tis reconcileable with these principles, or to many other fundamental maxims of the British constitution, as well as the natural and civil rights, which by the laws of their country, all British subjects are intitled to, as their best inheritance and birth-right, that all the northern colonies, who are without one representative in the house of Commons, should be taxed by the British parliament.

That the colonists, black and white, born here, are free born British subjects, and entitled to all the essential civil rights of such, is a truth not only manifest from the provincial charters, from the principles of the common law, and acts of parliament; but from the British constitution, which was reestablished at the revolution, with a professed design to lecture the liberties of all the subjects to all generations.[20]

---

19   See Locke on Government. B. II. C. xi.
20   See the convention, and acts confirming it.

In the 12 and 13 of Wm. cited above, the liberties of the subject are spoken of as their best birth-rights—No one ever dreamt, surely, that these liberties were confined to the realm. At that rate, no British subjects in the dominions could, without a manifest contradiction, be declared entitled to all the privileges of subjects born within the realm, to all intents and purposes, which are rightly given foreigners, by parliament, after residing seven years. These expressions of parliament, as well as of the charters, must be vain and empty sounds, unless we are allowed the essential rights of our fellow-subjects in Great-Britain.

Now can there be any liberty, where property is taken away without consent? Can it with any colour of truth, justice or equity, be affirmed, that the northern colonies are represented in parliament? Has this whole continent of near three thousand miles in length, and in which and his other American dominions, his Majesty has, or very soon will have, some millions of as good, loyal and useful subjects, white and black, as any in the three kingdoms, the election of one member of the house of commons?

Is there the least difference, as to the consent of the Colonists, whether taxes and impositions are laid on their trade, and other property, by the crown alone, or by the parliament? As it is agreed on all hands, the Crown alone cannot impost them. We should be justifiable in refusing to pay them, but must and ought to yield obedience to an act of parliament, tho' erroneous, 'till repealed.

I can see no reason to doubt, but that the imposition of taxes, whether on trade, or on land, or houses, or ships, on real or personal, fixed or floating property, in the colonies, is absolutely irreconcileable with the rights of the Colonists, as British subjects, and as men. I say men, for in a state of nature, no man can take my property from me, without my consent: If he does, he deprives me of my liberty, and makes me a slave. If such a proceeding is a breach of the law of nature, no law of society can make it just—The very act of taxing, exercised over those who are not represented, appears to me to be depriving them of one of their most essential rights, as freemen; and if continued, seems to be in effect an entire disfranchisement of every civil right. For what one civil right is worth a rush, after a man's property is subject to be taken from him at pleasure, without his consent? If a man is not his *own assessor* in person, or by deputy, his liberty is gone, or lays intirely at the mercy of others.

I think I have heard it said, that when the Dutch are asked why they enslave their colonies, their answer is, that the liberty of Dutchmen is confined to Holland; and that it was never intended for Provincials in America, or anywhere else. A sentiment this, very worthy of modern Dutchmen; but if their brave and worthy ancestors had entertained such narrow ideas of liberty, seven poor and distressed provinces would never have asserted their rights against the whole Spanish monarchy, of which the present is but a shadow. It is to be hoped, none of our fellow subjects of Britain, great or small, have borrowed this Dutch maxim of plantation politics; if they have, they had better return it from whence it came; indeed they had. Modern Dutch or French maxims of state, never will suit with a British constitution. It is a maxim, that the King can do no wrong; and every good subject is bound to believe his King is not inclined to do any. We are blessed with a prince who has given abundant demonstrations, that in all his actions, he studies the good of his people, and the true glory of his crown, which are inseparable. It would therefore, be the highest degree of impudence and disloyalty to imagine that the King, at the head of his parliament, could have any, but the most pure and perfect intentions of justice, goodness and truth, that human nature is capable of. All this I say and believe of the King and parliament, in all their acts; even in that which so nearly affects the interest of the colonists; and that a most perfect and ready obedience is to be yielded to it, while it remains in force. I will go further, and readily admit, that the intention of the ministry was not only to promote the public good, by this act; but that Mr. Chancellor of the Exchequer had therein a particular view to the "ease, the quiet, and the good will of the Colonies," he having made this declaration more than once. Yet I hold that 'tis possible he may have erred in his kind intentions towards the Colonies, and taken away our fish and given us a stone. With regard to the parliament, as infallability belongs not to mortals, 'tis possible *they* may have been misinformed and deceived. The power of parliament is uncontroulable, but by themselves, and we must obey. They only can repeal their own acts. There would be an end of all government, if one or a number of subjects or subordinate provinces should take upon them so far to judge of the justice of an act of parliament, as to refuse obedience to it. If there was nothing else to restrain such a step, prudence ought to do it, for forceably resisting the parliament and the King's laws, is high treason. Therefore let the parliament lay what burthens they please on us, we must, it is our duty to submit and patiently bear them, till they will be pleased to relieve us. And tis to be presumed, the wisdom and justice of that august assembly, always will afford us relief by repealing such acts, as through mistake, or other human infirmities, have been suffered to pass, if they can be convinced that their proceedings are not constitutional, or not for the common good.

The parliament may be deceived, they may have been misinformed of facts, and the colonies may in many respects be misrepresented to the King, his parliament, and his ministry. In some instances, I am well assured the colonies have been very strangely misrepresented in England. I have now before me a pamphlet, called the "administration of the colonies," said to be written by a gentleman who formerly commanded in chief in one of them. I suppose this book was designed for public information and use. There are in it many good regulations proposed, which no power can enforce but the parliament. From all which I infer, that if our hands are tied by the passing of an act of parliament, our mouths are not stoped, provided we speak of that transcendent body with decency, as I have endeavoured always to do; and should any thing have escaped me, or hereafter fall from my pen, that bears the least aspect but that of obedience, duty and loyalty to the King & parliament, and the highest respect for the ministry, the candid will impute it to the agony of my heart, rather than to the pravity of my will. If I have one ambitious wish, 'tis to see Great-Britain at the head of the world, and to see my King, under God, the father of mankind. I pretend neither to the spirit of prophecy, nor any uncommon skill in predicting a Crisis, much less to tell when it begins to be *"nascent"* or is fairly midwiv'd into the world. But if I were to fix a meaning to the two first paragraphs of the *administrations of the colonies*, tho' I do not collect it from them, I should say the world was at the eve of the highest scene of earthly power and grandeur that has been ever yet displayed to the view of mankind. The cards are shuffling fast thro' all Europe. Who will win the prize is with God. This however I know *detur digniori*. The next universal monarchy will be favourable to the human race, for it must be founded on the principles of equity, moderation and justice. No country has been more distinguished for these principles than Great-Britain, since the revolution. I take it, every subject has a right to give his sentiments to the public, of the utility or inutility of any act whatsoever, even after it is passed, as well as while it is pending.—The equity and justice of a bill may be questioned, with per-fect submission to the legislature. Reasons may be given, why an act ought to be repeal'd, & yet obedience must be yielded to it till that repeal takes place. If the reasons that can be given against an act, are such as plainly demonstrate that it is against *natural* equity, the executive courts will adjudge such acts void. It may be questioned by some, tho' I make no doubt of it, whether they are not obliged by their oaths to adjudge such acts void. If there is not a right of private judgement to be exercised, so far at least as to petition for a repeal, or to determine the expediency of risking a trial at law, the parliament might make itself arbitrary, which it is conceived it can not by the constitution.—I think every man has a right to examine as freely into the origin, spring and foundation of every power and measure in a commonwealth, as into a piece of curious machinery, or a remarkable phenomenon in nature; and that it ought to give no more offence to say, the parliament have erred, or are mistaken, in a matter of fact, or of right, than to say it of a private man, if it is true of both. If the assertion can be proved with regard to either, it is a kindness done them to show them the truth. With regard to the public, it is the duty of every good citizen to point out what he thinks erroneous in the commonwealth.

I have waited years in hopes to see some one friend of the colonies pleading in publick for them. I have waited in vain. One priviledge is taken away after another, and where we shall be landed, God knows, and I trust will protect and provide for us even should we be driven and persecuted into a more western wilderness, on the score of liberty, civil and religious, as many of our ancestors were, to these once inhospitable shores of America. I had formed great expectations from a gentleman, who published his first volume in quarto on the rights of the colonies two years since; but, as he foresaw, the state of his health and affairs have prevented his further progress. The misfortune is, gentlemen in America, the best qualified in every respect to state the rights of the colonists, have reasons that prevent them from engaging: Some of them have good ones. There are many infinitely better able to serve this cause than I pretend to be; but from indolence, from timidity, or by necessary engagements, they are prevented. There has been a most profound, and I think shameful silence, till it seems almost too late to assert our indisputable rights as men and as citizens. What must posterity think of us. The trade of the whole continent taxed by parliament, stamps and other internal duties and taxes as they are called, talked of, and not one petition to the King and Parliament for relief.

I cannot but observe here, that if the parliament have an equitable right to tax our trade, 'tis indisputable that they have as good an one to tax the lands, and every thing else. The taxing trade furnishes one reason why the other should be taxed, or else the burdens of the province will be unequally born, upon a supposition that a tax on trade is not a tax on the whole. But take it either way, there is no foundation for the distinction some make in England, between an internal and an external tax on the colonies. By the first is meant a tax on trade, by the latter a tax on land, and the things on it. A tax on trade is either a tax of every man in the province, or 'tis not. If 'tis not a tax on the whole, 'tis unequal and unjust, that a heavy burden should be laid on the trade of the colonies, to maintain an army of soldiers, custom-house officers, and fleets of guard-ships; all which, the incomes of both trade and land would not furnish means to support so lately as the last war, when all was at stake, and the colonies were reimbursed in part by parliament. How can it be supposed that all of a sudden the trade of the colonies alone can bear all this terrible burden. The late acquisitions in America, as glorious as they have been, and as beneficial as they are to Great-Britain, are only a security to these colonies against the ravages of the French and Indians. Our trade upon the whole is not, I believe, benefited by them one groat. All the time the French Islands were in our hands, the fine sugars, &c. were all shipped home. None as I have been informed were allowed to be bro't to the colonies. They were too delicious a morsel for a North American palate. If it be said that a tax on the trade of the colonies is an equal and just tax on the whole of the inhabitants: What then becomes of the notable distinction between external and internal taxes? Why may not the parliament lay stamps, land taxes, establish tythes to the church of England, and so indefinitely. I know of no bounds. I do not mention the tythes out of any disrespect to the church of England, which I esteem by far the best *national* church, and to have had as ornaments of it many of the greatest and best men in the world. But to those colonies who in general dissent from a principle of conscience, it would seem a little hard to pay towards the support of a worship, whose modes they cannot conform to.

If an army must be kept in America, at the expence of the colonies, it would not seem quite so hard if after the parliament had determined the sum to be raised, and apportioned it, to have allowed each colony to assess its quota, and raise it as easily to themselves as might be. But to have the whole levied and collected without our consent is extraordinary. 'Tis allowed even to *tributaries*, and those laid under *military* contribution, to assess and collect the sums demanded. The case of the provinces is certainly likely to be the hardest that can be instanced in story. Will it not equal any thing but down right military execution? Was there ever a tribute imposed even on the conquered? A fleet, an army of soldiers, and another of taxgatherers kept up, and not a single office either for securing or collecting the duty in the gift of the tributary state.

I am aware it will be objected, that the parliament of *England*, and of Great Britain, since the union, have from early days to this time, made acts to bind if not to tax Ireland: I answer, Ireland is a *conquered* country. I do not, however, lay so much stress on this; for it is my opinion, that a *conquered* country has, upon submission and good behaviour, the same right to be free, under a conqueror, as the rest of his subjects. But the old notion of the *right of conquest*, has been, in most nations, the cause of many severities and heinous breaches of the law of nature: If any such have taken place with regard to

Ireland, they should form no precedent for the colonies. The subordination and dependency of *Ireland* to Great Britain, is expresly declared by act of parliament, in the reign of G. 1st. The subordination of the *Colonies* to Great Britain, never was doubted, by a Lawyer, if at all; unless perhaps by the author of the administration of the colonies: He indeed seems to make a moot point of it, whether the colony legislative power is as independent "as the legislative Great Britain holds by its constitution, and under the great charter." —The *people* hold under the great charter, as 'tis vulgarly expressed from our law-books: But that the King and parliament should be said to hold under *Magna Charta*, is as new to me, as it is to question whether the colonies are *subordinate* to Great Britain. The provincial legislative is unquestionably subordinate to that of Great Britain. I shall endeavour more fully to explain the nature of that subordination, which has puzzled so many in their enquiries. It is often very difficult for great lovers of power and great lovers of liberty, neither of whom may have been used to the study of law, in any of its branches, to see the difference between subordination, absolute slavery and subjection, on one side; and liberty, independence and licenciousness, on the other. We should endeavour to find the middle road, and confine ourselves to it. The laws, the proceedings of parliament, and the decisions of the judges, relating to *Ireland*, will reflect light on this subject, rendered intricate only by art.

"Ireland being of itself a distinct dominion, and no part of the kingdom of England (as directly appeareth by many authorities in Calvin's case) was to have Parliaments holden there as in England."

4 Inst. 349.

Why should not the colonies have, why are they not entitled to their assemblies, or parliaments, at least, as well as a conquered dominion?

"Wales, after the conquest of it, by Edward, the first, was annexed to England, jure proprietatis, 12 Ed. 1. by the statute of Rutland only, and after, more really by 27 H. 8. and 34, but at first received laws from England, as Ireland did; but writs proceeded not out of the English chancery, but they had a Chancery of their own, as Ireland hath; was not bound by the laws of England, unnamed until 27 H. 8. no more than Ireland is.

Ireland in nothing differs from it, but having a parliament *gratia Regis* (i.e. upon the old notion of conquest) subject (truly however) to the parliament of England. None doubts Ireland as much conquered as it; *and as much subject to the parliament of England, if it please.*"

Vaughan. 300.

A very strong argument arises from this authority, in favour of the *unconquered* plantations. If since Wales was annexed to England, they have had a representation in parliament, as they have to this day; and if the parliament of England does not tax *Ireland*, can it be right they should tax *us*, who have never been *conquered*, but came from England to *colonize*, and have always remained *good subjects* to this day?

I cannot find any instance of a tax laid by the English parliament on *Ireland*. "Sometimes the King of England called his Nobles of Ireland, to come to his parliament of England, &c. and by special words, the parliament of England may bind the subjects of Ireland"—3 Inst. 350—.

The following makes it clear to me, the parliament of Great Britain do not tax *Ireland*, "The parliament of Ireland having been prorogued to the month of August *next, before they had provided for the maintenance of the government in that kingdom, a project* was set on foot here to supply that defect, by retrenching the drawbacks upon goods exported thither from England. According to this scheme, the 22d, the house in a grand committee, considered the present laws with respect to drawbacks upon tobaccoes, muslins, and East India silks, carried to Ireland; and came to two resolutions, which were reported the next day, and with an amendment to one of them agreed to by the house, as follows, Viz. 1. That three pence pr pound, part of the drawback on tobacco to be exported from Great Britain for Ireland, be taken off.

2. That the said diminution of the drawback do take effect upon all tobacco exported for Ireland, after the 24 of March 1713, and continue until the additional duty of three pence half penny per pound upon tobacco in Ireland, expiring on the said 24th of March, be *regranted*: And ordered a bill to be brought in, upon the said resolutions."

Proceedings of House of Commons, Vol. 5. 72.

This was constitutional; there is an infinite difference between taking off British drawbacks, and imposing Irish or other Provincial duties.

"Ireland is considered as a provincial government, subordinate to, but no part of the Realm of England," Mich. 11. G. 2. in case of Otway and Ramsay—"Acts of parliament made here, (i.e. in England) extend not to Ireland, unless particularly named; much less judgments obtained in the courts here; nor is it possible they should, because we have no officers to carry them into execution there." ib.

The first part seems to be applicable to the plantations in general, the latter is not; for by reason of charter reservations and particular acts of parliament, some judgments in England may be executed here, as final judgments, before his Majesty in council on a plantation appeal, and so from the admiralty.

It seems to have been disputed in Ireland, so lately as the 6 Geo. 1. Whether any act of the British parliament bound Ireland; or at least it was apprehended, that the undoubted right of the British parliament to bind Ireland, was in danger of being shaken: This, I presume, occasioned the act of that year, which declares, that "the kingdom of Ireland ought to be subordinate unto and dependent upon the Imperial Crown of Great Britain, as being inseparably united thereto. And the King's Majesty, with the consent of the lords and commons of Great Britain in parliament, hath power to make laws to bind the people of Ireland."—This parliamentary power must have some bounds, even as to *Ireland*, as well as the colonies who are admitted to be subordinate *ab initio* to Great Britain; not as *conquered*, but as *emigrant* subjects. If this act should be said to be a declaration not only of the general, but of the universal power of parliament, and that they may tax Ireland, I ask, Why it has never been done? If it had been done a thousand times, it would be a contradiction to the principles of a free government; and what is worse, destroy all subordination consistent with *freedom*, and reduce the people to *slavery*.

To say the parliament is absolute and arbitrary, is a contradiction. The parliament cannot make 2 and 2, 5; Omnipotency cannot do it. The supreme power in a state, is *jus dicere* only;—*jus dare*, strictly speaking, belongs alone to God. Parliaments are in all cases to *declare* what is parliament that makes it so: There must be in every instance, a higher authority, viz. GOD. Should an act of parliament be against any of *his* natural laws, which are *immutably* true, their declaration would be contrary to eternal truth, equity and justice, and consequently void: and so it would be adjudged by the parliament itself, when convinced of their mistake. Upon this great principle, parliaments repeal such acts, as soon as they find they have been mistaken, in having declared them to be for the public good, when in fact they were not so. When such mistake is evident and palpable, as in the instances in the appendix, the judges of the executive courts have declared the act "of a whole parliament void." See here the grandeur of the British constitution! See the wisdom of our ancestors! The supreme *legislative*, and the supreme *executive*, are a perpetual check and balance to each other. If the supreme executive errs, it is informed by the supreme legislative in parliament: If the supreme legislative errs, it is informed by the supreme executive in the King's courts of law. —Here, the King appears, as represented by his judges, in the highest lustre and majesty, as supreme executor of the commonwealth; and he never shines brighter, but on his Throne, at the head of the supreme legislative. This is government! This, is a constitution! to preserve which, either from foreign or domestic foes, has cost oceans of blood and treasure in every age; and the blood and the treasure have upon the whole been well spent. British America, hath been bleeding in this cause from its settlement: We have spent all we could raise, and more; for notwithstanding the parliamentary reimbursement of part, we still remain much in debt. The province of the *Massachusetts*, I believe, has expended more men and money in war since the year 1620, when a few families first landed at Plymouth, in proportion to their ability, than the three Kingdoms together. The same, I believe, may be truly affirmed, of many of the other colonies; tho' the *Massachusetts* has undoubtedly had the heaviest burthen. This may be thought incredible: but materials are collecting; and tho' some are lost, enough may remain, to demonstrate it to the world. I have reason to hope at least, that the public will soon see such proofs exhibited, as will show, that I do not speak quite at random.

Why then is it thought so heinous by the author of the administration of the colonies, and others, that the colonists should aspire after "a one whole legislative power" not independent of, but subordinate to the laws and parliament of Great-Britain? . . . It is a mistake in this author, to bring so heavy a charge as *high treason* against some of the colonists, which he does in effect in this place,[21] by representing them as "claiming in fact or indeed, the same full free independent unrestrained power and legislative will, in their several corporations, and under the King's commission, and their respective charters, as the government and legislature of Great-Britain holds by its constitution and under the great charter." No such claim was ever tho't of by any of the colonists. They are all better men and better subjects; and many of them too well versed in the laws of nature and nations, and the law and constitution of Great-Britain, to think they have a right to more than a *provincial subordinate legislative*. All power is of GOD. Next and only subordinate to him, in the present state of the well-formed, beautifully constructed British monarchy, standing where I hope it ever will stand, for the pillars are fixed in judgment, righteousness and truth, is the King and Parliament. Under these, it seems easy to conceive subordinate powers in gradation, till we descend to the legislative of a town council, or even a private social club. These have each "a one whole legislative" subordinate, which, when it don't conteract the laws of any of its superiors, is to be indulged. Even when the laws of subordination are transgressed, the superior does not destroy the subordinate, but will negative its acts, as it may in all cases when disapproved. This right of negative is essential, and may be inforced: But in no case are the essential rights of the subjects, inhabiting the subordinate dominions, to be destroyed. This would put it in the power of the superior to reduce the inferior to a state of

---

21   Page 39 of the administration.

slavery; which cannot be rightfully done, even with *conquered* enemies and *rebels*. After satisfaction and security is obtained of the former, and examples are made of so many of the latter, as the ends of government require, the rest are to be restored to all the essential rights of men and of citizens. This is the great law of nature: and agreeable to this law, is the constant practice of all good and mild governments. This lenity and humanity has no where been carried further than in Great Britain. The Colonies have been so remarkable for loyalty, that there never has been any instance of rebellion or treason in them. This loyalty is in very handsome terms acknowledged by the author of the administration of the colonies. "It has been often suggested that care should be taken in the administration of the plantations, lest, in some future time, these colonies should become independent of the mother country. But perhaps it may be proper on this occasion, and, it is justice to say it, that if, by becoming independent, is meant a revolt, nothing is further from their nature, their interest, their thoughts. If a defection from the *alliance* of the mother country be suggested, it ought to be, and can be truly said, that their spirit abhors the sense of such; their attachment to the protestant succession in the house of Hanover, will ever stand unshaken; and nothing can eradicate from their hearts their natural and almost mechanical, affection to Great Britain, which they conceive under no other sense nor call by any other name than that of *home*. Any such suggestion, therefore, is a false and unjust aspersion on their principles and affections; and can arise from nothing but an intire ignorance of their circumstances."[22] After all this loyalty, it is a little hard to be charged with claiming, and represented as aspiring after, independency. The inconsistency of this I leave. We have said that the loyalty of the colonies has never been suspected; this must be restricted to a just suspicion. For it seems there have long been groundless suspicions of us in the minds of individuals. And there have always been those who have endeavoured to magnify these chimerical fears. I find Mr. Dummer complaining of this many years since.

"There is, says he, one thing more I have heard often urged against the charter colonies, and indeed tis what one meets with from people of all conditions and qualities, tho' with due respect to their better judgments, I can see neither reason nor colour for it. 'Tis said that their increasing numbers and wealth, joined to their great distance from Britain, will give them an opportunity, in the course of some years, to throw off their dependence on the nation, and declare themselves a free state, if not curb'd in time, by being made *entirely subject to the crown*."[23]

22   Administration, p. 25, 26.
23   Defence. 60.

This jealousy has been so long talked of, that many seems to believe it really well grounded. Not that there is danger of a "revolt," even in the opinion of the *author of the administration*, but that the colonists will by fraud or force avail themselves, in "fact or in deed," of an independent legislature. This, I think, would be a revolting with a vengeance. What higher revolt can there be, than for a province to assume the right of an independent legislative, or state? I must therefore think this a greater aspersion on the Colonists, than to charge them with a design to revolt, in the sense in which the Gentleman allows they have been abused: It is a more artful and dangerous way of attacking our liberties, than to charge us with being in open rebellion. That could be confuted instantly: but this seeming indirect way of charging the colonies, with a desire of throwing off their dependency, requires more pains to confute it than the other, therefore it has been recurred to. The truth is, Gentlemen have had departments in America, the functions of which they have not been fortunate in executing. The people have by these means been rendered uneasy, at bad Provincial measures. They have been represented as factious, seditious, and inclined to democracy whenever they have refused passive obedience to provincial mandates, as arbitrary as those of a Turkish Bashaw: I say, Provincial mandates; for to the King and Parliament they have been ever submissive and obedient.

These representations of us, many of the good people of England swallow with as much ease, as they would a bottle-bubble, or any other story of a cock and a bull; and the worst of it is, among some of the most credulous, have been found Stars and Garters. However, they may all rest assured, the Colonists, who do not pretend to understand themselves so well as the people of England; tho' the author of the Administration makes them the fine compliment, to say, they "know their business much better," yet, will never think of independency. Were they inclined to it, they know the blood and the treasure it would cost, if ever effected; and when done, it would be a thousand to one if their liberties did not fall a sacrifice to the victor.

We all think ourselves happy under Great-Britain. We love, esteem and reverence our mother country, and adore our King. And could the choice of independency be offered the colonies, or subjection to Great-Britain upon any terms above absolute slavery, I am convinced they would accept the latter. The ministry, in all future generations may rely on it, that British America will never prove undutiful, till driven to it, as the last fatal resort against ministerial oppression, which will make the wisest mad, and the weakest strong.

These colonies are and always have been, "entirely subject to the crown," in the legal sense of the terms. But if any politician of "[24]tampering activity, of wrongheaded inexperience, misted to be meddling," means, by "curbing the colonies in time," and by "being made entirely subject to the crown;" that this subjection should be absolute, and confined to the crown, he had better have suppressed his wishes. This never will nor can be done, without making the colonists vassals of the crown. Subjects they are; their lands they hold of the crown, by common soccage, the freest feudal tennure, by which any hold their lands in England, or any where else. Would these gentlemen carry us back to the state of the Goths and Vandals, and revive all the military tenures and bondage which our fore-fathers could not bear? It may be worth nothing here, that few if any instances can be given, where colonies have been disposed to forsake or disobey a tender mother: But history is full of examples, that armies, stationed as guards over provinces, have seized the prey for their general, and given him a crown at the expence of his master. Are all ambitious generals dead? Will no more rise up hereafter? The danger of a standing army in remote provinces is much greater to the metropolis, than at home. Rome found the truth of this assertion, in her Sylla's, her Pompey's and Caesars; but she found it too late: Eighteen hundred years have roll'd away since her ruin. A continuation of the same liberties that have been enjoyed by the colonists since the revolution, and the same moderation of government exercised towards them, will bind them in perpetual lawful and willing subjection, obedience and love to Great-Britain: She and her colonies will both prosper and flourish: The monarchy will remain in sound health and full vigor at that blessed period, when the proud arbitrary tyrants of the continent shall either unite in the deliverance of the human race, or resign their crowns. Rescued, human nature must and will be, from the general slavery that has so long triumphed over the species. Great-Britain has done much towards it: What a Glory will it be for her to complete the work throughout the world!

The author of the Administration (page 54) "describes" the defects of the "provincial courts," by a "very description," the first trait of which is, "The ignorance of the judges." Whether the description, or the description of the description, are *verily* true, either as applied by Lord Hale, or the Administrator, is left to the reader. I only ask, who makes the judges in the provinces? I know of but two colonies, viz. Connecticut and Rhode-Island, where they are chosen by the people. In all other colonies, they are either immediately appointed by the crown, or by his Majesty's governor, with the advice of what the Administrator calls, the "governor's council of state." And if they are in

---

24 Administration. 34.

general such ignorant creatures, as the Administrator describes them, 'tis the misfortune, not the fault, of the people, in the colonies. However, I believe, justice in general, is as well administered in the colonies, as it will be when every thing is devolved upon a court of admiralty, general or provincial. The following is very remarkable. "In those popular governments, and where every executive officer is under a dependence for a temporary, wretched, and I had almost said arbitrary support, on the deputies of the people."[25]

Why is the temporary support found fault with? Would it be wise to give a governor a salary for a longer time than his political life? As this is quite as uncertain as his natural life, it has been granted annually. So every governor has the chance of one year's salary after he is dead. All the King's officers, are not even in the charter provinces "dependent on the people" for support. The judges of the admiralty, those mirrors of justice, to be trusted, when none of the common law courts are, have all their commissions from home. These, besides other fees, have so much per cent on all they condemn, be it right or wrong, *and this by act of parliament*. Yet so great is their integrity, that it never was suspected that 50 per cent, if allowed, would have any influence on their decrees.

Custom-house officers universally, and Naval-officers, in all but two or three of the colonies, are, I believe, appointed directly from home, or by instruction to the Governor: and take just what they please, for any restraint they are under by the provincial acts. But on whom should a Governor depend for his honorable support, but the people? Is not the King fed from the field, and from the labor of his people? Does not his Majesty himself receive his aids from the free grant of his parliament? Do not all these originate in the house of commons? Did the house of Lords ever originate a grant? Do not our law books inform us that the Lords only assent or dissent, but never so much as propose an amendment, on a money bill? The King can take no more than the Parliament will give him, and yet some of his Governors have tho't it an insufferable hardship, that they could not take what they pleased. To take leave of the administrator, there are in his book some good hints, but a multiplicity of mistakes in fact, and errors in matters of right, which I have not time to mention particularly.

Ireland is a conquered kingdom; and yet have tho't they received very hard measure in some of the prohibitions and restrictions of their trade. But were the colonies ever conquered? Have they not been subjects and obedient, and loyal from their settlement? Were not the settlements made under the British laws and constitution? But if the colonies were all to be considered

---

25   Administ. 56.

as conquered, they are entitled to the essential rights of men and citizens. And therefore admitting the right of prohibition, in its utmost extent and latitude; a right of taxation can never be infer'd from that. It may be for the good of the whole, that a certain commodity should be prohibited: But this power should be exercised, with great *moderation* and impartiality, over dominions, which are not *represented*, in the national parliament. I had however rather see this carried with a high hand, to the utmost rigor, than have a tax of one shilling taken from me without my consent. A people may be very happy; free and easy among themselves, without a particular branch of foreign trade: I am sure these colonies have the natural means of every manufacture in *Europe*, and some that are out of their power to make or produce. It will scarcely be believed a hundred years hence, that the American manufactures could have been brought to such perfection, as they will then probably be in, if the present measures are pushed. One single act of parliament, we find has set people a thinking, in six months, more than they had done in their whole lives before. It should be remembered, that the most famous and flourishing manufactures, of wool, in *France*, were begun by *Lewis* 14, not an hundred years ago; and they now bid fair to rival the *English*, in every port abroad. All the manufactures that Great-Britain could make, would be consumed in America, and in her own plantations, if put on a right footing; for which a greater profit in return would be made, than she will ever see again for woollen sent to any part of Europe.

But tho' it be allow'd, that liberty may be enjoy'd in a comfortable measure, where *prohibitions* are laid on the trade of a kingdom or province; yet if *taxes* are laid on either, *without* consent, they cannot be said to be free. This barrier of liberty being once broken down, all is lost. If a shilling in the pound may be taken from me against my will, why may not twenty shillings; and if so, why not my liberty or my life? Merchants were always *particularly* favor'd by the common law—"All merchants, except enemies, may safely come into *England*, with their goods and merchandize"—2 Inst. 28.—And why not as well to the *plantations*? Are they not entitled to all the British privileges? No. they must be confined in their imports and exports to the good of the metropolis. Very well, we have submitted to this. The act of navigation is a good act, so are all that exclude foreign manufactures from the plantations, and every honest man will readily subscribe to them. Moreover, "Merchant strangers, are also to come into the realm and depart at pleasure; and they are to be friendly entertained." 2 Ri. C. 1. But to promote the manufactures of *England*, 'tis tho't best to shut up the *colonies* in a manner from all the world. Right as to Europe: But for God's sake, must we have no trade with other colonies?

In some cases the trade betwen *British* colony and colony is prohibited, as in wool, &c. Granting all this to be right, is it not enough? No. duties and taxes must be paid without any *consent or representation* in parliament. The common law, that inestimable privilege of a jury, is also taken away in all trials in the colonies, relating to the revenue, if the informers have a mind to go the admiralty; as they ever have done, and ever will do, for very obvious reasons. "It has ever been boasted, says Mr. Dummer in his defence of the charters, as the peculiar privilege of an Englishman, and the security of his property, to be tryed by his country, and the laws of the land: Whereas this admiralty method deprives him of both, as it puts his estate in the disposal of a single person, and makes the civil law the rule of judgment; which tho' it may not properly be called foreign being the law of nations, yet 'tis what he has not consented to himself, nor his representative for him. A jurisdiction therefore so founded, ought not to extend beyond what *necessity* requires"—"If some bounds are not set to the jurisdiction of the admiralty, beyond which it shall not pass, it may in time, like the element to which it ought to be confin'd, grow outrageous, and overflow the banks of all the other courts of justice." I believe it has never been doubted by one sound, common lawyer of England, whether a court of admiralty ever answer'd many good ends; "the court of King's bench has a power to restrain the court of admiralty in England; and the reasons for such restraining power are as strong in New England as in Great-Britain," and in some respects more so; Yet Mr. Dummer mentions, a clamour that was raised at home by a judge of the admiralty for New England, who complain'd "that the common law courts by granting prohibitions, weaken, and in a manner suppress the authority of this court, and all the good ends for which it was constituted." Thus we see, that the court of admiralty long ago discover'd, no very friendly disposition towards the common law courts here; and the records of the house of Representatives afford us a notable instance of one, who was expelled the house, of which he had been an unworthy member, for the abusive misrepresentations of the province, by him secretly made.

Trade and traffick, says Lord Coke, "is the livelihood of a merchant, the life of the commonwealth, wherein the King and every subject hath interest; for the merchant is the good Bailiff of the realm, to export and vent the native commodities of the realm, and to import and bring in, the necessary commodities for the defence and benefit of the Realm—2 Inst. 28. reading on Magna Charta. C. 15—And are not the merchants of British America entitled to a livelihood also? Are they not British subjects? Are not an infinity of commodities carried from hence for the *benefit of the realm*, for which in return come an infinity of *trifles*, which we could do without? Manufactures we must go into if our trade is cut off; our country is too cold to go naked in, and we shall soon be unable to make returns to England even for necessaries.

"When any law or custom of parliament is broken, and the crown possessed of a precedent, how difficult a thing is it to restore the subject again to his former freedom and safety?" 2. Inst. *on the confirmation of the great charter*—which provides in these words: "And for so much as divers people of our realm, are in fear, that the aids and talks which they have given to us before time, towards our wars, and other business of their own grant and good will (howsoever they were made) might *turn to a bondage* to them and their heirs, because they might be at another time found in the rolls, and likewise for the prices taken throughout the realm by our ministers; We have granted for us and our heirs, that we shall not draw such aids, talks nor prices *into a custom*, for any thing that hath been done heretofore, be it by roll, or any other precedent that may be founden."

By the first chapter of this act, the great charter is declared to be the common law. I would ask, whether we have not reason to fear, that the great aids, freely given by these provinces in the late war, will in like manner turn *to our bondage*, if they are to be kept on and *increased* during a *peace*, for the maintenance of a *standing army* here?—If tis said those aids were given for *our own* immediate defence, and that England spent millions in the same cause; I answer: The names of his present Majesty, and his royal Grand-father, will be ever dear to every loyal British American, for the protection they afforded us, and the salvation, under God, effected by their arms; but with regard to our fellow-subjects of Britain, we never were a whit behind hand with them. The New England Colonies in particular, were not only settled without the least expence to the mother country, but they have all along defended themselves against the frequent incursions of the most inhuman Salvages, perhaps on the face of the whole earth, at *their own cost*: Those more than brutal *men*, spirited and directed by the most inveterate, as well as most powerful enemy of Great Britain, have been constantly annoying our infant settlements for more than a century; spreading terror and desolation and sometimes depopulating whole villages in a night: yet amidst the fatigues of labor, and the horrors of war and bloodshed, Heaven vouchsaf'd its smiles. Behold, an extensive territory, settled, defended, and secured to his Majesty, I repeat it, *without the least expence to the mother country*, till within twenty years past! —When *Louisbourg* was reduced to his late Majesty, by the valor of his *New-England subjects*, the parliament, it must be own'd, saw meet to refund *part* of the charges: And every one knows the importance of *Louisbourg*, in the consultations of Aix *la Chapple*; but for the loss of our young men, the riches and strength of a country, not indeed slain by the enemy, but overborn by the uncommon hardships of the siege, and their confinement in garrison afterwards, there could be no recompence made.—In the late war, the *northern colonies* not only rais'd their full quota of men, but they went even beyond their ability: they are still deeply in debt, notwithstanding the parliamentary grants, annually made them, *in part* of their expences, in the common, *national, cause*: Had it not been for those grants, they had all been bankrupt long ago; while the *sugar colonies*, have born little or no share in it: They indeed sent a company or two of *Negroes* and *Molattoes*, if this be worth mentioning, to the sieges of Gaudaloupe, Martineco and the Havanna: I do not recollect any thing else that they have done; while the flower of *our* youth were annually pressed by ten thousands into the service, and there treated but little better, as we have been told, than hewers of wood and drawers of water. Provincial acts for impressing were obtained, only by letters of requisition from a secretary of state to a Governor; requiring him to use his influence to raise men; and sometimes, more than were asked for or wanted, were pressed, to give a figure to the Governor, and shew his influence; a remarkable instance of which might be mentioned. I would further observe, that Great-Britain was as immediately interested in the late war in America, as the colonies were. Was she not threatned with an invasion at the same time we were? Has she not an immense trade to the colonies? The British writers say, more than half her profitable trade is to *America*: All the profits of our trade center there, and is little enough to pay for the goods we import. A prodigious revenue arises to the Crown on American exports to Great-Britain, which in general is not murmured at: No manufacture of Europe besides British, can be lawfully bro't here; and no honest man desires they ever should, if the laws were put in execution upon all. With regard to a few Dutch imports that have made such a noise, the truth is, very little has been or could be run, before the apparatus of guardships; for the officers of some ports did their duty, while others may have made a monopoly of smuggling, for a few of their friends, who probably paid them large contributions; for it has been observed, that a very small office in the customs in America has raised a man a fortune sooner than a Government. The truth is, the acts of trade have been too often evaded; but by whom? Not by the American merchants in general, but by some former custom-house officers, their friends and partizans. I name no man, not being about to turn informer: But it has been a notorious grievance, that when the King himself cannot dispense with an act of parliament, there have been custom-house officers who have practiced it for years together, in favor of those towards whom they were graciously disposed.

But to return to the subject of taxation: I find that "the lords and commons cannot be charged with anything for the defence of the realm, for the safe-guard of the sea, &c. unless by their *will* in parliament

    Ld. Coke, on Magna Charta, Cap. 30.

"Impositions neither in time of war, or other the greatest necessity or occasion, that may be, much less in the time of peace, neither upon foreign or inland commodities, of what nature soever, be they never so superfluous or unnecessary, neither upon merchants, strangers, nor denizens, may be laid by the King's absolute power, without assent of parliament, be it never for so short a time."

    Viner Prerogative of the King.
    Ea. 1. cites 2 Molloy. 320. Cap. 12 sec. 1.

"In the reign of Edward 3, the black Prince of Wales having *Aquitain* granted to him, did lay an imposition of suage or socage a *soco*, upon his subjects of that dukedom, viz. a shilling for every fire, called hearth silver, which was of so great discontentment and odious to them, that it made them revolt. And nothing since this time has been imposed by pretext of any prerogative, upon merchandizes, imported into or exported out of this realm, until Queen Mary's time." 2 Inst. 61.

Nor has any thing of that kind taken place since the revolution. King Charles 1. his ship-money every one has heard of.

It may be said that these authorities will not serve the colonists, because the duties laid on them are by parliament. I acknowledge the difference of fact; but cannot see the great difference in equity, while the colonists are not represented in the house of commons: And therefore with all humble deference I apprehend, that 'till the colonists are so represented, the spirit of all these authorities will argue strongly in their favour. When the parliament shall think fit to allow the colonists a representation in the house of commons, the equity of their taxing the colonies, will be as clear as their power is at present of doing it without, if they please. When Mr. Dummer wrote his defence of the charters, there was a talk of taking them away, by act of parliament. This defence is dedicated to the right honourable the Ld. Carteret, then one of this Majesty's principal secretaries of state, since Earl of Granville. His third proposition is, that "it is not for the interest of the crown to resume the charters, if forfeited." This he proves; as also that it would be more for the interest of Great Britain to enlarge rather than diminish, the privilege of all the colonists. His last proposition is, that it "seems inconsistent with justice to disfranchise the charter colonies by an act of parliament."

"It seems therefore, says he, a severity without a precedent, that a people, who have the misfortune of being a thousand leagues distant from their sovereign, a misfortune great enough in itself, should, unsummoned, unheard, in one day, be deprived of their valuable privileges, which they and their fathers have enjoyed for near a hundred years." 'Tis true, as he observes, "the legislative power is absolute and unaccountable, and King, lords and commons, may do what they please; but the question here is not about *power*, but *right*" (or rather equity) "and shall not the supreme judicature of all the nation do right?" "One may say, that what the parliament cannot do justly, they cannot do at all. *In maximis minima est licentia.* The higher the power is, the greater caution is to be used in the execution of it; because the sufferer is helpless and without resort." I never heard that this reasoning gave any offence. Why should it? Is it not exactly agreable to the decisions of parliament and the determinations of the highest executive courts? But if it was thought hard that charter privileges should be taken away by act of parliament, is it not much harder to be in part, or in whole, disfranchised of rights, that have been always tho't inherent to a British subject, namely, to be free from all taxes, but what he consents to in person, or by his representative? This right, if it could be traced no higher than Magna Charta, is part of the common law, part of a British subjects birthright, and as inherent and perpetual, as the duty of allegiance; both which have been bro't to these colonies, and have been hitherto held sacred and inviolable, and I hope and trust ever will. 'Tis humbly conceived, that the British colonists (except only the conquered, if any) are, by Magna Charta, as well entitled to have a voice in their taxes, as the subjects within the realm. Are we not as really deprived of that right, by the parliament assessing us before we are represented in the house of commons, as if the King should do it by his prerogative? Can it be said with any colour of truth or justice, that we are represented in parliament?

As to the colonists being represented by the provincial agents, I know of no power ever given them but to appear before his Majesty, and his ministry. Sometimes they have been directed to petition the parliament: But they none of them have, and I hope never will have, a power given them, by the colonists, to act as representatives, and to consent to taxes; and if they should make any concessions to the ministry, especially without order, the provinces could not by that be considered as represented in parliament.

Hibernia habet Parliamenta et faciunt leges et nostra statuta non ligant eos quia non mittant milites ad Parliamentum, sed personae eorum sunt subjecti Regis, sicut inhabitantes Calinae Gasconiae et Guienae.
12 Rep. 111. cites R. 3. 12.—

"Ireland hath parliaments, and makes laws, and our statutes do not bind them, *because they send no Knights to parliament*; but their persons are subjects, of the King, as the inhabitants of Guiene, Gascony, &c."

Yet, if specially named, or by general words included as within any of the King's dominions, Ireland, says Ld. Coke, might be bound. 4 Inst. 351.

From all which, it seems plain, that the reason why Ireland and the plantations are not bound, unless named by an Act of Parliament, is, because they are *not represented* in the British parliament. Yet, in special cases, the British parliament has an undoubted right, as well as power, to bind both by their acts. But whether this can be extended to an indefinite taxation of both, is the greater question. I conceive the spirit of the British constitution must make an exception of all taxes, until it is tho't fit to unite a dominion to the realm. Such taxation must be considered either as uniting the dominions to the realm, or disfranchising them. If they are united, they will be intitled to a representation, as well as Wales; if they are so taxed without a union, or representation, they are so far disfranchised.

I don't find anything that looks like a duty on the colonies before the 25th of C. 2. c. 7. imposing a duty on enumerated commodities. The liberty of the subject was little attended to in that reign. If the nation could not fully assert their rights till the revolution, the colonies could not expect to be heard. I look on this act rather as a precedent of power, than of right and equity; if 'tis such, it will not affect my argument. The act appointing a tax on all mariners, of a certain sum per month, to be deducted out of their wages, is not to be compared with this. Mariners are not inhabitants of any part of the dominions: The sea is their element, till they are decrepit, and then the hospital is open for all mariners who are British subjects without exception. The general post-office established thro' the dominions, is for the convenience of trade and commerce: It is not laying any burthen upon it; for besides that it is upon the whole cheaper to correspond in this way than any other, every one is at liberty to send his own letters by a friend. The act of the 6th of his late Majesty, tho' it imposes a *duty* in terms, has been said to be designed for a *prohibition*; which is probable from the sums imposed; and 'tis pity it had not been so expressed, as there is not the least doubt of the just and equitable right of the parliament to lay prohibitions thro' the dominions, when they think the good of the whole requires it. But as has been said, there is an infinite difference between that and the exercise of unlimited power of taxation, over the dominions, without allowing them a representation:—It is said that the duties imposed by the new act will amount to a prohibition: Time only can ascertain this. The utility of this act is so fully examined in the appendix that I shall add nothing on that head here. It may be said that the colonies ought to bear their proportion of the national burdens: 'Tis just they should, and I think I have proved they have always done it freely and chearfully, and I know no reason to doubt but that they ever will.

Sometimes we have been considered only as the corporations in England: And it may be urged that it is no harder upon us to be taxed by parliament for the general cause than for them, who besides are at the expence of their corporate subordinate government.[26] I answer. 1. Those corporations are *represented* in parliament. 2. The colonies are and have been at great expence in raising men, building forts, and supporting the King's civil government here. Now I read of no governors and other officers of his Majesty's nomination, that the city of London taxes its inhabitants to support; I know of no forts and garrisons that the city of London has lately built at its own expence, or of any annual levies that they have raised for the King's service and the common cause. These are things very fitting and proper to be done by a subordinate dominion, and tis their duty to do all they are able; but it seems but equal they should be allowed to assess the charges of it themselves. The rules of equity and the principles of the constitution seem to require this. Those who judge of the reciprocal rights that subsist between a supreme and subordinate state or dominion, by no higher rules than are applied to a corporation of button-makers, will never have a very comprehensive view of them. Yet sorry am I to say it, many elaborate writers on the *administration* of the *colonies*, seem to me never to rise higher in their notions, than what might be expected from a secretary to one of the *quorum*. If I should be ranked among this number, I shall have this consolation, that I have fallen into what is called very good company, and among some who have seen very high life below stairs. I agree with the Administrator, that of whatever revenues raised in the colonies, if they must be raised without our consent, "*the first and special appropriation of them ought to be to the paying the Governors, and all the other Crown officers*;" for it would be hard for the Colonists to be obliged to pay them after this. It was on this principle that at the last assembly of this province, I moved to stop every grant to the officers of the crown; more especially as I know some who have built very much upon the fine salaries they shall receive from the plantation branch of the revenue. Nor can I think it "injustice to the frame of human nature,"[27] to suppose, if I did not know it, that with similar views several officers of the Crown in some of the colonies have been pushing for such an

---

26   See Administration of the Colonies.
27   Adm. p. 57.

act for many years. They have obtained their wish, and much good it will do them: But I would not give much for all that will center neat in the exchequer, after deducting the costs attending the execution of it, and the appropriations to the several officers proposed by the Administrator. What will be the unavoidable consequence of all this, suppose another war should happen, and it should be necessary to employ as many provincials in America as in the last? Would it be possible for the colonies, after being burthened in their trade, perhaps after it is ruined, to raise men? Is it probable that they would have spirit enough to exert themselves? If 'tis said the French will never try for America, or if they should, regular troops are only to be employed, I grant our regular troops are the best in the world, and that the experience of the present officers shews that they are capable of every species of American service; yet we should guard against the worst. If another tryal for Canada should take place, which from the known temper of France, we may judge she will bring on the first fair opportunity, it might require 30 or 40,000 regulars to secure his Majesty's just rights. If it should be said, that other American duties must then be levied, besides the impossibility of our being able to pay them, the danger recurs of a large standing army so remote from home. Whereas a good provincial militia, with such occasional succours from the mother country, as exigencies may require, never was, and never will be attended with hazard. The experience of past times will show, that an army of 20 or 30,000 veterans, half 3000 miles from *Rome*, were very apt to proclaim *Cesars*. The first of the name, the assassin of his country owed his false glory, to stealing the affections of an army from the commonwealth. I hope these hints will not be taken amiss; they seem to occur from the nature of the subject I am upon: They are delivered in pure affection to my King and country, and amount to no reflection on any man. The best army, and the best men, we may hereafter have, may be led into temptation; all I think is, that a prevention of evil is much easier than a deliverance from it.

The sum of my argument is, That civil government is of God: That the administrators of it were originally the whole people: That they might have devolved it on whom they pleased: That this devolution is fiduciary, for the good of the whole; That by the British constitution, this devolution is on the King, lords and commons, the supreme, sacred and uncontroulable legislative power, not only in the realm, but thro' the dominions: That by the abdication, the original compact was broken to pieces: That by the revolution, it was renewed, and more firmly established, and the rights and liberties of the subject in all parts of the dominions, more fully explained and confirmed: That in consequence of this establishment, and the acts of succession and union his

Majesty GEORGE III. is rightful king and sovereign, and with his parliament, the supreme legislative of Great Britain; France and Ireland, and the dominions thereto belonging: That this constitution is the most free one, and by far the best, now existing on earth: That by this constitution, every man in the dominion is a free man: That no parts of his Majesty's dominions can be taxed without their consent: That every part has a right to be represented in the supreme or some subordinate legislature: That the refusal of this, would seem to be a contradiction in practice to the theory of the constitution: That the colonies are subordinate dominions, and are now in such a state, as to make it best for the good of the whole, that they should not only be continued in the enjoyment of subordinate legislation, but be also represented in some proportion to their number and estates, in the grand legislature of the nation: That this would firmly unite all parts of the British empire, in the greatest peace and prosperity; and render it invulnerable and perpetual.

APPENDIX

The City of *Boston*, at their Annual Meet— in *May*, 1764, made Choice of *Richard Dana, Joseph Green,*
    Nathaniel Bethune, John Ruddock, Esq'rs; and Mr. *Samuel Adams*, to prepare Instructions for their REPRESENTATIVES.
The following Instructions were reported by said Committee, and unanimously Voted.
To *Royal Tyler*[28], *James Otis, Thomas Cushing,* and *Oxenbridge Thacher,* Esq'rs.
    GENTLEMEN,
    Your being chosen by the freeholders and inhabitants of the town of *Boston,* to represent them in the General Assembly the ensuing year, affords you the strongest testimony of that confidence which they place in your integrity and capacity. By this choise they have delegated to you the power of acting in their public concerns in general, as your own Prudence shall direct you; always reserving to themselves the constitutional right of expressing their mind, and giving you such instruction upon particular matters, as they at any time shall judge proper.
    We therefore your constituents take this opportunity to declare our just Expectations from you.

---

28   Now of the honourable Board; in whose room was returned Mr. *Thomas Gray,* Merchant.

That you will constantly use your power and influence in maintaining the invaluable rights and privileges of the province, of which this town is so great a part: As well those rights which are derived to us by the royal charter, as those which being prior to and independent on it, we hold essentially as free-born subjects of Great-Britain;

That you will endeavour, as far as you shall be able, to preserve that independence in the house of representatives, which characterizes a free people; and the want of which may in a great measure prevent the happy effects of a free government: Cultivating as you shall have opportunity, that harmony and union there, which is ever desirable to good men, when founded in principles of virtue and public spirit; and guarding against any undue weight which may tend to disadjust that critical balance upon which our happy constitution, and the blessings of it do depend. And for this purpose, we particularly recommend it to you to use your endeavours to have a law passed, whereby the seats of such gentlemen as shall accept of posts of profit from the Crown, or the Governor, while they are members of the house, shall be vacated, agreeable to an act of the British parliament, 'till their constituents shall have the opportunity of re-electing them if they please, or of returning others in their room.

Being members of the legislative body, you will have a special regard to the morals of this people, which are the basis of public happiness; and endeavour to have such laws made, if any are still wanting, as shall be best adapted to secure them: And we particularly desire you carefully to look into the laws of excise, that if the virtue of the people is endangered by the multiplicity of oathes therein enjoined, or their trade and business is unreasonably impeded or embarrassed thereby, the grievance may be redressed.

As the preservation of morals, as well as property and right, so much depends upon the impartial distribution of justice, agreeable to good and wholesome law: And as the judges of the land do depend upon the free grants of the general assembly for support; it is incumbent upon you at all times to give your voice for their honourable maintenance, so long as they, having in their minds an indifference to all other affairs, shall devote themselves wholly to the duties of their own department, and the further study of the law by which their customs, precedents, proceedings, and determinations are adjusted and limited.

You will remember that this province hath been at a very great expence in carrying on the war; and that it still lies under a very grievous burden of debt: You will therefore use your utmost endeavor to promote public frugality as one means to lessen the publick debt.

You will join in any proposals which may be made for the better cultivating the lands, and improving the husbandry of the province: and as you represent a town which lives by its trade, we expect in a very particular manner, that you make it the object of your attention, to support our commerce in all its just rights, to vindicate it from all unreasonable impositions, and promote its prosperity—Our trade has for a long time laboured under great discouragements; and it is with the deepest concern that we see such further difficulties coming upon it, as will reduce it to the lowest ebb, if not totally obstruct and ruin it. We cannot help expressing our surprize that when so early notice was given by the agent, of the intentions of the ministry, to burthen us with new taxes, so little regard was had to this most interesting matter,

that the court was not even call'd together to consult about it 'till the latter end of the year; the consequence of which was, that instructions could not be sent to the agent, tho' solicited by him, 'till the evil had got beyond an easy remedy.

There is now no room for further delay: We therefore expect that you will use your earliest endeavours in the General Assembly, that such methods may be taken as will effectually prevent these proceedings against us. By a proper representation, we apprehend it may easily be made to appear that such severities will prove .detrimental to Great Britain itself; upon which account we have reason to hope that *an* application, even for a repeal of the act, should it be already pass'd, will be successful. It is the trade of the colonies, that renders them beneficial to the mother country; Our trade, as it is now, and always has been conducted, centers in Great Britain, and in return for her manufactures, affords her more ready cash, beyond any comparison, than can possibly be expected by the most sanguine promoters of these extraordinary methods. We are in short ultimately yielding large supplies to the revenues of the mother country, while we are labouring for a very moderate subsistence for ourselves. But if our trade is to be curtail'd in its most profitable branches, and burdens beyond all possible bearing laid upon that which is suffer'd to remain, we shall be so far from being able to take off the manufactures of Great Britain, that it will be scarce possible for us to earn our bread.—

But what still heightens our apprehensions is, that these unexpected proceedings may be preparatory to new taxations upon us: For if our trade may be taxed, why not our lands? Why not the produce of our lands, and every thing we possess or make use of? This we apprehend annihilates our

charter right to govern and tax ourselves—It strikes at our British privileges, which as we have never forfeited them, we hold in common with our fellow subjects who are natives of Britain: If taxes are laid upon us in any shape without our having a legal representation where they are laid, are we not reduc'd

from the character of free subjects to the miserable state of tributary slaves?

We therefore earnestly recommend it to you to use your utmost endeavors to obtain in the general assembly, all necessary instruction and advice to our agent at this most critical juncture; that while he is setting forth the unshaken loyalty of this province and this town—its unrival'd exertion in supporting his Majesty's government and rights in this part of his dominions-its acknowledg'd dependence upon and subordination to Great-Britain; and the ready submission of its merchants to all just and necessary regulations of trade; he may be able in the most humble and pressing manner to remonstrate for us all those rights and privileges which justly belong to us either by charter or birth.

As his Majesty's other northern American colonies are embark'd with us in this most important bottom, we further desire you to use your endeavors, that their weight may be added to that of this province: that by the united application of all who are aggrieved, All may happily obtain redress.

Substance of a Memorial presented the House, in Pursuance of the above Instructions; and by them voted to be transmitted to Jasper Mauduit,

Esq; Agent for this Province;[29] to be improved as he may judge proper.

The publick transactions from William the I. to the revolution, may be considered as one continued struggle between the prince and the people, all tending to that happy establishment, which Great-Britain has since enjoyed.

The absolute rights of Englishmen, as frequently declared in parliament, from Magna Charta, to this time, are the rights of *personal security, personal liberty,* and of *private property.*

The allegiance of British subjects being natural, perpetual and inseparable from their persons, let them be in what country they may; their rights are also natural, inherent and perpetual.

By the laws of nature and of nations, the voice of universal reason, and of God, when a nation takes possession of a desert, uncultivated, and uninhabited country, or purchases of Savages; as was the case with far the greatest part of the British settlements; the colonists transplanting themselves, and their posterity, tho' separated from the principal establishment, or mother country, naturally become part of the state with its ancient possessions, and intitled to all the essential rights of the mother country. This is not only confirmed

---

29 Only as a State drawn up by one of the House.

by the practice of the antients, but by the moderns ever since the discovery of America. Frenchmen, Spaniards, and Portugals are no greater slaves abroad than at home; and hitherto Britons have been as free on one side of the atlantic as on the other: And it is humbly hoped that his Majesty and the Parliament, will in their wisdom be graciously pleased to continue the colonists in this happy state.

It is presumed, that upon these principles, the colonists have been by their several charters declared natural subjects, and entrusted with the power of making *their own local laws,* not repugnant to the laws of England, and with *the power of taxing themselves.*

Their legislative power is subject by the same charter to the King's negative as in Ireland. This effectually secures the *dependence* of the colonies on Great-Britain—By the *thirteenth* of *George* the *second, chapter the ninth,* even foreigners having lived seven years in any of the colonies, are deemed natives on taking the oaths of allegiance, &c. and are declared by the said act to be his Majesty's natural born subjects of the kingdom of Great-Britain, to all intents, constructions and purposes, as if any of them had been born within the kingdom. The reasons given for this naturalization in the preamble of the act are, "that the increase of the people is the means of advancing the wealth and strength of any nation or country; and that many foreigners and strangers, from the lenity of our government, the purity of our religion, the benefit of our laws, the advantages of our trade, and the security of our *property,* might be induced to come and settle in some of his Majesty's colonies in America; if they were partakers of the advantages and priviledges, which the natural born subjects there enjoy."[30]

The several acts of parliament and charters declaratory of the rights and liberties of the colonies are but in affirmance of the common law, and law of nature in this point. There are says my Lord Coke, regularly three incidents to subjects born. (1.) Parents under the actual obedience of the King. (2.) That the place of his birth be within the King's dominions. (3.) The time of his birth to be chiefly considered: For he cannot be a subject born of one kingdom, that was born under the allegiance of the King of another kingdom; albeit afterwards the kingdom descends to the King of the other kingdom. See Calvin's case, and the several acts of parliament and decisions on naturalization, from Edward the third to this day. The common law is received and practiced upon here, and in the rest of the colonies; and all antient and modern acts of parliament that can be considered as part of, or in amendment of the common law, together with all such acts of parliament as expresly name

---

30   13 G. 2. C. 7.

the plantations; so that the power of the British parliament is held as sacred and as uncontroulable in the colonies as in England. The question is not upon the general power or right of the parliament, but whether it is not circumscribed within some equitable and reasonable bounds? 'Tis hoped it will not be considered as a new doctrine, that even the authority of the parliament of *Great-Britain* is circumscribed by certain bounds, which if exceeded their acts become those of meer *power* without *right,* and consequently void. The judges of England have declared in favour of these sentiments, when they expressly declare; that *acts of parliament against natural equity, are void.* That *acts against the fundamental principles of the British constitution are ooid.*[31] This doctrine is

31   A very important question here presents itself, J t essentially belongs to the society to make laws both in relation to the manner in which it desires to be governed, and to the conduct of the citizens: This is called the *Legislative Power.* The nation may entrust the exercise of it to the Prince, or to an assembly; or to the assembly and the Prince jointly; who have then a right of making new and abrogating old laws. It is here demanded whether, it their power extends so far as to the fundamental laws, they may change the constitution of the state? The principles we have laid down lead us to decide this point with certainty, that the authority of these legislators does not extend so far, and that they ought to consider the fundamental laws as sacred, if the nation has not in very express terms given them the power to change them. For the constitution of the state ought to be fixed; and since that was first established by the nation, which afterwards trusted certain persons with the legislative power, the fundamental laws are excepted from their commission. It appears that the society had only resolved to make provision for the state's being always furnished with laws suited to particular conjunctures, and gave the legislature for that purpose, the power of abrogating the ancient civil and political laws, that were not fundamental, and of making new ones: But nothing leads us to think that it was willing to submit the constitution itself to their pleasure.
When a nation takes possession of a distant country, and settles a colony there, that country though separated from the principal establishment, or mother country, naturally becomes a part of the state, equally with its ancient possessions. Whenever the political laws, or treaties make no distinction between them, every thing said of the territory of a nation, ought also to extend to its colonies. D'Vattel.
"An act of parliament made against natural equity, as to make a man judge in his own cause, would be void. *For jura naturae sun! immutabilia* Hob. 87 Trin. 12. Jac. Day v. Savage S. C. and P. cited Arg. 10 Mod. 115. Hill. 11 Ann. C. B in the case of Thornby and Fleetwood, "but says, that this must be a clear case, and judges will strain hard rather than interpret an act void, ab initio." *This is granted, but still their authority is not boundless, if subject to the controul of the judges in any case.* "Holt, Chief justice thought what Lord Coke says in Doctor Bonham's case a very reasonable and true saying, that if an act of parliament should ordain that the same person should be both party and judge in his cause, it would be a void act of parliament, and an act of parliament can

agreable to the law of nature and nations, and to the divine dictates of natural and revealed religion. J t is contrary to reason that the supreme power should have right to alter the constitution. This would imply that those who are intrusted with Sovereignty by the people, have a right to do as they please. In other words, that those who are invested with power to protect the people, and support their rights and liberties, have a right to make slaves of them. This is not very remote from a flat contradiction. Should the parliament of Great Britain follow the example of some other foreign states[32], and vote the King absolute and despotic; would such an act of parliament make him so? Would any minister in his senses advise a Prince to accept of such an offer of power? It would be unsafe to accept of such a donation, because the parliament or donors would grant more than was ever in their power lawfully to give. The law of nature never invested them with a power of surrendering their own liberty; and the people certainly never intrusted any body of men with a power to surrender theirs in exchange for slavery.[33]

---

do no wrong tho' it may do several things that look pretty odd; for it may discharge one from the allegiance he lives under, and restore to the state of nature; but it cannot make one that lives under a government both judge and party per Holt. C. J 12 Mod. 687, 688 Hill. 13 W. 3 B. R in the case of the city of London v. Wood ... It appears in our books, that in several cases the common law shall controul acts of parliament and sometimes adjudge them to be utterly void; for when an act of parliament is against common *right* and *reason,* or repugnant or impossible to be performed, the common law shall controul it, and adjudge it to be void, and therefore 8 E. 3.30. Thomas Tregor's case upon the statute of W. 2. Cap. 38. and Art Sup Chart 9 Herle said that sometimes statutes are made contrary to law and right, which the makers of them perceiving will not put them in execution. 8 Rep. 118 Hill 7 J. Dr. Bonham's case.

32   Sweden, Denmark, France, &c.

33   "But if the whole state be conquered, if the nation be subdued, in what manner can the victor treat it without transgressing the bounds at justice? What are his rights over the conquest? Some have dared to advance this monstrous principle that the conqueror is absolute master of his conquest; that he may dispose of it as his property, treat it as he pleases, according to the common expression of *treating a state as a conquered country;* and hence they derive one of the sources of despotic government: But enough of those that reduce men to the state of transferable goods, or use them like beasts of burden, who deliver them up as the property or patrimony of another man. Let us argue on principles countenanced by reason and becoming humanity. The whole right of the conqueror proceeds from the just defence of himself, which contains the support and prosecution of his rights. Thus when he has totally subdued a nation with whom he had been at war, he may without dispute cause justice to be done him, with regard to what gave rise to the war, and require payment for the expence and damage he has sustained; he may according to the exigency of the case

It is now near three hundred years since the continent of North-America was first discovered, and that by British subjects.[34] Ten generations have passed away thro' infinite toils and bloody conflicts in settling this country. None of those ever dreamed but that they were intitled, at least, to equal priviledges with those of the same rank born within the realm.

British America has been hitherto distinguished from the slavish colonies around about it, as the fortunate Britons have been from most of their neighbours on the continent of Europe. It is for the interest of Great-Britain that her colonies should be ever, thus distinguished. Every man must willfully blind himself that don't see the immense value of our acquisitions in the late war; and that tho' we did not retain all at the conclusion of the peace that we obtained by the sword; yet our gracious Sovereign, at the same time that he has given a divine lesson of equitable moderation to the Princes of the earth, has retained sufficient to make the British arms the dread of the universe, and his name dear to all posterity.

To the freedom of the British constitution, and to their increase of commerce, 'tis owing that our colonies have flourished without diminishing the inhabitants of the mother country; quite contrary to the effects of plantations made by most other nations, which have suffered at home, in order to aggrandize themselves abroad. This is remarkably the case with Spain. The subjects of a free and happy constitution of government, have a thousand advantages to

---

impose penalties on it as an example, he may should prudence so dictate disable it from undertaking any pernicious designs for the future. But in securing all these views the mildest means are to be preferred. We are always to remember, that the law of nature permits no injury to be done to an enemy unless in taking measures necessary for a just defence, and a reasonable security. Some princes have only imposed a tribute on it; others have been satisfied of striping it of some privileges, dismembring a province, or keeping it in awe by fortresses; others as their quarrel was only with the sovereign in person, have left a nation in the full enjoyment of all its rights, only setting a sovereign over it. But if the conqueror thinks proper to retain the sovereignty of the vanquished state, and has such a right; the manner in which he is to treat the state still flows from the same principles. If the sovereign be only the just object of his complaint, reason declares that by his conquest he acquires only such rights as actually belonged to the dethroned sovereign, and on the submission of his people he is to govern it according to the laws of the state. If the people do not voluntarily submit, the state of war subsists." "When a sovereign as pretending to have the absolute disposal of a people whom he has conquered, is for inslaving them, he causes the state of war to subsist between this people & him."
Mr. De Vattel B. 3. C. 10 sec. 201.

34   The Cabots discovered the Continent before the Spaniards.

colonize above those who live under despotic princes. We see how the British colonies on the continent, have out-grown those of the French, notwithstanding they have ever engaged the Savages to keep us back. Their advantages over us in the West-Indies are, among other causes perhaps, partly owing to these, (1.) A capital neglect in former reigns, in suffering them to have a firm possession of so many valuable islands, that we had a better title to than they. (2.) The French unable to push their settlements effectually on the continent, have bent their views to the islands, and poured vast numbers into them. (3.) The climate and business of these islands is by nature much better adapted to Frenchmen and to Negroes, than to Britons. (4.) The labour of slaves, black or white, will be ever cheaper than that of freemen, because that of the individuals among the former, will never be worth so much as with the latter; but this difference is more than supplied; by numbers under the advantages above-mentioned. The French win ever be able to sell their West-India produce cheaper than our own islanders; and yet while our own islanders can have such a price for theirs, as to grow much richer than the French, or any other of the King's subjects in America, as is the case, and what the northern colonies take from the French, and other foreign islands, centers finally in returns to Great-Britain for her manufactures, to an immense value, and with a vast profit to her: It is contrary to the first principles of policy to clog such a trade with duties, much more to prohibit it, to the risque if not certain destruction of the fishery. I t is allowed by the most accurate British writers on commerce, Mr. Postlethwait in particular, who seems to favour the cause of the sugar islands, that one half of the immense commerce of Great-Britain is with her colonies. It is very certain that without the fishery seven eights of this commerce would cease. The fishery is the center of motion, upon which the wheel of all British commerce in America turns. Without the American trade, would Britain, as a commercial state, make any great figure at this day in Europe? Her trade in woolen and other manufactures is said to be lessening in all parts of the world, but America, where it is increasing, and capable of infinite increase, from a concurrence of every circumstance in its favour. Here is an extensive territory of different climates, which in time will consume, and be able to pay for as many manufactures as Great Britain and Ireland can make, if true maxims are persued. The French for reasons already mentioned, can underwork, and consequently undersell the English manufactures of Great-Britain in every market in Europe. But they can send none of their manufactures here; and it is the wish of every honest British American that they never may; 'tis best they never should; we can do better without the manufactures of Europe, save those of Great-Britain, than with them: But without the French West-India produce we cannot; without it our fishery must infallibly be ruined. When that is gone our own islands will very poorly subsist. No British manufactures can be paid for by the colonists. What will follow? One of these two things, both of which it is the interest of Great-Britain to prevent. (1.) The northern colonists must be content to go naked, and turn Savages. Or (2.) Become manufacturers of linnen and woolen, to Cloath themselves; which if they cannot carry to the

perfection of Europe, will be very destructive to the interests of Great-Britain. The computation has been made, and that within bounds, and it can be demonstrated, that if North-America is only driven to the fatal necessity of manufacturing a suit of the most ordinary linnen or woolen for each inhabitant annually, which may be soon done, when necessity the mother of invention shall operate, Great-Britain & Ireland will loose two millions per annum, besides a diminution of the revenue to nearly the same amount. This may appear paradoxical, but a few years experience of the execution of the sugar act will sufficiently convince the parliament not only of the inutility, but destructive tendency of it, while calculations may be little attended to. That the trade with the colonies has been of surprizing advantage to Great-Britain, notwithstanding the want of a good regulation is past all doubt. Great-Britain is well known to have increased prodigiously both in numbers and in wealth since she began to colonize. To the growth of the plantations Britain is in a great measure indebted for her present riches and strength. As the wild wastes of America have been turned into pleasant habitations, and flourishing trading towns; so many of the little villages and obscure boroughs in Great-Britain have put on a new face, and suddenly started up, and become fair markets, and manufacturing towns, and opulent cities. London itself, which bids fair to be the metropolis of the world, is five times more populous than it was in the days of Queen Elizabeth. Such are the fruits of the spirit of commerce and liberty. Hence it is manifest how much we all owe to that beautiful form of civil government, under which we have the happiness to live.

It is evidently the interest, and ought to be the care of all those intrusted with the administration of government, to see that every part of the British empire enjoys to the full the rights they are intitled to by the laws, and the advantages which result from their being maintained with impartiality and vigour. This we have been reduced to practice in the present and preceeding reigns; and have the highest reason from the paternal care and goodness that his Majesty, and the British Parliament, have hitherto been graciously pleased to discover to all his Majesty's dutiful and loyal subjects, and to the colonists in particular, to rest satisfied, that our priviledges will remain sacred and inviolate. The 'connection between Great-Britain and her colonies is so natural and strong, as to make their mutual happiness depend upon their mutual support. Nothing can tend more to the destruction of both, and to forward the measures of their enemies, than sowing the seeds of jealously, animosity and dissention between the mother country and the colonies.

A conviction of the truth and importance of these principles, induced Great-Britain during the late war, to carryon so many glorious enterprises for the defence of the colonies; and those on their part to exert themselves beyond their ability to pay, as is evident from the parliamentary reimbursements.

If the spirit of commerce was attended to, perhaps, duties would be every where decreased, if not annihilated, and prohibitions multiplied. Every branch of trade that hurts a community, should be prohibited for the same reason that a private gentleman would break off commerce with a sharper or an extorsive usurer. 'Tis to no purpose to higgle with such people, you are sure to loose by them. 'Tis exactly so with a nation, if the balance is against them, and they can possibly subsist without the commodity, as they generally can in such cases, a prohibition is the only remedy; for a duty in such case, is like a composition with a thief, that for five shillings in the pound returned, he shall rob you at pleasure; when if the thing is examined to the bottom, you are at five shillings expence in travelling to get back your five shillings, and he is at the same expence in coming to pay it, so he robs you of but ten shillings in the pound, that you thus wisely compound for. To apply this to trade, I believe every duty that was ever imposed on commerce, or in the nature of things can be, will be found to be divided between the state imposing the duty, and the country exported from. This as between the several parts of the same kingdom or dominions of the same Prince, can only tend to embarrass trade, and raise the price of labour above other states, which is of very pernicious consequence to the husbandman, manufacturer, mariner and merchant, the four tribes that support the hive. If your duty is upon a commodity of a foreign state, it is either upon the whole useful and gainful, and therefore necessary for the husbandmen, manufacturer, mariner or merchant, as finally bringing a profit to the state by a balance in her favour; or the importation will work a balance against your state. There is no medium that we know of. –If the commodity is of the former kind, it should be prohibited; but if the latter, imported duty free, unless you would raise the price of labour by a duty on necessaries, or make the above wise composition for the importation of commodities you are sure to lose by. The only test of a useful commodity is the gain upon the whole to the state; such should be free; the only test of a pernicious trade is the loss upon the whole, or to the community, this should be prohibited. If therefore it can be demonstrated that the sugar and molasses trade from the northern colonies to the foreign plantations is upon the *whole* a loss to the *community,* by which term is here meant the three kingdoms and the British dominions taken collectively, then and not 'till then should this trade be prohibited. This never has been proved, nor can be; the contrary being certain, to wit, that the nation upon the whole hath been a vast gainer by this trade, in the vend of and pay for its manufactures; and a great loss by a duty upon this trade will finally fall on the British husbandman, manufacturer, mariner & merchant, and consequently the trade of the nation be wounded, and in constant danger of being eat out by those who can undersell her.

The art of underselling, or rather of finding means to undersell, is the grand secret of thrift among commercial states, as well as among individuals of the same state. Should the British sugar islands ever be able to supply Great-Britain and her northern colonies with those articles, it will be time enough to think of a total prohibition; but until that time, both prohibition and duty will be found to be diametrically opposite to the first principles of policy. Such is the extent of this continent, and the increase of its inhabitants, that if every inch of the British sugar islands was as well cultivated as any part of Jamaica, or Barbadoes, they would not now be able to supply Great-Britain, and the colonies on this continent. But before such further improvements can be supposed to take place in our islands, the demands will be proportionably increased by the increase of the inhabitants on the continent. Hence the reason is plain why the British sugar planters are growing rich, and ever will, because the demand for their produce has and ever will be greater than they can possibly supply, so long as the English hold this continent, and are unrivalled in the fishery.

We have every thing good and great to hope from our gracious Sovereign, his Ministry and his Parliament; and trust that when the services and sufferings of the British American colonies are fully known to the mother country, and the nature and importance of the plantation trade more perfectly understood at home, that the most effectual measures will be taken for perpetuating the British empire in all parts of the world. An empire built upon the principles of justice, moderation and equity, the only principles that can make a state flourishing, and enable it to elude the machinations of its secret and inveterate enemies.

P. S. By ancient and modern gods, P. 10, I mean, all idols, from those of Old Egypt, to the canonized monsters of modern Rome; and by king-craft and priest-craft, civil and ecclesiastic polity, as administred in general till the revolution. I now recollect that I have been credibly informed that the British Sugar Colonists are humane towards their slaves, in comparison with the others. Therefore in page 29, let it be read, foreign Sugar-islanders and foreign Creoles.

FINIS

Considerations on Behalf of the Colonists in a Letter to a Noble Lord (1765)

The following Pamphlet was sent to the Publisher, by an unknown Person, from Boston, in New England; with a Request to print it as soon as possible: finding after a careful Reading, it not to contain any Thing apparently, or particularly offensive to any Party, or Body of Men, he should have thought himself inexcuseable, if he had been the Means of withholding it from the Public.

A
LETTER, &.

My Lord,

    I have read the *Opusculum* of the celebrated Mr. J_____s, called "Objections to the taxation of the colonies by the legislature of Great-Britain, briefly considered." In obedience to your lordships commands, I have thrown a few thoughts on paper, all indeed that I have patience on this melancholy occasion to collect. The gentleman thinks it is "absurd and insolent" to question the expediency and utility of a public measure. He seems to be an utter enemy to the freedom of enquiry after truth, justice and equity. He is not only a zealous advocate for pusilanimous and passive obedience, but for the most implicit faith in the dictatorial mandates of power. The "several patriotic favorite words *liberty, property, Englishmen*, &" are in his opinion of no use but to "make strong impressions on the more numerous part of mankind who have ears but no understanding." The times have been when the favorite terms *places, pensions,* French *louis d'ors* and English *guineas,* have made very undue impressions on those who have had votes and voices, but neither honor nor conscience—who have deserved of their country an ax, a gibbet or a halter, much better than a star or garter. The grand aphorism of the British constitution, that *"no Englishman is or can be taxed but by his own consent in person or by his deputy"* is absurdly denied. In a *vain* and most *insolent* attempt to disprove this fundamental principle he exhibits a curious specimen of his talent at chicanery and quibbling. He says that "no man that he knows of is taxed by his own consent." It is a maxim at this day, that the crown by royal prerogative alone can levy no taxes on the subject. One who had any "understanding as well as ears" would from thence be led to conclude that some men must consent to their taxes before they can be imposed.

It has been commonly understood, at least since the glorious revolution, that the consent of the British Lords and Commons, i.e. of all men within the realm, must be obtained to make a tax legal there. The consent of the lords and commons of his majesty's ancient and very respectable kingdom of Ireland, has also been deemed necessary to a taxation of the subjects there. The consent of the two houses of assembly in the colonies has till lately been also thought requisite for the taxation of his majesty's most dutiful and loyal subjects, the colonists. *Sed tempora mutantur.*

I would ask Mr. J_____ s, if when a knight of a shire, or burgess of a borough, civil, military, or errant, possessed of a real estate, votes for a land tax, he does not tax himself and consent to such tax? And does he not by thus voting, tax himself as an *identic* individual, as well as some of his silly neighbours, who "may have ears but no understanding," and be therefore in great danger at a future election of chusing an empty *individuum vagum* to manage their highest concerns. Tis much to be lamented that these people with "ears but without understanding" by certain vulgar low arts, may be as easily led to elect a state auctioneer or a vote seller as the wisest and most upright man in the three kingdoms. We have known some of them cry Hosanna to the man who under God and his king had been their saviour, and the next day appear ready to crucify him. However, when a man in Europe or America votes a tax on his constituents, if he has any estate, he is at the same time taxing himself, and that by *his own consent;* and of all this he must be conscious unless we suppose him to be void of common sense.

No one ever contended that "the consent of the very person he chuses to represent him," nor that "the consent of the majority of those who are chosen by himself, *and* others of his fellow subjects to represent them," should be obtained before a tax can be rightfully levied. The pitiful chicanery here, consists wholly in substituting *and* for *or.* If for *and,* we read *or,* as the great Mr. J _____ s himself inadvertently reads it a little afterwards, the same proposition will be as strictly true, as any political aphorism or other general maxim whatever, the theorems of Euclid not excepted; namely, *"that no Englishman, nor indeed any other freeman, is or can be rightfully taxed, but by his own actual consent in person, or by the majority of those who are chosen by himself or others his fellow subjects to represent the whole people."*

Right reason and the spirit of a free constitution require that the representation of the whole people should be as equal as possible. A perfect equality of representation has been thought impracticable; perhaps the nature of human affairs will not admit of it. But it most certainly might and ought to be more equal than it is at present in any state. The difficulties in the way of a perfectly equal representation are such that in most countries the poor people can obtain none. The lust of power and unreasonable domination are, have been, and I fear ever will be not only impatient of, but above, controul. The Great love pillows of down for their own heads, and chains for those below them. Hence 'tis pretty easy to see how it has been brought about, that in all ages despotism has been the general tho' not quite universal government of the world. No good reason however can be given in any country why every man of a sound mind should not have his vote in the election of a representative. If a man has but little property to protect and defend, yet his life and liberty are things of some importance. Mr. J_____ s argues only from the vile abuses of power to the continuance and increases of such abuses. This it must be confessed is the common logic of modern politicians and vote sellers. To what purpose is it to ring everlasting changes to the colonists on the cases of Manchester, Birmingham and Sheffield, who return no members? If those now so considerable places are not represented, they ought to be. Besides the counties in which those respectable abodes of tinkers, tinmen, and pedlars lie, return members, so do all the neighbouring cities and boroughs. In the choice of the former, if they have no vote, they must naturally and necessarily have a great influence. I believe every gentleman of a landed estate, near a flourishing manufactory, will be careful enough of its interests. Tho' the great India company, as such, returns no members, yet many of the company are returned, and their interests have been ever very carefully attended to.

Mr. J_____s says, "by far the major part of the inhabitants of Great Britain are nonelectors". The more is the pity. "Every Englishman, he tells us, is taxed, and yet not one in twenty is represented." To be consistent, he must here mean that not one in twenty, votes for a representative. So a small minority rules and governs the majority. This may for those in the saddle be clever enough, but can never be right in theory. What *ab initio* could give an absolute unlimitted right to one twentieth of a community, to govern the other nineteen by their sovereign will and pleasure? Let him, if his intellects will admit of the research, discover how in any age or country this came to be the fact. Some favourite modern systems must be given up or maintained by a clear open avowal of these *Hobbeian* maxims, viz. That dominion is rightfully founded on force and fraud.—That power universally confers right.—That war, bloody war, is the real and natural state of man—and that he who can find means to buy, sell, enslave, or destroy, the greatest number of his own species, is right worthy to be dubbed a modern politician and an hero. Mr. J_____ s has a little contemptible flirt at the sacred names of Selden, Locke, and Sidney. But their ideas will not quadrate with the half-born sentiments of a courtier. Their views will never center in the *paricranium* of a modern politician. The characters of their writings cannot be affected by the crudities of a ministerial mercenary pamphleteer. He next proceeds to give us a specimen of his agility in leaping hedge and ditch, and of paddling through thick and thin. He has proved himself greatly skilled in the ancient and honourable sciences of horse-racing, bruising, boxing, and cock-fighting. He offers to "risk the merits of the whole cause on a single question." For this one question he proposed a string of five or six.—To all which I say he may be a very great statesman, but must be a very indifferent lawyer. A good lawyer might risque the merit of a cause on answers, but never would rest it on mere interrogatories. A multiplicity of questions, especially such as most of Mr. J_____s's only prove the folly and impertinent of the querist. Answers may be evidence, but none results from questions only. Further, to all his queries, let him take it for a full answer, that his way of reasoning would as well prove that the British house of commons, in fact, represent all the people on the globe, as those in America. True it is, that from the nature of the British constitution, and also from the idea and nature of a supreme legislature, the parliament represents the whole community or empire, and have an undoubted power, authority, and jurisdiction, over the whole; and to their final decisions the whole must and ought peaceably to submit. They have an undoubted right also to unite to all intents and purposes, for benefits and burthens, a dominion, or subordinate jurisdiction to the mother state, if the good of the whole requires it. But great tenderness has been shown to the customs of particular cities and boroughs, and surely as much indulgence might be reasonably expected towards large provinces, the inhabitants of which have been born and grown up under the modes and customs of a subordinate jurisdiction. But in a case of necessity, the good of the whole requires, that not only private interests, but private passions, should give way to the public. But all this will not convince me of the reasonableness of imposing heavy taxes on the colonists, while their trade and commerce are every day more than ever restricted. Much less will it follow, that the colonists are, in fact, represented in the house of commons. Should the British empire one day be extended round the whole world, would it be reasonable that all mankind should have their concerns managed by the electors of old Sarum, and the "occupants of the Cornish barns and ale-houses", we sometimes read of? We who are in the colonies, are by common law, and by act of parliament, declared entitled to all the privileges of the subjects within the realm. Yet we are heavily taxed, without being, in fact, represented.—In all trials here relating to the revenue the admiralty courts have jurisdiction given them, and the subject may, at the pleasure of the informer, be deprived of a trial by his peers. To do as one would be done by, is a divine rule. Remember Britons, when you shall be taxed without your consent, and tried without a jury, and have an army quartered in private families, you will have little to hope or to fear! But I must not lose sight of my man, who sagaciously asks "if the colonists are English when they solicit protection, but not Englishmen when taxes are required to enable *this country* to protect them?" I ask in my turn, when did the colonists solicit for protection? They have had no occasion to solicit for protection since the happy accession of our gracious Sovereign's illustrious family to the British diadem. His Majesty, the father of all his people, protects all his loyal subjects of every complexion and language, without any particular solicitation. But before the ever memorable revolution, the Northern Colonists were so far from receiving protection from Britain, that every thing was done from the throne to the footstool, to cramp, betray, and ruin them: yet against the combined power of France, Indian savages, and the corrupt administration of those times, they carried on their settlements and under a mild government for these eighty years past, have made them the wonder and envy of the world.

These colonies may, if truly understood, be one day the last resource, and best barrier of Great Britain herself. Be that as it may, sure I am that the colonists never in any reign received protection but from the king and parliament. From most others they had nothing to ask, but everything to fear. Fellow subjects in every age, have been the temporal and spiritual persecutors of fellow subjects. The Creoles follow the example of some politicians, and ever employ a negroe to whip negroes. As to "that country", and "protection from that country," what can Mr. J_____s mean? I ever thought the territories of the same prince made one country. But if, according to Mr. J_____s, Great Britain is a distinct country from the British colonies, what is that *country* in nature more than this country? The same sun warms the people of Great Britain and us; the same summer chears, and the same winter chills.

Mr. J_____s says, "the liberty of an Englishman is a phrase of so various a signification, having, within these few years, been used as synonymous terms for *blasphemy, bawdy, treason, libels, strong beer, and cyder,* that he shall not here presume to define its meaning." I commend his prudence in avoiding the definition of *English Liberty;* he has no idea of the thing.

But your lordship may, if you please, look back to the most infamous times of the Stuarts, ransack the history of all their reigns, examine the conduct of every debauchee who counted for one in that parliament, which Sidney says, "drunk or sober," passed the five mile act, and you will not find any expressions equal in absurdity to those of Mr. J_____s. He sagely affirms, "that there can be no pretence to plead any exemption from parliamentary authority." I know of no man in America who understands himself, that ever pleaded or pretended any such exemption. I think it our greatest happiness in the true and genuine sense of law and the constitution, to be subject to, and controulable by, parliamentary authority. But Mr. J_____s will scribble about *"our American colonies."* Whose colonies can the creature mean? The minister's colonies? No surely. Whose then, his own? I never heard he had any colonies. *Nec gladio nec arcu, nec astu vicerunt.* He must mean his Majesty's American colonies. His Majesty's colonies they are, and I hope and trust ever will be; and that the true native inhabitants, as they ever have been, will continue to be, his Majesty's most dutiful and loyal subjects. Every garetteer, from the environs of Grub-street, to the purlieus of St. James's, has lately talked of *his* and *my* and *our* colonies, and of the *rascally colonists,* and of *yokeing* and *curbing* the *cattle,* as they are by some politely called, at "this present now and very nascent crisis".[35]

I cannot see why the American peasants may not with as much propriety speak of their cities of London and Westminster, of their isles, of Britain, Ireland, Jersey, Guernsey, Sark, and the Orcades, and of the "rivulets and run lets thereof,"[36] and consider them all but as appendages to their sheepcots and goose-pens. But land is land, and men should be men. The property of the former God hath given to the possessor. These are *sui juris,* or slaves and vassals; there neither is nor can be any medium. Mr. J_____s would do well once in his life to reflect that were it not for *our* American colonies, he might at this "present crisis", been but the driver of a baggage cart, on a crusade to the holy sepulchre, or sketching caracatura's while the brave were bleeding and dying for their country. He gives us three or four sophistical arguments to prove that "no taxes can be exactly equal." "If not exactly equal on all, then not just."

---

35   Pownall's Administration of the Colonies. Second Edition.
36   Terms used in our obsolete charters.

"Therefore no taxes at all can be justly imposed." This is arch. But who before ever dreamt that no taxes could be imposed, because a mathematical exactness or inequality is impracticable.

Having in his odd way, and very confused method considered the right and authority of parliament to tax the colonies, which he takes for granted instead of proving; he proceeds to shew the expediency of taking the present crisis by the fore top, and proceeding in the present manner, lest it should run away. As to the *"nascent* crisis, or present tense," it is as good a tense as any in grammar. And misers and politicians will, for their purposes, ever think it the best. If we must be taxed without our consent, and are able to pay the national debt, it is our duty to pay it, which some take for granted; why then I agree we had better pay it off at once, and have done with it. For this purpose, the "present identic very now, is better than any other now, or crisis, begotten, or about to be begotten; nascent, or about to be nascent; born or unborn."[37] If Mr. J_____s pleases, it shall be the great *Aera,* or TO NUN, of the colony administratrix.

Ultima cummoei venit jam carminis aetas
_____ _ *Nascitar Crisis.*

But as to the manner and reasons, it may not be amiss to offer a word or two. He asks with the *pathos* of a stage itinerant, if "any time can be more proper to require some assistance from *our* colonies, to preserve to themselves their present safety, than when *this country* is almost *undone* by procuring it." That that *country,* as he calls it, is almost undone, I shall not dispute; especially after I have the sagacious Mr. J_____'s opinion, to the same purpose. But he shows his ignorance, weakness, and wickedness, who imputes so tremendous an impending evil to procuring safety for the colonies. The colonies never cost Britain anything till the last war. Even now, if an impartial account was stated, without allowing one penny for the increase of European trade since the discovery of America, or for the employment yielded by the colonists to millions in Britain who perhaps might otherwise starve, the neat revenue that has accrued by means of *"our* American colonies" alone, would amount to five times the sum the crown ever expended for their settlement, protection, and defence, from the reign of queen Elizabeth to this day. In this calculate the whole expence of the last war is included, and supposed intirely chargeable to America, according to the visionary theorems of the Administrator, and Regulator.[38] I should think, however, that some small part of the national debt might be justly charged to the "procuring the present safety of Hanover,

---

37   P-n-n Parody.
38   Administration and Regulations of the colonies.

and other parts of high and low Dutchland." But, waving this, if it were all to be charged to America, the hundred and forty-nine millions were well laid out, and much better than any sum from the time of Julius Caesar, to the glorious revolution, the "nascent" aera of British liberty, glory, and grandeur. It was for the very being of Britain, as a great maritime, commercial, and powerful, state; none of which would she long be without the assistance of her colonies. It requires no penetration to foresee that should she lose these, which God forbid, she would in a few years, fall a sacrifice to France, or some other despotic power on the continent of Europe. The national debt is confessed on all hands, to be a terrible evil, and may, in time, ruin the state. But it should be remembered, that the colonists never occasioned its increase, nor ever reaped any of the sweet fruits of involving the finest kingdom in the world, in the sad calamity of an enormous overgrown mortgage to state and stock jobbers. No places nor pensions, of thousands and tens of thousands sterling, have been laid out to purchase the votes and influence of the colonists. They have gone on with their settlements in spite of the most horrid difficulties and dangers; they have ever supported, to the utmost of their ability, his majesty's provincial government over them, and, I believe are, to a man, and ever will be, ready to make grants for so valuable a purpose. But we cannot see the equity of our being obliged to pay off a score that has been much enhanced by bribes and pensions, to keep those to their duty who ought to have been bound by honour and conscience. We have ever been from principle, attached to his majesty, and his illustrious house. We never asked any pay: the heart-felt satisfaction of having served our king and country, has been always enough for us. I cannot see why it would not be well enough to go a nabob hunting on this occasion. Why should not the great Mogul be obliged to contribute towards, if not to pay, the national debt, as some have proposed? He is a Pagan, an East Indian, and of a dark complexion, which are full as good reasons for laying him under contribution, as any I have found abroad in the pamphlets and coffeehouse conferences, for taxing the colonists. There are, doubtless, good reasons to be assigned, or it would not be done, by my superiors; but I confess I cannot reach them, nor has Mr. J_____s afforded me the least assistance in this matter. Necessity, say the coffee-house politicians has no law. Then say I, apply the *sponge* at once! A few jobbers had better be left to hang and drown themselves, as was the case after the South Sea bubble, and a few small politicians had better be sent after them, than the nation be undone. This would, in the end, turn out infinitely more beneficial to the whole, than imposing taxes on such as have not the means of paying them. In the way revenue has been sometimes managed, the universe, would not long set bounds to the rapid increase of the national debt. If places, pensions, and dependencies shall be ever increased in proportion to new resources, instead of carefully applying such resources to the clearing off former incumbrances, the game may be truly infinite. I remember that the great duke of Sully, on a revision of the state of his master's finances; found that of one hundred and thirty millions annually extorted from the poor people, but thirty millions of those livres centred in his majesty's coffers. He proceeded in a manner worthy himself. Happily for Britain, the papists ruined France and their own cause, by the villainous assassination of one of the greatest, wisest, and best princes, that ever lived. Of course the power and influence of the best minister beyond all comparison, that ever existed, fell with the sovereign. He only lived to explain to France what she might have been. She has ever since been toiling to regain the lost opportunity; God be thanked, it is yet in vain, and if Britain pleases, ever will be.

Mr. J_____s asks, if "any time can be more proper to impose taxes on their *trade,* than when they are enabled to rival us in our manufactures, by the encouragement and protection *we* have given them?" who are WE? It is a miracle he had not affirmed, that the colonies rival Great Britain in trade also. His not asserting this, is the only glimmering of modesty or regard to truth, discoverable through his notable performance. As the colonists are British subjects, and confessedly on all hands entitled to the same rights and privileges, with the subjects born within the realm, I challenge Mr. J_____s or anyone else to give even the colour of a conclusive reason, why the colonists are not entitled to the same means and methods of obtaining a living with their fellow-subjects in the islands.

Can anyone tell me why trade, commerce, arts, sciences and manufactures, should not be as free for an American as for an European? Is there any thing in the laws of nature and nations, any thing in the nature of our allegiance that forbids a colonist to push the manufacture of iron much beyond the making a horse-shoe or a hob nail? We have indeed "files for our mattocks, and for our coulters, and for our forks, and for our axes, to sharpen our goads," and to break our teeth; but they are of the manufacture of Europe: I never heard of one made here. Neither the refinements of Montesquieu, nor the imitations of the servile Frenchified half thinking mortals, who are so fond of quoting him, to prove, that it is a law of Europe, to confine the trade and manufactures to the mother state, "to prohibit the colonists erecting manufactories," and "to *interdict* all commerce between them and other countries," will pass with me for any evidence of the rectitude of this custom and procedure.

The *Administrator* has worked these principles up to "fundamental maxims of police at this crisis." The *Regulator* hath followed him, and given broad hints that all kinds of American manufactures will not only be discountenanced, but even prohibited, as fast as they are found to interfere with those of Britain. That is, in plain English, we shall do nothing that they can do for us. This is kind! ... And what they cannot do for us, we are permitted to do for ourselves. Generous! ... However, I can never hear American manufactures seriously talked of, without being disposed to a violent fit of laughter. My contempt is inexpressible, when I perceive statesmen at home amusing the mob they affect to despise, with the imminent danger, from American manufactories.

Mr. J_____s complains that the plantation governors have broke all their instructions to procure a handsome subsistence, and betrayed the rights of their sovereign. Traitors, villains! Who are they? I never before heard of any such governors. I have had the honour to be acquainted with not a few governors, and firmly believe they would in general sooner break their own necks than their instructions. If Mr. J_____s has discovered such a knot of traitors and betrayers of their sovereign's rights, as he represents the plantation governors to be "they one and all",[39] for he makes no discrimination, it is his duty to give the proper information that they may be brought to condign punishment, and he himself stand unimpeached for misprision of treason. I promise him aid enough in most provinces to apprehend and secure such atrocious offenders as the betrayers of the rights of the best of kings. He may also rest assured, there is no colony but what would rejoice in seeing its governor rewarded according to his works, and duly exalted or depressed as he may deserve. But this man cannot, by any figure in any logic or rhetoric, but his own, justify the position that the colonists ought to suffer for the perfidy and treachery of such governors as he says have betrayed the rights of their sovereign. That the colonies have eventually suffered and may again, by the faults of some governors is not impossible. But punishing the colonists in their stead, would be a sample of justice like that of hanging the weaver for the cobbler, according to Butler.

The reverend, honourable and grave, our American judges, are also lugged in head and shoulders, and scandalously abused by Mr. J_____s. He has the audacity even to flout and sneer at those who wear long robes and full bottomed wigs, instead of greasy hats, shaggy hair, and ragged coats, as the manner of some yet is. He has the impudence to mention "costly perriwigs and robes of expensive scarlet," "as marks of the legal abilities of the American judges." What an ungentleman-like insinuation is this? as if he apprehended

---

39   *P-nl-n.

them to be destitute of all other law-like qualifications. What a reflection is this on those who appoint American judges? They are chosen by the people no where but at Rhode Island or Connecticut. There they never expect any salaries. Their judges have been in general men of fortune, honour, integrity, and ability, who have been willing to give a portion of their time to the public. For the judges in other colonies, the people are not answerable; if they are any of them weak or wicked, it is a sore calamity on the people, and needs no aggravation.—He says the judges are "so dependent on the humors of the assemblies, that they can obtain a livelihood no longer than *quamdiu se male gesserint.*" This makes the judges as bad as the governors, who for a morsel of bread, or a mess of pottage, he makes mercenary enough to "betray the rights of their sovereign." I would have Mr. J_____s, for his own sake, a little more careful of his treatment of American judges. I once knew an American chief justice take it into serious consideration, and consult the attorney-general of the province where he lived, whether his late majesty's attorney and sollicitor-general had not been guilty of a libel upon his court, in stating a favourite case before the king and counsel, in a manner that bore a little hard upon the provincial judicatory. I would also ask good Mr. J_____s if he certainly knows that any of our plantation governors and judges have lately complained home, that they cannot get a "livelihood" in America, but by *breaking* their instructions and oaths, and basely "betraying the rights of their sovereign"? Dare any of them openly avow such a complaint on either side the atlantic? If any of them have given such reasons, among others, in a sedulous application to the ministry, that America should have heavy duties and taxes imposed, let them come forth and declare it, and they will soon receive their reward. If there have been any complaints of this kind, to my great consolation, the authors are like to be sadly disappointed: for I cannot find my intention of applying any part of the new American revenue to the discharge of the provincial civil list. The present palliative indeed seems to be the appointing a number of influencial Americans to be STAMP masters; but I suspect this will be but a temporary pro-vision, and as a kind of reward to some who may have been but *too active* in bringing about the measure. When the present set shall die off, or be suspended, there can be no objection to the appointment of Europeans, as I wish it had been at first. Here I must make a general reflection that will not affect the good, the just, and the worthy, all others are at liberty to apply it to themselves. In many years experience in American affairs, I have found that those few of my more immediate countrymen the colonists, who have been lucky enough to obtain appointments from home, have been either gentlemen of true American quality, or of no quality or ability at all. The former have generally the pride of a Spaniard without his virtue, the latter are often as ignorant and impudent as the Scotch writers of the Critical Review.—Hence 'tis easy to see the colonists, as they ever have been, would be in *general* better treated, less subjected to the insolence of office from Europeans, than from colonists. I will go one step further, and venture to affirm, that if we look carefully into the history of these provinces, we shall find that in every grievance, every hardship in the restriction of our trade and commerce, some high or low dirty American has had a hand in procuring it for us.

The main object of the American revenue, according to Mr. J_____s, the *Administrator*, the *Regulator* and others, seems to be for the maintenance of a standing army here. For what? To protect and defend us, poor souls. Against whom? Why a few ragged Indians, thousands and ten thousands of whose fathers, without any European aid, when we most wanted it, were sent to the infernal shades. But "filial duty", the moral Mr. J_____s thinks will "require that we give some assistance to the distresses of our mother country." Dear mother, sweet mother, honored mother-country, I am her most dutiful son, and humble servant! But what better assistance can be given to madam, than by yielding, as her American sons have, for more than a century, subsistence for half Britain? Take my word for once, my lord, every inhabitant in America maintains at least two lazy fellows in ease, idleness, or luxury, in mother Britain's lap. We have nothing we can call our own, but the toil of our hands and the sweat of our brows. Every dollar that is exported hence to lodge in madam's great pocket, returns no more to us, *jacilis descensus Averni.* The coarsest coat of the meanest American peasant, in reality contributes towards every branch of our gracious and ever adored sovereign's revenue. The consumer ultimately pays the tax, and 'tis confessed on all hands, and is the truth, that America, in fact or eventually, consumes one half the manufactures of Britain. The time is hastening when this fair daughter will be able, if well treated, to purchase and pay for all the manufactures her mother will be able to supply. She wants no gifts, she will buy them, and that at her mother's own price, if let lone. That I may not appear too paradoxical, I affirm, and that on the best information, the Sun rises and sets every day in the sight of five millions of his majesty's American subjects, white, brown and black. I am positive I am within bounds, let the *Administrator* and *Regulator* compute as they please in their rapid flight thro' our western hemisphere. The period is not very remote when these may be increased to an hundred millions. Five millions of as true and loyal subjects as ever existed, with their good affections to the best civil constitution in the world, descending to unborn miriads, is no small object. God grant it may be well attended to! Had I the honor to be minister to the first, the best monarch in the universe, and trustee for the bravest people, except perhaps one, that ever existed, I might reason in this manner, "the Roman Eagle is dead, the British Lion lives! strange revolutions! the savage roving Britons who fled before Julius Caesar, who were vanquished by his successors *Hengist* and *Harsa,* who cut the throats of the *Lurdanes,* and fell under the Norman bondage, are after all the masters of the sea, the lords of the ocean, the terror of Europe, and the envy of the universe! can Britain rise higher? Yes, how? Never think yourself in your zenith, and you will rise fast enough. Revolutions have been; they may be again; nay, in the course of time they must be. Provinces have not been ever kept in subjection. What then is to be done? Why it is of little importance to my master, whether a thousand years hence, the colonies remain dependant on Britain or not; my business is to fall on the only means to keep them ours for the longest term possible. How can that be done? Why in one word, it must be by nourishing and cherishing them as the apple of your *eye.* All history will prove that provinces have never been disposed to independency while well treated. Well treated then they shall be." To return, the colonists pride themselves in the real riches and glory their labours procure for the best of kings: liberty is all they desire to retain for themselves and posterity.

I could wish my lord, that the colonists were able to yield ten times the aids for the support of the common cause ever yet granted by, or required of, them. But to pay heavy provincial taxes in peace and in war, and also *external and internal* parliamentary *assessments,* is absolutely out of the people's power. The burden of the *stamp* act will certainly fall chiefly on the middling, more necessitous, and labouring people. The widow, the orphan, and others, who have few on earth to help, or even pity them, must pay heavily to this tax. An instance or two will give some idea of the weight of this imposition. A rheam of printed bail bonds is now sold for about fifteen shillings sterling; with the stamps, the same quantity will, I am told, amount to near one hundred pounds sterling. A rheam of printed policies of assurance, is now about two pounds sterling; with the stamps it will be one hundred and ninety pounds sterling. Many other articles in common use here, are in the same proportion. The fees in the probate offices, with the addition of the stamps, will, in most provinces, be three times what has been hitherto paid. Surely these, and many other considerations that must be obvious to all who are versed in the course of American business, are far from being any evidence of the boasted equality and equity, of this kind of taxation. I do not mean to insinuate that there is, or hath been, any thing intentionally wrong, in the views of administration; far from it, I detest the thought. I am convinced that every Englishman, as 'tis his interest, really wishes and means well to the colonies, and I shall ever have full confidence in the wisdom and rectitude of the present truly British administration. But I have a very contemptible opinion of divers vile informers and informations, that have been transported and re-transported, within these seven years. I know some of the former to be most infamous fellows, and not a few of the latter to be most infernal falsehoods. How many low and insignificant persons, have, on their landing in Britain, been instantaneously metamorphosed into wise politicians, or suddenly transformed into hugeously sage *connoisseurs* in the *administration* of the colonies at this crisis? Some have had the assurance on their return to assert, that they were permitted to attend, and even frequent, lord Greenlaurel's levy, and dine with duke Humphry? *Credat Judeus Appella.* Two hopeful young brother surgeons, who lately went over, wrote to their friends, that they had laid aside all thoughts of going into an ordinary hospital of invalids having had overtures from the Critical Reviewers, to assist them in a new project of theirs, for dissecting the colonies and all writers in their favour. An apothecary, a quack and a fortune-hunter, not long since arrived, say they were closeted by this, and that, and t'other great man, who made most marvellous shrewd enquiries concerning the luxurious taste of our cods, crabs, muscles, eels, and smelts. They even add, that as a reward for their important discoveries and informations, in the nature of American shrimps and serpents, they are to be admitted members of the society for the encouragement of arts, &. One swears he has obtained ample promises of high preferment, as soon as ever the *finance tres grande toute novelle et admirable* shall receive its long predicted completion in America. Another says, he is to be farmer general of a tax of his own projecting, on all colony gold finders. A third says, he shall accept of nothing less than the place of *Intendant extraordinaire* of the much expected duty on all North American manufactured mouse traps, he having given the first hint.—But be these things as they may: this however, is certain, that a set of fribbling people, and some others in the colonies, who are become to the last degree detestable to all true Americans, affect to use their sage advice, and surprising influence, in order to conciliate good and worthy men to measures, which if ever so just and salutary, these contemptible persons would bring into disgrace.

 Mr. J_____s says, "imposing taxes on *our* colonies has been called harsh and arbitrary." By whom? I never heard one man of sense and knowledge, in the laws and British constitution, call the parliamentary authority arbitrary. The power and authority of parliament is not to be questioned. Nay, after all the bustle, the authority of that august body really never has been questioned by one of the colony writers, when duly attended to. The mode of exercising this authority, and the manner of proceeding, may in some instances have been thought a little hard and grevous, and may be again, notwithstanding what Mr. J_____s has said. He objects to the assertion of some, that "it would have seemed less hard if the administration or the parliament had been pleased to settle the respective *quota* of each colony, and left it to each one to assess the inhabitants, as easily to themselves as might be, on penalty of being taxed by parliament in case of any unreasonable noncompliance with the just requisitions of the crown, of which the parliament is, and must, in the nature of things, be the final judge."—Mr. J_____s asks, "what would have been the consequence of this?" I answer, neither he nor I can tell. It will be time enough to answer this when the experiment is made; but I believe there would have been found a chearful compliance on the part of the colonies, and that they would exert their utmost abilities. He most insolently asks if the "assemblies have shown so much obedience to the orders of the crown, that we could reasonably expect they would tax themselves on the arbitrary commands of a minister?" I hope he holds the proper difference between the lawful commands of our sovereign, the just orders of the crown, and "the arbitrary commands of a minister," though he has so strangely tacked them together? 'Tis our indispensible duty to yield every aid in our power to our gracious prince, and to the state, and to obey the just orders of the crown: but the arbitrary commands of a minister, are no more obligatory, than the bulls of the pope. However, I have seen the time when the flower of our youth have been annually impressed and dragged forth by thousands and tens of thousands, to certain misery and want, if not death and destruction. I have also seen immense provincial taxes levied, and all these things effected, by a (no English) speech of a governor, the military mandate of a general, or, if possible, the more haughty dictate of a minister. What have we got by all our compliances? Precisely what by many wise and good men, was foreseen and foretold, we should get. Canada is conquered, the colony trade is more than ever restricted, we are taxed without our *actual* consent in person, or any representation *in fact,* and in many instances are to be tried without a jury. The remains of those tribes of savages, the French used to keep in pay, to scalp us, and cut our throats, are, in the estimation of some great men, more respectable than his majesty's ancient, and ever loyal colonists.

Mr. J_____s asks if it would be "possible to settle the quota's of an American tax with justice?" Why not? The whole used to be commensurate with all the parts. Is it not nearly as easy to say what each part ought to pay, as to determine what ought to be paid by the whole? The gentleman will not insinuate that administration can ever act so preposterous a part, as to guess what the whole should pay, as must be the case, if ignorant of the ability of each part. He also asks, if "anyone of the colonies would submit to their quota, if ever so just?" What doubt can there be of the loyalty and submission, passive obedience, and non-resistance, of the colonies, in all cases and contingences, so far as the laws of God, of nature, and of their country require? I have none. Is not the obligation to submission the same in one case as in the other? If an act of parliament says *A* shall pay ten shillings, and *B* ten shillings, would any man in his right mind say it was less binding, than if *A* and *B* were by the same authority ordered conjointly to pay twenty. His odious comparison of "the Roman tyrants," is left with its author, with this single remark: that "the choice of a dose, a dagger, or a halter is most certainly preferable to the sudden obtrusion of either singly, without time allowed to say a short *pater noster.*" The gentleman has made himself quite merry with the modest proposal some have made, though I find it generally much disliked in the colonies, and thought impracticable, namely-an *American representation in parliament.* But if he is now sober, I would humbly ask him, if there be really and naturally any greater absurdity in this plan, than in a Welsh and Scotch representation? I would by no means, at any time be understood to intend by an American representation, the return of half a score ignorant, worthless persons, who like some colony agents, might be induced to sell their country and their God, for a golden calf. An American representation, in my sense of the terms, and as I ever used them, implies a thorough beneficial union of these colonies to the realm, or mother country, so that all the parts of the empire may be compacted and consolidated, and the constitution flourish with new vigor, and the national strength, power and importance, shine with far greater splendor than ever yet hath been seen by the sons of men. An American representation implies every real advantage to the subject abroad, as well as at home.

It may be a problem what state will be of longest duration, greatest glory, and domestic happiness. I am not at leisure fully to consider this question at present. Time shall show. I can now only say, it will be that state, which, like Great-Britain, Heaven shall have favoured with every conceivable advantage, and gave it wisdom and integrity enough to see and embrace an opportunity, which once lost, can never be regained. Every mountain must be removed, and every path be made smooth and strait. Every region, nation and people, must to all real intents and purposes, be united, knit, and worked into the very bones and blood of the original system, as fast as subdued, settled or allied. Party views and short sighted politicians, should be discarded with the ignominy and contempt they deserve.

Mr. J_____s seems to be seized with an immense pannic lest "a sudden importation of American eloquence" should interfere with those who are fond of monopolizing the place and pension *business*. He even insinuates that it would cost more to pay our orators, than a standing army *here*. I will ease him of this difficulty. There would not be many worth the high prices of Britain. When trimmers, time servers, scepticks, cock fighters, architects, fiddlers and castle builders, who commonly sell cheap, were bought off, there might not be more than three or four worth purchasing; and if they should sell as cheap in Britain as I have known some of them in America, it would fall infinitely short of the blood and treasure a standing army may one day cost. From any danger therefore Mr. J_____s is in, from "the sudden importation of American eloquence", he may speechify and scribble for or against administration, abuse the colonies, turn and return, shift, wind and change as usual, no man will trust him, and 'tis hoped that in *secula seculorum* by the eternal fitness of things, and the constructure of the cells of his *cerebellum*, and moral aptitude, he will be kept down just where he is and ought to be, He seems to have no idea of revenue, but that of drawing money into the public coffers, *per fas aut nefas*, meerly to squander away ad *libitum*. Riches returning from the four winds of the earth in heavier showers than the poets ever dreamt of, into the pockets of the worthy and opulent British merchant will, according to him, give a griping minister too much trouble before he has extracted and "squeezed it out again by various domestic taxes". His own words: "Perhaps" says he "in the mean time, it may enable the merchant, by augmenting his influence, together with his wealth, to plunge us into new wars and new debts, for his private advantage." By this 'tis plain Mr. J_____s's plan is to stop the rivulets, and leave the cistern dry. Do you not see this, British colonists, British merchants, and British manufacturers? Consider this, before it is too late! it is the sum total of Mr. J_____s's political logic and arithmetic! It is too absurd to require a more particular refutation. He concludes, *ad captandum*, both the great and small vulgar, thus; "it is", says he, "to be hoped, that in this great and important question, all parties and factions, or in the more polite and fashionable term, all connections will cordially unite; that every member of the British parliament, whether in or out of humour with the administration, whether he has been turned out because he opposed, or whether he opposed because he has been turned out, will endeavour to the utmost of his power to support this measure. A measure which must not only be approved by every man who has any property or common sense, but which ought to be required by every *English* subject of an *English administration.*" —I thought all subjects were now British, and the administration too. I cannot tell whether the *exhorter* was ever "turned out because he opposed, or opposed because he was turned out;" but certainly among other species of readers, he has omitted to address himself to the hopeful young men and promising candidates for preferment, who have as it were perished in *embrio,* by discovering too great an insolence and avidity of power, by assuming the advowson, nomination and induction of their fellow servants, before they themselves have been taken into place.

My Lord, we have heard much said of a *virtual representation.* What can it mean? If a society of a thousand men are united from a state of nature and all meet to transact the business of the society they are on a perfect level and equality, and the majority must conclude the minority. If they find themselves too numerous to transact their business, they have a right to devolve the care of their concerns on a part of the society to act for the whole. Here commences the first idea of an *actual* trust or representation in *fact.* The trustees councilor senate, so chosen are in fact representatives of and agents for the whole society. If the society agrees to have but one trustee, representative or agent, he is a *monarch.* If they make choice of a councilor senate, they are joint agents, trustees or representatives of the whole community. Upon so simple a principle are all governments originally built. When a man chuses to act for himself he has no representative, agent or trustee. When the individuals of a community chose to take care of their own concerns, they are in no wise represented; but being their own factors in person, form that society which the learned wrangle about under the name of a *democracy.* When two or more are appointed joint factors, agents for, trustees and representatives of, the whole society, they are called noble, and politicians denominate this form an *aristocracy.* When the trust is as above observed devolved on one, it is called a *monarchy,* i.e. one great or chief man is in fact trustee, representative of, and agent for the whole state. And he has a right to act for them so long as he may be chosen to act by the society. Which society being originally the constitutents of their agent or representative, have an absolute right and power to lay him under such limitations and restrictions as they may think reasonable. In all this we find no mystery, no occasion for occult qualties, no want of the terms *virtual representation* as distinguished from a *representation in fact,* or any other jargon. If the society find each of the simple forms of administration inconvenient or dangerous, as they all are, and agree on a *mixture* of those simple forms, as it is commonly expressed, but in plainer English, to have different divisions, ranks and orders of trustees or representatives, they proceed thus. When they chuse a monarch or senate, they entrust him or them with the necessary powers of government, to act for the good and welfare of the whole society. So in a government constructed like that of Great-Britain, the society hath made two divisions of the supreme power: the first is the *supreme legislative,* consisting of three ranks of branches, viz., King, lords and commons. The *supreme executive,* which is solely monarchial, and admits of no division or different ranks. Both these divisions, and all the ranks of the former, derive their power originally from the whole community. This at least is all the idea a philosopher can form. As to the *jus divinum,* the indefeasible inheritance, the indelible character, and other nonsense of the schools, they are only for the entertainment of old women, and changelings.—The King's share in the legislative and executive trusts by the British constitution is perpetual, and his royal dignity is hereditable. So are the titles of the house of Lords. The honorable house of Commons, the third rank or branch of our universal legislative, are elective, and the *deliciae populi.* God grant they may be always viewed in this light. These several branches and divisions are all subject to further alterations, limitations and restrictions from time to time. In the original idea and frame of our happy constitution, it was immaterial as to the succession to the crown, whether the heir apparent, were Pagan, Turk, Jew, Infidel or Christian. But now Papists, and all but Protestants, are very justly excluded from the succession, as for the best reasons they are from a seat in either house of the august parliament of Great-Britain.—The number of the two houses of parliament, is not by nature nor by any thing I can discover in the British constitution, definite. The families of the peers may be extinct. The constitution, has on such events left it to the crown to supply the vacancies by new families and new creations. And as reason requires, when places have grown to be considerable, they have been called to a share in the legislature of their country by a precept to return members to the great council of the nation. So when a territory hath been conquered, as was the case of Wales, or united, as was the kingdom of Scotland, they have had their full share in the *legislative.* The wisdom of ages hath left Ireland to be governed by its own parliaments, and the colonies by their own assemblies, both however, subordinate to Great-Britain, and subject to the negative of both the supreme legislative and supreme executive powers there.[40] Is not this

---

40   The charters generally reserve to the crown a negative on all colony laws. The parliament repeal such as they think fit. So that a colony bill is in effect subject to four negatives, viz. the governor and council here, and his majesty in his privy council at home, and after all the parliament.

a sufficient subordination? The fears of our independency must be affected or imaginary. We all acknowledge ourselves to be not only controulable by his majesty's negative on all our acts, but more especially so by that august, and by all true British subjects, ever to be dearly esteemed and highly reverenced body, that high court the parliament of Great-Britain. In all this, however, we find nothing of *virtual representation*.

The parliament of 1st of James 1st, "upon the knees of their hearts (as they express it) agnize their most constant faith, obedience and loyalty to his majesty and his royal progeny, as in that high court of parliament, where all the whole body of the realm, and every particular member thereof either in person or by representation upon their own free elections, are by the laws of this realm, deemed to be personally present." But as much prone as those times were to mystick divinty, school philosophy, academick politicks, and other nonsense, they say not a word of the *virtual representation* of Ireland or the other dominions. There can be no doubt but the supreme legislature may if they please unite any subordinate dominion to the realm. It has not been yet asserted that the colonists are in *fact represented* in the house of commons, nor I believe will any man seriously affirm it. The truth is, the colonists are no more represented in the house of Commons than in the house of Lords. The king in his executive capacity, *in fact* as well as *law,* represents all his kingdoms and dominions: and king, lords and commons, conjointly, as the supreme legislature, *in fact* as well as in *law,* represent and act for the realm, and all the dominions, if they please. It will not follow from thence, that if all subordinate legislature and privileges are reassumed, without any equivalent allowed, but it will be a case of very singular hardship.[41] The inhabitants of the British nations, and of the dominions of the British crown, in Europe, Asia, Africa and America, are in my idea but one people, fellow subjects of the most gracious sovereign on earth, joint heirs to the rights and privileges of the best civil constitution in the world, and who I hope e'er long to see *united* in the most firm support of their Prince's true glory, and in a steady and uniform pursuit of their own welfare and happiness.

It may perhaps sound strangely to some, but it is in my most humble opinion as good *law* and as good *sense* too, to affirm that all the plebeians of Great-Britain are in fact or virtually represented in the assembly of the Tuskarora's, as that all the colonists are in fact or virtually represented in the

---

41   It is no where said in any act or resolution of parliament, nor in any law book, that the British house of Commons, in fact or in law, virtually represent the colonists.

honourable house of Commons of Great-Britain, separately considered as one branch of the supreme and universal legislature of the whole empire.

    These considerations I hope will in due time have weight enough to induce your lordship to use your great influence for the repeal of the *Stamp Act*. I shall transmit your lordship, by the next mail, a simple, easy plan for perpetuating the British empire in all parts of the world. A plan however that cost me much thought before I had matured it. But for which I neither expect or desire any reward in this world, but the satisfaction of reflecting that I have contributed my mite to the service of my king and country. The good of mankind is my ultimate wish.

I am, my Lord,
Your Lordship's most obedient,
and humble Servant,
F.A.

Boston, Sept. 4, 1765.

SOURCES & NOTES

Throughout the book, I've attempted to minimize the need for source notes by stating in the text the essential source information. For letters, the sender, receiver, and date of the letter are typically cited in the text, and for news papers, the paper's name and publication date are cited. In most cases, anyone interested in reviewing the source can do so from this information.

Below, in cases where specific information or quotes are used, particularly out of context, the particular source page is given. More commonly, though, entire sources are used in order to not only gather information but also to understand the people involved and the circumstances in which they acted. In these instances, the source is noted without reference to a particular page. Sources are listed in the order in which they are utilized for each chapter.

Sources and notes are also updated and appended on the book's website: www.jamesotis.net. A significant number of primary and secondary sources are available on the website for download.

The following sources are oft referenced, but no number of references can adequately reflect how extensively they were utilized in constructing the narrative.

> Otis Papers, Special Collections, Butler Library, Columbia University, New York
> Massachusetts Historical Society, Boston, Massachusetts
> Francis Bernard Papers, Sparks Manuscripts, Houghton Library, Harvard University, Cambridge
> *Journals of the House of Representatives of Massachusetts*
> *Report of the Record Commissioners of the City of Boston, Volume 16*
> *Boston Gazette*
> *Boston Evening-Post*

The single greatest source of information regarding James Otis is William Tudor's *The Life of James Otis, of Massachusetts: containing also, notices of some contemporary characters and events, from the year 1760 to 1775* (Wells and Lilly, 1823). Tudor was able to interview a few who knew Otis and others of the period, including John Adams. Tudor's work does suffer from the general urge of the era to idolize the founders, but, for the era, it is an unusually fair biography. Inevitably, every Otis biography is to a great degree a retelling of Tudor's work. John Clark Ridpath's book, *James Otis, the Pre-Revolutionist; A Brief Interpretation of the Life and Work of a Patriot* (The University Association, 1898) is largely a retelling of the essential facts as set forth by Tudor. Two sources also invaluable in constructing the general narrative are John Water's *The Otis Family in Provincial and Revolutionary Massachusetts* (University of North Carolina Press, 1968) and Hugh F. Bell's unpublished thesis *James Otis of Massachusetts, The First Forty Years, 1725-1765* (Cornell, 1970). While *Arsonist* fundamentally differs from *Otis Family* and *First Forty Years* in focus, interpretation, and narrative analysis, both books represent impressive and essential scholarship. Alice Vering's unpublished dissertation (*James Otis*, University of Nebraska, 1954), provides some basic facts but is otherwise far less helpful (and fundamentally more subjective) than other sources. The essential narrative of the Boston town meetings and the General Assembly are set forth in the *Journals of the House of Representatives of Massachusetts* and in *Report of the Record Commissioners of the City of Boston, Volume 16* (Boston Town Records 1758-1769). Ellen Elizabeth Brennan's "James Otis: Recreant and Patriot" (The New England Quarterly, Vol. 12, No. 4, Dec., 1939) is typically cited in Otis-related papers and books written in the 1960s and 70s and regarded as essentially sound and insightful; clearly, *Arsonist*'s focus and analysis is entirely opposed to Brennan's conclusions and the conclusions of those who essentially agreed with her, including nearly everything written about Otis in the 1960s and 70s. James R. Ferguson's "Reason in Madness: The Political Thought of James Otis" (*The William and Mary Quarterly*, Third Series, Vol. 36, No. 2 (Apr., 1979) is a regrettable example of uncritical acceptance of Brennan's thesis. Richard A. Samuelson's "The Constitutional Sanity of James Otis: Resistance Leader and Loyal Subject" (*The Review of Politics*, Vol. 61, No. 3, Summer, 1999) is more temperate in its treatment of Brennan's thesis but resorts to interpreting Otis's writings wholly outside of the context and turmoil in which they were created and exhibits a limited breadth of knowledge regarding Otis's life.

ARSONIST

Overture

For the 50ᵗʰ anniversary of the Declaration of Independence in 1826, Thomas Jefferson wrote: May it be to the world, what I believe it will be ... Jefferson to Roger Weightman, June 24 1826, in *The Jeffersonian cyclopedia: a comprehensive collection of the views of Thomas Jefferson classified and arranged in alphabetical order under nine thousand titles relating to government, politics, law, education, political economy, finance, science, art, literature, religious freedom, morals, etc.* John P. Foley, ed. Funk & Wagnalls company, 1900. Page 245.

This is a deluded generation, veiled in ignorance, that though popery and slavery be riding in upon them, do not perceive it ... *The terrific register: or, Record of crimes, judgments, providences, and calamities.* Sherwood, Jones, and co., 1825. Page 186.

It has been argued that the American Revolution "does not appear to resemble the revolutions of other nations in which people were killed, property was destroyed, and everything was turned upside down. ...
The Radicalism of the American Revolution, Gordon S. Wood. Vintage Books, 1993. Page 3.

Traditional economic models that focus on labor, capital, population and technology cannot explain what happened in the West in the second half of the 18ᵗʰ century. For an exceptional treatment of this idea, see *Bourgeois Dignity: Why Economics Can't Explain the Modern World*, Deirdre N. McCloskey. University of Chicago Press, 2010.

Chapter One
The time is which we have long foreseen

William Richard Cutter, *New England Families, Genealogical and Memorial: a record of the achievements of her people in the making of commonwealths and the founding of a nation*, 4 vols. Lewis historical publishing company, 1913. The main Otis entry is on page 1991 (vol 4), though the name is referenced throughout.

William Richard Cutter, *Genealogical and personal memoirs relating to the families of the state of Massachusetts*, 4 vols. Lewis historical publishing company, 1910. The main Allen entry is on page 693 (vol 2) though other entries appear for other spellings.

Glastonbury information in part from "Visitation Act Books" 1617 and 1618, Bath and Wells, Somerset Record Officer, Taunton, England.

Genealogical and other early colonial information: "Genealogical and Historical Memoir of the Otis Family," New England Historical and Genealogical Register, II (1848), 281-296. Somerset Record Office, Taunton. Exeter Diocesan Record Office. Plymouth Registry of Deeds (Plymouth, MA, USA). Records of the Inferior Court of Common Pleas (Plymouth), Minute Books of Common Pleas (Barnstable), Records of the Superior Court of Judicature, Suffolk Court files (Suffolk County Court House, Boston). Barnstable Registry of Probate (Barnstable), Plymouth Registry of Probate (Plymouth), Suffolk Registry of Probate (Boston). Barnstable Town Records (Town Hall, Hyannis). Particularly the *First Book of Records for the Proprietors of the Common Lands in Barnstable*, Hyannis, pages 16- 29.

Sources regarding colonial Massachusetts Bay, the people involved and the culture in which they lived, particularly the 17th century, include:

Samuel Deane, *History of Scituate, Massachusetts, From Its First Settlement to 1831* (James Loring 1831)

Thomas Bouve, Edward Bouve, John Long, Walter Bouve, Francis Henry, *History of the Town of Hingham, Massachusetts*, 3 vols. (Published by the Town 1893)

Amos Otis, *Genealogical Notes of Barnstable Families*. (Barnstable, 1888).

Biographical Memoir of Rev. John Lothropp, Massachusetts Historical Society, Collections. (1814), pp 163-178.

Donald Trayser, *Barnstable, Three Centuries of a Cape Cod Town* (Hyannis, 1939)

Simeon L. Deyo, *History of Barnstable County, Massachusetts* (New York, 1890)

Frederick Freeman, *The History of Cape Cod: The annals of the Thirteen Towns of Barnstable County.* Printed for the author by Geo C. Rand & Avery, 1862

Nathaniel B. Shurtleff (ed.), *Records of the Colony of New Plymouth in New England*, 8 vols. {Boston, 1855-1861}, I, 57, 108, 120, 121.

ARSONIST

William Haller, Jr., *The Puritan Frontier–Town-Planting in New England Colonial Development 1630-1660* (New York, 1951), pages 20-24.

Justin Winsor, "Abstracts of Early Plymouth Wills." (New England Historical and Genealogical Register, V, 1853), page 260.

The New England Historical & Genealogical Register, Volume 4. New England Historic Genealogical Society. S.G. Drake, 1850. Pages 201-221.

C. Benjamin Richardson, *The Historical Magazine, and Notes and Queries Concerning the Antiquities, History, and Biography of America.* Oxford University, 1868. Pages 277-278. (Louisburg referenced on page 279).

John L. Sibley, *Biographical Sketches of Graduates of Harvard University*, 3 vols. Cambridge, 1873-1885.

Ethan Allen Doty, *Doty-Doten family in America: descendants of Edward Doty, an emigrant by the Mayflower, 1620.* E.A. Doty, 1897.

William H. Whitmore (ed.), *The Massachusetts Civil List* (Albany, 1870).

On business liquidity: "Winthrop Papers," Massachusetts Historical Society, Collections, 6th Series, V, Pt. 6, 246; letter from Jonathan Sewall to John Otis, September 20, 1723, Otis Papers, Massachusetts Historical Society; Court Files Suffolk, 10705, 11803, and 11232.

Horatio Otis, "Genealogical Memoir," New England Historical and Genealogical Register, II (1848), 285-286

Charles Otis, "Description of Otis Estate," Otis Papers, Special Collections, Butler Library, Columbia University, New York.

"Barnstable, Mass. Vital Records," The Mayflower Descendant, Vol. 32 (1934), pages 153-154.

Samuel Sewall, *Diary of Samuel Sewall: 1699-1714.* Massachusetts Historical Society, 1879.

NATHAN A. ALLEN

Chapter Two
Storms & tempests are consequent

According to the Probate Records of Barnstable County, (Barnstable Court House), Record IV, page 475, John Otis III owned three slaves at the time of his death in 1727 that were listed under "swine" in his estate inventory.

"Young Jim" was often used in Barnstable to differentiate James Otis from his father, and "Jemmy" was used not only in Barnstable but also during his adult life in Boston. See Amos Otis, *Genealogical Notes of Barnstable Families*; also see "Jemmibullero," *Boston Evening-Post*, May 13, 1765.

James Thacher, *History of the Town of Plymouth* (Boston, 1835), pages 302-305.

Henry C. Kittredge, *Cape Cod – Its people and their History.* (Boston, 1930), Chapter 9.

John A. Schutz, *Legislators of the Massachusetts General Court, 1691-1780: a biographical dictionary* (UPNE, 1997),

Samuel Eliot Morison, *The Life and Letters of Harrison Gray Otis: Federalist*, 2 vols. (Boston, 1913). Vol 1 pages 15-17.

William Weeden, *Economic and Social History of New England, 1620-1789*, 2 vols. New York, 1963 and 1890 , vol II, Cap. 13

Nathaniel B. Shurtleff (ed.), *Records of the Governor and Company of the Massachusetts Bay*, 5 vols. (Boston, 1853-1854), II, 203 and *Records of the Colony of New Plymouth in New England*, 12 vols. (Boston, 1855-18 1), XI, 14 , 233, 237; V, 107-108, 237, 246-247.

Robert Middlekauff, *Ancients and Axioms; Secondary Education in Eighteenth Century New England* (New Haven, 1963). Chapter 2.

Benjamin Bangs Diary, Massachusetts Historical Society, Boston, Mass.,

Samuel Pearce May, *The Descendants of Richard Sares (Sears) of Yarmouth, Mass., 1638-1888,* Munsell's sons, 1890.

Samuel Eliot Morison, *Three Centuries of Harvard* (Cambridge, 1937).

Samuel Batchelder, *Bits of Harvard History* (Cambridge, 1924).

Josiah Quincy, *The History of Harvard University*, 2 vols. (Cambridge, 1840), Vol I, pages 230-264, 398-399.

Vicesimus Knox, Marcus Tullius Cicero, Pliny (the Younger), William Melmoth, et, al., *Elegant epistles: being a copious collection of familiar and amusing letters, selected for the improvement of young persons, and for general entertainment.* F.C. and J. Rivington, 1822. Page 180.

Benjamin Martyn, Andrew Kippis, *The life of the first Earl of Shaftesbury: from original documents in the possession of the family, Volume 1*. R. Bentley, 1836

Peter Oliver, *Origin and Progress of the American Rebellion* (Stanford, 1961), 40-45.

W. G. Brooks, "Rank of Students in Harvard," Massachusetts Historical Society, Proceedings. IX (1366-1867), 252-255.

Faculty College Record and Room Assignment Records, Harvard Archives.

David Bederman, "The Classical Constitution: Roman Republic Origins of the Habeas Suspension Clause." (*Southern California Interdisciplinary Law Journal,* Vol. 17:405, 2008) Pages 405-456.

Edwin A. Miles, "The Young American Nation and the Classical World." (*Journal of the History of Ideas,* Volume 35, Issue 2, Apr. - Jun., 1974). Pages 259-274.

James Otis, Jr. to James Otis, Sr., September S, 1740, Otis Papers, Massachusetts Historical Society.

The Allyne name appears variously as Allen, Allin, Allyn, and Allyne; "Records of Wethersfield," New England Historical and Genealogical Register, XV (1861), pages 241-246 and many other places in the Genealogical Register.

John Langdon Sibley, Clifford Kenyon Shipton, Conrad Edick Wright, Edward William Hanson, *Biographical Sketches of Graduates of Harvard University, in Cambridge, Massachusetts* (Charles William Sever, University Bookstore, 1873-1886). *Sketches* includes biographies of many of those involved in this narrative.

Tutor Flynt's Diary. Houghton Library, Harvard University, Cambridge (January 17, 1741).

James Otis, Jr. to James Otis, Sr., February 7, 1743. James Otis, Jr. to James Otis, Sr., April 4, 1743.
James Otis, Jr. to James Otis, Sr., May 9, 1743. James Otis, Jr. to James Otis, Sr., June 3, 1743. James Otis, Sr. to James Otis, Jr., Boston, June 10, 1748. Joseph Otis to James Otis, Sr., Barnstable, January 8,
1750. James Otis, Jr. to James Otis, Sr., Plymouth, January 3, 1750, Otis Papers, Special Collections, Butler Library, Columbia University, New York.

James Otis, Sr. to James Otis, Jr., May 2, 1743, Otis Papers, Massachusetts Historical Society.

James Otis, Jr. to James Otis, Sr., June 17, 1743, Harvard University Archives.

"A Satyrical Description of Commencement. Calculated to the Meridian of Cambridge in New England,"
Chapin Library, Williams College.

James Otis, Jr., to James Otis, Sr., June 17, 1743, Waterston Collection, Massachusetts Historical Society, Boston.

Barnstable Town Records, II, 115, 119, 142.

Journals of the House of Representatives of Massachusetts, December 12, 1744, pages 120-135 and Journals of the House, 1745-1746. May 29, 1745, pages 3-4, June 7, 1745, page 20, July 23, 1745, page 73, January 4, 1746, page 139, and April 25, 1746, page 245. Generally, all Massachusetts House activity is referenced from the *Journals of the House of Representatives of Massachusetts*.

William Douglass, *A Summary, Historical and Political of the First Planting, Progressive Improvements and Present State of the British Settlements In North America*, 2 vols (Boston, 1755).

John A. Schutz, *William Shirley, King's Governor of Massachusetts*. (Early American History and Culture at Williamsburg, Va., by the University of Noth Carolina Press, 1961).

Justin Winsor, History of the town of Duxbury, Massachusetts: with genealogical registers. Crosby & Nichols, 1849.

James Otis, Jr., to James Otis, Sr., July, 1745, Otis Papers, Massachusetts Historical Society.

James Otis, Jr., to James Otis, Sr., October 2, 1745, Otis Papers, Massachusetts Historical Society.

J. K. Reeves, "Jeremy Gridley, Editor," The New England Quarterly, XVII (1944), pages 265-281.

Sir William Blackstone, Commentaries on the laws of England: In four books. Printed at the Clarendon Press, 1770.

Henry R. Spencer, *Constitutional Conflict in Provincial Massachusetts* (Columbus, 1905), pages 55-59.

John Adams to Charles Cushing, April 1, 1756, quoted in Kinvin Wroth, and Hiller B. Zobel, eds.,
Legal Papers of John Adams, 3 vols. (Cambridge, 1965).

Jonathan Sewall to Thomas Robie, September 1773, printed in Massachusetts Historical Society, Proceedings, 2nd Ser., X (1896), page 409.

F. W. Grinnell, "The Bench and Bar in Colony and Province (1630-1776)," *Commonwealth History of Massachusetts*, Albert B. Hart, ed., 5 vols. (New York, 1928), II, 161. .

Charles Henry James Douglas, *The Financial History of Massachusetts: From the Organization*
of the Massachusetts Bay Colony to the American Revolution. (Cornell University, 1892)

James Otis, Jr., to James Otis, Sr., December 1, 1746, Otis Papers, Special Collections, Butler Library,
Columbia University, New York.

John Adams's worrying about the abatement of his first writ, Lyman H. Butterfield, ed., *Diary & Autobiography of John Adams*, 4 vols. (Cambridge, 1961). Vol I, pages 64-65 (December 29, 1758).

Oxenbridge Thacher Papers, Massachusetts Historical Society, Boston.

James Otis, Sr., first appears as "Colonel" in *Journals of the House of Representatives of Massachusetts*, August 30, 1747. The location of the original appointment documents is unknown.

Evarts Boutell Greene, *The Provincial Governor in the English Colonies of North America*. 1898.

Dockets of the Plymouth County Inferior Court of Common Pleas, Court House, Plymouth, 1745-1749. (Particularly Vol. 9.) March term, 1748; Record, Vol. 9, 465, 474-475.

William T. Davis, *Ancient Landmarks of Plymouth* (Boston, 1899), 190

Francis R. Stoddard, Jr., "The Old Warren House at Plymouth," The Massachusetts Magazine, IV (1911), 104-109.

Polly Lang, "America's Oldest Courthouse," Boston Herald Traveler, July 7, 1968

Books of the Superior Court of Judicature, Office of the Clerk of the Supreme Judicial Court for Suffolk
County, Fourteenth Floor, Suffolk County Court House, Boston. Vol. 10, Plymouth, 1748 Term, New
Entry no. 23; Superior Court Record (1747-1750), page 116.

Early Court Files and Miscellaneous Papers, Office of the Clerk of the Supreme Judicial Court. Court
File 67989.

Journals of the House of Representatives of Massachusetts, January 6, 1748 [1749], page 172, 1715-1761 (Second Session), Reprinted by Massachusetts Historical Society (Boston, 1919, 1967). 1761 (Third Session) 1765-1766, Early American Imprints, 1639-1800, ed. Clifford K. Shipton.

Bernhard Knollenberg, ed., "Thomas Hollis and Jonathan Mayhew, Their Correspondence, 1759-1766." (1949)

Emory Washburn, *Sketches of the Judicial History of Massachusetts* (Boston, 1840), pages 151-164, 186-225, 276-290.

John Henry Wigmore, Ernst Freund, William Ephraim Mikell, *Select Essays in Anglo-American Legal History,* 3 vols. Little, Brown, and Company, 1907-9. Vol III, pages 259-303, 417-445.

Jonathan Mayhew, *A Discourse concerning Unlimited Submission and Non-Resistance to the Higher Powers: With some Reections on the Resistance made to King Charles I. And on the Anniversary of his Death: In which the Mysterious Doctrine of that Prince's Saintship and Martyrdom is Unriddled* (1750). University of Nebraska-Lincoln, 2008.

George Washington, *The Journal of Major George Washington* (1754). University of Nebraska-Lincoln, 2007.

Statement of Account, James Otis to James Otis, Junior, December, 1748 to June, 1759, and James Otis corrections thereto, Otis Papers, Columbia.

George L. Beer, *British Colonial Policy* 1754-1765 (New York, 1907).

Peter Oliver to James Otis, Sr., Boston, August 3, 1750, Otis Papers, Massachusetts Historical Society.

Boston Evening-Post, January 8, January 2 , February 5, May 14,1750.

Boston Gazette, September 4, 1750.

Boston News-Letter, September 6 and September 20, 1750.

James Otis, Jr. to James Otis, Sr., September 10,1750, Otis Papers, Massachusetts Historical Society.

John Adams to Thomas Jefferson, May 3, 1816. Charles Francis Adams, editor, *The Works of John Adams, Second President of the United States: Life of John Adams* (Little, Brown, 1856)
, X, 214.

William Fletcher, *The state of the action brought by William Fletcher against William Vassall, for defaming him: trial in the Superiour Court at Boston, August term, A.D. 1752 : and now pending by appeal to His Majesty in council*, 1753.

Fletcher v. Vassall, Plaintiff's Declaration, Court Files, Suffolk, 68,677.

William Fletcher to John Cushing, May 1, 1752, Cushing Papers, Massachusetts Historical Society, Boston.

Sup. Ct. Minute Books, Suffolk County, November 1752 Term, Cases 26 and 140.

James Otis, Jr. to William Vassall, September 1, September 28, and October 22, 1753, MS American 1250, Houghton Library, Harvard University, Cambridge.

The Respondent's Case, 2; British Museum Add. MS., 36,217, Folios 44,72, 73, 736, 78-83.

Order in Council, Court Files Suffolk, 73,510 (3), 72,594.

Petition of William Vassall, Massachusetts Archives, State House, Boston, XLIV, 8-9; Court Files Suffolk, 73,510

Agreement, John Tudor and William Fletcher, March 21, 1761, Dana Family Papers, Massachusetts Historical Society.

Essex Institute historical collections, *Abstracts of English Shipping Records Relating to Massachusetts Ports* , Essex Institute historical collections, Volumes 1-40 (Salem, 1905).

George Louis Beer. *The Old Colonial System, 1660-1754.* (The Macmillan company, 1913)

William Bourne to James Otis, Jr., March 1, 1754, Court Files Suffolk, 72423.

Halifax Gazette, September 28, 1754, November 8, 1754.

Thomas Beamish Akins, editor. Selections from the public documents of the province of Nova Scotia: Pub. under a resoltion of the House of assembly passed March 15, 1865 *Volume 1 of Nova Scotia archives Public Archives of Nova Scotia* (C. Annand, 1869)

Vice-Admiralty Proceedings, Public Archives of Nova Scotia, 492, 171

Beamish Murdoch, *A History of Nova-Scotia or Acadia*, 3 vols. (Halifax, 1866)

Commander Kinsey Report, Colonial Office Papers, Class 217, Public Archives of Canada

Parkman Papers, Massachusetts Historical Society, Boston; Lawrence to Governor Shirley, November 5, 1754. Volume 40. Massachusetts Archives, Vol. 65, 48-50. Acts and Resolves, III, 814, Province Laws, 1754-55.

Boston News-Letter, December 11, 1754 (arrival of the ship *Delap*)

James Otis, Sr. to Joseph Otis, December 18, 1754, Otis Papers, Massachusetts Historical Society.

Samuel Adams Drake, Walter Kendall Watkins, Annie Haven Thwing, *Old Boston Taverns and Tavern Clubs*. (W. A. Butterfield, 1917)

Philip Henry Stanhope (Lord Mahon), *History of England from the peace of Utrecht to the peace of Versailles: 1713-1783*, 7 vols. (J. Murray, 1836)

Chapter Three
I will kindle a fire

Ellen Elizabeth Brennan , "James Otis: Recreant and Patriot." (The New England Quarterly, Vol. 12, No. 4, Dec., 1939). Pages 691-725.

Michael Harris, "Historians Assess the Impact of Print on the Course of American History; The Revolution as a Test Case." (Library Trends, Oct 1973)

Samuel Mather to Samuel Mather, Jr., April 26, 1760 and June 7, 1760, *Samuel Mather's Letters to his Son*, Massachusetts Historical Society, Boston.

Boston News-Letter, August 7, 1760, April 7, 1763.

Edward Channing, Archibald Cary Coolidge, eds, *The Barrington-Bernard correspondence and illustrative matter, 1760-1770: drawn from the "Papers of Sir Francis Bernard" (sometime governor of Massachusetts-Bay).* (Harvard University, 1912)

Edmund S. Morgan and Helen Morgan, *The Stamp Act Crisis – Prologue to Revolution* (New York 1965)

Albert Carlos Bates, editor, *The Fitch papers: correspondence and documents during Thomas Fitch's governorship of the colony of Connecticut, 1754-1766* (Connecticut Historical Society, 1920)

Peter Orlando Hutchinson, editor, *The diary and letters of His Excellency Thomas Hutchinson: captain-general and governor-in-chief of Massachusetts Bay in North America* (S. Low, Marston, Searle & Rivington, 1883)

Charles Francis Adams, editor, *The Works of John Adams, Second President of the United States: Life of John Adams* (Little, Brown, 1856)

Boston Gazette. September 15, 1760, March 9, 1761, January 4, 1762, April 4 and April 11, 1763.

Jonathan Mayhew, *Two discourses delivered October 25th. 1759: Being the day appointed by authority to be observed as a day of public thanksgiving, for the success of His Majesty's arms, more particularly in the reduction of Quebec, the capital of*

Canada. (Printed and sold by Richard Draper, in Newbury-Street; Edes & Gill, in Queen-Street; and Thomas & John Fleet, in Cornhill, 1759)

Alden Bradford, *Memoir of the life and writings of Rev. Jonathan Mayhew, D. D.: pastor of the West Church and Society in Boston, from June, 1747, to July, 1766* (C. C. Little & Co., 1838)

Massachusetts. Superior Court of Judicature, Josiah Quincy, Horace Gray, *Reports of cases argued and adjudged in the Superior Court of Judicature of the Province of Massachusetts Bay, between 1761 and 1772* (Little, Brown, 1865)

Ellen Elizabeth Brennan, *Plural office-holding in Massachusetts, 1760-1780: its relation to the "separation" of departments of government* (The University of North Carolina Press, 1945)

Thomas Hancock to Thomas. Pownall , September 24 , 1760. Hancock Papers, Baker Library Harvard University, Cambridge

Samuel P. Savage Papers, Massachusetts Historical Society; see particularly Thomas Lechmere to Benjamin Barrons June 20, 1761.

Charles Paxton papers, Massachusetts Historical Society.

Arthur M. Schlesinger, "The Colonial Newspapers and the Stamp Act." The New England Quarterly, Vol. 8, No. 1 (Mar., 1935), pp. 63-83.

William Gordon, *The history of the Rise, progress, and Establishment, of the Independence of the United States of America: including an account of the late war ; and of the thirteen colonies, from their origin to that period.* (Printed for the Author, 1788)

Israel Williams Papers, Massachusetts Historical Society.

Thomas C. Barrow, Trade and empire; the British customs service in colonial America, 1660-1775. Harvard University Press, 1967

Lawrence Averell Harper, The English navigation laws: a seventeenth-century experiment in social engineering. Columbia University Press, 1939

William Threipland Baxter, The house of Hancock: business in Boston, 1724-1775. Harvard University Press, 1945.

Court Files Suffolk, 100515b, printed in Quincy.

Charles Janeway Stillé, The life and times of John Dickinson, 1732-1808. The Historical Society of Pennsylvania, 1891

Maurice Henry Smith, *The Writs of Assistance Case* (University of California Press, 1978).

John Rowe Letter Book, Baker Library, Harvard University, Cambridge. Letters to William Catherwood, July 6 and July 27, 1761.

Anne Rowe Cunningham, editor, *Letters and diary of John Rowe: Boston merchant, 1759-1762, 1764-1779*. (W.B. Clarke Co., 1903)

Boston Post-Boy and Advertiser, March 20, 1760.

Chapter Four
the Resentor & the popular Conductor

Ellis Ames, Abner Cheney Goodell, Melville Madison Bigelow, editors, *The acts and resolves, public and private, of the province of the Massachusetts bay: to which are prefixed the charters of the province. With historical and explanatory notes, and an appendix. Published under chapter 87 of the Resolves of the General court of the commonwealth ..., Volume 1, Part 1* (Wright & Potter, printers to the state, 1896)

Frank Edward Manuel, Fritzie Prigohzy Manuel, *James Bowdoin and the Patriot Philosophers*. (American Philosophical Society, 2004)

Esther Forbes, *Paul Revere and the World He Lived In* (Houghton Mifflin Harcourt, 1999)

John Henry Cary, *Joseph Warren; Physician, Politician, Patriot* (Univ. of Illinois Press, 1961)

R. A. Ryerson Political Mobilization and the American Revolution: The Resistance
Movement in Philadelphia, 1765 to 1776 (*William and Mary Quarterly*, Third Series, Volume 31, Issue 4, Oct., 1974). Pages 565-588.

Otis Papers, Special Collections, Butler Library, Columbia University, New York. James Otis, Sr. to Joseph Otis, May 30, 1762.Samuel Allyne Otis to Joseph Otis, May 31, 1762.

Massachusetts Historical Society, Boston, Massachusetts. James Otis Sr. to Joseph Otis, October 20, 1761.

G.B. Warden, "The Caucus and Democracy in Colonial Boston," New England Quarterly 43 (1970), Pages 19-45.

Gary B. Nash, "The Urban Crucible: Social Change, Political Consciousness, and the Origins of the American Revolutions" (Cambridge, Mass.: Harvard University Press, 1979).

Minute Books of the Superior Court of Judicature Barnstable. May Term 1761 and Plymouth, May Term 1761.

William Tudor, *The Life of James Otis of Massachusetts* (Boston, 1823).

Henry Russell Spencer, *Constitutional conflict in provincial Massachusetts: a study of some phases of the opposition between the Massachusetts governor and General court in the early eighteenth century.* (Fred J. Heer, 1905)

Journals of the House of Representatives of Massachusetts. May 27 , 1761 , pages 5-16. June 2, 1761, pages 20-23; June 3, 1761, page 25; June 4, 1761, page 26. November 12, 1761, page 114. November 13, 1761, pages 116-120; February 2, 1762, page 220; February 10, 1762, pages 239; February 10, 1762, page 242; February 19, 1762, page 262; February 24, 1762,page 278; March 4, 1762, page 290; March 5, 1762, page 292; March 6, 1762, pages 294-7; April 19, 1762, page 319.

Report of the record commissioners of the city of Boston, Volume 16. *City documents*, Boston (Mass.). (Rockwell and Churchill, 1886) 48, 53, 54, 56, 57

Boston Evening-Post: May 18, 1761, December 14, 1761.

Boston Gazette: October 12, 1761; December 21 and 28, 1761; February 15, 1762 (intimations of prosecuting Otis for his publications); December 23, 1765.

Hutchinson Correspondence. Hutchinson to William Bolan, December 14, 1761 & January 11, 1762.

Charles Henry James Douglas, *The Financial History of Massachusetts: From the Organization of the Massachusetts Bay Colony to the American Revolution.* (1892)

Robert Treat Paine Papers, Massachusetts Historical Society. Samuel Eliot to Robert Treat Paine, January 22, 1762; Robert Treat Paine to Jonathan Sewall, February 17, 1762

Chapter Five
mad people have overturned empires

Journals of the House of Representatives of Massachusetts. June 4, 8, 9, 11, 12, 15, 1762, pages 42-43, 48, 57, 65-67, 70, 76-77. September 14, 1762, page 100. January 12-13, 1763, pages 125-127. January 17, 1763, page 138. January 18, 1763, pages 143-145. January 21, 1763, page 162. January 27, 1763, page 173. January 29, 1763, page 189. January 31, 1763, page 193. February 1, 1763, pages 194-195. February 5, 1763, page 213. February 15, 1763, page 248. February 23, 1763, pages 273-277.

Edward Channing, Archibald Cary Coolidge, eds, *The Barrington-Bernard correspondence and illustrative matter, 1760-1770: drawn from the "Papers of Sir Francis Bernard" (sometime governor of Massachusetts-Bay).* Harvard University, 1912. Letters of June 7, 1762 and July 17, 1762.

Report of the record commissioners of the city of Boston, Volume 19. *City documents,* Boston (Mass.). Pages 204-207. Volume 16, pages 79-88.

Richard A. Samuelson, "The Constitutional Sanity of James Otis: Resistance Leader and Loyal Subject." (*The Review of Politics*, Vol. 61, No. 3, Summer, 1999). Pages 493-523.

Robert Treat Paine Papers, Massachusetts Historical Society. Samuel Quincy to Robert Treat Paine, February 9, 1763. Thacher to Robert Treat Paine, December 9, 1963. Jonathan Sewall to Robert Treat Paine, February 11, 1762. Thacher to Robert Treat Paine, August 23, 1763.

Records of the Superior Court of Judicature, Suffolk Court files (Suffolk County Court House, Boston). 1762, pages 385, 415.

Massachusetts Historical Society, Boston, Massachusetts. Samuel Allyne Otis to Joseph Otis, April 13, 1762. James Otis, Jr. to Jasper Mauduit, October 28, 1762. James Otis, Jr. to Jasper Mauduit, October 28, 1762. James Otis, Jr. to Jasper Mauduit, February 14, 1763. Samuel Mather to Samuel Mather, Jr., June 30, 1763. Agreement between John Murray and James Otis, February 8, 1763, Harrison Gray Otis Papers.

Otis Papers, Special Collections, Butler Library, Columbia University, New York. Samuel Allyne Otis to Joseph Otis, February 14, March 8 and June 18, 1763. Samuel Allyne Otis "Invoice" to "James & Jos. Otis, Esqrs." Dated May 31, 1763.

James Otis, Esq., *A Vindication of the Conduct of the House of Representatives.* (Edes & Gill, 1762) Reprinted in this edition.

Boston Gazette: January 31, 1763. February 21, 1763, February 28, 1763, March 28, 1763, April 4, 1763, April 11, 1763.

Boston Evening-Post: February 14, 1763, March 21, 1763, March 28, 1763.

Boston News-Letter: April 7, 1763.

Moses Coit Tyler, *The Literary History of the American Revolution, 1763-1783*, 2 vols. G. P. Putnam's Sons, 1897

James R. Ferguson, "Reason in Madness: The Political Thought of James Otis" (*The William and Mary Quarterly*, Third Series, Vol. 36, No. 2 (Apr., 1979). Pages 194-214.

Chapter Six
Troubles in this Country take their rise from one Man

William Gordon, *The history of the Rise, progress, and Establishment, of the Independence of the United States of America: including an account of the late war ; and of the thirteen colonies, from their origin to that period.* (Printed for the Author, 1788)

Thomas Hutchinson, *The History of the Province of Massachusetts Bay: from 1749 to 1774*. (J. Murray, 1828)

Boston Gazette: January 17, 1963; February 28, 1763, March 28, 1763, January 30, 1764, February 6, 1764.

Oliver Morton Dickerson, *American Colonial Government 1696-1765: a study of the British board of trade in its relation to the American Colonies, Political, Industrial, Administrative* (The Arthur H. Clark Company, 1912)

Office of the Clerk of the Supreme Judicial Court for Suffolk County, Fourteenth Floor, Suffolk County Court House, Boston. 1764 Term; Inferior Court Record.

Richard Frothingham, *Life and times of Joseph Warren*. (Little, Brown & Company, 1865)

Justin Winsor, *Narrative and Critical History of America: The United States of North America*. (Houghton, Mifflin and Company, 1888)

Jared Sparks Collection of American Manuscripts, Houghton Library, Harvard College Library, Harvard University, Cambridge (http://oasis.lib.harvard.edu/oasis/deliver/~hou01965)

Oliver Morton Dickerson, *The Navigation Acts and the American Revolution* (University of Pennsylvania Press, 1951)

Colin Nicolson, editor, *The Papers of Francis Bernard: Governor of Colonial Massachusetts, 1760-1769* (Colonial Society of Massachusetts, January 30, 2008))

William H. Whitmore (ed.), *The Massachusetts Civil List* (Albany, 1870). Pages, 61, 104-106.

Thomas C. Barrow, *Trade and Empire: The British Customs Service in Colonial America, 1660-1775* (IUniverse, June 21, 1999)

Massachusetts Historical Society, Boston, Massachusetts. Charles Chauncy to Jasper Mauduit, October 12, 1762. Jasper Mauduit to James Bowdoin, August 27, 1762 and April 7, 1763. James Otis, Jr to Jasper

Mauduit, February 14, 1763. Jasper Mauduit to Timothy Ruggles, April 8, 1763 and December 30, 1763.

Thomas Cushing to Jasper Mauduit, October 28, 1763, Thomas Cushing to Jasper Mauduit, January 1764 and February 11, 1764. Arthur Savage, Jr, to Samuel P. Savage, January 12, 1765.

Samuel Gardner Drake, *The history and antiquities of the city of Boston: from its settlement in 1630 to the year 1670. With notes, historical and critical; also an introductory history of the discovery and settlement of New England.* (L. Stevens, 1854)

Journals of the House of Representatives of Massachusetts. April 20, 1762, page 319. January 26-27, 31, 1764, pages 231-236 and 251-252. May 30, 1764, pages 4-6. June 1 through 8, 1764, pages 14-53. June 13 and 14, 1764, pages 72-82. Otis to Rhode Island Assembly, June 25, 1764.

Report of the Record Commissioners of the City of Boston, 39 vols:. (Boston, 1886-1909). Vol. 26, Page 88.

William V. Wells, *The Life and Public Services of Samuel Adams V3: Being a Narrative of His Acts and Opinions, and of His Agency in Producing and Forwarding the America* (Kessinger Publishing, LLC, 2008)

Otis Papers, Special Collections, Butler Library, Columbia University, New York. James Otis, Jr. to James Otis, Sr, not dated.

Bernard Bailyn, *Pamphlets of the American Revolution, 1750-1776, Volume 1* (Belknap Press of Harvard University Press, 1965)

Emer de Vattel, *Le droit des gens: Translation of the edition of 1758, by Charles G. Fenwick, with an introduction by Albert de Lapradelle* (Carnegie institution of Washington, 1916)

Jeremiah Dummer, A Defence of the New-England Charters, Volume 1, Issue 1 (Printed for J. Almon, 1765)

Chapter Seven
the Terror of Election

Otis Papers, Special Collections, Butler Library, Columbia University, New York. James Otis, Jr. to James Otis, Sr., July 14, 1764. James Otis, Jr. to James Otis, Jr., not dated. Samuel Allyne Otis to Joseph Otis, December 5, 1764. Samuel Allyne Otis to Joseph Otis, August 16, 1765.

Massachusetts Historical Society, Boston, Massachusetts. James Otis, Sr to Joseph Otis, Plymouth, April 8, 1764. Thomas Cushing to Jasper Mauduit, September 12, 1763. Thomas Hutchinson to Israel Williams, April 15, 1763. Thomas Whately to John Temple, London, August 14, 1764. Jasper Mauduit to Andrew Oliver, May 26, 1764. Oxenbridge Thacher Papers. Thomas Cushing to Jasper Mauduit, March 29, 1764. Thomas Cushing to Jasper Mauduit, November 17, 1764. James Otis, Sr to Harrison Gray, Barnstable, December 10, 1764. Edmund Trowbridge to William Bollan, Novermber 1764. John Watts to Robert Monckton, October 12, 1765.

Boston Gazette. January 28, 1761. *March 18, 1765.* April 23, 1764. October 1, 1764. October 8, 1764. April 22, 1765. July 22 and 29, 1765. August 5, 12, 19 and 26, 1775. September, 2, 1765. January 20, 1766.

Massachusetts. Superior Court of Judicature, Josiah Quincy, Horace Gray, *Reports of cases argued and adjudged in the Superior Court of Judicature of the Province of Massachusetts Bay, between 1761 and 1772* (Little, Brown, 1865)

Ezra Stiles, Franklin Bowditch Dexter, *Extracts from the Itineraries and other Miscellanies of Ezra Stiles, D. D., LL. D., 1755-1794: with a selection from his correspondence.* (Yale university press, 1916)

Jared Ingersoll, Jared Ingersoll Papers (BiblioLife, 2010)

Journals of the House of Representatives of Massachusetts. February 1, 1764, pages 203-206. February 4, 1764, pages 210-211. October 18, 1764, page 96. October 24-25, 1764, pages 132-135. May 30, 1765, page 11. June 8 and 25, 1765, page 108-111.

Report of the Record Commissioners of the City of Boston, 39 vols. (Boston, 1886-1909). Vol. 30, page 423. Vol. 26, page 141-152.

John Cary, *Joseph Warren: Physician, Politician, Patriot* (University of Illinois Press, 1961)

Hancock Papers, Baker Library, Harvard University. John Hancock to Harrison, January 21, 1765.

James Otis, Esq., *The Rights of the British Colonists Asserted and proved.* (Edes & Gill, 1764) Reprinted in this edition.

Boston Evening-Post: September 9, 1765. November 4, 1765.

"An Act for granting and applying certain Stamp Duties, and other Duties, in the British Colonies and Plantations in America ..." *Anno Quinto Georgii III. Regis.* Pages 499-520. (Boston: printed by Richard and Samuel Draper and Green and Russell, 1765)

William B. Sprague, *Annals of the American Pulpit* (Robert Carter & Brothers, 1865)

David Meade, *Chaumiere papers: containing matters of interest to the descendants of David Meade, of Nansemond County, Va., who died in the year 1757* (Horace O'Donoghue, Brief and Abstract Printer, 1883)

Massachusetts Historical Society, Boston, Massachusetts. James Freeman notebook, 1745-1765. Letter from Cyrus Baldwin to Loammi Baldwin, 15 August 1765, Miscellaneous Bound Manuscripts.

Hezekiah Niles, *Principles and acts of the Revolution in America: or, An attempt to collect and preserve some of the speeches, orations, & proceedings, with sketches and remarks on men and things, and other fugitive or neglected pieces, belonging to the men of the revolutionary period in the United States.* (Printed and pub. for the editor, by W.O. Niles, 1822)

NATHAN A. ALLEN

Chapter Eight
a damned faction

Boston Gazette, March 18, 1766.

Eben Edwards Beardsley, *Life and times of William Samuel Johnson, LL.D.: First Senator in Congress from Connecticut, and President of Columbia College, New York* (Hurd and Houghton, 1876)

Pauline Maier, "Reason and Revolution: The Radicalism of Dr. Thomas Young." *(American Quarterly* Vol. 28, No. 2, Special Issue: An American Enlightenment, Summer, 1976.) Pages 229-249.

The Colonial Society of Massachusetts, *The Memoir of Thomas Young (1731-1777)* (1906). Pages 5-7, 27-31.

David Freeman Hawke, "Dr. Thomas Young - Eternal Fisher in Troubled Waters: Notes for a Biography," *New-York Historical Society Quarterly* 64:1 (January 1970), pp.7-29

Bruce Henry, "Dr. Thomas Young and the Boston Committee of Correspondence." (*Huntington Library Quarterly* Vol. 39, No. 2, Feb., 1976), Pages 219-221.

Colonial Society of Massachusetts, Publications of the Colonial Society of Massachusetts, Volume 11. (The Society, 1910)

Boston Gazette. Monday September 11, 1769.

James M. Farrell, "The Writs of Assistance and Public Memory: John Adams and the Legacy of James Otis." (The New England Quarterly, Vol. 79, No. 4, Dec., 2006). Pages 533-556.

The correspondence of King George the Third with Lord North from 1768 to 1783, Volume 1 (J. Murray, 1867)

David Freeman Hawke, "Dr. Thomas Young - Eternal Fisher in Troubled Waters: Notes for a
Biography." *New-York Historical Society Quarterly* 64:1 (January 1970),

The Colonial Society of Massachusetts, *Circulating Libraries in Boston, 1765-1865* (1907).

Oscar Sherwin, "Sons of Otis and Hancock." (The New England Quarterly, Vol. 19, No. 2, June 1946). Pages 212-223. John Mein appears on pages 196-199.

Alfred F. Young, "George Robert Twelves Hewes (1742-1840): A Boston Shoemaker and the Memory of the American Revolution." (*William and Mary Quarterly*, Third Series, Volume 38, Issue 4, Oct., 1981) Pages 561-623.

Treasury Papers, Class I, Bundle 442, Library of Congress transcripts.

Acts of the Privy Council, Colonial, VI.

Newport Mercury. September 17, 1764. November 16, 1764. November 19, 1764. January 7, 28, 1765. February 4, 1765.

Records of the Colony of Rhode Island, Vols. 4-6. (A. C. Greene and brothers, state printers, 1859-1861)

Providence Gazette. February 23, 1765. March 2 and 9, 1765. April 8, 1765.

John Wilkes, *The Correspondence of the Late John Wilkes: With His Friends*. (R. Phillips, by T. Gillet, 1805)

Massachusetts Historical Society, John Adams, Samuel Adams, James Warren, *Warren-Adams letters: being chiefly a correspondence among John Adams, Samuel Adams, and James Warren ... 1743-1814*, Volume 72. (The Massachusetts Historical Society, 1917)

Danske Dandridge, *American Prisoners of the Revolution*. (1910)

Treaty of Paris, 1783; International Treaties and Related Records, 1778-1974; General Records of the United States Government, Record Group 11; National Archives.

Effects

Mercy Otis Warren, Jeffrey H. Richards, Sharon M. Harris, *Mercy Otis Warren: Selected Letters* (University of Georgia Press, 2009)

Justin Winsor, *Narrative and Critical History of America: The United States of North America.* (Houghton, Mifflin and Company, 1888)

United States Senate, History.

Compton, Nancy. "Ruggles & Allied Families Genealogy"

Chandler Bullock, *The Bathsheba Spooner Murder Case.* (Worcester, Mass: American Antiquarian Society, 1939.)

Peleg W. Chandler, "Trial of Mrs. Spooner and Others." (*American Criminal Trials*. Vol. 2. Boston: T. H. Carter, 1844.)

Murdered by His Wife, by Deborah Navas (University of Massachusetts Press, 1999).

Lucius Robinson Paige, *History of Hardwick, Massachusetts: With a genealogical register* (Houghton, Mifflin and company, 1883)

Shirley Ruggles Sullivan Germain, *Brigadier-General Timothy Ruggles and Descendants* (Shirley Germain, 2001)

Edward Alfred Jones, *The loyalists of Massachusetts: their memorials, petitions and claims* (The Saint Catherine Press, 1930)

Thomas Jefferson Randolph, Ed., *Memoir, Correspondence, And Miscellanies, From The Papers Of Thomas Jefferson* (September 30, 2005, EBook #16781)

Maurice Henry Smith, "Charles Paxton: Founding Stepfather." (1982)

James Henry Stark, *The Loyalists of Massachusetts and the other side of the American Revolution* (J.H. Stark, 1907)

Ledyard Bill, *The History of Paxton Massachusetts* (reprint: BiblioLife, 2009)

INDEX

A Vindication of the Conduct of the House of Representatives, 173, 175, 176, 179, 343

A Vindication of the British Colonies Against the Aspersions of the Halifax Gentleman in His Letter to a Rhode-Island Friend, 240, 241, 244, 246

Adams, John, 46, 51, 53, 63, 68, 96, 110, 112, 122, 125, 135, 137, 161, 177, 180, 182, 191, 214, 217, 251, 285, 306, 313, 328, 335

Adams, Sam, 33, 99, 201, 203, 204, 206, 218, 266, 271, 275, 283, 287, 302, 304, 308, 312, 319, 322

Allen, James, 151, 159, 184

Allyne, Joseph, 19

Allyne, Mary, 24

Amer-Indian, 5, 9, 44

Andros, Edmund, 9, 10, 12

Apthorp, Charles, 74, 233

Apthorp, Charles Ward, 337

Arminianism, 36, 162, 211

Arminius, Jacobus, 211

Auchmuty, Robert, 29, 68, 146, 178, 181, 320

Bare Cove, 1

Barnstable, 5, 7, 8, 11, 15, 16, 20, 25, 26, 40, 43, 47, 54, 139, 196, 325, 333, 334

Barnstaple, 1, 2

Barons, Benjamin, 114, 116, 144, 145, 323

Bay of Fundy, 79, 80

Belcher, Jonathan, 19, 38, 79, 81, 82, 83, 88

Belshazzar, 189

Bernard, Francis, 103, 104, 106, 108, 109, 110, 112, 115, 116, 118, 129, 131, 143, 145, 154, 156, 157, 159, 163, 165, 170, 171, 172, 176, 192, 196, 200, 208, 221, 229, 230, 237, 239, 251, 254, 256, 261, 271, 272, 273, 274, 280, 284, 289, 292, 293, 295, 298, 299, 302, 307, 309, 311, 314, 320, 322, 337

Bienseance de la Conversation entre les Hommes, 49, 50, 327

Black Regiment, 33, 42, 160, 161, 179, 198, 207, 235, 269, 270, 295

Blackburn, Joseph, 87, 342

Blackstone, William, 242, 243, 244, 246, 266, 267

Bollan, William, 92, 126, 147, 158, 198, 238, 320

Boston bench, 13, 136, 137, 141, 142, 163, 191, 203, 204, 206, 231, 275, 334

Bourne, Sylvanus, 94, 163

Bowdoin, James, 29, 33, 146, 152, 230, 339
Brattle Street Church, 33, 192
Brief Remarks, 247, 248, 249
British Coffee House, 67, 117, 176, 312, 322, 324,

Castle William, 105, 133, 172, 231, 280, 284, 288, 311, 320, 322
Caucas Clubb, 135, 136,
Charles II, 9, 123, 160, 168
Chauncy, Charles, 160, 178, 207, 235
Choate, John, 29, 30, 37, 142
Church of England, 9, 113, 158, 161
Circular Letter of 1768, 306, 307, 308, 309, 310, 314
Coke, Edward, 124, 223, 245, 246, 300
Commentaries (Blackstone), 243, 244, 246, 247
Confederacy, 36, 129, 137, 142, 144, 163, 207, 270, 295, 336
consent, 5, 132, 138, 162, 201, 203, 210, 212, 218, 219, 220, 222, 223, 246, 265, 266, 276, 283, 284, 291, 292, 300, 301, 305, 306, 325, 341
Considerations on Behalf of the Colonists in a Letter to a Noble Lord, 262, 264, 304, 306, 307
Copley, John Singleton, 108, 164, 341
Corbet, Michael, 313, 314, 318
Country Justice, 46
Cushing, Thomas, 33, 74, 99, 137, 161, 181, 191, 200, 203, 206, 228, 231, 232, 236, 237, 254, 257, 294, 312, 339

Dana, Richard, 68, 69, 201
DeBerdt, Dennis, 304
Declaration of Independence, 123, 125, 210, 246, 306, 307
Dickinson, John, 244, 277, 278, 286

Dillingham, John, 58, 59, 60, 61, 64
Dominion of New England, 9, 14
Dorchester, 5, 105
Dr. Bonham's Case, 124, 245
Dummer, Jeremiah, 218, 219, 241

East Anglia, 2, 3, 4
Edes and Gill, 127, 172, 192, 209, 240, 248, 290, 308, 313
Edwards, Jonathan, 227
ejectment, 64, 65
entailed estates, 64, 65, 168, 169
Evening-Post (Boston), 69, 79, 127, 136, 148, 150, 152, 185, 186, 187, 189, 190, 247, 252, 261, 275

Faneuil Hall, 74, 104, 136, 190, 319
fee simple estates, 168, 169
feudal (feudalism), 5, 8, 10, 33, 41, 45, 49, 50, 51, 64, 65, 66, 104, 111, 113, 123, 138, 142, 151, 167, 168, 169, 174, 182, 189, 212, 214, 216, 243, 244, 245, 263, 326, 327, 339, 341
Fletcher, William, 70, 71, 72, 73, 74, 75, 76, 77, 78
Flucker, Thomas, 95, 99, 100, 130, 137, 142
France, 49, 50, 78, 79, 86, 101, 103, 110, 131, 157
Franklin, Benjamin, 181, 216, 217
Freeman, James, 267-272, 280

Gage, Thomas, 276, 277, 310, 311, 313, 328, 333
Gazette (Boston), 127, 131, 139, 146, 148, 151, 153, 163, 172, 184, 185, 186, 190, 196, 200, 201, 203, 210, 227, 230, 238, 246, 247, 252, 253, 262, 266, 275, 288,

290, 291, 292, 295, 298, 300, 307, 308, 310, 312, 313, 321, 322, 323, 324
General Court, 6, 12, 13, 15, 19, 26, 29, 30, 39, 43, 47, 48, 54, 77, 92, 94, 99, 121, 136, 142, 143, 154, 156, 163, 171, 172, 184, 198, 199, 200, 201, 202, 203, 204, 205, 206, 228, 230, 235, 236, 256-260, 272, 274, 292, 297, 303,
George II, 101, 157, 177, 337
Glastonbury, 1, 4, 10, 21, 336
Glorious 92, 309, 314, 337
Glorious Revolution, 10, 16, 124, 175, 176, 211, 223
Gorum, John, 8, 9, 10, 12, 15, 16, 20
Gorum, Ralph, 8
Governor's Council, 12-14, 29-31, 56, 106, 180, 293, 296, 299, 302
Gray, Elizabeth, 233, 341
Gray, Harrison, 128, 138, 192, 201, 233, 293, 334, 336
Gray, Thomas (poet), 97-98, 101, 132
Gray, Thomas (politician), 206-207, 254
Great Awakening, 35-36, 63
Greek (language), 26, 27, 33, 97-98, 189
Grenville, George, 197-199, 201, 203, 206, 209, 229, 248, 250, 268, 280
Gridley, Jeremiah, 49-52, 68, 72-76, 78, 96, 104, 120-123, 146, 168, 180
Grotius, Hugo, 211-212

H.M.S. *Vulture*, 79, -81, 84
Halifax, 12, 77-86, 340
Hamilton, Alexander, 335, 338
Hancock, John, 108, 234, 280, 299, 309, 319-321, 326-328, 330, 339, 341

Hancock, Thomas, 87, 92-93, 100, 144, 147, 230
Harrington, James (*Oceana*), 212
Harvard College, 18-20, 26-28, 32-36, 40-42, 50-54, 108, 111, 139, 156, 160, 182, 189, 202
Henry, Patrick, 244, 261, 328,
Hewes, George, 326-327
Hingham, 2-8, 336
HMS Romney, 319
hogreeve, 14, 43, 88, 99
Hopkins, Stephen, 239-240, 246-247
House Journal, 171, 173, 180, 192, 206, 257
House of Representatives, 12-13, 44, 51, 60, 67, 77, 85, 88-89, 99, 114, 117, 170, 173, 205, 257-259, 283, 305
Hovey, John, 80-85
Howard, Martin, 239, 246
Hulton, Henry, 303, 322, 327
Hutchinson, Edward, 29, 68
Hutchinson, Eliakim, 68
Hutchinson, Foster, 34, 100, 153, 201
Hutchinson, Thomas, 37, 39, 49, 60, 68-69, 77, 93, 95, 100, 104-105, 108, 110, 113, 117, 127, 154, 156, 177-178, 186, 190, 199-202, 225, 236, 254, 269-270, 296, 299, 302, 314, 338

Inferior Courts of Common Pleas, 47, 111, 181, 288

Jackson, Richard, 159, 172, 179, 192, 198, 199-200, 222, 235-239, 279, 299, 308, 320-321
Jamaica, 68, 70, 139, 242,
James II, 10, 168, 285
Jefferson, Thomas, 214, 246, 306, 335
Jemmiwilliad, 301

Jemmy (James Otis, Jr.)
  assassination attempt, 323-325
  black Regiment (working with), 160-161, 172, 294-295
  childhood, 24-26
  Corbet Murder Trial, 313-314
  education, 27-32, 34-35, 40-43, 48-49, 50
  enlightenment 36
  feudal experience, 34
  Fletcher v. Vassall, 70-77, 86
  Great Awakening, 36
  James Otis, Junior v. John Turner, 64-66
  law practice, 52-53, 55-56, 62, 66-68, 70, 138
  marriage, 86-88, 228, 315, 336
  media, 148-149, 152-153, 183-191, 196
  Nancy and Sally, 80-85
  Oliver v. Sale, 169
  Otis v. Leonard, 94-96
  Paxton Case (1760), 113-118, 127-130
  Petition of Lechmere, 118-126, 146
  political activity & strategy, 137-138, 142-143, 147, 155-159, 168, 170-171, 172, 179-180, 206-207, 235, 237-239, 247, 249-252, 253, 254-256, 261, 267, 270, 284-285, 289, 292-293, 297-298, 300-301, 304, 311-312
  political philosophy, 174, 176-177, 197, 205, 208-220, 223, 239, 241-242, 246-247, 262-267, 288, 304-308
  Rudiments of Latin Prosody, 97-98
  Russell v. Dillingham, 57-61
  Samuel Veazie v. The Inhabitants of the Town of Duxborough, 63-64
  set the Province in a flame, 113
  smear attempts, 181-182, 189-190, 252, 299, 301, 321, 323

The Paxton Case (1760), 113-118, 127-130
Political Activity, 137
Petition of Lechmere, 118-126
Jenyns, Soame, 262, 267
Jersey, 329-330

Kent, Benjamin, 60, 63, 67, 69, 96, 100, 127, 169, 201
Kidd, William "Captain", 15, 31, 129, 175, 309
King Arthur, 1, 336

Land Bank, 18-19, 28-32, 36-40, 66, 85, 95, 124-125, 204, 207, 301, 309
Latin (language), 26-27, 33, 97-98, 113, 123
Lechmere, Thomas, 114-118, 120, 130
Lillibullero, 252
Lincoln, Benjamin, 63, 232, 336
Locke, John, 33, 43, 125, 132, 148-150, 173, 175-176, 212, 216, 223, 306
Lord Bute, 197
Lord Hillsborough, 302, 308-311, 314, 322, 324
Lothrop, John, 4-5, 16, 27, 34
Louisbourg, 42, 44-45, 48-49, 53, 60, 78, 85, 89-90, 184, 339

Madras, India, 45, 78, 90, 339
Malcolm, Daniel, 296, 309, 337,
Masaniello, 187
Mauduit, Jasper, 160-162, 165, 171-172, 178-180, 184-186, 198-209, 228-229, 231-232, 235-238, 295
Mayhew, Jonathan, 33, 42, 70-71, 74, 105, 111, 156, 160-161, 179, 186, 198, 207, 235, 269, 271-272, 294-295, 328,
Mene, Mene, Tekel Upharsin, 189-190

496

mob, 249-250, 267-273, 277-278, 280-281, 283-290, 296, 301, 303, 309-311, 316-320, 322-324, 327, 338
Molasses Act, 114, 199-203, 337
Montesquieu, 153, 176, 214,
Mount Desert Island, 157-158, 230, 235, 251, 300, 337
Musquash Cove, 80-85

Nancy and Sally, 79-85
Navigation Acts, 17, 290

Old South Church, 87, 311, 319
Oliver, Andrew, 104-108, 111, 171, 256, 268, 293, 300, 338, 341
Oliver, Peter, 42, 46, 55, 90-91, 100, 106-109, 113, 161, 164, 167, 198, 270, 293, 328, 338, 341
Osgood farm, 325, 331
Otis, James III, 315, 330
Otis, James Jr., see *Jemmy*
Otis, James Sr., 19-23, 24-26, 34, 44-46, 53, 60-64, 73, 85-86, 89-95, 97, 100, 104-106, 109-115, 119, 137-138, 140-143, 149, 151, 157-158, 163-165, 179-180, 190, 195-196, 209, 251, 254, 293-295, 298-299, 315, 333, 341
Otis, John III, 8, 17, 23, 46
Otis, John IV, 89, 91
Otis, John Jr., 1, 6-9
Otis, Mary, 233
Otis, Mercy, 87, 141, 335, 341
Otis, Polly, 227, 336
Otis, Richard, 1-2
Otis, Ruth, 87-88, 178, 228, 315, 319, 336
Otis, Samuel Allyne, 19, 23, 54, 138-141, 144, 147, 164, 188, 190, 192, 232-234, 292, 315, 325, 333-336, 341

Oxford, 104, 242, 309

Paxton, Charles, 105, 113-122, 126-128, 130-132, 146, 310, 318, 322-323, 339
Petition of Lechmere, 118-126, 146
piracy, 14-15, 81-84, 170
Plymouth, 3-7, 9-12, 15, 17, 18-19, 25-27, 55-57, 62-66, 86, 93, 254-256, 335-336
Plymouth Colony, 6-7, 12, 18, 26, 55
Polly, 317
population demographics, 244
Pownall, Thomas, 91-93, 99-100, 103, 129, 131, 215, 218, 236-237, 248, 290, 302
Prat, Benjamin, 33, 51, 52, 75-76, 78, 96, 137, 169
Privy Council, 76-77, 155, 221, 297
Pufendorf, Samuel, 211-212
Puritan, 1-2, 4, 6, 20, 42, 47, 269, 319
pursuit of happiness, 205, 306-307

Quakers, 286

Revere, Paul, 108, 309, 337, 340
Robinson, John, 316-318, 322-325, 333
Ruggles, Timothy, 63-64, 100, 137-138, 142, 163-165, 171, 192-193, 257-260, 276-279, 283, 338
Russell, Jonathan, 11, 16, 18, 20
Rutledge, John, 275, 277-278

Scituate, 4-9, 14
Second Treatise of Government (Locke), 173, 216
Seven Years' War, 86, 101, 131, 197
Sewall, Stephen, 57, 101, 104-105
Shirley, William, 19, 38-39, 44, 69-70, 77, 79, 88-93, 109-110, 119, 172
Sidney, Algernon, 160, 207

Silver Bank, 29-30
slavery, 23, 36, 54-55, 123, 169, 173, 176, 182, 199-201, 206, 208-209, 214-217, 223, 228, 238, 269, 285, 294, 300, 325, 342
smallpox, 73, 201, 204, 206, 227-228, 329
Smith, John, 7
Society for the Propagation of the Gospel, 36, 160, 162, 186
Sons of Liberty, 186, 267, 269, 280, 286-288, 296, 309, 318, 321-322, 328, 338
Stamp Act, 208-209, 217, 229, 239, 243, 244, 248, 254-262, 264-281, 284-293, 296, 310, 335
Sugar Act, 198-208, 216-218, 222-223, 229, 235, 239

Temple, John, 220, 229, 316-318,
Thacher, Oxenbridge, 33, 51, 69, 95-96, 99-100, 121-122, 146, 152-154, 163, 169, 181, 191, 202-204, 222, 230-231, 254, 261, 275, 328
The Rights of the British Colonies Asserted and Proved, 206-225, 227, 240-241
The Rudiments of Latin Prosody, 97-98
Treaty of Aix-la-Chapelle, 79
Treaty of Paris, 331
Trowbridge, Edmund, 68-69, 71-78, 115, 120, 128, 162, 169, 179-180, 293

Tyler, Royall, 33, 99-100, 136-137, 161, 163-164, 186, 191, 202-203, 206
Tyler, Wat, 187

Vassall, William, 70-78, 86
Vattel, Emmerich de, 212
Veazie, Samuel, 63-64

Washington, George, 49-50, 85-86, 89, 212, 227, 327, 334-335, 338-339, 341
Watts, Samuel, 29, 31, 37-38
Wesley, John, 36, 212
West Country, 1-4
Whately, Thomas, 203, 209, 229, 248, 250
Wheelwright, Nathaniel, 233-235, 336
Whitefield, George, 35-36, 201
Whitehall, 13, 40, 42, 45, 83, 198, 200-210, 229, 233, 243-248, 250, 256, 265-267, 272, 276, 291, 296, 304, 310, 314, 337
Wigglesworth, Edward, 35-36
William III, 15, 160
Writs of Assistance, 109-110, 118-126, 132, 146-147, 158-159, 193, 196, 213, 251, 281, 297, 341

Yorke, Charles, 76
Young, Thomas, 286-288

Made in the USA
Lexington, KY
14 December 2011